THOMAS AQUINAS
and the
GREEK FATHERS

THOMAS AQUINAS
and the
GREEK FATHERS

EDITED BY

Michael Dauphinais, Andrew Hofer, OP,
and Roger Nutt

SAPIENTIA PRESS
OF AVE MARIA UNIVERSITY

Sapientia Press
of Ave Maria University
5050 Ave Maria Blvd.
Ave Maria, FL 34142
800-537-5487

Distributed by:
The Catholic University of America Press
c/o HFS
P.O. Box 50370
Baltimore, MD 21211
800-537-5487

Cover Design: Kachergis Book Design
Cover Image: Madonna and Child c. 1265 by Coppo di
Marcovaldo (1225–1276). St. Martino dei Servi, Orvieto.
Courtesy of Wikimedia Commons.

Printed in the United States of America.

Library of Congress Control Number: 2018959215

ISBN: 978-1-932589-82-1

In thanksgiving to a dear priest, teacher, scholar, and friend, who opened up for others the pathways of wisdom found in contemplation of the eternal Triune God who revealed himself in Scripture, a revelation received and developed by the fathers and Aquinas and communicated in the one, holy, catholic, and apostolic Church, this book is dedicated to

FR. MATTHEW L. LAMB

Contents

List of Abbreviations

Works of Aquinas

CAI	*Catena in John*
CAL	*Catena in Luke*
CAM	*Catena in Matthew*
CAMR	*Catena in Mark*
CEG	*Contra Errores Graecorum*
Comp. Theol.	*Compendium Theologiae*
De Pot.	*De Potentia*
De Trin.	Commentary on Boethius's *De Trinitate*
De Ver.	*De Veritate*
De Virt.	*De Virtutibus*
Quodl.	*Quodlibet*
ScG	*Summa contra Gentiles*
ST	*Summa Theologiae*

Other Abbreviations

CCCM	Corpus Christianorum Continuatio Mediaevalis
CCSL	Corpus Christianorum Series Latina
CSEL	Corpus Scriptorum Ecclesiasticorum Latinorum
GCS	Die Griechischen Christlichen Schriftsteller
PG	Patrologia Graeca
PL	Patrologia Latina
Sent.	Peter Lombard's *Four Books of the Sentences*

Foreword

The context of the theology of Thomas Aquinas seems rather easy to sketch. Raised by Benedictines as the son of an Italian nobleman, Aquinas came in contact with Dominican preachers while a young student at the newly founded University of Naples. He became a Dominican, and his brilliance was immediately evident. In Paris and Cologne, he studied under and assisted Albert the Great, while commenting on Peter Lombard's *Sentences* and also upon biblical books such as Isaiah. While still young, he became a Master of the Sacred Page at the University of Paris. He lectured on Paul, the Gospel of John, and other biblical books. He led disputations and commented upon Aristotle's corpus. He composed two brilliant *Summae*, the second of which is filled with biblical and patristic citations that demonstrate his powerful grasp of the full spectrum of Christian thought. He was familiar with the best insights of the preceding two centuries of medieval Christian theology. He was deeply conversant in the Christian philosophical tradition, and his outlook was Aristotelian but also heavily indebted to Platonic themes such as participation. At the pope's request, he investigated the East-West theological divisions and produced his *Catena Aurea*. He was among the first Latin theologians to read the *Acta* of the ecumenical councils, deepening his sensitivity to the achievements of the Greek Fathers. He lived a life of communal liturgical prayer, preaching, and contemplation. Around the age of forty-nine, while he was in the midst of vast projects of dictation involving many scribes at once, he suddenly stopped writing, deeming his work to be "straw" in comparison with what he had seen. He died within a year. Throughout his life, his work as a university teacher (and as a founder of a Dominican studium) was stimulated by his prayer and his devotion to the Eucharist.

This may seem to be largely all the context that one needs, but I suggest that more is needed. To understand Aquinas aright—and to understand the period of eschatological fervor in which he came of age (as the popularity of Joachim of Fiore shows)—one needs to begin at the beginning. Though it may seem a detour, therefore, I think that a foreword to a book on Aquinas and the Greek Fathers needs to expose the New Testament understanding of the human situation after Christ's Pasch. This will help us to perceive not only what Aquinas had most in common with the Greek Fathers, but also what we today have most in common with Aquinas and the Greek Fathers.

In the Gospel of John, Jesus makes clear that he is the Son of the Father, and that with the Father he will send the Holy Spirit upon his disciples after he has been glorified by his Cross and Resurrection. Jesus teaches, "When the Spirit of truth comes, he will guide you into all the truth.... He will glorify me, for he will take what is mine and declare it to you. All that the Father has is mine; therefore ... he will take what is mine and declare it to you" (Jn 16:13–15). After his resurrection, Jesus breathes his Spirit upon his disciples and says, "Receive the Holy Spirit. If you forgive the sins of any, they are forgiven; if you retain the sins of any, they are retained" (Jn 20:22–23). Jesus thereby commissions them to share in his mission of spreading the inaugurated kingdom of mercy, grace, and truth.

In the Gospel of Matthew, the risen Jesus declares that all authority in heaven and on earth has been given to him. He sends forth his disciples to preach and baptize, so that people might believe unto salvation and be incorporated into his inaugurated kingdom. In the Book of Acts, the risen and ascended Christ completes the inauguration of his kingdom by pouring forth his Spirit upon his gathered disciples at Pentecost. The sign of their possession of the Spirit is that they are able to proclaim the Gospel in the languages of the nations. As the Gospel spread, the first community of Christians "devoted themselves to the apostles' teaching and fellowship, to the breaking of bread and the prayers" (Acts 2:42).

At first, the disciples thought that the risen Jesus, as the Messiah, was going to accomplish immediately the restoration of Israel, which they understood to include the ingathering of the Jews exiled throughout the nations (especially the members of the ten northern tribes) and the temporal reign of the Messiah in Jerusalem. But Jesus is restoring Israel differently. He does not will simply to come and reign in Jerusalem; rather, he wishes to draw the entire human race to himself, to his status of sitting at the right hand of the Father, so that in the coming new creation all the redeemed will share in the life of God. He is restoring Israel by means of a new Exodus to the Promised Land of the new Jerusalem, but each of these categories has been transformed by Jesus. God is constituting a Bride, the Church of Christ, that will descend from heaven at the eschatological consummation of the kingdom. The perfected kingdom will need no light from the sun, nor will it need a temple, because God will be all in all.

A key element of this new Exodus journey is the Spirit's guidance of the proclamation of the saving Gospel. Paul reminds his recalcitrant Corinthian congregation, "According to the commission of God given to me, like a skilled master builder I laid a foundation, and another man is building upon it. Let each man take care how he builds upon it. For no other foundation can any one lay than that which is laid, which is Jesus Christ" (1 Cor 3:10–11). As an Apostle, Paul is among the "stewards of the mysteries of God" (1 Cor 4:1). It matters whether the true Gospel is handed on, because the truth of the Gospel contains the truth about God, the truth about Christ, the truth about the Church, and the truth about humanity. In the Gospel of John, Jesus teaches his followers that "if you continue in my word, you are truly my disciples, and you will know the truth, and the truth will make you free"; he adds, "if the Son makes you free, you will be free indeed" (Jn 8:31–32, 36). We must continue in Jesus's word. In his inaugurated kingdom, we receive the truth about Jesus that reveals the truth about God and about our lives. Jesus teaches in the Gospel of Matthew, "Every one then who hears these words of mine and does them will be like a wise man who built his house upon the rock" (Mt 7:24). We need to hear Jesus's words and to understand them rightly, in order to build our houses "upon the rock."

The point is that truth—doctrine—is important for the Church of Christ. In the Gospel of John, Jesus teaches that if we obey his commandment of love, then we are his friends, truly sharing his life. This is sometimes taken to mean that love is all we need. But Jesus himself goes on to explain, "No longer do I call you servants, for the servant does not know what his master is doing; but I have called you friends, for all that I have heard from my Father I have made known to you" (Jn 15:15). He has made known divine truth to us; he has taught us not only by deeds, but also by words that express the truth of the Father.

As Jesus goes on to say, however, God's truth fuels an eschatological trial in the world. Jesus endures the trial first, on our behalf, in his Passion. But his followers endure it, too, as part of the new Exodus that Jesus is leading. The Holy Spirit enables Jesus's followers to follow the path of the Cross—which is the path of self-sacrificial love—and thereby to share in his resurrection. Jesus teaches his disciples, "Remember the word that I said to you, 'A servant is not greater than his master.' If they persecuted me, they will persecute you; if they kept my word, they will keep yours also" (Jn 15:20). The ongoing eschatological trial means that the Church is constantly challenged to hold on to the words of Jesus and to understand the truth of the Gospel. Paul speaks of just such a challenge when he complains to the Galatians, "I am astonished that you are so quickly deserting him who called you in the grace of Christ and turning to a different gospel—not that there is another gospel, but there are some who trouble you and want to pervert the gospel of Christ" (Gal 1:6–7).

In the Book of Acts, we see the Church passing through severe troubles, and coming through them owing to the aid of the Holy Spirit. A major controversy arose about whether circumcision was necessary for salvation. In Antioch, Paul and Barnabas faced fellow Christians who argued against their position. To resolve the issue, representatives of the opposed parties were sent by the Antiochene Church "to go up to Jerusalem to the apostles and elders about this question" (Acts 15:2). In the council that followed, several people speak, and finally Peter and James speak. The council sets forth its conclusion in the form of a letter, the key portion of which states that "it has seemed good to the Holy Spirit and to us to lay upon you no greater burden than these necessary things: that you abstain from what has been sacrificed to idols and from blood and from what is strangled and from unchastity" (Acts 15:28–29). The Holy Spirit guides the Council of Jerusalem to teach about the truth of the Gospel and about what following Christ requires.

The above provides a significant part of the context for why the Greek Fathers are particularly important to Thomas Aquinas and to all theologians today. Namely, when we read Scripture, we perceive that the Holy Spirit does not stop with the Council of Jerusalem, but rather continues to guide the inaugurated kingdom during the patristic period. Many councils took place in the patristic period. At these decisive ecumenical councils, and in the arguments that followed them, the leading bishop-theologians spoke Greek. Athanasius, who had been present at the Council of Nicaea (325), was a key figure in the ensuing debates. Gregory of Nazianzus presided over the Council of Constantinople (381) for a time. Cyril of Alexandria gave crucial leadership at the Council of Ephesus (431). Many further such examples could be named.

Nor should the importance of the second and early third centuries, during which many of the most significant theologians spoke Greek, be overlooked. Church historian John McGuckin has noted that "it is possible to see more or less the entirety of the second century as a prolonged battle about belonging and exile, core identity and secessionist deviation. Who, or what, was the core? Where were the boundaries?"[1] The key questions were doctrinal: was the truth of God, Christ, the Church, and humanity what the Gnostic Christians held? Or were the Gnostics wrong? In the second century as in the first, the Holy Spirit was ensuring that "the gospel of Christ" would be faithfully communicated for the salvation of the world.

The eminent Thomist Gilles Emery has pointed out that "the believer's knowledge of the Trinity rests on the revelation that takes place in the words and in the historical events to which the words are connected," namely, the events of the Incarnation of the Son and his life in the flesh, and the sending of the Spirit to the Church at Pentecost.[2] These events are depicted in the New Testament. Christ and the Church are the center of the whole of inspired Scripture, which the Spirit inspired to teach saving truth to every generation. Because Scripture is written down within the Church and is meant to be proclaimed liturgically, it is evident that Scripture must be interpreted within the Church. Christian life involves an ongoing struggle to interpret and perform Scripture rightly. An example of this struggle among Christians consists in the fourth-century work to define Trinitarian doctrine. The answers often seem scripturally evident to us now but obviously did not seem so evident then.

Emery shows that the way forward was sketched preeminently by the Cappadocian Fathers: Basil, Gregory of Nazianzus, and Gregory of Nyssa. He shows that the Cappadocians provided the foundations for the declaration of the Second Council of Constantinople (553) that Christians must confess "that the Father, Son and Holy Spirit have one nature (*phusis*, *natura*) or substance (*ousia*, *substantia*), that they have one power (*dunamis*, *virtus*) and authority (*exousia*, *potestas*), that there is a consubstantial (*homoousios*, *consubstantialis*) Trinity, one deity to be adored in three hypostases (*hupostaseis*, *subsistentiae*) or persons (*prosopa*, *personae*)."[3] This teaching is the heart of Scripture's teaching about God. It required a tremendous effort, nonetheless, for the Greek Fathers to overcome the widespread cultural assumption that only the Father could

---

1. John Anthony McGuckin, *The Path of Christianity: The First Thousand Years* (Downers Grove, IL: IVP Academic, 2017), 105.

2. Gilles Emery, OP, *The Trinity: An Introduction to Catholic Doctrine on the Triune God*, trans. Matthew Levering (Washington, DC: Catholic University of America Press, 2011), 2.

3. Cited in Emery, *The Trinity*, 83.

be God and that worshipping a divine Trinity would be the same as worshipping three gods, thereby dividing the Godhead and turning God into three finite entities. Emery affirms that "the Word of God [Scripture], interpreted by the Church, is directly homogeneous to the faith, and it is this Word that grounds the conviction of the Catholic Church."[4] It was the task of the Greek Fathers, in this early epoch of the inaugurated kingdom, to struggle nobly and sometimes desperately to help the Church arrive at a Trinitarian teaching true to Scripture and liturgical practice. Emery speaks of "the 'Trinitarian Christian culture' that was formed at the end of antiquity."[5]

Even if the greatest fourth-century theologians spoke Greek, Augustine and other Latin-speaking theologians also provide much insight into Trinitarian doctrine. Khaled Anatolios has exposed this fruitful conjunction of East and West in his *Retrieving Nicaea*, which devotes major chapters to Athanasius, Gregory of Nyssa, and Augustine.[6] Anatolios shows that their work was focused not solely on the doctrine of the Trinity but indeed on the whole of Christian doctrine. As he says, "orthodox trinitarian doctrine emerged as a kind of meta-doctrine that involved a global interpretation of Christian life and faith" and that called forth a true and salvific performance of "the entirety of Christian existence."[7] Lewis Ayres's *Nicaea and Its Legacy* likewise includes a chapter on Augustine while otherwise devoting almost all its attention to the Greek East. Ayres finds in the Greek Fathers a set of foundational "accounts of theological language, of the reading of Scripture, of analogical reasoning, and of the doctrine of God"—as well as of Christology, anthropology, and salvation.[8] He rightly bemoans the fact that many modern theologians have "barely engaged with" the central exponents of pro-Nicene Trinitarian theology.[9]

To Thomas Aquinas, the Greek Fathers matter because the Holy Spirit guided the Church in the formation of its Trinitarian culture, expressive of the truth of Scripture. Because the ascended Christ is guiding his inaugurated kingdom, the achievements of the past are never simply past. In their efforts of interpreting and proclaiming the faith, the Church

4. Emery, *The Trinity*, 143.

5. Emery, *The Trinity*, xvi.

6. Khaled Anatolios, *Retrieving Nicaea: The Development and Meaning of Trinitarian Doctrine* (Grand Rapids, MI: Baker Academic, 2011).

7. Anatolios, *Retrieving Nicaea*, 8.

8. Lewis Ayres, *Nicaea and Its Legacy: An Approach to Fourth-Century Trinitarian Theology* (Oxford: Oxford University Press, 2004), 2.

9. Ayres, *Nicaea and Its Legacy*, 7.

Fathers discerned not mere signposts, authentic only for their day, but rather truths of the Gospel that are salvifically true today. The Church Fathers were not engaged in an effort to accommodate the Scriptures to their culture, so as to leave an exemplar of Christian practice that, while time-bound, might inspire later Christians to undertake similar projects of correlating Christ with culture. Rather, as Aquinas recognized, the Fathers were participating in Christ's commission of spreading the truth of the Gospel in faith and life. The Holy Spirit guided the fourth-century councils to endow the Church with a permanent heritage of Gospel truth, richly doctrinal and pastoral at the same time.

For Aquinas, therefore, the Fathers are cherished authorities upon whose wisdom later theologians must constantly draw. To refuse to attend reverently to the Fathers would be tantamount to denying the work of the Holy Spirit in leading the Church into the truth of Christ. In his *Thomas Aquinas and His Predecessors*, Leo Elders articulates the perspective that guided Aquinas and that should guide every Thomist: "The writings of the Fathers are directly related to Scripture, since they were composed under the inspiring influence of the same Holy Spirit.... There is a continuity of thought between them [the Fathers] as representatives of the authority of the apostles and the Bible."[10] There is no excuse for a dogmatic or moral theologian trained in Aquinas to fail to draw deeply upon the Greek Fathers.

Yet, given human limitations, one cannot read everything. For Aquinas, there was also the difficulty of acquiring manuscripts and the added difficulty of not being educated in Greek, at a time when many Greek texts were not translated into Latin. How much knowledge of the Greek patristic inheritance did Aquinas actually have?

Elders points us to three figures: John Chrysostom, Pseudo-Dionysius, and John Damascene. We know with certitude that Aquinas drew heavily upon each of these Greek Fathers. Because Damascene mediated the Cappadocian tradition, Aquinas had more contact with the Cappadocians than otherwise might have been the case, but he rarely quotes them. Aquinas's reading of Origen and of the documents of the ecumenical councils also proved instructive, as the present volume shows. Ultimately, however, can his thought be said to draw sufficiently from the Greek Fathers, by comparison with his enormous debts to Augustine and the Latin tradition?

---

10. Leo J. Elders, *Thomas Aquinas and His Predecessors: The Philosophers and the Church Fathers in His Works* (Washington, DC: Catholic University of America Press, 2018), 101–2.

Seeking an answer to this question is one purpose of the present volume. Without doubt, therefore, *Thomas Aquinas and the Greek Fathers* makes a major and overdue historical and theological contribution to Thomistic studies, one that demonstrates the range and scope of Aquinas's patristic debts.

Yet in an equally important way, the present volume also stands as a pressing invitation to all theologians, Thomist or otherwise. The reason that theologians must learn to read the Fathers—and to read Aquinas himself—is because the Holy Spirit guides the Church into the truth of the Gospel in every epoch. Clearly, the Holy Spirit has done this in a uniquely determinative way in the patristic period. Aquinas helps us to understand and to digest dogmatically this work of the Spirit, since otherwise we might become lost in the theological weeds of tallying—without being able to adjudicate—the various instances where different Fathers contradict each other.

Thus this book is no mere museum piece or demonstration of scholarship lacking interior motivation other than desire for professional reward. On the contrary, the labor of the present volume possesses profound contemporary theological and spiritual import. It implicitly calls theologians and bishops to recognize that it is not possible to develop doctrine without undertaking the scholarly work of seeking to know the true doctrine of the Gospel. Without enduring doctrinal truth, Christians could only gesture toward the ineffable, having left divine revelation (and divine friendship!) far behind.

In sum, amid the inevitable tribulations of our own epoch, Aquinas and the Greek Fathers invite us to participate in the cruciform proclamation of the truth of the Gospel. To answer this invitation, we must begin by reading Scripture with the Fathers, not least the Greek Fathers who shaped the Church's enduring, foundational Trinitarian culture. One could not ask for a better way to learn how to do so than by learning from a medieval spiritual master who faced precisely this challenge.

Matthew Levering

THOMAS AQUINAS
and the
GREEK FATHERS

Introduction

ROGER W. NUTT

Two of the earliest accounts of St. Thomas Aquinas's life include slightly different versions of an anecdote related to his interest in the Greek Fathers of the Church. Thomas's first biographer, William of Tocco, relates that in response to a question from a student, Aquinas voiced a preference for John Chrysostom on Matthew over the whole city of Paris. The alternative version comes from Bartholomew of Capua, an authoritative witness to Aquinas's life at his canonization. According to Bartholomew, the student suggested that, were Thomas to own Paris, he could sell it back to the king of France in order to build his Dominican brothers new convents, to which Thomas replied that he would prefer Chrysostom on Matthew.[1] Scholars, of course, dispute the authenticity of this delightful anecdote, but the recognition that Thomas so loved Chrysostom's work that he would forsake great wealth to possess it certainly encapsulates the spirit of the international conference "Thomas Aquinas and the Greek Fathers," which was held in early 2018 on the campus of Ave Maria University under the co-sponsorship of the Aquinas Center for Theological Renewal at Ave Maria University and the Thomistic Institute of the Pontifical Faculty of the Immaculate Conception at the Dominican House of Studies. This volume is the fruit of that gathering.

If the great figures of "second scholasticism" and "neo-scholasticism" focused on the philosophical principles of Thomas's thought, it is also true that, since the early part of the twentieth century, scholarship on

1. For a summary of this story and its sources, see Pasquale Porro, *Thomas Aquinas: A Historical and Philosophical Profile*, trans. Joseph G. Trabbic and Roger W. Nutt (Washington, DC: Catholic University of America, 2016), 176–77.

1

St. Thomas's *Catena Aurea* and the later parts of the *Summa Theologiae* has begun to unearth the unique influence that the Fathers of the Church had on his mind and theological thinking.[2] Wider scholarship on Aquinas as a reader of the Fathers has likewise grown significantly in the last sixty-plus years.[3] Nonetheless, while he remains readily known as a deep reader of Augustine and commentator on Latin authors like Boethius and Peter Lombard, renowned for his sentences of the Fathers, Thomas's study of Dionysius under Albert the Great in Cologne, for example, is less taken into account, as is his own commentary on Dionysius's *The Divine Names*.[4]

In particular, the intensified use of Greek patristic sources in Thomas's theological work—especially his Christology[5]—during and after the Orvieto period (1261–65) is only now becoming more widely appreciated.[6] Commenting directly on Aquinas's composition of the *Catena*, Pasquale Porro makes the following observation: "Here it is fitting to recall that the justly accepted image of Thomas as a dogmatic theologian and reader of philosophy should not be allowed to eclipse his great interest in Greek patristic thought. In the *Catena*, 57 Greek Fathers are quoted (compared to 22 Latin Fathers), some of whom were practically unknown in the

2. See L.-J. Bataillon, "Saint Thomas et les Pères. De la Catena à la Tertia pars," in *Ordo sapientiae et amoris: Image et message de saint Thomas d'Aquin à travers les récentes études historiques herméneutiques et doctrinales. Hommage au Professeur Jean-Pierre Torrell op à l'occasion de son 65e anniversaire*, Studia Friburgensia 78, ed. C. J. Pinto de Oliveira (Fribourg: Editions Universitaires de Fribourg, 1993), 15–36.

3. See, e.g., C. G. Geenen, "Saint Thomas et les Pères," in *Dictionnaire de théologie catholique*, vol. XV/I, ed. V. Vacant, J.-E. Mangenot, and E. Amann (Paris: Letouzey at Ane, 1946), coll. 738–61.

4. Bernhard Blankenhorn's remarkable tome *The Mystery of Union with God: Dionysian Mysticism in Albert the Great and Thomas Aquinas* (Washington, DC: Catholic University of America Press, 2016) significantly addresses the deficiencies in attention paid to this area of Aquinas's thought.

5. See *Question disputée: L'union du Verbe incarné (De unione Verbi incarnati)*, ed. Marie-Hélène Deloffre (Paris: Vrin, 2000), 30. See also Corey Barnes, *Christ's Two Wills in Scholastic Thought: The Christology of Aquinas and Its Historical Contexts* (Toronto: Pontifical Institute of Medieval Studies, 2012), passim. "Briefly put," Barnes argues, "Aquinas follows the formulations of early church councils and patristic authors, especially Cyril of Alexandria, professing that the person or hypostasis of the Word assumed into union with itself a perfect human nature consisting of a body and rational soul joined together" (200).

6. See Jean-Pierre Torrell, OP, *Saint Thomas Aquinas*, vol. 1, *The Person and the Work*, trans. Robert Royal (Washington, DC: Catholic University of America Press, 1996), 103. For an extensive treatment of the Orvieto period, the papal library that Thomas had access to there, and the emergence of fresh Greek patristic sources in his thought during this period, see Porro, *Thomas Aquinas*, 116–84, esp. 176.

West before Thomas's use of them."[7] In fact, as James Weisheipl points out, "Thomas d'Aquino was the first Latin Scholastic writer to utilize verbatim the acts of the first five ecumenical councils of the Church, namely in the *Catena aurea* ... and in the *Summa theologiae*."[8]

Contemporary theologian Gilles Emery has also devoted especial attention to how Aquinas's knowledge of Greek patristic theology, read through Latin translations, "visibly makes its mark in the structure [of his] Christology."[9] In particular, the use of Greek sources, Emery explains, "designates Thomas as a pioneer: He was the first Latin Scholastic," for example, "truly to exploit Constantinople II in Christology and exegesis. His knowledge of the Third Council of Constantinople," moreover, "is no less evident."[10] Emery likewise traces an indebtedness to Cyril of Alexandria in a deep way.

Just as Cyril has a strong sense of the unity of the person or hypostasis of Christ, so does St. Thomas: his Christology, against all Nestorianism, starts with the person or hypostasis of the Word who unites to himself a human nature. Cyril conceives the union according to the hypostasis as a substantial *appropriation* by which the Word makes humanity his own; St. Thomas follows him even in his vocabulary.[11] Other Greek patristic sources that were even better known to the Latin schoolman, such as the *De Fide Orthodoxa* of John Damascene, are even more pervasive.

In turn, it is important to ask: What value is there in pursuing the presence and influence of the Greek Fathers in Aquinas's thought? The essays in this volume attest that the relation of Thomas's mind to the Fa-

---

7. Porro, *Thomas Aquinas*, 176.

8. James Weisheipl, *Friar Thomas D'Aquino: His Life, Thought, and Works* (Washington, DC: Catholic University of America Press, 1983), 164. For Thomas's reliance upon these types of sources and their influence on his Christology in his disputed question on the hypostatic union, see Thomas Aquinas, *De unione verbi incarnati*, trans. Roger W. Nutt (Leuven: Peeters Press, 2015), 6–42.

9. Gilles Emery, "A Note of St. Thomas and the Eastern Fathers," in *Trinity, Church, and the Human Person: Thomistic Essays*, trans. Jennifer Harms and John Baptist Ku (Naples, FL: Sapientia Press of Ave Maria University, 2007), 193–207, at 194.

10. Emery, "Note of St. Thomas," 195. Emery recommends the essential study of Martin Morard, "Thomas d'Aquin lecteur des conciles," *Archivum Franciscanum Historicum* 98 (2005): 211–365. Emery points out that in several key theological loci of Aquinas's work, citations from the Greek Fathers often double those from their Latin counterparts. Emery notes, too, that Aquinas's understanding of the "structure" of the hypostatic union is "fundamentally" Greek (202) and that his use of the term "instrument" (*organum*) to explain the causal merit of Christ's humanity is particularly indebted to the Greek Fathers.

11. Emery, "Note on St. Thomas," 202–3.

thers—especially the Greek Fathers—has significant ecclesial, doctrinal, and ecumenical implications.

In particular, there are a number of contributions that we hope to make with this volume. First there is, of course, the enduring stereotype of Aquinas, despite the growing scholarship noted above and throughout this book that he did not know the theology of the Greek Fathers well— or at least that he preferred philosophical principles over theological authorities. We hope that this project further contributes to the confutation of false stereotypes and highlights how Aquinas's special reverence for the Greek Fathers exercised a fundamental influence upon the very shape of his thought.

Furthermore, there is a danger to the life of the Church and ecumenical progress so long as, to use a term from Andrew Hofer's concluding chapter, "false dichotomies" between St. Thomas and the Fathers persist. Certain contemporary systematic theologians, for example, ignorant of both how Greek patristic thought informed Aquinas's theology as well as the Greek Fathers' thought itself concerning key fundamental Christian doctrines, often level criticisms against Aquinas that unwittingly extend to the Greek Fathers and even some of the most basic tenets of the Christian faith itself. Though often portrayed as happy dismissals of Aquinas's philosophical excesses in favor of a less systematic and more biblically vivacious approach to theology among the Fathers, these criticisms inoculate against the very Fathers on whose behalf they portend to advocate.

To give one example, French sacramental theologian Louis-Marie Chauvet strongly objects to Aquinas's teaching on sacramental efficacy in terms of instrumental causality as extending from the instrumentality of Christ's human nature. In Chauvet's mind, Aquinas's discussion of the sacraments as instrumental causes is a mechanistic philosophical imposition that reduces the sacraments from their proper spiritual order to crude objects. In particular, Chauvet seems to read something like "tool of production" into Aquinas's use of the term "instrument" and proposes that this entire line of thinking be jettisoned. Chauvet alleges that the instrumental causality spelled out by Aquinas is the product of "the technico-productionist scheme oriented toward the finished product, the guaranteed outcome, the necessary first cause or the ultimate significance serving as the highest reason."[12] "Because of its distinctive metaphysical bent," Chauvet charges, "Western thought is unable to represent to itself

---

12. Emery, "Note on St. Thomas," 26.

the relations between subjects or of subjects with God in any way other than one according to a technical model of cause and effect."[13] And, while recognizing that Aquinas views the sacraments in light of his Christology, Chauvet deems that Aquinas's doctrine leaves "his sacramental theology static."[14] In sum, a perceived flaw—especially manifest, according to Chauvet, in Aquinas's sacramental doctrine—in other words reduces the spiritual significance of the Incarnation and the sacraments.

As it were, though one can certainly understand how an isolated first glance at terminology such as "instrumental cause" can lead, in a post-Newtonian world, to thoughts of material force and productivity, a scholar of Chauvet's repute and capacity should know better. His position is fundamentally unfair to Aquinas's teaching and, indirectly, to the Greek Fathers from whom Aquinas derived his doctrine of instrumentality. Indeed, a patrologist as historically and sober minded as Aloys Grillmeier can be found underscoring the use of the term *organum*/"instrument" by the likes of Athanasius himself:

In the word [organon], Athanasius sums up the whole significance of the Logos-sarx relationship. Here his deep insight into the conjunction of the divine Word with the flesh becomes particularly clear: the flesh becomes an agent moved directly and physically by the Logos. It is in this sense that we should understand the summary sentence: "He became man; for this cause also he needed the body as a human instrument." Athanasius wishes to make two points here: first the unity of subject in Christ and second the difference between the instrument and the agent. The organon concept allows him to stress the living power of the Logos in redemption and at the same time to emphasize his transcendence without relinquishing any of the closeness of the community of the Logos and sarx.[15]

A passage like this on Athanasius leaves those reading Chauvet's rejection of Aquinas's understanding of instrumentality scratching his head. Much the same could be said about Athanasius's understanding as well. Neither Athanasius's nor Aquinas's use of the term "instrument" can be fairly characterized as "static" or "productionist" when contemplated in

13. Louis-Marie Chauvet, *Symbol and Sacrament: A Sacramental Reinterpretation of Christian Existence*, trans. Patrick Madigan and Madeleine Beaumont (Collegeville, MN: Liturgical Press, 1995), 22.

14. Chauvet, *Symbol and Sacrament*, 456.

15. Aloys Grillmeier, SJ, *Christ in the Christian Tradition*, vol. 1, *From the Apostolic Age to Chalcedon (451)*, trans. John Bowden, rev. ed. (Atlanta: John Knox Press, 1975), 205–6.

proper context. Learning the connections between Thomas's mind and the minds of the Greek Fathers can save contemporary theology from cheating itself of fertile resources by means of these false dichotomies.

Third and most importantly, the essays in this volume all provide insight and material for scholars and students of theology who wish to learn more about the deep connections and points of continuity, and at times discontinuity, that exist between Aquinas and his Greek patristic teachers—and the implications that these inroads have for current and future theological engagement. Dominic Legge considers the Greek influence on Aquinas's doctrine of the Transfiguration. Differing from what will be seen in Palamas, Legge argues, Aquinas follows Chrysostom and Cyril of Alexandria in maintaining that the light of the Transfiguration is not the uncreated light of Christ's divine nature, but rather a visible light showing forth the glorification of Christ's body, and hence revealing the truth of his humanity and its supernatural glorification. Contrary to the opinion that Aquinas was not positively engaged with or concerned about Origen's contribution to the Church's theological patrimony, Jörgen Vijgen's chapter unearths nearly 1,110 explicit references to Origen in Thomas's writings. Khaled Anatolios accentuates notes of convergence and complementarity between Aquinas's and Athanasius's understanding of the salvific work of Christ. John Baptist Ku presents a comparison between Aquinas and Gregory Nazianzen on the question of God the Father as the principle/cause of God the Son, with surprising finds. Gerald Boersma examines the nuanced manner in which Aquinas relates to the Greek Fathers, who dealt explicitly or implicitly with Eunomianism, on the possibility and manner of the vision of the divine essence. Brian Dunkle considers the *Catena Aurea* and the Third Part of the *Summa Theologiae* in order to demonstrate that Chrysostom helps Aquinas describe Christ's humanity as model and paradigm for human action, progress, and perseverance. Stephen Fields traces Thomas's doctrine of analogy through his balanced appropriation of the apophatic and kataphatic movements of the Pseudo-Areopagite's theology. Bernhard Blakenhorn identifies similarities between the accounts of mystical union offered by Aquinas and Maximos the Confessor vis-à-vis their respective Christologies. Marcus Plested affirms the "Greek patristic turn" taken by Aquinas during and after Orvieto by situating Aquinas's reception of John of Damascus's teaching on the Transfiguration in closer proximity to that of the Palamites than the teaching of the anti-Palamites. John Sehorn writes on Thomas's teaching on giving latria to images of Christ, and how this can be considered in light of Nicaea II (787), whose acta Aquinas did not have. Jane Sloan Peters's careful study of the *Catena Aurea in Ioannem* and *Lectura Super Ioannem* reveals a somewhat hidden yet significant influence of the Byzantine exegete Theophylact of Ochrid on Aquinas's exegesis of John. As a capstone to the volume's chapters, Joseph Wawrykow traces developments in Aquinas's eucharistic theology, finding certain themes derived from John Chrysostom, Cyril of Alexandria, Pseudo-Dionysius, and John Damascene in his advanced teaching, which assist Aquinas to make clear the immediacy and poignancy of the encounter with Christ in the Eucharist and the spiritual benefits of fruitful reception.

At the same time, this collection of essays is offered as a modest springboard for further research in this rich area of theological exploration. Much exciting work remains available for scholars of diverse interests and perspectives. In general, an ethos of conviviality surrounded the conference that led to this volume, whose ethos we hope to capture, at least somewhat, in these pages.

In regard to the conference and production of this volume, we wish to extend a word of thanks to all of the conference participants and the contributors to this volume. We thank our volume's copy editor, Ashleigh McKown, and we extend gratitude to Elly A. Brown for compiling the bibliography and to Grace De Salvo for producing the index. The multifaceted contributions of Fr. Andrew Hofer and Michael Dauphinais to the organization of the conference and the editorial work on the volume were indispensable to any modicum of success realized by the conference and this volume. The support staff of the Thomistic Institute and the Aquinas Center for Theological Renewal are deserving of special recognition for their faithful and tireless work in preparation for and in hosting the event. Mrs. Grace De Salvo's contributions merit special mention. Last, Fr. Matthew L. Lamb (†2018), founding chair of the Patrick F. Taylor Graduate Programs in Theology at Ave Maria University and a regular participant in the Aquinas Center's annual conferences, passed from this life just weeks prior to this event. He was looking forward to the conference—both the topic itself and for the chance to spend time with the many friends and colleagues who attended—and his teaching and voluminous writings reflect an enduring and contemplative love for the work, inter alia, of Athanasius and Aquinas. His physical presence—often manifest in delightfully long, penetrating questions during the question-and-answer periods—at this conference was sorely missed, but his influence and friendship were most certainly not forgotten. In gratitude for his faithful years of priestly and scholarly service to the Church and the Catholic academy, we dedicate this volume to his memory—*Requiescat in pace*!

1

Christ and the Trinity at the Transfiguration
Aquinas and the Greek Fathers

DOMINIC LEGGE, OP

When reading the Gospel accounts of the Transfiguration, one cannot help but conclude that it is one of the most striking and profound mysteries of Christ's earthly life. It seems as if the three apostolic witnesses have been brought up a high mountain to glimpse something that is no longer earthly, but rather of heaven: Christ radiates with splendor, a bright cloud overshadows them, and they hear the Father's voice bearing witness to his only begotten Son.

In patristic and medieval theology, one can typically observe two axes of theological reflection on the theophany of the Transfiguration. The first axis is Trinitarian, a theophany of the divine persons: the Father's voice, the beloved Son, and in some authors (though not all), the luminous cloud signifies the Holy Spirit. The second axis is Christological: it is a theophany of Christ, who is true God and true man, a manifestation of the divine Son present in human form, as he radiates a divinized glory—or, for some, the very eternal light of the divine nature. Some patristic and medieval authors interpret the Transfiguration principally along one axis or the other, or emphasize one and acknowledge the other only in passing.

In Thomas Aquinas's theological reading of the Transfiguration, we find both dimensions or axes. St. Thomas offers a distinctive and powerful account of this mystery that is at once both Christological and Trinitarian, and not only as two separate domains or axes. The Transfiguration is a good example of Aquinas's Trinitarian Christology at work: the luminous mystery of the Trinity is manifested *through* Christ, the eternal Son sent by the Father *as man* in the power of the Spirit; as man who is true God incarnate, Christ leads us up into the heart of the Trinitarian mystery and, through all that he does and suffers, reveals it and gives us a share in it. Aquinas not only draws on the Church Fathers (both Greek and Latin), but also is perhaps best described as offering a rich and original theological synthesis of them, a synthesis that is both highly traditional and showcases Aquinas's genius for integrating diverse traditions into an overarching unity of theological vision. It yields a reading that is at the same time both traditional and patristic, and also distinctively Thomistic.

Let's begin with the Trinitarian axis. For St. Thomas, the Transfiguration is clearly a theophany or revelation *of the three divine persons of the Trinity*. This view is indeed found in some Fathers, but, perhaps surprisingly, it is missing in many. A good number do not mention the Holy Spirit at all, perhaps because they are concerned principally with the identity of Christ and the relation between the Father and the Son. As far as I've been able to discover, there is no mention of the Holy Spirit at the Transfiguration in Basil, Gregory of Nazianzus, Gregory of Nyssa, John Chrysostom, Cyril of Alexandria, Leo, nor Gregory the Great.[1] Origen thinks one *could* identify the cloud with the Spirit, but says it might also signify the Father or the Son.[2] Ambrose and Jerome, in contrast, do expressly identify all three persons at Mt. Tabor.[3] For Aquinas, however, the most important source may well be John Damascene, who—in a sermon that Aquinas quotes in treating of the Transfiguration—sees the

---

1. I reviewed the texts of each Church Father in two different collections of primary sources: John Anthony McGuckin, *The Transfiguration of Christ in Scripture and Tradition* (Lewiston, NY: Edwin Mellen Press, 1986), 146–248, and Brian E. Daley, trans., *Light on the Mountain: Greek Patristic and Byzantine Homilies on the Transfiguration of the Lord* (Yonkers, NY: St. Vladimir's Seminary Press, 2013). For Leo the Great, I reviewed his one extant text (Sermon 51) treating of the Transfiguration. St. Leo the Great, *Sermons*, trans. Jane Patricia Freeland and Agnes Josephine Conway (Washington, DC: Catholic University of America Press, 1996), 218–24.

2. Origen, *Commentary on Matthew* 12.36–43, in *Light on the Mountain*, 55–66.

3. See St. Ambrose, *Expositio Evangelii Secundum Lucam*, c. 7, and the text reprinted in McGuckin, *Transfiguration of Christ*, 263–69. For Jerome, see the text quoted in Thomas C. Oden and Christopher A. Hall, eds., *Ancient Christian Commentary on Scripture*, vol. 2, *Mark* (Downers Grove, IL: InterVarsity Press, 1998), 120.

Holy Spirit in the luminous cloud and draws an express parallel to the Spirit's appearance in the form of a dove at Christ's baptism.[4]

Even more importantly for St. Thomas, however, the Transfiguration is seen most clearly as a Trinitarian theophany under the rubric of the divine missions. This is extremely significant, because the divine missions play an architectonic role in Aquinas's theology.[5] By means of the divine missions, the Trinitarian mystery of God in himself is not only *revealed* in the dispensation of salvation, but also is *active* in drawing creation back into the Trinity. Aquinas holds that, in the divine missions, the very processions of the Word and the Spirit are extended into time and made present in the world as those persons are sent by the Father according to some created effect, and that they also are the vectors of the return of creatures to God according to the pattern of the eternal processions of the persons. The created effect of a divine mission might be invisible—their personal presence in the soul—but, above all in the Incarnation, the divine persons are sent *visibly*. Thus, Jesus is the Son incarnate, true God and true man, sent by the Father according to a true—and visible—human nature. This is the created effect of the Son's visible mission. And in the dispensation of Christ, there are also visible missions of the Holy Spirit, where the Holy Spirit's invisible presence is revealed and manifested by means of a visible sign.

The visible missions are therefore both a revelation of the divine persons, making known the invisible things of God, and the historical events that found the economy of grace (since all grace comes to us through, and in virtue of, Christ's incarnation). These dimensions are interrelated: the visible missions *manifest* the mystery of the Triune God, and *save* us as they draw us into that mystery. This double aspect of manifestation and salvation is a fundamental trait of the entire dispensation of salvation. (The significance of all this for Aquinas's interpretation of the Transfiguration is major; I return to it in a moment.)

Speaking of the divine missions in Trinitarian theology is traditional —it is a central and structuring theme of Augustine's *De Trinitate*, and

---

4. John Damascene, *Homily on the Transfiguration*, PG 96 at col. 564. Cf. *ST* III, q. 45, a. 2 co.

5. See, e.g., Gilles Emery, "*Theologia* and *Dispensatio*: The Centrality of the Divine Missions in St. Thomas's Trinitarian Theology," *The Thomist* 74 (2010): 515–61; idem, "Missions invisibles et missions visibles: le Christ et son Esprit," *Revue Thomiste* 106 (2006): 51–99; Dominic Legge, *The Trinitarian Christology of St. Thomas Aquinas* (Oxford: Oxford University Press, 2017), 11–58.

henceforth it is commonly treated in the West. For example, the missions feature prominently in Peter Lombard's *Sentences* in Book I's treatment of the Trinity, where he introduces them especially in connection with the Holy Spirit, and consequently they feature in the thought of most medieval scholastics. One might think, therefore, that it is a particularly Latin and Western mode of Trinitarian reflection. Yet, in fact, it has an important pedigree among the Greek Fathers.

That the Son and the Holy Spirit are "sent" (Latin: *missio*) is of course a fundamental truth of faith revealed in the New Testament. Yet in the Arian crisis, precisely this truth gave rise to an important theological question among the Fathers. Those who argued that the Son had a subordinate status in comparison to the Father claimed the language in the Scriptures about the sending of the Son as evidence for their view. They argued that one sends a subordinate, not an equal, and so if the Son is sent by the Father, the Son must be less than the Father. Consider this text, from a letter written by Eusebius of Caesarea to Euphration, which scholars have generally dated to before the Council of Nicaea:[6]

The Son of God himself, who quite clearly knows all things, knows that he is different from, less, and inferior to the Father, and with full piety also teaches us this when he says, "The Father who sent me is greater than me" (Jn 14:28).[7]

In response to this challenge, then, it was extremely important for theologians to articulate an account of the sending of divine persons—that is, what will later be called a doctrine of the divine missions—that does not imply any subordination but rather the eternal procession of one person from another, and a manifestation or proper activity of that person in the world.

The seminal figure here is not Augustine, but Athanasius. In his Orations against the Arians, he argues that the Word was "in the beginning" with the Father and that "He is afterwards sent" in the economy for the

---

6. David M. Gwynn, *The Eusebians: The Polemic of Athanasius of Alexandria and the Construction of the "Arian Controversy"* (Oxford: Oxford University Press, 2007), 64; Rowan Williams, *Arius: Heresy and Tradition*, rev. ed. (Grand Rapids, MI: William B. Eerdmans, 2001), 58–59.

7. G. C. Hansen and E. Klostermann, *Eusebius Werke, Band 4: Gegen Marcell. Über die kirchliche Theologie. Die Fragmente Marcells*, Die griechischen christlichen Schriftsteller 14, 2nd ed. (Berlin: Akademie Verlag, 1972). For the English translation, see Glen L. Thompson, "Fragments of a Letter of Eusebius of Caesarea to Euphration of Balanea," Fourth-Century Christianity, accessed January 20, 2018, http://www.fourthcentury.com/index.php/urkunde-3/.

restoration of creation.[8] Reflection on the divine missions is central to this work of Athanasius. What is more, in both his first Oration against the Arians and in his first Letter to Serapion, Athanasius speaks expressly of the mission of the Holy Spirit in time, sent by Christ for the sanctification of the human race.[9]

It has likewise been documented that Augustine was familiar with at least a portion of Athanasius's Orations against the Arians precisely on this question of the divine missions, leading us to wonder whether Augustine's reflections on the divine missions in his *De Trinitate* transmit to the Latin West a pro-Nicene Athanasian influence regarding the divine missions—an influence felt also in the thought of St. Thomas.[10]

Let us return to Aquinas. When St. Thomas situates the Transfiguration in the whole of the dispensation of salvation, he identifies it as one of the most significant moments in Christ's earthly life because it is a manifestation not only of the truth of the visible mission of the Son—that the true identity of Jesus is the incarnate Son of the Father—but also because, at the Transfiguration, the Holy Spirit is sent visibly to Christ as man. Of course, Aquinas insists that Christ as man possessed the fullness of the Holy Spirit from the first moment of his conception, but this was an invisible mission. The *visible* sending of the Spirit upon Christ occurred by means of signs visible to his disciples in order to manifest what Jesus already possessed.

What is unique in Aquinas is not the view that the Holy Spirit is visibly sent to Christ—both Augustine (and Athanasius before him)[11] had already accounted for such a visible mission with the dove descending on Jesus at his baptism. But they speak of only one such visible mission. Aquinas adds that there is a second visible mission of the Spirit to Christ at the Transfiguration—this view is, as best as I can discover, first articulated by St. Thomas and is an original contribution of his thought.[12]

8. Athanasius, *Orations against the Arians* II.51, as published in John Henry Newman and Archibald Robertson, trans., *Nicene and Post-Nicene Fathers*, vol. 4, 2nd ed. (Peabody, MA: Hendrickson, 1994).

9. Athanasius, *Orations against the Arians* I.46–47; First Letter to Serapion, nos. 19–20, 23–24, 30, 33.

10. Jean-Louis Maier, *Les missions divines selon saint Augustin* (Fribourg: Editions Universitaires Fribourg Suisse, 1960), 35–37.

11. Athanasius, *Orations against the Arians* I.46–47. Although Athanasius does not use the term "divine mission" or "visible mission," he expressly identifies the descent of the Holy Spirit in visible form on Jesus at the Baptism, and also the giving of the Holy Spirit by Christ to the Apostles as he breathed on them on the evening of the Resurrection.

12. If I have been able to find any precedent for Aquinas's view, however, it is a rather oblique statement in John Damascene's Homily on the Transfiguration—a text Aquinas

This second visible mission of the Spirit plays an important role in Aquinas's overarching account of the dispensation of salvation, because it means that there is a total of four visible missions of the Holy Spirit: two to Christ (at the baptism of Christ and at the Transfiguration), and two to the Apostles (in Christ's breath in the upper room on the evening of Easter Sunday, and at Pentecost). These four visible missions manifest the genealogy of the propagation of grace, given first to Christ's humanity, then handed on from him to the Apostles, and which comes down to us in the sacraments and teaching of the Church. Aquinas explains this at length and repeatedly throughout his career: it is found in his *Sentences* commentary, in the *Summa Theologiae*, and in his *Commentary on John*, from which the following quotation is taken:

> It should be noted that the Holy Spirit was sent upon Christ first in the appearance of a dove at [his] baptism (Jn 3:5), and in the appearance of a cloud at the transfiguration (Mt 17:5). The reason for this is that the grace of Christ, which is given through the Holy Spirit, was to be derived to us through the propagation of grace in the sacraments (and thus he descended at the baptism in the appearance of a dove, which is a fruitful animal), and through teaching (and thus he descended in a luminous cloud). Hence also Christ is there shown [to be] a teacher, so it says "Listen to him." But the Holy Spirit first descended on the Apostles in [Christ's] breath, to designate the propagation of grace in the sacraments, of which they were ministers. For this reason, he says: "Whose sins you will forgive, will be forgiven" (Jn 20:23), and "Go therefore and baptize them in the name of the Father, and of the Son, and of the Holy Spirit" (Mt 28:19). Second, [the Holy Spirit descended on the Apostles] in tongues of fire, to signify the propagation of grace through teaching. Thus, Acts 2:4 says that when they were filled with the Holy Spirit, they immediately began to speak.[13]

---

quotes in his discussion of the Transfiguration in the *Summa Theologiae*. Damascene does not say that the manifestation of the Holy Spirit by the luminous cloud was a visible mission to Christ, but he does draw a parallel between the Spirit's appearance in the form of a dove (at Christ's baptism) and the cloud as a sign of the Spirit's presence at the Transfiguration. Aquinas, of course, goes much further, even working out an elegant parallelism between the visible mission of the Spirit to Christ at the Transfiguration for the propagation of grace by teaching and the visible mission of the Spirit upon the Apostles at Pentecost, empowering them to preach to the nations.

13. *In Ioan.* c. 20, lect. 4 (no. 2539): "Notandum autem, quod super Christum Spiritus sanctus missus est primo quidem in columbae specie in baptismo, supra III (5), et in specie nubis in transfiguratione; Matth. XVII, 5. Cuius ratio est, quia gratia Christi, quae datur per Spiritum sanctum, derivanda erat ad nos per propagationem gratiae in sacramentis: et sic descendit in specie columbae in baptismo, quae est animal fecundum; et per doctrinam, et sic descendit in nube lucida. Unde et ibi ostenditur doctor; unde dicit: *Ipsum audite.* Super Apostolos autem

Just as Christ as man received two visible missions of the Holy Spirit—one manifesting him at his baptism as endowed with the Spirit to give grace through the sacraments, and the other, at his transfiguration, showing him as graced by the Spirit for the sake of teaching (this is why the Father's voice at the Transfiguration adds the injunction "Listen to him")—so also the Apostles receive from Christ two visible missions of the Spirit, which makes them qualified to be his ministers in this twofold path of the propagation of grace.

In the *Summa Theologiae*, St. Thomas emphasizes that these two pairs of visible missions of the Spirit play a special role in the foundation of the Church, which is to say, of the New Covenant itself.[14] They manifest not only in the presence of the divine persons according to a "personal" or "private" gift to individuals, but also in a "public" grace, brought about by Christ's life in the flesh and especially by his passion,[15] given for the good of the whole world. He writes: "It is not necessary that an invisible mission always be manifested by some visible exterior sign, but, as 1 Cor. 12 says, 'the manifestation of the Spirit' is given to someone 'for the good,' namely, of the Church."[16] Thomas continues: "therefore a visible mission of the Holy Spirit especially should be made to Christ and to the Apostles and to others of the first saints, in whom the Church was in a certain way founded."[17] Those who receive a visible mission of the Spirit—first Christ as man and then his Apostles—are thus "those through whom many graces are diffused, insofar as through them the Church was planted."[18]

---

primo descendit in flatu, ad designandam propagationem gratiae in sacramentis, cuius ipsi ministri erant; unde dicit *Quorum remiseritis peccata, remittuntur eis.* Matth. ult., 19: *Euntes ergo baptizate eos in nomine Patris et Filii et Spiritus sancti.* Secundo vero in igneis linguis ad significandam propagationem gratiae per doctrinam. Unde dicit Act. II, 4, quod postquam repleti sunt Spiritu sancto, statim coeperunt loqui." See also I *Sent.* d. 16, q. 1, a. 3; *ST* I, q. 43, a. 7, ad 6.

14. See Emery, "Missions invisibles et missions visibles," 64–66.

15. See *ST* III, q. 46, a. 3; q. 48, a. 1, ad 3: "[P]assio Christi habuit aliquem effectum quem non habuerunt praecedentia merita, non propter maiorem caritatem, sed propter genus operis, quod erat conveniens tali effectui." See also *Compendium Theologiae* I, c. 231; *Quodlibet* II, q. 1, a. 2. On this, see Jean-Pierre Torrell, *Le Christ en ses mystères: La vie et l'oeuvre de Jésus selon saint Thomas d'Aquin*, vol. 2 (Paris: Desclée, 1999), 292–95.

16. *ST* I, q. 43, a. 7, ad 6: "[N]on est de necessitate invisibilis missionis, ut semper manifestetur per aliquod signum visibile exterius: sed, sicut dicitur I *Cor.* 12, *manifestatio Spiritus datur alicui ad utilitatem*, scilicet Ecclesiae."

17. *ST* I, q. 43, a. 7, ad 6: "ideo specialiter debuit fieri missio visibilis Spiritus Sancti ad Christum et ad Apostolos, et ad aliquos primitivos Sanctos, in quibus quodammodo Ecclesia fundabatur."

18. I *Sent.* d. 16, q. 1, a. 2: "per eos plures gratia diffusa est, secundum quod per eos Ecclesia plantata est."

The Transfiguration, then, is a Trinitarian mystery, in Aquinas's view, principally because it manifests the Trinitarian shape of our salvation in Christ—and, more specifically, the role of *revelation* or *teaching* in that economy of salvation. On Mt. Tabor, Christ is manifested as the one who saves us through his revelatory teaching, and this saving revelation comes down to us through the Apostles' preaching after they receive the Spirit at Pentecost. What is more, elsewhere, Aquinas is clear that this is how the Son's teaching saves us—he sends the Spirit to the Church, so that as we receive his saving revelation through the Church's proclamation, and we receive the Spirit himself, sent by the Son, through whom we come to know the Father by the knowledge of faith.[19]

On this point, then, Aquinas is building on the insights of Athanasius, Augustine, and Damascene (whom he cites and sometimes quotes), with respect to the importance of the mission of the Holy Spirit to Christ as man, and again to the sending of the Holy Spirit from Christ to the world. But Aquinas is, to my knowledge, quite original in reading the Transfiguration as Trinitarian, and more specifically as a visible manifestation of how the Spirit empowers Christ as man to teach with divine authority—indeed, with the authority that originates in the Father who sends him—and a teaching that not only is a fundamental aspect of the Church's mission but also reflects the Trinitarian structure of the whole economy of salvation in Christ. To put it simply, we see at work here Aquinas's distinctive and powerful synthesis of Trinitarian theology and Christology.

From this overarching perspective of the Transfiguration as a visible mission, let us now turn to the features of the Transfiguration itself. Here again, we find Aquinas offering a reading that is derived from the Fathers, to which he adds his own original insights.

If one were to offer a broad-brush summary of the Greek Fathers on the Transfiguration, one might say they speak of it as a manifestation of the glory of Christ's divinity. Here, however, care is warranted, lest the shading given to the Transfiguration by the influential fourteenth-century Greek theologian Gregory Palamas color the reading of earlier Greek Fathers.[20] Palamas famously asserts that the traditional teaching of the Fathers is that, at the Transfiguration, the Apostles beheld not some created glory of Christ, but the ineffable, eternal, and immaterial divine light of Christ's divine nature, of the Godhead itself.

19. *In Ioan.* c. 17, lect. 6 (no. 2269).
20. See, e.g., Georges Habra, *La transfiguration selon les pères grecs* (Paris: Editions S.O.S., 1973).

[He] revealed this brightness not as a different light [than his divine nature], but as what he already had in an invisible way. He had the brightness of the divine nature, hidden beneath his flesh. So, then, that light is the light of the divinity, and it is uncreated.... [T]hat light was not perceptible light, nor did those who saw it simply see with the eyes of sense, but with eyes transformed by the power of the Holy Spirit.[21]

There are many other similar passages in Palamas, and the sense of them seems to be that this light is simply the uncreated light of Christ's divine nature. He sees the Transfiguration as a kind of direct unveiling of Christ's Godhead to the Apostles, not by means of a visible or sensible light that could be seen by their "eyes of sense," but rather in an entirely supernatural way (and thus their experience is an exemplar of the hesychast's mystical contemplation). Palamas's emphasis is decidedly on Christ's divinity, even to the point that he says that, in this light, Christ "became invisible to the Apostles' eyes because of an excess of brightness."[22] Consequently, he describes the light of the Transfiguration as "not perceptible,"[23] "ineffable,"[24] "indescribable,"[25] "immaterial light that has no evening, the light that is eternal and is not only beyond perception but even beyond the mind,"[26] "uncreated,"[27] "unchangeable,"[28] and "the light of the Godhead."[29] Palamas

---

21. Gregory Palamas, *Homily 34 on the Transfiguration*, as translated in *Light on the Mountain*, 363 (no. 13).

22. Palamas, *Homily 35*, in *Light on the Mountain*, 373 (no. 11). Palamas does suggest that Christ's body "possessed" this light. He says the "divine brilliance" was "common to the Godhead of the Word and to his flesh (376 [no. 16]). "[His] glory, naturally coming forth from his divinity and possessed in common by his body, was revealed on Thabor through the unity of his hypostasis. So it was also through this light that 'his face shone like the sun'" (*Homily 34*, 362 [no. 11]). His body on Mt. Tabor was "as a lamp," which, "instead of [shining with] light," was radiant with "the glory of the divinity" (365 [no. 15]).

Do these statements that mean that, at the Transfiguration, the body of Jesus manifested a creaturely participation in the uncreated light of his divine nature? If yes (Palamas's meaning is not entirely clear), then perhaps there is room to read Palamas in a way that tends to converge with Aquinas's account of Christ's human glory at the Transfiguration. Yet questions remain. Palamas denies that there was a sensible light shining from Christ's body. It is difficult to articulate how a body, as a body, could "be radiant" or "shining" with an incorporeal and immaterial light, so it is hard to know how to interpret his references to the transfigured glory of Christ's body precisely as a visible body.

23. Palamas, *Homily 34*, in *Light on the Mountain*, 363–64 (no. 13).

24. Palamas, *Homily 34*, in *Light on the Mountain*, 361 (no. 10).

25. Palamas, *Homily 34*, in *Light on the Mountain*, 361 (no. 10).

26. Palamas, *Homily 34*, in *Light on the Mountain*, 363 (no. 12).

27. Palamas, *Homily 34*, in *Light on the Mountain*, 363 (no. 12).

28. Palamas, *Homily 34*, in *Light on the Mountain*, 365 (no. 15).

29. Palamas, *Homily 34*, in *Light on the Mountain*, 365 (no. 15).

certainly thinks creatures can receive various degrees of participation in this light,[30] but the Transfiguration's light itself is simply the fullness of the divinity of Christ, "the manifestation of the divine,"[31] source of our reception of the divine light and of beatitude.[32]

Thus, for Palamas, the divine light of the Transfiguration becomes a key feature of the economy, and the heart of the mystical life. Brian Daley puts it thus: "The image of Christ ... now revealed to the disciples in the heavenly light that is personally proper to him ... becomes here a central symbol of the object of the hesychast's prayer and contemplation .... [as he]—like the three disciples on Mount Thabor—comes to glimpse the uncreated light that flows from the divine nature and embodies in perceptible form God's 'energies.'"[33]

A review of the exegesis of a range of prominent Greek Fathers on the Transfiguration shows, however, that the Greek Fathers are generally less forceful and direct on this point than Palamas, and considerably more diverse in their understanding of the light of Tabor.[34] For example, while St. Gregory of Nazianzus speaks rhetorically in praise of "light, the divinity that showed itself upon the mountain to the disciples, a little too strong for their eyesight,"[35] he also holds that Christ "radiate[s] in his form," thereby revealing the Godhead.[36] One might wonder whether Gregory principally intends to stress the revelation of Christ's divine identity by this brilliant light, rather than claiming—as Palamas insists— that the light itself is uncreated.

There is another line of interpretation in the Greek Fathers that con-

30. Palamas, *Homily 35*, in *Light on the Mountain*, 375–77 (nos. 15–16). See also *Homily 34*, in *Light on the Mountain*, 362 (no. 11): "the righteous, too ... becoming wholly divine light, as offspring of the divine light, they shall gaze on the one who outshines them in a divine and ineffable way."

31. Palamas, *Homily 34*, in *Light on the Mountain*, 375 (no. 13).

32. For example: "'Like the sun,' [Matthew] says, not that one should imagine that light as something perceptible—let us shun the mental blindness of those who cannot imagine anything higher than what appears to the senses—but that we might know that what the sun is to those who live by the senses and see through sense-perception, this Christ, as God, is for those who live by the Spirit and see in the Spirit, and for those in the image of God there is no need of any other light for seeing God.... What need is there, after all, for a second light for those who have the greatest light?" Palamas, *Homily 34*, in *Light on the Mountain*, 361 (no. 10).

33. Daley, *Light on the Mountain*, 353.

34. McGuckin, *Transfiguration of Christ*, 105.

35. Oration 40.6, in St. Gregory of Nazianzus, *Festal Orations*, trans. Nonna Verna Harrison (Crestwood, NY: St. Vladimir's Seminary Press, 2008), 102.

36. Gregory of Nazianzus, *De Moderatione in Disputando*, Orat. 32.18, as translated in McGuckin, *Transfiguration of Christ*, 171.

ceives the Transfiguration principally as a manifestation of the future glory of the Resurrection—that is, as a theophany revealing the mystery of the renewal of creation through Christ. Thus, John Chrysostom does not expressly identify the light on Mt. Tabor with the uncreated and immaterial light of Christ's divinity, as Palamas does; rather, he emphasizes that the disciples saw an anticipation of "the full radiance of the age to come. The splendour here was a condescension rather than a true manifestation of what it will be like."[37] And again, in Homily 56 on Matthew, he expressly compares Christ's transfigured glory with the future glory of Christ at the Second Coming, revealed by Jesus to strengthen the disciples for his coming passion: "Since [Jesus] has said a great deal about danger and death ... wishing to give assurance even to their sense of sight, and to reveal what that glory is in which he is going to come again ... he reveals the Kingdom to them visually."[38] But what is revealed there is not yet the full glory of his future coming: "[On the mountain,] to spare the disciples, he only revealed as much of his glory as they could bear; but he will come later on in the very glory of the Father."[39] Even the saints will radiate with the brightness of this glory on the last day, Chrysostom adds.[40]

Cyril of Alexandria later follows the same line as Chrysostom and, when one carefully reads his texts, is even more clear that he does not think of the light of the Transfiguration as the uncreated light of Christ's divine nature, but rather a visible light showing forth the glorification of Christ's body. He writes:

> It is my belief that his transfiguration did not happen by a laying aside of the human form of the body, but rather by certain luminous glory clothing him, which therefore changed the dishonourable character of the flesh into a far nobler appearance.... [I]n the time of the resurrection a kind of divine transformation will take place, a change in glory rather than a change in form, and then the body clothed in divine glory will be radiant ... And so we see that the transfiguration was an example of that glory that is to come, given to the disciples and revealed in a bodily way to fall under the scope of mortal eyes, even though they could not bear the immensity of the radiance.[41]

---

37. John Chrysostom, *Ad Theodorum Lapsum* 1.11, as translated in McGuckin, *Transfiguration of Christ*, 172.

38. John Chrysostom, *Homily 56 on Matthew* (no. 1), as translated in Daley, *Light on the Mountain*, 69–70. According to Daley, this homily likely dates to around 390 AD.

39. John Chrysostom, *Homily 56 on Matthew* (no. 4), 79.

40. John Chrysostom, *Homily 56 on Matthew* (no. 4), 80.

41. Cyril of Alexandria, *Commentary on Luke* 9.122, as translated in McGuckin, *Transfiguration of Christ*, 181.

For Cyril, then, we see a notable emphasis on the humanity of Christ, who is the Son in person in virtue of the hypostatic union. Like John Chrysostom, he holds that the light of the Transfiguration foreshadows Christ's resurrected glory, revealing the radiance that a divinized human nature will have at the Resurrection. There is, at the Transfiguration, a visible revelation takes place *through* Christ's human form.

Thomas Aquinas self-consciously stands in this same line of interpretation: in Aquinas, the light of the Transfiguration is not the splendor of Christ's divine nature—that remains invisible of itself. And Aquinas insists that the disciples did not see a "spiritual" or "imaginary" vision (e.g., it was not infused into their minds nor into their imaginations), but one that they beheld with their human eyes, which were dazzled by the brightness of Christ's radiance.[42] Consequently, he reads this as a miraculous revelation of *Christ's human glory*—or, more specifically, how his humanity is elevated unto God and made radiant *as a divinized human nature*, in virtue of the hypostatic union and the habitual grace that flows from it. In fact, we know that Aquinas was familiar with the texts of Chrysostom and Cyril quoted just above, because he quotes them, too, above all in his express treatments of the Transfiguration in his mature works. In his Matthew commentary, Aquinas extensively quotes and paraphrases Chrysostom, to the point that his text might be seen largely a commentary on Chrysostom's Homily 56.[43] And question 45 of the *Tertia Pars*, composed shortly after the Matthew commentary, seems to build on this same material.[44]

42. In his youthful *Sentences* commentary, Aquinas specifically insists that the brightness (*claritas*) of Christ's body was "true," not "imaginary," as one medieval gloss had suggested—it was real and was seen by the bodily eyes of the disciples, "a sensible *claritas* [splendor or brightness], truly existing in Christ's body, to show forth the splendor which he had promised to the saints after the future resurrection, when he said 'Then the just shall shine like the sun in the kingdom of their Father' (Mt 13:43)." III *Sent.* d. 16, q. 2, a. 1: "claritas illa fuit claritas sensibilis, secundum veritatem in corpore Christi existens, ad ostensionem claritatis quam promiserat in Sanctis post resurrectionem futuram, dicens: '*Fugebunt justi tamquam sol in regno patris eorum*,' Mat., XIII, 43." See also III *Sent.* d. 16, q. 2, a. 1, ad 4 (explaining how the eyes of the disciples would not be overpowered by the glory of Christ's body at the Transfiguration).

43. *In Matt.* c. 17, lect. 1, nos. 1418–30. See also *ST* III, q. 45, a. 3, ad 3–4. For Aquinas's quotation of Cyril's *Commentary on Luke*, see *Catena Aurea in Lucam* c. 9, lect. 6, and *ST* II-II, q. 189, a. 10, ad 2.

44. To be sure, this is not an unusual reading in the medieval West, and we do not know at what point Aquinas encountered the texts of Chrysostom and Cyril. In his youthful *Sentences* commentary, where he first takes this position, Aquinas does not cite those Fathers; his text seems rather to be reacting to opinions from a gloss, and he uses Bede as an authority

This aspect of Aquinas's account thus operates principally on a Christological axis: the splendor or *claritas* of Christ reveals both the truth of his human nature and also its unity with the divinity. But even here, there is an important Trinitarian note, thanks to Aquinas's theology of the divine missions, as we shall see.

In the *Summa Theologiae*, Aquinas explains the reason for this manifestation of Christ's human splendor: it has to do with strengthening his disciples for his coming journey to the Cross. This is the famous interpretation of Leo the Great, and his influence may well be in the background, even if St. Thomas did not know Leo's Sermon 51 directly (as seems to be the case—he never refers to it). But this is also the interpretation of John Chrysostom, whose homily on the Transfiguration is clearly a prominent source for Aquinas's exegesis here. Aquinas's rich text is worth quoting in full:

> Our Lord, after foretelling his passion to His disciples, exhorted them to follow [him] to his passion. But, if one is to go straight along the way, he must have some foreknowledge of the end, just as an archer will not shoot his arrow straight unless he first see the target he is to aim at.... And this is especially necessary when the way is hard and rough, and the journey difficult, but delightful the end. Now through his passion, Christ came to arrive at glory, not only of his soul, which He had from the first moment of his conception, but also of his body; according to Luke 24:26: "Was it not necessary for Christ to suffered these things, and so to enter into His glory?" He also leads those who follow in the footsteps of his passion to this [glory], as Acts 14:21 says: "Through many tribulations we must enter into the kingdom of God." And hence it was fitting that he should show His disciples the glory of His clarity (which is what it means for him to be transfigured), to which he will configure those who belong to him, as Philippians 3:21 says: "he will reform the body of our lowliness, configured to the body of His glory." Thus Bede says: "By His loving foresight He allowed them to taste for a short time the contemplation of eternal joy, so that they might bear persecution bravely."[45]

---

for this point; see III *Sent.* d. 16, q. 2, a. 2, obj. 1. Starting with his Matthew commentary (in roughly 1260), Aquinas begins to quote from the very texts of John Chrysostom and Cyril excerpted above, and especially Chrysostom.

45. *ST* III, q. 45, a. 1: "Dominus discipulos suos, praenuntiata sua passione, induxerat eos ad suae passionis sequelam. Oportet autem ad hoc quod aliquis directe procedat in via, quod finem aliqualiter praecognoscat: sicut sagittator non recte iaciet sagittam nisi prius signum prospexerit in quod iaciendum est. Unde et Thomas dixit, *Ioan.* 14: *Domine, nescimus quo vadis: et quomodo possumus viam scire?* Et hoc praecipue necessarium est quando via est difficilis et aspera, et iter laboriosum, finis vero iucundus. Christus autem per passionem ad hoc pervenit ut gloriam obtineret, non solum animae, quam habuit a principio suae conceptionis, sed etiam corporis: secundum illud *Luc.* 24.: *Haec oportuit Christum pati, et ita intrare in*

There are three notable elements in this text. First, Aquinas is explicating the *reason* for this extraordinary manifestation of Christ's glory, and so his focus is on Christ's *revelation* and *instruction* to his followers. They cannot be expected to "go along the way" of the Cross unless they know the ultimate destination: not suffering and death, but Christ's glorification—and ultimately their glorification as well. Second, that future glory of Christ will be in both soul and body—that is, of the whole of Christ's humanity. (His soul was always glorious, Aquinas avers, in part because he always enjoyed the beatific vision, but he merited the glorification of his body by his passion.) This is why it is so important for Thomas to insist that the *claritas* of the Transfiguration pertained to Christ's human body. Third, Christ brings his followers to the same kind of glory that they see at the Transfiguration—and he does this as they follow his footsteps on the way to the passion. The Christian life is a life of being configured to Christ in his passion, thus sharing in his exaltation.

A fourth principle hovers just in the background of this text: Christ's glorification at the Resurrection is the efficient and exemplar cause of our future glorification.[46] On this point, the influence of the Greek patristic tradition is clear, and especially Athanasius and Cyril as filtered through John Damascene, in the Greek patristic theology of how Christ's humanity operates as an instrument of his divinity, on which Aquinas especially relies on this point. But Pseudo-Dionysius is also an important influence on Aquinas's thinking on exemplar causality, and Aquinas quotes him elsewhere in speaking of the exemplar causality of Christ's resurrection.[47]

How is Christ's body glorified at the Transfiguration? Aquinas explains:

The splendor (*claritas*) that Christ assumed in the transfiguration was the splendor of glory with respect to its essence, but not with respect to its mode of being. For the splendor of a glorified body is derived from the splendor of its soul, as Augustine says. And likewise, the splendor of the body of Christ in the transfiguration was derived from his divinity, as Damascene says, and from the glory of his soul.[48]

---

gloriam suam. Ad quam etiam perducit eos qui vestigia suae passionis sequuntur: secundum illud Act. 14: *Per multas tribulationes oportet nos intrare in regnum caelorum.* Et ideo conveniens fuit ut discipulis suis gloriam suae claritatis ostenderet (quod est ipsum transfigurari), cui suos configurabit: secundum illud *Philipp.* 3: *Reformabit corpus humilitatis nostrae, configuratum corpori claritatis suae.* Unde Beda dicit, *super Marcum, Pia provisione factum est ut, contemplatione semper manentis gaudii ad breve tempus delibata, fortius adversa tolerarent.*"

46. *ST* III, q. 56, a. 1, ad 3.

47. See, e.g., *ST* III, q. 56, a. 1.

48. *ST* III, q. 45, a. 2: "claritas illa quam Christus in transfiguratione assumpsit, fuit

22

Note the principles of Aquinas's argument. He cites Augustine for the principle that a glorified body is glorious because of the splendor of its soul—and this point has a special resonance in Aquinas, holding as he does that the soul is the form and principle of life and unity of the body. He then cites John Damascene, on a point that seems to run in a different direction: that the splendor was indeed of Christ's body, but it was "derived from his divinity." This sounds closer to the view of Gregory of Nazianzus and seems to suggest the manifestation of Christ's divine nature through this light.

What is fascinating is that Aquinas cites these two authorities in immediate succession, and not as contrary positions but as if their harmonization were evident. He adds to Damascene's quotation, giving us an important indication of how he reads them together: the *claritas* "was derived from his divinity, as Damascene says, *and from the glory of his soul*." After explaining that, during Christ's earthly life, the glory of his soul did not normally overflow into his body "due to a certain divine dispensation, so that he would fulfill the mysteries of our redemption in a passible body,"[49] Aquinas returns to the synthesis of these two authorities:

Splendor was derived to the body of Christ in the transfiguration from the divinity and his soul, not in the mode of a quality immanent in and affecting his body in itself, but rather in the mode of a passing passion, like when the air is illuminated by the sun.[50]

Aquinas's point is threefold: first, the source of this bodily splendor is his divinity *and* his soul; second, it is really in his body and emanating from it; and third, it is not a stable dimension of his bodily existence during his earthly life but a miraculous and temporary one. Aquinas thinks that this is fully harmonious with Damascene's position—earlier in the *Tertia Pars*, he quotes Damascene on precisely this third point, which Thomas thinks is an aspect of the truth of the unity of natures in Christ. The beatitude of Christ's soul, he explains, was not derived to his body during his

---

claritas gloriae quantum ad essentiam, non tamen quantum ad modum essendi. Claritas enim corporis gloriosi derivatur ab animae claritate: sicut Augustinus dicit, in Epistola *ad Dioscorum*. Et similiter claritas corporis Christi in transfiguratione derivata est a divinitate ipsius, ut Damascenus dicit, et a gloria animae eius."

49. *ST* III, q. 45, a. 2: "ex quadam dispensatione divina factum est, ut in corpore passibili nostrae redemptionis expleret mysteria."

50. *ST* III, q. 45, a. 2: "Sed ad corpus Christi in transfiguratione derivata est claritas a divinitate et anima eius, non per modum qualitatis immanentis et afficiens ipsum corpus: sed magis per modum passionis transeuntis, sicut cum aer illuminatur a sole."

earthly life (aside from the Transfiguration) because, "as Damascene says, the good pleasure of the divine will permitted his flesh to suffer and to do what was proper to it."[51] This is a key aspect of the Incarnation for Aquinas, and a core Chalcedonian insight that gives a special poignancy to the momentary revelation of glory in the Transfiguration: Christ has a true human nature, and it is not yet glorified during his earthly sojourn even though his soul was perfectly united to God. His flesh really does what is proper to flesh, and his divinity does what is proper to the divinity. The reason is soteriological, and Aquinas says it is from the Church Fathers:

The infirmity assumed by Christ did not impede the end of the incarnation, but promoted it to the greatest degree ... And although through these infirmities his divinity was hidden, yet his humanity was manifested, which is the way of coming to the divinity ... Indeed, the ancient Fathers desired in Christ not some bodily strength, but rather spiritual strength, through which he vanquished the devil and healed human infirmity.[52]

Yet we should not overlook the innovation that Aquinas has added to Damascene's view. The glory of the Transfiguration is not only from his divinity, but also "from the divinity *and his soul.*" What does this mean? Aquinas's explanation is fascinating and especially important for our theme—in a certain sense, here we are at the crux of the two axes, Trinitarian and Christological, of his account. Or, better, we discover that they are different dimensions of the same mystery, which is at once Trinitarian and Christological, or even a mystery of Trinitarian Christology. Listen to how he explains it in his parallel account of the Transfiguration in his *Commentary on Matthew*:

It says: "and his face shone like the sun." Here he revealed future glory, where bodies will be bright and gleaming (*clara et splendentia*). And this *claritas* was not from the essence, but from the interior *claritas* of a soul filled with charity.... Whence there was a certain refulgence in the body.[53]

---

51. *ST* III, q. 14, a. 1, ad 2: "secundum illud quod dicit Damascenus, quod *beneplacito divinae voluntatis permittebatur carni pati et operari quae propria.*"

52. *ST* III, q. 14, a. 1, ad 4: "[I]nfirmitas assumpta a Christo non impedivit finem incarnationis, sed maxime promovit ... Et quamvis per huiusmodi infirmitates absconderetur eius divinitas, manifestabatur tamen humanitas, quae est via ad divinitatem perveniendi ... Desiderabant autem antiqui Patres in Christo, non quidem fortitudinem corporalem, sed spiritualem, per quam et diabolum vicit et humanam infirmitatem sanavit."

53. *In Matt.* c. 17, lect. 1 (no. 1424): "Dicit ergo *Et resplenduit facies eius sicut sol.* Hic futuram gloriam revelavit, ubi erunt corpora clara et splendentia. Et haec claritas non erat ab essentia, sed ex claritate interioris animae plenae caritate ... Unde erat quaedam refulgentia in corpore."

The clarity of Christ's body was not "from the essence" or nature of Christ's humanity. Aquinas holds that Christ's humanity was not changed in a direct way by the union with the divinity; his human nature remains what it is, with the characteristics proper to it. In fact, this is one reason why Christ's habitual grace is such an important dimension of Aquinas's Christology. According to Aquinas—and this is a point often misunderstood—the hypostatic union of itself does *not* directly qualify or modify Christ's humanity—it does not of itself directly elevate and empower it to do the things that he must do as savior of the world. It only does so *indirectly*—namely, through Christ's habitual grace, which is a distinct and subordinate principle proportioned to and at work in Christ's humanity. Christ's habitual grace is uniquely full, and it flows into his humanity as a necessary consequence of the hypostatic union, somewhat like a proper accident. But that grace is really and formally distinct from the grace that this humanity be united to the person of the Son without any preceding merits, which is the grace of union. In contrast, Christ's habitual grace involves the divinization of his human nature in a human way, by participation.[54]

So St. Thomas is claiming that Christ's *claritas* at the Transfiguration came from his divinity *through* the glory of his soul—and he specifies: "this *claritas* was ... from the interior *claritas* of a soul filled with charity." Charity, of course, is the heart of habitual or sanctifying grace. Even more significantly, it is a capital truth of Aquinas's theology that charity is the created effect according to which the Holy Spirit dwells in the soul in person, and that the first and principal cause of charity in the soul is in the personal presence of the Spirit. When Thomas says that Christ's radiant splendor at the Transfiguration comes was "from his divinity and his soul" and was a splendor "from the interior splendor of a soul filled with charity," he is in fact saying that the splendor radiating from Christ's body at the Transfiguration was *the effect of the Holy Spirit* indwelling in Christ as man.

This is a point of profound importance, and it brings us back to why Aquinas calls the Transfiguration a visible mission of the Holy Spirit to Christ. The Holy Spirit is manifested to the Apostles by the visible sign of the luminous cloud. But what is that cloud signifying? Not simply the general presence of the Holy Spirit, but the Spirit's presence *in Christ's humanity*. And at the same time, Christ's own humanity radiates with

---

54. *In Ioan.* c. 3, lect. 6 (no. 544).

splendor, which is the effect in Christ's human soul, and thence in his human body, of the Spirit's indwelling.

At the same time, Aquinas understands this mission of the Holy Spirit to Christ as man as entailed by the hypostatic union. Because Christ is the Son of God in person, when he is sent as man into the world, he comes breathing forth Love to his own sacred humanity. It is inconceivable to Aquinas that you could have a mission of the Son without an accompanying mission of the Holy Spirit, just as it is inconceivable that the consubstantial divine persons be separated from one another.

At this point, we can now see the full extent to which the Transfiguration is a mystery at once Trinitarian and Christological in Aquinas. It presupposes the visible mission of the Son sent by the Father as man, and it manifests the sending of the Holy Spirit to Christ's humanity. And at the same time, Christ's body is radiant with splendor first (though indirectly) because, as Damascene says, it is united to the divinity; and second (and directly) because it is filled with the interior splendor of charity, the effect in Jesus of the Holy Spirit's presence.

How does St. Thomas's view compare to Palamas's account of the Transfiguration? On the one hand, Aquinas is clear that the three disciples saw a sensible light that emanated from Christ's body, which was miraculously manifested to their bodily eyes as a glorified human body. That would seem in direct tension with Palamas's view that the disciples did not see a sensible light, but rather "saw" the ineffable, incorporeal, and uncreated light of Christ's divine nature. Yet perhaps there is more common ground here than might appear at first glance. Aquinas does think that the ultimate root and source of this human glory at the Transfiguration is Christ's divinity, which was the true source of the splendor on Mt. Tabor. The perfect light of glory—the light by which Christ has the beatifying vision of the divine essence in the highest part of his mind at every moment of his life—caused the glory of his divinity to penetrate his soul and to overflow into his body, so that it became radiant—a kind of lamp of divine glory. In fact, in a different context, Aquinas cites John Chrysostom while commenting on John 1:14 ("And the Word became flesh and dwelt among us, full of grace and truth; we have beheld his glory, glory as of the only Son from the Father") to make the point that the Apostle John saw "the divine light" as if shining in the "cloud" of Christ's flesh.

It is as if to say: The incarnation of the Word not only conferred on us the benefit of being made sons of God, but also that we would see [his] glory. For weak and infirm eyes are not able to see the sun's light, but they are able to see it when it shines in a cloud or on some opaque body. Now before the incarnation of the Word, human minds were impotent to see the divine light in itself, the light which enlightens every rational nature. And so, in order that it might be more easily perceived and contemplated by us, he covered it with the cloud of our flesh.[55]

Thomas doesn't stop there. He then cites Augustine to make a point with a striking affinity to Palamas (and also to Origen):[56]

The spiritual eyes of men not only were naturally deficient for the contemplation of the divine light, but also were such from the defect of sin ... Thus, that the very divine light could be seen by us, he healed the eyes of men, making from his flesh an eye-salve of his flesh, so that with the salve of his flesh the Word might heal our eyes, corrupted by the concupiscence of the flesh.... Moses and the other prophets saw in enigmas and figures the glory of the Word that was to be manifested to the world at the end of their times ... But the apostles saw the very *claritas* of the Word through his bodily presence. "All of us, gazing on the Lord's glory [with unveiled faces, are being transformed from glory to glory into his very image]" (2 Cor 3:18). And "blessed are the eyes that see what you see. For many kings and prophets longed to see what you see, and did not see it" (Lk 10:23).[57]

In this text, Aquinas may not have in mind the Apostles' sight of the transfigured Christ (though he does mention it a few paragraphs later); he may be making a more general point about how, through the visible human nature of Christ, the spiritual eyes of fallen human beings were healed and elevated so as to be able to rise to the contemplation of the

---

55. *In Ioan.* c. 1, lect. 8 (no. 181): "Quasi dicat: Non solum hoc beneficium collatum est nobis per incarnationem Verbi, scilicet quod efficiamur filii Dei, sed etiam quod videamus gloriam. Oculi enim debiles et infirmi lucem solis non possunt videre; sed tunc eam videre possunt, cum in nube vel in aliquo corpore opaco resplendet. Ante incarnationem enim Verbi mentes humanae erant invalidae ad videndum in seipsa lucem divinam, quae illuminat omnem rationalem naturam; et ideo ut a nobis facilius cerni contemplarique posset nube nostrae carnis se texit."

56. Cf. Origen, *Commentary on Matthew* 12.36–43, in *Light on the Mountain*, 53–66.

57. *In Ioan.* c. 1, lect. 8 (nos. 182–3): "Spirituales enim oculi hominum non solum naturaliter deficiebant a contemplatione divinae lucis, sed etiam ex defectu peccati ... Ut ergo ipsa divina lux posset a nobis videri, sanavit oculos hominum, faciens de carne sua salutare collirium, ut sic oculos ex concupiscentia carnis corruptos Verbum collirio suae carnis curaret ... Moyses enim et alii Prophetae Verbi gloriam manifestandam mundo in fine temporum speculabantur, in aenigmatibus et figuris; ... Apostoli autem ipsam Verbi claritatem per praesentiam corporalem viderunt. II Cor. III, v. 18: *Nos autem revelata facie* etc.; et Lc. c. X, 23: *Beati oculi qui vident quae vos videtis. Multi enim reges et prophetae voluerunt videre quae vos videtis et non viderunt.*"

divine light. He also might have in mind our future beholding of the glorified Christ, as the quotation of 2 Corinthians might suggest. In any case, it is clear is that, for Aquinas, the splendor of the Word is mediated to the disciples *through* the flesh of Christ, just as, more generally, Aquinas argues that the Incarnation brings us through visible realities to the invisible mysteries of God.[58] This is not simply the same position as Palamas on the manifestation of the divine nature of Christ, but perhaps Aquinas might be closer to Palamas than is sometimes thought, inasmuch as he teaches that the Incarnation manifests the divine light of the Word to the minds of believers.

There is a final text in Aquinas on the Transfiguration that I cannot fail to mention, because it connects this Trinitarian-Christological revelation to our filial adoption and thus our return to the Trinity according to the pattern of the Trinitarian processions—a central feature of Aquinas's articulation of the dispensation of salvation as a whole.

Aquinas recapitulates and summarizes all this in his concluding article in the *Summa Theologiae* on the Transfiguration. That mysterious event manifests our future conformity in glory to the natural Son of God, "when we will be like him because we shall see him as he is" (Jn 3:2).[59] This is why the Father's voice is not only heard at Christ's baptism, which instituted the sacrament by which we receive what Thomas calls "the imperfect conformity" to the Son "of the grace of a wayfarer,"[60] but also resounded at the Transfiguration, which foreshadowed

the splendor of [our] future glory, and so ... it was fitting in the transfiguration that the Father's testimony manifest the natural filiation of Christ, because he alone, together with the Son and the Holy Spirit, is perfectly conscious of [the Son's] perfect generation.[61]

He continues:

in the transfiguration, which is the sacrament of our second regeneration [namely, not by grace in this life but by glory], the whole Trinity appeared, the Father in the voice, the Son in the man, and the Holy Spirit in the bright cloud, because

---

58. *ST* III, q. 1, a. 1.

59. *ST* III, q. 45, a. 4. Aquinas himself quotes Jn 3:2 on this point.

60. *ST* III, q. 45, a. 4.

61. *ST* III, q. 45, a. 4: "in transfiguratione autem praemonstrata est claritas futurae gloriae, ideo ... in transfiguratione conveniens fuit manifestare naturalem Christi filiationem testimonio Patris: quia solus est perfecte conscius illius perfectae generationis, simul cum Filio et Spiritu Sancto."

... in the resurrection, the whole Trinity will give to his elect the splendor of glory and rest from every evil, which is designated by the luminous cloud.[62]

We are saved by—indeed, glorified by—the Trinity as we are conformed by the Holy Spirit to the natural sonship of Christ.

In elaborating his teaching on the Transfiguration, I hope to have provided at least a glimpse of how Aquinas draws from and builds on the Greek Fathers in a way that is both quite traditional but also produces a synthesis that is distinctive. In the end, it produces an echo of Aquinas's beautiful teaching that the divine missions in time follow the order of the eternal processions in God, and that our return to God likewise is configured to this pattern—a pattern that operates on both a Trinitarian and a Christological axis. Thus the Father sends the Son as man, and the Father and Son send the Holy Spirit to Christ's humanity. Empowered by the Spirit, the incarnate Word then wins our salvation by what he does and suffers, and after his glorious resurrection, he pours out the Holy Spirit in full upon the Apostles and indeed upon the world. As we receive that Spirit, we are configured to Christ the natural Son, and thus made adopted sons and daughters of the Father—and so we will shine, we firmly hope, with a glory like what Christ revealed at his transfiguration.

---

62. *ST* III, q. 45, a. 4, ad 2: "ita etiam in transfiguratione, quae est sacramentum secundae regenerationis, tota Trinitas apparuit, Pater in voce, Filius in homine, Spiritus Sanctus in nube clara; quia ... in resurrectione dabit electis suis claritatem gloriae et refrigerium ab omni malo, quae designantur in nube lucida."

2

Aquinas's Reception of Origen

A Preliminary Study

JÖRGEN VIJGEN

Introduction: Context, Challenges, and Methodology

Origen Adamantius of Alexandria (ca. 185/86 to ca. 253/54) is undoubtedly one of the principal Greek interlocutors of St. Thomas and the only pre-Nicean Greek Christian writer to whom he devotes considerable attention. In fact, the *Corpus Thomisticum* contains 1,093 explicit references to Origen. This places him in third place after John Chrysostom (347–407) and Pseudo-Dionysius, but before John Damascene (ca. 675/76–749) and on equal par with the Latin Father Ambrosius of Milan (ca. 340–97), whom St. Thomas mentions 1,186 times.

Although these numbers need to be critically examined,[1] their

---

1. A comprehensive examination must await the critical edition. A few examples may suffice. Eight references in his *Commentary on John* derive from John Scotus Eriugena and in particular from his homily *Vox spiritualis aquilae.* See Carmelo G. Conticello, "San Tommaso ed i Padri: La 'Catena aurea super Ioannem,'" *Archives d'Histoire Doctrinale et Littéraire du Moyen Âge* 57 (1990): 31–92, here 72. Thomas seems to be aware of the uncertainty of its authorship (*In Ioh.* 1, l. 2, no. 86: "In quadam autem homilia quae incipit, vox spiritualis aquilae, et attribuitur Origeni"). On several occasions, he attributes the phrase "Deus est pronior ad miserendum quam ad puniendum" to the Glossa ordinaria on Jeremiah, but this actually stems from Origen's Homily I on Jeremiah, no. 1 (PG 13, 255A; SC 232, 197). In the *Scriptum*, in the context of refuting the idea that the accomplishment of Christ's conception should be attributed to the Father, Aquinas attributes to Origen the saying "sicut generatio filii aeterna est a patre sine matre, ita generatio ejus temporalis est a matre sine patre" (*In III*

30

chronological division in the entire *Corpus Thomisticum* already indicates two things. First, Origen is continuously present in Thomas's writings, with a marked increase in his writings after 1261–62, when he started working, at the request of Pope Urban IV, on his *Catena Aurea* on the four Gospels. Second, Origen is present not only in writings that typically result from the *Magister in Sacra Pagina*'s threefold task of *lectio*, *disputatio*, and *predicatio* but also in pastoral and occasional writings and writings that are the result of Thomas's own initiative.

Contemporary Thomist scholarship has contributed considerably in establishing, both historically and in the context of what has been called "Ressourcement Thomism," Thomas's indebtedness to the Church Fathers in general and the Greek Fathers in particular.[2] Marcus Plested has even suggested that one "can go so far as to characterize his entire theology as being *ad mentem patrum*."[3] Almost simultaneously with Plested's "new image of Thomas" as a theologian deeply steeped in his patristic sources, some of the most prominent twentieth-century theologians like Henri de Lubac, Jean Daniélou, and Hans Urs von Balthasar, often associated with the *nouvelle théologie*, took part in the "rediscovery" of Origen in the twentieth century.[4] Henri de Lubac's classic *Exegèse Médiévale*, published in four volumes between 1959 and 1964, and containing a still valuable and detailed account of the transmission of Origen's work in the Latin West,[5]

Sent., d. 4, q. 1, a. 1, qc. 2, arg. 3, ed. Moos, 157). This is in fact a saying by Augustine in his *Sermo* 189.IV.4 (PL 38, 1006); see also *Sermo* 196.I.1 (PL 38, 1016). Aquinas never uses this phrase in his later writings.

2. For a good introduction on Thomas's reception of the Church Fathers, see Leo Elders, "Thomas Aquinas and the Fathers of the Church," in *Theological Innovation and the Shaping of Tradition: The Reception of the Church Fathers in the West from the Carolingians to the Maurists*, ed. Irena Backus (Leiden: Brill, 1996), 337–66.

3. Marcus Plested, *Orthodox Readings of Aquinas* (Oxford: Oxford University Press, 2012), 20. The entire first chapter of his book (pp. 9–28) gives an excellent *status quaestionis*. See also Gilles Emery, "Saint Thomas d'Aquin et l'Orient chrétien," *Nova et Vetera* 74, no. 4 (1999): 19–36.

4. See Monique Alexandre, "La redécouverte d'Origène au XX siècle," in *Les Peres de l'Èglise dans le monde d'aujourd'hui*, ed. Cristian Badilita and Charles Kannengiesser (Paris: Beauchesne, 2006), 54–94. Among the reasons for this rediscovery of Origen, Alexandre mentions, at least in the case of Daniélou, the *dénonciation de la sclérose neo-thomiste* but also the *hégémonie grandissante de la méthode historico-critique* (60). Löser has argued that von Balthasar tried to achieve a *Rehabilitierung* of Origen and "Rekatholisierung des Origenesbildes." See Werner Löser, *Im Geiste des Origenes: Hans Urs von Balthasar als Interpret der Theologie der Kirchenväter* (Frankfurt: Josef Knecht Verlag, 1976), 83–99.

5. Henri de Lubac, "The Latin Origen," in *Medieval Exegesis*, vol. 1, trans. by M. Sebanc (Grand Rapids, MI: William B. Eerdmans, 1998), chap. 4, 161–224.

originated from notes collected when writing an earlier book on Origen's understanding of Scripture and his exegetical methods.[6]

A comprehensive account of Thomas's knowledge and use of and his indebtedness to Origen, however, faces a number of difficulties. A first difficulty arises from the lack of a critical edition of many of Thomas's works, which makes the identification of his sources a difficult task. Once these sources have been identified, however, a question arises: To what extent did Thomas have a direct access to Origen's writings? It seems, for instance, that two of the most important sources for Thomas's knowledge of Origen are Jerome's *Epistula* 124 to Avitus[7] and Augustine's *De Civitate Dei*, 11.23 and 21.17.[8] And even if he had such a direct access, one cannot infer that he had access to the entire work as such, given the extensive use of *florilegia* and *catenae*[9] as well as the custom at the time to commission, for practical and financial reasons, partial translations of Greek texts rather than entire works. A third difficulty that arises stems from one of the characteristic features of Origen's theological enterprise. One can find numerous instances where he propounds an interpretation while hoping that someone else might provide a better solution in the future. He even urges his audience not to hesitate to adopt a better solution once they come across one.[10] Expressions such as "to the extent we understood this"[11] or his admission that "we make these comments while somehow in private"[12] because other interpretations (ἐκδοχαί) are possible, or his admission that what he offers is not a "definitive resolution,"[13] occur frequently throughout his writings. In fact, with regard to his most contro-

6. Henri de Lubac, *Histoire et esprit: L'intelligence de l'écriture d'après Origène* (Paris: Aubier Montaigne, 1950).

7. PL 22, 1059A–1072B.

8. CCSL 48, 341–43, and 783–85.

9. See Charles Kannengieser, *Handbook of Patristic Exegesis* (Leiden: Brill, 2006), Part B, chap. 10, XI: "*Catenae*: 'Chains' of Biblical Interpretation," 978–87; and H. A. G. Houghton, ed., *Commentaries, Catenae, and Biblical Tradition: Papers from the Ninth Birmingham Colloquium on the Textual Criticism of the New Testament in Conjunction with the COMPAUL Project* (Piscataway, NJ: Gorgias Press, 2016).

10. Origenes, *Peri Archon* II, 6, 7: "Si quis sane melius aliquid poterit invenire, et evidentioribus de Scripturis sanctis assertionibus confirmare quae dicit, illa potius quam haec recipiantur." In what follows, I use the Latin-German edition: Origenes, *Vier Bücher von den Prinzipien*, 2nd ed., ed. Herwig Görgemanns and Heinrich Karpp (Darmstadt: Wissenschaftlichen Buchgesellschaft, 1985).

11. Origenes, *Comm. Matt.* 15, 37 (GCS 40, Origenes Werke 10, 460): ὡς ἐχωρήσαμεν.

12. Origenes, *Comm. Joh.* X, 46 (SC 157, 412; FOCT 80, 266).

13. *Comm. Matt.* 13, 30 (GCS 40/10, 266).

versial positions regarding eschatology, he explicitly states that they are offered in the style of a disputation rather than of strict definition.[14] This distinction between what he calls speaking *dogmatikos* and speaking *gymnastikos*—that is, by way of an exercise of the mind[15]—was recognized by his early defenders such as Pamphilius[16] as well as Athanasius[17] and the Cappadocians.[18] For this reason, some contemporary scholars go so far as to deny that Origen is a systematic theologian and prefer to call the theology of our Alexandrian gymnast a *théologie en recherche*[19] or "experimental theology."[20] In an age of *catenae* and partial translations, this feature of Origen's theology poses a difficulty in determining the correctness of a reader's interpretation. A further difficulty is related to the complex transmission and translation of Origen's writings into the Latin West. Not only is this transmission partial, but also the trustworthiness of the translations, particularly in the case of Rufinus's translations, have been the object of fierce discussions. By his own admission in the preface of his translation of *Peri Archon*, he employed techniques that are, according to contemporary standards, questionable. Not only does he sometimes abbreviate the text or give a translation *ad sensum*, but he also, because he thought Origen's critics had tampered with the Greek text, suppresses contradictory elements, attempts to clarify Origen's thought where he finds it obscure, and tries to restore Origen's authentic thought from other texts of Origen.[21] A final difficulty is related to the controversial nature of Origen's writings. The so-called First Origenist Controversy toward the end of the fourth century and the Second Origenist Controversy in the middle of the sixth century took issue with some of Origen's posi-

---

14. *Peri Archon* I, 6, 1: "Quae quidem a nobis etiam cum magno metu et cautela dicuntur, discutientibus magis et pertractantibus quam pro certo ac definitio statuentibus."

15. *Comm. Matt.* 15, 33 (GCS 40/10, 448); see also 14, 12 (GCS 40/10, 305)

16. Pamphilius, *Apologia pro Origene*, Praefatio (PL 17, 543C): "quae cum exponit, frequenter addere solet et profiteri se non haec quasi definitiva pronuntiare sententia, nec statuto dogmate terminare, sed inquirere pro viribus."

17. Athanasius, *De Decretis Nicaenae Synodis* 27.1 (PG 25, 466B).

18. See Panayiotis Tzamalikos, *Origen: Philosophy of History and Eschatology* (Leiden: Brill, 2007), 22.

19. Henri Crouzel, *Origène* (Paris: Lethielleux, 1985), 216–33.

20. Freddy Ledegang, *Mysterium Ecclesiae: Images of the Church and Its Members in Origen* (Leuven: Peeters, 2001), 5.

21. *Peri Archon*, Praef. I, 3; for more on Rufinus's method of translation, see Ronald E. Heine's introduction to Origen, *Homilies on Genesis and Exodus*, Fathers of the Church 71 (Washington, DC: Catholic University of America Press, 1981), 27–39.

tions, especially in the areas of protology and eschatology, resulting in a series of anathemas against Origen, first by Emperor Justinianus I in 543 and subsequently by the Second Council of Constantinople in 553.[22] For many scholastic authors, these condemnations became the interpretative lens through which they received Origen's thought.

The approximately 1,100 explicit references to Origen in Thomas's writings undoubtedly cause his readers to notice another interpretative lens through which Thomas receives Origen's thought. Thomas seems to consider Origen both a formidable opponent as a theologian as well as a trusted interlocutor in exegetical matters. This nuanced relation to Origen comes to the fore when Thomas vehemently rejects the errors he ascribes to Origen and at the same time refers to him as a *doctor fidei, doctor ecclesiae,* and *doctor sanctus.* Already in his Letter to Tranquillinus, written in 396 or 397, Jerome advised to follow 1 Thessalonians 5:21 ("Prove all things: hold fast that which is good") and select what is good and avoid what is bad in his writings. "For while the ability of his teaching must not lead us to embrace his wrong opinions, the wrongness of his opinions should not cause us altogether to reject the useful commentaries which he has published on the holy scriptures."[23] In his *Dialogues,* Sulpicius Severus (ca. 363 to ca. 425) writes about Origen in the context of the First Origenist Controversy: "I am amazed that one and the same man could differ so much from himself. In the part that is acceptable he has no equal since the Apostles, but in that which has justly been censured no one can be found who has made more disgraceful errors (*deformius ... errasse*) shown to have erred more egregiously."[24] This remark by Sulpicius resembles the oft-employed phrase "Ubi bene dixit, nemo melius; ubi male, nemo peius." "When Origen spoke well, no one has ever said it better, when he spoke badly, no one has ever spoken worse." After referring to Jerome's advice to Tranquillinus and quoting this adagium, Cassiodorus (c. 485 to c. 585) writes: "We must read him cautiously and judiciously to draw the healthful juices from him while avoiding the poisons of his perverted faith which are dangerous to our way of life. The comment Vergil made while he was reading Ennius[25] is applicable also to Origen. When

---

22. Elizabeth A. Clark, *The Origenist Controversy: The Cultural Construction of an Early Christian Debate* (Princeton, NJ: Princeton University Press, 1992). For the text of these lists, see the edition quoted at 811n10, nos. 14–31.

23. Hieronymus, *Epist.* 51 (PL 22, 606).

24. Sulpicius Severus, *Dialogi* 1, 6 (PL 20, 188B; FCOT 7, 169).

25. Virgil is referring to the epic poem *Annales* by Quintus Ennius (ca. 239 to ca. 169 BC).

asked by someone what he was doing Vergil replied, 'I am looking for gold in a dung-heap (*aurum in stercore quaero*).'"[26]

To what extent do these and other evaluations of Origen's thought, and in particular the juxtaposition of Origen the theologian and Origen the exegete, apply to Aquinas's reception of Origen as well? To answer this question, and given the difficulties listed above, a preliminary analysis of Aquinas's explicit references to Origen is a necessary and much needed first step. In this essay, I do this in two ways. First, I order and analyze systematically the topics in which Aquinas mentions and uses Origen. As a framework for such ordering, I have chosen the order of the various treatises as they can be found in the *Summa Theologiae*. Second, I examine the function of Origen's contribution to Aquinas's scriptural exegesis, focusing on Aquinas's commentaries on the Gospels of John and Matthew and the Psalms.

A Systematic Overview and Analysis

The Use of Philosophy

In his commentary on Boethius's *De Trinitate*, St. Thomas discusses the role of philosophy as a tool for doing theology (*sacra doctrina*). As is well known, he distinguishes between a threefold use of philosophy: to demonstrate the preambles of faith, to enable a clearer understanding of the mysteries of faith, and to answer objections to the faith. The legitimacy of these uses is based on the guiding principles that grace does not destroy but perfects nature and that God is the author of both natural and supernatural truths, and hence a conflict between these truths is a priori impossible. It is obvious that this view is far removed from the position of, for instance, Tertullian, who thought there is a clandestine complicity between heresy and philosophy insofar as a heresy is ultimately provoked by introducing philosophical categories to explain the content of the faith. For him, "philosophy is the ancestor of heretics" (*patriarchae haereticorum philosophi*).[27] In even stronger terms, Walter of St. Victor (ob. 1180) writes against the "four labyrinths of France" (*Contra quatuor Labyrinthos Franciae*)—that is, Peter Abelard, Peter Lombard, Peter of

---

26. Cassiodorus, *Institutiones* I, 1, 8, ed. R. Mynors, trans. James W. and Barbara Halporn (Oxford: Clarendon Press, 1937), 14.

27. Tertullianus, *Adversus Hermogenem* VIII, 3 (CCSL 1, 404, 14–15). See also *De Praescriptione Hereticorum* VII, 3 (CCSL 1, 192, 14–15): *Ipsae denique haereses a philosophia subornantur.*

Poitiers, and Gilbert of la Porrée—saying that they were so much animated by the Aristotelian spirit (*aristotilico spiritu*) that, in treating the mysteries of the Holy Trinity and the Incarnation of Christ, these authors "vomited" many heresies and propagated numerous erroneous doctrines.[28] St. Thomas is aware, however, of possible misuses of philosophical reasoning. This can happen in at least two ways. If philosophy is viewed as the measure for doing theology, one is willing to believe only those truths that are established by philosophical reasoning.[29] The second way in which philosophical reasoning can be misused occurs "by using doctrines contrary to faith, which are not truths of philosophy, but rather error, or abuse of philosophy, as Origen did."[30] If no conflict between natural and supernatural truths is in principle possible, the appearance of a conflict from the perspective of natural truths must be due to a false or abusive understanding of a particular natural truth. Throughout his writings, one notices that St. Thomas links the formal content of Origen's positions in several areas to the fact that he followed "the Platonists." This connection or even accusation that Origen was a Platonist or at least a crypto-Platonist seems to be a *doctrina recepta* from as early as the writings of St. Jerome[31] but is ultimately reducible to Origen's own praise of Plato and his use of Platonic doctrines in numerous areas.[32]

Doctrine of God

Is God's Foreknowledge the Cause of Things?   Thomas encounters in Peter Lombard's *Sentences*, Book I, d. 38, a. 1, an objection ascribed to Origen to the effect that because a thing will be, it is known by God before it exists. This would seem to imply that things are the cause of God's knowledge. He mentions Origen's phrase in his *divisio textus* but does not respond to it.[33] In fact, as we will see elsewhere, the *Scriptum* is characterized by

---

28. Palémon Glorieux, ed., "Le '*Contra quatuor labyrinthos Franciae*,'" *Archives d'histoire Doctrinale et Littéraire du Moyen Âge* 27 (1952): 187–355, here 201: "dum ineffabilia sancta Trinitatis et incarnationis scolastica levitate tractarent, multas hereses olim vomuisse et adhuc errores pullulare?"

29. See, e.g., Petrus Abelardus, *Introductio ad Theologiam* (PL 178, 1050D; CCCM 13, 430): "nec quia Deus id dixerat creditor, sed quia hoc sic esse convincitur, recipitur."

30. *De Trin.*, q. 2, a. 3 (LE 50, 99, 162–65).

31. See Hieronymus, *Apologia adversus libros Rufini* III, no. 40 (PL 23, 486; CSEL 54, 400).

32. See Ilaria L. E. Ramelli, "Origen, Patristic Philosophy, and Christian Platonism Re-Thinking the Christianisation of Hellenism," *Vigiliae Christianae* 63 (2009): 217–63.

33. *In I Sent.*, d. 38, q. 1, pr. (ed. Mandonnet, 897).

the fact that Thomas leaves many topics, which he later develops in referencing Origen, unaddressed or does not engage with Origen, although Peter Lombard's text offered occasions to do so. In this case, both in *De Ver.*, q. 2, a. 14 (1256–59), as well as in *ST* I, q. 14, a. 8, the phrase from Origen's *Commentary on Romans* 8:30 forms the first objection, and in both instances Thomas defends Origen.[34] What Origen is denying is that because "something is known by God it must necessarily take place." Origen's phrase "Because it is to be, it is known by God" should be read as giving the reason for concluding (*causa inferendi*) that God knows it or as the cause of consequence (*causa consequentiae*) and not as the cause of the divine knowledge (*causa essendi*). In other words, if X is going to happen, it follows that God foreknows X, but this does not mean that X is the cause of God's foreknowledge.

Trinity: The Inferiority of the Son and the Holy Spirit   Thomas mentions this topic for the first time in his *Super Boethium de Trinitate* (1257–59), where he offers a severe criticism of Origen. The text is worth quoting in full:

Origen, moreover, following the teachings of the Platonists, thought that after the same manner the doctrine of the true faith ought to be interpreted, because it is said, "There are three who give testimony in heaven" (1 Jn 5:7). And so, as the Platonists supposed that there were three principal substances, Origen held that the Son was a creature and less than the Father, in that book which is entitled *Peri Archon* ("Concerning the Principles"), as is made clear by Jerome in a certain epistle regarding the errors of Origen. And since Origen himself taught at Alexandria, Arius drank in his error from the things he wrote. On this account Epiphanius says that Origen was the father and font of Arius.[35]

A few lines earlier, Thomas already indicated Augustine's *De Civ. Dei* 10.23 and 10.29 as his source for the Platonic position regarding the existence of three principal substances.[36] Jerome's epistle to which Thomas refers is Jerome's *Letter 124* to Avitus, a letter that contains numerous translated passages from *Peri Archon* in an attempt to dispel Avitus's perplexity. Jerome warns Avitus that, when reading *Peri Archon*, "you will have to walk among scorpions and serpents" (*inter scorpiones, et colubros incedendum*),

---

34. *De Ver.*, q. 2, a. 14, obj. 1 (LE 22.1.2, 91, 1–9); Origenes, *In Rom.* VII, 8 (PG 14, 1126C).

35. *De Trin.*, q. 3, a. 4 (LE 50, 116, 124–35).

36. *De Trin.*, q. 3, a. 4 (LE 50, 115, 111).

referring to Luke 10:19. In this letter, Jerome claims that Origen held that "except God the Father alone there is nothing uncreated."[37] Jerome is also one of the principal sources for the claim that Origen was a follower of Plato or at least a crypto-Platonist.[38] Finally, Jerome translated Ephiphanius's letter to the bishop of Jerusalem wherein Epiphanius warns him as follows: "Arii patrem et aliarum haereseon radicem et parentem laudare non debetis."[39] Given these secondary sources to which Aquinas himself refers, it is unlikely that Aquinas had at that time a firsthand knowledge of Origen's position.[40]

While Thomas does not mention this topic in his *Summa contra Gentiles*, a few years later, in 1266, something remarkable occurs in his commentary on Dionysius's *De Divinis Nominibus*. The depiction of the Trinity as *trina unitas* "quae est simul Deus et simul bonum" in chapter 1 of Dionysius's text is seen as indicating that within the Trinity there is "not some grade (*gradus*) or order but that all three are *per se* and simultaneously and equally God and simultaneously and equally the good itself, in which the Son is not the shadow of the goodness as Origen and Arius said."[41] In chapter 2, in commenting on Dionysius's claim that all the names proper to God are always applied "not partially but to the whole, perfect, integral and first Deity" ("non particulariter sed in tota et perfecta et integra et prima Deitate"), Thomas expounds on these qualifications of the Deity. Regarding the word "first," he writes that it is used to signify "that the Deity of the three persons is not a participated Deity. For 'first' is said of what is unparticipated as Deity *per se* and Goodness *per se*." He continues, referring to the qualifications "whole," "perfect," "integral," and "first" by saying, "And it seems that these words are formulated (*posita*) to exclude the error of Origen and Arius, who posited that the deity of the Son was a participated Deity."[42] In other words, Dionysius, the disciple of St. Paul, had Origen and Arius in mind when criticizing them! Even if one takes into account that for Thomas, Dionysius is foremost a Platonist, his chronology is remarkable.

37. Hieronymus, *Epist.* 124 (PL 22, 1060).

38. Hieronymus, *Apologia adversus Libros Rufini* III, no. 40 (PL 23, 486; SC 303, 318–21).

39. Hieronymus, *Epist.* 51, no. 3 (PL 22, 520).

40. For another indication, see *In I Sent.*, d. 6, q. 1, a. 2, arg. 3 (ed. Mandonnet, 167).

41. *In De Div. Nom.*, c. 1, l. 3 (ed. Marietti, no. 81). Possibly a distorted reading of Origen's comments in *Peri Archon* II, 6, 7, where Origen reflects on Lam 4:20 ("Spiritus vultus nostri Christus dominus, cuius diximus quod in umbra eius vivemus in gentibus"), is the foundation for this reproach.

42. *In De Div. Nom.*, c. 2, l. 1 (ed. Marietti, no. 116).

In the *Prima Pars* (finished before September 1268), Thomas mentions Origen two times in this regard; that is, Arius and his source Origen are said to hold that the Son and the Father differ in substance, but these remarks are merely an aside to other topics.[43]

In the *Commentary on John* (1270–72), containing ninety-one explicit references to Origen, forty-one appear in his discussion of chapter 1 of John's Gospel. While such a considerable presence of Origen and many other heterodox positions in chapter 1 may be surprising to a contemporary reader, one should keep in mind that for St. Thomas, Scripture has an apologetic function. Precisely regarding the first four clauses of the Prologue ("In the beginning was the Word; and the Word was with God; and the Word was God. He was in the beginning with God"), Aquinas writes: "If one considers these four propositions well, he will find that they clearly destroy all the errors of the heretics and of the philosophers."[44] One of the earliest references immediately goes to the heart of Thomas's criticism of Origen, who asks why John says "In the beginning was the Word" and not "the Word of God." Thomas responds that although there are many participated truths, there is only one absolute Truth or one absolute Wisdom, which is Truth or Wisdom by its very essence. Now the divine Word is of itself the Word (*per se ipsum*), and it is precisely to signify this *per se ipsum* that John speaks about the Word without any addition.[45] Although the distinction between "absolutely" and "by participation" is clearly that of Aquinas, he is dependent upon Origen for the identification of the Word with Truth and Wisdom. Both also emphasize the absoluteness and the oneness of the Word as becomes clear from both the *Catena Aurea* and Origen's text. For Thomas, this is emphasized by the fact that the Greek manner of speaking affixes an article to a name to signify the elevated nature of the thing. For this reason, the passage says *ho logos*, and if it were expressed in Latin, it would have said *ly verbum*.[46] The distinction between "absolutely" and "by participation" is nevertheless central to Aquinas's criticism of Origen. This becomes apparent in

---

43. See *ST* I, q. 32, a. 1, ad 1; *ST* I, q. 34, a. 1, ad 1.

44. *In Ioh.* 1, l. 2, no. 64. Regarding Thomas's method of juxtaposing Scripture and errors in explaining the individual articles of faith, Gilles Emery writes: "Cette méthode est révélatrice de la function de l'Ecriture pour Thomas: celle-ci s'oppose, comme par avance, aux erreurs commises contre la foi, et elle contient ce qui permet de les écarter." *Thomas d'Aquin, Traités: Les raisons de la foi; Les articles de la foi et Les sacraments de l'Eglise* (Paris: Cerf, 1999), 202.

45. *In Ioh.* 1, l. 1, no. 33; *CAI* 1, 4 (ed. Marietti, 330); see Origenes, *Comm. in Ioan.* II, 4, nos. 37–46 (PG 14, 116B; SC 120bis, 234–38).

46. *In Ioh.* 1, l. 1, no. 33.

Aquinas's observation on John 1:1c, "the Word was God": "[The] Word is called God absolutely because he is God by his own essence, and not by participation, as men and angels are." Thomas immediately continues by identifying the central error of Origen. Led astray by the Greek manner of speaking, Origen argued that the absence of an article before the word "God" in John 1:1c (*Et Deus erat Verbum*) indicates that the Word was not God by essence but by participation and therefore held the Son to be inferior (*minorem*) to the Father.[47] With John Chrysostom, Aquinas argues, however, that in other passages where the divinity of the Son is clearly affirmed, the article is indeed used. For Aquinas, this "misunderstanding" (*turpiter erravit*) by Origen resulted in the "blasphemous" (*blasphemavit*) and "clearly false" view that the Son is inferior to the Father (*Patet igitur esse falsum quod Origenes finxit*).[48] The passage in Origen on which Thomas seems to draw is indeed ambiguous insofar as it speaks of the Word as that "which is made God by participation in his divinity,"[49] but Origen is also adamant in wanting to uphold the divinity of the Word. Commenting on John 1:9, "He was the true light," Thomas will return to this error ("Christ was not true God, but God by participation") and attribute it explicitly to both Arius and Origen.[50]

In commenting on John 1:3, "All things were made through him," Aquinas continues to use the adjectives "blasphemous" and "heretical" to describe two of Origen's errors. The first is "that the Holy Spirit was included among all the things made through the Word; from which it follows that he is a creature," and, as if to emphasize that this really was Origen's position, he repeats *et hoc posuit Origenes*.[51] The second concerns an erroneous interpretation of the use of the preposition "through" (*per*) in "all things were made through him," as if it signifies inferiority on the part of the Son, who is acted upon as a minister or an instrument by the Father, who is a superior.[52] Origen indeed writes about the Holy Spirit as being "the first in rank of all the things which have been made

---

47. *In Ioh.* 1, l. 1, no. 58; see Origenes, *Comm. in Ioan.* II, 2, no. 17–18 (PG 14 109A–B; SC 120bis, 222–24)

48. *In Ioh.* 1, l. 1, nos. 58–59. See *CAI* I, 3 (ed. Marietti, p. 329), for the text of Chrysostom.

49. Origenes, *Comm. Joh.* II, 2, no. 17 (SC 120bis, 222: μετοχῇ τῆς ἐκείνου θεότητος θεοποιούμενον; FOCT 80, 99).

50. *In Ioh.* 1, l. 5, no. 126.

51. *In Ioh.* 1, l. 2, no. 74: "Secundo vitandus est error Origenis, qui dicit spiritum sanctum, inter omnia, factum esse per verbum, ex quo sequitur ipsum esse creaturam: et hoc posuit Origenes." See Origenes, *Comm in Ioan.* II, 10, no. 75 (PG 14, 128A–B; SC 120bis, 258).

52. *In Ioh.* 1, l. 2, no. 75; see *Comm in Ioan* II, 10, no. 72 (PG 14, 125c).

by the Father through Christ"[53] as well as being "inferior (ὑποδεέστερος) to him through whom he was made."[54] Such phrases are, at least from a post-Nicean perspective, ambiguous. For Thomas, this could only mean that the Son or the Holy Spirit would have received not the same power from the Father but another and created one (*sed aliam et creatam*). He reproaches Origen for having taught that the Son or the Holy Spirit are ministers or instruments of the Father in such strong words that he accuses him of being deranged (*deliravit*),[55] a qualification that Aquinas uses only once in his entire oeuvre. In letters by Theophilus of Alexandria and Epiphanius, translated by Jerome, one finds both of them questioning Origen's sanity in similar words.[56] The central issue for Thomas has to do with the identity of the power (*virtus*) between the one who gives and the one who receives.[57] One learns from his *Commentary on John* that Thomas, despite his increased knowledge of Origen, whether firsthand or not, and despite an explicit but rudimentary awareness of the historical development of dogma,[58] continues to view Origen's position as what has been named "subordinationism" and as such a forerunner of Arius's position.[59]

Creation

The Distinction among Created Things and the Origin of the Soul   One of the topics in which Origen occurs frequently concerns creation. The most extensive discussion can be found in *ScG* II, chaps. 44 and 83 (1261–62), dealing with the distinction among created things and the origin of the soul, respectively.

For Thomas, Origen's intention was to oppose the manicheian doctrine of two contrary principles, good and evil. This doctrine was supposed to explain the diversity and distinction among things such as the distinction between luminous and dark bodies or between people who were born as pagans and those who were born as Christians. Origen was therefore compelled to replace the doctrine of two contrary principles, and he did so by way of the doctrine that all diversity in things results

---

53. Origenes, *Comm. Joh.* II, 10, no. 75 (SC 120bis, 258; FCOT 81, 114).

54. Origenes, *Comm. Joh.* II, 10, no. 86 (SC 120bis, 264; FCOT 81, 116).

55. *In Ioh.* 1, l. 2, no. 76.

56. Hieronymus, *Epist.* 51, no. 4 (PL 22, 521); *Epist.* 96, no. 6 (PL 22, 777).

57. *In Ioh.* 1, l. 2, no. 76.

58. See his prologue to *Contra Errores Graecorum* (LE 40A 71, 16–44).

59. On the difficulties in using the term "subordinationism" for pre-Nicene theologies as that of Origen, see Lewis Ayres, *Nicaea and Its Legacy: An Approach to Fourth-Century Trinitarian Theology* (Oxford: Oxford University Press, 2004), 20–30.

from a diversity of merits. Originally, God, out of his goodness alone, made all creatures equal, that is, spiritual and rational. By their free choices, some spiritual creatures adhered more or less to God, while others withdrew themselves more or less from God. As a result, "diverse grades in spiritual substances were established by the divine justice, so that some were angels of diverse orders, some human souls in various conditions, some demons in their differing states. And because of the diversity among rational creatures, Origen stated that God had instituted diversity in the realm of corporeal creatures so that the higher spiritual substances were united to the higher bodies, and thus the bodily creature would subserve, in whatever other various ways, the diversity of spiritual substances."[60] Comparing this text with *Peri Archon* II, 9, 6, one can notice that Aquinas's account, while brief, is certainly not false. He is equally correct about Origen's apologetic intention.[61] Aquinas, however, fails to notice the tentative nature of Origen's response.[62] The same needs to be said about Origen's attempt to offer a more concrete explanation for the hierarchy among spiritual creatures. Origen's argument in *Peri Archon* II, 8, that a *decessus* or *devolutio mentis* into the soul (*anima*) has occurred, is offered as an invitation for the reader to reflect upon the matter, and not as a more or less fixed doctrine.[63]

In his earlier writings, such as the *Scriptum* or *De Veritate*, Aquinas remains remarkably silent on Origen's views on creation and related questions.[64] In his later writings, however, similar reproaches to the ones in the *Summa contra Gentiles* occur frequently.[65] St. Thomas's response has

60. *ScG* II, chap. 44; for similar texts, see *ST* I, q. 47, a. 2, and *ST* I, q. 65, a. 2.

61. See *Peri Archon* II, 9, 5 (ed. cit. 408).

62. See *Peri Archon* II, 9, 6 (ed. cit. 412).

63. See *Peri Archon* II, 8, 4 (ed. cit. 396): "Verum tamen quod diximus mentem in animam verti vel si qua alia quae in hoc videntur aspicere, discutiat apud se qui legit diligentius et pertractet; a nobis non putentur velut dogmata esse prolata, sed tractandi more ac requirendi discussa." See also *Peri Archon* II, 8, 5 (ed. cit. 398).

64. In this regard, it is telling that Thomas mentions Origen's position on the preexistence of the soul in the *divisio textus* of *In III Sent.*, d. 6, q. 1 (ed. Moos, 218) without, however, discussing it.

65. In his *Super Primam Decretalem*, it is said that the *error Origenis* consisted in holding that God in the beginning created only spiritual creatures and that only after some sinned they received material bodies as a punishment for their sins (LE E 34, l. 419–E35, l. 430). In *De Articulis Fidei*, we find his error to be that all the souls were created at the same time as the angels and according to what they have done in this state—some are called by God *per gratiam*, others are left in their infidelity (LE 42 E 38, 674–82). In *Contra Errores Graecorum*, we can read that Origen held that, because all are created equal by God, there are no ranks in

two parts. He shows first that Origen's theory to replace the Manichean position is metaphysically unsound, and second that Origen's theory about the soul is false.

With regard to the first, Aquinas develops a lengthy purely philosophical response in *ScG* II, chap. 44, to show that diversity implies inequality; that is, the formal distinction in things, by which things differ specifically, requires inequality. The metaphysical foundation is Aristotle's insight in *Metaphysics* VII, 3 (1043v34) that "the forms of things are like numbers in which species vary by addition or subtraction of unity."[66] On this basis, Aquinas writes: "Since multitude without diversity cannot exist, if from the beginning any multitude at all of rational creatures existed, then there must have been some diversity among them. And this means that one of those creatures had something which another had not. And if this was not the consequence of a diversity in merit, for the same reason neither was it necessary that the diversity of grades should result from a diversity of merits."[67] In other words, given the necessity of multitude and inequality in creation, Origen's initial question of how inequality in creation is to be squared with the goodness and justice of God becomes superfluous.[68]

With regard to the second part, Aquinas offers a series of responses. If a particular soul would only be united to a particular body on the basis of a free choice and its corresponding merit, such a union would not be natural but accidental. The existence of such an accidental union is impossible for several reasons. For instance, a species cannot result

---

angels (LE 40 A 84, 7–10). An account similar to the one in *ScG* II, chap. 44, can be found in *De Pot.*, q. 3 (1265–66), on creation. With Gennadius of Massilia, the author of *De Ecclesiasticis Dogmatibus*, chap. XIV, Thomas judges the position that human souls were created at the beginning together with other intellectual natures to be a fiction (a. 9). The same can be said of the claim that inequality among rational creatures is a result of free will (a. 16; see also *Q. D. de Anima*, q. 7). He is equally adamant in his rejection that the soul was thrown into a body as into a prison (a. 10), a position that for Thomas is a result of the Platonic position that the soul is already a complete species in itself and hence the body soul union a mere accidental one (*Q. D. de Anima*, q. 2, ad 14: LE 20, 458–21, 466). One can find similar positions in his *Summa Theologiae*.

66. *ScG* II, chap. 44; *De Pot.*, q. 10, a. 5; *ST* I, q. 47, a. 2.

67. *ScG* II, chap. 44.

68. Elsewhere he emphasizes that inequality among creatures is a result of God's wisdom and goodness. See *De Pot.*, q. 3, a. 16, ad 19: "This argument which is used by Origen is not very convincing. There is no injustice in dealing unequally with equal persons except when one is giving them their due: and this cannot be said of the first creation of things. That which is given out of pure liberality may be given more or less liberally as the giver wills and as his wisdom dictates." See also *De Pot.*, q. 3, a. 18.

from an accidental union; if so, "white man" or "clothed man" would be a species.[69] Moreover, if merits and demerits can be increased or diminished, as Origen held, it would be possible for a soul to be united again to another human or even a celestial body. "Obviously, this idea is both erroneous as regards philosophy, according to which determinate matters and determinate movable things are assigned to determinate forms and determinate movers, and heretical according to faith, which declares that in the resurrection the soul resumes the same body that it has left."[70]

The preexistence of the soul, implicit in Origen's position as summarized in *ScG* II, chap. 44, receives an equally extensive philosophical rejection in *ScG* II, chap. 83. For our purposes, we should note that Aquinas presents Origen's position as a *via media* between "those who profess the Catholic faith" and those who, as a consequence of their view that the world is eternal, think the human soul also exists from eternity. In the latter position, Aquinas sees converging not only "Platonists" but also Latin Averroïsts and even Aristotle himself. The *via media*, which holds that human souls are not eternal but "that they were created with, or rather before, the visible world," was, according to St. Thomas, first expounded by Origen and subsequently defended by many of his followers, imbued as they were with the "teachings of the Platonists." Moreover, St. Thomas notes that "the theory, indeed, survives to this day among heretics, the Manicheans, for example, siding with Plato in proclaiming the eternity and transmutation of souls."[71] In his response, Aquinas starts by asking how the soul and body are united to each other if the soul is created without the body. Various possibilities are eliminated. Such a union cannot be the result of violence, because what is brought about by violence is unnatural and the union of body and soul would therefore also be unnatural, "which is obviously false" (*quod patet esse falsum*). Neither can this union be natural, because given that "a natural appetite immediately issues in act if no obstacle stands in the way," the soul's existence at some time separated from the body, which would be the result of violence. This position is "incongruous" because "the violent and the unnatural, being accidental, cannot be prior to that which is *secundum naturam*." Neither is it possible that the union is the result of a free choice. For if, as the Platonists hold, the separate soul enjoys a higher state of existence, a voluntary entrance into a lower state can only occur as the result of deception, which

69. See also *ScG* II, chap. 83.
70. *ScG* II, chap. 44.
71. *ScG* II, chap. 83.

is impossible given that the separate soul already contemplates truth. A final possibility would be that the union is the result of a divine decree. Aquinas considers this position to not be in conformity with the order of divine wisdom. For if every creature in particular and all creatures collectively are seen by God as good, as it is written in Genesis 1:10 and 1:31, then a reduction of the soul to a lower state would be inconsistent on the part of God's divine wisdom. It is at this point that St. Thomas introduces Origen's position. He writes: "Origen said that they were united to bodies by divine decree, but as a punishment. For Origen thought that souls had sinned before bodies existed, and that according to the gravity of their sin, souls were shut up in bodies of higher or lower character, as in so many prisons."[72] Aquinas's response is unambiguous: *Sed haec positio stare non potest.* In his lengthy response, he refers to his rejection of Origen's position regarding the distinction in things in chapter 44 and adds another series of objections. The core element of Origen's position—that is, the union of soul and body is a result of divine punishment—can easily be refuted. From his position two things would follow. *Primo,* the union of body and soul is not a good of nature but contains something penal in character, and *secundo,* the union of body and soul is merely accidental. If from evil good does not come forth except by accident and the union is the result of sin, it follows that the union is an accidental good. This conclusion Aquinas equates with the idea that the production of man was a matter of chance. For Aquinas, these conclusions that follow from Origen's position are contrary to divine wisdom as expressed in Genesis 1:31 ("God saw all the things that He had made, and they were very good") and Wisdom 11:21 ("It [God's wisdom] ordered all things in number, weight, and measure"). St. Thomas, however, sees a more far-reaching problem. For if St. Thomas and the Platonists both agree that the ultimate end of man is the contemplation of truth, then the more pressing question becomes whether the body is advantageous or whether it is a hindrance in realizing this end. If the latter is the case, then Origen's position might be plausible. Consequently, in a lengthy section of chapter 83, he explores in detail the truth of the Platonic position regarding the acquisition of knowledge. He argues for the position that the intellect has as its natural object being (*ens*) upon which the knowledge of principles

---

72. *ScG* II, chap. 83. For texts supporting this position, see Origenes, *Peri Archon* I, 5, 3, and the texts added to I, 8 (ed. cit. 267–79). For a concise discussion, see Anders-Christian L. Jacobsen, "Origen on the Human Body," in *Origeniana octava: Origen and the Alexandrian Tradition,* vol. 1, ed. L. Perrone (Leuven: Peeters, 2003), 649–56.

is founded; that is, "if, for instance, we had not perceived some whole by our senses, we would be unable to understand the principle that the whole is greater than its parts."[73] The final sections of chapter 83 reject the possibility of transmigration of the soul, that is, the possibility that the same soul would be united to different bodies throughout time. Although Thomas sees this theory as connected to the preexistence of the soul and therefore proposed by adherents of the preexistence of the soul, he does not attribute it to Origen, and correctly so according to contemporary scholarship.[74] Rather, he sees it as a consequence of the doctrine of the eternity of the world, and in particular of the eternal coming into being of human beings, for from this position it follows "that an infinite number of human bodies have come into being and passed away throughout the whole course of time."[75] Such a doctrine is, however, equally absent in Origen or at least highly disputed within scholarship on Origen.[76]

For various reasons, one should not underestimate the importance of this lengthy discussion on Origen in chapters 44 and 83 of his *Summa contra Gentiles*. Not only will the arguments return in much the same way in his later writings, but, more importantly, the discussion enables St. Thomas to emphasize both the possibility of finding divine goodness and wisdom in all of creation, including the body-soul union as well as the philosophical demonstrability of these divine attributes. Moreover, it becomes clear that in Aquinas's opinion, Origen's position remains tempting to this day—that is, to the thirteenth century—but it would be presumptuous to claim that this would not be the case anymore.[77] This explains, I suggest, why he devotes so many pages to the refutation of Origen as he does in the *Summa contra Gentiles*. In other words, it is likely that Aquinas had contemporary heterodox positions in mind when writing these chapters.[78] Internal and external evidence corroborates this

---

73. *ScG* II, chap. 83. See Horst Seidl, "Über die Erkenntnis erster, allgemeiner Prinzipien nach Thomas von Aquin," in *Thomas von Aquin: Werk und Wirkung im Licht neuerer Forschungen*, ed. Albert Zimmermann (Berlin: De Gruyter, 1988), 103–16.

74. See John A. McGuckin, ed., *Westminster Handbook to Origen* (Louisville, KY: Westminster John Knox Press, 2004), 206.

75. *ScG* II, chap. 83.

76. See the extensive discussion in chap. 1 of Panayiotis Tzamalikos, *Origen: Cosmology and Ontology of Time* (Leiden: Brill, 2006), 21–38.

77. *ScG* II, chap. 83: "Quae quidem opinio usque hodie apud haereticos manet."

78. As such, this is another indication of the apologetic goal of the *Summa contra Gentiles*. See L. Elders, "Les destinataires de la Somme contre les gentils," in *S. Tommaso Filosofo : Ricerche in occasione dei due centenari accademici*, ed. Antonio Piolanti (Vatican City: Libreria Editrice Vaticana, 1995), 287–304.

suggestion. In *ScG* II, chap. 83, Thomas explicitly links Origen to those who defend the eternity of the world and to Averroes's position on the unity of the intellect. Both topics were already controversial at the time of writing *ScG* II (1261–62),[79] and Aquinas devoted separate works to these topics in the wake of the 1270 condemnation of radical Aristotelianism.[80] External evidence comes from the fact that nowhere in the *Scriptum* (composed before 1256) does he discuss Origen's position on the preexistence of the soul. This seems to indicate that in the early 1250s, Thomas considered Origen's position and its actuality not to be a matter of concern. Further external evidence comes to mind when reading an occasional work such as *De Articulis Fidei et Ecclesiae Sacramentis*, composed around the same time (1261–65) as *ScG* II. In this work, he sets out to discuss briefly (*breviter*) and at the request of the archbishop of Palermo the articles of faith and the sacraments as well its corresponding errors, which need to be avoided.[81] It is remarkable that in such a "pastoral" work Aquinas enumerates at length century-old errors, often quoting verbatim from Augustine's *De Haeresibus*. It is certainly true that St. Thomas's interest in discussing so extensively errors opposed to the faith stems from his awareness that, as 1 Corinthians 11:19 ("for there must be factions (*haereses*) among you in order that those who are genuine among you may be recognized") suggests, errors often present an occasion for more careful analysis, clearer understanding, and more effective preaching of the truth.[82] Notwithstanding this systematic context of Aquinas's interest in heresies, it is probable that as Dominican friar[83]

79. See, e.g., *In II Sent.*, d. 17, q. 2, a. 1 (ed. Mandonnet, 420–30).

80. See the introduction to *De Unitate Intellectus* in LE 43, 247–51, and to *De Aeternitate Mundi* in LE 43, 54–57. See also John F. Wippel, *Metaphysical Themes in Thomas Aquinas* (Washington, DC: Catholic University of America Press, 1984), 191–214.

81. *De Articulis Fidei et Ecclesiae Sacramentis* (LE 42, 245, 1–13).

82. See *In I Cor.* 11:19, no. 628. One example Aquinas himself gives concerns the error of Arius. This caused subsequent writers to emphasize the unity of the divine essence (prologue to *Contra Errores Graecorum*) and the addition of a separate article of the Creed (*Genitum, non factum, consubstantialem Patri*). See *ST* II-II, q. 1, a. 8, ad 3.

83. One recalls that the Dominican Order, from its inception, was commissioned to preach and act against the Cathars. See John Inglis, "Emanation in Historical Context: Aquinas and the Dominican Response to the Cathars," *Dionysius* 17 (1999): 95–128. An indication that this was also a concern for St. Thomas can be found in his treatises in defense of the religious life. See, e.g., *Contra Impugnantes*, c. 6: "Hic autem error per successiones errantium usque ad hodierna tempora pervenit; et in haereticis quibusdam qui Cathari nominantur, permansit, et adhuc permanet, sicut patet in quodam tractatu cuiusdam Desiderii haeresiarchae Lombardi nostri temporis, quem edidit contra Catholicam veritatem: in quo inter cetera condemnat statum eorum qui relictis omnibus egere volunt cum Christo. Nuper autem,

he had contemporary unorthodox positions, which were often seen as deriving from Origen's positions,[84] in mind.[85] A final reason why Thomas's discussion in *ScG* II, chaps. 43 and 83, is important has to do with the remaining references to Origen in the work. Aquinas's rejection of many of these are based on the arguments developed in *ScG* II, chaps. 43 and 83. He returns to and develops, for instance, the arguments from chapter 44 to the effect that the difference between human souls and spiritual substances is not based on merit, as Origen thought, but is natural.[86] The preexistence of the soul of Christ is rejected on the basis of the impossibility of the preexistence of the soul in general.[87] The claim that some men are converted on the basis of works done by their soul before being united to their bodies is also rejected on this basis.[88]

---

quod est horribilius, antiquus error renovatus est ab his qui fidem defendere videbantur; et more errantium in peius procedentes" (LE 41A 96, 236–47).

84. The Cistercian monk Caesarius of Heisterbach (ca. 1180 to ca. 1240), in his *Dialogus Miraculorum*, d. V, c. XXI, written ca. 1220, explicitly links the Albigensian heresy to Origen: "Quaedam haeresiarchae eorum, quae in Periarchon scripsisse fertur Origenes, plurima etiam, que de suo corde finxerant adiicientes" (ed. Josef Stahl, vol. 1 [Cologne: Heberle, 1851], 300). See also Heinrich Fichtenau, *Heretics and Scholars in the High Middle Ages, 1000–1200* (University Park: Pennsylvania State University Press, 1998), 105–6, for connections between the Cathars and Origen.

85. Thomas was certainly aware of some of the heresies of his time, as is evident from the remark in *De Articulis Fidei* about the error of *quorundam modernorum hereticorum*, who thought that in the Resurrection souls would be united with celestial bodies and not with their own bodies (LE 42, 249, 290–297), or from the explicit reference in the same work to the Poor of Lyons, a heretical group closely related to the Waldensians (LE 42, 255, 288–56, 287). He also knew and used the treatise *Adversus Catharos et Valdenses Libri Quinque*, written ca. 1241 by Moneta de Cremona, as well as the *Summa de Catharis*, written ca. 1250 by Raynier Sacconi, OP. See the introduction by René-Antoine Gauthier to *Saint Thomas d'Aquin, Somme contre les gentils* (Paris: Cerf, 1993), 136–40, and John Inglis, "Emanation in Historical Context: Aquinas and the Dominican Response to the Cathars," *Dionysius* 17 (1999): 95–128. For a defense of Origen, see Henri Crouzel, "Origène est-il la source du Catharisme?," *Bulletin de littérature ecclésiastique* 80 (1979) : 3–28.

86. *ScG* II, chap. 95.

87. *ScG* IV, chap. 33.

88. *ScG* III, chap. 161. The three remaining references occur in *ScG* II, chap. 91; III, chap. 62; and III, chap. 89. The first has to do with the claim that Origen "held that no substance, save the divine Trinity, can subsist apart from a body." This is rejected on philosophical grounds, i.e., the existence of per se subsistent souls. The second passage attributes to Origen the claim that "souls and angels, after beatitude, could again return to unhappiness." This is rejected on the basis that happiness requires the natural desire to come to rest. The third passage claims Origen thought God merely causes in us the power of willing but not the willing as such. This is rejected on the basis of (1) Scripture (Isa 26:2, "O Lord, you have wrought all our works in us"); (2) the argument that if every bodily motion is caused by the

Given the influence of his arguments developed in *ScG* II, chaps. 43 and 83, a passage from his treatise *De Substantiis Separatis*, composed in Paris or in Naples in 1272–73, is remarkable. The fact that this treatise contains an entire chapter explicitly directed against Origen's claim that all spiritual creatures are created equal by God is, given what we have seen so far, not remarkable. Nor is his account of Origen's position or Aquinas's refutation remarkable in light of *ScG* II, chaps. 44 and 83. Therefore we can briefly summarize Origen's position as it appears in *De Substantiis Separatis* as follows. Given that an author who is one and from whom no diversity can proceed, all things were first produced by God as equal. Bodies cannot be made equal to non-bodily substances; hence there were no bodies at first. Diversity entered creation as a result of the diversity of the will of non-bodily substances, that is, their freedom of choice. Ultimately, those who had turned in a lesser way from God were bound to nobler bodies, and those who turned away more were bound to less noble bodies. In his response, Thomas is unsurprisingly adamant when he calls the *ratio* of this position *vana* and the position itself *impossibile*. Thomas grants, however—and this is the remarkable part—that there might be some truth in Origen's position. He writes:

But in things which differ materially, nothing prevents things that have the same form from being equal. For diverse subjects can participate in the same form either equally or by excess and defect. Consequently, it would be possible for all spiritual substances to be equal, if, having specifically the same form, they differed only in matter. And perhaps this is what Origen thought them to be (*forte tales eas esse Origenes opinabatur*) by not distinguishing noticeably between spiritu-

---

first motion, then in the more perfect order of spiritual things every movement of the will must be caused by the first will; (3) finally *Eudemian Ethics*, Book VIII, where he argues for the impossibility of an infinite regress regarding every act of understanding, willing, and choosing and the superiority of the first mover. "Therefore, God is the first principle of our acts of counsel and of will." This is the first time Thomas refers to the *Eudemian Ethics*. The passage to which he refers (1248a25–34), together with *Magna Moralia* 1206b30–1207b19, will later be described by Thomas as the *Liber de Bona Fortuna*. This text will play a key role in his mature understanding of the gifts of the Holy Spirit as well as in his understanding of the efficacy of the inspiration of the Holy Spirit for entering the religious life (see *Contra Retrah.* c. 9; LE 41C 57, 63–78). For the textual and historical sources, see Valérie Cordonier, "Sauver le Dieu du Philosophe: Albert le Grand, Thomas d'Aquin, Guillaume de Moerbeke et l'invention du 'Liber de bona fortuna,'" in *Christian Readings of Aristotle from the Middle Ages to the Renaissance*, ed. L. Bianchi (Brepols: Turnhout, 2011), 65–114; Valérie Cordonier and Carlos Steel, "Guillaume de Moerbeke traducteur du 'Liber de bona fortuna' et de l'Ethique à Eudème," in *The Letter before the Spirit: The Importance of Text Editions for the Study of the Reception of Aristotle*, ed. A. M. I. van Oppenraay (Leiden: Brill, 2012), 401–46.

al and corporeal natures. But because spiritual substances are immaterial, there must be an order of nature among them.[89]

Although in the end Thomas maintains his position that spiritual substances are truly spiritual, and hence there can be no differentiation on the basis of matter, he gives us here an example of an *expositio reverentialis*, insofar as he seems aware that Origen does not defend a strict distinction between the corporeal and the spiritual but allows for the existence of subtle (*quoddam subtile*) bodies, as is the case with demons, distinguished from "solid and palpable bodies," as Origen says in *Peri Archon* I, 1.[90]

Further Questions Dealing with Creation: The Bodies of Angels and Demons   Thomas frequently takes issue with a claim found in *Peri Archon* I, 6, 4, which says that "It is proper to the nature of God alone, that is, of the Father and of the Son and of the Holy Spirit, that it be understood to exist without material substance and without any association of a corporeal adjunct." This claim seems to imply that angels and demons have bodies naturally united to them. Every time Thomas discusses this question, he affirms that it seems (*videtur*) to be the position Origen held, but he also attributes this position to an uncritical adoption by Origen of the views of "the Platonists"[91] or to Origen being "deceived" by "the ancient philosophers."[92] The clearest statement in this respect and one that confirms that Thomas is clearly aware that Origen practices, in the words of Henri Crouzel, a *théologie en recherche*, comes from *De Pot.*, q. 6, a. 6. There he writes: "On many points Origen adopts the views of the Platonists: thus, he seems to have been of the opinion that all created incorporeal substances are united to bodies: and yet he does not state this positively, but suggests it as by no means certain, and at the same time mentions the other view."[93]

The Waters above the Heavens   Genesis 1:2 seems to indicate that certain waters are placed above the heavens. Thomas allows for a multiplicity of responses to the general question of whether the creation of formless matter

89. *De Subst. Separ.*, chap. 12 (LE 40D, 63, 66–73).

90. *Peri Archon* I, Praef. 8; see also *Peri Archon* II, 2, 2.

91. *De Pot.*, q. 6, a. 6.

92. *ST* I, q. 51, a. 1, ad 1; see also *De Spir. Creat.*, a. 5, ad 1 (LE 24.2, 62, 259–62); *De Malo*, q. 16, a. 1 (LE 23, 282, 268–71; *De Subst. Separ.*, chap. 19 (LE 40D, 74, 5–12).

93. *De Pot.*, q. 6, a. 6, ad 2: "Ad secundum dicendum, quod Origenes in pluribus Platonicorum opinionem sectatur; unde huius opinionis fuisse videtur quod omnes substantiae creatae incorporeae sint corporibus unitae, quamvis etiam hoc non asserat, sed sub dubitatione proponat, aliam etiam opinionem tangens."

preceded the creation of things so long as two rules of interpretation are upheld. First, one should not obstinately defend matters of which one is ignorant because then such a defense becomes a stumbling block to others, and the faith is made ridiculous. Second, one interpretation should not be seen as to exclude other interpretations so long as an interpretation does not destroy the literal sense.[94] Yet the view that Thomas, again relying on Jerome's Letter 51,[95] attributes to Origen—that is, that the waters above the heavens denote spiritual natures—cannot be reconciled with the text because "it is not competent to the nature of a spiritual being to occupy a situation, as though the firmament intervened between them and the lower corporeal waters, according to the Scriptures [Gn 1:6]."[96] In the *Summa*, Origen is reproached with the same view, to which Thomas responds by invoking the authority of Basil. Psalm 148:4 ("Let the waters that are above the heavens praise the name of the Lord") does not indicate that the waters themselves are spiritual creatures "but that 'the thoughtful contemplation of them by those who understand fulfils the glory of the Creator.'"[97]

The Animation of the Celestial Bodies   The question of whether celestial bodies are animated occupied Thomas on several occasions. Each time he mentions Origen's position affirming the animation of celestial bodies in *Peri Archon* I, 7, 3. Noteworthy in this regard is the fact that, when listing the variety of positions of philosophers and others on this question, Thomas attributes the term *doctor fidei* or *doctor ecclesiae* to Origen.[98] He defends the position that celestial bodies are animated in the sense that these bodies "are moved by the direct influence and contact of some spiritual substance."[99] In the *Summa*, Thomas explicitly harmonizes the difference of opinions of philosophers and Church Fathers by saying that it is ultimately a matter of semantics.[100]

94. *De Pot.*, q. 4, a. 1.

95. See Hieronymus, *Epist.* 51, no. 5 (PL 22, 523).

96. *De Pot.*, q. 4, a. 1, ad 5.

97. *ST* I, q. 68 a. 2. Quotation from Basilius's *In Hexaem.*, hom. III, no. 9 (PG 29,76A; SC 26, 237).

98. *ST* I, q. 70, a. 3. See also *Q. D. de Anima*, a. 8, ad 3 (LE 24.1, 70, 357–60); *De Spir. Creat.*, a. 6 (LE 24.2, 68, 178). On the terminology of *patres*, *doctores*, and *sancti* in Thomas, see Juan José de Miguel, "Los padres de la iglesia en la criteriología teológica de Santo Tomás de Aquino," *Scripta Theologica* 7 (1975): 125–61.

99. *ST* I, q. 70, a. 3.

100. *ST* I, q. 70, a. 3: "Unde inter ponentes ea esse animata, et ponentes ea inanimata, parva vel nulla differentia invenitur in re, sed in voce tantum."

The Definition of Conscience   On three occasions, Thomas uses Origen's description of conscience as *spiritus corrector et paedagogus animae* from his *Commentary on Romans*[101] as an objection to the question whether conscience is an act. The use of *spiritus* seems to entail either that it is a potency or that it belongs to the essence of the soul and is therefore not an act. In the *Scriptum*, he responds that *spiritus* is here taken as a spiritual operation and therefore does not refer to the essence of the soul. In *De Veritate*, *spiritus*, he says, is taken to mean an instinct or impulse of the spirit, while in the *Summa* he responds that *spiritus* is the same as mind, that is, a certain pronouncement of the mind (*quoddam mentis dictamen*).[102]

Is Paradise a Corporeal Place?   Regarding the question of whether Paradise a corporeal place, Thomas begins in the *Scriptum* by claiming that, for Origen, "omnia quae de Paradiso dicuntur, allegorice de Paradiso spirituali interpretanda esse." This has been rejected as erroneous, he says, by Epiphanius in a letter translated by Jerome.[103] His own position at the time is that Paradise is indeed situated at a specific place on earth (*in determinata parte terrae situm*). Later, in the *Summa*, his position remains unchanged insofar as Paradise is a real existing place, but the juxtaposition of the historical and the spiritual, and therefore any mention of Origen, disappears in favor of a more nuanced reading, under the influence of Augustine. Thomas reads Augustine's position in *De Civ. Dei* 13.21—"'nothing prevents us from holding, within proper limits, a spiritual paradise; so long as we believe in the truth of the events narrated as having there occurred'"—as saying that "we must hold to the historical truth of the narrative as a foundation of whatever spiritual explanation we may offer."[104]

The Government of Angels   In *De Ver.*, q. 5, a. 8, and in *ST* I, q. 110, a. 1, Thomas uses a remark from Origen's Homily on Numbers 22:23 ("When the donkey saw the angel of the Lord standing in the road with a drawn sword in his hand, it turned off the road into a field"[105]) in support of the

---

101. Origenes, *In Rom.* II, 9 (PG 14, 893B).

102. See *In II Sent.*, d. 24, q. 2, a. 4, arg. 1 + ad 1 (ed. Mandonnet, 611 + 613); *De Ver.*, q. 17, a. 1, arg. 8 + ad 8 (LE 22.2, 514, 51–56); *ST* I, q. 79, a. 13, obj. 1 + ad 1.

103. *In II Sent.*, d. 17, q. 3, a. 2 sol. (ed. Mandonnet, 438). See Hieronymus, *Epist.* 51, no. 5 (PL 22, 522).

104. *ST* I, q. 102, a. 1.

105. *De Ver.*, q. 5, a. 8, s.c. 4 (LE 22.1.2, 157, 142–47). Origenes, *In Num. Hom. 14 Rufine interprete* (PG 12, 680B).

view that material creatures are governed by God's providence through angels.

The Guardian Angel Origen provides Thomas with two opinions on the time of appointment of man's guardian angel, that is, at the time of birth or at the time of baptism. Thomas sides with the former opinion, approved by Jerome, because the guardianship of the human being is in conformity with divine providence according to which "all things … movable and variable are moved and regulated by the immovable and invariable";[106] that is, the guardian angel and its guardianship are benefits that God bestows on the human being as a rational being, whose nature is received at birth.[107]

The Moral Life

Charity and Sin In *De Virtutibus*, written around the same time as the *Secunda Secundae* (1271–72), in the first objection to the question of whether charity can exist together with mortal sin, Aquinas quotes from *Peri Archon* I, 3, 8, where Origen says: "I do not think that anyone who has continually stayed in the highest and perfect state would suddenly fall from that height, but he must need fall away little by little."[108] If, however, a mortal sin is committed suddenly, it seems that, on the authority of Origen, charity can exist simultaneously with mortal sin. In his response, Aquinas places Origen's words in the correct context by paraphrasing the complete passage from *Peri Archon* I, 3, 8, thereby showing that he has Origen's text at hand. Aquinas notes that Origen's words should be understood to mean "that it does not easily happen that a perfect man would suddenly commit a mortal sin at once, but through negligence; and many venial sins would be disposed finally to fall into mortal sin." And Origen mentions negligence as the cause of a smaller fall from which a person can recover.[109] Aquinas uses the same text in *ST* II-II, q. 14,

---

106. *ST* I, q. 113, a. 1.

107. *ST* I, q. 113, a. 5; *CAM* 18, 3 (ed. Marietti, 271); Origenes, *Comm. Matt.*, 13, 27 (GCS 40/10, 254).

108. *De Virt.* q. 2, a. 6, obj. 1: "Dicit enim Origenes in I periarchon: non arbitror quod aliquis ex his qui in summo perfectoque perstiterunt gradu, ad subitum evacuetur ac decidat; sed per partes et paulatim eum diffluere necesse est." Compare this to *Peri Archon* I, 3, 8 (ed. cit., 184): "qui in summo perfectoque constiterunt gradu, arbitror quod ad subitum quis evacuetur ac decidat, sed paulatim et per partes defluere eum necesse est."

109. *Peri Archon* I, 3, 8: "ita ut fieri possit interdum, si brevis aliquis lapsus acciderit,

a. 4, to corroborate his claim that "never or scarcely ever does it happen that the perfect sin all at once against the Holy Spirit" because this sin is either the result of habit or it presupposes for the most part other sins or at least previous dispositions. The same text is used in *De Virtutibus*, q. 2, a. 13, obj. 1, and *ST* II-II, q. 24, a. 12, obj. 1, in asking whether charity can be lost by a single act of a mortal sin. This time, he refers to the complete text from *Peri Achon* I, 3, 8, including the passage where Origen mentions the possibility of a smaller fall from which recovery is possible. This text seems to deny that charity can be lost by a single act of a mortal sin. In both *De Virtutibus* and the *Summa*, Aquinas again offers a defense of Origen. The first part of the text can be understood as referring to a previous negligence that disposes someone to sin. The second part of the text might indicate that "when he [Origen] speaks of a man being emptied and falling away altogether, he means one who falls so as to sin through malice; and this does not occur in a perfect man all at once."[110] Here we should recall that, for Thomas, "one does not fall suddenly into sin from certain malice, and that something is presupposed,"[111] which could be either a corrupt disposition, arising from a habit acquired by custom or a bodily condition, or the removal of an obstacle.[112] Raising the question of "whether the object to be loved out of charity is a rational nature," he quotes from the prologue to Origen's *Commentary on the Song of Songs* that loving God and loving other goods is the same thing.[113]

---

ut cito resipiscat atque in se revertatur, non penitus ruere, sed revocare pedem et redire ad statum suum ac rursum statuere posse id, quod per neglegentiam fuerat elapsum."

110. *ST* II-II, q. 24, a. 12.

111. *ST* II-II, q. 78, a. 3, ad 2.

112. In *ST* II-II, q. 78, a. 3, he gives the following example: "if a man be prevented from sinning, not through sin being in itself displeasing to him, but through hope of eternal life, or fear of hell, if hope give place to despair, or fear to presumption, he will end in sinning through certain malice, being freed from the bridle, as it were." In *De Virt.*, q. 2, a. 13, ad 1, Aquinas finds additional support in Aristotle's *Nicomachean Ethics*. He writes: "quia etiam, ut philosophus dicit in I Ethic., non est facile iusto ut opus iniustum operetur statim, sicut iniustus facit, scilicet ex electione." The source is EN V, 1137a17–23, and the text should therefore be in "in V. Ethicorum." (I thank Iacopo Costa of the Leonine Commission for this information.) I take Aquinas to mean that, whereas the just person is disposed to do just actions in accordance with rational choice, the unjust person acts out of a disproportionate excess or deficiency so that the just person will not suddenly perform unjust actions.

113. *De Virt.*, q. 2, a. 7, obj. 3: "Praeterea, Origenes dicit super cantica, quod unum est diligere Deum et quaecumque bona. Sed Deus diligitur ex caritate. Ergo, cum omnes creaturae sint bonae, omnes sunt diligendae ex caritate, et non solum rationalis natura." See Origenes, *Super Cantica*, Prologus, no. 35 (PG 13, 70C; SC 375, 116): "Unum enim atque idem est diligere Deum, et diligere bona."

If God, however, is to be loved in charity and all creatures are good, all creatures and not just rational creatures are to be loved in charity. Again, Aquinas shows he knows the context of this phrase when he writes that "all goods are in God as in a first principle" (*sicut in primo principio*) and that this is how Origen understood the identity between loving God and loving other goods.[114]

The Sin of Adam and Eve The same text from *Peri Archon* I, 3, 8—that someone who "stands on the highest step of perfection cannot fail or fall suddenly"—is used as a *sed contra* in *ST* II-II, q. 163, a. 3, where Aquinas asks whether the sin of Adam and Eve was more grievous than other sins. For if our first parents stood on this highest step of perfection, their sin was not the greatest of sins. In his response, Aquinas argues that *simpliciter*—that is, with regard to the species of sin—our first parent's sin was not the greatest because the pride of denying God is greater than the pride of coveting God's likeness inordinately. But *secundum quid*—that is, with regard to the circumstances—their sin was the greatest because of their state of perfection.

Is the Devil the Cause of Sin? The devil, who is also for Origen created good, as Thomas recognizes,[115] can only cause sin indirectly. On the three occasions Thomas discusses this question, he quotes the same passage from *Peri Archon*: "Origen proves this (*probat*) from the fact that even if the devil were no more, men would still have the desire for food, sexual pleasures and the like; which desire might be inordinate, unless it were subordinate to reason, a matter that is subject to free-will."[116]

The Sin of Peter Thomas knows of the discussion between Jerome and Augustine regarding the question of whether Peter sinned when capitulating to those "who were of the circumcision," as St. Paul writes in Galatians 2:12. Thomas sides with Augustine that Peter did indeed sin venially. Among the "stronger" (*validius*) arguments by Augustine, Thomas mentions the fact that "Jerome adduces on his own behalf seven doctors,

---

114. *De Virt.*, q. 2, a. 7, ad 3. See Origen's use of *principaliter* and *primum* in the context of love of God at PG 13, 70B; SC 375, 114–16.

115. For Thomas, both Augustine and Origen are authorities for the position that the devil was created good. See *De Subst. Separ.*, chap. 20 (LE 40D, 78, 174–77); Origenes, *Peri Archon* I, 5, 4, concurs with Augustine in *De Civ. Dei* 11.15.

116. *ST* I, q. 114, a. 3; *ST* I-II, q. 80, a. 4; *De Malo*, q. 3, a. 5. Source: *Peri Archon* III, 2, 2.

four of whom, namely, Laudicens, Alexander, Origen, and Didymus, Augustine rejects as known heretics."[117] This remark is a sign of Augustine's influence on the overall picture of Origen as a heretic.[118]

The Law   Thomas's reflections on the Law are hardly influenced by Origen. Regarding the question of whether the precepts of the decalogue are suitably distinguished from one another, he mentions Origen's view that four pertain to God and six to our neighbor, but sides with (*et hoc melius est*) Augustine's position that three refer to God and seven to our neighbor.[119] In the *Scriptum*, he asks whether the use of the sacraments of the Old Law, by which Thomas has above all the animal sacrifices in mind, were meritorious. Thomas mentions Origen's opinion in his Homily 17 on the Book of Numbers that God permitted these sacrifices for the same reason he permitted the bill of repudiation to Moses. The objection adds, however, that the bill was always evil and never meritorious (*semper malus fuit, et nunquam meritorious*).[120] Aquinas favors the opinion that the use of such sacrifices could be meritorious if done out of charity. In his response to the objection, he refers to Peter Lombard's view that, insofar as these sacrifices are offered to idols, they are displeasing to God and therefore not meritorious.[121]

Merit   As can be expected from Origen's claim that diversity in rational creatures is the result of merit, Origen is prominently present in the question of merit itself, although not in the *Summa Theologiae*. With regard to this topic, Romans 9:11–12, where it is said of Esau and Jacob that "though they were not yet born and had done nothing either good or bad ... the elder will serve the younger," figures prominently in Thomas's rejection of Origen's position.[122] In his *Commentary on Romans*, he

117. *In Gal.* 2, 11–15, l. 3, no. 88.

118. This sin of Peter is to be distinguished from his sin of denying to know Christ. Thomas (*In Matt.* 26:74, no. 2300) observes that there are "certain writings" that seem to excuse Peter from sinning mortally in this case. Thomas believes that Peter did sin mortally, however, "not due to malice but to fear of death."

119. *ST* I-II, q. 100, a. 4; Origenes, *Hom. VII in Exod.*, no. 2 (PG 12, 351).

120. *In IV Sent.*, d. 1, q. 1, a. 5, qc. 2, arg. 4 (ed. Moos, 40). Origenes, *Hom. XVII in Num.*, no. 1 (PG 12, 703).

121. *In IV Sent.*, d. 1, q. 1, a. 5, qc. 2, arg. 4 (ed. Moos, 43). A possible source is Petrus Lombardus, *In Epistolum ad Hebraeos*, c. 10 (PL 192, 480A).

122. *Ad Rom.*, c. 9, l. 2., no. 758. In *ScG* II, chap. 44, Rom 9:11–12 is used as a scriptural rejection of Origen's position that the union of body and soul was decreed by God as a result of previous sins. Thomas responds: "That notion also clearly clashes with apostolic doctrine. For

links Origen to the "Pelegian heresy" because both have in common the opinion that grace is given according to one's preceding merits, whether in this life, as Pelagius believed, or in another life, as Origen believed.[123] Both also understood Exodus 33:19 ("For the Lord says to Moses: 'I will have mercy on whom I have mercy, and I will have compassion on whom I have compassion'"), quoted in Romans 9:15, as meaning "that one is counted worthy of mercy on account of preexisting works." Nor can Romans 9:15, Thomas continues, be said to refer to merits subsequent to grace, as when God foresaw that a person would make good use of the grace He gives. This is so because, just as in natural things God causes both their forms and their activities so that any activity would cease if he would cease to act, so also both the infusion and the use of grace is from God.[124] The only reason for God to show mercy is therefore his will.[125] In his *Commentary on John*, Aquinas again claims that Origen said that our preceding merits are the cause of our election. Christ's words in John 15:16, "You did not choose me, but I chose you," are clearly opposed (*sed contra hoc est*) to such a claim.[126]

Religion   Aquinas's treatise on religion in the *Summa* contains a few important references to Origen. In the context of the high priest's words to Jesus in Matthew 26:63 ("And the high priest said to him: I adjure thee by the living God that you tell us if you are the Christ the Son of God"), Origen remarks: "a man who wishes to live according to the Gospel need not adjure another, for if it be unlawful to swear, it is also unlawful to

---

St. Paul says of Jacob and Esau, that 'when they were not yet born, nor had done any good or evil, it was said that the elder shall serve the younger' (Rom 9:11–17). Hence, before this was said, their souls had not sinned at all, yet the Apostle's statement postdates the time of their conception, as Genesis (25:23) makes clear."

123. *Ad Rom.*, c. 9, l. 3., no. 771.

124. At this point, as elsewhere in his later writings, Aquinas finds additional support in a fragment of Aristotle's *Eudemian Ethics*, known as *Liber de Bona Fortuna*.

125. In *Ad Rom.*, c. 9, l. 3., no. 773, Aquinas gives some insightful examples: "For it is clear that distributive justice has its field in things given as due; for example, if some persons have earned wage, more should be given to those who have done more work. But it has no place in things given spontaneously and out of mercy; for example, if a person meets two beggars and gives one an alms, he is not unjust but merciful. Similarly, if a person has been offended equally by two people and he forgives one but not the other, he is merciful to the one, just to the other, but unjust to neither. For since all men are born subject to damnation on account of the sin of the first parent, those whom God delivers by His grace He delivers by His mercy alone; and so He is merciful to those whom He delivers, just to those whom He does not deliver, but unjust to none."

126. *In Ioh.*, 15, l. 3, no. 2022.

adjure."[127] Thomas uses this phrase as an objection to the claim that supplication (*obsecratio*) is a part of prayer. In the corpus of the article, he
explains that there are three things needed for prayer. First, there needs
to be a "raising up of one's mind to God," and this is precisely what prayer
means. Second, there should be a petition as in an intercessory prayer.
Third, there needs to be a reason for what is asked for, and this can be
either on the part of God or on the part of the one who asks. On the
part of God, it is his sanctity, and this is called *obsecratio* or supplication,
which literally means pleading through sacred things (*per sacra contesta-
tio*); on the part of the one who asks, it is the gratitude we express through
thanksgiving. An example of *obsecratio* or supplication is therefore when
one prays "Through Thy nativity, deliver us, O Lord." Or each time one
ends a prayer with words like "Through Christ our Lord." In his response
to Origen, Thomas writes: "Supplication (*obsecratio*) is an adjuration not
for the purpose of compelling, for this is forbidden, but in order to im-
plore mercy."[128] He uses the same text from Origen when asking whether
it is lawful to adjure a man. Aquinas makes the distinction between putting oneself under an obligation by invoking God's name, doing the same
to another, and doing the same to another who is one's subject. Only the
first and third possibilities are lawful, because in the second case, "one
usurps over another a power which he has not," and this Origen had in
mind, Aquinas thinks.[129] He again defends Origen when asking whether
it is lawful to adjure the demons. He distinguishes once again between
two ways of adjuring: "one by way of prayer or inducement through reverence of some holy thing: the other by way of compulsion." The former
is not lawful because it gives the impression of some benevolence toward
the demons. The latter is lawful for some purposes—for instance, to prevent them from harming our soul or body—but not to learn from them
or obtain something from them. Origen's rejection of adjuring, Aquinas says, refers to the first way, that is, by way of prayer or inducement
through reverence of some holy thing or "by way of a friendly appeal."[130]
Further on in the same treatise in the *sed contra* of *ST* II-II, q. 95,
a. 2, Aquinas rejects divination as a species of superstition on the basis of

127. *ST* II-II, q. 83, a. 17, obj. 1; *CAM* 26.16 (ed. Marietti, 396); Origenes, *CMtS* on Mt
26:63, no. 110 (GCS 38/11, 229).
128. *ST* II-II, q. 83, a. 17, ad 1. In his own *Commentary on Matthew*, he does not mention
this phrase at the passage in question (Mt 26:63).
129. *ST* II-II, q. 90, a. 1, obj. 1 + ad 1.
130. *ST* II-II, q. 90, a. 2, obj. 1 + ad 1.

a passage from Origen's Homilies on the Book of Numbers, in which Origen ascribes seeking knowledge of the future to the work of demons.[131] This is the first of five instances in which Origen is quoted in a *sed contra* in the *Summa*.[132] This means that in these cases, as Leo Elders has observed, Origen serves as the foundation of the theological elaboration in the *corpus*.[133]

The Virtue of Humility   In *ST* II-II, q. 161, a. 1, Aquinas recognizes that Aristotle nowhere discusses humility or at least does not list humility among the virtues. In an excellent instance of *expositio reverentialis*, he argues that Aristotle was merely concerned with the virtues of the civic life in which the subjection toward one and other has a central place, whereas humility chiefly regards "the subjection of man to God, for Whose sake he humbles himself by subjecting himself to others."[134] It is remarkable that of all the biblical and patristic texts available to him on this topic, Thomas in the *sed contra* turns to one of Origen's homilies on Luke 1:48 ("Quia respexit humilitatem ancillæ suæ") in support of the virtuousness of humility. This is all the more remarkable given that only here, in question 161, Thomas refers to this passage from Origen. A look at the complete passage as it appears in Origen as well as in Thomas's *Catena* on Luke[135] sheds some light. There, in searching for the meaning of humility, Origen writes that "even the philosophers" write about the humility that God looks upon which "they call ἀτυφία (modesty) or μετριότης (moderation)."[136] Such an attempt to convey a positive meaning

131. *ST* II-II, q. 95, a. 2, s.c. Aquinas's text mistakenly refers to *Peri Archon*. See Origenes, *In Hom. XVI in Num.*, no. 7 (PL 12, 697B).

132. The other instances are *ST* II-II, q. 161 a. 1 s.c.; *ST* II-II, q. 161 a. 4 s.c. (on humility); *ST* II-II, q. 163 a. 3 s.c. (on the sin of the first man); *ST* II-II, q. 189 a. 5 s.c. (on whether children should be received in religion).

133. Leo Elders, "Structure et fonction de l'argument Sed contra dans la Somme théologique," *Divus Thomas* 80 (1977): 245–60, reprinted in *Autour de saint Thomas d'Aquin: Recueil d'études sur sa pensée philosophique et théologique, tome II. L'agir moral; Approches théologiques* (Paris: Fac-Editions, Uitgeverij Tabor, 1987), 147–66, here 165.

134. *ST* II-II, q. 161, a. 1, ad 5.

135. *CAL* 1.16 (ed. Marietti, p. 20): "Origenes in Lucam. Sed quid humile atque deiectum habebat quae Dei filium gestabat in utero? Sed considera quoniam humilitas in Scripturis una de virtutibus praedicatur, quae a philosophis atyphia, sive metriotis, dicitur. Sed et nos possumus eam appellare quodam circuitu, cum aliquis non est inflatus, sed ipse se deicit." Origenes, *Hom. VIII in Luc.*, no. 4 (PG 13, 1821B; SC 87, 170–71; FOCT 94, 35).

136. See the notes on p. 35 of Lienhard's English translation in *Origen, Homilies on Luke*, Fathers of the Church 94, translated by by Joseph T. Lienhard (Washington, DC: Catholic University of America Press, 1996), for more on these connotations in secular Greek.

of ταπεινότης or humility, which in secular Greek had the connotation of vileness and lowness in position, must have appealed to Thomas, who is known for the reverence with which he approached Greek philosophers and theologians.[137] Something identical occurs in the same q. 161, a. 4, asking whether humility is a part of modesty or temperance. Again, Thomas refers in the *sed contra* to the same homily and to the passage where Origen explicitly connects humility to modesty. This twofold use of Origen as an authority in one question, in both cases referring to the same homily, might indicate that at the time of writing this question he had direct access to this homily in the Latin translation by Jerome but also that the choice of authoritative texts occurred on the basis of which text was accessible on that particular occasion.

The Religious Life   The final topic to be treated in this section concerns the religious life and in particular the mendicant way of life. Given that this way of life was a matter of conflict in the thirteenth century,[138] a conflict in which Thomas himself participated, the use of Origen, known for his errors and described by Thomas himself as a "known heretic"[139] in his lectures on Galatians, is remarkable.

In his *De Perfectione* (1269–70) regarding poverty, Thomas argues that the renunciation of earthly possessions in Matthew 19:21 does not in itself make one perfect but is a way (*via*) toward perfection, which, ultimately, quoting St. Jerome, consists in following Christ. Moreover, following Christ's counsel does not make someone perfect at once (*in ipso tempore*) but is to be understood, following Origen, "that from that time, his contemplation of God begins to attract him to all virtues."[140] In the *Summa Theologiae*, Aquinas uses this thought to argue that the religious state is perfect in a prescriptive manner rather than in a descriptive manner; in other words, those in a religious state are not perfect but "tend toward perfection," and some are "beginners" and others "proficient."[141] The importance of Origen can also be gathered from the fact that Aquinas prefaces his defense of the religious life in *Contra Retra-*

---

137. For two examples, see the prologue to *Contra Errores Graecorum* and *In De Div. Nom.*, c. 14, l. 4, no. 1008.

138. See Ulrich Horst, *Evangelische Armut und Kirche: Thomas von Aquin und die Armutskontroversen des 13. und beginnenden 14. Jahrhunderts* (Berlin: Akademie Verlag, 1995).

139. *In Gal.* 2, 11–15, l. 3, no. 88.

140. *De Perfect.*, c. 8 (LE 41B 73, 97–103); see also *CAM* 19, no. 5 (ed. Marietti, 287); Origenes, *Comm. Matt.* XV, 17 (GCS 40/10, 398; PG 13, 1303). LE mistakenly has 1309A.

141. *ST* II-II, q. 186, a. 1, ad 3.

hentium (1270–71) with a large quote from one of Origen's homilies on Exodus. He sees the attacks on the religious life, and in particular on the counsels, prefigured in Exodus 5:4 in the words of the Pharaoh, who said to Moses and Aaron: "'Why do you, Moses and Aaron, draw off the people from their work?'" Aquinas approvingly quotes Origen, who remarks that also today the "friends of the Pharaoh" are accusing those who want to enable others to enter the religious life of deceiving and leading astray the young.[142] One of the objections claimed is that one should first have mastered the commandments before practicing the counsels. This claim would exclude the very young from entering the religious life. Aquinas rejects this argument on the basis of the life of Christ, Scripture, and the customs that resulted from Scripture, but he also detects, with Origen, a false moral and intellectual superiority at work in the objection to prevent the "unlearned" (*minus adhuc eruditos*) to enter the religious life: "We ought to bear this [the life of Christ and in particular that Christ himself became a child] in mind, lest, in our esteem for our own superior wisdom, we should despise the little ones of the Church, forbidding the children to go to Jesus."[143] In his concluding remarks on this objection in *Contra Retrahentium*, Aquinas shows the extent to which he takes Origen seriously as an exegete. Aquinas starts with boldly saying that objections to the claim that one should first have practiced the commandments before being able to follow the counsels can be easily refuted by drawing on St. Jerome.[144] He argued that if the young man in Matthew 19 had indeed fulfilled the commandments, there should have been no reason for him to go away sad when Christ said to him to sell everything and give it to the poor. Jerome concludes, therefore, that when the young man said "All these things have I kept from my youth," the young man must have lied. At this point, Aquinas inserts a comment by Origen, which seems to undermine the position of Jerome. Origen recounts that the Gospel of the Hebrews,[145] a lost apocryphal writing of which fragments are preserved in Origen's writings, among others, says that the young man first hesitated

---

142. *Contra Retrah.*, c. 1 (LE 41C, 40, 100–109); Origenes, *In Exod. Hom.* III, no. 3 (PG 12, 315A; SC 321, 106).

143. *Contra Retrah.*, c. 3 (LE 41C, 43, 94–102); *CAM* 19, 14 (ed. Marietti, 284); Origenes, *Comm. Matt.* XV, 8 (GCS 40/10, 370; PG 13, 1275). For other uses of this text on the same topic, see *Quodl.* III, q. 5, a. 1 (LE 25.2, 256, 111–19); *Quodl.* IV, q. 12, a. 1 (LE 25.2, 350, 374–84); and *ST* II-II, q. 189, a. 5, s.c.

144. See Hieronymus, *Super Matthaeum* III, 18, on Mt 19:20 (PL 26, 137B).

145. On the passage of the young man in Origen's *Commentary on Matthew*, see P. Luomanen, *Recovering Jewish-Christian Sects and Gospels* (Brill: Leiden, 2012), 177–90.

(literally "scratched his head," *scalpere caput suum*).[146] Origen concludes that it is possible that the young man practiced the commandments in an imperfect way and therefore was not lying to Christ. Aquinas follows this opinion, in part because it is supported by others such as Chrysostom and Bede.[147] What is more important, however, is that it shows that, even if the young man only practiced the commandments to a certain extent (*aliqualiter*), such a practice is not necessary for the exercise of the counsels. On the contrary, "the way of perfection is open both to sinners and to innocent souls," as is attested by the fact that Matthew did not practice the commandments but "was called from the habits of sin to the practice of the Counsels."[148]

Another remarkable instance can be found in *ST* II-II, q. 186, a. 10, where it is asked whether a religious sins more grievously than a secular by the same kind of sin. Given the importance and the high demands that Aquinas (and the Catholic Church) attaches to the religious life, one should not be surprised to find an affirmative answer to this question. Aquinas argues that, because of the counsels, which are not mere divine precepts, and because of the divine favors a religious person has received, and finally because of the fact that a religious is in some respect a public figure whose way of life is noticed by the people, when a religious sins against the counsels, he sins out of contempt. Therefore, in general, any sin by a religious is more grievous than when the same sin is performed by a layperson. It is, however, surprising that Aquinas also holds the opposite, that is, that sins by a religious person are in a certain respect less grievous than when they are performed by a layperson: "if a religious, not out of contempt, but out of weakness or ignorance, commit[s] a sin that is not against the vow of his profession, without giving scandal (for instance if he commits it in secret) he sins less grievously in the same kind of sin than a secular." Why is this so? In the case of a minor sin, the good works of the religious "absorb as it were" (*quasi absorbetur*) that sin. In the case of a mortal sin, a religious more easily recovers from it. This happens for two reasons. Not only is a religious helped by his fellow religious to rise again from sin, but also a religious has the right intention toward God. At this point, for the first and only time, Aquinas quotes Origen's homily

146. *Contra Retrah.*, c. 7 (LE 41C, 49, 15–26); *CAM* 19.5 (ed. Marietti, 286); Origenes, *Comm. Matt.* XV, 14 (GCS 40/10, 389; PG 13, 1294–96).

147. See *CAMR* 10.3 (ed. Marietti, 510).

148. *Contra Retrah.*, c. 7 (LE 41C, 49, 35–42). The same argument is used in *ST* II-II, q. 189, a. 1, ad 1.

on Psalm 36:24 ("When he shall fall, he shall not be bruised"). There, Origen, to corroborate his claim that the just man knows how to make amends and recover himself, introduces St. Peter, who, "even as he who had said: 'I know not the man,' shortly afterwards when the Lord had looked on him, knew to shed most bitter tears."[149]

Christ

The principal point of contention regarding Christ is undoubtedly Origen's view on the Incarnation as the assumption of a body by the pre-existent soul of Christ.[150] Thomas, echoing the position of the Synod of Constantinople in 543, attributes this view to Origen in both the *Summa contra Gentiles* and in the *Summa Theologiae*; in the *Scriptum*, he seems unaware of this view or at least does not address Origen's position. In the *Summa contra Gentiles*, he refutes Origen's position as plainly false (*unde patet falsum esse Origenis dogma*) on the basis of the impossibility in general of the preexistence of the soul. In the *Summa Theologiae*, he uses a strictly theological argument and argues for the unfittingness (*inconveniens*) of the possible logical consequences of Origen's position. The first logical consequence would entail that Christ's soul had its own subsistence before the assumption. This position opens up two further possibilities, neither of which are acceptable. Either the assumption leaves the subsistence of Christ's soul intact or the assumption would destroy the subsistence of the soul, which is unfitting. In the former case, there would be two subsistent subjects in Christ: the Word and the soul. Although Thomas does not say so explicitly, it is clear that the preexistence of Christ's soul would result in Nestorianism. The second logical consequence would entail the union with the Word from the very moment of the creation of Christ's soul followed by Christ's assumption of his body. This position seems to resemble more correctly Origen's actual position. For Thomas, however, this would result in Christ's soul "not being of the same nature as ours."[151] Whereas Origen explicitly holds that the nature of Christ's soul is not essentially different from other souls and that it is

---

149. *ST* II-II, q. 186, a. 10. Origenes, *Hom. IV in Ps. 36*, no. 2 (PG 12, 1351D; SC 411, 190). Note that repentance occurs because Christ looked at Peter. In his commentary on Mt 26:75, Aquinas numbers three motives of repentance: the cock—i.e., the preacher; Peter's remembering, which is a consequence of the words of a preacher; and Luke's remark in Lk 22:61: "The Lord looked on Peter."

150. See Origenes, *Peri Archon* II, 6, 4–5.

151. *ST* III, q. 6, a. 3. See also *In Heb.*, c. 1, l. 4, no. 63.

precisely the preexistence of Christ's soul that accounts for the belief that Christ's soul was indeed like our souls,[152] Thomas's reasoning results in precisely the opposite result. If indeed the soul is created at the very moment of its embodiment, as Thomas holds, preexistence of the assumed soul would imply that the beginning of Christ's soul would differ from the beginning of the souls of other men, which in turn would entail that Christ's soul would be of a different nature than our souls. Nowhere does Thomas hint at the fact that Origen proposed all this as an opinion and invited his readers to propose better arguments if needed.[153] In his *Commentary on John*, he claims that a misinterpretation of John 3:13, "the One who came down from heaven, the Son of Man," resulted in Origen's claim that Christ's preexisting human soul descended from heaven and took flesh from the Virgin. Aquinas's rejection of this position resembles his method in *Summa contra Gentiles*: "But this also conflicts with the Catholic faith, which teaches that souls do not exist before their bodies."[154]

The twenty references in the unfinished *Tertia Pars* all occur in the area of Christology. Apart from the first reference, discussed above, all occur in answers to objections and deal with the interpretation of scriptural passages for which Origen is seen to be helpful. Even if Aquinas prefers a different interpretation, he is willing to allow for the validity of Origen's interpretation. This occurs, for instance, with regard to the statement in Mark 13:32 that only the Father knows day and hour. Aquinas prefers to say that the Son did know but was not willing to reveal it. He allows, however, for Origen's opinion that Christ is referring to his Body, the Church, which is ignorant of the time.[155] Another example is the difficulty posed by Luke 2:46–47, where it is said that Christ was asking questions in the temple. This seems to indicate that Christ learned something from these teachers. One of Origen's homilies on the Gospel of Luke, as translated by Jerome, gives a sufficient answer. "As Origen says: 'Our Lord asked

152. See *Peri Archon* II, 6, 5. Origen argues that the perfection of Christ's love resulted in the free choice between good and evil becoming an immutable habit. According to R. Williams, the immutable adherence to the good could take place only in the preexistence because the rejection of the preexistence of the soul would make Christ's human soul a sort of concurrence to the Logos, a position that would result in Apollinarianism. See Rowan Williams, "Origen on the Soul of Jesus," in *Origeniana Tertia*, ed. Richard Hanson and Henri Crouzel (Rome: Edizioni dell'Ateneo, 1985), 131–37.

153. See *Peri Archon* II, 6, 7.

154. *In Ioh.*, 3, l. 2, no. 467.

155. *ST* III, q. 10, a. 2, ad 1; *In Matt.* 24:36 (ed. Marietti, no. 1983); *CAM* XXIV, no. 11 (ed. Marietti, 357). Origenes, *CMtS* XXIV, 36, no. 55 (GCS 38/11, 126).

questions not in order to learn anything, but in order to teach by questioning. For from the same well of knowledge came the question and the wise reply.' Hence the Gospel goes on to say that 'all that heard Him were astonished at His wisdom and His answers.'"[156] One can find a particular instance in *ST* III, q. 46, a. 11, where it is asked whether it was fitting for Christ to be crucified among thieves. The second objection quotes a phrase from Origen's *Commentary on Matthew*: "It was not men's lot to die with Jesus, since He died for all," which seems to deny its fittingness. Aquinas, however, points to the context of the phrase in question, that is, that which immediately follows: "It was not fitting that anyone else should die with Christ from the same cause as Christ: hence Origen continues thus in the same passage: 'All had been under sin, and all required that another should die for them, not they for others.'"[157] It is interesting to see not only that Thomas, by providing the correct context of Origen's phrase used in the objection, explicitly rescues Origen from an erroneous reading, but also that this is the only instance in his works wherein he uses this passage from Origen's *Commentary on Matthew*. Neither in his *Catena Aurea* on Matthew nor in his *Commentary on Matthew* did Aquinas mention Origen in this context. It seems reasonable to say, therefore, that in his willingness to exonerate Origen, Thomas did not rely solely on his knowledge accumulated in his *Catena Aurea* but read Origen afresh.

The only disagreement occurs when Thomas investigates what happened when, at the moment of Christ's death, darkness filled the whole earth, as one reads in Matthew 27:45. Origen's opinion that this was caused because clouds came between the sun and the moon is mentioned extensively by Aquinas.[158] It is rather the authority of Dionysius that leads him to give more credence to his opinion. "On this point, however, credence is to be given rather to Dionysius, who is an eyewitness as to this having occurred by the moon eclipsing the sun."[159] Both in the *Summa* and in his *Commentary on Matthew*, where Thomas recounts the same position, he has the intellectual honesty to mention Origen's objection

---

156. *ST* III, q. 12, a. 3, ad 1. Origenes, *Hom. XIX in Luc.*, no. 6 (PG 13, 1851; SC 87, 279).

157. *ST* III, q. 46, a. 11, ad 2. Origenes, *CMtS* XXVI, 35, no. 88 (GCS 38/11, 204; PG 13, 1740): "cum Iesu enim mori pro nobis omnibus moriente, ut nos vivamus, hominum non erat, quoniam omnes fuerant in peccatis et omnes opus habebant, ut pro eis alius moreretur non ipsi pro aliis."

158. Origenes, *CMtS* XXVII, 45, no. 134 (GCS 38/11, 274–76; PG 13, 1782).

159. *ST* III, q. 44, a. 2, ad 2; *In Matt.* 27:45 (ed. Marietti, no. 2377). The source for Dionysius is his *Epist. VII Ad Polycarpum* § 2 (PG 3, 1081).

that, if it were such a great miracle, why wasn't there an astrologist who re-corded it?[160] In both passages, Aquinas writes that, because it was not the time for an eclipse, astronomers were not expecting one. In the *Summa* he adds, "But in Egypt, where clouds are few on account of the tranquility of the air, Dionysius and his companions were considerably astonished so as to make the aforesaid observations about this darkness."[161]

Eschatology

In Thomas's first systematic work, the *Scriptum*, references to Origen are rare and do not give rise to lengthy discussions, as will be the case in lat-er works. Nor is Thomas interested in investigating Origen's orthodoxy. He makes an exception, however, for Origen's positions in eschatological questions.[162] It is in the *Scriptum*, in fact, that one finds Thomas for the first time explicitly ascribing to Origen doctrinal errors that have been "rejected by the Church."[163]

The Fate of Demons and Those Who Are in Hell   The first time this oc-curs is in the question of whether prayers profit those who are in hell. In a long response, he reviews and rejects a number of opinions. A final opin-ion, which he contemplates, has to do with the idea that prayers profit the damned, if it is understood as neither diminishing nor interrupting their punishment, nor as diminishing their sense of punishment, but as withdrawing some matter of grief, that is, the knowledge of themselves as outcasts for whom nobody cares, from the damned. He rejects this opinion on the authority of Augustine, who writes that "the spirits of the departed are where they see nothing of what men do or of what happens

160. *ST* III, q. 44, a. 2, ad 2. *In Matt.* 27:45 (ed. Marietti, no. 2378).
161. *ST* III, q. 44, a. 2, ad 2.
162. It is as if Thomas already realized what Hans Urs von Balthasar wrote about es-chatology being the *Wetterwinkel* of theology. See Hans Urs von Balthasar, "Umrisse der Eschatologie," in *Verbum caro: Skizzen zur Theologie I* (Einsiedeln: Johannes Verlag, 1960, 276–300, here 276: "Die Eschatologie ist der 'Wetterwinkel' in der Theologie unserer Zeit. Von ihr her steigen jene Gewitter auf, die das ganze Land fruchtbar bedrohen: verhageln oder erfrischen. Wenn für den Liberalismus des 19. Jahrhunderts das Wort von Troeltsch gelten konnte: 'Das eschatologische Bureau ist meist geschlossen,' so macht dieses im Gegenteil seit der Jahrhundertwende Überstunden." First published as "Eschatologie," in *Fragen der Theologie heute*, ed. B. J. Feiner, J. Trütsch, and F. Böckle (Einsiedeln: Benziger, 1957), 403–21.
163. *In IV Sent.*, d. 46, q.2, a. 3, qc. 1 (ed. Parma, 1148). On two previous occasions, he had ascribed an error to Origen, but the first instance is secondhand (*In II Sent.*, d. 17, q. 3, a. 2, ed. Mandonnet, 438), and the second instance merely mentions the error in the *divisio textus* (*In III Sent.*, d. 6, q. 1, ed. Moos, 218) without developing it further.

to them in this life."[164] Aquinas grants the possibility of an extraordinary revelation to the damned so that they gain knowledge about the prayers offered for them, but ultimately considers all this to be "a matter of uncertainty" (*verbum omnino incertum*). It is therefore safer (*tutius*) to simply say, he concludes, that prayers do not profit the damned.[165]

In the course of this discussion, Aquinas considers the possibility that at least before the time of the final judgment and for those who, although now in hell, during their lifetime were actual members of the Church and had the faith, received the sacraments and performed works generically good, prayers by the Church are of some assistance. This opinion contains the difficulty, however, that, since punishment of hell is infinite in duration but finite in intensity,[166] "a multiplicity of prayers would take away that punishment altogether, which is the error of Origen (*error Origenis*)."[167]

A more extreme position regards the possibility that by divine mercy even the punishment of the demons can be terminated. Here we encounter a second instance of an *error Origenis*, namely, the opinion that, as Augustine recounts in his *De Civitate Dei*,[168] by God's mercy demons are one day to be liberated (*liberandi sunt*) from their punishments.[169] In his *Scriptum*, Aquinas gives two reasons why this error "has been rejected by the Church." First, it manifestly goes against the authority of Scripture and in particular against Revelations 20:10 ("the devil who had deceived them was thrown into the lake of fire and sulphur where the beast and the false prophet were, and they will be tormented day and night for ever and ever)." In his Hebrews commentary, Aquinas uses Hebrews 2:14b ("that through death he might destroy him who has the power of death, that is, the devil") to argue against Origen that neither the devil's substance nor his malice is destroyed "so that the devil would become good at some time," but that it is his power that is destroyed.[170] Second, it ultimately entails a restriction of God's mercy, because Origen also held that the angels and the souls of the blessed will one day pass from their state of beatitude to the misery of this life.[171]

---

164. Augustinus, *De Cura pro Mortuis Gerenda* 13, 16 (PL 40, 604).

165. *In IV Sent.*, d. 45, q. 2, a. 2, qc. 1 (ed. Parma, 1123).

166. Later in *In IV Sent.*, d. 46, q. 1, a. 3 co, he gives the following reason: "cum non possit esse poena infinita per intensionem, quia creatura non est capax alicujus qualitatis infinitae, requiritur quod sit saltem duratione infinita" (ed. Parma, 1142).

167. *In IV Sent.*, d. 45, q. 2, a. 2, qc. 1 (ed. Parma, 1123).

168. Augustinus, *De Civ. Dei* 21.17 (CCSL 48, 783, 7–10).

169. *In IV Sent.*, d. 46, q. 2, a. 3 qc. 1 (ed. Parma, 1148).

170. *In Heb.*, c. 2, l. 4., no. 141.

171. *In IV Sent.*, d. 46, q. 2, a. 3, qc. 1 (ed. Parma, 1148): "Unde sicut ponebat daemones

A less extreme position entertains the possibility that at least human beings by divine mercy will not have to undergo eternal punishment. This time, and again on the basis of Augustine's *De Civitate Dei*, Aquinas does not ascribe this view to Origen as such but regards it as a conclusion drawn from Origen's error. Aquinas finds this view "entirely unreasonable" (*omnino irrationabilis*). He writes: "Because just as the demons are obstinate in their malice and therefore ought to be punished for eternity, so also the souls of men who die without charity for 'death is to men, what the fall is to the angels,'" quoting from John of Damascene's *De Fide Orthodoxa*.[172]

In *ST* I, q. 64, he combines these last two positions—that is, on the fate of demons and the fate of humans—and ascribes them both to Origen. This time, however, the textual corroboration is better, for he implicitly refers to Origen's position that every intelligent creature, because of their free will, has the faculty to direct itself toward good or toward evil.[173] Aquinas seems to think that for Origen this applies to both demons and angels and saints to such an extent that there always remains for them the possibility to change their moral and ontological status either in heaven or in hell. As in the *Scriptum*, he refutes this idea on the basis of both Scripture and reason. In terms of the scriptural foundation, he quotes not Revelations 20:10, as he did in the *Scriptum*, but Matthew 25:46 ("And they will go away into eternal punishment, but the righteous into eternal life"). He explicitly opposes Origen's error to the "Catholic faith," that is, "the will of the good angels is confirmed in good, and the will of the demons is obstinate in evil." The second argument holds that "everlasting stability is of the very nature of true beatitude" and hence should be affirmed of angels and saints.[174] Already in *De Ver.*, q. 24, a. 8, regarding the related question of whether the free choice of a creature can be confirmed in good by grace, he emphasized *contra Origenes* that the happiness of saints and angels cannot come to an end because *immutabilitas et securitas sit de ratione beatitudinis*. Otherwise, their happiness

---

et animas damnatorum quandoque a poena liberandas, ita ponebat Angelos et animas beatorum quandoque a beatitudine in huius vitae miserias devolvendas." It is difficult to find textual corroboration for the necessity (*liberandas, devolvendas*) that Thomas ascribes to Origen's position. It seems, in fact, that Origen merely argued for the possibility of such an event; see *Peri Archon* I, 6, 3. See also Jerome, *Epist.* 124, 3 (PL 22, 1062).

172. *In IV Sent.*, d. 46, q. 2, a. 3, qc. 2 (ed. Parma, p. 1149). Johannes Damascenus, *De Fide Orthodoxa* 2.4 (PG 94, 877C).

173. See *Peri Archon* I, 6, 3, and I, 8, 3.

174. *ST* I, q. 64, a. 2.

would not be true happiness, something that Aquinas finds inadmissible.[175] In his Sermon 19 *Beati qui habitant*, dated probably between 1261 and 1264, he corroborates the claim that stability essentially belongs to beatitude by referring to Aristotle's remark in *NE* I (1100b4–7) that a happy person is not a chameleon, now happy and then miserable again.[176] Elsewhere he defines *stabilitas* as *confirmatio in bono*[177] or *firmitas ad bona*.[178] In his *Super Psalmos*, Aquinas frequently links *stabilitas* to immutability and eternity. This happens, for instance, when commenting on Psalm 32 (33):11: "The counsel of the Lord stands for ever"[179] or on Psalm 34 (35):18: "in the mighty throng I will praise thee."[180] In his commentary on the well-known passage from Psalm 42 (43):3 ("ipsa me deduxerunt, et adduxerunt in montem sanctum tuum, et in tabernacula tua"), Aquinas writes, "all this refers to the heavenly fatherland on which we should fix our desire and which we should ardently pursue; and he designates this when he says 'in montem sanctum tuum.' Exodus 15:17 says: 'Thou shalt bring them in, and plant them in the mountain of thy inheritance' because it is there that the perfect stability exists."[181]

Now, if such a stability pertains to the angels, the mere possibility of their fall becomes unintelligible or so it seems. Aquinas recognizes clearly this conundrum. In his *Expositio super Iob* (1263–65), commenting on Job 4:18 ("Even those who serve him are not stable and in his angels, he found evil"), he writes that the fall of the angels seems astonishing (*mirum videtur*), especially if one examines their contemplative and active powers. With respect to their contemplative power, "there should have been *stabilitas* in the angels." Why this is so can be shown by recalling the fundamentals of his metaphysics as he himself does at this point. Whereas the cause of mutability is potency, the cause of immutability is act. Now, what is more completed by act has a firmer hold on unity (*firmius stat in uno*). As potency is to act, so the will is to the good. The will of a creature is compared to the will of the Creator as potency to act. From this, one should conclude that the more a created will cleaves to his Creator, the more confirmed it is in the good (*stabiliuntur in bono*). In the case of the angels,

---

175. *De Ver.*, q. 24, a. 8 (LE 22.3, 700, 67–81).
176. *Sermo XIX 'Beati qui habitant'* (LE 44.1, 300, 77–80).
177. *ST* I, q. 62, a. 1, s.c.
178. *Super Psalmo* 45, no. 4.
179. *Super Psalmo* 32, no. 10.
180. *Super Psalmo* 34, no. 14.
181. *Super Psalmo* 42, no. 2.

this means that "since the angels seem to cling more to God and in closer proximity than other creatures, in that they contemplate him more exactly, they seem to be the more stable (*stabiliores*) than other creatures." Nevertheless, they fell, or, in the words of Aquinas, *tamen non fuerunt stabiles*![182]

With respect to the active power of the angels, the conundrum becomes even more apparent. Aquinas writes: "As the rule more approaches the true measure of straight, so much the less crookedness does it have. God, in whom the prime righteousness exists, directing all things by his providence, disposes lower creatures through higher ones. Hence, as they are sent by God to direct others, there seems to be little or no perversity possible in the higher creatures who are called angels." Nevertheless, there is! This means for us human beings that if even angels, who by their nature are more prone to cling to God, fail to possess *stabilitas*, there is not a single man who can be called *stabilis*, and if even angels in their mission to direct lower creatures can hardly possess any depravity but nevertheless do, "one must believe that depravity could be found in any man."[183]

At this point, it becomes clear why I have devoted so much space to this passage from Aquinas's *Commentary on Job*. The bleak view of the "human condition"—an expression he uses in this context—should not lead us, so Aquinas warns us, to "fall into the error of Origen who asserts that even now all created spirits are not steadfast and can be seduced into depravity. For some gained by grace the favor to cling to God unchangeably by seeing him in his essence. In this way, even some men, although they are lower in nature than the angels are granted by grace immunity from the depravity of mortal sin even in this life."[184]

Regarding the duration of beatitude, he recalls "the error of Plato and his followers in which even Origen fell,"[185] that is, souls that have merited beatitude return to a body after a number of years and again are subjected to "the miseries of this life" and therefore stop to possess beatitude, a position already attributed to Origen in his *Scriptum*.[186] Thomas rejects this view on the basis of three arguments. First, the view goes against the natural desire of the soul, which is not satisfied unless it gains perpetual

182. *In Iob*, c. 4 (LE 26.2, 31, 408–37).
183. *In Iob*, c. 4 (LE 26.2, 32, 450–51).
184. *In Iob*, c. 4 (LE 26.2, 32, 452–60).
185. *Sermo XIX 'Beati qui habitant'* (LE 44.1, p. 300, 95–301, 97). The Leonine edition gives as a source Hieronymus, *Contra Joannem Hierosolymitanum* 6 (PL 23, 384BC) and *Epist.* 124, 3 (PL 22, 1061). Jerome paraphrases *Peri Archon* I, 4, 1, or I, 5, 3, depending on the edition (ed. cit., 202).
186. *In IV Sent.*, d. 46, q. 2, a. 3, qc. 1 (ed. Parma, 1148).

beatitude. Second, it goes against the perfection of grace, which fills the soul entirely; otherwise, beatitude would not be a perfect good. Third, it goes against the equity of divine justice, because perfect charity entails the impossibility of becoming removed from the *fruitio Dei*.[187] The first and the third argument one also finds in the *Summa Theologiae*, where Aquinas again attributes this error to Origen, following "certain Platonists." The third argument finds a more complete expression there as well: "since the withdrawal of happiness is a punishment, it cannot be enforced by God, the just Judge, except for some fault; and he that sees God cannot fall into a fault, since rectitude of the will, of necessity, results from that vision as was shown above [in q. 4, a. 4]."[188] In the *Summa contra Gentiles*, a text contemporaneous to *Sermo XIX*, Aquinas devotes an entire chapter to this question, again connecting Plato to Origen. Given the philosophical nature of the first three books, the argument from natural desire plays a key role. He also offers an argument that clarifies that *stabilitas* or "the highest immutability," as he calls it, is not something static. When arguing that one cannot become weary of the delight in the vision of God because tiredness is a result of the use of the body, he writes: "nothing that is contemplated with wonder can be tiresome, since as long as the thing remains in wonder it continues to stimulate desire. But the divine substance is always viewed with wonder by any created intellect, since no created intellect comprehends it. So, it is impossible for an intellectual substance to become tired of this vision."[189] For the created intellect, therefore, wonder and desire remain, even when seeing God.

Years later, in his *De Malo*, q. 16, a. 5 (1269–71), he asks whether the free choice of devils can return to good after their sin. As in the *Scriptum* and *De Ver.*, q. 24, a. 10, Thomas's account of Origen's position is very much influenced by Augustine's *De Civ. Dei* 21.17. The scriptural basis for rejecting this position is identical to *ST* I, q. 64, namely, Matthew 25:46 ("And they will go away into eternal punishment, but the righteous into eternal life"). Now, however, Aquinas engages in a detailed analysis of what intrinsically belongs to the power of free choice, because he thinks that it is from the fact that Origen failed to consider this that his error arose. What belongs intrinsically to the power of free choice is that "it can be for different things," something that belongs exclusively to beings possessing intellect and will and that is exemplified by the difference of

---

187. *Sermo XIX 'Beati qui habitant'* (LE 44.1, 301, 101–41).
188. *ST* I-II, q. 5, a. 4.
189. *ScG* III, chap. 62.

means chosen for the sake of ends. Angels and human beings, therefore, while they cannot not desire happiness, can choose different means to that end. The difference between good and evil, however, does not intrinsically belong to the power of free choice, because even a nature capable of defect can have free choice, and to be deficient in its activity does not belong to the nature of a power. In the case of a will that strives for evil, such a deficiency of the intellect occurs because evil can only be desired insofar as it is understood under the aspect of the good. Thomas concludes therefore: "And so nothing prevents there being a power of free choice that so strives for good that it is in no way capable of striving for evil, whether by nature, as in the case of God, or by the perfection of grace, as in the case of the saints and the holy angels."[190] Nor does a difference of change—that is, not willing what one previously willed or willing what one previously did not will—belong intrinsically to the nature of free choice, but is an incidental result of being a changeable nature that can undergo changes through internal causes (acquisition of new knowledge or the influence of emotions or habits on the will) or external causes (God changing the will of a human being from evil to good). Next, Thomas applies these distinctions to the case of the angels. It belongs intrinsically to the angels' nature "to have actual knowledge of everything they can know naturally"; that is, the angels' intellect "is permanently disposed regarding everything it knows by nature." Given that "the will is proportioned to the intellect, it follows that their will is also by nature irrevocable regarding what belongs to the natural order." Regarding the angels' potentiality for moving toward supernatural things, he reasons as follows. Given that, following Aristotle (*Physics* III, 2, 201b31–32), change belongs to things having potentiality, angels can only move from the order of nature to supernatural things by either turning toward or turning away from them. In other words, once actualized in the angels' first choice, a subsequent change from the supernatural to the natural is no longer possible. Moreover, any addition "to something is added to it according to the mode of its nature," and the angels' nature is, as already established, irrevocable with regard to what belongs to the order of nature. Hence it follows "that angels persist irrevocably in turning from or toward a supernatural good." All this belongs to the internal causes that, because angels after their first choice no longer have a changeable nature, no longer have an effect on the angels' nature. The same applies, however, to the external causes. Given that "the

---

190. *De Malo*, q. 16, a. 5 c. (LE 23, 305, 266–70).

condition of wayfarer is ended for them" after their first choice, they are immutable in either good or evil. An infusion on the part of God of more grace to "recall them from the evil of their first turning away from him" would for Thomas therefore be contrary to God's wisdom.[191]

The topic of a possible salvation for the demons or the damned figures prominently in Thomas's commentaries on the *Corpus Paulinum*. Among the nineteen explicit references to Origen, fifteen are formulated negatively and attribute to him an error or misunderstanding by way of expressions such as *erravit Origenes, incidit in errorem, cavendus est error Origenis, Origenes non intelligens*, and the like. Eight of these fifteen references deal with his eschatology. In commenting on 1 Corinthians 15:26–27 ("The last enemy to be destroyed is death. For God has put all things in subjection under his feet"), Thomas introduces a digression (*Sciendum est autem*) in which he presents Origen's position in *Peri Archon* as saying that the punishments of the damned are cleansing and therefore not eternal. Ultimately, Origen "wanted that all in hell will be converted to Christ at some time and be saved, including the devil." Thomas rejects this position briefly[192] and firmly on the basis of an argument from authority: "Sed hoc est haereticum et damnatum in Concilio."[193] Another important passage for Origen's position is Philippians 2:10 ("at the name of Jesus every knee should bow, in heaven and on earth and under the earth"). This passage is again wrongly interpreted by Origen as if it implies that even the demons will be subjected to Christ in virtue of Christ's charity. Aquinas's counterargument is Matthew 25:41 ("Depart from me, you cursed, into the eternal fire prepared for the devil and his angels").[194] Commenting on Ephesians 1:10 ("to re-establish all things in Christ"; ἀνακεφαλαιώσασθαι τὰ πάντα ἐν τῷ Χριστῷ), he warns his listeners: "Beware of the error Origen fell into, as if the damned angels were to be redeemed through Christ; this was only a figment of his imagination."[195]

---

191. *De Malo*, q. 16, a. 5 (LE 23, 305, 301–06, 340).

192. The distinction between the subjection that occurs *per conversionem peccatorum ad Deum* and the subjection of those who are subject to Christ but *numquam convertuntur ad Christum* becomes clearer in his commentaries on Eph 1:22 and Phil 2:10 as well as on Heb 1:13.

193. *In I Cor.*, 15, 26, l. 3, no. 946. A possible source is *Peri Archon* III, 6, 5. A similar strategy can be found in *De Rationibus Fidei*, c. 9 (LE 40B 69, 16–20), where he ascribes to Origen the position that all the pain after death is purifying and rejects this position on the basis of what "the Holy, Catholic and Apostolic Church confesses."

194. *In Phil.* 2:10, l. 3, no. 72.

195. *In Eph.* 1:10, l. 3, no. 29: "Ubi cavendus est error Origenis, ne per hoc credamus Angelos damnatos redimendos esse per Christum, ut ipse finxit."

Another figment of Origen's imagination that Thomas deplores under the influence of Jerome concerns the consequences of a new redemption of the demons by Christ, for this would entail Christ having to suffer anew for their redemption.[196] Ephesians 1:22 ("he has subjected all things under his feet") again offers occasion to mention the error of Origen, which he again refutes on the basis of Matthew 25:41 as well as Matthew 25:46 ("And these shall go into everlasting punishment").[197] In his commentary on the passages from Ephesians and Philippians, however, Thomas also engages in a more argumentative criticism of Origen. Similar to *De Malo*, q. 16, a. 5, he blames Origen for failing to make the necessary distinctions. In this case, it regards the distinction between a voluntary and an involuntary subjection to Christ. A voluntary subjection to Christ acknowledges Christ as Savior, whereas an involuntary subjection to Christ acknowledges Christ as Judge who accomplishes his will. The former applies to the just, the latter to the wicked.[198] A somewhat different distinction, which Origen failed to notice, occurs in his *Commentary on Hebrews* 1:13 ("But to what angel has he ever said, 'Sit at my right hand, till I make your enemies a stool for your feet'"?), that is, the distinction between subjection *per voluntatem subditorum* and subjection *per voluntatem domini*. In the former, the subjection occurs "as good ministers are subject to their master, as to their king; in this way, only the good are subject to Christ." In the latter, "some force is exerted on the subjects," and this "is how the wicked are subject to Christ" "because Christ will accomplish His will in their regard by punishing them, who refused to do His will here."[199] In his Romans commentary,

---

196. *De Articulis Fidei* I (LE 42, 252, 518–23): "Secundus error est qui imponitur Origeni, quod sit iterum pro salute hominum et daemonum passurus; contra quod dicitur Ro. VI, 9: 'Christus resurgens ex mortuis, iam non moritur; mors illi ultra non dominabitur.' Et contra hos errores dicitur in Symbolo: 'tertia die resurrexit a mortuis.'" See Hieronymus, *Epist.* 124, 12 (PL 22, 1070). Jerome goes on to cite from *Peri Archon* IV, 3, 13.

197. Mt 24:46 is also used in *De Articulis Fidei*, c. 1 (LE 42, 249, 339–45) to reject Origen's denial of an eternal punishment and his claim that purification of the damned is possible and saints and good angels can return to evil.

198. *In Eph.* 1:22, l. 8, no. 67. See also *In Phil.* 2:10, l. 3, no. 72.

199. *In Heb.* [rep. vulgata], c. 1, l. 6., no. 82. In support of universal salvation, Thomas attributes the following to Origen: "just as being subject to the light is nothing more than being enlightened, so, since Christ is truth, justice and goodness and whatever else He can be called, to be subjected to the Savior is nothing less than to be saved." I have been unable to identify this, and neither has the Leonine Commission. Father Gilles de Grandpré, whom I thank, informed me that no printed edition contains a reference for this quote. A marginal note in an edition of his Pauline commentaries, printed in Lyon in 1689, merely refers to *Peri Archon* I, 6, and III, 5–6. See also *In Heb.* [rep. vulgata], c. 2, l. 4., no. 141.

Thomas thinks it is necessary to explicitly deny that Romans 11:32 ("For God has consigned all men to unbelief, that he may have mercy upon all") applies to demons as well as *secundum errorem Origenis*.[200] The rejection of this position is so important for Thomas that he thinks the Church added a passage on two occasions into her foundational doctrinal documents to ensure that Origen's position was explicitly rejected. He thinks that the Fathers at the Nicene Council added *propter nos homines* into the Nicene Creed to exclude Origen's position that demons would also be saved by Christ's incarnation and passion.[201] Similarly, to exclude Origen's position, the Council Fathers at Lateran IV (1215) in its decree *Firmiter* added "eternal punishment with the devil ... eternal glory with Christ."[202]

Further Points of Disagreement   Regarding the manner in which the separated soul suffers, Thomas mentions the following argument. Given that a passion in its proper sense entails an alteration in which "one contrary form is received and the other is driven out," and given that this is only to be found in bodily things subject to generation and corruption, "everything said in the Scriptures about the bodily pains of the damned is to be understood metaphorically." Thus bodily pains and delights are to be understood as spiritual ones. Origen, he says, "seems (*videtur*) to have been of this opinion."[203] Elsewhere Thomas is less uncertain: *et hec fuit opinio Origenis*.[204] Aquinas rejects this opinion as contrary to the resurrection of the body and prefers the opinion of Augustine, who held that punishment occurs by way of corporeal fire.[205]

---

200. *Ad Rom.*, c. 1,1 l. 4., no. 932.

201. See *Comp. Theol.* I, 220 (LE 42, 173, ll. 8–11). See also *Expositio in Symbolum Apostolorum*, art. 3.

202. *Super Primam Decretalem* (LE 40E, 38, 674–77): "Et quia Origenes posuit quod poena damnatorum non erit perpetua, similiter nec gloria beatorum, ideo ad hoc excludendum dicit 'et illi cum Diabolo poenam aeternam, et isti cum Christo gloriam sempiternam.'"

203. *De Ver.*, q. 26, 1 (EL 22.3, 748, 214–25). The editors refer to *Peri Archon* II, 10, 4, and Jerome's *Epist.* 124. In both texts, however, the bodily is not opposed to the spiritual, but rather the effect of sin in guilty consciences is being put forward.

204. *Q. D. de Anima*, q. 21 (EL 24.1, 179, 196).

205. Augustinus, *De Civ. Dei* 21.10 (CSEL 48, 775–76). In his earlier *De Genesi ad Littera Libri Duodecim* XII, 32, Augustine had written: "Est ergo prorsus inferorum substantia, sed eam spiritualem arbitror esse, non corporalem" (PL 34, 480; CSEL 28.1, 427). Thomas replies, "dicendum, quod Augustinus loquitur opinando, et non determinando, sicut frequenter facit in libro illo" (*In IV Sent.*, d. 44, q. 3, a. 2, qca 1, ad 2, editio Parma, 1104). Later he writes that, in the passage from *De Civitate Dei*, Augustine revokes his earlier position (*Q. D. de Anima*, q. 21, ad 19, LE 24.1, 182, 401–4).

The manner in which the separated soul acquires knowledge offers another occasion to disagree briefly with Origen. Thomas defends the view that the separated soul has a knowledge of natural things through an influx of higher intelligible species, but the separated soul can know them only generally and indistinctively (*in quadam universitate et confusio*) "in the manner in which things are known through universal principles." He adds that this knowledge is acquired "all at once by an influx and not successively by instruction, as Origen says."[206]

In another question related to the resurrected body, Thomas mentions that Origen writes about some who held that eventually even the saints will lay aside the bodies they had resumed at the Resurrection, for only then are they perfectly like God and are able to live in perfect happiness. For Thomas, this opinion is both contrary to the faith and to reason: "For there can be no perfect happiness where nature itself is not perfect. And since the union of soul and body is natural, besides being substantial and not accidental, the soul's nature cannot be perfect unless it be united to the body."[207] Here, one has an indication that Thomas is using Rufinus's translation, for he makes it sound as though the claim of an incorporeal final state is not Origen's own position, whereas in the same passages translated by Jerome in his Letter 124, he presents this claim as being that of Origen.[208]

Apokatastasis   The related topic of apokatastasis as such receives far less attention than one would expect. In his *De Potentia* (1265–66), Thomas notes that some have ascribed to Origen the view that "at the final consummation all corruptible creatures will be reduced to nothing," but he remarks that Origen did not assert this as his own view but rather as a view held by others.[209] Commenting on the quotation from Haggai 2:7 in Hebrews 12:26 ("His voice then shook the earth; but now he has promised, 'Yet once more I will shake (*movebo*) not only the earth but also the heaven'"), Thomas, following St. Paul's, or the author's, own analysis of the words "yet once more" (*adhuc semel*), lays much stress on its correct

---

206. *Q. D. de Anima*, q. 18 (LE 24.1, 158, 344). See *Peri Archon* I, 6, 3: "eruditionibus primo angelicis tum deinde etiam superiorum graduum virtutibus, ut sic per singular ad superior provecti usque ad ea quae sunt 'invisibilia' et 'aeterna' perveniant." The context, however, is that of a process of reparation over many ages (*saeculis*).

207. *De Pot.*, q. 5, a. 10.

208. Compare *Peri Archon* II, 3, 3, with Hieronymus, *Epist.* 124, 5.

209. *De Pot.*, q. 5, a. 4. A possible source is *Peri Archon* II, 3, 7, where three opinions are listed, among which the annihilation of all that exists *within* the fixed spheres.

interpretation. Following the explanation by the author of Hebrews, who writes that the *adhuc semel* of Haggai 2:7 indicates a "translatio mobilium tamquam factorum, ut maneant ea, quae sunt immobilia" (Heb 12:27), Thomas comments that the change in question is one from a "state of movability and corruptibility," indicated by the use of *adhuc*, to "a state of incorruption and immutability," indicated by the use of *semel*. If the author of Hebrews meant to say that after such a change things would have remained in a state of changeableness, Aquinas points out, "he would not have said, once more (*semel*), but 'again and again' (*iterum et iterum*). This is against Origen who believed that the world will be renewed in an infinitude of time and be recovered."[210]

The Function of Origen in Aquinas's Biblical Commentaries

The *Commentary on John*

Aquinas's *Commentary on John* contains ninety-one explicit references to Origen,[211] forty-one of which occur in chapter 1, and only eight of which occur in the context of attributing an error to Origen.[212] In fact, together with Augustine (426 references) and John Chrysostom (259 references), Origen is one of Aquinas's principal patristic interlocutors,[213] and at one

---

210. *In Heb.* [rep. vulgata], cap. 12, l. 5., no. 721: "Consequenter cum dicit *quod autem dicit*, etc., exponit verba prophetiae, et facit magnam vim in hoc quod dicit *adhuc semel*. Quod enim dicit *adhuc*, ostendit quod mobilia sunt. Sed quod dicit *semel*, ostendit quod a statu mobilitatis et corruptibilitatis mutanda sunt ad statum incorruptionis et immutabilitatis. Si enim post motionem illam remanerent in statu mutationis, non diceret *semel*, sed iterum et iterum, quod est contra Origenem, qui voluit quod mundus in infinitum renovabitur ac recuperabitur."

211. By way of comparison, Albert's commentary contains three references to Origen, and Bonaventure's commentary only one. One has also to consider the many implicit references. Here are two examples: in no. 252 regarding Bethabora, a possible alternative for Bethany in Jn 1:28, Thomas mentions the spiritual meaning of Bethabora as "the house of preparation." See *CAI* 1.20 (ed. Marietti, 347). Similarly, in no. 674, regarding the fact that for a second time a visit to Cana is mentioned in Jn 4:46, he gives a spiritual sense in which the two visits indicate the two comings of Christ. See *CAI* 4.11 (ed. Marietti, 394).

212. Nos. 59, 59, 75, 75, 76, and 126 deal with the Trinity; no. 467 with the preexistence of Christ's human soul; and no. 2022 with preceding merits as the cause of election.

213. Regarding Origen's *Commentary on John*, of the original thirty-two books, reaching to Jn 13:33, only nine are preserved in more or less complete form in the original Greek. In addition, there are fragments preserved, some of whose authenticity is questioned. The critical edition can be found in *Die Griechischen Christlichen Schriftsteller 10*, Origenes Werke 4 (Leipzig: J. C. Hinrichs, 1903). The first Latin translation was published in Venice in 1551 by

point Aquinas lists Origen among the saints.[214] The references to Origen can be divided according to the function they have in the commentary. A *first function* is to provide an additional spiritual sense. This occurs, for instance, in commenting on John 2:19 ("Destroy this temple and in three days I will raise it up again"), which, in the anagogical sense, can be understood as referring to the Church, which in the final resurrection "will be made certain of the things we now hold through faith in a dark manner."[215] A second example concerns the meaning of *gazophylaciim* in John 8:20 ("Jesus spoke these words in the treasury where he was teaching in the temple"), where Aquinas draws on Origen to explain that "treasury" signifies that "the coins, that is, the words of his teaching, are impressed with the image of the great King."[216] *Second*, on a number of occasions, he presents Origen's view as what I would call a "valid option," offering an additional interpretation but without taking sides. For instance, the "light of men" in John 1:4b can refer to humans primarily as John Chrysostom thought or to every rational creature, including angels as Origen thought.[217] Or Christ's question in John 13:12 (*scitis quid*

Ambrogio Ferrari. For the moment, we do not know which Latin translation was the source for Thomas. Timothy F. Bellamah writes: "In all likelihood, Thomas' source was a Greek *florilegium*, several of which are known to have contained excerpts from this work. To be sure, Thomas did not read Greek, but we have clear evidence indicating that he commissioned the translations of several other Greek sources he employed for the *Catena aurea*. It is therefore not unreasonable to suppose that he was similarly responsible for the translation of Origen's comments on John." "The Interpretation of a Contemplative: Thomas' Commentary *Super Iohannem*," in *Reading Sacred Scripture with Thomas Aquinas: Hermeneutical Tools, Theological Questions and New Perspectives*, ed. J. Vijgen and Piotr Roszak (Turnhout: Brepols, 2015), 229–55, here 235–36. In an email of December 14, 2017, he confirmed these findings and added: "Unless there should appear a surprising discovery of a previously unknown commentary on John that also employs Origen's commentary, Thomas must be credited with the first use of it. I am now persuaded that the best explanation is that he personally commissioned the translation he used."

214. *In Ioh.* I, l. 4, no. 119. Another illustration of the importance of Origen is the fact that on two occasions (no. 11 and no. 114) he gives an etymological interpretation of the name "John" as "in whom is grace." In *CAI*, he attributes this etymology to Origen, in *CAL*, however, to Bede. The source for *CAL* is Beda, *In Lucae Euangelium Expositio* I, 1 (CCSL 120, 25). See also Hieronymus, *Liber Interpretationis Hebraicorum Nominum* (CCSL 72, 136). But also John Scotus Eriugena, *Homilia super "In principio erat uerbum,"* II (CCCM 166, 5).

215. *In Ioh.* II, l. 3, no. 415. *CAI* 2:19, no. 5 (ed. Marietti, 365) Origen, *Comm. Joh.* X, no. 304 (FOTC 80, pp. 23). See also nos. 289, 373, 404, and 601 for other uses of this function.

216. *In Ioh.* VIII, l. 2, no. 1164. *CAI* 8:20, no. 4 (ed. Marietti, 449); Origen, *Comm. Joh.* XIX, no. 12 (FOTC 89, p. 169).

217. *In Ioh.* I, l. 3, no. 98. *CAI* 1:4 no. 8 (ed. Marietti, 333); Origen, *Comm. Joh.* II, nos. 141–43 (FOTC 80, p 132).

fecerim vobis?) can also have an imperative sense, as in "Know what I have done to you," so as to arouse the understanding of the disciples.[218] On a number of occasions when listing these valid options, Thomas emphasizes that Augustine and Origen are of the same opinion.[219] This function of a valid option is by far the one Aquinas uses the most. According to Gilbert Dahan, it is one of the major characteristic features of medieval exegesis. He calls this feature "a machine-gunning hermeneutic" (*mitraillage herméneutique*), which consists in accumulating different exegeses in order to try to find the richness of a biblical text, albeit in the awareness that one can never reduce the transcendent Word to human words.[220]

Third, on other occasions he gives such a valid option but indicates which is the better one. This occurs famously, for instance, when interpreting John 1:3c–4a: "What was made in him was life" (*quod factum est in ipso vita erat*). Augustine's punctuation—that is, "what was made," comma, "in him was life"—intends to show that whatever is in God as in the Word is life itself. In the commentary, this is presented as a valid option, but from *ST* I, q. 18, a. 4, we know that this is Aquinas's preferred solution. The punctuation by Origen—that is, "what was made in him," comma, "was life"—emphasizes that the Son is life in himself so as to become life for us and give us life.[221] Chrysostom's reading, which has no punctuation at all and emphasizes the continuous production of things by the Word's intellect and will and not by a necessity of his nature, is mentioned as well. Regarding this reading, Aquinas writes: "Chrysostom is held in such esteem by the Greeks in his explanations that they admit

---

218. *In Ioh.* XIII, l. 3, no. 1773. *CAI* 13:12 no. 3 (ed. Marietti, 506) Origen, *Comm. Joh.* XXXIII, no. 113 (FOTC 89, p. 364).

219. See, e.g., *In Ioh.* I, l. 1, no. 36; *In Ioh.* I, l. 2, no. 87.

220. Gilbert Dahan, "Les Pères dans l'exégèse médiévale de la Bible," *Revue des Sciences Philosophiques et Théologiques* 91 (2007), 109–27, here 120. This "flexibility" is not to be confused with an "individual, charismatic intervention" but inscribes itself within a "predefined tradition": Gilbert Dahan, "Tradition patristique, autorité et progrès dans l'exégèse médiévale," in *Les réceptions des Pères de l'Église au Moyen Âge*, vol. 1, ed. Rainer Berndt and Michel Fédou (Münster: Aschendorff Verlag, 2013), 349–68, here 364. Regarding this openness of Aquinas's biblical exegesis, Piotr Roszak writes about "a multi-level exegesis, that, like rays, goes out in many directions at the same time": "Between Dialectics and Metaphor: Dynamics of Exegetical Practice of Thomas Aquinas," *Angelicum* 90 (2013): 507–34, here 518. See also the distinction Gilbert Dahan draws between a typically modern "passive reading" of a text and a typically medieval "active reading" of a text: *Lire la Bible au Moyen Âge: Essais d'herméneutique médiévale* (Geneva: Droz, 2009), 9–54.

221. *In Ioh.* II, l. 2, no. 92; *CAI* 1:4 no. 7 (ed. Marietti, 332–33); Origen, *Comm. Joh.* II, no. 128 (FOTC 80, p. 128).

no other where he expounded anything in Holy Scripture. For this reason, this passage in all the Greek works is found to be punctuated exactly as Chrysostom did."[222] In another passage, Thomas explicitly assigns to Origen a lesser interpretation. Commenting on John 8:41, where the Jews say to Christ, "We were not born of fornication," he mentions Origen, who thought these words were directed to Christ, suggesting that it was he who was the product of adultery. Thomas prefers (*Sed melius potest dici*), however, a reading inspired by Augustine[223] and based on the spousal imagery of God being the spiritual spouse of the soul individually and Judea collectively. Within this imagery, fornication receives the meaning of abandoning the true God and turning toward idols, as is also suggested by Hosea 1:2 ("for the land by fornication shall depart from the Lord"). Thomas paraphrases the claim in John 8:41, therefore, as follows: "It was like saying: although our mother, the synagogue, may now and then have departed from God and fornicated with idols, yet we have not departed or fornicated with idols."[224]

A *fourth function* consists in corroborating an interpretation. For instance, regarding John 4:44 ("Jesus himself had testified that a prophet has no honor in his own country"), Aquinas employs Chrysostom to argue that this statement is true insofar as it deals with the majority of cases, which does not exclude exceptions in some individual cases where prophets were indeed honored in their own land. At this point he adds an additional corroboration by referring to a passage by Origen, not found in the *Catena Aurea*, where it is said that this statement holds true not only for the prophets among the Jews but also for the prophets among the Gentiles.[225] In other words, Thomas uses Origen to argue for a pattern in human behavior; namely, once there is a high degree of familiarity among persons, it is likely that persons will revere each other less than when there was no such familiarity.

The *fifth function* consists in using Origen as an explanatory tool to deal with questions that can arise from the text. Often these passages are

222. *In Ioh.* II, l. 2, no. 94. See also no. 200 for other uses of this function.

223. Augustinus, *In Ioannis Evangelium Tractatus* CXXIV, tr. 42, 7 (PL 35, 1702; CCSL 36, 368): "Et quia consuetudo Scripturarum est, quas legebant, fornicationem spiritualiter appellare, cum diis multis et falsis anima tanquam prostituta subiicitur, ad hoc responderunt: Dixerunt itaque ei, Nos ex fornicatione non sumus nati, unum patrem habemus Deum." This passage is also mentioned in *CAI* 8.10 (ed. Marietti, 456).

224. *In Ioh.* VIII, l. 5, no. 1232; for the passage by Origen, see *CAI* 8.10 (ed. Marietti, 456).

225. *In Ioh.* IV, l. 6, no. 666; Origenes, *Comm. Joh.* XIII, no. 376 (FOTC 89, p. 149).

introduced with *Sciendum autem*,[226] *Attendendum est autem*,[227] *Sed attendendum*,[228] *Ubi attende*,[229] or just by *Si vero quaeratur*.[230] So he draws, for instance, on Origen to explain the multiple meanings of *principium* in John 1:1 ("In the beginning").[231] Jesus's statement in John 8:19 ("You know neither me nor my Father") occasions Aquinas to draw on Origen's remark that some misunderstood this phrase as if the Father of Christ was not the God of the Old Testament.[232] Jesus's washing the feet of his disciples can raise the question of why he did not begin by washing the feet of Peter. Origen himself raised this question, and Aquinas concurs with his answer; that is, just as a doctor begins to take care of those who need it the most, Christ only at the end came to Peter, "who needed it less than the others."[233] A final example is another question raised by Origen, namely, whether Judas ate from the piece of bread he received in John 13:30. Aquinas again follows Origen in giving two possibilities: either Judas did not eat the bread because the devil had already entered the heart of Judas, for 2 Corinthians 6:15 says "What accord has Christ with Belial?," and Thomas adds 1 Corinthians 10:21—"You cannot drink from the cup of the Lord and the cup of the demons"[234]—or Judas did eat from it, but the bread became "a source of harm for after the bread entered into him so did Satan." Both Origen and Aquinas refer implicitly to 1 Corinthians 11:29, where St. Paul writes about unworthily receiving the bread of Christ and thus bringing judgment upon himself.[235]

A combination of these functions is also possible. For instance, in commenting on John 2:20 ("This temple took forty-six years to build"), Thomas combines functions one, two, and five: the addition of a spiritual

226. *In Ioh.* VIII, l. 6, no. 1161.
227. *In Ioh.* VIII, l. 6, no. 1243.
228. *In Ioh.* XIII, l. 2, no. 1749.
229. *In Ioh.* XIII, l. 5, no. 1823.
230. *In Ioh.* XIII, l. 2, no. 1753.
231. *In Ioh.* I, l. 1, no. 34; *CAI* 1: 1, no. 1 (ed. Marietti, 327). Origenes, *Comm. Joh.* I, nos. 90–105 (FOTC 80, pp. 52–55).
232. *In Ioh.* VIII, l. 2, no. 1161: "Sciendum autem, secundum Origenem, quod ex hoc verbo aliqui sumentes occasionem erroris, dixerunt patrem Christi non fuisse Deum veteris testamenti"; *CAI* 8: 19, no. 4 (ed. Marietti, 448); Origenes, *Comm. Joh.* XIX, no. 12 (FOTC 89, p. 169).
233. *In Ioh.* XIII, l. 2, no. 1752; *CAI* 13: 7–10, no. 2 (ed. Marietti, 504); Origenes, *Comm. Joh.* XXXII, nos. 68–69 (FOTC 89, p. 355).
234. *In Ioh.* XIII, l. 5, no. 1823; *CAI* 13: 21–30, no. 4 (ed. Marietti, 509–510); Origenes, *Comm. Joh.* XXXII, nos. 303–9 (FOTC 89, pp. 398–99).
235. Origenes, *Comm. Joh.* XXXII, no. 309 (FOTC 89, p. 399).

sense, the valid option function, and the explanatory tool option. Thomas discusses at length Augustine's view that the number forty-six can refer to the temple of Christ's body. First, however, he raises a question about the literal meaning of the number forty-six given that 1 Kings 6:38 says that Solomon needed seven years to build the temple. He gives two possible explanations: either the text is not referring to the temple built by Solomon but to the rebuilding of the temple by Zerub'babel as mentioned in Ezra 5:2, or—and this seems to have been Origen's position though Thomas does not mention him—the text refers to the temple built by Solomon but takes into account the first time David spoke to the prophet Nathan about this project, as mentioned in 2 Samuel 7, so that until the final completion, the building of the temple lasted forty-six years. The terminology used in this passage illustrates these functions: *Sed contra hoc est* to introduce the problem, *vel dicendum* to introduce a valid option, and *potest referri ad* to introduce an additional spiritual meaning.[236]

The *Commentary on the Psalms*

The first two functions occur in the eighteen references to Origen in Aquinas's *Commentary on the Psalms* 36, 37, and 38.[237] We can find the first function in Psalm 36:19b ("in the days of famine they shall be filled"), for instance. The days of famine can, according to Origen, refer to the future life where the unjust will experience hunger.[238] The function of a valid option can be found, for instance, in Aquinas's commentary on Psalm 37:12 ("My friends and my neighbors have drawn near, and stood against me"). This can be understood as referring to the person of Christ, who talks about himself or about his members, and in this case the neighbors are the Jews. Or the verse can be applied, as Origen thought, to every sinner who used to be Christ's friend but now opposes him.[239]

236. *In Ioh.* 2, l. 2, nos. 406–9. For the references to Alcuin, who distinguishes between the Temple of Solomon and the Temple of Zerub'babel, and the position of Origen, see *CAI* 2.5 (ed. Marietti, 364). The references to Alcuin in *CAI* do not derive, however, from the *Commentary on John* by Alcuin (ob. 804) but from a *Glosae super Iohannem*, probably compiled by Anselm of Laon in the early twelfth century. See Alexander Andree, Tristan Sharp, and Richard Shaw, "Aquinas and 'Alcuin': A New Source of the Catena Aurea on John," *Recherches de Théologie et Philosophie Médiévales* 83 (2016): 3–20. Anselmi Laudunensis, *Glosae super Iohannem* (Turnhout: Brepols, 2014) (CCCM 267).

237. The fact that the references to Origen all occur in Ps 36–38 and that Origen's nine homilies on them have been transmitted to the West in a Latin translation by Rufinus might be an indication that Thomas had firsthand access to Rufinus's translation.

238. *In Psalm.* 36, 19; Origenes, *Hom. III, 10 in Ps. 36* (PG 12, 1346; SC 411, 164–67).

239. *In Psalm.* 37, 12; Origenes, *Hom II, 1 in Ps. 37* (PG 12, 1381–82; SC 411, 300–307).

The *Commentary on Matthew*

In his *Commentary on Matthew*, which has ninety-five explicit references to Origen[240] mostly in chapters 16–27, we find Aquinas briefly mentioning the error of Origen, who thought good angels could sin. This occurs in the context of explaining the passage from the *Pater Noster*: *sicut in caelo et in terra.*[241] He rejects this position by quoting Psalm 103:21, where it is said of the angels that they do the Lord's word. We also find Aquinas again mentioning and rejecting the idea that, for Origen, election depends on merit.[242] These are the only two instances where Thomas attributes an error to Origen; they occur, moreover, in Books 6 and 11, of which no commentary by Origen has been transmitted. Thomas also recalls the possibility of misunderstanding Matthew 19:12 ("Et sunt eunuchi, qui castraverunt seipsos propter regnum caelorum") and tells the story, which Eusebius initiated,[243] about Origen's self-castration, but he does not seem to pay much attention to the trustworthiness of the story, instead focusing on its consequences.[244]

The *first function*—that is, providing an additional spiritual sense—can be found for instance in Thomas's *Commentary on Matthew* 19:13. The reason why the disciples rebuked the children who wanted Jesus to impose his hands on them can, following Origen, indicate that the perfect, signified by the disciples, easily become indignant when they meet uncultivated men (*rudes*) in the Church. This shows that they are ignorant of the fact that Christ wants all men to be saved, for St. Paul says

---

240. Regarding Origen's *Commentary on Matthew*: Of the original twenty-five books, Books X–XVII, corresponding to Mt 13:36–22:33, are preserved in the original Greek. An edition can be found in PG 13 and the critical edition in GCS 40, Origenes Werke 10 (Leipzig: J. C. Hinrichs, 1935). An ancient, anonymous (sometimes thought to be made by a friend of Cassiodorus) Latin translation exists of Book XII, chap. 9, to Book XXV, corresponding to Mt 16:13–27:66. A comparison between the Greek and the Latin is therefore possible for Book XII, chap. 9, to Book XVII. The Latin translation, corresponding to 16:13–22:33, is called the *Vetus Interpretatio* and printed in PL 13 facing the Greek. The Latin translation, corresponding to 22:34–27:66, is called *Commentatorium Series* and divided into 145 chapters. It can be found in PL 13, 1599–800 and the critical edition in GCS 38, Origenes Werke 11 (Leipzig: J. C. Hinrichs, 1933).

241. *In Matt.* [*rep. Petri de Andria*], c. 6, vs. 10.

242. *In Matt.* 11, 25, no. 955.

243. Eusebius, *Hist. Eccl.* VI, 8, 1–3.

244. *In Matt.* 19, 12, no. 1568: Quidam male intellexerunt verbum istud, dicentes scindenda esse genitalia, et leguntur hoc quidam fecisse, de quibus dicitur fuisse Origenes. Sed istud reprobatum est, et separari debent a clero, capit. ex parte, et capitul. significavit, extra de corp. Vit. [Decr. I, 20,3]."

in Romans 1:14: "To the Greeks and the barbarians I am a debtor."[245] A further example regards the gold, altar, and temple of Matthew 23:16–23. Origen and Thomas understand it as an invitation to reflect on the correct way of interpreting Scripture. The gold or the contemplative life based upon meditating Holy Scripture, no matter how reasonable a certain interpretation of Holy Scripture might be, is worthless "unless it be in the Temple, that is to say, unless it be confirmed in Holy Scripture." Moreover, if the contemplative life is not lived out from upon the altar—that is, from a pure heart possessing the fire of devotion—any service and offering is without value.[246] A final example can be found in Matthew 26. Peter's threefold denial in Matthew 26:69–75 can signify three things. It can, following Remigius of Auxerre, signify the threefold temptation man faces: the temptation of the concupiscence of the flesh, the temptation of earthly things, and the temptation of the demons.[247] Or these can, following Augustine, signify the three denials of "all the heretics," that is, the divinity of Christ, his humanity, or both.[248] Finally, following Origen, these can signify the three persecutions the Church was going to face: by the Jews, by the Gentiles, and by the heretics.[249]

Whereas the *second function* of a valid option can be found in several instances,[250] the *third function*, by which Thomas indicates his own preference, seems far less present. There seems to be only one instance. Regarding the woman who pours precious ointment on Jesus's head in the house of Simon the leper in Matthew 26:6–7, several Church Fathers ask whether it is the same woman as in Luke 7. Thomas mentions extensively

245. *In Matt.* 19, 13, no. 1575; *CAM* 19:13, no. 4 (ed. Marietti, 284); Origenes, *Comm. Matt.* XV, 7 (GCS 40/10, 366–67).

246. *In Matt.* 23, 19–23, no. 1868; *CAM* 23:19–23, no. 6 (ed. Marietti, 336); Origenes, *CMtS* XXIII, no. 18 (GCS 38/11, 32–33).

247. Remigius is not mentioned in *In Matt.* but in *CAM* 26:69–74, no. 17 (ed. Marietti, 398).

248. *In Matt.* 26, 71–75, no. 2299 (ed. Marietti, 352): "Vel aliter, secundum Augustinum, dicendum est, quod per istas tres negationes omnium haereticorum error signatur. Quidam enim Christi divinitatem negabant, ut Photinus; quidam autem humanitatem, ut Eunomius; quidam utrumque, ut Arius qui inaequalem patri dicebat filium." A comparison with the source reveals that in his Matthew commentary (but not in *CAM*) Thomas adds names to Augustine's text in *Quaestiones Evangeliorum* I, q. 45 (CCSL 44B, 35, 2–6): "Quod petrus necdum solidatus in fide dominum ter negauit, uidetur ipsa trina eius negatio prauum errorem hereticorum designasse. nam error hereticorum de christo tribus generibus terminatur: aut enim de diuinitate eius aut de humanitate aut de utroque falluntur."

249. *CAM* 26:69–74, no. 17 (ed. Marietti, 398); Origenes, *CMtS* XXVI, no. 114 (GCS 38/11, 240).

250. See his commentary on Mt 16:20, 19:8, 21:23, 22:40, and 24:31.

Origen's reasons for why he thinks there must have been two different women but finds Augustine's arguments that it is indeed the same woman more persuasive.

Whereas the *fourth function* seems to be entirely absent, the *fifth function*—that is, the use of Origen as an explanatory tool to deal with questions that can arise from the text—is present on several occasions. For instance, Matthew 24:24 contains a difficulty insofar as it suggests that at Christ's Second Coming the false Christs and false prophets might even deceive the elect. Thomas turns to Origen, who writes that this is said hyperbolically to indicate the strength of these false prophets and the extent of divine predestination preventing them from being seduced by these false prophets.[251] Matthew 25:14 ("For even as a man going into a far country") poses the difficulty that it seems to introduce a comparison (*sicut*), but without providing the second part of the comparison. Thomas inserts a digression, introduced by *notandum quod*, in which Origen argues that we are not dealing with a comparison. Rather, the man—that is, Christ—goes into a far country—that is, heaven—not as God but as a man.[252]

Noteworthy in the *Commentary on Matthew* is the fact that several references are grouped together into one passage. For instance, the parable of the talents in Matthew 25:14–30 contains nine references to Origen, and the parable of the ten virgins going out to meet the bridegroom and bride in Matthew 25:1–13 contains ten references to Origen. Even more noteworthy is that in the latter case, Thomas seems to prefer a literal reading that he attributes to Origen. The cry at midnight, for instance, does not refer to the voice of Christ at the final judgment as "all others" think but refers to the present life when a shout by a preacher or an internal inspiration causes men to rise from their negligence and vainglory and begin to correct their deeds and turn back to Christ.[253] Likewise, the request for oil refers to the present life in which it happens that those who recognize that they have spent their lives in vain start to ask others for their help and prayers.[254] Or it happens that when a sinner sees a just man,

251. *In Matt.* 24:24, no. 1947; *CAM* 24:23–28, no. 6 (ed. Marietti, 351); Origenes, *CMtS* XXIV, no. 47 (GCS 38/11, 97).

252. *In Matt.* 25:14, no. 2033; *CAM* 25:14, no. 2 (ed. Marietti, 366); Origenes, *CMtS* XXV, no. 65 (GCS 38/11, 152–53). For another example of this function, see no. 1394.

253. *In Matt.* 25:6, no. 2021: "De ista dicit Origenes aliter quam alii, et magis secundum litteram." See also nos. 2022–23.

254. *In Matt.* 25:8, no. 2024.

he asks him for advice.[255] Thomas, in fact, emphasizes that for Origen this literal sense suffices and is "more clear" (*planior littera*) because "he [Origen] holds that all this takes place in this world."[256] Origen's insistence on the literal sense as well as his particular explanations of Matthew 25:1–13 mentioned above, however, are not only absent from Thomas's *Catena Aurea* but also, at least to my knowledge, from Origen's *Commentary on Matthew*.[257]

Conclusion

In his *Scriptum*, St. Thomas leaves many topics, which he later discusses in referencing Origen, unaddressed. Only the question of the fate of the demons and the damned will, from his earliest writings onward, be a recurrent theme in which he disagrees with Origen. Although Peter Lombard certainly gave him occasions to do so, Thomas apparently did not feel the need to address these topics or had not acquired enough knowledge of Origen to critically engage with him. Once he started writing his *Summa contra Gentiles* and preparing his *Catena Aurea*, this changed significantly, as the number of references also attest.

The number and scope of the topics wherein he engages Origen are impressive.

Among these, Origen's claims regarding the inferiority of the Son and the Holy Spirit to the Father, the preexistence of the soul (of Christ), the diversity in creation as the result of preceding merits, the soul-body union by divine decree as a punishment, and the temporary nature of punishment for demons and damned are evaluated by Thomas as untenable and contrary to Church doctrine. On various occasions in these debates, Thomas reduces his disagreement with Origen to the latter's Platonism. The doctrine of apokatastasis as such receives little attention.

On at least two occasions (*ST* I, q. 70, a. 3, and *De Subst. Separ.*, chap. 12) and on two different topics (animation of celestial bodies and diversity in creation), Origen receives a charitable reading, and on one occasion (*De Pot.*, q. 6, a. 6), regarding the bodies of angels and demons, Thomas shows that he is aware of Origen's theological enterprise as a *théologie en recherche* (H. Crouzel).

---

255. *In Matt.* 25:9; no. 2026.
256. *In Matt.* 25:9; no. 2026.
257. See *CAM* 25:1–13 (ed. Marietti, 363–66); Origenes, *CMtS* XXV, nos. 63–64 (GCS 38/11, 145–51).

Thomas clearly regards Origen as an authority, as can be gathered from the fact that Thomas assigns to him the titles "doctor" and "sanctus" and uses him on several occasions in the *sed contra* of the *Summa Theologiae*. As such, Thomas, if needed, will defend Origen, and he does so by looking at the context of a passage ascribed to Origen.

While the references to Origen in his commentary on the *Corpus Paulinum* are rare and, to a significant extent, negative, the huge number of references in his commentaries on the Gospels of John and Matthew and on the Psalms show a profound knowledge of Origen's biblical commentaries on these books of the Bible. The five different functions of Origen in these biblical commentaries show Thomas to be an avid reader and a keen interpreter of Origen, willing to engage him afresh and not merely relying on the texts compiled in the *Catena Aurea*.

The motives for Thomas's engagement with Origen can be traced back to the ambiguous reception of his writings in the Latin West, following the anathemas of 543 and 553. It seems equally the case, however, that, as Martin Morard has pointed out, Thomas's considerable knowledge of the Greek Fathers, including Origen, might be inspired by efforts to come to reconciliation with the Orthodox world. This would have led Thomas to augment his references to Greek authors to propose a theology rooted in both traditions.[258]

With regard to Origen in particular, however, I would add that Thomas seems aware of the influence of ideas, inspired by Origen, in heretical movements of his time. Ultimately, however, it is Thomas's exercise of his ministry as a theologian that moves him to seriously study Origen's positions. In one of his Quodlibetal questions, dated Easter 1271, he describes the goals of this ministry as follows. It consists in both removing doubt about the truth of a matter as well as instructing students in an understanding of this truth. In the former case, one must use, above all, the authorities accepted by both parties. In the case of the Greeks, he writes, "one has to debate with them on the basis of the authority of the New or the Old Testament and the doctors they accept." In the latter case, one must rely on arguments to show the reasons for the truth of the faith.[259] Both strategies are present in his engagement with Origen and allow Thomas to nuance to some extent the *doctrina recepta* regarding Origen. In short, therefore, one should conclude that Thomas, with all

---

258. Martin Morard, "Thomas d'Aquin, lecteur des conciles," *Archivium Franciscanum Historicum* 98 (2005): 211–365, here 352.

259. *Quodl.* IV, q. 9, a. 3 [18] (LE 25.2, 339, 17–340, 46).

the means available to him, took St. Jerome's advice to take 1 Thessalonians 5:21 ("Prove all things: hold fast that which is good") to heart in reading Origen.

Acknowledgments

This chapter uses information gathered through the grant "Identity and Tradition: The Patristic Sources of Thomas Aquinas' Thought" (2017–20), funded by the National Science Center (NCN) in Poland, allotted following decision no. DEC-2016/23/B/HS1/02679.

The author would like to thank Matthew Levering for his help and support. The author dedicates these pages to Father Johannes Tercic in gratitude of his friendship and inspiration.

3

The Ontological Grammar of Salvation and the Salvific Work of Christ in Athanasius and Thomas Aquinas

KHALED ANATOLIOS

Introduction

While it has only recently fallen out of scholarly fashion to posit a stark opposition between Eastern and Western Trinitarian theologies, asserting a binary contrast between Western and Eastern approaches to soteriology is still very much in vogue. The fundamental terms of this contrast go back to Adolf Harnack, who characterized the Greek patristic conception of salvation variously as "naturalistic," "physical," and "mystical." According to Harnack, this Eastern conception identified the fundamental human predicament as death, rather than sin, and posited the resolution to this predicament in the deifying union of humanity and divinity, which took place through the Incarnation of the Logos.[1] Harnack regarded this

1. Adolph von Harnack, *History of Dogma*, vol. 5, trans. J. Millar (Boston: Roberts, 1897–99), esp. 1–22. For more recent examples of this contrast, see Dennis Edwards, "Roman Catholic Theologies," in *Creation and Salvation*, vol. 2, *A Companion on Recent Theological Movements*, ed. Ernst M. Conradie (Zürich: Lit Verlag, 2012), 64–65; Karl Rahner, "Dogmatic Questions on Easter," in *Theological Investigations*, vol. 4, trans. K. Smyth (London: Darton, Longman and Todd, 1966), 129; Donald Fairbairn, "Patristic Theology: Three Trajectories," *Journal of the Evangelical Theological Society* 50, no. 2 (2007): 294. Recent presentations of Eastern soteriology as centered on the overcoming of death, rather than sin, include the following: Andrew Louth, *Introducing Eastern Orthodox Theology* (Downers Grove, IL:

soteriological approach with undisguised disdain. He considered deification to be a philosophical rather than biblical concept, in which "the simple content of the Gospel was obscured."[2] Commenting on the putative Greek patristic emphasis on the Incarnation, he quipped: "The fact is that one cannot think in realistic fashion of the 'deus homo factus' without thinking oneself out of it."[3] Fortunately, in Harnack's view, the Western tradition preserved the authentic biblical conception of salvation as a matter of sin, forgiveness, and moral living. Since Harnack's time, the essential contents of this contrast have been largely preserved, though the nomenclature has changed somewhat. Harnack's qualification of the Eastern conception of salvation as "physical" is now generally rendered as "ontological," while his description of the Western approach as "ethical" has been generally replaced with the pejoratively intended characterizations of "juridical" and "forensic." Of course, the more striking development is the reversal of Harnack's valuation of these approaches. It is now the Eastern "ontological" approach that wins the lion's share of approbation, while the Western putatively "juridical" construal is widely derided.

The prevalent use of this hermeneutical binary is deeply problematic for at least three reasons. First, the opposition between the categories of the "ontological" on the one hand and the "ethical" or juridical on the other is fundamentally antithetical to the logic of scriptural revelation. Over against the criterion of whether the problem with which salvation deals is the moral one of sin or the ontological condition of death, for example, it is quite clear in the Scriptures that sin and death are entirely intertwined and that if we must speak of an original causal relation between them, it is sin that leads to death.[4] It is equally clear that the salvation

---

InterVarsity Press, 2013), 70: "the resurrection is seen as the conquest of Christ over death, and so it is death, rather than sin, that is central to the Orthodox understanding of the consequences of Adam's disobedience"; Paul Evdokimov, *Orthodoxy* (London: New City Press, 2011), 96: "That is why in the East atonement is usually discussed in physical and ontological terms rather than ethical and juridical terms"; Sergius Bulgakov, *The Lamb of God*, trans. B. Jakim (Grand Rapids, MI: W. B. Eerdmans, 2008), 362.

2. Von Harnack, *History of Dogma*, 2:318.

3. Von Harnack, *History of Dogma*, 2:285.

4. In Gn 3:2, the divine commandment not to eat of the tree of the knowledge of good and evil is accompanied by the threat that disobedience to the commandment will lead to death. In the subsequent narrative, Adam and Eve do not immediately die after their act of disobedience. Nevertheless, their sin brings about mortality (cf. Gn 3:22–23). This understanding is also found in the Wisdom literature: cf. Ws 1:12–16. This is the understanding assumed by Paul: cf. Rom 5:12, 5:23, 7:13; 1 Cor 15:21. On the grappling of the early phases of the Jewish and Christian traditions with the apparent lack of immediate fulfillment of the

gained for us by Christ is grounded in his divine-human constitution, but it is also actualized throughout his life and in his death and resurrection. The result of Christ's salvific work is that we gain both the forgiveness of sins and participation in the life of the Triune God.

A second problem with this hermeneutical binary is that it falsifies both traditions in a way that obscures their commonality and complementarity. Now, it is sometimes said that every cliché has some truth to it. It may well be true that the Eastern theological tradition tends to articulate the mystery of salvation in a more ontological key, while the Western tradition is inclined toward a more ethical and transactional focus on the drama of sin and forgiveness. But it is undeniably and demonstrably true that both traditions, in their most paradigmatic and authoritative expressions, achieve a synthesis of the ontological and ethical dimensions of salvation. An accurate and judicious apprehension of the commonality and complementarity of the two traditions, therefore, cannot be gained by a caricatured contrast between an Eastern ontological approach and a Western "ethical" approach, but rather by attending to the *interplay* of these two registers in both traditions.

The third major problem with this interpretive binary is that its implicit logic, which often becomes quite explicit, leads ultimately to the positing of a tension between the divine attributes whose resolution typically involves a denigration of divine justice. The construction of this tension undermines the classic patristic and medieval trope, prevalent in both East and West, of understanding the logic of salvation as a manifestation and dramatization of the co-inherence of the divine attributes.[5] Instead, we have the modern continuation through this binary of a certain strand of Reformation theology in which salvation is ascribed to the triumph of God's mercy over God's justice.[6] Among the more intelligent

---

divine threat of death as following upon the disobedience, see James L. Kugel, *The Bible as It Was* (Cambridge, MA: Harvard University Press, 1999), 67–72.

5. The paradigmatic patristic example of this approach is Gregory of Nyssa, *Catechetical Orations*, in *Christology of the Later Fathers*, Library of Christian Classics, ed. Edward R. Hardie, trans. Cyril C. Richardson (Philadelphia: Westminster, 1954). In the medieval era, both the Western and Eastern traditions emphasized the co-inherence of God's justice and mercy in Christ's work of redemption. Cf. *ST* III, q. 46, a. 1; Gregory Palamas, *Serm.* 16 (P. K. Chrestou, Γρηγορίου τοῦ Παλαμᾶ ἅπαντα τὰ ἔργα, vol. 9 [Ἕλληνες Πατέρες τῆς Ἐκκλησίας 72. Θεσσαλονίκη: Πατερικαὶ Ἐκδόσεις Γρηγόριος ὁ Παλαμᾶς, 1985]: 26–596, retrieved from http://stephanus.tlg.uci.edu.proxy.library.nd.edu).

6. For a classic formulation of the "duel" between divine justice and mercy in Christ, see Martin Luther's *Lectures on Galatians* 3:13, in *Luther's Works*, vol. 26, *Lectures on Galatians*

of such construals, we can cite the case of the magisterial Orthodox theologian Georges Florovsky. Florovsky, presuming the binary we have just criticized, of the ontological and ethical, protests:

> In any case, no merely ethical categories will do. The moral, and still more the legal or juridical conceptions, can never be more than colorless anthropomorphism … Nor does the idea of Divine justice alone, *justitia vindicativa*, reveal the ultimate meaning of the sacrifice of the Cross. The mystery of the Cross cannot be adequately presented in terms of the transaction, the requital, or the ransom … Finally, there could hardly be any retributive justice in the Passion and death of the Lord … Nor is this to be explained by the idea of a substitutional satisfaction, the *satisfactia vicaria* of the scholastics…. Does justice really restrain Love and Mercy, and was the Crucifixion needed to disclose the pardoning love of God, otherwise precluded from manifesting itself by the restraint of vindicatory justice? If there was any restraint at all, it was rather a restraint of love … The Cross is not a symbol of justice, but the symbol of Love Divine.[7]

To counteract both the distorted historical judgment represented in the standard contrast between the Eastern and Western soteriological traditions as well as the problematic theological presuppositions that are inscribed in this contrast, we can hardly do better than attend to the soteriological thinking of two of the most paradigmatic figures in the Eastern and Western traditions, St. Athanasius of Alexandria and St. Thomas of Aquino, respectively. In this chapter, I make a modest overture toward an assessment of the commonality and complementarity of their respective soteriologies, and show how both the commonality and complementarity between them speak against the logic of the standard contrast between Eastern and Western soteriologies. The point of commonality that I highlight is the similarity of the ontological grammar of God's relation to creation that is foundational to both their soteriologies. Given this common ontological ground, however, I further indicate a point of complementarity in their respective accounts of the content of Christ's

---

1535 Chapters 1–4, ed. Jaroslav Pelkians (St. Louis, MO: Concordia, 1963), 276–91. For a discussion of this aspect of Luther's thought, see Ed Schroeder, *Gift and Promise: The Augsburg Confession and the Heart of Christian Theology*, ed. Ronald Neustadt and Stephen Hitchcock (Minneapolis: Fortress Press, 2016), 53: "Thus, for Luther, legal justice and divine mercy clash on Good Friday … Not coordination, but conquest is the upshot of Christ's being made a curse for us." See also the nuanced discussion in Adonis Vidu, *Atonement, Law, and Justice: The Cross in Historical and Cultural Contexts* (Grand Rapids, MI: Baker Academic, 2014), 89–132.

7. Georges Florovsky, "Redemption," in *Collected Works*, vol. 3, *Creation and Redemption* (Belmont: Nordland, 1976), 101–3.

sacrifice. Athanasius's account of Christ's sacrifice is largely confined to an ontological register, while that of Aquinas builds on the ontological foundation that he shares with Athanasius while further specifying the content of Christ's sacrifice in terms of a description of Christ's psychological interiority. Aquinas's development of this more interiorized and more concretely existential conception of Christ's sacrifice not only may but also must be considered as a necessary extension and elaboration of Athanasius's ontological framework.

My account of the commonality and complementarity of the understanding of Christ's sacrifice in Athanasius and Aquinas thus proceeds in two parts. The first part presents the commonality of the ontological grammar whereby the relation of being between God and creation determines the soteriologies of both theologians. The second part considers the complementarity of the two accounts of Christ's salvific work within their common ontological framework.

Part I: The Ontological Grammar of Salvation in Athanasius and Aquinas

Athanasius's Ontological Grammar

Given the putative contrast between an Eastern "ontological" approach and a Western "juridical" approach, it is valuable to see how the soteriologies of both Athanasius and Aquinas share a common ontological grammar and how, for both thinkers, divine justice is integral, and not extrinsic, to that ontological grammar. In both cases, we have soteriologies that are built upon a common conception of the God-world relation as determined by the actualization of divine goodness precisely through the interplay of divine mercy and justice. Let us see first how this works in Athanasius.[8] In his classic treatise *Against the Greeks—On the Incarna-*

---

8. This section on "Athanasius's Ontological Grammar" summarizes material that is developed in greater detail in Khaled Anatolios, "*Creatio ex nihilo* in Athanasius of Alexandria's *Against the Greeks-On the Incarnation*," in *Creation ex nihilo: Origins, Development, Contemporary Challenges*, ed. Gary Anderson (Notre Dame, IN: University of Notre Dame Press, 2017), 119–49, and idem, "Creation and Salvation in St. Athanasius of Alexandria," in *On the Tree of the Cross: George Florovsky and the Patristic Doctrine of Atonement*, ed. Matthew Baker, Seraphim Danckaert, and Nicholas Marinides (Jordanville, NY: Holy Trinity Seminary Press, 2016), 59–72. See also idem, *Athanasius: The Coherence of His Thought* (London: Routledge, 1998), 26–84; idem, *Athanasius*, Early Church Fathers (New York: Routledge, 2004), esp. 39–43; idem, *Retrieving Nicaea: The Development and Meaning of Trinitarian Doctrine* (Grand Rapids, MI: Baker Academic, 2011), 99–108.

tion, Athanasius constructs an ontological grammar of salvation by way of describing the continuity between God's work of creation and God's work of salvation. The description of this continuity is integral to the apologetic intent of this treatise, which is to demonstrate the inherent rationality of Christian faith. Christian faith is not "irrational" precisely because the seemingly absurd notion that the God of the universe died on the Cross for human salvation is in fact consistent with the fundamental terms of the ontological relation between God and creation. For Athanasius, the most fundamental of these terms is divine goodness, which is the most radical motive for the divine work of creation. In his frequent references to divine goodness throughout *Against the Greeks—On the Incarnation*, Athanasius repeatedly echoes the Platonic characterization of the generous and non-jealous nature of the Good, as well as Neoplatonic language that characterizes the Good God as "beyond being."[9] But he also transforms and qualifies the Platonic conception in significant respects, of which two are particularly noteworthy. First, he uses the doctrine of *creatio ex nihilo* to inform the Christian understanding of divine goodness with a more extensive and radical content than was the case in the Platonic tradition. The Platonists demonstrated divine goodness by referring to the demiurgic act of granting form to disordered matter, while Athanasius echoes Plato's affirmation that "the good can never have any jealousy of anything" (ἀγαθῷ δὲ οὐδεὶς περὶ οὐδενὸς οὐδέποτε ἐγγίγνεται φθόνος), only to extend the scope of divine liberality so as to signify the granting of *being itself* to what did not previously exist.[10] Second, over against the Plotinian conception of the good as not being consciously inclined toward what is inferior to it, Athanasius depicts divine goodness as intentionally oriented toward creation.[11] Moreover, to borrow a modern terminological framework that is sometimes applied to the divine attributes, we can

---

9. For examples of Athanasius's emphasis on divine goodness, see, inter alia, Athanasius, *CG*, 2, 8, 35, 41; Athanasius, *On the Incarnation*, 3. For the characterization of God as "beyond being," see *CG* 2, 40. As E. P. Meijering points out, this ostensibly Neoplatonic formulation actually has a "Middle Platonic" sense in Athanasius, in which God is still identified with being itself, albeit as beyond created being. See E. P. Meijering, *Athanasius, Contra Gentes: Introduction, Translation, and Commentary,* Philosophia Patrum 7 (Leiden: Brill, 1984), 16.

10. Plato, *Timaeus*, 29E–30A, in *The Collected Dialogues of Plato: Including the Letters*, Bollingen Series 71, ed. Edith Hamilton and Huntington Cairns (Princeton, NJ: Princeton University Press, 1961), 1162.

11. For Plotinus, the Good or the One, is beyond both knowing and not knowing inasmuch as intellection cannot be predicated of it (Plotinus, *Enneads* VI.9.6). As such, it is present to all things, but it cannot be said to "know" creatures precisely in their finitude.

say that in Athanasius, divine liberality is characterized in terms that are not only metaphysical but also "ethical"; divine goodness is depicted specifically as love of humanity, *philanthropia*.[12] Divine goodness does not only diffuse itself in emanated effects of which it is not conscious, but it is also intentionally preoccupied with bridging the gap between creation's contingent being and God's perfect possession of being.

Athanasius's interpretations of the notions of both divine mercy and justice are also grounded in his efforts to differentiate the Christian account of divine goodness from the Platonic account. For Athanasius, the crucial distinguishing element in the Christian account is the affirmation of a divine intentional activity that compensates for creation's inherent lack of a hold on its own being. Because Athanasius identifies this compensation with divine mercy, he uses the language of mercy to describe even the divine act of creation itself. In *On the Incarnation*, it is applied specifically to the creation of human beings, to whom God grants a maximal compensation for the contingency of their being by making them participants in the Word's eternal imaging of the Father:

God is good—or rather, he is the source of goodness. But the good is not jealous of anything. Because he does not jealously begrudge being to anything, he made all things from non-being through his own Word, our Lord Jesus Christ. Among all the things upon the earth, he was especially *merciful* (ἐλεήσαϛι) toward the human race. Seeing that by the logic of its own origin it would not be capable of always remaining, he granted it a further gift. He did not create human beings merely like all the irrational animals upon the earth, but made them according to his own Image, and granted them participation in the power of his own Word.[13]

What, then, of divine justice? Athanasius does not deal with justice expressly as a divine attribute, but rather economically, in its manifestation in divine law, and with special reference to the biblical narrative of creation in Genesis 1–3. In the opening chapters of *On the Incarnation,* after describing the original creation of human beings according to God's image, he immediately proceeds to refer to the divine commandment to refrain from eating of the tree of the knowledge of good and evil. In doing so, it might appear that he is simply following the general order of the narrative of Genesis. But the original and striking move that Athanasius makes is that he does not narrate the acts of creation and that of divine law-giving as two separate acts in a sequence, but effectively includes the

12. *Inc.*, 2.
13. *Inc.*, 3, my translation.

latter within the former. The giving of the Law is rendered as intrinsic to the divine act of creation and thus as constitutive of the creative manifestation of divine goodness and generosity. Placed in this framework of *creatio ex nihilo*, the function of divine law, for Athanasius, is precisely to secure the gift of the human creature's originating movement from nothing into being:

> Knowing again that the free choice of human beings could turn either way, he preemptively secured the gift that he gave by a law and a fixed place. When he brought them into his own paradise, he gave them a law, so that if they guarded the gift and remained good, they would retain the life of paradise ... but if they transgressed ... they would suffer the corruption of death in accordance with their nature, and would no longer live in paradise. From then on, they would die outside of it, and would remain in death and corruption.[14]

The overlap between Athanasius's descriptions of the act of divine law-giving and the working of divine mercy in the act of creation is quite striking. Most fundamentally, both are manifestations of the divine goodness, and specifically under the aspect of protecting creatures from relapsing into nothingness. Athanasius speaks of divine *mercy* as compensating for humanity's ontological vulnerability by granting human beings participation in the divine image, who is the Word. At the same time, he presents the divine Law precisely as a safeguard for the preservation of the working of divine mercy. The Law, for Athanasius, is simply an explicit and, as it were, public announcement of the project of divine mercy, an announcement that is also a plea addressed to human freedom not to frustrate this divine mercy. While Aristotle had spoken of justice in a political and social framework as the distribution of honor or property to the citizens of a state, Athanasius's much more radically metaphysical framework, which is always configured by the doctrine of *creatio ex nihilo*, leads him to depict justice as God's distribution to human beings of a share in the upholding of their own being. According to this understanding, the Law is neither in tension with the "grace" of divine goodness and mercy, nor something heteronymous to the being of humanity, nor even subsequent to the establishment of humanity's being but entirely integral to it. Divine law is, rather, a manifestation of the ontology of *creatio ex nihilo* as entirely and comprehensively gift, and it is an expression of the divine solicitude for the integrity and endurance of that gift.

14. *Inc.*, 3, my translation.

Aquinas's Ontological Grammar

Turning now to Aquinas, we can admit that the ontological grammar of his soteriology is not as compact and its logical relation to his soteriology is not as transparent as what we find in Athanasius's *On the Incarnation*. In the *Tertia Pars* of the *Summa*, Thomas explicates the rationale of Christ's salvific work in terms of God's goodness, justice, and mercy.[15] But this is done in a rather cursory manner, without a clear presentation of how these divine attributes determine the God-world relation and thus establish the ontological grammar of Aquinas's conception of salvation. Nevertheless, we do find the basic elements of this ontological grammar in the *Prima Pars*, where Aquinas treats the divine attributes, and the similarities to Athanasius in Aquinas's treatment of divine goodness, mercy, and justice are striking. Just as we saw in Athanasius, Aquinas speaks of divine goodness as foundational to the metaphysics of participation in the ontological relation between God and creatures. In this regard, Aquinas does not explicitly rely on Athanasius, but he draws upon another Greek theologian, Dionysius, to explicate divine goodness in terms of *creatio ex nihilo* and an ontology of participation. In *ST* I, q. 6, a. 1, resp., "Whether God is good," Aquinas explains:

To be good belongs pre-eminently to God. For a thing is good according to its desirableness. Now everything seeks after its own perfection; and the perfection and form of an effect consist in a certain likeness to the agent, since every agent makes its like; and hence the agent itself is desirable and has the nature of good. For the very thing which is desirable in it is the participation of its likeness. Therefore, since God is the first effective cause of all things, it is manifest that the aspect of good and of desirableness belong to Him; and hence Dionysius (*Div. Nom.* IV) attributes good to God as to the first efficient cause, saying that, God is called good as by Whom all things subsist.[16]

---

15. *ST* III, q. 46, a. 1.

16. "Respondeo dicendum quod bonum esse praecipue Deo convenit. Bonum enim aliquid est, secundum quod est appetibile. Unumquodque autem appetit suam perfectionem. Perfectio autem et forma effectus est quaedam similitudo agentis, cum omne agens agat sibi simile. Unde ipsum agens est appetibile, et habet rationem boni, hoc enim est quod de ipso appetitur, ut eius similitudo participetur. Cum ergo Deus sit prima causa effectiva omnium, manifestum est quod sibi competit ratio boni et appetibilis. Unde Dionysius, in libro de Div. Nom., attribuit bonum Deo sicut primae causae efficienti, dicens quod bonus dicitur Deus, sicut ex quo omnia subsistunt" (*ST* I, q. 6, a. 1). All English translations of *ST* are from Thomas Aquinas, *Summa Theologiae*, ed. John Mortensen and Enrique Alacrón, trans. Laurence Shapcote, OP, *Latin-English Edition of the Works of St. Thomas Aquinas* (Lander, WY: Aquinas Institute for the Study of Sacred Doctrine, 2012).

With regard to the understanding of divine mercy, the most striking commonality between our two thinkers is again the way that they insert divine mercy into the foundational ontological structure of the God-world relation. Consequently, they both speak of God's mercy not only in the work of salvation but also in the work of creation, as denoting the very act of granting being to creatures. We have already seen how Athanasius speaks of divine mercy as compensating for humanity's inherent nothingness by granting them "the greater gift" of being made in his own image. Aquinas makes a similar move. In *ST* I, q. 21, a. 3, "Whether mercy can be attributed to God," Aquinas first defines God's mercy in a fairly conventional way as God's inclination to remove the defects and dispel the misery of his creatures. A little later in article 4 of the same question, "Whether in every work of God there are mercy and justice," however, Aquinas confronts the objection that God's mercy is not applicable to the work of creation. His response to that objection echoes, without directly quoting, Athanasius. "The idea of mercy," he says, "is preserved in the change of creatures from non-existence to existence."[17] Just as in Athanasius, creation itself here is conceived as an act of divine mercy, and thus divine mercy is made intrinsic to the ontological structure of the God-world relation.

Divine justice is also intrinsic to the ontological structure of the God-world relation in Aquinas, as it was for Athanasius. In *ST* I, q. 21, a. 1, "Whether there is justice in God," Aquinas concedes that we cannot attribute to God the commutative justice that seeks to uphold a relation of equivalence within a mutual exchange. But we can attribute to God a distributive justice according to which a benefactor or ruler "gives to each what his rank deserves" (resp.). Here again, Aquinas assimilates his own position to that of Dionysius:

As then the proper order displayed in ruling a family or any kind of multitude evinces justice of this kind in the ruler, so the order of the universe, which is seen both in effects of nature and in effects of will, shows forth the justice of God. Hence Dionysius says (*Div. Nom.* VIII, 4): "We must see that God is truly just, in seeing how He gives to all existing things what is proper to the condition of each; and preserves the nature of each in the order and with the powers that properly belong to it."[18]

---

17. "Et salvatur quodammodo ratio misericordiae, inquantum res de non esse in esse mutatur" (*ST* I, q. 21, a. 4, ad. 4) (*Works of Thomas Aquinas*, 13:241).

18. "Sicut igitur ordo congruus familiae, vel cuiuscumque multitudinis gubernatae,

The problem with defining justice as giving to each what is "proper" or "due" to it is that it seems to exclude the operation of divine justice in the original act of creation, in which there is no preexistent entity to which anything can be "proper" or "due." This is exactly the objection that will come up later in *ST* I, q. 21, a. 4. In responding to this objection, Aquinas does not hearken back to his original explication, in question 21, article 1, of God's distributive justice as giving each thing what is proper to it. Instead, he draws upon a further specification and elaboration of that definition that he had developed in the following article (q. 21, a. 2), in which divine justice is ultimately equated with the arrangement of divine wisdom. The question of that article asks whether the justice of God is truth. Aquinas responds that the equation of mind and thing that constitutes truth is configured in opposite ways, depending on whether the thing is the measure of the mind, which is the case with creatures, or whether the mind is the measure of the thing, which is the case with the Creator. Therefore the justice of God is truth, not ultimately because it conforms to the things that are created but rather because it conforms to the mind of God that created those things. Thus the original definition of divine justice as giving to each created thing what is proper to it is now deepened into the formulation that divine justice gives to each created thing what is proper to it *according to divine wisdom*:

> But when the mind is the rule or measure of things, truth consists in the equation of the thing to the mind ... Therefore God's justice, which establishes things *in the order conformable to the rule of His wisdom*, which is the law of His justice, is suitably called truth. Thus we also in human affairs speak of the truth of justice.[19]

The cursory comparison that we have undertaken of the basic ontological grammars of Athanasius and Aquinas is sufficient to indicate their fundamental commonality. The most salient common features are, first, that in both cases, God's goodness, mercy, and justice (and truth) are entirely intertwined and co-inherent and, second, that in both cases

---

demonstrat huiusmodi iustitiam in gubernante; ita ordo universi, qui apparet tam in rebus naturalibus quam in rebus voluntariis, demonstrat Dei iustitiam. Unde dicit Dionysius, VIII cap. de Div. Nom., oportet videre in hoc veram Dei esse iustitiam, quod omnibus tribuit propria, secundum uniuscuiusque existentium dignitatem; et uniuscuiusque naturam in proprio salvat ordine et virtute" (*ST* I, q. 21, a. 1) (*Works of Thomas Aquinas*, 13:235–36).

19. "Quando igitur res sunt mensura et regula intellectus, veritas consistit in hoc, quod intellectus adaequatur rei ... Iustitia igitur Dei, *quae constituit ordinem in rebus conformem rationi sapientiae suae*, quae est lex eius, convenienter veritas nominatur. Et sic etiam dicitur in nobis veritas iustitiae" (*ST* I, q. 21, a. 2, resp.; my italics) (*Works of Thomas Aquinas*, 13:237).

it is really divine goodness that is the primary and overarching category. For Athanasius, God's goodness is the ultimate explanation for both the act of creation and the economy of salvation, such that the "rationality" of Christian faith is manifest precisely in showing how the Christian accounts of both creation and salvation present a maximalist rendering of divine goodness. In the divine work of creation, God's mercy is the enactment of divine goodness in relation to creation's inherent nonbeing, while God's justice safeguards the terms of that enactment. Similarly, for Aquinas, all God's dealings with humanity can be encompassed within the category of the "communication of perfections," which is an enactment of divine goodness, while the other attributes denote specifications of the different aspects of that enactment:

It must, however, be considered that to bestow perfections appertains not only to the divine goodness, but also to his justice, liberality, and mercy; yet under different aspects. The communicating of perfections, absolutely considered, appertains to goodness ... ; in so far as perfections are given to things in proportion, the bestowal of them belongs to justice ... in so far as perfections given to things by God expel defects, it belongs to mercy.[20]

The articulation of this ontological grammar in Athanasius and its reiteration in Aquinas constitute the foundational logic of a classic mode of soteriological thinking that has been largely lost in modern theology, namely, the explanation of the Christian economy of salvation as consistent with the co-inherence of the divine attributes. Within this mode of explanation, the denigration of divine justice is completely unintelligible. For both Athanasius and Aquinas, God's justice is constitutive of the ontological structure of the God-world relation in a way that is not in competition with mercy, but derived from and ordered to divine mercy. For Athanasius, divine justice, in the form of divine law, safeguards the gifts of divine mercy, while for Aquinas, too, "the work of divine justice always presupposes and is founded upon the work of mercy" (*ST* I, q. 21, a. 4, resp.). Far from substantiating the alleged contrast between an Eastern

20. "Sed considerandum est quod elargiri perfectiones rebus, pertinet quidem et ad bonitatem divinam, et ad iustitiam, et ad liberalitatem, et misericordiam, tamen secundum aliam et aliam rationem. Communicatio enim perfectionum, absolute considerata, pertinet ad bonitatem, ut supra ostensum est. Sed inquantum perfectiones rebus a Deo dantur secundum earum proportionem, pertinet ad iustitiam, ut dictum est supra. Inquantum vero non attribuit rebus perfectiones propter utilitatem suam, sed solum propter suam bonitatem, pertinet ad liberalitatem. Inquantum vero perfectiones datae rebus a Deo, omnem defectum expellunt, pertinet ad misericordiam" (*ST* I, q. 21, a. 3, resp.) (*Works of Thomas Aquinas*, 13:238).

ontological approach and a Western juridical one, we find in Athanasius and Aquinas a common ontological grammar in which the conception of divine justice is completely integrated with those of divine goodness and mercy.

Part II: The Complementarity of the Accounts of Christ's Salvific Work in Athanasius and Aquinas

Let us now turn our attention to the complementary ways in which this common ontological framework informs the accounts of Christ's salvific work in Athanasius and Aquinas. Modern accounts of Athanasius's soteriology have typically bypassed the integrated ontological framework sketched above, in which divine justice and mercy are coordinated manifestations of divine goodness, and simply focused on Athanasius's metaphysics of participation and his emphasis on creation *ex nihilo*. By this reductive path, they arrive at the conclusion, which simply reiterates Harnack's characterization of the Greek Fathers, that salvation, for Athanasius, is merely the reinjection of divine life into human nature through the Incarnation. In this vein, we have the disdainful conclusion of R. P. C. Hanson that "The fact is that his doctrine of the Incarnation has almost swallowed up any doctrine of the Atonement, rendered it unnecessary. Once the *Logos* has taken human flesh on himself, in a sense, certainly in principle, redemption is accomplished."[21] Over against this assessment, however, is the massive and straightforward evidence of the text itself. There, Athanasius tells us that Christ's death is "the chief point of our faith";[22] that Christ's incarnation was intended to bring about the forgiveness of human sins;[23] that it was through this death that the debt of corruption that humanity had incurred through sin was canceled;[24] that Christ suffered and died "on behalf of all;"[25] and, quoting Isaiah 53, that Christ was wounded for our transgression[26] and offered himself as a sacrificial sheep for our salvation.[27]

21. R. P. C. Hanson, *The Search for the Christian Doctrine of God: The Arian Controversy 318–381 AD* (Edinburgh: T&T Clark, 1988), 450.

22. τὸ κεφάλαιον τῆς πίστεως ἡμῶν (*Inc.*, 19); cf. *Inc.*, 22.

23. *Inc.*, 14.

24. *Inc.*, 9, 20.

25. *Inc.*, 7, 8, 9, 10, 20, 21, 25, 31.

26. *Inc.*, 34.

27. *Inc.*, 37.

In his critique of Athanasius, Hanson concedes that "Athanasius believes in the Atonement, in Christ's death as saving, but he cannot really
explain why Christ should have died. When in chapters 19 and following
of the *De Incarnatione* he begins trying to explain the necessity of Christ's
death, he can only present a series of puerile reasons unworthy of the rest
of the treatise."[28] This comment represents a gross misreading of the *De
Incarnatione*. In chapter 19 and following of the *De Incarnatione*, Athanasius is not at all trying to explain the *necessity* of Christ's death. He is
rather attempting to explain the fittingness of the *circumstances* of Christ's
death: why he died on the Cross, why he was dead for three days, and so
on. The explanation of Christ's death is found in the earlier chapters of
the treatise and is entirely bound up with the ontological framework we
have just sketched. For Athanasius, just as creation has its ultimate motive
and rationale in divine goodness, and just as sin is essentially a repudiation of divine goodness that threatens to destroy the created effects of
that goodness, so salvation is essentially the reiteration of divine goodness
in the face of human sin. In that reiteration, God's mercy is reenacted in a
manner that is consistent with divine justice, that is, with the fundamental law of creation's being as a participation in divine being. According to
this ontological law, which is also proclaimed in the positive law of God's
commandments, sin must lead to death because the human withdrawal
from God that is sin not only brings about but also essentially consists
in a decline from being, which is death. Therefore Athanasius insists that
the "debt of sin" must be paid for salvation to be made possible. "It was
absurd (ἄτοπον)," says Athanasius, "for the law to be annulled before being fulfilled." As I have explained elsewhere, for Athanasius, the absurdity
of the notion of salvation without death is that it posits a salvation that is
entirely unreal because it fundamentally contradicts the basic character of
created reality as a participation in divine being, such that the creature's
withdrawal from that participation is equivalent to the forfeiture of its
own being.[29]

For Athanasius, however, Christ does not accomplish salvation merely by dying, but rather by dying an incorruptible death, a death unto resurrection. The crucial characterization of this incorruptible death in the
De Incarnatione is that of "offering."[30] The notion of Christ's sacrifice of
self-offering is grounded in the epistle to the Hebrews, the most quoted

28. Hanson, *Search for the Christian Doctrine of God*, 450.
29. Anatolios, "Creation and Salvation in St. Athanasius of Alexandria," 69–71.
30. See Anatolios, *Athanasius*, 56–61.

biblical book in the *De Incarnatione*. Insofar as this notion provides an implicit explanation for the saving efficacy of Christ's death, it does so by way of its logical relation to the ontological framework we have been sketching. If sin is simultaneously a withdrawal from God and from being itself, and thus manifests itself in death, then Christ's salvific death is an entrance into our withdrawal from being and the reversal of that withdrawal by his self-offering. Christ can accomplish this simultaneous entrance into and reversal of our withdrawal from being because he is, in his divinity, the eternal Image of the Father whose sharing in the life of the Father and whose living-unto-the-Father is immutable and indestructible. Thus, in Christ, we retrieve our lost participation in the life of the Father, and our withdrawal from God is reinverted by our self-offering to the Father in Christ. In this way, our salvation also renews and perfects God's enactment of his goodness, mercy, and justice in the original act of creation.

Aquinas

Nevertheless, it is true that Athanasius does not explicate the inner content of Christ's sacrifice of self-offering, in terms of Christ's own subjectivity. The distinctive virtue of his approach is precisely the seamlessness and consistency of the logic of his ontological framework. But it is at this juncture that we can turn to Aquinas for help in extending Athanasius's ontological conception of Christ's self-offering in a more concretely existential and ethical mode.[31] By an "ethical" mode of soteriological explanation, I mean what is generally meant by this qualification in modern descriptions of Western soteriology as preoccupied with what Christ does to address the demands of divine justice and thereby bring about the forgiveness of human sins. We have already seen that such a perspective is not altogether absent in Athanasius, even if it is subsumed within an emphatically ontological framework in which the objective facts of Christ's incarnation, death, and resurrection restructure the order of being between God and creation.

When we turn to Aquinas, we find a much more developed ethical

---

31. For a "personalist" reading of Aquinas's soteriology, focusing especially on Aquinas's understanding of satisfaction, see Romanus Cessario, *The Godly Image: Christ and Salvation in Catholic Thought from St. Anselm to Aquinas* (Petersham, MA: St. Bede's, 1990). For an excellent comprehensive treatment of the various motifs of Aquinas's soteriology, see Jean-Pierre Torrell, *Pour nous les hommes et pour notre salut: Jésus notre redemption.* (Paris: Cerf, 2014).

trajectory of soteriological reflection, but I contend that this trajectory does not supplant the ontological framework that he fundamentally has in common with Athanasius but is an outgrowth of that framework. This outgrowth, and the resultant synthesis of ontological and ethical trajectories that I claim we find in Aquinas, is not merely the result of his individual genius. It was made possible by the development of the dogmatic tradition of Christological doctrine that largely postdated Athanasius.[32] In the Council of Ephesus, we have the dogmatic basis for an ontological Christology, based on Cyril's emphasis on the hypostatic union, which Athanasius already largely anticipated. But in the Third Council of Constantinople (680–81), which affirmed the two wills of Christ, we have the dogmatic basis for a functional and ethical Christology that focuses on what Christ *does*, both divinely and humanly, to effect our salvation. Before Aquinas, we already have in the Greek tradition—in the figures of Maximus the Confessor and John Damascene, for example—the beginnings of this synthesis of ontological and ethical perspective. Within this synthesis, we find the combination of a Cyrillian stress on the hypostatic union, which is altogether complete at the moment of Jesus's human conception, as well as a consideration of the theandric quality of all of Christ's actions and his willed sufferings. This Christological synthesis necessarily contains within itself a synthesis of ontological and ethical dimensions of soteriology.

It was this dogmatic Greek patristic synthesis that Aquinas inherited and developed in his own way. There is plenty of material in the secondary literature that further elaborates on Aquinas's reliance on the conciliar Christological tradition, though it seems to me that the particular significance of Constantinople III for his Christology and soteriology merits more attention than it has received.[33] But rather than reiterating this material, I attend to one distinctive expression of the ethical trajectory of Aquinas's soteriology, which is the notion of Christ's vicarious repentance for human sin.[34] The lack of attention to this theme is under-

---

32. See, further, Khaled Anatolios, "The Soteriological Grammar of Conciliar Christology," *The Thomist* 78, no. 2 (2014): 165–88.

33. For an excellent overview of this question, along with the pertinent bibliography, see Corey L. Barnes, "Thomas Aquinas's Chalcedonian Christology and Its Influence on Later Scholastics," *The Thomist* 78, no. 2 (2014): 189–217.

34. While Aquinas's doctrine of Christ's vicarious contrition is generally overlooked by modern commentators, one significant exception is the insightful treatment of Christ's dereliction by Bruce Marshall. Marshall offers the following apt summary of Thomas's understanding of Christ's vicarious contrition: "Out of love for the Father and for sinners, Jesus

standable, since it is not a notion that Aquinas makes much of. Yet, if I am reading the pertinent passages correctly, it is explicitly there, and I argue that it is also implicitly contained in some of his more noted motifs, such as satisfaction and sacrifice. It also strikes me as a theme that has great promise for our contemporary challenges and difficulties in articulating the mystery of Christ's salvific work. Aquinas's treatment of this theme offers an example of the enduring value and vitality of an ethical trajectory of soteriological reflection that is securely anchored in the ontological framework sketched above.

The explicit formulation of this theme is found in *ST* III, q. 46, a. 6, where Aquinas asks "Whether the pain of Christ's Passion was greater than all other pains."[35] The obvious rebuttal to this proposal, which is the first objection to be cited by Aquinas, is that there are accounts of martyrs who have endured pain that seems to be both more intense and more prolonged than that suffered by Christ. In his response to this objection, Aquinas adduces four causes for the uniqueness and superior extent of Christ's suffering. Christ's suffering was greater than that of any other human being, first, with regard to the sources of his suffering, which in their physical aspect during the Crucifixion constituted the infliction of pain on "nervous and highly sensitive parts of the body," while in their interior aspect encompassed "all the sins of the human race" (resp.). Second, Christ's suffering was greater than any other's with respect to the physical and interior susceptibility of the sufferer, inasmuch as Christ's body enjoyed "a most perfect constitution" that was therefore preeminently sen-

---

accepts responsibility for all the sorrow human beings owe to God for the total reality of sin, for all the sins of every sinner … In his passion Jesus undertakes one great act of contrition for the sins of the world, an act of the deepest possible human sorrow for sin, rooted in the greatest possible *caritas* … Jesus does not lament any sins of his own, but the sins of others, of all those who are at least potentially his members (that is, of every human being). This does not diminish, but increases, his suffering. As every penitent knows, contrition is always painful, and the peculiar suffering it brings—voluntary self-humiliation out of sorrow for sin—in fact increases the more the sorrow springs from love for God, freely given.…. Jesus' sorrow for sin is purely voluntary (since he has no sins of which he needs to repent), supremely rooted in love, and extends to every single sin. He alone 'truly bears our griefs' (Isa 53:4), and this is one way in which his suffering is like no other (cf. Lam 1:12) … What Jesus suffers in his own person, in particular the contrition he offers for ours sin, is part and parcel of his sacrifice, of his perfect offering of himself to the Father in love." Bruce D. Marshall, "The Dereliction of Christ and the Impassibility of God," in *Divine Impassiblity and the Mystery of Human Suffering*, ed. James F. Keating and Thomas Joseph White, OP (Grand Rapids, MI: W. B. Eerdmans, 2009), 272–73.

35. *Works of Thomas Aquinas*, 19:489–92.

sitive to its own demise, while the perfections of his soul also rendered him most capable of apprehending all the causes of human sadness. Third, Christ's sufferings were unique and exceeded all others because he did not allow any of his own higher powers to mitigate his suffering, whereas all other human suffering is qualified to some extent by the consoling effect of these higher powers. Fourth, the magnitude of Christ's suffering is preeminent insofar as Christ voluntarily accepted the amount of pain proportionate to the whole extent of human sin.

Embedded in Aquinas's account of the preeminence of Christ's suffering is a clear affirmation that a significant element of this suffering is Christ's interior pain and sadness, which are caused by human sin. The *responsio* says: "The cause of his interior pain was, first of all, all the sins of the human race, for which He made satisfaction by suffering; hence He ascribes them, so to speak, to Himself saying (Ps 21:2): 'the words of my sins' (*verba delictorum meorum*)."[36] In his response to the second objection in this article, Aquinas describes Christ's appropriation of human sin as contrition and identifies this contrition as the content of Christ's satisfaction. The second objection had stipulated that because, according to the Stoics, strength of soul mitigates pain, the greatest pain could not exist in Christ, to whom must be attributed the most perfect strength of soul. Moreover, the same objection continues, the Aristotelian principle that moral virtue determines the mean with respect to the passions should lead us to assume that Christ's virtue would have fixed that mean perfectly and not allowed him to experience any excess of suffering or sadness. It is in his response to this objection that Thomas explicit depicts Christ's interior suffering as contrition, using the classic text of Christian repentance, 2 Corinthians 7:10: "The sorrow that is according to God works repentance ... unto salvation." Combining this Pauline text with the testimony of Augustine, Thomas contends that Christ's suffering of vicarious repentance should be understood as not only a moral virtue in itself, but also as constituting "satisfaction" for sin.

But, in truth, some sadness is praiseworthy, as Augustine proves, namely, when it flows from a holy love; this occurs when a person is saddened over his own or another's sins. Furthermore, it is employed as a useful means for the satisfaction of sins (*ut utilis ad finem satisfactionis pro peccatis*), according to the saying of the Apostle: "The sorrow that is according to God produces repentance that leads to salvation" (2 Cor 7:10). And so Christ, to satisfy for the sins of all people, suffered

---

36. *Works of Thomas Aquinas*, 19:490.

the most profound sadness, absolutely speaking, but not so great that it exceeded the rule of reason.[37]

Aquinas's exposition of Christ's contrition continues in his response to the fourth objection of the same article. This objection had stated that because pain is proportionate to loss, and because the sinner's loss of the life of grace is greater than Christ's loss of the life of nature in his suffering, then the sinner must suffer a greater pain than Christ in keeping with the greater loss that he incurs. Aquinas's response to this objection leads him to distinguish between Christ's suffering over his own loss of the life of nature and his suffering through the appropriation of all the sins of all of humanity. It is the latter suffering of Christ, not the former, that is greater than all other human suffering. Citing the description of the suffering servant in Isaiah 53, Thomas once again explicitly speaks of the representative suffering of Christ as a contrition that transcends all other human experiences of repentance:

Christ grieved not only over the loss of his own bodily life, but also over the sins of all others. And this grief in Christ surpassed all grief of every contrite heart ("qui dolor in Christo excessit omnen dolorem cuiuslibet contriti"), both because it flowed from a greater wisdom and charity, by which the pang of contrition is intensified, and because He grieved at one time for all sins, according to Isa 53.4: "Surely he has carried our sorrows."[38]

The understanding of Christ's salvific satisfaction as representative repentance is again implied in Aquinas's response to the sixth objection, wherein we also find the assumption that divine justice is "satisfied" by Christ's vicarious contrition over human sin. The sixth objection had stipulated that it would have been redundant for Christ to suffer more than any other human being, since the hypostatic union is sufficient to make Christ's slightest pain efficacious for obtaining humanity's salvation.

---

37. "Sed secundum rei veritatem, tristitia aliqua laudabilis est, ut Augustinus probat, in XIV de Civ. Dei, quando scilicet procedit ex sancto amore, ut puta cum aliquis tristatur de peccatis propriis vel alienis. Assumitur etiam ut utilis ad finem satisfactionis pro peccato, secundum illud II Cor. VII, quae secundum Deum est tristitia, poenitentiam in salutem stabilem operatur. Et ideo Christus, ut satisfaceret pro peccatis omnium hominum, assumpsit tristitiam maximam quantitate absoluta, non tamen excedentem regulam rationis" (*ST* III, q. 46, a. 6, ad 2) (*Works of Thomas Aquinas*, 19:491; slightly altered).

38. "Qui dolor in Christo excessit omnem dolorem cuiuslibet contriti. Tum quia ex maiori sapientia et caritate processit, ex quibus dolor contritionis augetur. Tum etiam quia pro omnium peccatis simul doluit, secundum illud Isaiae LIII, vere dolores nostros ipse tulit" (*ST* III, q. 46, a. 6, ad 4) (*Works of Thomas Aquinas*, 19:491).

Aquinas's rejoinder to this objection is that Christ's work of salvation was accomplished not only as an act of power but also according to the dictates of justice, in consideration of which Christ assumed the quantity of suffering that was adequate for "so great a satisfaction."[39] The suffering in question has been designated by Aquinas throughout this article as consisting of Christ's vicarious contrition on behalf of sinful humanity. It is this vicarious contrition that Aquinas is here again equating with satisfaction and that he claims to be commensurate with the requirements of divine justice.

We see, then, that in this article Aquinas not only explicitly affirms that Christ suffered a vicarious and salvific contrition for human sin, but also insinuates this vicarious contrition into his more pervasive theme of Christ's satisfaction of divine justice. Moreover, there are hints in this article, which are further explicated in the subsequent article on Christ's enjoyment of the beatific vision during his Passion, that Christ's vicarious contrition on behalf of human sin is enabled precisely because of the perfection of his human wisdom and charity that is the ontological result of the hypostatic union and his habitual grace, virtues, and gifts. There is surely a lot more to be said about this theme and the validity of my identification and interpretation of it. But for now, I let my brief and admittedly tantalizing presentation of it stand merely as a glimpse of how an ethical explanation of Christ's salvific work could be intelligible and compelling in itself, while still being grounded in an ontological Christological vision.

Conclusion

In lieu of a standard conclusion that repeats in summary form what has gone before, I would like to "go back to the future," as it were, and suggest three ways in which our consideration of the commonality and complementarity of the thinking of Athanasius and Aquinas on Christ's salvific work can inform contemporary soteriological reflection.

First, the common witness of Athanasius and Aquinas demonstrates the value of a clear ontological framework as a foundation for soteriological thinking. This framework explicates the ontological structure of the God-world relation as determined by the co-inherence of the divine

---

39. "Ad tantam satisfactionem" (*ST* III, q. 46, a. 6, ad 6) (*Works of Thomas Aquinas*, 19:492).

attributes and thus derives the intelligibility of the Christian mystery of salvation from the congruence between the drama of Christ's salvific work and the doctrine of God.

Second, both Athanasius and Aquinas demonstrate the necessity, fittingness, and intelligibility of seeing divine justice as integral to this ontological framework and thus also demonstrate the necessity, fittingness, and intelligibility of understanding the Christian mystery of salvation as corresponding to divine justice. The setting up of a competition or a contradiction between divine mercy and justice, or the denigration of a soteriological mode of reasoning as "juridical," is thereby rendered invalid. Much more valid and intelligible is the mode of reasoning we find explicitly in Aquinas's work, in which the satisfaction of divine justice is considered to constitute the greatest kind of mercy.

Third, and finally, the complementarity between the conceptions of Christ's salvific work that we find in Athanasius and Aquinas demonstrate the complementarity and continuity between a soteriological mode of reflection that draws on a Christological focus on the hypostatic union and one that draws on a Christological focus on the two wills of Christ. The fruition of the Christological teaching of the Church does not give us an option between these two modes of Christological reflection but rather demands their integration. Therefore we must ground our soteriological reasoning both in the affirmation of the ontological transformation of human nature through its assumption by the Word, as we find in Athanasius, as well as in a more concretely detailed consideration of the existential process by which Christ enacted this transformation in all that he did and suffered, such as we find in Aquinas. Moreover, it is entirely appropriate that our modern attentiveness to the realms of personal interiority, subjectivity, and self-consciousness should stimulate us to extend our contemplation of Christ's salvific work into a consideration of how Christ's thinking and feeling contributed to the working out of human salvation. Both Athanasius's global characterization of Christ's stance of self-offering and Aquinas's concrete depiction of the salvific efficacy of Christ's representative contrition for human sins provide invaluable material for such a contemplation.

4

Divine Paternity in the Theology of SS. Gregory Nazianzen and Thomas Aquinas

JOHN BAPTIST KU, OP

Without pretending to come anywhere near an exhaustive treatment of this topic, this essay compares the understanding of God the Father as the principle of God the Son in the thought of St. Gregory of Nazianzus and St. Thomas Aquinas.[1] God the Father can be known distinctly in three ways: (1) insofar as he is unoriginate, or proceeds from no one and has no

---

1. For more on the Father in the theology of Aquinas, see John Baptist Ku, *God the Father in the Theology of St. Thomas Aquinas* (New York: Peter Lang, 2013), and Emmanuel Durand, *Le Père, Alpha et Oméga de la vie trinitaire* (Paris: Cerf, 2008). For more on the Father in the theology of Nazianzen, see Domingo García Guillén, *Padre es Nombre de Relación: Dios Padre en la teología de Gregorio Nacianceno* (Rome: Gregorian and Biblical Press, 2010).

I use these editions of Nazianzen's texts: *Orations* 20, 23, and 25 (PG 35), *Orations* 29, 30, and 31 (J. Barbel, *Gregor von Nazianz: Die fünf theologischen Reden* [Düsseldorf: Patmos-Verlag, 1963]), *Orations* 34 and 40 (PG 36), and *Letter 101 to Cledonius* (P. Gallay, *Grégoire de Nazianze: Lettres théologiques*, Sources chrétiennes 208 [Paris: Cerf, 1974], 36–94).

For Aquinas's texts, I use the Leonine Commission's critical edition of Aquinas's works whenever possible: (*ST, ScG, Comp. Theol., CEG, In Boetii de Trin., Super Decretalem, De 108 Articulis*). For works for which there is yet no critical edition, I consult the most recent version of the Marietti edition as the second-best choice (*De Pot., In Ioan., In ad Rom., In ad Cor., In ad Eph., In ad Gal.*). Because there is no Leonine or Marietti edition of Aquinas's commentary on Peter Lombard's *Sentences*, I use the Mandonnet-Moos edition for his commentary on the first three books of the *Sentences* and the Parma edition for the commentary

principle—on account of which he is said to have innascibility; (2) insofar as he is the principle of the Son—on account of which he has paternity; and (3) insofar as he is the principle of the Holy Spirit—on account of
which he has spiration. There is no way to tell the Father apart from the
other divine persons besides these three notions. One cannot distinguish
the persons by any pure perfections in God, because the persons possess
all perfections equally.

This chapter considers the second of these notions—the Father's paternity. Three central points emerge in considering the Father's paternity
that enable us to assess the consonance of the theology of the Theologian
and the Common Doctor, namely, (1) how the Father is or is not the *cause*
of the Son, (2) whether and how the Son *receives* his divinity from the Father, and (3) how the Father is or is not *greater* than the Son. Incidentally,
Gregory does not apply the term "monarchy" to God the Father—at least
not unambiguously—and Thomas avoids using the term for either the
Father or the whole Trinity.[2]

My exposition unfolds in five parts, comprising two introductory sections followed by three sections dealing with the three points mentioned
above. The introductory sections offer a cursory consideration of Aquinas's reception of Nazianzen and a few examples of some general differences in manners of speaking between these two Doctors of the Church.

---

on the fourth book—as the Mandonnet-Moos edition includes only the first three books and
distinctions 1–22 of Book 4.

Translations of Latin are my own. For translations of the Greek, I rely on the following,
which I have lightly edited: *Orations* 20, 23, and 25 (*St. Gregory of Nazianzus: Select Orations*,
Fathers of the Church 107, trans. Martha Vinson [Washington, DC: Catholic University
of America Press, 2003]), *Orations* 29 and 30 (Frederick W. Norris, *Faith Gives Fullness to
Reasoning*, trans. Lionel Wickham and Frederick Williams [New York: E. J. Brill, 1991]),
Oration 34 (Philip Schaff and Henry Wace, eds., *From Nicene and Post-Nicene Fathers*, vol. 7,
rev. ed., trans. Charles Gordon Browne and James Edward Swallow [Buffalo, NY: Christian
Literature, 1894]).

2. Gregory uses *monarchy* to refer to the divine essence *in each of the divine persons* (*Oration* 29.2, Barbel line 6), *in the Son from the Father* (*Oration* 25.15, PG 35.1220.24), *as that
in which the persons have unity* (*Oration* 31.14, Barbel line 9; *Oration* 40.41, PG 36.417.27),
and *as overemphasized by the Sabellians or Jews* (*Oration* 25.8, PG 35.1208.45; *Oration* 25.18,
PG 35.1224.12; *Oration* 31.17, Barbel line 9; *Oration* 38.8, PG 36.320.25; *Oration* 45.4, PG
36.628.42). Christopher Beeley interprets *monarchy* to refer to the Father; see his "Divine
Causality and the Monarchy of God the Father in Gregory of Nazianzus," *Harvard Theological Review* 110, no. 2 (2007): 206–8. Richard Cross recognizes that the word *monarchy* is
associated with the divine essence or the whole Trinity; see his "Divine Monarchy in Gregory
of Nazianzus," *Journal of Early Christian Studies* 14, no. 1 (2006): 116.

Aquinas's Reception of Nazianzen

Thomas Aquinas had access to some of Gregory Nazianzen's works in translation, and he mentions the Cappadocian Father by name fifty-one times in his whole corpus, but twenty-five of these are in the *Catena Aurea*.[3] Thus, in the context of his own theological argument, Thomas refers to Gregory on twenty-six occasions. Three of these cases refer to a fact about the life of Nazianzen, namely, that St. Jerome was a disciple of his, and that he was an example of a monk who taught and a religious who defended himself against detractors.[4] That leaves twenty-three occurrences where Aquinas invokes Nazianzen's theological opinion.[5] In eleven of these cases, Aquinas quotes text verbatim and with reasonable accuracy.[6] Three of these eleven cases, all from the *Contra Errores Graecorum*, concern the Trinity.

Aquinas shows the deep respect he has for Gregory in *ST* I, q. 61, a. 3, where when he rules out an opinion that Gregory held, he concludes that the rejected opinion "is not to be judged erroneous, especially on account of the opinion of Gregory Nazianzen, whose authority on Christian teach-

---

3. By 400, Rufinus had translated nine of Nazianzen's orations (2, 6, 16, 17, 26, 27, 38, 39, and 41) into Latin that would have been available to Aquinas in whole or part. See Augustus Engelbrecht, ed., *Tyranii Rufini Opera*, Pars I, *Orationum Gregorii Nazianzeni Novem Interpretatio*, vol. 46, *Corpus Scriptorum Ecclesiasticorum Latinorum* (Vienna: F. Tempsky, 1910).

4. In *De Subst. Separ.*, chap. 18; *Contra Impugnantes* II, chap. 1, corp.; and *Contra Impugnantes* IV, chap. 2, corp. In his *De Viris Illustribus*, 117, Jerome testifies that Gregory taught him Scripture and that Gregory lived the life of a monk.

5. Gregory is invoked in discussions on angels (I *Sent.*, d. 37, q. 3, a. 1, corp.; II *Sent.*, d. 2, q. 1, a. 3, corp. and obj. 1; *ST* I, q. 61, a. 3, corp.; *De Pot.*, q. 3, a. 18, obj. 1), Christ's human nature (*ST* III, q. 2, a. 1, obj. 3; *ST* III, q. 2, a. 3, ad 1; *ST* III, q. 16, a. 7, obj. 3; *ST* III, q. 17, a. 1, ad 2; *ST* III, q. 31, a. 2, ad 2), genealogy in Scripture (*ST* III, q. 31, a. 3, ad 2), Christ's baptism (*ST* III, q. 39, a. 1, corp.; *ST* III, q. 39, a. 2, corp.; *ST* III, q. 39, a. 3, ad 1), Church law (*ST* III, q. 39, a. 3, ad 3), the six days of creation (*De Subst. Separ.*, chap. 18, corp.), the Holy Spirit (*CEG* I, chap. 8, corp.; *CEG* I, chap. 9, corp.; *CEG* II, chap. 24, corp.; *CEG* II, chap. 27, corp.), and unleavened bread (*CEG* II, chap. 39, corp.).

6. The translated quotations in the *Contra Errores Graecorum* at least retain the sense. Thomas's quotation of *Oration 42* is the one exception, where the correspondence is clear but loose; however, the part of the text relevant to the argument correctly reports the sense. *Letter 101 to Cledonius*, 20–21, is quoted in *ST* III, q. 2, a. 3, ad 1; *ST* III, q. 16, a. 7, obj. 3; and *ST* III, q. 17, a. 1, ad 2. *Oration* 39.15, PG 36.352.25–27, is quoted in *ST* III, q. 39, aa. 1 and 2. *Oration* 39.14, PG 36.352.16–24, is quoted in *ST* III, q. 39, a. 3, ad 3. *ST* III, q. 39, a. 3, ad 1, refers to *Oration* 40.29, *PG* 36.400.32–35, and then *Oration* 40.19, *PG* 36.384.23–25. *CEG* I, chap. 8, and *CEG* II, chap. 27, quote *Oration* 31.8, Barbel lines 9–12. *CEG* II, chap. 39, corp., quotes *Oration* 1.1, PG 35.397.13–17. And *CEG* II, chap. 24, corp., quotes *Oration* 42.15, PG 36.476.19–20.

ing is so great that no one has ever dared to raise an objection to his words, as neither to the instruction of Athanasius, as Jerome says."[7]

Difference in Manner of Speech

There are marked differences in the writing styles of these two authors. Here I include three miscellaneous cases just to give sense of their different flavors. First, Aquinas avoids looser poetic and metaphorical speech, such as one finds in Gregory's *Oration* 30: "But by what he suffered as man, he as the Word and the Counselor persuades [the Father] to be patient."[8] Now, Gregory would concede that, properly speaking, the Father and the Son have one unchanging will, as he affirms elsewhere.[9] But Aquinas is more careful in distinguishing what is proper analogous speech versus what is metaphorical, such as we read concerning the attribution of anger to the Almighty: "Because it is proper to the angry person to punish, [God's] punishment is metaphorically called anger."[10]

Second, Gregory's rhetorical style is more biting. Frederick Norris describes the context:

The general tone of the first oration is ψόγος, "invective." That form of rhetoric was common to the fourth century C.E. Although it involved ridicule of the opponents, it was considered to be one aspect of the persuasive art, at least for the audience sitting in judgment. The modern reader may be offended by Nazianzen's incessant attack, but these *Theological Orations* are mild in comparison with his treatises against Julian (*Orations* 4 and 5). They breathe fire.[11]

---

7. This precise wording cannot be found in Jerome. For Jerome's praise of Gregory, see his aforementioned *De Viris Illustribus*, 117, and his *Apologia adversus Libros Rufini*, 1.13. Rufinus writes of Gregory Nazianzen: "Than his life, none can be found more commendable and holy, than his eloquence, none more renowned and illustrious, than his faith, none more pure and orthodox, than his knowledge, none fuller and more complete. He stands alone in that not even those who indulge in the usual disagreements with one another as to factions and schools could challenge his faith, but this reward he has achieved with God and the church of God, that whoever would dare to contest his doctrine in anything, by this very act he reveals himself the more clearly as a heretic; for everyone who does not concur in the faith of Gregory gives evident proof that he is not of orthodox belief." *Praefatio in Gregorii Nazianzeni Orationes, ad Apronianum*, in M. Monica Wagner, "Rufinus the Translator: A Study of His Theory and His Practice as Illustrated in His Version of the *Apologetica* of St. Gregory Nazianzen" (PhD diss., Catholic University of America, 1945), 24–25.

8. *Oration* 30.14, Barbel lines 16–17: ἀλλ' οἷς πέπονθεν, ὡς ἄνθρωπος, πείθει καρτερεῖν, ὡς λόγος καὶ παραινέτης.

9. For instance, in *Oration* 30.12 and 16.

10. *ST* I, q. 3, a. 2, ad 2.

11. Frederick Norris, *Faith Gives Fullness to Reasoning* (New York: E. J. Brill, 1991), 85.

It is difficult to restrict oneself to only a couple of the Theologian's delicious insults, but as illustrations, we could point to *Oration* 20, where the author explains: "I am repeating myself because your crassly materialistic cast of mind frightens me,"[12] and *Oration* 40, where he delivers this ultimatum:

But if you still halt and will not receive the perfectness of the Godhead, go and look for someone else to baptize—or rather to drown you: I have no time to cut the Godhead, and to make you dead in the moment of your regeneration, that you should have neither the gift nor the hope of grace, but should in so short a time make shipwreck of your salvation.[13]

There is a widespread impression that Aquinas is a stolid diplomatic author, with the one notable exception of judging David of Dinant to have most stupidly (*stultissime*) asserted that God is prime matter.[14] In fact, in a few passages of his *Commentary on John*, Aquinas is a bit impatient with Origen, who "disgracefully erred," "blasphemed," and "raved."[15] And he does end two works with similarly worded personal challenges to contemporary critics of religious life:

This is all that occurs to me, at present, to write against the pernicious and erroneous teaching that deters men from entering religious life. If anyone should wish to contradict what I have written, let him not prattle before boys [students], but let him write and share his writing in public, so that intelligent persons may judge what is true, and what is false may be refuted by the authority of the truth.[16]

Even so, Aquinas is helplessly tame by comparison. Both Gregory and Aquinas write with great ardor about God, but their rhetorical styles are different, and an accurate theological analysis must take note of this.

Is the Father the Cause, or αἰτία, of the Son?

The divine person who is the principle not from a principle is named the Father on account of his begetting of the Son. At first glance, Gregory and Thomas appear to hold different views on a potentially significant point, namely, whether the Father is the cause (αἰτία, *causa*) of the Son. Upon further examination, however, their profound agreement on the Father's status in begetting the Son is brought into relief.

---

12. *Oration* 20.7.
13. *Oration* 40.44.
14. *ST* I, q. 3, a. 8, corp.
15. *In Ioan.* 1:1 (lect. 1, #58), 14:10 (lect. 3, #1895), and 1:3 (lect. 2, #76).
16. *Contra Retrah.*, chap. 16. Similarly, *De Unitate Intellectus*, chap. 5 (#124).

Nazianzen on the Father as Cause

Gregory clearly refers to the Father as the *cause* (αἰτία) of the Son at least a dozen times in his writings: he asserts that the Father is the cause of the Son and Spirit;[17] the Son and the Spirit are related to God as to a cause;[18] the Father is the source of the other divine persons in the sense of a cause;[19] God, the first cause, is the source of divinity in the other persons;[20] in respect of being the cause, the Father is greater than the Son;[21]

17. *Oration* 23.7, PG 35.1160.1: "But if, no matter how highly you exalt the Son or the Spirit, *you do not proceed to place them above the Father or alienate them from him as their cause* (οὐχ ὑπὲρ τὸν Πατέρα θήσεις, οὐδὲ τῆς αἰτίας ἀποξενώσεις), but attribute their noble generation and marvelous procession to him, I shall simply ask you … who dishonors God more, the one who regards him as the source of the kinds of beings you yourself introduce, or the one who regards him as the source not of such, but of those which are like him in nature and equal to him in honor, the kind that our doctrine professes?" (emphasis mine).

18. *Oration* 20.7, PG 35.1073.3: "The one God, in my view, would be preserved if *both Son and Spirit come back to one cause* (εἰς ἓν αἴτιον καὶ Υἱοῦ καὶ Πνεύματος ἀναφερομένων) neither being merged nor fused together, but according to one and the same divinity, if I may so phrase it, as well as movement and will and identity of being." *Oration* 20.6, PG 35.1072.37: "Nor by the same token, should we be so partial to Christ that we fail to preserve this very distinction, his sonship, for *whose son would he in fact be if there were no causal relationship between his Father and himself* (τίνος γὰρ ἂν καὶ εἴη Υἱὸς, μὴ πρὸς αἴτιον ἀναφερόμενος τὸν Πατέρα)? Nor again should we diminish the Father's status as source, proper to him as Father and generator since he would be the source of small and worthless things *were he not the cause of deity contemplated in Son and Spirit* (μὴ θεότητος ὢν αἴτιος τῆς ἐν Υἱῷ καὶ Πνεύματι θεωρουμένης)." *Oration* 25.15, PG 35.1220.34: "Paradoxically, they are not without beginning, and, in a sense, they are: they are not in terms of causation, since they are indeed from God although they are not subsequent to him, just as light is not subsequent to the sun, but they are without beginning in terms of time since they are not subject to it" (Οὐκ ἄναρχα γὰρ, καὶ ἄναρχά πως· ὃ καὶ παράδοξον. Οὐκ ἄναρχα μὲν γὰρ τῷ αἰτίῳ· ἐκ Θεοῦ γὰρ, εἰ καὶ μὴ μετ᾽ αὐτὸν, ὡς ἐξ ἡλίου φῶς· ἄναρχα δὲ τῷ χρόνῳ. Οὐ γὰρ ὑπὸ χρόνον; emphasis mine).

19. *Oration* 20.7, PG 35.1073.11: "And the individual properties will be maintained if, in the case of the Father, we think and speak of him as being both source and without source" (I use the term in the sense of *causal agent* [ἀρχῆς δὲ, ὡς αἰτίου], fount, and eternal light). *Oration* 20, PG 35.1073.25: "The Son is not without source if you understand 'Father' to mean causal agent, since *the Father is the source of the Son as causal agent* (ἀρχὴ γὰρ Υἱοῦ Πατὴρ ὡς αἴτιος), but if you take source in the temporal sense, he too is without source because the Lord of all time does not owe his source to time" (emphasis mine).

20. *Oration* 23.6, PG 35.1157.33: "In fact, God is the object of proportionately more honor than his creatures are, to the degree that it is more in keeping with the greater majesty of *the first cause to be the source of divinity* (τῇ πρώτῃ αἰτίᾳ, θεότητος εἶναι ἀρχὴν) rather than of creatures and to reach the creatures through the medium of divinity rather than the reverse, that is, for divinity to acquire substantive existence for their sakes, as our very subtle and high-flown thinkers imagine" (emphasis mine).

21. *Oration* 29.15, Barbel line 1: "If we say that the Father is *qua cause superior to the Son*

the Father is the cause but not prior in time to the Son and Spirit;[22] the Father has causality but the Son does not;[23] and the Father is the Cause, the Son is the Creator, and the Spirit is the Perfecter.[24]

Therefore it could seem like Gregory has a rather different theology of the Father than Thomas, who insists that the Father is called a principle but *not a cause* of the Son or the Spirit[25] in order to avoid thinking of the Son or Spirit as having been made.[26] Aquinas is aware of the Eastern Fathers' use of the term, and judges that when Chrysostom calls the Father a cause, he does so "improperly."[27]

But the judgment that this term is improper appears in Thomas's *Commentary on the Sentences*, an early work (1252–56); this conclusion will mature into the opinion in the *Contra Errores Graecorum* (1263–64) that the Greeks use different language than the Latins but mean the same thing:

> This is not to be interpreted, however, as if the aforementioned saints who used such terms as cause and caused meant to imply that the divine persons did not have the same nature, or that the Son was a creature. They wished to indicate merely the origin of the persons, as we do when we use the term principle.[28]

(ὅτι τῷ αἰτίῳ μείζων ὁ πατὴρ τοῦ υἱοῦ), they add the minor premise *but he is cause by nature* and hence conclude that *he is superior by nature*" (first italicization mine).

22. *Oration* 29.3, Barbel line 14: "So *because they have a cause they are not unoriginate* (οὐκ ἄναρχα οὖν τῷ αἰτίῳ). But clearly a cause is not necessarily prior to its effects—the Sun is not prior to its light. *Because time is not involved, they are to that extent unoriginate* (καὶ ἄναρχά πως τῷ χρόνῳ)—even if you do scare simple souls with the bogey-word; for things which produce Time are beyond time" (emphases mine).

23. *Oration* 34.10, PG 36.252.1: "But if all that the Father has belongs likewise to the Son, except causality" (δὲ πάντα ὅσα ἔχει ὁ Πατὴρ, τοῦ Υἱοῦ ἐστι, πλὴν τῆς αἰτίας).

24. *Oration* 34.8, PG 36.249.4: "The Former is called God, and subsists in Three Greatest, namely, *the Cause, the Creator, and the Perfecter* (αἰτίῳ, καὶ δημιουργῷ, καὶ τελειοποιῷ); I mean the Father, the Son, and the Holy Ghost, who are neither so separated from one another as to be divided in nature, nor so contracted as to be circumscribed by a single person."

25. *I Sent.*, d. 12, q. 1, a. 2, ad 1: *pater dicitur principium, sed non causa*. *I Sent.*, d. 29, q. 1, a. 1, corp.: *pater non est causa filii, sed principium*. *I Sent.*, d. 29, q. 1, a. 1, ad 2: "quamvis pater dicatur principium filii, non tamen dicendus est causa." *ST* I, q. 33, a. 1, ad 1: "Graeci utuntur in divinis indifferenter nomine causae, sicut et nomine principii, sed Latini doctores non utuntur nomine causae, sed solum nomine principii." *CEG* I, chap. 1: "Apud Latinos autem non est consuetum quod pater dicatur causa filii vel spiritus sancti, sed solum principium vel auctor."

26. *De Pot.*, q. 10, a. 1, ad 8: "unde ne cogamur filium vel spiritum sanctum factos dicere, patrem non dicimus causam eorum." *CEG* I, chap. 1: "unde patrem non dicimus esse causam, ne aliquis intelligat filium esse factum."

27. *I Sent.*, d. 29, q. 1, a. 1, ad 2: "quamvis pater dicatur principium filii, non tamen dicendus est causa, nisi improprie, sicut Chrysostomus utitur nomine causae, dicens patrem causam filii."

28. *CEG* I, chap. 1: "Nec tamen intelligendum est, quod sancti praedicti, qui nomine

Aquinas's ecumenism is not mere diplomacy. In support of his assertion, let us consider three cases—two from *Oration* 30 and one from *Oration* 23 —where Gregory pushes back on problematic implications of calling the Father a cause, showing that Gregory shares Aquinas's concerns.

In discussing the two natures of Christ in *Oration* 30, Gregory determines that, in his divinity, the Son is *not caused* but is absolute and unoriginate—in the sense of uncreated:

> Whatever we come across with a causal implication we will attribute to the humanity; what is absolute and free of cause we will reckon to the Godhead.[29]

In the next line, Gregory notes that this is because *cause* is connected to *creation*—which observation addresses Aquinas's concern exactly. For Gregory, too, the idea of being caused cannot apply to the Son in any way that would suggest his being created by the Father; we should rather deploy the term "begotten," which is not connected with "cause" or "creation":

> "Created" has a causal implication, has it not? The text [of Prv 8:22] in fact runs: "He created me as the beginning of his ways for his works." ... But the expression, "begets me," has no causal implication.... What objection will there be to Wisdom's being called a "creature" in respect to earthly generation, but "offspring" with regard to the primal and less comprehensible one?[30]

Thus, because *cause* is connected to creation, we should think of the Son's eternal proceeding from the Father as a begetting, not a being caused. So, although there might be some ambiguity in Nazianzen's use of the term *cause*, his doctrine is clear enough. Namely, while the Father is understood in some way to be the cause (αἰτία) of the Son as his principle, the Son in his divinity is not in any way caused as a creature. The Cappadocian Father affirms later in *Oration* 30 that the Son is uncaused, or beyond all cause:

> The statement: "I live because of the Father" [Jn 6:57], corresponds with this fact—meaning not that his living and being are restricted by the Father, but that he exists outside time and *beyond all cause* (ἀναιτίως).[31]

---

causae et causati utuntur in divinis personis, intendant diversitatem naturae inducere, aut filium esse creaturam. Sed per hoc volunt ostendere solam originem personarum, sicut nos nomine principii."

29. *Oration* 30.2, Barbel lines 17–19: ὃ μὲν ἂν μετὰ τῆς αἰτίας εὑρίσκωμεν, προσθῶμεν τῇ ἀνθρωπότητι· ὃ δὲ ἁπλοῦν καὶ ἀναίτιον, τῇ θεότητι λογισώμεθα.

30. *Oration* 30.2, Barbel line 19: ἆρ᾽ οὖν οὐ τὸ μὲν Ἔκτισεν εἴρηται μετὰ τῆς αἰτίας;... τὸ δὲ Γεννᾷ με χωρὶς αἰτίας. ... τίς οὖν ἀντερεῖ λόγος, κτίσμα μὲν λέγεσθαι τὴν σοφίαν κατὰ τὴν κάτω γέννησιν, γέννημα δὲ κατὰ τὴν πρώτην καὶ πλέον ἄληπτον;

31. *Oration* 30.11, Barbel lines 9–11: καθ᾽ ὃ καὶ λέγεται καὶ τό· Ἐγὼ ζῶ διὰ τὸν πατέρα. οὐχ ὡς

The context of this discussion is Gregory's dispute with the Eunomians over whether the Son is coequally God with the Father. Accepting that the Father is the cause of the Son, Gregory argues in *Oration* 23 that it is no affront to the Father that the Son should be equally divine, but on the contrary, the Son's full divinity affirms the Father's infinite power:

In fact, God is the object of proportionately more honor than his creatures are, to the degree that it is more in keeping with the greater majesty of the first cause to be the source of divinity rather than of creatures and to reach the creatures through the medium of divinity rather than the reverse, that is, for divinity to acquire substantive existence for their sakes, as our very subtle and high-flown thinkers imagine.... But if, no matter how highly you exalt the Son or the Spirit, you do not proceed to place them above the Father or alienate them from him as their cause, but attribute their noble generation and marvelous procession to him, I shall simply ask you, my friend, you who are so fond of the expressions "unbegotten" and "without source," who dishonors God more, the one who regards him as the source of the kinds of beings you yourself introduce, or the one who regards him as the source not of such, but of those which are like him in nature and equal to him in honor, the kind that our doctrine professes?[32]

Aquinas on the Father as Cause

So, Gregory can be brought closer to Thomas regarding calling the Father the cause of the Son, but can Thomas be brought closer to Gregory? While Aquinas eschews the term *cause* for the Father with respect to the Son, he readily asserts in four works that the Father produces (*producere*) the Son.[33] And in what way should the Father be understood to *produce*

ἐκεῖθεν αὐτῷ τοῦ ζῆν καὶ τοῦ εἶναι συνεχομένου, ἀλλ' ὡς ἐκεῖθεν ὑπάρχοντος ἀχρόνως καὶ ἀναιτίως (emphasis mine).

32. *Oration* 23.6–7, PG 35.1157.36–1160.7: Καίτοι ὅσῳ τιμιώτερον Θεὸς κτισμάτων, τοσούτῳ μεγαλοπρεπέστερον τῇ πρώτῃ αἰτίᾳ, θεότητος εἶναι ἀρχήν, ἢ κτισμάτων· καὶ διὰ θεότητος μέσης ἐλθεῖν ἐπὶ τὰ κτίσματα, ἢ τοὐναντίον, τούτων ἕνεκεν ὑποστῆναι θεότητα, ὃ δοκεῖ τοῖς λίαν ἐξεταστικοῖς τε καὶ μετεώροις. Εἰ μὲν γὰρ ἐμέλλομεν, Υἱοῦ καὶ Πνεύματος τὴν ἀξίαν ὁμολογοῦντες, ἢ ἄναρχα ταῦτα εἰσάγειν, ἢ εἰς ἑτέραν ἀρχὴν ἀνάγειν, δέος ἂν ἦν ὄντως μὴ ἀτιμασθῇ Θεός, ἢ κινδυνεύσῃ παρ' ἡμῶν τὸ ἀντίθεον. Εἰ δὲ ὅσον ἂν ἐξαίρῃς τὸν Υἱόν, ἢ τὸ Πνεῦμα, οὐχ ὑπὲρ τὸν Πατέρα θήσεις, οὐδὲ τῆς αἰτίας ἀποξενώσεις, ἀλλ' ἐκεῖσε ἀνάγεις τὸ καλὸν γέννημα, καὶ τὴν θαυμασίαν πρόοδον· προσερήσομαί σε ὀλίγον, φιλαγέννητε σὺ καὶ φιλάναρχε, πότερος Θεὸς ἀτιμάζει μᾶλλον, ὁ τοιούτων τιθεὶς ἀρχήν, οἵων αὐτὸς εἰσάγεις, ἢ ὁ μὴ τοιούτων, ἀλλ' ὁμοίων τὴν φύσιν, καὶ ὁμοδόξων, καὶ οἵων ὁ ἡμέτερος βούλεται λόγος;

33. *ST* I, q. 42, a. 2, corp.: "actio qua pater producit filium, non est successiva, quia sic filius Dei successive generaretur, et esset eius generatio materialis et cum motu, quod est impossibile." *Super Decretales*, no. 2, corp.: "Pater enim generando filium, dedit ei substantiam

the Son? By way of efficient causality. This indeed brings Thomas closer to Gregory.

Thomas answers this question in three places. In *CEG* I, chap. 1, Aquinas considers our original question *how it is to be understood that . . . the Son has [everything] from the Father as something caused from a cause.* He replies that this production or causation may not be understood "in the manner of a formal or material or final cause but only by way of an originating cause, which is an efficient cause."[34] Now, because "we find that this [efficient cause] is always of a diverse essence from that of which it is the cause," Aquinas rules out the use of *cause*.[35] But the mode of causality is in some way inescapably efficient.

Thomas offers the same analysis in several passages in his commentary on Peter Lombard's *Sentences*. There he distinguishes between real relations and merely logical relations in God. If the Father and the Son are to be distinct in the real order and not only according to our way of knowing, then the relations must be real, which means that the procession that gives rise to these relations must be by way of efficient causality:

> But in God there can only be a relation (*habitudo*) according to a twofold genus of cause—only one of which is a real relation, namely through the mode of an efficient or originating cause, as the Father is said to be the principle of the Son— and the other relation of a principle can be indicated in God according to reason

suam, cum generare nihil aliud sit quam ex substantia sua alium producere." *Comp. Theol.* I, chap. 223, corp.: "Est enim de ratione patris ut ex sua natura filium sibi connaturalem producat." *De 108 Articulis*, q. 12: "Sicut igitur Deus pater filium non voluntate, sed natura produxit, ita de spiritu sancto sentiendum est."

34. *CEG* I, chap. 1: "pater non posset intelligi causa filii per modum causae formalis vel materialis vel finalis, sed solum per modum causae originantis, quae est causa efficiens." He articulates the same in I *Sent.*, d. 32, q. 2, a. 2, qla. 1, corp.—"una [habitudo] . . . est habitudo realis, scilicet *per modum causae efficientis vel originantis*, sicut pater dicitur principium filii"—and in I *Sent.*, d. 34, q. 1, a. 2, corp.—"ut tamen efficiens large sumatur, quia in divinis non est aliquid faciens et factum: sed est ibi origo unius personae ab alia. Et ita patet quod omnis constructio in divinis respectu divinorum, vel est secundum habitudinem *causae efficientis, ut cum dicitur filius patris*; vel secundum habitudinem causae formalis, ut cum dicitur: tres personae sunt unius essentiae" (emphasis mine).

This passage shows that Thomas's position is not relegated to his early work of commenting on the *Sentences*. The *Contra Errores Graecorum* was begun in 1263, only two years prior to the *Summa Theologiae*.

35. *CEG* I, chap. 1: "Hanc autem semper invenimus secundum essentiam diversam ab eo cuius est causa." By "diverse essence," he means *not the numerically same essence*. Obviously, human parents are the efficient causes of their offspring with whom they share the *specifically* same essence.

only and not really, namely, the relation of form, as when we say that the Father is God through his deity.[36]

In another passage from the *Sentences Commentary*, Aquinas specifies that *efficient* is to be taken broadly, and he offers a different example of a formal relation:

But the relation (*habitudo*) of an efficient cause is fitting to God both with respect to creatures and with respect to that which is in him—however, not of being (*esse*) to person but of person to person that is in him. Nevertheless this relation (*habitudo*) is not founded on a grasp of the intellect but on a relation (*relatio*) that is real, where "efficient" is taken broadly—because in God there is not something making and something made, but here there is the origin of one person from another. And so it is clear that every comparison in God with respect to God is either according to the relation (*habitudo*) of an efficient cause, as when we say, the Son of the Father, or according to the relation (*habitudo*) of a formal cause, as when we say, three persons are of one essence.[37]

Interestingly, Gregory rules out the idea that the Father *produces* the Son:

If there is an active producer, there must be a production and [the Eunomians] will declare themselves surprised at the idea of an identity between creator and created.[38]

---

36. I *Sent.*, d. 32, q. 2, a. 2, qla. 1, corp.: "In divinis autem non potest esse nisi habitudo secundum duplex genus causae; quarum una tantum est habitudo realis, scilicet per modum causae efficientis vel originantis, sicut pater dicitur principium filii; alia vero habitudo principii potest designari in divinis secundum rationem tantum et non realiter, scilicet habitudo formae, ut cum dicimus quod pater est deus per deitatem suam."

37. I *Sent.*, d. 34, q. un., a. 2, corp.: "Habitudo autem causae efficientis competit Deo et respectu creaturae et respectu ejus quod in ipso est, non quidem esse ad personam, sed personae ad personam, quae ab ipso est; nec tamen ista habitudo fundatur supra acceptionem intellectus, sed supra relationem, quae in re est; ut tamen efficiens large sumatur, quia in divinis non est aliquid faciens et factum: sed est ibi origo unius personae ab alia. Et ita patet quod omnis constructio in divinis respectu divinorum, vel est secundum habitudinem causae efficientis, ut cum dicitur filius patris; vel secundum habitudinem causae formalis, ut cum dicitur: tres personae sunt unius essentiae."

Aquinas could have said that *efficient causality* here is to be taken analogously, but it seems that he did not find that specification clarifying. After all, any comparison between God and creatures is at closest analogous. And in the case of generation, on one hand, the Father's production of the Son far exceeds human generation in that the Son's similitude is so perfect that he is not specifically but even numerically the same in nature as the Father; and on the other hand, the Father's act of generating the Son produces positively no *effect* at all—unlike earthly causes that produce an effect with every act absolutely without exception.

38. *Oration* 29.16, Barbel lines 6–8: οὐ γὰρ ὁ ἐνεργῶν, ἐκεῖ πάντως καὶ τὸ ἐνεργούμενον. καὶ πῶς τῷ πεποιηκότι ταὐτὸν τὸ πεποιημένον, θαυμάζειν φήσουσι.

So, Nazianzen allows for the use of *cause*, but Aquinas does not. Aquinas permits the use of *produces*, however, which Nazianzen rejects. And by *produces*, Aquinas means somehow according to the mode of efficient causality.

Although Arians were much less of a threat in Aquinas's time, his vigorous defense of the Son's equality suggests that Aquinas viewed the conceptual threat of subordinationism as relevant. For instance, he writes that "the Father is not more like himself than he is to the Son"[39] and "the divine essence is not more the Father's than the Son's."[40] But if the Son receives his being from the Father and is produced by the Father, there is something like the mode of efficient causality here. That is, it is not as if the three persons simply exist in relationships to each other in the logical order or in a symmetrical perichoresis. No, the relations are real because they arise from real processions of one person from another, which are real actions.[41]

Aquinas clarifies the two aspects of this mystery, in a passage where he rules out calling the Father the Son's cause, with the assertion that the Father gives *the Son* his very being, but the Father does not have the order of a principle to the Son's *being*:

But we find this in the origin of divine persons that the whole essence of one is received into the others so that the essence of the three is numerically the same, and the same being. And therefore to signify the order of such an origin, the word "cause" is not fitting for two reasons: first, because every cause is either outside the essence of the thing, as the agent or end, or it is part of the essence, as matter or form; second, because every cause has the order of a principle to the being of the thing caused that is constituted by the cause. But the Father does not have any order of principle to the being of the Son, as neither to his own being, since the being of each is one and the same. Thus the Father is not the cause of the Son but the principle, because principle indicates an order of origin absolutely, not by determining any mode that is alien to the origin of persons. For we find a principle that is not outside the essence of the principled, as the *terminus from which* is called the principle of motion and as the dawn is called the principle of the day.[42]

---

39. *ST* I, q. 36, a. 4, ad 3: "sicut pater non est similior sibi quam filio."

40. *ST* I, q. 42, a. 1, ad 3: "essentia divina non magis est patris quam filii."

41. See *ST* I, q. 28, a. 1.

42. I *Sent.*, d. 29, q. 1, a. 1, corp.: "Hoc autem invenimus in origine divinarum personarum quod tota essentia unius accipitur in alia, ita quod una numero est essentia trium, et idem esse. Et ideo ad significandum ordinem talis originis, non competit nomen causae propter duo: primo, quia omnis causa vel est extra essentiam rei, sicut efficiens et finis; vel pars essentiae,

To sum up then, the Father is the principle of the Son: he produces the Son in the manner of an efficient cause, but he is not a cause in that the Son is not an effect that depends on the cause and is less than the cause in power and perfection. The Son receives the divine essence from the Father, but not by the Father's choice. The Father produces the Son by nature; that is, in knowing himself, the Father produces a concept that is another *I* and no less the divine essence than the Father is.

Affirming the full divinity of the Son, these two great Doctors see no other way to affirm the truth of the mystery of the Trinity than to declare that the Father is the *cause* of the Son (Gregory) or *produces* the Son *by way of efficient causality* (Thomas); the Son *receives his very being*, which is nothing less than the Father's own being, from the Father. Nazianzen and Aquinas are of one mind on this point despite the difference in vocabulary.

As regards the term *cause*, one might ask whether it is even a difference in vocabulary and not simply a question of translation. Translators generally render αἰτία in English as "cause," and Aquinas himself understood the Greek Fathers to be using the equivalent of Latin's *causa*.[43] However, given Gregory's qualifications ruling out any difference in power or perfection between the Father and the Son, a better rendering of αἰτία in this precise context might be *author* (*auctor*). Aquinas applies this term to the Father to mean *unoriginate principle*, which is precisely what Gregory means when he states that the Father is the αἰτία of the Son:

But the word "author" adds to the meaning of a principle that it is not from another; and therefore the Father alone is said to be an *author*, although the Son too is called a *principle* notionally.[44]

---

sicut materia et forma. Secundo, quia omnis causa habet ordinem principii ad esse sui causati quod per ipsam constituitur. Pater autem non habet aliquem ordinem principii ad esse filii, sicut nec ad esse suum, cum unum et idem sit esse utriusque: unde pater non est causa filii, sed principium; quia principium dicit ordinem originis absolute, non determinando aliquem modum qui ab origine personarum alienus sit. Invenitur enim aliquod principium quod non est extra essentiam principiati, sicut punctus a quo fluit linea; et quod non habet aliquam influentiam ad esse principiati, sicut terminus a quo dicitur principium motus, et sicut mane dicitur principium diei."

43. Aquinas names Chrysostom in I *Sent.*, d. 29, q. 1, a. 1, ad 2, and III *Sent.*, d. 11, q. 1, a. 1, obj. 5, and speaks of the "Greeks" in *De Pot.*, q. 10, a. 1, ad 9; *ST* I, q. 33, a. 1, ad 1; and *CEG* I, chap. 1, corp., specifying in the last Theodoret, Athanasius, and Basil.

44. I *Sent.*, d. 29, q. 1, a. 1, corp.: "Sed nomen auctoris addit super rationem principii hoc quod est non esse ab aliquo; et ideo solus Pater auctor dicitur, quamvis etiam Filius principium dicatur notionaliter."

For a consideration of Thomas's use of *auctor*, see John Baptist Ku, "Thomas Aquinas's

For Thomas, author does not mean cause: "for source and authority in God signify nothing other than the principle of origin."[45] While it would perhaps be anachronistic to use *author* in translating αἰτία in Gregory's writings on God the Father, that is clearly the sense Gregory intends.[46]

The Son Receives Everything from the Father

So, Gregory and Thomas agree on what calling the Father *the cause of the Son* does not mean, but do they agree on what it does mean? Indeed they do. Let us consider three passages concerning the Father's begetting from *Oration* 30 and then turn to Aquinas. According to Nazianzen, the Son, even in his divinity, can be said to receive (λαμβάνειν) everything from the Father:

The fifth point to be mentioned is that he *receives* life [Jn 5:26], judgment [Jn 5:22 and 27], inheritance of the Gentiles [Ps 2:8], power over all flesh [Jn 17:2], glory [Rv 5:12], disciples [Jn 17:6]—everything. This "receiving" belongs to his manhood. Yet it would not be absurd to ascribe it to the Deity.[47]

In the next line, Gregory observes that the Son receives everything from the Father, but the Son is begotten *by nature* not by choice:

You will not be ascribing him acquired properties, but properties which have existed with him from the outset, not by a principle of grace but by a condition of his nature.[48]

Nazianzen traces out the implications of this full receiving that is not a gift, with reference to Scripture: because the Son receives everything

---

Careful Deployment of *auctor* and *auctoritas* in Trinitarian Theology," *Angelicum* 90, no. (2013): 677–710.

45. *ST* I, q. 33, a. 4, ad 1: "nam fontalitas et auctoritas nihil aliud significant in divinis quam principium originis." See also: I *Sent.*, d. 15, q. 1, a. 2, corp.; I *Sent.*, d. 15, q. 2, a. 1, corp.; I *Sent.*, d. 15, q. 4, *divisio textus*; I *Sent.*, d. 16, *expositio textus*; I *Sent.*, d. 19, a. 2, ad 2; II *Sent.*, d. 13, a. 5, ad 4; *ScG* IV, chap. 24 (no. 3); *ST* I, q. 33, a. 1 and 2; *ST* I, q. 33, a. 4, ad 1; *De Pot.*, q. 10, a. 1, ad 9; *De Pot.*, q. 10, a. 4, corp. and ad 14; *CEG* I, chap. 2; *CEG* II, chap. 23; *In Boetii de Trin.* II, q. 3, a. 4, ad 1; *In Ioan.* 14:28 (lect. 8 no. 1971); *In ad Gal.* 3:5 (lect. 2, no. 127).

46. For more on this term, See John P. Egan, "αἴτιος/'Author,' αἰτία/'Cause' and ἀρχή/ 'Origin': Synonyms in Selected Texts of Gregory Nazianzen," *Studia Patristica* 32 (1997): 102–7.

47. *Oration* 30.9, Barbel lines 1–4: λεγέσθω τὸ λαμβάνειν αὐτὸν ζωήν, ἢ κρίσιν, ἢ κληρονομίαν ἐθνῶν, ἢ ἐξουσίαν πάσης σαρκός, ἢ δόξαν, ἢ μαθητάς, ἢ ὅσα λέγεται. καὶ τοῦτο τῆς ἀνθρωπότητος. εἰ δὲ καὶ τῷ θεῷ δοίης, οὐκ ἄτοπον (emphasis mine). And *Oration* 20.10, PG 35.1077.13–14, states that the Son "receives his being" (ἐξ αὐτοῦ τε ὑπάρχοντος).

48. *Oration* 30.9, Barbel lines 4–5: οὐ γὰρ ὡς ἐπίκτητα δώσεις, ἀλλ' ὡς ἀπ' ἀρχῆς συνυπάρ-χοντα, καὶ λόγῳ φύσεως, ἀλλ' οὐ χάριτος.

from the Father, the Father and the Son have all in common, and the Son can do nothing on his own but only does what he sees the Father doing:

It cannot be the case that the Son does anything which the Father does not do. For all that the Father has, is the Son's and vice versa [Jn 16:17, 17:10]. Nothing belongs only to one, because all things belong to both; *even existence per se, though it comes to the Son from the Father*, belongs to both and both alike.[49]

Gregory's understanding of the Son's receiving everything from the Father is in exact accord with Thomas's view. In at least fifty-three places in ten different works, Aquinas affirms the principle that while "the Father and the Son are equals in life, they are distinguished because the Father gives and the Son receives."[50] For example, the Father gives (*dare*) to the Son: being (*esse*),[51] the divine nature,[52] substance,[53] glory,[54] power,[55] and

---

49. *Oration* 30.11, Barbel lines 5–8: οὕτως ἀδύνατον καὶ ἀνεγχώρητον ποιεῖν τι τὸν υἱόν, ὧν οὐ ποιεῖ ὁ πατήρ. πάντα γὰρ ὅσα ἔχει ὁ πατήρ, τοῦ υἱοῦ ἐστίν· ὡς ἔμπαλιν τὰ τοῦ υἱοῦ τοῦ πατρός· οὐδὲν οὖν ἴδιον, ὅτι κοινά. ἐπεὶ καὶ αὐτὸ τὸ εἶναι κοινὸν καὶ ὁμότιμον, εἰ καὶ τῷ υἱῷ παρὰ τοῦ πατρός.

50. *In Ioan.*, chap. 5, lect. 5: "Sunt enim aequales in vita pater et filius; sed distinguuntur, quia pater dat, filius accipit."

51. I *Sent.*, d. 9, q. 2, a. 1, ad 2: "And therefore the Son receives being from the Father, nor does he have it from himself, but from eternity, he receives from the Father" ("et ita filius accepit esse a patre, nec habet esse a se, sed ab aeterno a patre accepit esse"). I *Sent.*, d. 9, expositio: "Praeterea, Deus per hoc quod dat esse creaturae, dicitur creator, et per hoc quod dat esse filio, dicitur pater." I *Sent.*, d. 16, expositio: "Et quamvis patri attribuatur auctoritas a sanctis, tamen filio non attribuitur subauctoritas, sed est per abusum loquentium praesumptum; et hoc sonant verba Hilarii dicentis quod *major est donans, sed non est minor, cui unum esse donatur. Innascibilitatis imaginem.* Sic expone: cui, scilicet filio, pater *impartit,* idest dat, esse: *imaginem innascibilitatis,* idest sui innascibilis; et hoc *sacramento nativitatis,* idest sacra et secreta nativitate." *ScG* IV, chap. 8, no. 5: "Ex hac ergo datione generatio ipsa intelligitur, secundum quam pater filio veram divinitatem dedit. Idem etiam ostenditur ex hoc quod omnia sibi dicit esse data a patre." *De Pot.*, q. 7, a. 10, ad 3: "Ad tertium dicendum, quod pater dat esse filio sui generis, cum sit agens univocum; non autem tale esse dat Deus creaturae; et ideo non est simile."

52. I *Sent.*, d. 5, expositio: "Pater per generationem dat naturam suam filio"; and also *ScG* IV, chap. 8, no. 5; *ST* III, q. 7, a. 11, ad 1; *De Ver.*, q. 29, a. 3 corp.; *CEG* I, chap. 4, corp.; *In Ioan.*, chap. 3, lect. 6, and chap. 16, lect. 4; and *In ad Eph.*, chap. 3, lect. 4.

53. *Super Decretales*, no. 2, corp.: "pater ab aeterno dedit substantiam filio"; and *In Ioan.*, chap. 16, lect. 4.

54. *In Ioan.*, chap. 17, lect. 6: "Sed pater natura dedit filio claritatem, non voluntate, quia genuit eum per naturam."

55. I *Sent.*, d. 20, q. 1, prol.: "Verum est quod pater potentiam filio dedit"; and *In Ioan.*, chap. 1, lect. 2: "Quia ergo pater eamdem virtutem, quamhabet, dat filio, per quam filius operatur."

the power to give life;[56] and the Son receives (*accipere*): the numerically same being (*esse*),[57] the divine nature,[58] the whole substance,[59] the whole form (*figura*),[60] power,[61] the same power to act,[62] the power to judge,[63] and the power to spirate the Holy Spirit.[64] Thus we find no difference in thought or formulation here: the Son receives everything, even his very being, from the Father—but by nature, not by the Father's free choice.[65]

56. *In ad I Cor.*, chap. 15, lect. 3: "*sicut pater habet vitam in semetipso, ita et filio dedit vitam habere,* id est vivificandi virtutem."

57. I *Sent.*, d. 9, q. 2, a. 1, ad 2: "et ita filius accepit esse a patre, nec habet esse a se, sed ab aeterno a patre accepit esse." *De Pot.*, q. 10, a. 1, ad 14: "Filius autem accipit a patre idem numero esse et eamdem naturam numero quam pater habet."

58. I *Sent.*, d. 30, q. 1, a. 3, ad 3: "quia secundum unum et eumdem modum et eamdem rationem pater dat, et filius accipit naturam divinam." *ScG* IV, chap. 7, no. 24: "Unde patet quod sola Ecclesiae Catholicae fides vere confitetur generationem in Deo, dum ipsam generationem filii ad hoc refert quod filius accepit divinam naturam a patre." *ScG* IV, chap. 8, no. 6: "Per hoc ergo quod filius sua nativitate a patre naturam divinam acceperit." *ST* I, q. 45, a. 6, ad 2: "Ad secundum dicendum quod, sicut natura divina, licet sit communis tribus personis, ordine tamen quodam eis convenit, inquantum filius accipit naturam divinam a patre, et spiritus sanctus ab utroque." *De Pot.*, q. 10, a. 1, ad 14: "Filius autem accipit a patre idem numero esse et eamdem naturam numero quam pater habet."

59. *In Ioan.*, chap. 16, lect. 4: "filius dicitur de substantia patris, quia accipit totam substantiam patris."

60. *In Ioan.*, chap. 6, lect. 3: "Quando autem sigillum in cera imprimitur, cera retinet totam figuram sigilli, sicut et filius totam figuram patris accepit."

61. I *Sent.*, d. 20, q. 1, a. 2, ad 3: "et ideo quantam potentiam pater habet, tantam accipit filius ab eo."

62. *In ad Rom.*, chap. 11, lect. 5: "Hoc autem modo de quo nunc loquimur, dicuntur omnia esse facta a patre per filium, secundum illud Io. I, 3: *omnia per ipsum facta sunt:* non ita quod pater habeat a filio hoc quod facit res, sed potius, quia virtutem faciendi filius accipit a patre, non tamen instrumentalem, aut diminutam, aut aliam, sed principalem et aequalem, et eamdem."

63. *ST* III, q. 59, a. 1, ad 2: "auctoritas iudicandi est apud patrem, a quo filius accepit potestatem iudicandi."

64. *De Pot.*, q. 10, a. 4, ad 10: "filius a patre accipit virtutem spiritum sanctum spirandi."

65. As Khaled Anatolios observes, this is a unity of being as opposed to merely a unity of will. In his *Retrieving Nicaea* (Grand Rapids, MI: Baker Academic, 2011), Anatolios astutely discerns this distinction: "Alexander, Athanasius, and the Cappadocians, despite undeniable differences and developments, all designated the relation between Father and Son in terms of unity of being. Arius, Asterius, Eusebius, and Eunomius, again despite all their divergences, insisted that the relations between Father and Son pertained to will, not to being" (31). In *ST* I, q. 41, a. 2, Thomas clarifies that the Father generates the Son *by will* only in the sense of desiring it concomitantly with the existing reality. That is, the Father wills the Son in the same way that the Father wills to be God. If the Father generated the Son by free will, the Son would be a creature, who could have not existed.

Is the Father Greater Than the Son?

Along the same fault line, we find Nazianzen's understanding that the Father is *greater* than the Son and the Spirit but only with respect to being a cause; he is not greater in nature:

It is impossible for the same thing to be, in a like respect, greater than and equal to the same thing. Is it not clear that the *superiority belongs to the cause and the equality to the nature?* ... But someone else might persist with our argument and say that *derivation from the uncaused does not mean inferiority to the uncaused.* He will share in the glory of the unoriginate because he derives from the unoriginate.[66]

Gregory simply accepts this manner of speaking as a given—likely because of John 14:28: "the Father is greater than I"—and he takes the Eunomians to task for misinterpreting it to mean that the Father is greater in nature. Such reasoning involves a semantic error:

If we say that the Father is qua cause superior to the Son, they add the minor premise, "but he is cause by nature" and hence conclude that "he is superior by nature...." The fallacy here arises from arguing, as the logicians call it, "from the particular to the general." We concede, of course, that it belongs to the nature of the cause to be superior, but they infer that the superiority belongs to the nature—which is like our saying "X is a dead man" and their drawing the inference that "Man," without qualification, is dead.[67]

Gregory wishes to assert the Father's unique dignity while also defending the Son's equality. And he is not impressed by the appeal to Christ's human nature to account for the Father's being greater than the Son:

Of course, the explanation that the Father is greater than the Son considered as man is true, but trivial. Is there anything remarkable about God's being greater than man?[68]

66. *Oration* 30.7, Barbel 4–10: τὸ γὰρ αὐτὸ τοῦ αὐτοῦ ὁμοίως μεῖζον καὶ ἴσον εἶναι τῶν ἀδυνάτων· ἢ δῆλον ὅτι τὸ μεῖζον μέν ἐστι τῆς αἰτίας, τὸ δὲ ἴσον τῆς φύσεως.... τάχα δ᾽ ἂν εἴποι τις ἄλλος τῷ ἡμετέρῳ λόγῳ προσφιλονεικῶν, μὴ ἔλαττον εἶναι τὸ ἐκ τοιαύτης αἰτίας εἶναι τοῦ ἀναιτίου. τῆς τε γὰρ τοῦ ἀνάρχου δόξης μετέχοι ἄν, ὅτι ἐκ τοῦ ἀνάρχου (emphasis mine).

67. *Oration* 29.15, Barbel lines 1–3, 11–15: Ἐὰν δὲ λεγόντων ἡμῶν, ὅτι τῷ αἰτίῳ μεῖζων ὁ πατὴρ τοῦ υἱοῦ, προσλαβόντες τὴν Τὸ δὲ αἴτιον φύσει πρότασιν, ἔπειτα τὸ Μεῖζον τῇ φύσει συνάγωσιν.... ἀλλ᾽ οἶμαι, παρὰ τὸ πῇ καὶ ἁπλῶς ὁ παραλογισμὸς οὗτος, ὡς τοῖς περὶ ταῦτα τεχνολογεῖν σύνηθες. ἡμῶν γὰρ τὸ μεῖζον τῇ τοῦ αἰτίου φύσει διδόντων, αὐτοὶ τὸ τῇ φύσει μεῖζον ἐπάγουσιν· ὥσπερ ἂν εἰ καὶ λεγόντων ἡμῶν, ὅτι ὁ δεῖνα νεκρὸς ἄνθρωπος, ἁπλῶς ἐπῆγον αὐτοὶ τὸν ἄνθρωπον.

68. *Oration* 30.7, Barbel lines 12–14: τὸ γὰρ δὴ λέγειν, ὅτι τοῦ κατὰ τὸν ἄνθρωπον νοουμένου μεῖζων, ἀληθὲς μέν, οὐ μέγα δέ. τί γὰρ τὸ θαυμαστόν, εἰ μεῖζων ἀνθρώπου θεός;

In *Oration* 40, Gregory states that he fears the word *source* (ἀρχή) more than the word *greater* (μέγας).[69] Although this might strike modern Western ears as odd, it confirms from yet another angle that the Father's causality in generation in no way makes the Son an effect.

Given Aquinas's fierce defense of the Son's equality to the Father, it is somewhat shocking to see how close his language is to Gregory's concerning the Father's being greater than the Son. The Angelic Doctor asserts that the Father is not more like himself than he is to the Son and that the divine essence is not more the Father's than the Son's; we could add to this Thomas's insistence that "the Father is in no way prior to the Son"[70] as well as his judgment that Origen blasphemed and was delirious because he spoke of the Son in a subordinationist manner.[71] One would expect the Doctor who writes thus to strictly rule out speaking of the Father as greater than the Son. But throughout his works, including his most mature writings such as the *Summa Theologiae* and the *Commentary on John*, Thomas repeats St. Hilary's expression that "the Father is greater but the Son is not less."[72]

In the *De Potentia*, where he disapproves of calling the Son and Spirit *principled* or attributing *subauthority* to them, Aquinas offers Hilary's expression as a correct example.[73] Thus Thomas holds a nuanced position,

---

69. *Oration* 40.43, PG 36.420.22–25.

70. I *Sent.* d. 9, q. 2, a. 1, corp.; I *Sent.*, d. 12, q. 1, a. 1, s.c. 2; and *CEG* I, chap. 2, corp.

71. *In Ioan.* 1:1 (lect. 1, #58), *In Ioan.* 1:3 (lect. 2, #76), and *In Ioan.* 14:10 (lect. 3, #1895).

72. I *Sent.*, d. 16, q. 1, prologue; *De Pot.*, q. 10, a. 1, ad 9; *CEG* I, chap. 2, corp.; *In Ioan.*, chap. 14, lect. 8; *ST* I, q. 33, a. 1, ad 2: "pater maior est; sed minor non est filius."

73. *De Pot.*, q. 10, a. 1, ad 9: "Now although the Father is said to be the principle of the Son and the Holy Spirit, nevertheless it does not seem to be said indifferently that the Son or the Holy Spirit is principled, although the Greeks use even this mode of speaking, and it can be allowed reasonably among the discerning. Nevertheless we ought to flee those expressions that imply any lesser status so that they will not be attributed to the Son or the Holy Spirit, in order to avoid the error of the Arians—as Hilary, although he allowed that the Father was greater than the Son on account of the authority of origin, nevertheless did not allow that the Son should be less than the Father, to whom equal being was given by the Father. Similarly, the words *subauthority* or *principled* should not be applied to the Son, although the words *authority* and *principle* are allowed for the Father." ("Quamvis autem pater dicatur esse principium filii et spiritus sancti, non tamen videtur indifferenter dicendum, quod filius sit principiatum, vel etiam spiritus sanctus, licet etiam hoc modo loquendi Graeci utantur, et possit apud sane intelligentes concedi; tamen ea quae minorationem aliquam importare videntur, refugere debemus, ne filio vel spiritui sancto attribuantur, propter Arianorum errorem vitandum; sicut Hilarius, etsi concedat patrem esse maiorem filio propter auctoritatem originis, non tamen concedit quod filius sit minor patre cui est aequale esse donatum a patre. Et similiter non est extendendum nomen subauctoritatis vel principiati in filio, licet nomen auctoritatis, vel principii concedatur in patre.")

respectful of this patristic manner of speaking. He offers his most complete interpretation of Hilary in the *Scriptum*:

And therefore if we compare the Father to the Son with respect to that which is given to the Son by the Father, neither is the Father said to be greater nor is the Son said to be less. But if we compare with respect to the meaning of giving, thus the dignity of someone giving is not taken away from the Father, by reason of which he is said to be greater, as *greater* conveys more the perfection of dignity than the comparison of greatness. But because the Son perfectly receives whatever the Father has, no lesser status is fitting to him. And therefore even no word of lesser status can be fitting to the Son.[74]

This reliance on Hilary aligns Aquinas more closely with Nazianzen's position and steps away from Augustine's preference to speak of the Father's being greater than the Son by virtue of the Son's humanity—an interpretation that did not impress Nazianzen. Augustine emphasizes this in his *De Trinitate*:

For the Father is God with the Son, but the Son alone is Christ, especially since the Word already made flesh mentions his lowliness according to which the Father is greater, as he says, "For the Father is greater than I."[75]

This puts Gregory and Thomas in agreement not only of understanding but even of refined and arduous articulation of a deep mystery of the faith.

Conclusion

In this chapter, I compared the understanding of God the Father's paternity in the thought of St. Gregory of Nazianzus and St. Thomas Aquinas. I verified a profound agreement in the thought of these two great theo-

74. I *Sent.*, d. 16, q. 1, expos.: "Et ideo si comparemus patrem ad filium quantum ad id quod filio a patre datur, neque pater major neque filius minor dicitur. Si autem quantum ad rationem dationis, sic dignitas dantis patri non subtrahitur, ratione cujus major dicitur, ut major magis sonet perfectionem dignitatis, quam comparationem magnitudinis. Sed quia filius perfecte recipit quidquid pater habet, nulla minoratio sibi convenit: et ideo etiam nullum nomen minorationis filio potest convenire."

75. Augustine, *De Trin.*, bk. 6, ch. 9, line 35: "cum filio enim pater deus; solus autem filius christus est maxime quia iam uerbum caro factum loquitur secundum quam humilitatem eius etiam maior est pater sicut dicit: quoniam pater maior me est, ut hoc ipsum deum esse quod illi cum patre unum est caput sit hominis mediatoris quod ipse solus est." Augustine also addresses the Father's being greater in *De Trin.*, bk. 1, ch. 7, line 13; bk. 1, ch. 8, lines 8 and 23; bk. 1, ch. 9, line 3; bk. 1, ch. 11, line 6; bk. 2, ch. 1, line 27; bk. 2, ch. 6, line 1; bk. 6, ch. 3, line 37.

logians. Namely, (1) the Son, though perfectly equal to the Father and in no way a creature, (2) receives everything that he has from the Father, who produces him according to a mode of efficient causality, and (3) the Son is in no way less than the Father, but the assertion that the Father is greater than the Son can be correctly said to mean that the Father is the principle of the Son.

This inquiry produced two surprising discoveries. First, while Gregory is content to call the Father the cause (αἰτία) of the Son, he does not believe that one should say that the Father is the producer (ἐνεργής) of the Son. Conversely, while Thomas definitively rules out referring to the Father as the cause (*causa*) of the Son, he freely speaks of the Father's producing (*producere*) the Son, and he holds that the Father produces the Son in the manner of an efficient cause—taking *efficient* broadly. Second, Nazianzen finds it more dangerous to call the Father the source (ἀρχή) of the Son than to say that he is greater (μέγας) than the Son, and Aquinas allows that the Father is greater than the Son, if greater is taken only to mean that the Father has the dignity of being a giver with respect to the Son.

Separated by nine hundred years and two thousand miles, living in different cultures and writing in different languages, these two holy men naturally articulated their doctrines in diverse ways. But they are unmistakably two sons born of the same mother Church, who has handed on to them the same revelation from God.

5

Aquinas and the Greek Fathers on the Vision of the Divine Essence

GERALD P. BOERSMA

Thomas Aquinas seemed well aware that the teaching of the Greek Fathers regarding the saints' vision of the divine essence runs, at least prima facie, contrary to his own position. In *ST* I, q. 12, Aquinas deals at length with the question of whether a created intellect can see the essence of God.[1] His interlocutors, quoted in the objections of the first article, are John Chrysostom and Pseudo-Dionysius.[2] Chryostom is cited first: when the Apostle John writes "No man hath seen God at any time," the Apostle establishes a categorical line of demarcation between the creature and the Creator. Neither prophets nor angels have seen God: "For how can a creature see what is increatable?"[3] Also in the first objection, Dionysius is seen to advance a similar position: "Neither is there sense, nor image, nor opinion, nor reason, nor knowledge of him."[4] The third objection points

1. I have used the Benziger Bros. edition of the *Summa Theologiae* (1947), translated by the Fathers of the English Dominican Province. The Latin text is from *Sancti Thomae de Aquino Opera omnia: Iussu impensaque, Leonis XIII. P.M. edita* (Rome: Ex Typographia Polyglotta S. C. de Propaganda Fide, 1882).

2. Similarly, in *ST* I-II, q. 3, a. 8, the question of "Whether man's happiness consists in the vision of the divine essence" is posed. Dionysius is quoted in the first objection to the effect that man is united to God as to something altogether unknown (*ST* I-II, q. 3, a. 8, obj. 1).

3. *ST* I, q. 12, a. 1, obj. 1: *qualiter videre poterit quod increabile est?* Cf. Chrysostom, Homily 14 *in Joan.*

4. *ST* I, q. 12, a. 1, obj. 1. Cf. Pseudo-Dionysius, *On the Divine Names*, 1.

to Dionysius's teaching that God is not something existing (*existens*) but superexistence (*supra existentia*). As such, there is simply no correlation between the divine essence and the finite intellect: "God is not intelligible; but above all intellect."[5]

The *sed contra* is a terse and unambiguous appeal to Scripture: "We shall see him as he is" (*sicuti est*) (1 Jn 3:2). In the body of the article, Thomas distinguishes between that which is *in itself* knowable and how it might be known to the knower. Because act is knowable and God is *actus purus*, he is, in principle, supremely knowable. Nevertheless, he remains unknown *to us*. The plenitude of his knowability cannot be received by paltry finite intellects, just as the plenitude of the sun, which is in itself supremely visible, cannot be received by the bat by reason of the sun's excess of light.[6]

Thomas continues by responding to the opinion of "some" who, in fidelity to the explicit teaching of the Eastern Fathers, hold that "no created intellect can see the essence of God." Thomas disagrees with this thesis for two reasons. First, he holds that ultimate beatitude consists in the perfection of the intellect, which is nothing less than seeing God. (This is in an argument that will be developed to much greater lengths when discussing happiness in the *prima secundae*.) Second, human beings have a natural desire to know the causes of things, but this desire would remain void (*inane*) if the intellect could not reach the first cause.[7]

There is, undeniably, a profound difference between the Eastern Fathers and Aquinas on the question of the possibility of the vision of the divine essence. Thomas holds that, yes, the intellectual vision of God's essence is the reward of the blessed, whereas many Eastern Fathers maintain that it is impossible for any creature ever to see the divine essence. My contention is that, despite what seems, prima facie, diametrically opposed conclusions regarding the possibility of the vision of the divine essence,

5. *ST* I, q. 12, a. 1, obj. 3: "Ergo non est intelligibilis; sed est supra omnem intellectum."

6. Cf. *ST* I, q. 88, a. 3. Thomas Gilby comments, "God is wholly lucid in himself, yet not to us, creatures of the night, who blink at divine truth like owls in sunshine.... The objective truth in creatures is turbid compared with limpid divinity—if only we could see it." Thomas Gilby, "Introduction," in Thomas Aquinas, *Summa Theologiae*, vol. 3, *Knowing and Naming God, 1a. 12–13*, ed. Herbert McCabe (Cambridge: Cambridge University Press, 2006), xx–xxi.

7. *ST* I, q. 12, a. 1. Thomas is equally incisive in the *Summa contra Gentiles*: "It is impossible for a natural desire to be incapable of fulfillment" (*ScG* I, chap. 51.1). I have used Thomas Aquinas, *Summa contra Gentiles III*, vol. 3, pt. I, trans. Vernon J. Bourke (Notre Dame, IN: University of Notre Dame Press, 1975).

Thomas and the Greek Fathers share a fundamental theological concern in their approach to the vision of God. Both are intent to safeguard the Creator/creature distinction. They do so in distinct ways.

Thomas follows the Eastern Fathers in maintaining that the vision of God does not admit of comprehensive knowledge. For Thomas, the blessed "attain" to the divine essence but do not "comprehend" God (in the manner that God knows himself). The Greek Fathers, by contrast, deny even that the blessed "attain" to the divine essence. For the Eastern Fathers such as Basil of Caesarea, Gregory of Nyssa, and John Chrysostom, the blessed participate in the "condescension" of the divine energies but never attain to the divine essence. Despite this important difference, Thomas insists with the Greek Fathers that the divine essence is per se inaccessible to any creature by his natural power. It is only by the wholly gratuitous character of the *lumen gloriae* that the intellectual creature can be elevated to a vision of the divine essence. As such, Thomas's teaching on the *lumen gloriae* serves the same theological purpose that the Eastern Fathers have in maintaining the blessed experience only the "condescension" of the divine energies, and not the divine essence, namely, to preserve the primordial distinction between Creator and creature.

The Eastern Fathers and Aquinas on the Incomprehensibility of the Divine Essence

At least on the face of it, Thomas's argument is starkly opposed to that of Dionysius and Chrysostom. These Eastern Fathers hold that no created intellect can see the essence of God, while Thomas holds that the fulfillment of the rational creature consists in nothing less than the vision of the divine essence. Of course, in the reply to the first objection in question 12, Thomas insists that he has no quarrel with either Chrysostom or Dionysius, for they are speaking of a particular type of knowledge, namely, *comprehension*.[8] Later in question 12, Thomas elaborates on the distinction between the vision of knowledge, which belongs to the beatitude of the saints, and the vision of comprehension, which God has of himself. Here, in his reply to the objections referencing Chrysostom and Dionysius, Thomas maintains that these Eastern Fathers preclude only the vision of comprehension.

8. *ST* I, q. 12, a. 1, rep. obj. 1: "Both of these authorities speak of the vision of comprehension."

But the distinction between these two types of vision seems foreign to Chrysostom, who rules out any knowledge or vision of God *simpliciter*. In the third of a series of homilies titled *On the Incomprehensibility of God*, Chrysostom writes,

Let us call upon him then, as the ineffable God who is beyond our intelligence, invisible (τὸν ἀόρατον), incomprehensible (τὸν ἀκατάληπτον), who transcends the power of mortal words. Let us call on him as the God who is inscrutable to angels, unseen by the Seraphim, inconceivable to the Cherubim, invisible to the principalities, to the powers, and to the virtues, in fact, to all creatures without qualification, because he is known only to the Son and the Spirit (ὑπὸ δὲ Ὑιοῦ καὶ Πνεύματος μόνου γνωριζόμενον).[9]

Commenting on the Apostle Paul's description of God dwelling in "unapproachable light, whom no man has ever seen or can see" (1 Tm 6:15–16), Chrysostom remarks that the Apostle does not say that God *is* an unapproachable light but *dwells* in unapproachable light: "So that you may learn that if the dwelling is unapproachable, much more so is the God who dwells in it."[10] Chrysostom explains that the word "unapproachable" entails an even greater remove than "incomprehensible":

A thing is said to be incomprehensible (ἀκατάληπτον) when those who seek after it fail to comprehend it, even after they have searched and sought to understand it. A thing is unapproachable (ἀπρόσιτον) which, from the start, cannot be investigated nor can anyone come near to it. We call the sea incomprehensible (ἀκατάληπτον) because, even when divers lower themselves into its waters and go down to a great depth, they cannot find the bottom. We call that thing unapproachable (ἀπρόσιτον) which, from the start cannot be searched out or investigated.[11]

Chrysostom clearly holds that God is not only incomprehensible, but also unapproachable. Thomas, by contrast, holds that the divine essence is

<hr />

9. Chrysostom, Homily 3.5, trans. Paul Harkins, Fathers of the Church 72 (Washington, DC: Catholic University of America Press, 1982): Καλῶμεν τοίνυν αὐτὸν τὸν ἀνέκφραστον, τὸν ἀπερινόητον Θεόν, τὸν ἀόρατον, τὸν ἀκατάληπτον, τὸν νικῶντα γλώττης δύναμιν ἀνθρωπίνης, τὸν ὑπερβαίνοντα θνητῆς διανοίας κατάληψιν, τὸν ἀνεξιχνίαστον ἀγγέλοις, τὸν ἀθέατον τοῖς Σεραφίμ, τὸν ἀκατανόητον τοῖς Χερουβίμ, τὸν ἀόρατον ἀρχαῖς, ἐξουσίαις, δυνάμεσι καὶ ἁπλῶς πάσῃ τῇ κτίσει, ὑπὸ δὲ Ὑιοῦ καὶ Πνεύματος μόνου γνωριζόμενον. The Greek text is from the *Thesaurus Linguae Graecae*, accessed October 23, 2018, http://stephanus.tlg.uci.edu.

10. Chrysostom, Homily 3.11.

11. Chrysostom, Homily 3.12: Τὸ μὲν γὰρ ἀκατάληπτον λέγεται, ὅταν ἐρευνηθὲν καὶ ζητηθὲν μὴ καταληφθῇ παρὰ τῶν ζητούντων αὐτό· ἀπρόσιτον δέ ἐστιν, ὃ μηδὲ ἐρεύνης ἀνέχεται τὴν ἀρχήν, μηδὲ ἐγγὺς αὐτοῦ γενέσθαι τις δύναται. Οἷον ἀκατάληπτον λέγεται πέλαγος, εἰς ὃ καθιέντες ἑαυτοὺς οἱ κολυμβηταὶ καὶ πρὸς πολὺ καταφερόμενοι βάθος, τὸ πέρας ἀδυνατοῦσιν εὑρεῖν· ἀπρόσιτον δὲ ἐκεῖνο λέγεται, ὃ μήτε τὴν ἀρχὴν ζητηθῆναι δυνατόν, μηδὲ ἐρευνηθῆναι.

known to the blessed even if not fully comprehended. Thomas maintains that we can even say God is comprehended by the blessed if by that we mean the blessed *attain* him. In q. 12, a. 7, Thomas explains that if comprehension entails perfect knowledge (knowing something insofar as it can be known), it is certainly impossible to comprehend God, even for the blessed. Yet if we do not take "comprehension" in the strict and proper sense of the term, but in the sense of "attaining" to an end (*attingere*), then we can affirm that the blessed comprehend God. The teleological character of the intellectual vision of God seems to necessitate, for Thomas, some sense of finality and arrival proper to comprehension: "For he who attains to anyone is said to comprehend him when he attains to him" ("Qui enim attingit aliquem, quando iam tenet ipsum, comprehendere eum dicitur").[12]

On the face of it, these two positions seem irreconcilable. Thomas maintains that if we take *comprehendere* in the sense of *attingere*, we can affirm that the blessed comprehend and certainly have knowledge of the divine essence, inasmuch as the intellects of the blessed know the divine essence and are fulfilled by that end. Chrysostom, by contrast, rejects not only comprehension but also approachability. Thomas's affirmation of *attingere* seems the diametrical contrary to Chrysostom's insistence that God is unapproachable (ἀπρόσιτον).

The challenge of the apparent opposition between Thomas and the Greek Fathers was not lost on the scholastic commentatorial tradition. To some, it seemed that Thomas's distinction between the vision of comprehension and the vision of knowledge introduced a nicety foreign to the Eastern Doctors. Gabriel Vasquez (1549–1604) thought of Thomas as defending the indefensible. Vasquez holds that Chrysostom (and many other Fathers) clearly (and wrongly) taught that the divine essence is not seen by the blessed. Further, Vasquez believed the attempt to save the Fathers with the distinction between the vision of comprehension and the vision of knowledge cannot be maintained on the plain reading of the patristic witness.[13] In contrast, Vasquez's contemporary and fellow Jesuit Francisco Suárez (1548–1617) insisted that Thomas's distinction between

---

12. *ST* I, q. 12, a. 7, rep. obj. 1. As a proof text, Thomas quotes Song 3:4: "I held (*tenui*) him and will not let him go." Thomas's use of the Canticle to inform *attingere* suggests that he is not speaking here of a knowledge of scientific demonstration, but of a participatory unitive knowledge conceived in love. "I held (*tenui*) him and will not let him go" bespeaks the consummation of love arriving at or resting in the beloved in such a way that one's desire is fulfilled.

13. Gabriel Vasquez, *Disputatio* XXXVII. Cf. Michael J. Lapierre, *The Noetical Theory of Gabriel Vasquez, Jesuit Philosopher and Theologian (1549–1604): His View of the Objective Concept* (Lewiston, NY: Mellen Press, 1999).

comprehension and knowledge should be maintained, lest a great number of the Fathers be understood to have taught wrongly on this fundamental question.[14]

It is worth exploring the context within which the Eastern Fathers after the Eunomian controversy insist that the divine essence is not seen by any creature. Several Eastern Fathers of the fourth and fifth centuries are responding to the rationalism of Eunomius (355–93), who hailed from the region of Cappadocia and was briefly bishop of Cyzicus. Eunomius and his disciples identified with the radical wing of the Arian party. They insisted on a distinction of substance between the Father and the Son. The Father, they argued, is ingenerate, the one named "He who is" (Ex 3:14), and is the "sole true God" (Jn 17:3). The Son, by contrast, is the product of the will of the incorporeal Father. The Eunomians maintained that the generation or creation (which to them were identical terms) of the Son indicates a second, inferior divine substance.[15] With their customary, logical rigor, they would take their Nicene opponents through a process of dialectical interrogation. Are Father and Son distinct? If two are named, how are they distinguished? Is not one generate and the other ingenerate? If the essence of the Father is that he is "unbegotten," is not the contrary essence of the Son to be "begotten"?[16]

The response of the Cappadocian Fathers was first to castigate the overweening hubris of Eunomian rationalism; they challenged the Eunomian assumption that dialectics could disclose the mystery of the eternal generation of the Son. Second, the Cappadocians insisted that the divine essence is utterly incomprehensible. Human knowledge cannot even fully account for the substance of an ant; how could the Eunomians possibly claim to scale the heights of knowledge so as to understand the immortal, invisible, and eternal substance?[17] Gregory of Nyssa contends,

This is the true knowledge of what is sought; this is the seeing that consists in not seeing, because that which is sought transcends all knowledge, being separated on all sides by incomprehensibility as by a kind of darkness. Wherefore John the sublime, who penetrated into the luminous darkness, says, "No one has ever seen

14. Francisco Suárez, *De Deo*, 1.2, chap. 7, no. 15–19 (Mainz, 1607). Cf. Vladimir Lossky, *The Vision of God* (Bedfordshire: Faith Press, 1973), 12–20.

15. Eunomius, *Apology* 12, in Richard Paul Vaggione, ed., *Eunomius: The Extant Works* (New York: Oxford University Press, 1987), 49. Cf. Richard Paul Vaggione, *Eunomius of Cyzicus and the Nicene Revolution* (New York: Oxford University Press, 2000).

16. Cf. Gregory of Nyssa, *Against Eunomius*, 1.19.

17. Cf. Gregory of Nyssa, *Against Eunomius*, 10.1.

God" [Jn. 1:18], thus asserting that knowledge of the divine essence is unattainable (πάσῃ νοητῇ φύσει τῆς θείας οὐσίας τὴν γνῶσιν ἀνέφικτον).[18]

Gregory's elder brother and fellow bishop, St. Basil, explains that we come to know God's greatness, power, goodness, providence, and justice, "but not His very essence (οὐκ αὐτὴν τὴν οὐσίαν) ... his operations (ἐνέργειαι) come down to us, but His essence (οὐσία) remains beyond our reach."[19] Similarly, John Chrysostom insists that we only know God's "condescension" (συγκατάβασις) and that the divine essence is incomprehensible to human nature.[20] Speaking of the vision of the angels in the divine presence, Chrysostom maintains,

Yet they did not see the pure light itself nor the pure essence (οὐσίαν) itself. What they saw was a condescension (συγκατάβασις) accommodated to their nature. What is this condescension? God condescends whenever he is not seen as he is, but in the way one incapable of beholding him is able to look upon him.[21]

John of Damascus and Pseudo-Dionysius carefully follow the Cappadocian Fathers, insisting that the divine essence per se is incomprehensible. God's essence is never seen, but intellectual creatures ought to purify themselves so as to receive the divine condescensions in this life and, to a greater degree, in the next. The distinction between the divine "condescension" (συγκατάβασις) and the divine essence (οὐσία) would be developed by later Eastern theologians into the distinction between the divine energies and the divine essence—a theology codified in Gregory Palamas.

The textbook version of this history depicts the Eastern and Western traditions as incompatible. Vladimir Lossky's description is illustrative of this narrative:

We find ourselves confronted by two formulae neatly opposed, the first of which resolutely denies all possibility of knowing the essence of God, while the second explicitly insists on the fact that it is the actual essence of God which must be the object of beatific vision.[22]

18. Gregory of Nyssa, *The Life of Moses*, 2.163, in Abraham Malherbe, trans., *Classics of Western Spirituality: St. Gregory of Nyssa. The Life of Moses* (New York: Paulist Press, 1978), 95.

19. Basil of Caesarea, *Ep.* 234, in Philip Schaff and Wace Henry, eds., *Nicene and Post-Nicene Fathers: A Select Library of the Christian Church. Second Series*, vol. 8, *Basil: Letters and Select Works* (Peabody, MA: Hendrickson, 1995), 274.

20. Cf. Chrysostom, Homily 3.13.

21. Chrysostom, Homily 3.15: Καίτοι γε οὐκ ὑπὸ ἄκρατον ἑώρων τὸ φῶς, οὐδ' αὐτὴν ἀκραιφνῆ τὴν οὐσίαν, ἀλλὰ συγκατάβασις ἦν τὰ ὁρώμενα. Τί δέ ἐστι συγκατάβασις; Ὅταν μὴ ὡς ἔστιν ὁ Θεὸς φαίνηται, ἀλλ' ὡς ὁ δυνάμενος αὐτὸν θεωρεῖν οἷός τέ ἐστιν.

22. Lossky, *Vision of God*, 10–11.

In this rendering, the Eastern tradition—following the Cappadocians, John Chrysostom, John of Damascus, and eventually Gregory Palamas—maintains that the divine essence cannot seen by the blessed. In contrast, the Western tradition, building on Augustine and stated with precision by Thomas, insists that a vision of the divine essence is the reward of the blessed. In Constantinople, a series of councils (1341, 1351, and 1368) taught that the divine essence is inaccessible and known neither to saints nor to angels. In contrast, so it is argued, a different position held sway in the Roman See: the controversy surrounding Pope John XXII's opinion that the beatific vision would occur only after the general resurrection resulted in a condemnation by John's successor, Benedict XII. In the Papal Bull, *Benedictus Deus* (1336), Benedict XII definitively decreed that the saints

have seen and see the divine essence with an intuitive vision and even face to face, without the mediation of any creature by way of object of vision; rather the divine essence immediately manifests itself to them, plainly, clearly and openly, and in this vision they enjoy the divine essence.[23]

According to this narrative, then, theological developments leading to the High Middle Ages result in two irreconcilable positions, each pitted against one another.

Aquinas on the Vision of the Divine Essence

Perhaps, however, these formulae are not as irreconcilable as it seems at first glance. A second look at the teaching of St. Thomas on the vision of the divine essence is instructive. In answer to the question of "Whether any created intellect by its natural powers can see the Divine essence,"[24] Aquinas is explicit that no creature can in any way see the divine essence by its own natural powers.[25] In the body of the article, Thomas contends

23. "Vident et videbunt divinam essentiam visione intuitiva et etiam faciali, nulla mediante creatura in ratione obiecti visi se habente, sed divina essentia immediate se nude clare et aperte eis ostendendo; quodque sic videntes eadem divina essentia perfruuntur." See Benedictus XII, "Benedictus Deus," January 29, 1336, https://w2.vatican.va/content/benedictus-xii/la/documents/constitutio-benedictus-deus-29-ian-1336.html.

24. *ST* I, q. 12, a. 4.

25. Thomas is categorical: "It is impossible for any created intellect to see the essence of God by its own natural power." *ST* I, q. 12, a. 4. Cf. *De Ver.*, q. 8, a. 3, co: "Nature does not transcend its limits. Now, the divine essence surpasses any created nature. Consequently, the divine essence cannot be seen by any natural cognition." Robert W. Mulligan, trans., *De Veritate* (Chicago: Regnery, 1952).

that neither sense knowledge, nor intellectual abstraction, nor even angelic knowledge can ascend to a knowledge of the divine substance. To know *esse subsistens* is natural to the divine intellect alone. In this respect, at least, Thomas's position tracks that of the Eastern Fathers: the divine essence per se is, according to Thomas as well, incomprehensible and inaccessible to the natural created intellect.

Nevertheless, as Thomas sees it, the clear teaching of Scripture is that beatitude consists in the direct, face-to-face vision of God, *sicuti est* (1 Jn 3:2). Further, Thomas holds (1) that the perfection of the intellect consists in seeing God and (2) that natural desire to know the causes of things only finds its end in God:

For as the ultimate beatitude of man consists in the use of his highest function, which is the operation of his intellect; if we suppose that the created intellect could never see God, it would either never attain to beatitude or its beatitude would consist in something else beside God, which is opposed to faith.... Further the same opinion is also again reason. For there resides in every man natural desire to know the cause of any effect which he sees.... Hence it must be absolutely granted that the blessed see the essence of God.[26]

The nature of the vision of the divine essence is not just an interesting theological appurtenance for Thomas. His entire anthropology and theory of human action hinge on this question. Only if human happiness is a possibility does Thomas's extensive treatment of moral theology—the extrication of vice and the growth in virtue through the assistance of law and grace—make any sense. And yet human happiness cannot rest in any created good; human felicity is realized only in the intellectual vision of God.

In question 12, Thomas leads the reader into what seems an irresolvable paradox: the happiness of the intellectual creature lies in the direct vision of the divine essence, but such a vision is beyond the capacity of the intellectual creature. Thomas writes, "Therefore the created intellect cannot see the essence of God, unless God by his grace unites Himself to the created intellect, as an object made intelligible to it."[27] Here, Thomas introduces the *lumen gloriae* as the mode by which God elevates the created intellect, uniting it to himself. The light of glory enables a participation by

---

26. *ST* I, q. 12, a. 1. Elsewhere Thomas maintains, "For perfect happiness the intellect needs to reach the very Essence of the First Cause" (*ST* I-II, q. 3, a .8).

27. *ST* I, q. 12, a. 4: "Non igitur potest intellectus creatus Deum per essentiam videre, nisi inquantum Deus per suam gratiam se intellectui creato coniungit, ut intelligibile ab ipso."

grace in God's own light, since it elevates and strengthens the intellect to a direct and immediate vision of the divine essence. In Thomas's language, the *lumen gloriae* is "perfectio quaedem intellectus confortans ipsum ad videndum Deum."[28] The doctrine of the *lumen gloriae* both resolves the paradox raised in question 12 regarding the seeming impossibility of human fulfillment and answers the principal objection of the Greek Fathers that no finite creature can see the infinite Creator. Thomas can affirm with the Eastern Doctors that it is impossible for a creature by nature to see the divine essence while also affirming that the *lumen gloriae* so elevates the rational creature that the fulfillment of human nature is possible. Admittedly, a fundamental difference remains in that the Greek Fathers reject the possibility that grace can so elevate the intellectual creature to render him capable of a vision of the divine essence.

Aquinas and the *Lumen Gloriae*

The boundless abyss between the divine essence and the created intellect, so starkly articulated by the Eastern Fathers, is affirmed in Thomas's teaching. And yet, for Thomas, the grace of the *lumen gloriae* allows the creature to participate in the vision of the divine essence in a manner that neither divinizes the creature in such a way as to render it coterminous with God nor reduces the divine essence to a species comprehended by created intellect.

Thomas describes the *lumen gloriae* as a "similitude of God on the part of the visual faculty" that strengthens the intellect to see God.[29] Whereas corporeal sight involves a likeness of the thing seen made present to the seer, the vision of glory does not involve any likeness. God is not an external object whose similitude is impressed on the mind. No created form can be the similitude that represents the divine essence. Rather, the beatific vision entails that the one seeing is immediately and intimately united to the divine essence in and by the *lumen gloriae*. In fact, the divine

28. *ST* I, q. 12, a. 5, ad 2.
29. *ST* I, q. 12, a. 2. The light of glory by which the blessed see the divine essence is an "abiding form" (*forma immanens*) or habit (*ST* II-II, q. 175, a. 3, rep. obj. 2). This is distinct from the temporal vision of either the Apostle Paul, who was caught up to the third heaven, or Moses, who saw God face-to-face. Thomas explains that they were "beatified not as to the habit, but only to the act of the blessed" (*ST* II-II, q. 175, a. 3, rep. obj. 3). In contrast to the blessed, Paul and Moses experienced the light of glory as a "transitory passion" (*passio transeuns*) (*ST* II-II, q. 175, a. 3, rep. obj. 2).

essence becomes the intelligible form of the created intellect.[30] The mode of this vision enabled by the *lumen gloriae* is unlike all other finite vision: "If the divine essence is seen, it must be done as [God's] intellect sees the divine essence itself through itself, and in such a vision the divine essence must be both what is seen and that whereby it is seen."[31] Thus God is not only the object of beatific vision but also the medium of the vision, so that the blessed do not see God *in* or *through* a likeness, but immediately and directly. The creature is not thereby absorbed into God; rather, the *lumen gloriae* raises the creature to a greater likeness of God. Thomas Gilby clearly summarizes Thomas teaching on the *lumen gloriae*:

No representation can match the very being of God. Hence all signs are past and done with if we know him face to face even as we are known; then no likeness objectively mirrors him and divinity itself supplies the epistemological role of a *species*: of the *species impressa*, for God's essence clasps the mind closely, *copuletur ei*, and is there the intelligible form, *ipsa essentia divina fit forma intelligibilis intellectus*; and of the *species expressa*, for the mind does not conceive a word of its own, for the divine essence is so united to the mind as to be what is actually seen, through its very self making the mind actually seeing, *ut intellectus in actu per seipsam faciens intellectum in actu*. And so we know, not the last ebb of things in the evening light of our own mental words, but their full tide in the dawn light of the Word of God.[32]

For Thomas, the essential characteristic of the *lumen gloriae* is a disposition given to the intellectual creature enabling him by grace to participate in God's own knowledge of himself. This knowledge is direct, immediate, and intimate in a manner fundamentally distinct from all finite ways of knowing.

Aquinas's Epistemology: A Disposition to Divine Glory

Thomas's understanding of the beatific vision is a species of his broader theory of cognition. As such, it is fruitful to briefly sketch Thomas's epistemology. Thomas often repeats that knowledge consists of the thing known present in the knower according to the mode of the knower.[33] A

---

30. *ST* I, q. 12, a. 2. Cf. *De Ver.*, q. 8, a. 3, co.

31. *ScG* III, q. 51, a. 2: "Si Dei essentia videatur, quod per ipsammet essentiam divinam intellectus ipsam videat: ut sit in tali visione divina essentia et quod videtur, et quo videtur."

32. Gilby, "Introduction," xxvi–xxvii.

33. Cf. *ST* I, q. 12, a. 4.

known reality becomes *present* to the knower in three different ways, however:

A thing is known in three ways: first, by the presence of its essence in the knower (*per praesentiam suae essentiae in cognoscente*), as light can be seen in the eye; and so we have said that an angel knows himself—secondly, by the presence of its similitude (*per praesentiam suae similitudinis*) in the power which knows it, as a stone is seen by the eye from its image being in the eye—thirdly, when the image of the object known is not drawn directly from the object itself, but from something else (*a re alia*) in which it is made to appear, as when we behold a man in a mirror.[34]

The first way of knowing—the immediate presence of the essence of the thing known in the knower—is the knowledge proper to beatitude. Thomas goes on to explain that in this life creatures cannot know God in this way.[35] Rather, it is the third way of knowing—a vision of the reflection of the known thing and not the essence of the object itself—by which we come to know God *in via*. Thomas references Romans 1:20 to explain the reflected vision one has of the divine vestiges in this life. Between these two extremities of immediate knowledge of an essence and knowledge of the reflection of an essence, Thomas posits a second knowledge in-between these two. This is the type of knowledge that angels have of God. This knowledge is like the knowledge of abstraction in which the mind adverts to the immaterial form to come to a knowledge of the reality perceived before it: "For since God's image is impressed on the very

---

34. *ST* I, q. 56, a. 3. Thomas presents the same epistemological delineation in *De Ver.*, q. 8, a. 3, co., and in *De Ver.*, q. 8, a. 3, ad 17, where he writes, "A thing is seen in three different ways. First, it is seen through its essence (*per essentiam*), in the way in which a visible essence itself is joined to sight when the eye sees light. Second, it is seen through a species (*per speciem*), as takes place when the likeness of a thing is impressed on my sense of sight when I see a stone. Third, it is seen 'through a mirror' (*per speculum*); and this takes place when the thing's likeness, through which it is known, is not caused in the sight by the thing itself directly but by that in which the likeness of the thing is represented, just as sensible species are caused in a mirror." These three gradations of sight correspond respectively to the mode of knowing proper to God, angel, and man.

35. Any knowledge obtained *in via* is, according to Thomas, obtained by way of an impress on the intellect of the likeness of that which is known: "The known is a perfection of the knower, not by its substance (*secundum illam rem quae cognoscitur*) (for the thing is outside the knower), but rather by the likeness by which it is known; for a perfection exists in the perfected—and the likeness of the stone, not the stone, exists in the soul" (*De Ver.*, q. 2, a. 3, ad 1). Cf. *ScG* I, chap. 54; *ScG* I, chap. 57; *ScG* IV, chap. 11; *ST* I, q. 12, a. 7, ad 3; *ST* I, q. 14, a. 1, ad 3; *ST* I, q. 14, a. 12, co.; *ST* I, q. 84, a. 2, co.; *De Ver.*, q. 2, a. 5, ad 15; and *Sentencia libri De anima*, Book 1, lect. 4, para. 43.

nature of the angel in his essence, the angel knows God in as much as he is the image of God."[36]

The intellectual vision of the divine essence proper to beatitude conforms to the first type of knowledge, by which the divine essence is itself present in the knower. Of course, this knowledge far exceeds the nature of creaturely knowing. For any nature to be raised above its natural capabilities, it needs to be disposed thereto by that which is above its nature.[37] Thomas gives the example of air, which, if it is to receive the higher form of fire, must be prepared by some disposition of fire to receive such a form.[38] He continues,

But when any created intellect sees the essence of God, the essence of God itself becomes the intelligible form of the intellect. Hence it is necessary that some supernatural disposition should be added (*dispositio supernaturalis ei superaddatur*) to the intellect in order that it may be raised up to such a great and sublime height. Now since the natural power of the created intellect does not avail to enable it to see the essence of God, as was shown in the preceding article, it is necessary that the power of understanding should be added by divine grace. Now this increase of the intellectual powers is called the illumination of the intellect, as we also call the intelligible object itself by the name of light of illumination. And this is the light spoken of in the Apocalypse (Rv 21:23): "The glory of God hath enlightened it"—viz. the society of the blessed who see God. By this light the blessed are made "deiform"—i.e. like to God, according to the saying: "When He shall appear we shall be like to Him, and [Vulg.: 'because'] we shall see Him as He is" (1 Jn 2:2).[39]

The intellectual creature cannot, by his own power, be raised to the vision of the divine essence.[40] The real distinction between Creator and creature

---

36. *ST* I, q. 56, a. 3.

37. *ScG* III, chap. 52, 2: "A lower nature cannot acquire that which is proper to a higher nature except through the action of the higher nature to which the property belongs."

38. In the *Summa contra Gentiles*, Thomas evinces similar examples: water cannot be hot except through the action of fire (III, chap. 52, 2), and water does not tend upward unless moved by something else (III, chap. 52, 6). The latent potency in water awaits the dispositive form of fire to move the water toward heat. This movement or potency cannot be realized apart from the active agency of the higher nature—in this case fire, which communicates its own substance. Thomas holds, "The form proper to any being does not come to be in another being unless the first being is the agent of this event, for an agent makes something like itself by communicating its form to another thing" (ScG III, chap. 52, 3).

39. *ST* I, q. 12, a. 5.

40. In *De Ver.*, q. 8, a. 3, ad 12, Thomas distinguishes between irrational creatures, which by their own nature achieve their own natural end, from rational creatures whose end is beatitude but who can attain this end only by assistance. To attain beatitude through one's own power is exclusive to God.

entails a radical incommensurability on the part of the creature with a vision of the divine essence. Nevertheless, Thomas suggests that human and angelic intellects have a certain disposition, propensity, or aptness *to be raised* to the vision of God in a manner that neither physical vision nor nonrational creatures could possibly be disposed. In *De Veritate*, Thomas describes the disposition of the intellect as a capacity for perfection and a "potency suitable" (*propria potentia*) to receiving the intelligible form of the divine essence.[41] Corporeal sight, a rock, or a dog is in no way ordered to an intellectual vision of the divine essence. Corporeal sight only apprehends individual matter, and so sensory knowledge only obtains to singulars,[42] but intellectual vision is not constrained in this way. The intellect is marked by the power for abstraction. What the eyes see as a singular the mind can know as the expression of a universal:

> The sense of sight, as being altogether material, cannot be raised up to immateriality. But our intellect, or the angelic intellect inasmuch as it is elevated above matter in its own nature, can be raised up above its own nature to a higher level by grace.[43]

For Thomas, it is this capacity for intellectual abstraction that entails a potency open to being strengthened and elevated by the disposition of supernatural grace (i.e., the *lumen gloriae*) to know the divine essence.[44]

Nature and Grace in Relation to the *Lumen Gloriae*

Thomas's conception of the intellectual vision of the divine essence is contingent upon his broader framing of nature and grace. The elevation

---

41. *De Ver.*, q. 8, a. 3, co: "In order that God be seen through His essence, the divine essence must be united with the intellect in some way as an intelligible form. However, what is to be perfected can be united with a form only after a disposition is present which makes the subject to be perfected capable of receiving such a form, because a definite act takes place only in a potency suitable for it. For example, a body is united with a soul as with its form only after it has been organized and disposed. Similarly, there must be some disposition produced in the intellect by which it is made perfectible by this form, the divine essence. This disposition is brought about by an intellectual light."

42. *ST* I, q. 12, a. 4, rep. obj. 3.

43. *ST* I, q. 12, a. 4, rep. obj. 3.

44. Cf. *ST* II-II, q. 175, a. 4: "The Divine essence cannot be seen by man through any cognitive power other than the intellect. Now the human intellect does not turn to intelligible objects except by means of the phantasms which it takes from the senses through the intelligible species; and it is in considering these phantasms that the intellect judges of and coordinates sensible objects. Hence in any operation that requires abstraction of the intellect from phantasms, there must be also withdrawal of the intellect from the senses."

by grace of the created intellect is not impossible per se; rather, its created nature exists in such a way that by the assistance of grace it can be so elevated.[45] In fact, Thomas insists categorically, *homo est capax visionis divinae essentiae*.[46] Thomas's teaching on the beatific vision underscores the continuity of nature and grace:

The divine substance is not beyond the capacity of the created intellect in such a way that it is altogether foreign to it (*omnino extraneum*), as sound is from the object of vision, or as immaterial substance is from sense power; in fact, the divine substance is the first intelligible object and the principle of all intellectual cognition. But it is beyond the capacity of the created intellect, in the sense that it exceeds its power.[47]

The examples used in the passage are revelatory of how Thomas understands the elevation of intellectual vision within his broader teaching on grace—most tersely expressed as *gratia non tollit naturam, sed perficit*.[48] Unlike sound, which has no correlation to vision, the elevation of the intellect by the *lumen gloriae* to a sight of the divine essence is continuous with its nature. With a slight variation on his succinct maxim that grace perfects nature, Thomas writes of beautitude, "Glory perfects nature, it does not destroy it."[49]

The commensurate relation between nature and grace in Thomas's account of beatitude safeguards the genuinely human character of the saints' vision of God. Thomas emphasizes that the created intellect does not cease to be human should it be elevated by grace to a vision of the divine essence.[50] That this is a concern to him is evident from the objections

45. Cf. *ScG* III, chap. 52, 7: "Man's happiness, which is called life everlasting, consists in this divine vision, and we are said to attain it by God's grace alone, because such a vision exceeds all the capacity of a creature and it is not possible to reach it without divine assistance."

46. *ST* I-II, q. 5, a. 1, co.

47. *ScG* III, chap. 54, 8: "Divina enim substantia non sic est extra facultatem creati intellectus quasi aliquid omnino extraneum ab ipso, sicut est sonus a visu, vel substantia immaterialis a sensu, nam divina substantia est primum intelligibile, et totius intellectualis cognitionis principium: sed est extra facultatem intellectus creati sicut excedens virtutem eius."

48. *ST* I, q. 1, a. 8, ad 2.

49. *In IV Sent.*, d. 49, q. 2, a. 3, ad 8: *gloria perficit naturam, et non destruit*. See also *De Ver.*, q. 8, a. 5, ad 3, and *De Ver.*, q. 9, a. 3, ad 2.

50. Gilby, "Introduction," xxiii, expresses the commensurate relation between nature and grace in Thomas's teaching on the vision of God:

There is no abrupt chasm between nature and grace, and when [Thomas] sees in natural desire a stretching out to God himself he is not indulging a wish-fulfillment fantasy, which is quite out of keeping with his cast of mind. All he is saying is that the vision is possible, not that it is likely, and that the yearning itself is a prophecy of what can be, not a promise of what

with which he engages in question 12, article 4, concerning whether a rational creature's natural powers are sufficient to see the divine essence. The third objection contends that just as corporeal sense cannot be elevated to grasp an incorporeal substance, so too the created intellect cannot be elevated to see the divine essence.[51] In short, the objection proposes that the created intellect is fundamentally unsuited for the vision of God. In his response, Thomas disputes the parallelism. While it is true that corporeal sense cannot be elevated to grasp an incorporeal substance without ceasing to be corporeal sense, the relation between the intellect and the divine essence is not construed in this manner:

> The sense of sight, as being altogether material, cannot be raised up to immateriality. But our intellect, or the angelic intellect, inasmuch as it is elevated above matter in its own nature, can be raised up above its own nature to a higher level by grace. The proof is, that sight cannot in any way know abstractedly what it knows concretely; for in no way can it perceive a nature except as this one particular nature; whereas our intellect is able to consider abstractedly what it knows concretely. Since therefore the created intellect is naturally capable of apprehending the concrete form, and the concrete being abstractedly, by way of a kind of resolution of parts; it can by grace be raised up to know separate subsisting substance, and separate subsisting existence.[52]

The intellect's ability to *abstract* to a universal from the particular presented to it by the senses suggests that the nature of the created intellect has a propensity, directionality, or aptness for elevation to a vision of the divine essence. Although it belongs only to God to know the divine essence by nature, the created intellect is capable of being raised by grace to participate in the knowledge God has of his own essence.[53] In Thomas's account,

---

will be. For it is not daydreaming or a sophisticated projection, but an inborn and inescapable craving, and this, he holds, cannot be pointless, *inane*, not because his was an optimistic temperament, apt to translate fiction into fact, but because quite dispassionately he reckoned that potentiality and 'intentions' could not be accounted for without corresponding actualities and ends. Nothing would stir in time were there no complete possession of life in eternity

In the same vein, Michael Waddell notes, "Thomas does not say that knowledge of what exceeds our mode of being is altogether beyond us; he only says that knowledge of what exceeds the mode of the knower's being is *above the nature* of the knower.... To be sure, this participation rises above the level of what is natural to humans, but this does not mean that it rises above what is 'human' altogether." "Aquinas on the Light of Glory," *Tópicos* 40 (2011): 118–19.

51. *ST* I, q. 12, a. 4, obj. 3.

52. *ST* I, q. 12, a. 4, ad 3.

53. In this respect, Thomas's language regarding the character of the *lumen gloriae* is

however, the accent falls on the fact that this capacity is wholly contin-gent upon divine grace to be realized.[54] Nor does the intellectual creature cease to be human by such participation. Michael Waddell expresses this principle: "The light of glory perfects the power that is seminally present in the created intellect's natural capacity to look upon abstracted forms and separated being, and enables the created intellect to participate in an act that is essential to the divine intellect."[55] As such, Thomas's teaching on the *lumen gloriae* posits a profound degree of continuity between nat-ural acts of knowing (by way of abstraction) and glorified knowledge that correlates to his broader teaching on the continuity of nature and grace.[56]

We see in this treatment both an affirmation of the continuity of grace fitted to created nature and the newness and change of this elevation. On the one hand, it is because the human person already participates in the divine likeness that he is capable of receiving "a more sublime form."[57] Thomas gives the following example: "Light can only become the act of a body if the body participates somewhat in the diaphanous."[58] Just as only a diaphanous object is capable of illumination (without destroying its nature), so too only a creature in the divine likeness is capable of be-atification. In this case, elevation by grace is fitting and perfective of its nature. Thomas writes,

It is impossible for this [divine] essence to become the intelligible form of a cre-ated intellect unless by virtue of the fact that the created intellect participates in the divine likeness. Therefore, this participation in the divine likeness is necessary so that the substance of God may be seen.[59]

---

instructive. He uses verbs like "increase," "added," "raised," "elevated," "strengthened," "super added," and "perfecting." All suggest an essential congruity between the nature of the intel-lectual creature and the grace of beatific vision.

54. Steven A. Long articulates the nuance of Thomas's position on this score: "The pow-ers of intellect and will thus constitute a natural translucence to God within the creature, without yet constituting the least trace of actual motion toward beatific vision as such on the part of the creature. For the least such motion will require a supernatural principle to operate within the human person so as to begin to uplift the human faculties from their natural objects and assume them within the divine itinerary of salvation, ordering them to the inner being of God." "Obediential Potency, Human Knowledge, and the Natural Desire for God," *International Philosophical Quarterly* 37 (1997): 50.

55. Waddell, "Aquinas on the Light of Glory," 123.

56. Cf. Waddell, "Aquinas on the Light of Glory," 120: "It is as though Thomas finds the seeds of glorified knowing lying dormant in natural acts of knowing."

57. *ScG* III, chap. 53, 3.

58. *ScG* III, chap. 53, 2.

59. *ScG* III, chap. 53, 2.

The participation of the blessed in the vision of God is predicated on their created *nature* in the divine likeness that is capable of such elevation.[60]

At the same time, Thomas is clear that the elevation by the *lumen gloriae* is not simply an *intensification* of the created intellect's nature; rather, a *new* form is bestowed. By way of explanation, Thomas notes that a power may be elevated in two ways. First, this may happen simply through the intensification of that power. Thus hot water can be made even hotter, and, despite the intensification of heat, it remains the same species. But a power may also be elevated by the imposition of a new form. Thus the power of a diaphanous object (such as a stained-glass window) is elevated by the reception of a new form of light. Upon the reception of light, the diaphanous object actually *becomes* light in a way that it was not before. Of course, there must be a certain capacity (proper to diaphanous objects) to receive this new form. Similarly, the intellectual creature has by nature a certain capacity or potency to receive the new form of the *lumen gloriae*.[61] The nuance of this exposition avoids positing the new form of the *lumen gloriae* as either totally foreign to the created nature or as a simple intensification of its innate natural powers. Thomas's teaching on the grace of the *lumen gloriae* avoids both extrincicism and naturalism. When the divine essence becomes the intelligible species of the created intellect, this involves a genuine change (*mutatio*) for that intellect, but it remains that created intellect.[62]

The Thomistic theory of obediential potency provides a conceptual framing that affirms both the authentically human character of the vision of the divine essence and the fact that such a vision obtains only through the elevation of grace. Obediential potency thus refers to the potency proper to a creature whose effects can be realized only by the active agency of divine power.[63] Again, this active divine agency does not do

---

60. Thomas uses the language of potency and act to articulate the transformed disposition to receive the form of the divine essence. Cf. *ScG* III, chap. 53, 3: "Nothing is receptive of a more sublime form unless it be elevated by means of a disposition to the capacity for this form, for a proper act is produced in a proper potency. Now, the divine essence is a higher form than any created intellect."

61. Cf. Waddell, "Aquinas on the Light of Glory," 122.

62. *ScG* III, chap. 53, 4: "Quae quidem mutatio aliter esse non potest nisi per hoc quod intellectus creatus aliquam dispositionem de novo acquirat." Thomas holds, "This change (*mutatio*) can only come about by means of the created intellect acquiring some new disposition" (*ScG* III, chap. 53, 4).

63. The best entry into the topic is Long, "Obediential Potency," 51–52. Long explains the Thomistic thesis as follows:

violence to the nature of the creature but is, on the contrary, the necessary condition that allows the creature to realize his end. As such, there is, for St. Thomas, a difference in *kind* between the elevation of the created intellect by the *lumen gloriae* to a vision of the divine essence and the fact that (for example) "God is able from these stones to raise up children to Abraham" (Mt 3:9). The grace of divine filiation entails that the intellectual creature raised to a vision of God remains human, indeed now fully human. The (hypothetical) divine filiation of stones would render them no longer stones. Intellectual creatures are constituted by an obediential potency ordering them to elevation to the vision of God in a way that stones are not. The application of the theory of obediential potency to Thomas's teaching on the saints' vision of the divine essence offers the necessary conceptual distinctions to affirm both the gratuity of beatitude and the fact that such a vision is congruent with the desire of the human heart.

Conclusion

Few theological differences between Eastern and Western Christianity are posed in as stark and neatly opposed manner as the question regarding

---

Obediential potency is simply the potency of a creature towards acts achieved only with the assistance of divine causality. As a stained-glass window can irradiate colored light only with the assistance of light, so the human soul can directly contemplate God only with the assistance of God. Subrational beings lack any obediential potency for beatific knowledge of God because they lack intellective nature. All this makes it abundantly clear that one is not dealing merely with the extrinsic susceptibility of creatures to divine miracle, that is, with natures being supernaturally transmuted. Rather, what is involved is the constellation of a created nature's passive potencies in relation to the active agency of God. In this way acts of a creature can proceed from a supernatural principle without ceasing to be true acts of the creature.

For Thomas, obediential potency must be distinguished from a divine miracle. In *De Ver.*, q. 10, a. 11, co, Thomas describes the vision of God experienced by Moses and Paul *in via* as "miraculous," whereas the vision of God in glory is not a miracle but an expression of obediential potency. Thomas explains that just as Peter walking on the water is a miracle of the body, so too Paul, seeing the divine essence in this life, is a miracle of the mind. The nature of a miracle is "to produce effects, the dispositions for which they do not have within themselves" (*De Ver.*, q. 10, a. 11, co). Obediential potency, by contrast, expresses effects (contingent upon the action of grace) that are congruous with innate dispositions. Thus, in this life, no obediential potency obtains for either walking on water or seeing God, whereas the purified and glorified soul does stand in obediential potency to receive the vision of the divine essence.

the possibility of the vision of the divine essence. For the East, following the teaching of the Eastern Doctors, the vision of the divine essence is accessible to no creature. In their rejection of the rationalism of Eunomius, the Cappadocian Fathers, John Chrysostom, and John of Damascus insist that God is radically ineffable and incomprehensible—not only incomprehensible, but also unapproachable (ἀπρόσιτον). The Eastern tradition came to insist that only the divine operations or energies (ἐνέργειαι) can be known; the divine essence (οὐσία) is known to God alone. The Western tradition, so it is often thought, charted a different theological path, finding its consummation in Thomas Aquinas. The intellectualism of St. Thomas and his reliance on Aristotelian teleology allegedly led to a different theological conclusion holding sway in the West. St. Thomas would affirm that intellectual creatures can by grace see (*attingere*) the divine essence. The very nature of the rational creature is such that it cannot find fulfillment apart from the vision of the divine essence.

I have suggested that a careful analysis of Thomas's teaching on the *lumen gloriae* challenges this neat antithesis. Thomas is certainly aware of a tension between his own position and that of the Eastern Fathers and a substratal difference remains between them with respect to the possibility of the intellectual creature's vision of the divine essence. Nevertheless, the same concern that animates the Eastern Fathers in their insistence that the divine essence is inaccessible to all creatures is equally the *ratio* undergirding Thomas's treatment of the *lumen gloriae*, namely, to preserve the transcendence of God and the real distinction between Creator and creature. Thomas maintains that if God is to be seen, the creature must be raised to participate in the manner by which God sees himself. This is an utterly gratuitous gift, completely beyond the nature of creaturely capability. By the disposition of the *lumen gloriae*, the blessed see God immediately and not through any similitude or by the impress of any likeness, in a way that is impossible to comprehend in this life. While the vision of the divine essence is unlike any finite mode of knowing, the intellectual creature's ability to abstract suggests a certain disposition (or obediential potency) to be elevated by grace to the vision of God. As such, the intellectual vision of God is, in St. Thomas's account, something *new*, but not radically *foreign* to the rational creature. While the vision of God lies beyond any creaturely capability, it remains fitting to the created intellect and fulfilling of the desires of the human heart. Thomas's teaching on the grace of the *lumen gloriae* allows him to affirm that the desire for perfect happiness, which is nothing other than the direct vision of the divine essence, is not void, but capable of fulfillment. But the doctrine of the *lumen gloriae* also allows him to affirm with the Greek Fathers that the divine essence is unapproachable to any creature by nature; to see God *sicuti est* remains strictly gratuitous.

Acknowledgements

The author is grateful to Michael Dauphinais for the invaluable direction he gave in the early stages of writing this essay. He also thanks Hans Boersma, Fr. Andrew Hofer, and Sean Robertson for their perceptive suggestions, which did much to improve this essay.

6

Thomas Aquinas's Use of John Chrysostom in the *Catena Aurea* and the *Tertia Pars*

BRIAN DUNKLE, SJ

If we judge by acclaim and statistics, Thomas ranked John Chrysostom (ca. 349–407) foremost among the Greek Fathers.[1] In his *Commentary on John*, Thomas observes that among the Greeks, Chrysostom possesses such authority as an expositor of Scripture that they do not admit other interpretations if Chrysostom has given one.[2] A famous legend reports that he would trade the city of Paris for a complete copy of Chrysostom's *Incomplete Commentary on Matthew*.[3] And, as I discuss below, Thomas cites Chrysostom more than any other Greek source.

1. The classic study of Chrysostom's reception is Chrysostome Baur, *S. Jean Chrysostome et ses oeuvres dans l'histoire littéraire* (Louvain: Bureaux du Recueil, 1907); on Thomas, see 74.

2. *Super Io.* c. 1, l.2: "Et quia apud Graecos Chrysostomus est tantae auctoritatis in suis expositionibus, quod ubi ipse aliquid exposuit in sacra Scriptura, nullam aliam expositionem admittant."

3. A pseudonymous work. For the account, found in the biography of William of Tocco (*Acta Sanctorum* 7 mars, t. 1, Paris 1865, c. 671A + 711B), see J. van Banning, "Saint Thomas et l'Opus Imperfectum in Matthaeum," in *Atti dell' VIII Congresso Tomistico Internazionale*, Studi Tomistici 17 (Vatican City: Congresso Tomistico Internazionale, 1982), 73–85, who establishes convincingly that the text of Chrysostom intended is the *Opus Imperfectum*; see the additional arguments in the preparatory volume for the Corpus Christianorum Latinorum edition of the text, *Opus Imperfectum in Matthaeum*, CCL 87B (Turnholt: Brepols, 1988), 179; on the *Opus Imperfectum* itself, see Franz Mali, *Das "Opus imperfectum in Matthaeum" und sein Verhältnis zu den Matthäuskommentaren von Origenes und Hieronymus* (Innsbruck: Tyrolia, 1991). On the desire for whole texts and *originalia* (as opposed to excerpts) in the

Yet if we look for Chrysostom in specific elements of Thomas's thought, we struggle to trace any clear and discernible influence. Even as scholars since Ignaz Backes have scrutinized the presence of the Greek Fathers in Thomas's later writings, especially the *Summa Theologiae*, the place of Chrysostom in Thomistic thinking remains underappreciated.[4] To be sure, tracking Chrysostom in Thomas is a challenge. First, one must identify and authenticate Thomas's references to Chrysostom; even what Thomas takes to be Chrysostom's *Opus Imperfectum* was shown long ago to be inauthentic, most likely the work of a fifth-century Latin-speaking Arian.[5] But there is also the problem of uncovering distinctively "Chrysostomian" ideas in Thomas's corpus. Unlike, say, his engagement with Augustine on the Trinity or with Cyril on the hypostatic union, Thomas does not rely directly on Chrysostom to develop particular doctrinal formulations.[6]

While Chrysostom may not figure prominently in the "doctrinal" portions of Thomas's corpus, in this chapter I argue that Aquinas does rely heavily on Chrysostom—or, at least, "Chrysostom"—precisely in those sections of his Christological writings that, until recently, have received little attention from scholars.[7] Thomas shows a lively engagement with Chrysostom in perhaps the most innovative Christological contributions

---

thirteenth century, see Mary Rouse and Richard Rouse, "*Statim Invenire:* Schools, Preachers, and New Attitudes to the Page," in *Authentic Witnesses: Approaches to Medieval Texts and Manuscripts* (Notre Dame, IN: University of Notre Dame, 1991), 191–219, and idem, "The Development of Research Tools in the Thirteenth Century," in *Authentic Witnesses,* 249–51.

4. Ignaz Backes, *Die Christologie des hl. Thomas v. Aquin und die griechischen Kirchenväter* (Paderborn: Schöningh, 1931), who has little to say about Chrysostom. One notable exception is Giuseppe Ferraro, "San Giovanni Crisostomo come fonte de san Tommaso: La sua esposizione dei testi pneumatologici nel commento del questo vangelo," *Angelicum* 62 (1985): 194–244, which focuses on Thomas's *Lectura* on John. Subsequent studies on specific Greek patristic and conciliar sources include Gottfried Geenen, "En marge du concile de Chalcédoine: Les texts du Quatrième Concile dans les oeuvres de Saint Thomas," *Angelicum* 29 (1952): 43–59; Martin Morard, "Une source de Saint Thomas d'Aquin: Le deuxième concile de Constantinople (553)," *Revue des Sciences Philosophiques et Théologiques* 81 (1997): 21–56, and other studies of Louis Bataillon, including "Note sur la documentation patristique de Saint Thomas à Paris en 1270," *Revue des Sciences Philosophiques et Théologiques* 47 (1963): 403–6.

5. Van Banning, *Opus Imperfectum,* 179.

6. On Cyril and Thomas, see Aaron Riches, "Theandric Humanism: Constantinople III in the Thought of St. Thomas Aquinas," *Pro Ecclesia* 23 (2014): 197; on Augustine and Thomas, see Gilles Emery, "Trinitarian Theology as Spiritual Exercise in Augustine and Aquinas," in *Aquinas the Augustinian,* ed. Michael Dauphinais, Barry David, and Matthew Levering (Washington, DC: Catholic University of America, 2007), 1–40.

7. See Joseph Boyle, "The Twofold Division of St. Thomas's Christology in the Tertia Pars," *The Thomist* 60 (1996): 47.

of his later career—namely, his compilation of the *Catena Aurea* as well as *ST* III, qq. 27–59, both of which emphasize the *acta et passa* of the Incarnate Word.[8] After offering some introduction to the two texts and their relationship to patristic sources, I argue that Aquinas draws on Chrysostom in particular to formulate his views on the teaching function of what Christ did and suffered. Chrysostom helps Aquinas describe Christ's humanity as *exemplum* for human action, progress, and endurance.

The *Acta et Passa* of Christ in the *Catena Aurea*

Thomas's reverence for the Fathers as theological authorities is well documented, but it is especially evident in the composition of his own scriptural gloss.[9] The *Glossa Continua Super Evangelia*, which came to be known as the *Catena Aurea* in the fifteenth century, contains extended excerpts from Greek and Latin Fathers that Thomas compiled to form a sequential commentary on the four Gospels.[10] Begun at the request of Urban IV in 1262 and eventually completed around 1264 (after the pope's death), the first volume on Matthew relies on previously available texts and translations, while the three subsequent volumes, composed from 1264 to 1268, contain Latin translations of many Greek sources that Thomas commissioned.[11] Thomas's innovative use of Greek sources in the *Catena* is widely noted and had an enduring influence on his later writings.[12] Thomas came

---

8. On the innovations of the *Tertia Pars*, see Leo Scheffczyk, "Die Stellung des Thomas von Aquin in der Entwicklung der Lehre von den *Mysteria vitae Christi*," in *Renovatio et Reformatio (Festschrift für Ludwig Hödl)*, ed. Manfred Gerwing and Godehard Ruppert (Münster: Aschendorff, 1985), esp. 51–58; Richard Schenk, OP, "Omnis Christi Actio Nostra Est Instructio: The Deeds and Sayings of Jesus as Revelation in the View of Thomas Aquinas," in *La doctrine de la révélation divine de Saint Thomas d'Aquin*, ed. Arturo Blanco and Leo Elders (Vatican City: Pontificia Accademia di S. Tommaso d'Aquino, 1990), 104–31; Jean-Pierre Torrell, *Saint Thomas Aquinas*, vol. 1 (Washington, DC: Catholic University of America, 1996), 261–66.

9. For an overview, see Leo Elders, "Thomas Aquinas and the Fathers of the Church," in *The Reception of the Church Fathers in the West: From the Carolingians to the Maurists*, vol. 1, ed. Irena Backus (Leiden: Brill, 1997), 337–66.

10. On the composition and the sources of the *Catena*, see Louis Bataillon, "La diffusione manoscrita e stampata dei commenti biblici di San Tommaso d'Aquino," *Angelicum* 71 (1994): 579–90.

11. *Cat. in Mc.*, *dedicatio*: "quasdam expositiones doctorum Graecorum in Latinum feci transferri"; Elders, "Thomas Aquinas and the Fathers," 348–49.

12. Elders, "Thomas Aquinas and the Fathers," 338, notes the contrast with earlier Latin theologians: "In his *Sentences* Peter Lombard quotes Augustine about 1000 times, Ambrose and Hilary respectively 90 and 85, Gregory and Jerome 55 and 50 times, but there are only 27 references to John Damascene and 17 to Chrysostom."

to rely on the *Catena* for much of his subsequent theological work.[13]

The composition of the *Catena* was, as James Weisheipl notes, a "turning point" in the development of Thomas's theology.[14] His later writings exhibit a greater attention to the work of the Fathers, a wider range of references to their thought, and more frequent insertion of extensive quotations. Moreover, the *Catena* itself became a *strumento di lavoro*, as Carmelo Conticello puts it, for many of his exegetical writings.[15] His *Commentary on John*, for instance, contains many of the Chrysostom quotations employed in *Catena*.[16] Thomas seems to have had the *Catena* close at hand as he composed his later treatises and commentaries.

Yet any scholar working with the *Catena* faces daunting obstacles. First, Thomas did not simply transcribe ancient texts. In *The Book of Memory*, Mary Carruthers includes an extended excerpt from "The Life of St. Thomas Aquinas" by Bernardo Gui, which attests to Thomas's extraordinary powers of recall as well as to his nontextual process of composition: "Consider, for example, that admirable compilation of Patristic texts on the four Gospels which he made for Pope Urban and which, for the most part, he seems to have put together from texts that he had read and committed to memory from time to time while staying in various

13. See Aidan Nichols, "Introduction," in *Catena Aurea of St. Thomas Aquinas* (Southampton: St. Austin, 1997), ix, who claims that Thomas always kept a copy of the *Catena* with him (although he provides no reference); see also Carmelo Conticello, "San Tommaso ed i Padri: *Archives d'Histoire Doctrinale et Littéraire du Moyen Âge* 65 (1990): 87, for a similar claim.

14. James A. Weisheipl, *Friar Thomas d'Aquino* (New York: Doubleday, 1974), 171, citing I. T. Eschmann, who calls it a turning point in "the history of Catholic dogma." See I. T. Eschmann, "A Catalogue of St. Thomas's Works: Bibliographical Notes," in Etienne Gilson, *The Christian Philosophy of St. Thomas Aquinas*, trans. L. K. Shook (New York: Random House, 1956), 397.

15. Conticello, "San Tommaso ed i Padri," 83. On Thomas's exegesis, see Thomas Prügl, "Thomas Aquinas as Interpreter of Scripture," in *The Theology of Thomas Aquinas*, ed. Rik Van Nieuwenhove and Joseph Wawrykow (Notre Dame, IN: University of Notre Dame Press, 2005), 386–415; Wilhelmus Valkenberg, *Words of the Living God: Place and Function of the Holy Scripture in the Theology of St. Thomas Aquinas* (Leuvens: Peeters, 2000).

16. For representative examples, see *Super Io., c.*1 l.15, *Cat. in Jn* 1:37–40 (Morard #269), *Super Io., c.* 7 l.2, and *Cat. in Jn* 7:14–18 (Morard #1053); "ed. #" refers to the numbering used in the Morard edition (see below). In the *Lectura* on John, he also contrasts interpretations from Augustine with those from Chrysostom; see, e.g., *Super Io., c.* 5 l.5, and *Super Io., c.* 10 l.1. Conticello, "San Tommaso ed i Padri," 61–70, includes a careful comparison of citations in *Super Io.* with the text of Burgundio's twelfth-century translation of Chrysostom. For a discussion of the varieties of citations in Thomas's corpus, see Wilhelmus Valkenberg, *Did Not Our Heart Burn? Place and Function of Holy Scripture in the Theology of St. Thomas Aquinas* (Utrecht: Publications of the Thomas Instituut te Utrecht, 1990), 46–70.

religious houses."[17] Thomas often condenses or even paraphrases the original patristic quotation to offer a summary of the insight; in these instances, we cannot be certain whether Thomas depended on the *originalia*, on earlier glosses, or on his prodigious memory.[18] Second, Thomas deliberately altered many of the quotations, as he notes in the dedicatory epistle to Urban IV: "I have added a few things to the words of certain authors ... Often much had to be omitted from the middle to avoid prolixity and to clarify the meaning, ... or the order had be changed."[19] Third, many of the glosses, especially Chrysostom's, are from spurious or pseudonymous works, which Thomas occasionally corrects when citing the same text elsewhere.[20]

In the past decade, Martin Morard of the L'Institut de Recherche et d'Histoire des Textes at France's Centre National de la Recherche Scientifique, in collaboration with Giuseppe Conticello and associated researchers, has improved on previous versions of the *Catena* by developing not only a more reliable text but also an extensive critical apparatus that includes texts of both the translations available to Aquinas as well as, when available, the Greek originals.[21] Furthermore, the project pays close attention to Thomas's rearrangement of the original's structure, often with impressive results for understanding Thomas's method of theology.[22] In

---

17. Mary Carruthers, *The Book of Memory: A Study of Memory in Medieval Culture* (Cambridge: Cambridge University Press, 1990), 3; translated by Kenelm Foster, *Biographical Documents for the Life of St. Thomas Aquinas* (Oxford: Blackfriars, 1949), 50. Carruthers adds, "It is important to note that in writing this work Thomas did not look up each quotation in a manuscript tome as he composed; the accounts are specific on this point. The texts were already filed in his memory, in an ordered form that is one of the basics of mnemonic technique" (6). See also *Ystoria sancti Thome de Aquino de Guillaume de Tocco (1323)*, ed. Claire le Brun-Gouanvic (Toronto: Pontifical Institute of Mediaeval Studies, 1996), 130–31 and 170–71, on Thomas's composition of the *Catena* as a mark of his prodigious memory.

18. See Beryl Smalley, *The Gospels in the Schools* (London: Hambledon, 1985), 257.

19. *Cat. in Mt prol.* (Morard #6, 8): "Pauca quidem certorum auctorum verbis, ... plerumque oportuit aliqua rescindi de medio ad prolixitatem vitandum necnon ad manifestiorem sensum, vel, secundum, congruentiam expositionis littere, ordinem commutari." All translations from the *Catena* are my own.

20. On Thomas's pseudepigraphical sources, see Gottfried Geenen, "Saint Thomas d'Aquin et ses sources pseudoépigraphiques," *Ephemerides Theologicae Lovaniensis* 20 (1943): 71–80.

21. The results, along with regular updates, are available at the Sacra Pagina website, accessed May 15, 2018, https://big.hypotheses.org/. I rely on Morard's version for my text and references (my references are by scriptural verse with Morard's number in parentheses).

22. The version available online currently includes an apparatus with the original Greek that is gradually increasing; the editors maintain that an integral critical edition is not their

examining excerpts in the *Summa*, for instance, one uncovers Thomas's sophisticated reworking of the original texts.[23] We have good reason, then, to suspect that Thomas chose his sources not simply to "decorate" his conclusions, but rather to develop and bolster his arguments.

Chrysostom in the *Catena*

Chrysostom is Thomas's favorite source in the *Catena Aurea*.[24] Even after he begins, when composing the *Catena on Mark*, to acquire additional translations from other Greek Fathers, he still relies heavily on Chrysostom. In compiling these references to Chrysostom, Thomas shows that he has consulted an impressive range of his works: while in the *Catena on Matthew* he relies almost exclusively (and understandably) on Chrysostom's *Homilies on Matthew* and the *Opus Imperfectum*, for the other three Gospels, he shows he read and quite often memorized extended passages from Chrysostom's sermons and biblical commentaries.[25]

In composing the *Catena*, Thomas acquired a much more expansive grasp of Chrysostom than he had in his early career. While Thomas quotes from Chrysostom as early as the *Scriptum*, citations are always brief and isolated.[26] In the *Catena*, by contrast, Thomas often couples citations from Chrysostom, especially to balance references to Chrysostom's homilies with references to the *Opus Imperfectum*.[27] In pairing the two

---

objective. The translation of Chrysostom's *Homilies on Matthew* is Burgundio's. Occasionally, Thomas uses a passage from the *Glossa* that includes a reference to Chrysostom (e.g., Mt 26:26 [Morard #4383]).

23. See, e.g., the close analysis of Fabio Gibiino and Martin Morard, "Catena in Lucam 7, 36–50 péricope de la pécheresse repentie: Un cas de traitement des sources," October 16, 2014, https://f-origin.hypotheses.org/wp-content/blogs.dir/4064/files/2017/09/Comment -Thomas-travaille-ses-sources_lexemple-de-la-p%C3%A9cheresse_repentie.pdf.

24. Leo J. Elders, "Santo Tomás de Aquino y los Padres de la Iglesia," *Doctor Communis* 48 (1993): 66.

25. Cf. *Sermone in passione*; see Backes, *Die Christologie*, 37–40, on range of Thomas's citations in his corpus.

26. Some from the *Scriptum* reappear in greater length in the *Catena*; see *Super Sent. Lib.* 4, d. 3, q. 1, a. 4, qc. 2, s.c. 2, quoting *Homily 24 on John*, and the *Cat. Jn* on Jn 3:4–8 (Morard #415). The *Summa contra Gentiles* contains no references to Chrysostom.

27. Thus, e.g., on Mt 4:5–6 (Morard #651 and #652), Thomas pairs *Op. Imp.* 5 with *Hom. in Mt.* 13. Thomas nowhere makes explicit any doubts about the *Opus Imperfectum's* authenticity, but in the dedicatory letter, he does note that the translation is *vitiosa* (Morard #7). The question of authenticity was raised by his contemporary, Vincent de Beauvais, in his *Speculum Historiale* 1.16.42.3; see Chrysostome, *S. Jean Chrysostome*, 66.

authoritative sources and creating an extended gloss, Thomas shows that he is interested in the *totus* Chrysostom.

To some extent, Chrysostom is put to service for the ends that Thomas mentions in his dedicatory letter to the *Catena*, that is, clarifying the literal and spiritual meaning of Scripture while confuting errors and confirming Catholic truth in order to provide a guide for Christian life.[28] Thomas occasionally cites Chrysostom to refute heretical understandings of Scripture. Thus Chrysostom's *Homily 6 on Matthew* is Thomas's source for identifying the Priscillianists as astrologers.[29] In the *Catena on John*, Chrysostom is cited to show that John 14:15–17 is anti-heretical, for it confirms the unity of the divine substance and the distinction of hypostases.[30] Hence Thomas is aware of Chrysostom as a "doctrinal" source. Nevertheless, if we compare the citations of Chrysostom with those of the second most cited source, Augustine, we find that Augustine is much more often invoked to establish a point of doctrine or to confute errors.[31]

By contrast, Thomas prefers to quote Chrysostom for material relevant to the pedagogical meaning of the events within the life of Christ.[32] As we shall see in the use of Chrysostom in the *Tertia Pars*, these citations show a special preference for Christ's *acta et passa* as ordered to the instruction of humanity. Thus in the materials cited to treat the beginning of Christ's ministry, after the baptism in Mark's Gospel (Mk 1:9–11), Thomas cites Chrysostom's *Homily 13 on Matthew*: "Because all that Christ worked and suffered was for our instruction."[33] The *Catenae on Luke* and *on Mark* contain similar programmatic citations from Chrysostom's materials.[34] To be sure, Thomas uses other authorities for similar ends,[35] but I argue that Chrysostom's prominence as an authority for instruction given through Christ's *acta et passa* reappears in the *Tertia Pars*.

Thomas's use of Chrysostom in the *Catena* depends in part on the types of sources at hand. In the *Catena on Matthew*, Thomas often follows

28. *Cat. in Mt prol.* (Morard #9).

29. *Cat. in Mt* 2:1–2 (Morard #84).

30. *Cat. in Io* 14:15–17 (Morard #474).

31. See, e.g., *Cat. in Mt* 6:17 (Morard #1294); *Cat. in Io* 5:18b–20 (Morard #722).

32. Conticello, "San Tommaso ed i Padri," 31–92, has a wealth of statistics.

33. "Quia Christus omnia ad doctrinam nostram operabatur." *Cat. in Mc* 1:12–13 (Morard #65).

34. *Cat. in Lc* 1:1–4 (Morard #8): "Dicit autem viderunt, quia hoc maxime robur nanciscitur credulitatis, quod addiscitur ab his qui presentialiter viderunt"; *Cat. in Mc* 1:23–28 (Morard #101): "Unde dogma salutiferum nobis datur."

35. Cf. Augustine's *Contra Faustum* cited at the beginning of the *Cat. in Mt* (Morard #2).

the *Opus Imperfectum* in sequence, dividing the original according to the corresponding scriptural passages.[36] Hence Thomas relies on Chrysostom in part because Chrysostom provides such extensive and ready material for the gloss. But the blend of citations from the range of Chrysostom's writings suggests that Thomas was not simply proceeding through his commentaries in sequence.

Chrysostom in *ST* III, qq. 1–26

When Thomas comes to compose the *Tertia Pars* near the end of his life, Chrysostom is a major influence.[37] Here again, Thomas's pattern of citations suggests that he viewed Chrysostom as less valuable for formulating the doctrine of the Incarnation and more valuable as an authority for treating the mysteries of Christ's life and suffering.

Chrysostom appears only seven times in qq. 1–26, the portion of *ST* III on the "mystery of the Incarnation itself," while he is cited regularly in qq. 27–59.[38] Moreover, in the opening "traditional" sections, the quotations are relatively decorative.[39] Thus in *ST* III, q. 1, a. 4, on whether the Incarnation was aimed more for the forgiveness of actual sins than for original sin, Chrysostom is invoked in the third argument and the response to the same argument, as though to correct a possible misunderstanding of Chrysostom's own words; in the end, Chrysostom is "neutralized" rather than invoked for support.[40] Unlike, say, John Damascene and the Acts of Chalcedon, two Greek sources central to explaining the dynamics of the hypostatic union, Chrysostom only really enters the *Tertia Pars* when Aquinas turns to narrate the *acta et passa* of the Incarnate Lord.[41]

We should also note that the material from Chrysostom that appears

---

36. See, e.g., the passages quoted for Matthew 1, which includes a text from the *Opus Imperfectum* for every verse in the chapter (except for vv. 22–23, which receive no comment in the *Opus Imperfectum*).

37. On Aquinas's use of patristic sources in the *Summa*, see also Ceslao Pera, *Le fonti del pensiero di S. Tommaso d'Aquino nella Somma Theologica* (Turin: Marietti, 1979), 29–64.

38. Seven times in *ST* III, qq. 1–26, vs. one hundred and five times in qq. 27–59. As Backes, *Die Christologie*, 38, notes, these references are surprisingly often to authentic works of Chrysostom.

39. Backes, *Die Christologie*, 56–66, identifies one class of citation as "Ornamente." For similar "decorative" references, see *ST* III, q. 6, a. 3, arg. 3; *ST* III, q. 10, a. 2, ad 1; *ST* III, q. 16, a. 11, ad 2; at *ST* III, q. 21, a. 4, ad 1, he is named with Ambrose and Origen; on the limits of the term "decorative," see Elders, "Thomas Aquinas and the Fathers," 345–46.

40. *ST* III, q. 1, a. 4, obj. 3, ad 3.

41. See, e.g., *ST* III, q. 1, a. 1, s.c., and *ST* III, q. 2, a. 1, and a. 2, s.c.

in the earlier questions of the *Tertia Pars* appears nowhere among the exegetical material in the *Catena*. In compiling quotations for the "doctrinal" portion of the *Tertia Pars*, Thomas seems to prefer the "doctrinal" Chrysostom, who appeared less frequently than the "exegetical" Chrysostom in the *Catena*.

Chrysostom in *ST* III, qq. 27–59

As many have noted, *ST* III, qq. 27–59, is an innovation in treating the Incarnation. While other *Summae* and *Sentences* commentaries (including the *Scriptum* and *Summa contra Gentiles*) focused extensively on theological principles such as the mode of union, Thomas introduced the *acta et passa* to explore the biblical record of the Word's life on earth.[42] The *Catena* became the main source for these explorations.

Many of the citations of Chrysostom in qq. 27–59 have parallels in the *Catena*.[43] While Thomas might have relied on his memory or *originalia* for some of these, examples suggest that he drew on the gloss. In *ST* III, q. 44, a.3, Thomas considers whether it was fitting for Christ to perform miracles on human beings. In each of the four responses to the objections, Thomas cites Chrysostom (twice in two cases).[44] Each case has a direct parallel in the *Catena* and includes examples from all four Gospel glosses, a virtuosic display of the breadth of Thomas's mastery of Chrysostom's exegetical writings as contained in the *Catena*.[45] Further evidence that Thomas drew from the *Catena* appears in *ST* III, q. 46, a. 11, ad 3, where Thomas responds to the suggestion that the Gospels of Luke and Matthew are inconsistent on the number of thieves who insulted Christ at the

---

42. Scheffczyk, "Die Stellung des Thomas von Aquin," 51–58; Boyle, "Twofold Division," 439–47.

43. On Thomas's use of the Fathers and the *Catena* in qq. 27–59, see Bataillon, "Saint Thomas et les Pères," 15–16; the chapter includes a helpful appendix charting the correspondences between citations in the *Tertia Pars* and the *Catena*; most of the citations of Chrysostom (c. 100) in qq. 27–59 have a parallel in the *Catena*.

44. *ST* III, q. 44, a. 3, ad 1–4.

45. Ad 1: *Cat. in Lc* 4:28–30 (Morard #832); ad 2: *Cat. in Mc* 8:22–26 (Morard #628) and *Cat. in Io* 2:5–11 (Morard #331); ad 3: *Cat. in Io* 5:14–18a (Morard #705); and *Cat. in Mt* 9:1–8 (Morard #1693); ad 4: *Cat. in Mt* 9:27–31 (Morard #1803). Moreover, one of these references is mistaken: the quotation on Jn 2:5–11 at *ST* III, q. 44, a. 3, ad 2, has been attributed Victor of Antioch. The same mistaken attribution occurs in the *Catena* (Morard #331), suggesting that it served as Thomas's source. It is much less likely that Thomas would have made such a mistake if he had been referring to the *originalia* of Chrysostom.

crucifixion (since Mt 27:44 mentions "thieves" insulting Christ, which would seem to contradict Luke's version of the good thief rebuking the bad). Thomas creates a composite citation, comprising excerpts from Chrysostom's *Contra Iudaeos et Gentiles*, his *Homily on Matthew 87*, and his *Homily on John 85*; the same combination appears in the *Catena on Luke*.[46] The parallel suggests that it served as an easy reference for Thomas as he composed this section. If this is the case, we can begin to see Thomas working out the details of his presentation on the life of Christ by drawing more extensively on patristic sources, especially Chrysostom.

As in the *Catena*, Thomas's citation of Chrysostom in *ST* III, qq. 27–59, shows that he has a firm grasp of the characteristic features of his source's thought. For *ST* III, q. 58, a. 4, ad 4, we find Chrysostom invoked to respond to whether it was proper to Christ alone to sit at the right hand of the Father; Thomas quotes Chrysostom and includes the characteristic term *condescendens* (συγκατάβασις) to explain Christ's response to the sons of Zebedee's request. In *ST* III, q. 27, a. 4, which I discuss below, Thomas cites Chrysostom's indictment of *inanis gloria*, a vice frequently condemned in works such as *De Inani Gloria et de Educandis Liberis*.

Thomas's Use of Chrysostom on Christ's Life as Teaching

As I suggested in the use of Chrysostom in the *Catena*, closer attention to Thomas's use of Chrysostom in the *Tertia Pars* shows a special preference for Chrysostom as a source for the pedagogical aims of Christ's *acta et passa*. In *ST* III, q. 45, a. 3—whether the witnesses to the Transfiguration were fittingly chosen—we find a thorough and continuous use of Chrysostom in explaining the presence of Moses and Elijah at the Transfiguration. Here, Thomas appropriates an extended excerpt from *Catena on Matthew*.[47] Each of the five reasons he supplies relates to the teaching motive of the Incarnation: that the "difference between servants and the Lord might appear" (*appareat*); to show that Moses was the giver of the Law and Elijah was zealous for the glory of the Lord in response to those Jews (*excluditur calumnia*) who claimed that Christ was a transgressor of the Law and a blasphemer of God; to show (*ostendat*) that he had power over life and death; to strengthen (*confirmaret*) the hearts of his disciples; and because he wanted his disciples to emulate (*volebat ut discipuli eius*

---

46. *Cat. in Lc* 23:33 (Morard #3510).
47. *Cat. in Mt* 17:1–4 (Morard #2744).

aemularentur) the meekness of Moses and the zeal of Elijah. Each of the reasons underscores the teaching aims of the Word's actions.

The language of "showing" and indicating "so that you might know" appears frequently in Aquinas's citations from Chrysostom. Throughout q. 46, on the Passion of Christ, Chrysostom's name appears often as Thomas explains the instructive ends of the crucifixion. Hence in *ST* III, q. 46, a. 10, ad 2, Chrysostom is invoked to explain why Christ's execution in the outdoors was fitting: the location teaches (*ut scias*) that Christ was offered for all and not for the Jews alone.[48] In *ST* III, q. 46, a. 9, ad 1, Christ's taking the Passover with his disciples shows (*demonstrans*) that he was not contrary to the Law until his final day.[49] In addition, citations from Chrysostom are much less common in the sections where Christ is not primarily "teaching," for instance, at the moment of his death. Hence, while Chrysostom may not be central to articulating the mystery of the Incarnation, he is essential to Thomas's explanation of the pedagogical end of the actions and sufferings of Christ.

Chrysostom's primary role as a guide for the life and works of Christ might also explain Thomas's willingness to correct his sources when they appear contrary to the faith.[50] There may be more room to disagree, as it were, on issues that do not pertain to the doctrine of the Incarnation itself. Hence in an often-noted reference, when Thomas discusses Mary's preservation from all actual sin in *ST* III, q. 27, a. 4, he considers Chrysostom's claim that Mary demonstrated vainglory when she spoke up from the crowds at Matthew 12:47 and at Cana (Jn 2:3). Thomas concludes that Chrysostom "went too far" (*excessit*) in these statements, a rare admission that one of his authorities was mistaken.[51] And for *ST* III, q. 59,

---

48. "Noluit dominus pati sub tecto, non in templo Iudaico, ne Iudaei subtraherent sacrificium salutare, ne putares pro illa tantum plebe oblatum. Et ideo foras civitatem, foras muros, ut scias sacrificium esse commune quod totius terrae est oblatio, quod communis est purificatio."

49. "Demonstrans quod usque ad ultimum diem non erat contrarius legi," citing *Homily 81 on Matthew*; likewise see *ST* III, q. 51, a. 3, on whether the body of Christ in the sepulcher was *incineratum*, where Aquinas quotes Chrysostom on the aim of the action: *ut noscas*.

50. Compare Thomas's correction of Augustine's reference to Christ as *homo dominicus*, which Augustine had already corrected in his own *Retractationes*; *ST* III, q. 16, a. 3, s.c.

51. *ST* III, q. 27, a. 4, ad 3. Here, Thomas also attempts to "save" Chrysostom's statement by suggesting that it might be understood to refer to the vainglory perceived (inaccurately) by the onlookers. But Thomas's approach is quite different from Kevin Madigan's claim about medieval use of patristic sources: "Medieval inheritors of deeply problematic opinions in the orthodox tradition, if they wished to preserve them somehow for subsequent use, had utterly

a. 2, there is extensive engagement with Chrysostom regarding Christ's judiciary power belonging to him *secundum quod est homo*. The disagreement with Chrysostom allows Thomas to draw on his conclusions regarding Christ's "capital grace" (which Thomas has already treated at *ST* III, q. 8, a. 1) to explain how the Word uses his assumed human nature for the purpose of exercising judgment. Thomas seems more willing to correct the statements of Chrysostom than those of his other authorities.

Chrysostom's Significance for the Composition of the *Tertia Pars*

Thomas's growing dependence on extended exegetical excerpts from Chrysostom corresponds to the basic structure of his work on the life of Christ. Comparing Thomas's sources in the questions on the Resurrection in the *Tertia Pars* (qq. 53–56) to those in the *Scriptum* (d. 21, q. 2) on the same topic, Pim Valkenberg argues that Thomas in the later work depends much less on many of the systematic-theological sources (e.g., the *Summa Alexandrini* and the *Summa Aurea* of William of Auxerre) that he employed in the earlier work and more directly on Scripture.[52] Moreover, Thomas increasingly tends to cite his *auctoritates* directly rather than through the medium of a gloss. This trend reflects the influence of direct engagement with the Fathers in compiling the *Catena*, which especially informs Thomas's method in composing qq. 27–59 on the life of Christ. Even more than in the earlier questions of the *Tertia Pars*, the Scripture narrative—that is, the sequence of the Gospels—provides the backbone of these questions, which in turn serve an almost exegetical purpose. Thomas's liberal use of patristic quotations render these later portions something of an extended commentary; one might even suggest that they resemble a second *Catena*, with extended glosses serving to elucidate the literal and spiritual meaning of the moments in the life of Christ in order to refute heretics and to support the Catholic truth. Recognizing the exegetical emphasis of these questions, we have a better sense of how the earlier questions on the mechanics of the Incarnation function as a "control" on the reading of the later questions and are informed by them

---

to evacuate the intention and meaning of an author's suspicious words." "On the High-Medieval Reception of Hilary of Poitiers's Anti-'Arian' Opinion: A Case Study of Discontinuity in Christian Thought," *Journal of Religion* 78 (1998): 217. Thomas is willing to entertain and reject Chrysostom's view, even if he offers a manner of hospitable interpretation.

52. Valkenberg, *Words of the Living God*, 206–9.

in turn. As Gilles Emery has demonstrated, in the *Summa Theologiae*, Thomas often concludes extensive treatments of Catholic doctrine with an investigation of the *dispensatio*, that is, a question treating the scriptural record of what God actualizes temporally.[53] But, as Emery makes clear, this in no way implies that the discussion of the narrative is just an "appendix" or an afterword to a doctrinal dispute. Rather, according to the *ordo disciplinae* in the *Summa Theologiae*, Thomas begins with the scriptural doctrine in terms of the *theologia* before proceeding to the scriptural *dispensatio*, from Christ in his nature to Christ in relation to us. At the same time, according to the order of discovery, we come to knowledge of theology through the scriptural *dispensatio*. We come to know Christ in relation to us before we know him in his divine nature. Scripture controls both projects, which differ only in their respective relation to human knowing. Thomas's use of Chrysostom reveals a similar interpenetration: in the doctrine of the early questions, which serves to clarify the precise nature of the what is at stake in the Incarnation, Chrysostom is relatively absent. And yet, in the order of discovery, the "exegetical" Chrysostom of *ST* III, qq. 27–59, illuminates the doctrine in qq. 1–26 precisely because he demonstrates the *dispensatio* aimed to *instruct* us for our salvation. Chrysostom is not at a "decorative" afterthought, but rather a sure guide in leading the reader to grasp the motive of the Incarnation.

Conclusion

We should not exaggerate the influence of Chrysostom's preaching and exegesis on Thomas to the extent that we would suggest that Thomas simply reprises his predecessor's claims over the course of the *Tertia Pars*. Thomas cites an awesome range of authors. Moreover, many of the insights and Christological claims that Thomas makes cannot be found in Chrysostom at all. Hence Chrysostom never examines the distinctions between the divine principle of the Incarnation and the terminus of the union in the Person of the Word in anything like a Thomistic grammar. Much of Chrysostom's Christology, unlike that of Thomas, is explicitly polemical, directed against the excesses of the Arians and the Apollinar-

---

53. See Gilles Emery, "*Theologia* and *Dispensatio*: The Centrality of the Divine Missions in St. Thomas's Trinitarian Theology," *The Thomist* 74 (2010): 515–61; and "Trinitarian Theology as Spiritual Exercise," in *Aquinas the Augustinian*, ed. Michael Dauphinais, Barry David, and Matthew Levering (Washington, DC: Catholic University of America Press, 2007), 1–40.

ians, and also pre-Nestorian.[54] Hence Thomas could not have generated his distinctive account of the nature of the Incarnation on the basis of Chrysostom alone. But the basic differences between Thomas's and Chrysostom's Christological project throw into relief their common point of emphasis: by means of his conjoined humanity, the Incarnate Word acted and suffered in order to show us how to act and suffer.[55]

Hence the singular source for Thomas's account of the Incarnation and the life of Christ in the *Tertia Pars* is Scripture, particularly the four Gospels.[56] As scholars continue to examine Thomas's innovative and consistent reliance on patristic sources in composing his theology, we do well to remember that Thomas was, in many ways, remarkably "original" only insofar as he was constantly returning to the biblical origins to refresh and renew his theology. While Chrysostom stands out among Thomas's aids in reading the Bible, from Thomas's perspective, only the Word of God can determine the place and function of all other authorities.

54. For an overview, see Mel Lawrenz, *The Christology of John Chrysostom* (Lewiston, NY: Mellen University Press, 1996).

55. Cf. *In Ioan.* c. 11, lect. 6: "omnis Christi actio nostra est instructio"; on Christ as the exemplar cause of our life of grace, see Dominic Legge, *The Trinitarian Christology of St Thomas Aquinas* (Oxford: Oxford University Press, 2017), 93–96.

56. *ST* I, q. 1, a. 8.

7

Analogy in Thomas and the
Pseudo-Areopagite

STEPHEN M. FIELDS, SJ

The much-touted problem of "ontotheology" in contemporary theology shows us why it is vital to maintain the equipoise of the apophatic and kataphatic dimensions of God's relations with the world. Although ontotheology's deepest modern roots lie in Kant's preclusion of metaphysics, they have been nourished more recently by Heidegger's avowal that Western metaphysics reduces the incomprehensibly infinite to the order of beings. As so defined, ontotheology is idolatrous on the one hand even as, on the other hand, it causes us to forget the rich symbolism of historical beings in their own right. Against these errors, both Protestants and Catholics are tending to envisage God, along with Paul Tillich, as the apophatic "abyss" beyond all symbols, such that, as in Jean-Luc Marion, God's act of being is not being at all.[1] Roger Haight's *Jesus, Symbol of God*, for instance, claims to offer a contemporary Christology that replaces Chalcedon's hypostasis of the Logos, which it judges anachronistic. The result, however, produces an essentially adoptionist Christology that attenuates, even eliminates, the intimacy of the divine's subsumption of

---

1. Paul Tillich, "Theology and Symbolism," in *Religious Symbolism*, ed. F. Ernest Johnson (New York: Institute for Religious and Social Studies, 1955), 107–16, at 114–15; Jean-Luc Marion, "Thomas Aquinas and Onto-theo-logy," in *Essential Writings*, ed. Kevin Hart, trans. B. Gendreau et al. (New York: Fordham University Press, 2013), 288–311, at 310.

materiality.[2] Louis-Marie Chauvet's *Symbole et sacrement: Une relecture sacramentelle de l'existence chrétienne* argues that the sacraments communicate grace merely by leaving a divine "trace" without causality.[3] David Power's *Sacrament: The Language of God's Giving*, while affirming that words communicate God's being through sacred signs, conspicuously lacks a natural relation between speech and reality.[4] These thinkers leave human reason gaping in an open-ended apophasis without an analogical bridge linking finite and infinite being.

Marion, for his part, aware that sacramentality constitutes the heart of the Catholic vision of reality, knows that a replacement is needed for this bridge to explain God's providential action, at least in the world of grace. He finds it in the Holy Spirit, who can cross "definitive and unsurpassable" distances, thus allowing the divine to mediate the holy in symbols to the faithful.[5] Significantly, the loss for Marion of a natural analogy between finite and infinite being for the Spirit's action to baptize seems taken for granted, and this is precisely the problem. Without it, we may well wonder how Christian theology can develop a viable hermeneutics by which it can do its work, which is to render the truths of revelation credibly intelligent to both believer and nonbeliever alike. Without a robust philosophical analogy, truth itself becomes an equivocal term, leaving only some type of fideism to warrant theology's claims. Because fideism truncates reason's created powers, Catholicism has traditionally viewed it as diminishing the rich meaning of "understanding" in Augustine's foundational principle *Crede, ut intellegas*.[6]

My purpose here is twofold. First, I show how two thinkers from the tradition, one Eastern and patristic and the other Western and high scholastic, balance the apophatic and kataphatic to fashion a middle ground between ontotheology and fideism. In the late fifth- or early sixth-century

2. Roger Haight, *Jesus, Symbol of God* (Maryknoll, NY: Orbis, 1999).

3. Louis-Marie Chauvet, *Symbole et sacrement: Une relecture sacramentelle de l'existence chrétienne* (Paris: Éditions du Cerf, 1987), 214–16.

4. David Power, *Sacrament: The Language of God's Giving* (New York: Crossroad, 1999).

5. Jean-Luc Marion, "The Prototype and the Image," trans. James K. A. Smith, in Marion, *Essential Writings*, 285.

6. Augustine, *Tractates on the Gospel of John* 29.6. See also Avery Dulles, "The Cognitive Basis of Faith," *Philosophy and Theology* 10, no. 1 (1998): 19–31; and "Criteria of Catholic Theology," *Communio: International Catholic Review* 22 (1995): 305–15. For an elaboration of the current chapter's introduction, see Stephen M. Fields, *Analogies of Transcendence: An Essay on Nature, Grace and Modernity* (Washington, DC: Catholic University of America Press, 2016), 253–69.

corpus attributed to Denys the Pseudo-Areopagite, Hans Urs von Balthasar finds an "explosive yet constructive originality" that adapts the analogy of being to the analogy of faith.[7] In Thomas Aquinas, we find a skillful integration of the analogies of proper proportionality and intrinsic attribution that makes reason capable of true judgments in both nature and grace.[8] Second, I consider more broadly the Common Doctor's relation to the great doctor of the mystical ascent, given that both thinkers share roots in the Neoplatonic metaphysics of participation.

According to Balthasar, whose reading of Denys guides this part of my study, the Areopagite sees the emerging world as an artifact entailing an analogy between its own spatiotemporality and its sublimely generating source. The cosmos of being dynamically proceeds from and returns to God, thus constituting a manifestation of its hidden origin. Between finite and infinite, this analogy establishes a *simultaneous* relation of affirmation and negation. Although God remains immanent in the world, all predicates drawn from it that affirm God must be denied, even to the point of "frenzy," because divinity exceeds rational reduction (165, no. 43, referring to "the end of the *Mystical Theology*"). Nonetheless, in Denys, even more than in Plotinus on whom he so depends, the mind's ascent to God by means of apophasis "is kindled only" by God's self-effusive descent to the world (165).[9] In fact, Denys underscores this descent so strongly that "any flight from the world is unthinkable, even for the most exalted mysticism" (166). As a result, Balthasar boldly asserts that Denys resists definition as "the advocate and architect of all negative theology, the mystical iconoclast, as he is generally thought to be" (179).

If the divine kataphasis establishes the analogy of being, still, because God's reality is utterly "inimitable," God and the world constitute a "like unlikeness and an unlike likeness" (180, 202).[10] This paradox, Balthasar

7. Hans Urs von Balthasar, "Denys," in *Studies in Theological Styles: Clerical Styles*, ed. John Riches, trans. Andrew Louth et al., vol. 2, *The Glory of the Lord: A Theological Aesthetics*, ed. Joseph Fessio SJ et al., 7 vols. (San Francisco, CA: Ignatius Press, 1984–91), 144–210, at 147; "Denys" is cited in the text.

8. Étienne Gilson, "Cajétan et existence," *Tijdschrift voor Philosophie* 15 (1953): 267–86; George P. Klubertanz, *St. Thomas Aquinas on Analogy: A Textual Analysis and Systematic Synthesis* (Chicago: Loyola University Press, 1960), 13.

9. Balthasar mentions other influences on Denys, like his teacher Hierotheus, and the Alexandrians Gregory of Nyssa, Philo, and Proclus. About these, Balthasar pays a moving tribute to Denys, who "does not want to borrow, but rather to return what has been borrowed to its true owner" (i.e., the true God revealed in Christ; 208).

10. Denys, *Epistolae* 2, 9.1, in J.-P. Migne, ed., *Patrologia cursus completus*, vol. 3, *Series*

claims, results from the distinction that Denys draws between God's self-communication, which grounds the finite order, and the reality of God, who communicates. God communicates being to the visible reality through, or means of, his own reality. This act of divine self-revelation bridges finite and infinite and thus establishes the simultaneous similarity and dissimilarity between them. At once, this act flows forth from God while it creates the cosmos that, in its contingency, stands radically other than God. Consequently, God's reality instrumentally causes creation and thus provides the basis for the divine names. But because creation exists "by God's *allowing* it *to share* ... that 'which cannot be shared,'" creation participates in God "'while not participating'" (186).[11] Here, in my opinion, Balthasar helps us to glimpse where for the first time Denys introduces something new into the schema of Plotinus: a notion of divine freedom radically other than that of the great student of Ammonius Saccas. Accordingly, we see what in Denys is perhaps the precise point of transition from the analogy of being to the analogy of faith. Through the mediation of grace alone "can the sensible symbols speak of God's" authentic freedom. In so doing, these symbols allow us to peer "through the sacred veil of time to perceive in rapt contemplation the eternal mysteries" (153, 184).

Denys develops his innovative doctrine of God by subordinating being to eros, by which he means extroverted love. Eros subsists in "equal rank and the same meaning" as the good and the beautiful (189, referring to *DN* IV). He thus fuses into Christian monotheism three predicates that Plotinus, by contrast, distributes between the One (the good) and Nous (being and beauty), even as he adds a fourth (eros).[12] In deference to the Plotinian One, Denys affirms that the name of God embracing all being is the good. But "the good," he avers, "is celebrated ... as beauty" because goodness "causes the consonance and splendor of all."[13] Moreover, the divine goodness is eros because it does not "abide in itself but

---

graeca, 161 vols. (Paris, 1857–66), 1068A–1069A, 1105D. Where available, Denys is cited with the pagination from Migne in parenthesis.

11. *Div. Nom.* II, 5 (644A), V, 8 (824C), XI, 6 (953C). For an analysis of the role of participation in Balthasar's study of Denys, see Junius Johnson, *Christ and Analogy: The Christocentric Metaphysics of Hans Urs von Balthasar* (Minneapolis, MN: Fortress Press, 2013), 91–95.

12. "Denys avoids speaking in a Plotinian way of a world-soul" (Psyche) (161).

13. *Div. Nom.* IV, 7 (701C), in Pseudo-Dionysius the Areopagite, *The Divine Names and Mystical Theology*, trans. John D. Jones (Milwaukee, WI: Marquette University Press, 1980), 138.

has moved [to] the generative thrusting forth of all beings," especially the Incarnation, its "preeminent ecstasis."[14] Eros, goodness, and beauty thus constitute "'the cause of all initiation,'" even as they "express the power of the primordial Godhead in radiance and affirmation" (196, 191).[15] It therefore follows that eros, goodness, and beauty mediate the being that creates; in them being subsists, and from them flow "'both being and well-being to all that is.'"[16] If God's goodness is loving, then God is free. If eros generates being, then being is freely loving. In the relation among goodness, beauty, eros, and being, Denys incorporates the philosophical analogy into the analogy of faith. In so doing, he augments what Plotinus, transforming Plato, bequeathed to Denys. Indeed, claims Balthasar, Denys's "Christianizing of the Neo-Platonic *milieu* [is but] a side-effect of his own properly theological endeavor" (149).

We see this Christianizing perhaps most forcefully in the adaptations that Denys's innovative genius makes to the Platonic ascent of the mind to transcendence. In its mounting ecstasy driven by eros, the soul, in contrast to Plato and Plotinus, imitates the free ecstasy of the divine, "which out of eros goes out of itself into the multiplicity of the world" (205). God's eros confers an aesthetic significance on creation absent in Platonism. Although Plotinus would agree that all existents "'carry within themselves ... the image of their causes [in the good and the beautiful, which] are transcendent to their effects,'" still Denys, by deriving all reality from the divine freedom, makes human beings capable of a mutual relation of love with their supreme artisan.[17] If this relation is consummated when the soul's ascent enters into mysticism, then, as Balthasar notes, Denys stands "far removed from Plato's 'conversion' from aesthetics to philosophy." By this, Balthasar means that any ascent into the transcendent "'much more'" can never abandon humanity's radical engagement with "form and what it expresses" (168). Even as the apophatic mystic is "peeling off" the layers of sensible existence, he must realize that God exceeds apophasis even as God exceeds kataphasis (206). Crucially, therefore, the ascent of the analogy of faith "demands both a deeper penetration *into* the [sen-

14. *Div. Nom.* IV, 10 (708B), in Jones, *Divine Names*, 142–43; Jones, "Introduction," in *Divine Names*, 15–103, at 59. Nonetheless, Balthasar refers to "Roques' systematic account," claiming that "christology appears as a kind of appendix" in Denys (162).

15. Denys, *De Coelesti Hierarchia* III.1 (164D). Citations of this text take vol. 58 of *Sources chrétiennes* as a basis: René Roques et al., eds. and trans., *La hiérarchie céleste* (Paris: Éditions du Cerf, 1958). Roques follows Migne's numbering and keeps to his lines.

16. Denys, *De Ecclesiastica Hierarchia* I.3 (373CD), 200.

17. *Div. Nom.* II, 8 (645 CD), 168–69, no. 52

sible form of beings] and also a more sublime transcendence *beyond* it." These two acts "are more fully integrated, the more perfectly [each act is] achieved" (169).

Yet how is this integration achieved? For sure, Denys posits the immanence of the incomprehensible in the comprehensible, because God, who transcends comprehension, "makes himself comprehensible in his communications" (185). Nonetheless, Balthasar subtly diagnoses in this paradox the same tension between the mind's flight to the eternal and its return into history that emerges in Plato. In Denys, both humanity's greatness and tragedy entail its immersion "in the aesthetics of the world of images [forms] and at the same time" the mind's irresistible exigency "to dissolve all images in the light of the unimaginable" (179). In Plato, the resolution entails an ontologically univocal merging between finite and infinite. (We see this in the *Timaeus, Laws,* and *Epinomis*.[18]) In Plotinus, it entails the mystical passing-over of the soul from form in its return to the One who transcends being, truth, and beauty.[19] Christianity precludes both solutions because, as Balthasar claims, no immediate knowledge of God, however analogous, is possible, at least in this life, not even for Moses and the Apostle Paul (206–7). Par excellence, the Incarnation mediates divine knowledge when it suddenly radiates "into the darkness of human existence" precisely to embrace form and give it divine value (193). In Christianity, therefore, philosophy left to itself remains impotent to give surcease to the dialectic in the core of Platonism.

Only the sacraments of the Church can lift the veil covering being's conundrum (166). In the Eucharist, for instance, the consecration of the natural elements results in an apophatic "destruction of the image for the sake of the pure content"—the real presence of Christ. When they are consumed and the finality of the sacrament is realized, a "mystical union" ensues that subsumes the human into the divine (183). Ultimately, then, Denys does accomplish the merging of the One and the many that Plato and Plotinus effect by pure metaphysics. But in Christianity, this quasi-univocity can only obtain by the One's freely self-revealed eros. As Balthasar trenchantly concludes, Denys adamantly resists any naive apophatic demythologizing, whether of the Eucharist or the Scriptures, that would supersede the kataphatic media sensibly containing the message (180–81). Thus Denys's

---

18. Hans Urs von Balthasar, "Plato," in *The Realm of Metaphysics in Antiquity*, trans. Brian McNeil, CRV, in *Glory of the Lord*, 4:166–215, at 210, 213, 214–15, citing *Timaeus* 33D, 34B; *Epinomis* 991E–992B.

19. Hans Urs von Balthasar, "Plotinus," in *Realm of Metaphysics*, 280–313, at 304–6.

Christian modification of Neoplatonism expands nature by suffusing it with grace, even as both nature and grace each retains its integrity.[20]

Now I turn to Thomas, who balances the kataphatic and apophatic by harmonizing the analogies of proper proportionality and intrinsic attribution. This harmony results from the Angelic Doctor's integration of an Aristotelian metaphysics of knowledge into a Neoplatonic metaphysics of participation. In the analogy of proper proportionality, the same quality is predicated of different subjects, because this quality belongs intrinsically to each subject, although in a manner appropriate to each. Thus, as Aristotle observes, soul is properly predicated of humanity, animals, and plants, although in differing levels of potential.[21] In intrinsic attribution, a quality is predicated principally of one subject (the prime analogate) and then of other subjects, because these bear a relation to the principal subject. Thus health is properly predicated of human beings and only secondarily of medicine, food, and blood because these enhance human health.[22]

The Common Doctor's analogy deals with the attribution of the transcendentals: being, truth, goodness, and beauty that determine finite realities but do not, in and of themselves, admit any finite determination. Consequently, they are often called "perfections." In the analogy of proper proportionality, the transcendentals intrinsically inhere in both infinite and finite modes of reality. In other words, God may be said to be good in his own right, and so may all finite realities simply because they exist. In the analogy of intrinsic attribution, God, as reality's infinite mode, is the prime analogate or principal subject of the perfections. As the unique being whose essence is infinite existence, God realizes the transcendentals in no determined sense. By contrast, finite modes of being embody the transcendentals according to their specifically determined essences. Thus, although a perfection inheres intrinsically in a finite essence, this essence embodies the perfection only as an image or likeness of the divine archetype.[23] According

20. For an elaboration of the first part of this chapter, see Stephen M. Fields, SJ, "From Classic to Patristic: Balthasar, Rahner, and the Origins of Analogy," in *Ressourcement after Vatican II: Essays in Honor of Joseph Fessio, SJ*, ed. Nicholas J. Healy Jr. and Matthew Levering (San Francisco, CA: Ignatius Press, in press).

21. Aristotle, *De Anima* 414e, 28*ff.*

22. Frederick Ferré, "The Logic of Analogy," in *The Challenge of Religion: Contemporary Readings in Philosophy of Religion*, ed. Frederick Ferré et al. (New York: Seabury Press, 1982), 104–13, at 106–7.

23. For Aquinas's treatment of the relation between intrinsic attribution and the metaphysics of participation, see *De Pot.* q. 3, a. 5; q. 7, a. 7, ad 2; *Summa contra Gentiles* II, chap. 15, 53; III, chap. 66, 97; *ST* I, q. 3, a. 8; q. 44, a. 1; q. 47, a. 1; q. 75, a. 5, ad 1 and 4; q. 79, a. 4; *In*

to the analogy of intrinsic attribution, any determined instance of a perfection implies the existence of its unlimited prime analogate.[24]

In *ST* I, q. 13, Thomas asserts that divine perfections are, in the first instance, relative. They pertain to God's operations in the world. They are inferred from their sensible manifestations in the order of historical realities. On this basis, they can be applied analogously to God as the most perfect and real being. When they are, such attributes are no longer relative but absolute. They pertain to God as he exists in himself. Precisely because the empirical world serves as the propaedeutic for divine predication, an important question arises: How can the relative attributes, conditioned by sensuous experience, be affirmed of God, when all we know of God's essence is *that* it is, not *what* it is? In *ST* I, q. 3, Thomas says that such an affirmation can be made literally. What is signified by the name goodness belongs to God and to finite objects, but the mode by which goodness signifies these beings differs. It signifies a creature in the sense of finitude, but God in the sense of infinity. Moreover, the perfection applies to God in its primary sense, asserts Thomas, because he possesses it with universal necessity. It applies to creatures only in a derived sense in virtue of their dependence and contingency.[25]

Stressing the difference in the mode of an attribute's signification allows Thomas to affirm a predicate's literal application to all subjects without collapsing infinite and finite modes of being. Because the predicate is neither univocal nor equivocal, it avoids pantheism on the one hand and blind fideism on the other, which would deny that a divine predicate possesses some epistemic relation to human understanding. But when Thomas is pressed as to the warranting ground of the differing mode of the predicate's signification, interpretive problems begin. Herbert McCabe, for instance, finds this ground in Thomas's belief that things point beyond themselves to the "no thing" that altogether transcends them. Thus, because words signify things, words can point beyond their finite mode of predication. Still, McCabe insists, it does not necessarily follow that our finite predicate should have the same literal meaning in God.[26]

Joannem, Prooemium; *Quodlibetales* 2.2.1. All are cited in *New Catholic Encyclopedia* (*NCE*), 1st ed., s.v. "Analogy," 1:464b, and in *Aquinas on Analogy*, appendices I and II.

24. See especially Aquinas's analysis of the perfection "living": *ST* I, q. 4, a. 2, in *NCE*, s.v. "Analogy," 1:465b.

25. Wilbur M. Urban, "Symbolism as a Theological Principle in St Thomas," in *Language and Reality: The Philosophy of Language and the Principles of Symbolism* (London: Allen and Unwin, 1939), 748–50.

26. Herbert McCabe, "Analogy," Appendix 4, in Thomas Aquinas, *Summa Theologiae*,

In response, Thomas denies that we can conceive any adequate notion of the divine perfections and that their predication depends on the affirmation of God's infinite existence.[27] The ground of this affirmation lies in the mind's *excessus*, by which it negates the finite to affirm the infinite. Excessus operating at the third degree of abstraction, which surpasses the abstraction of forms and of mathematics, gives us "an objectively valid knowledge" of God without representing God in quiddities and concepts.[28] In further seeking the ground of this excessus, another important question for interpretation arises: Can the human mind affirm universal propositions about infinite being without some manner of intrinsic connection to the transcendent absolute? In other words, we could well argue that, unless reason has a final cause that is implicitly infinite, it is impossible to claim that the predication of the names of God can rise above the mutable datum of their empirical ground. Thus, as Kant claims, while the predicates of God serve the useful purpose of satisfying the demands of reason's own immanent operations, they spuriously evanesce as analogously divine. I do not pursue this question here, but I have addressed it in detail elsewhere.[29]

As a summary, let us advance two theses that define the balance of the apophatic and the kataphatic in Thomas's doctrine of analogy. It is vital to note that these theses are necessarily dovetailed, because for Thomas, truth is the *adequatio rei et intellectus*: the conforming of the subject's mind to the objective reality that it knows. First, there is what we might call the deductive thesis. God is good, and finite realities are good, each as a result of its own act of existence. Yet God's infinite essence means that he is the prime analogate of goodness, because all other realities owe the

---

vol. 3, trans. and ed. English-speaking Dominican Provinces, 60 vols. (New York: McGraw-Hill, 1964–66), 106–7.

27. *NCE*, s.v. "Analogy," 1:465b, referring esp. to *ST* I, q. 4, a. 2.

28. Joseph Maréchal, *A Maréchal Reader*, ed. and trans. Joseph Donceel (New York: Herder and Herder, 1970), 149: selections from Maréchal, *Le Thomisme devant la philosophie critique*, vol. 5, *Le point de départ de la métaphysique* (Brussels: Édition universelle, 1926 [2nd ed. 1949]).

29. See Stephen M. Fields, SJ, "Contraries in One: Contingency, Analogy, and God in Transcendental Thomism," in *The Discovery of Being and Thomas Aquinas: Philosophical and Theological Perspectives*, ed. Christopher M. Cullen, SJ, and Franklin T. Harkins (Washington, DC: Catholic University of America Press, in press); and idem, "The Reception of Aquinas in Twentieth-Century Transcendental Thomism," in *The Oxford Handbook to the Reception of Aquinas*, ed. Marcus Plested and Matthew Levering (Oxford: Oxford University Press, in press). For a different perspective, see Steven A. Long, *Analogia Entis: On the Analogy of Being, Metaphysics, and the Act of Faith* (Notre Dame, IN: University of Notre Dame Press, 2011), esp. the final chapter.

cause of their existence to God, in whom they participate as image to Archetype. This participation implies no necessary emanation (as in Plotinus); on the contrary, it is free and spontaneous (as in Denys). Accordingly, God's creative act kataphatically establishes all subordinate grades of reality. These grades include even pure potency, as Thomas affirms in *Summa contra Gentiles* and *De Potentia*.[30] Yet, because it is a law of metaphysics that all determination entails negation, God's kataphatic act that establishes finite essences entails an apophatic difference, distance, and distinction between them and his infinite essence.[31] The analogy of the transcendental perfections is thus constituted by the mutual conditioning of kataphasis and apophasis whose tension is ontologically synthesized.

Second, there is what we might call the inductive thesis. It concerns the mind's act of excessus. This act is the condition for the possibility of the mind's affirming the analogical unity of intrinsic attribution and proper proportionality. Excessus effects the mind's affirmation of God as the prime analogate of the transcendentals, *precisely on the basis of* the mind's knowledge of their existence as finite objects. Significantly, this affirmation results from the mind's negating our finite grasp of the perfections when they are predicated of the Absolute. Through this negation, they are "*corrected*," so to speak, to make a true judgment about God.[32] In other words, in the very knowledge of finite perfections precisely as relative, we have some knowledge of their divine term precisely as universal. Put another way, in the very knowledge of contingency, we have knowledge of necessity. As Thomas reminds us in *De Potentia*, for instance: when we know God, we know "that he exceeds all that which we should be able to conceive of him."[33] In short, in Thomas's analogy, the apophatic moment of excessus is sandwiched between the kataphatic judgments of finite reality and its transcendental properties on the one hand and of infinite reality and its transcendental properties on the other hand, which infinite reality is apophatically irreducible to quiddities and concepts.

Having studied analogy in Denys and Thomas, let us now consider more broadly the relation between the Areopagite's thought and Aquinas's natural theology.[34] One immediate contrast emerges in his *Commen-*

---

30. *Summa contra Gentiles* II, chaps. 45–46; *De Pot.*, q. 3, a. 1, ad 12.
31. Hegel attributes this law to Spinoza, but it is surely implicit in Socrates; see G. W. F. Hegel, *Hegel's Logic*, trans. William Wallace (Oxford: Clarendon Press, 1975), 135.
32. Maréchal, *Reader*, 144.
33. *De Pot.*, q. 7, a. 5, ad. 14, in Maréchal, *Reader*, 145.
34. This section of this chapter is guided by Fran O'Rourke, *Pseudo-Dionysius and the*

tary on Denys's *Divine Names*. The Angelic Doctor understands as a positive quality the human mind's disposition to finite realities as the basis for all knowledge, whereas Denys sees it as a restriction (32). Thomas, although influenced by the maxim that he takes from Aristotle (nothing obtains in the intellect unless first presented to sensibility), nonetheless leans heavily on Denys when considering how the order of creation leads us to God. A trenchant passage from his *Commentary on the Sentences* of Peter Lombard illustrates this debt:

> Since a creature proceeds by exemplarity from God himself as from a cause which is by analogy in some way similar (because every creature imitates him according to the possibility of its nature), it is possible to arrive at God from creatures by three ways: causality, remotion, eminence. (*In I Sent.*, d. 3, q. 1, a. 3; O'Rourke, 41)

Of key importance here is the use of the threefold mode of the mind's ascent to God in *DN* 7, 3, to shed light on our previous discussion of Thomas's doctrine of analogy.

DN 7, 3, states that we mount to God "through the removal and excess of all things in the cause of all things."[35] For both thinkers, causality, removal, and excess operate as a synergy. By causation, we come, by means of finite realities, to affirm God as their absolute origin. But this affirmation must be purified so that, as Thomas commenting on Denys says, "none of those things which we observe in the order of creatures [are judged] to be God" (33).[36] Purification obtains as a moment properly called remotion (or removal), but it constitutes an intrinsic moment of *excessus*. This judges God's eminence as utterly transcending anything finite. In further commenting on *Divine Names*, Aquinas refines Denys's analysis by discriminating between those predicates of finite realities that cannot be applied to the absolute being and the perfections. These admit of no finite determination and thus appositely may be applied to God, even though they are represented in contingent beings (34).

We might conclude, therefore, that the sensitivity to the equipoise of

---

Metaphysics of Aquinas (Leiden: Brill, 1992). Alasdair MacIntyre, commenting on the cover of the paperback edition (Notre Dame, IN: University of Notre Dame Press, 2005), calls this "one of the two or three most important books on Aquinas published in the last fifty years."

35. Translations henceforth of *De Divinis Nominibus* are O'Rourke's.

36. Aquinas, *Commentary on DN*, VII, iv, 729. In citing this text, the first number indicates the chapter and the second the *lectio*. The third refers to the paragraph in the Ceslaus Pera, ed., *Commentary* (Turn: Marietti, 1950).

the apophatic and kataphatic that hallmarks Aquinas is owing to Denys's differentiated formulation of the organic unity of the mind's ascent. Two further texts of Aquinas, when read together, reiterate this sensitivity. *ST* I, q. 13, when considering the name "God," gives us a "unique" account of the divine's absolute transcendence as "removed from all" things and therefore as "existing above all that is" (40). But this robust apophatic statement must be read in light of the previous question. In *ST* I, q. 12, a. 12, Aquinas nuances his well-known position that we know only *that* God is, not *what* God is. From the relation of God to his creatures, we can come to know "whatever must belong to the first cause of all things which is beyond all that is caused" (37). Thomas thus lays the ground for subsequently considering, like Denys, the attributes and names of God that are entailed in *causa sua*. The fact remains: if God considered in himself stands in splendid ontological isolation, God has nonetheless from all eternity decided to enter into relation with us. Consequently, as Denys so often insists, apophasis must be used against itself, even as it must qualify kataphasis. Moreover, knowing *that* but not *what* God is posits, of course, true knowledge, and therefore constitutes a kataphatic judgment of reality.

In light of our analysis thus far, the relation of Denys's threefold ascent to analogy in Aquinas should be clear enough. But a word is needed, however brief, about the ascent's relation to exemplarity and participation. As to exemplarity, God, says Aquinas in his commentary on *Divine Names*, "going further than Denys," brings things into being according to an order that obtains in the divine mind (VII, iv, 733; O'Rourke, 33). As a result, beings are constituted as imperfect images of their infinite archetypes (VII, iv, 727; O'Rourke, 33). Exemplarity is thus a mode of formal causality that establishes the condition for the possibility of the material and efficient causality of the world. For its part, participation is derived from exemplarity while constituting its counterpart. It denotes the act of being of the finite image insofar as it causally depends on the act of being of its divine archetype. It is thus because of participation that we are able to harness finite causality to ascend to God precisely by the threefold method.[37]

All our claims about the mutuality of the apophatic and kataphatic having been made, still we need to consider whether one dimension pre-

---

37. For the influence of Denys's view of participation on Aquinas, compare *Div. Nom.*, I, 7, 25–26, and *ST* I, q. 13, a. 4 (O'Rourke, *Pseudo-Dionysius and the Metaphysics of Aquinas*, 45).

dominates in our thinkers' assessment of the mind's divine knowledge. An argument can be made for the apophatic, but it must be properly framed. Both Denys and Thomas are bent on avoiding what, as Christians, they consider the error of Neoplatonism. Plotinus resolves the problem of the One and the many by conceiving the mind's ascent as a passing-over from all form in its return to the One who utterly transcends being, truth, and beauty. Although these perfections lead us to the ultimate horizon, intellect itself must be abandoned for the "'upward leap,'" the "'dreadful yearning'" of a solitary encounter.[38]

By contrast, the incarnate Word obviates all such radical apophasis because of its own kataphasis that, as Athanasius says, "being incorruptible, quickened and cleansed the body, which is in itself mortal."[39] He is implying that the entire finite order, created externally to God, is brought within God, thus conferring on it a theosis analogous to the hypostatic union.[40] Thus in both Denys and Thomas, whereas the divine essence is utterly unthinkable, still the end, goal, and purpose of the finite universe are nothing less than to serve as a gift "through which we may know" God (33). Consequently, as Balthasar emphasizes, for Denys, no ascent, however intense its mysticism, can be conceived as totally escaping the world of material form divinized by Christ. Yet even as reason, through grace, enjoys an intense intimacy with the self-communicated essence of God that permits it to peer through time's sacred veil, the mind can never dissolve all images in the light of the unimaginable transcendent much-more. In short, Denys's supple and subtle theology of aesthetic form demands, paradoxically, the priority of the apophatic *precisely as a moment within the kataphatic*. However the participating symbols reveal the archetype that they signify, they always remain media translucent in their communication.

The same thesis applies to Aquinas. In *ST* I, q. 12, a. 1, he avers, for instance: "When we say that God is non-existent, this does not mean that he does not exist in any manner whatsoever: but that he transcends everything which exists, insofar as he is his own being" (56). While it is true that God "subsists superior to his participation" by creatures, when "we

---

38. Plotinus, *Enneads*, V.5.4, V.7.34; cited in Balthasar, "Plotinus," 304–5.

39. Athanasius, *On the Incarnation of the Word*, s. 17, trans. Archibald Robertson, in *Christology of the Later Fathers*, ed. Edward Rochie Hardy (Philadelphia: Westminster Press), 55–110, at 71.

40. Karl Rahner, *The Christian Commitment: Essays in Pastoral Theology*, trans. Cecily Hastings (New York: Sheed and Ward, 1963), 49.

remove from him even 'being' itself," we do so not absolutely or equivo-cally, but insofar as being "is found in creatures" (*In I Sent.*, d. 8, q. 1, a. 1, ad 4; O'Rourke, 58). For Thomas, therefore, whereas negations of all di-vine qualities "are absolutely true," still affirmations of them are "not false" but "only relatively true" (51). This vital nuance ensues from the nature of remotion that constitutes an intrinsic moment of excessus. Perfections are not *deficient* in their divine predication; rather, they are possessed "more *supereminently* than is spoken or understood" (*De Pot.,* q. 7, a. 5; O'Rourke, 52; emphasis mine). For this reason, remotion in the Angelic Doctor rests on "a positive foundation," such that God is *quasi ignoto*, not *omnino ignoto*, as some have rendered Denys (55).[41] Accordingly, the priority of apophasis in Aquinas obtains "after and not before, the exercise of 'proving, naming and knowing God'" (54).[42] In other words, knowledge can only be qualified as inadequate once it is affirmed.

Finally, let us consider our thinkers' contrasting handling of the re-lation of being to the perfections goodness and eros (extroverted love). In Denys, eros constitutes equal rank and the same meaning as goodness and beauty, even as being, while flowing forth from them, is subordinated to them. As a result, God is supremely free in his essence, even as created reality, grounded in his act of eros, emerges as supremely free, good, and beautiful. But because God's goodness, eros, and beauty transcend being, an analogy of being that would allow unaided reason to affirm God's exis-tence seems compromised. Here we confront an "aporia" in the Dionysian system: to express the divine transcendence to being, terms that refer to being are used, such as "who *is* beyond being" (202; emphasis mine). We might thus infer Denys to mean that, from the perspective of philosophy (but not grace), the apophatic enjoys an absolute priority.

Two comments shed light on this aporia's resolution. First, we must recall that for Denys the prime means of humanity's knowledge of God is the Incarnation. Because it yokes the divine perfections goodness, eros, and beauty to the worldly being that it subsumes into itself, it thereby im-bues all finite realities with a kataphatic luster proclaiming their infinite source. Denys is not expressly concerned with the autonomy of philos-ophy that we find in Aquinas. Second, however, although Denys is not unambiguous, he does *not* posit, in my opinion, an absolute philosophical dichotomy between being and the divine predicates. There is a sense that

41. *ST* I, q. 12, a. 13, and Eriugena's translation of a phrase in Denys's *Mystical Theology.*
42. Citing C. B. Daly, "The Knowableness of God," *Philosophical Studies* 9 (1959): 90–133, at 132.

being belongs to God in that his eros (goodness and beauty) instrumentally causes creation and thus provides some basis in nature (as opposed to grace) for the divine names. We might even say that Denys implies an analogy between being and the divine predicates. If being ensues from them, then being in some dim fashion must carry them, insofar as it is an ontological rule that the cause of effects must lodge immanently in them. Accordingly, Denys's use of the language of being to express God's transcendence to being is paradoxical, not contradictory (analogical, not equivocal). Furthermore, he has coherently enveloped the analogy of being within the analogy of faith.

For his part, Thomas does clarify the Dionysian ambiguity by positing a priori that only absolute being *qua* being "can cause what does not of itself exist" (204). When Denys speaks of the good as absolutely transcendent, he wants to distance God from relating in any manner whatsoever to finite being (202). Thus, unlike Aquinas, for Denys, it is often the case that "being is not in itself the fullness of perfection, but a received perfection" (203). But because for Thomas being is unequivocally *a fullness that is received*, it follows that goodness exercises no priority over being but is convertible with it. If for Aquinas God can be called "nonbeing," it is only because, as noted, he is being supereminently, not deficiently (205).

The convertibility of absolute being and goodness allows the Angelic Doctor to frame his own metaphysics incorporating eros into these two perfections. We must caution, however, that Thomas does not seem to consider eros a perfection. This is not to say that, according to natural reason or philosophy, the order of created being cannot be said to be loving. But Aquinas works his way to this claim, not by a direct analogy from finite instances of love to an infinite love, in the manner of the analogy of being. Rather, his argument first affirms inductively the existence of God (by means of the five ways), then affirms that God must be absolute intelligence and, as such, must possess a will that is absolutely free and not constrained by necessity, like the Neoplatonic One. Accordingly, should God "choose" to create a world, its existence would be wholly good because of the convertibility of being and goodness. By implication, it would also be loving because love, as the first act of the will, aims at the universal good, which is God himself as *causa sua* and *ens realissimum* (*ST* I, q. 12, a. 12; q. 19; q. 20, a. 1).

Two important corollaries follow. First, because God's eros does not terminate heteronomously in and as the world, God retains his absolute transcendence (unlike absolute Spirit in idealism). Second, because God creates freely out of and on account of his infinite goodness (*ex nihilo sui et subjecti*), and because love drives that goodness, it follows that unaided reason can affirm the immanence of love in the "generative thrusting forth of all beings," at least in some vestigial sense. Yet neither being nor goodness seems convertible with love. We might suggest that one reason for this inconvertibility is that being in Thomas is act, whereas eros, insofar as it yearns for completion in some yet-to-be-achieved end (except in God), is constituted by a dynamic potency. We might also mention in passing that, although Thomas affirms the insufficiency of reason alone to demonstrate the world's beginning in time, still unaided reason can assert the world's free creation, whether it be eternal or originating in time (*De Pot.*, q. 3, a. 17).

In conclusion, I have worked to tease out in Denys and Thomas the equipoise of the apophatic and kataphatic dimensions of God's relations with the world. I did so to pose a counterfoil to some contemporary theology that seeks to combat ontotheology. However worthy that seeking, it relies on a form of fideism. This results from attenuating, or eliminating, reason's natural bridge between God and the world. By contrast, Aquinas and the Areopagite avoid the extremes of both positions because they differentiate among causality, remotion, and eminence within the organic unity of the mind's ascent from finite to infinite. On its basis, they posit truth as properly analogical in both nature and grace (philosophy and theology). Analogy holds in synthesis the affirmations about God that are relatively true and the negations about God that are absolutely true.

This study leaves us with two penetrating questions to be pondered. Can we use natural reason to conceive eros as a perfection and so as convertible with being? If so, could eros provide a deeper means of accounting for the equipoise between the kataphatic and apophatic than being and goodness? Here we can only ever so briefly indicate an approach. One could note, for instance, that Karl Rahner offers a demonstration for the intrinsic freedom of creation directly from its own contingency rather than, as in Aquinas, from the intelligence and will of God first known in the analogy of being. Rahner thus posits inductively an analogy of freedom between finite and infinite. Insofar as freedom entails love (eros), he also posits an analogy of love. If it can be shown that being is itself intrinsically free and hence loving, then, on the basis of reason alone, eros could be said to constitute the inner core of the ontological relation between

God and the world.[43] If so, then God's eros would be kataphatically experienced with existence. Moreover, the eros that we directly experience would lead us analogically to the loving freedom of God that, like all love, is lodged in the mysterious depths of personhood. In the case of God, this personhood is infinitely unfathomable and hence paradigmatically apophatic.

43. Karl Rahner, *Hearer of the Word: Laying the Foundation for a Philosophy of Religion*, trans. Joseph Donceel (New York: Continuum, 1994), chap. 7, especially as developed in Fields, *Analogies of Transcendence*, chap. 6.

8

The Christocentric Mystical Theologies of Maximos the Confessor and Thomas Aquinas

BERNHARD BLANKENHORN, OP

Maximos the Confessor and Thomas Aquinas developed doctrines of the human being's perfect union with God that manifest striking links with their Christologies. This chapter offers a first comparative sketch of those connections from the perspective of a scholastic systematic theologian. My aim is not to argue that Maximos and Aquinas consciously developed theologies of union with God in light of their Christologies. Rather, I seek to exploit the doctrinal potential and implications of their texts.

A terminological clarification is in order. When I speak of union with God, I mean the perfection of graced knowledge and love of God in this life. For Aquinas, this comes about through the perfection and actualization of habitual charity as well as the intense motion of the Spirit in the gifts of understanding and wisdom. For Maximos, such union comes by divinization, especially the transformation of the heart. The confessor also evokes the Dionysian Moses who knows God by unknowing when he describes divinization.[1]

---

1. See Maximos the Confessor, *On Difficulties in the Church Fathers: The Ambigua*, vol. 1, trans. Nicholas Constas, Dumbarton Oaks Medieval Library 28 (Cambridge, MA: Harvard University Press, 2014), *Amb. John* 10, section 3, pp. 162–65. All citations of the *Ambigua to John* are from this edition.

To begin, I point to some key general doctrinal similarities between Maximos and Aquinas. I then briefly survey Aquinas's synergistic approach to the pilgrim's union with God. Next, I explore four themes in Thomas's Christology: (1) Christ's habitual created grace, (2) Christ's two operations and two wills, (3) his beatific vision during his earthly pilgrimage, and (4) the place of the mysteries of Christ in the *Summa Theologiae*. I argue that Thomas sets the doctrinal foundations for a vision of the spiritual life wherein Christ in his humanity stands as the model subject and object of union with God.[2] I then turn to Maximos to see whether his thought might lead in a similar direction. Here, I offer evidence that Maximos likely has a place for the knowledge of finite realities such as Christ's humanity at the height of noetic perfection. Furthermore, I propose that Maximos is best read as positing the will's active, graced cooperation with God at the summit of union, a synergy of divine and human wills that imitates (however poorly) the perfect operations of Christ's two wills.

As I proceed, it is crucial to distinguish between the roles of the intellect and the will. That is, the intellect's cooperation in union almost certainly entails the will's cooperation as well, but perhaps not vice versa. Finally, the reader will notice a certain asymmetry in this presentation. The section on Aquinas focuses on Christology, while the section on Maximos centers on the believer's divinization. I have already set out Thomas's vision of the pilgrim's perfect union elsewhere: the task that remains for me is to show the link with Aquinas's Christology.[3] For Maximos, I assume a basic knowledge of his Christology and look for possible Christological echoes in the confessor's exposition of divinization.[4]

Some Doctrinal Similarities

Numerous doctrinal parallels in Maximos and Aquinas give support to the comparison that follows. First, Maximos and Aquinas both firmly

---

2. More specifically, I argue that the Triune God and Christ in his humanity become inseparable objects of contemplation at the summit of the spiritual life. This is not to say that both must be the *conscious* objects in any realization of perfect contemplation, however.

3. Bernhard Blankenhorn, *The Mystery of Union with God: Dionysian Mysticism in Albert the Great and Thomas Aquinas*, Thomistic Ressourcement 4 (Washington, DC: Catholic University of America Press, 2015), chaps. 5–8.

4. For a good overview of Maximos's Christology, see Paul M. Blowers, *Maximus the Confessor: Jesus Christ and the Transfiguration of the World*, Christian Theology in Context (Oxford: Oxford University Press, 2016), chaps. 4, 6–7.

oppose any anthropological dualism. This is perhaps best illustrated by the centrality of the Transfiguration for Maximos's theology, especially his theology of the transformation of the human senses.[5] In Aquinas's works, a holistic anthropology comes to the fore in many places, perhaps most especially in his doctrine of the unicity of substantial form and its impact on his account of human operation.[6] For his part, Maximos fuses hylomorphism and the Platonic theme of the soul as a substance.[7] Each thinker corrects problematic tendencies in the Platonic anthropologies of his age (whether they be Origenist, Evagrian, or Neo-Augustinian).

Second, Maximos and Aquinas synthesize Aristotelian and Platonic philosophy in an original way. The place of Aristotle in Thomas's metaphysics is a given, yet the importance of Platonic traditions therein has gained much recognition among scholars in recent decades.[8] Aquinas's anthropology is more Aristotelian, yet not without important Augustinian and Dionysian influences.[9] An Aristotelian notion of nature and operation seems to have left its mark on Maximos.[10]

Third, Maximos and Aquinas hold for a clear grace/nature distinction and frequently apply it in their discussions of union. Both often insist that divinization lies beyond our natural capacities, and that grace does not suppress or destroy nature but rather elevates it.[11]

Fourth, both saints maintain the primacy of love in union with God. We can already see this in Maximos's *Centuries on Charity* and in his later

---

5. *Amb. John* 10, section 17, pp. 191–95.

6. Blankenhorn, *Mystery of Union with God*, 221–26.

7. Marius Portaru, "Classical Philosophical Influences: Aristotle and Platonism," in *The Oxford Handbook of Maximus the Confessor*, ed. Pauline Allen and Bronwen Neil (Oxford: Oxford University Press, 2015), 142–43.

8. Fran O'Rourke, *Pseudo-Dionysius and the Metaphysics of Aquinas* (Notre Dame, IN: University of Notre Dame Press, 2005); John F. Wippel, *Metaphysical Themes in Thomas Aquinas II*, Studies in Philosophy and the History of Philosophy 47 (Washington, DC: Catholic University of America Press, 2007), 272–89.

9. This is a driving theme in Blankenhorn, *Mystery of Union with God*, chap. 5.

10. Antoine Lévy, *Le créé et l'incréé: Maxime le Confesseur et Thomas d'Aquin, aux sources de la querelle palamienne*, Bibliothèque Thomiste 59 (Paris: Vrin, 2006); Philippe Gabriel Renczes, *Agir de Dieu et liberté de l'homme: Recherches sur l'anthropologie théologique de saint Maxime le Confesseur*, Cogitatio Fidei 229 (Paris: Cerf, 2003). For a critique, see Portaru, "Classical Philosophical Influences."

11. For Maximos, see Jean-Claude Larchet, "The Mode of Deification," in Allen and Neil, *Oxford Handbook of Maximus the Confessor*, 343–46; Renczes, *Agir de Dieu*, 322–29; For Thomas, see Blankenhorn, *Mystery of Union with God*, 216–21, 249–80; Richard Schenk, "From Providence to Grace: Thomas Aquinas and the Platonisms of the Mid-Thirteenth Century," *Nova et Vetera* (English ed.) 3 (2005): 307–20.

writings.[12] He thus nuances a Greek mystical tradition that tended to focus on noetic union (e.g., Evagrius, Pseudo-Dionysius).[13] Aquinas places charity at the center as he draws on the Johannine writings and Augustinian theology. Interestingly, the centrality of love allows both theologians to overcome elitism in the spiritual life, for the perfect knowledge of creatures (one that would require extensive learning) no longer constitutes a necessary, preliminary stage to union. For Maximos, the perfection of virtue constitutes a kind of shortcut to divinization.[14] Aquinas has a similar view, with an emphasis on virtue perfected by the Spirit's seven gifts.[15] Here, the unlearned saint can reach the summit of union. On a related issue, Maximos and Aquinas both developed an original account of habitual charity.[16]

Fifth, Maximos and Aquinas emphasize progress in all the virtues as essential stepping stones toward union. Many previous theologians certainly recognized the necessity of virtuous living, but our two Doctors devote great attention to this issue. Here, Maximos appropriates the Desert Fathers' spirituality, while Aquinas develops Aristotelian ethics in synthesis with an Augustinian vision of grace. Maximos's approach to virtue may be described as more monastic, and Aquinas's as more philosophical and analytic.[17]

Sixth, Maximos and Aquinas both see the need for God's immediate action in the soul for its attainment of perfect union, whether in this life or in the next. This doctrine helps them to highlight the primacy of grace in mystical ascent. Neither theologian thinks that such divine activity constitutes a violation of human freedom. They clearly have a noncompetitive vision of divine and human action.[18] This point will be crucial as I proceed in my argumentation.

---

12. Maximos the Confessor, *The Ascetic Life, the Four Centuries on Charity*, trans. Polycarp Sherwood (London: Longmans, Green, 1955), century 1, nos. 9 and 12; century 2, no. 52; Blowers, *Maximus the Confessor*, 267; Jean-Claude Larchet, *La divinisation de l'homme selon saint Maxime le Confesseur*, Cogitatio Fidei 194 (Paris: Cerf, 1996), 477–79.

13. Andrew Louth, *Maximus the Confessor*, Early Church Fathers (London: Routledge, 1996), 38, 43.

14. Larchet, *La divinisation de l'homme*, 492.

15. Blankenhorn, *Mystery of Union with God*, 246–47.

16. Renczes, *Agir de Dieu*, 267–86, 333; Blankenhorn, *Mystery of Union with God*, 285–91, 434–35; Anthony W. Keaty, "Thomas's Authority for Identifying Charity as Friendship: Aristotle or John 15?," *The Thomist* 62 (1998): 581–601.

17. Blowers, *Maximus the Confessor*, 262–83.

18. Blankenhorn, *Mystery of Union with God*, 259–69, 438–40; Renczes, *Agir de Dieu*, 140–41, 294. For Thomas's doctrine of noncompetitive causality, see esp. Michael J. Dodds,

Seventh, Maximos and Aquinas make much use of a Dionysian doctrine of contemplative ascent via affirmations and negations. At the same time, both theologians make significant modifications to that doctrine. For example, Maximos gives the names of Christ a much greater role in his theology than does the Areopagite, while Aquinas operates a kataphatic turn in the Dionysian tradition, following in the footsteps of his teacher, Albertus Magnus.[19]

Aquinas's Doctrine of Union:
An Overview

In my book *The Mystery of Union with God*, I argued that, for Aquinas, the mind's highest communion with God in this life remains participatory, meaning that it involves a properly human act of knowing (i.e., it is not just about receiving). I also maintained that this human cognitive act remains bound to concepts and images. That is, at the height of contemplation enabled by the Spirit's gifts of wisdom and understanding, the believer does not cease to gaze upon God through creatures.[20] As for the will, that perfect union with God clearly involves a human act of love enabled by habitual charity. The *imago Dei* attains its perfection by a properly creaturely imitation of the Triune exemplar.[21] The path of loving ascent to God also involves infused acts of charity at various points along the way, though Aquinas rarely discusses these, except in the context of eucharistic communion.[22] This should not surprise us, given the spirituality that we find in the *Office of Corpus Christi*.[23]

Aquinas sees habitual or created grace as foundational for the spiritual life. This very grace enables our active cooperation with God. Now, created grace cannot be separated from the invisible missions of Son and Spirit and their indwelling. Hence both created and uncreated grace are essential for any communion with God. The Spirit's seven gifts constitute

---

Unlocking Divine Action: Contemporary Science and Thomas Aquinas (Washington, DC: Catholic University of America Press, 2012), chap. 1.

19. Ysabel de Andia, "Transfiguration et théologie négative chez Maxime le Confesseur et Denys l'Aréopagite," in *Denys l'Aréopagite: Tradition et Métamorphoses* (Paris: Vrin, 2006), 178–81; Blankenhorn, *Mystery of Union with God*, 148–57, 296–316.

20. Blankenhorn, *Mystery of Union with God*, chap. 8.

21. *ST* I, q. 93, a. 7; Blankenhorn, *Mystery of Union with God*, 237–47.

22. *ST* III, q. 79, aa. 1 and 4.

23. See Paul Murray, *Aquinas at Prayer: The Bible, Mysticism and Poetry* (London: Bloomsbury, 2013).

seven created modifications of the soul's faculties, a supernatural elevation that renders those powers docile to the Spirit's unforeseeable movement. The gifts as *habitus* make possible a new cooperation with the Spirit, yet the activation of the gifts comes by God's gratuitous will. Increasing docility to the Spirit occurs precisely by growth in charity. Hence cognitive and affective (or loving) union advance hand in hand. Finally, even when we look beyond infused acts of charity or the Spirit's motion in the seven gifts, we cannot find graced human acts wholly autonomous from God's operation. Thanks to Aquinas's mature theology of divine action, God always moves in and with the human being.

Among the seven gifts, three directly apply to contemplation: understanding, knowledge, and wisdom. Aquinas grants a certain eminence to the gifts of wisdom and understanding.[24] Wisdom involves an act of truth judgment facilitated by the heart's inclination to God. Understanding places infused negations or remotions at the center. This gift helps believers to deepen their knowledge of what the mysteries of faith are not.[25] Here, the Spirit strips away errors and foreign additions from our mode of conceiving the Trinity, the Incarnation, and God's saving work. The Spirit smashes our conceptual idols. The Spirit's movement in the gift of understanding purifies our mind's reception of the truths of faith that have been concretized in Scripture and in various ecclesial mediations.

For Thomas, even at the summit of noetic union, the Spirit leads the believer in the contemplation of God manifested in the economy, not beyond it. The greatest revelatory events, especially Christ's passion and resurrection as well as Pentecost, present the most excellent divine effects whereby we can glimpse Christ and the Trinity.[26] The gift of understanding refines our grasp of these effects, effects such as Christ's resurrected body and the tongues of fire at Pentecost. In other words, the intellect's act still reaches completion by a return to phantasms, even at the summit of divine cognition. Aquinas never denies this principle of Aristotelian epistemology when he studies mystical cognition.[27] Thomas thus quietly brings history into the dark cloud.

Hence, for Thomas, perfect knowledge of God and his saving work

---

24. *ST* I-II, q. 68, a. 7.

25. *ST* II-II, q. 8, aa. 2 and 7.

26. *ST* I, q. 12, a. 13. See also Charles Journet, *Connaissance et inconnaissance de Dieu* (Paris: Egloff, 1943), 93.

27. See *ST* I, q. 84, a. 7; q. 86, a. 1; II-II, q. 15, a. 3; q. 180, a. 5, ad 2. For the role of phantasms in Aquinas's epistemology, see Blankenhorn, *Mystery of Union with God*, 226–30.

remains tied to concepts and images. To be precise, I imply a distinction between (1) the conscious use of images in a cognitive act and (2) the human attainment of understanding that employs concepts and images. The latter involves an act of truth judgment, which brings intellectual repose. Now, the mind's judgment remains blind without concepts. Furthermore, concepts that have no link with perfections or attributes found in corporeal beings remain too nebulous for the human mind in its pilgrim state.

Aquinas's Christology and Mystical Theology[28]

This brief summary of Aquinas's theology of union with God has accentuated two themes: (1) the intellect's and the will's active cooperation with divine grace, and (2) the abiding function of mediations in the mind's union with God. My next step is to argue that this vision of union makes perfect sense in light of some key features of Aquinas's Christology. My analysis limits itself to the mature Christology found in the *Summa Theologiae*, following the four themes mentioned in the introduction.

In *ST* III, q. 7, a. 1, Aquinas gives three reasons to posit the presence of habitual grace in Christ's human soul. His second reason is as follows: "[it is necessary to posit habitual grace in Christ] because of the nobility of his soul, whose operations must attain most intimately to God, by knowledge and by love. For this, it was necessary for the rational soul to be elevated by grace."[29] The term "attaining" signals the soul's actual union with God, which is more than a merely habitual union. The text highlights two key theological principles. First, union comes about via operation. That is, the mere fact of the hypostatic union does not suffice for the perfection of Christ's humanity. Rather, his human faculties must also be fully actualized. In Christ's humanity and in all creatures, being is for the sake of operation.[30] Second, the mere union of the two natures does not suffice to ensure the perfection of Christ's human operation. Rather, his soul needs a created grace that intrinsically modifies his natural operative capacity. This assures both the elevation of his faculties and that his operation will have a properly *human* mode as well as a *divinized* mode. The presence of the *divine* acts of knowing and loving in Christ is not enough for the perfection of his soul.

---

28. This section partly integrates and expands upon part of my essay "Mystical Theology and Christology in Aquinas," forthcoming with Leuven University Press.

29. *ST* III, q. 7, a. 1, corpus.

30. *ST* III, q. 9, a. 4, corpus.

Rather, his human nature needs to be perfected by properly human acts of cognition and volition, acts that cannot be merely natural. The Gospels display these perfect human deeds of Christ at every turn.

Behind Aquinas's exposition of Christ's habitual grace stands a well-developed doctrine of Christ's two natures, operations and wills. We find it in *ST* III, q. 19. Evidently, Aquinas's doctrine builds on the teaching of the Third Ecumenical Council of Constantinople, which in turn reflects the theology of Maximos.[31] Unfortunately, Thomas did not enjoy direct access to Maximos's corpus, yet there is no doubt that the acts of the ancient councils and the writings of John Damascene left their Maximian mark on Aquinas. Thomas treats the issue of two operations in question 19, article 1. He recounts an opinion condemned at Constantinople III. Then he explains Christ's two operations:

the action of a thing which is moved by another is two-fold, one which it has from its proper form, the other which it has insofar as it is moved by another. Thus, the operation of an ax according to its proper form is division [cutting]; but insofar as the ax is moved by the craftsman, its operation is to make a bench. Hence the operation which belongs to a thing by its form is proper to it; nor does this operation belong to the mover [of a thing], except insofar as he uses this kind of thing for his operation: thus to heat is the proper operation of fire, but not of a blacksmith, except insofar as he uses fire to heat iron. But that operation which only belongs to the thing insofar as it is moved by another is not beyond the operation of the one moving the thing; thus, to make a bench is not an operation of the ax separate from the operation of the craftsman, but rather the ax participates instrumentally in the operation of the craftsman. And therefore, wherever the mover and the thing moved have diverse forms or operative powers, the proper operation of the mover must be other than the proper operation of the thing moved; although the thing moved participates in the operation of the mover, and the mover makes use of the operation of the thing moved, and thus each acts in communion with the other.

Therefore, in Christ the human nature has its proper form and power whereby it acts; and similarly, the divine [nature]. Hence the human nature has its proper operation distinct from the divine [nature], and conversely. Nevertheless, the divine nature uses the operation of the human nature, as the operation of its instrument; and similarly, the human nature participates in the operation of the divine nature, as an instrument participates in the operation of the principal agent. And this is what Pope Leo says (*Ad Flavianum*): "Each form acts," namely, both the divine and the human nature in Christ, "in communion with the other,

---

31. Jean-Pierre Torrell, Notes to *Encyclopédie Jésus le Christ chez saint Thomas d'Aquin*, by Thomas Aquinas (Paris: Cerf, 2008), 1062–65.

[doing] what is proper [to each]: namely, the Word operates what belongs to the Word, and the flesh carries out what belongs to flesh."

… Hence it is with reason that the Sixth Council [Constantinople III] condemned this opinion [of one operation in Christ], and in its determination said: "We glorify two natural, indivisible, unconvertible, unconfused, and inseparable operations in the same Lord Jesus Christ, our true God," that is, the divine operation and the human operation.[32]

Thomas here both relies on Damscene and gives the doctrine of Christ's operations his personal touch.[33] The analogy with the artisan's activity dominates this text. Thomas is concerned with nature as a principle of operation. The nature or form of any agent shapes the effect of an action, whether an agent acts as principal or as instrumental cause. Every form has an operation proportioned to it. In the background stands an Aristotelian notion of nature, as a stable, intrinsic source of activity. Yet we can also see Thomas employing the triad of nature-power-operation, which both he and Maximos would have found in Dionysius.[34] Thomas holds that every agent has its *proper* operation. The theme of instrumental causality relies heavily on the notion of participation. In other words, we are looking at Aquinas's synthesis of the Greek Fathers, Aristotelian action theory, and Platonic metaphysics. Here, John Damascene (and through him Maximos), Proclus, and the *Liber de Causis* constitute key sources for Aquinas.[35] When one agent becomes an instrument that is used by a higher agent, its instrumental act goes beyond its own operative capacity. But the elevated operation made possible by the motion of the principal cause is not separate from the instrument's own operation. The proper operations of the two agents remain distinct, yet they do not act side by side. The instrument participates or shares in the operation of the principal agent, though without fusing their operative powers into one.

---

32. *ST* III, q. 19, a. 1, corpus. All translations of Aquinas are mine. They are based on the following edition: Thomas Aquinas, *Summa Theologiae* (Ottawa: Commissio Piana, 1941–54).

33. See John Damascene, *On the Orthodox Faith*, Book 3, chap. 15. The analogy with the burning iron can be found in Maximos as well (e.g., *Ambiguum* 5, in *On Difficulties in the Church Fathers*, 1:56–57). I am grateful to Andrew Hofer for these references.

34. Édouard Wéber, *La personne humaine au XIIIe siècle*, Bibliothèque Thomiste 46 (Paris: Vrin, 1991), 227–33, 256–59. Portaru, "Classical Philosophical Influences," 141, points to Maximos's non-Aristotelian, Platonic source for the doctrine but does not specify further.

35. The doctrine of primary and secondary causality partly comes from the *Liber de Causis*. See Thomas Aquinas, *Super librum de causis expositio*, 2nd ed., ed. Henri-Dominique Saffrey, Textes philosophiques du Moyen Âge 21 (Paris: Vrin, 2002), proposition 1.

Christ's human nature has its proper operation. This neither excludes nor diminishes the Son's divine nature from acting through his human nature, as he accomplishes his saving deeds. Thus there is an operative synergy, so that Christ wills with a human love that is moved by divine love. A noncompetitive metaphysic is already inscribed in the Christological dogmas of Chalcedon and Constantinople III. Thomas presents one way to account for that metaphysic.

All of this entails the following theological consequence: the highest divine action in the saving economy that we can imagine does not require a passive instrument in God's all-powerful hands. Rather, what we find at the heart of salvation is the highest creaturely activity that we can conceive: the human knowledge and love of Jesus of Nazareth, as well as all his virtuous deeds and sufferings. His human deeds are salutary because the divine nature also acts through them. His humanity poses no obstacle to our salvation; on the contrary, because his sacred humanity acts, his divine nature also acts.

The doctrine of instrumental causality is crucial for Thomas's Christology, and the same doctrine stands at the center of his theology of the Spirit's seven gifts in the lives of the faithful. Christ in his humanity is an active instrument moved and elevated by his divinity to perform operations that exceed the capacity of his created nature. By analogy, believers' acts of knowledge and love are elevated by the Spirit, yet without ceasing to be created acts. In Christ, two operations join to bring about a single effect, such as healing the sick.[36] Something similar happens in the Spirit's movement in the minds and hearts of the faithful, as he joins the soul to God in a new way.

The doctrine of Christ's two wills, illumined by the analogy of instrumentality, helps us to grasp well Aquinas's theology of Christ's habitual grace. Aquinas compares Christ's divine will moving his human will and God moving our human wills. We find it in *ST* III, q. 18, a. 1. The first objection argues that the first mover cannot move the will except by mode of violence. Aquinas respond to the objection in this way:

Whatever was in Christ's human nature, was moved by the command of the divine will, yet it does not follow that there was no motion of the will proper to the human nature, for the good wills of other saints are moved by God's will, "who operates in them to will and to perfect," as is said in Philippians 2:13. For although the will cannot be moved interiorly by another creature, still it can be moved

36. *ST* III, q. 19, a. 1, ad 3 and 5.

interiorly by God, as was said in the first part. And so also Christ followed the divine will according to his human will.[37]

The passage then continues with a quote of Augustine. Thomas follows the Latin Father as he reads in Philippians 2:13 the following teaching: God works within the will of each believer, and not alongside of it. By implication, the act of our will remains free. It seems that, for Aquinas, the doctrine of God's saving action in our wills is easier to grasp than the operative link between Christ's two wills. An Augustinian vision of divine operation and grace helps Thomas to conceptualize more clearly a doctrine of Christ's two wills that is in line with Constantinople III. This Augustinian doctrine underlies (1) Thomas's insistence that divine *auxilium* works in all our acts (a doctrine most fully worked out in *ST* I-II, q. 109) and (2) his theology of the Spirit's interior motion through the seven gifts (also developed earlier in the *Summa Theologiae*). Now, Philippians 2 as read by Thomas does not tell us whether the believer's will is active or passive before God. Instead, it signals the principle that divine-human cooperation in willing leaves human freedom intact.

My third theme is the beatific vision of Christ.[38] For Aquinas, Christ's vision during his earthly life was *sui generis*, and this in three ways. First, unlike the brief vision of God granted to Moses and Paul during their experience of rapture, Christ's vision was (and is) constant. Second, unlike the holy patriarch and the Apostle to the Gentiles, Christ's vision did not (and does not) exclude a simultaneous knowledge by the senses. In this way, Christ's beatific vision constitutes an anticipation of our future eschatological vision. Third, the beatific vision was necessary to ensure that Christ's human actions constituted adequate expressions of his personal unity, the unity of two natures in one hypostasis.[39]

The second point just made takes us directly to a doctrine of union with God. For Aquinas, the eschaton has already begun in Jesus. Here we see that unmediated human knowledge of the divine essence need not exclude nor diminish the knowledge of beings via intelligible forms or

---

37. *ST* III, q. 18, a. 1, ad 1.

38. Two theologians have recently argued for the viability and necessity of Christ's beatific vision during his earthly life. See Thomas Joseph White, *The Incarnate Lord: A Thomistic Study in Christology*, Thomistic Ressourcement 5 (Washington, DC: Catholic University of America Press, 2015), 236–74, and Simon Gaine, *Did the Saviour See the Father? Christ, Salvation and the Vision of God* (London: T & T Clark, 2015). See also Emmanuel Durand, *L'offre universelle du salut en Christ*, Cogitatio Fidei 285 (Paris: Cerf, 2012), 156–73.

39. *ST* III, q. 18, a. 1; White, *Incarnate Lord*, 251–56.

the knowledge of material creatures via phantasms. Thomas posits the simultaneous perfection of three types of knowledge in Christ, namely, beatific, infused, and acquired. Each kind of cognition complements the other.[40] Therefore concept- and image-bound cognition need not impede an elevated graced knowledge of God.

Thus the abiding link of the saints' highest graced knowledge with concepts and phantasms finds its model in the "both-and" or *et ... et* cognition of Christ, rather than the visionary transported to the heavenly throne room or to the third heaven. The spiritual, incarnated knowledge of Christ, the only kind that Jesus in his humanity ever had, can serve as the exemplar for the mystic.[41] This is the ultimate destiny of the saints, for in their resurrected state, they will contemplate the essence of God *and* Christ's glorified body in the new heaven and the new earth, a vision at once spiritual and physical, without competition or separation.[42]

The third Christological theme leads to the fourth. Aquinas was unique among the medieval scholastics in that he inserted a lengthy theological study on the life of Christ into a systematic presentation of his Christology. The questions on Christ's life are not simply treated as background material for a technical account of the hypostatic union or redemption. Rather, the astounding length of this section of the *Summa Theologiae* shows that Aquinas values the contemplation and analysis of the mysteries for their own sake. The frequent appeals to arguments from fittingness in these pages also show that Thomas is interested in much more than rigorous theological conclusions. In the *Tertia Pars*, Aquinas seeks to gaze upon the face of Christ with the help of Scripture, the patristic and conciliar tradition, and with the aid of a metaphysical theology that proceeds from the being of Christ to his action, so that knowledge of Christ's being may illumine our understanding of his action.

I propose that one reason for Thomas to present this lengthy "treatise" on the mysteries of Christ, with all the details of his saving acts and sufferings, is that these mysteries constitute platforms for mystical ascent. The knowledge of Christ's human life can continue to accompany the wayfarer even to the height of noetic union. The mysteries are a mystical ladder in Thomas, much as the divine names constitute the rungs of that

---

40. *ST* III, q. 9, aa. 3–4.

41. Here, one makes an evident exception for Christ's Holy Saturday experience, owing to the separation of his soul from his body.

42. Thomas Aquinas, *Scriptum super Sententiis*, Parma Edition 7.2 (Parma, 1857), Book IV, distinction 49, q. 2, a. 2, corpus.

ladder for Dionysius (as they do for Aquinas). Yet, unlike the Areopagite's Moses, Aquinas's mystic never needs to set that ladder aside. In a way, he cannot even do so, for in this life, he cannot understand anything without intelligible forms and the mind's return to phantasms. The massive section on the mysteries destroys false notions of Christ's person and his saving work, thus purifying the soul. It guides the intellect's indirect gaze upon Christ's divine nature by teaching the Gospel truth. That same teaching inflames the heart. Such contemplation flourishes under the movement of the Spirit, as he continues to pour out habitual and actual charity, as well as his movement in the seven gifts.

Maximos on Union with God and Christology

At first glance, Maximos's theology of union with God seems to leave little room for the specific kind of Christocentric, synergistic noetic union that follows from Aquinas's theology, because Maximos's doctrine of cognitive union sounds Dionysian.[43] Also, Jean-Claude Larchet holds that Maximos contrasts the active cooperation of Christ's human will with our divinization. According to Larchet, in our case, the will's divinization occurs by God's energy alone. In other words, the will's perfection takes place in mono-energistic fashion. I begin with the issue of cognitive perfection in Maximos.

Questions and Responses for Thalassios 25 offers a good example of Maximos's Dionysian doctrine. He refers to the intellect that attains "mystical theology." Here, the mind's spiritual head is the Logos, who is understood by way of unknowing. Here, there is no place for the senses, reason (i.e., the mind's motion) or things conceived. Purified of all sensible representations, the mind learns ineffable dogmas. It must be freed from the diversity and multitude of beings, so that it may attain a deifying identity and simplicity with the Monad, a gift that allows for an intense and permanent movement around God.[44] The latter theme evokes the Ar-

---

43. For a good survey, see Jean-Claude Larchet, "Introduction," in Maximos the Confessor, *Questions à Thalassios*, vol. 1, *Questions 1 à 40*, ed. J.-L. Larchet and Françoise Vinel, Sources Chrétiennes 529 (Paris: Cerf, 2010), 63–81.

44. Maximos the Confessor, *Questions à Thalassios*, vol. 1, q. 25, pp. 288.52–290.61 (the page numbers are followed by the line numbers indicated in the critical edition given in Sources Chrétiennes): "Et encore l'homme, c'est l'intellect qui se trouve à l'intérieur de la théologie mystique: sa tête sans voile, c'est le Christ, c'est-à-dire le Logos de la foi que l'on comprend dans l'inconnaissance par des mystagogies ne passant pas par la démonstration ou, pour le dire plus précisément, connu sans compréhension; au-dessus de lui, l'intellect,

eopagite's circular motion and recalls the eschatology of Gregory of Nyssa. In this text, Maximos describes a this-worldly reality. His focus is on the intellect, not the will. It is clear that one type of knowledge excludes the other: ineffable learning can only take place if one no longer gazes upon creatures. Maximos says that the head of this intellect is the Logos. Here, we might ask: In what way is Christ's humanity involved, beyond opening the path to this summit as mediator of divinization?

In *Questions and Responses for Thalassios* 25 and elsewhere, Maximos consistently espouses a Dionysian description of "mystical theology."[45] For example, in *Ambigua to John* 10, shortly after commenting upon the Transfiguration, Maximos meditates on the figure of Melchizedek, who "cognitively through contemplation left behind all that comes after God."[46] Then, "in a manner beyond knowledge, following the total negation of all beings from thought, he entered into God Himself, and was wholly transformed, receiving all the qualities of God."[47] In other words, Melchizedek no longer contemplates any creature but God alone. The mind's transcending of creatures is a precondition for radical transformation. A few pages later, we learn that Moses, too, separated himself from all intelligible and sensible objects so that he could see divine fire (and allusion to the theophany on Mt. Sinai).[48] Moses attained a wordless ecstasy as he "entered into the dark cloud and through unknowing converses with God in a manner beyond words."[49] Maximos clearly takes up the Dionysian narrative from the first chapter of the Areopagite's *Mystical Theology*. Yet the image of conversation is provocative, for it seems to suggest that Moses's human mind is active but in a higher mode. Apparently, Moses's mind has not simply been taken over by God's operation (as in Dionysius), since that would likely render the image of conversation problematic. But Maximos does not pursue this matter further.

The confessor clearly develops his doctrine of cognitive perfection in this life with an eye to eschatology. The former grants a foretaste of the latter, and the nature of the latter helps to shape our understanding of

---

lorsqu'il s'est exercé à la privation louable et éminente de lui-même et des êtres, totalement et d'une manière qui le rend particulièrement divin, ne place aucun être—ni sensibilité, ni raison, ni intellect, ni intellection, ni connaissance, ni rien qui soit connu, conçu, exprimé, rien qui soit sensible ou senti."

45. Larchet, "Introduction," in Maximos the Confessor, *Questions à Thalassios*, 1:131.

46. *Amb. John* 10, p. 217 (PG 91, 1141A).

47. *Amb. John* 10, p. 221 (PG 91, 1141C).

48. *Amb. John* 10, p. 233 (PG 91, 1148D–1149A).

49. *Amb. John* 10, p. 235 (PG 91, 1149C).

how the former functions. Here, Maximos takes an important step beyond Dionysius, who said little about our knowledge of God in the life to come. A key Maximian passage on eschatological union is found in *Questions and Responses for Thalassios 60*. The topic of question 60 is the manifestation of Christ the lamb at the end of time. First, Maximos recalls the Christocentric character of creation. All things were made in view of the perfect union of Christ's two natures. Maximos then considers two ways of knowing the divine. The first is in the order of relation. Here, the contemplative employs reason (or *logos*) and the mind's representations, and nothing more. Maximos says that this mode of knowing belongs to the present life. The second way is higher and eschatological. It occurs by experience alone, in separation from reason and noetic representations, for we will participate in the reality known. This union involves the gift of divinization, which will be constantly actualized. Maximos speaks of a "perception" (*aisthēsis*) of the reality known. Finally, he notes that this experience or perception excludes or destroys knowledge via relation. "The wise" teach that their coexistence is impossible. The first kind of knowledge advances by analogy from sensible beings and ascends toward the contemplation of God. Maximos also describes knowing by experience as something that occurs after reasoning.[50] He develops a doctrine of

50. Maximos the Confessor, *On the Cosmic Mystery of Jesus Christ*, trans. Paul M. Blowers and Robert Louis Wilken (Crestwood, NY: St. Vladimir's Seminary Press, 2003), 126–27: "The scriptural Word knows of two kinds of knowledge of divine things. On the one hand, there is relative knowledge, rooted only in reason and ideas, and lacking in the kind of experiential perception of what one knows through active engagement; such relative knowledge is what we use to order our affairs in our present life. On the other hand, there is that truly authentic knowledge, gained only by actual experience, apart from reason and ideas, which provides a total perception of the known object through a participation (*methexis*) by grace. By this latter knowledge, we attain, in the future state, the supernatural deification (*theōsis*) that remains unceasingly in effect. They say that the relative knowledge based on reason and ideas can motivate our desire for the participative knowledge acquired by active engagement. They say, moreover, that this active, experiential knowledge which, by participation, furnishes the direct perception of the object known, can supplant the relative knowledge based on reason and ideas. For the sages say that it is impossible for rational knowledge (*logos*) of God to coexist with the direct experience (*peira*) of God, or for conceptual knowledge (*noēsis*) of God to coexist with immediate perception (*aisthēsis*) of God. By 'rational knowledge of God' I mean the use of the analogy of created beings in the intellectual contemplation of God; by 'perception' I mean the experience, through participation, of the supernatural goods; by 'conceptual knowledge' I mean the simple and unitary knowledge of God drawn from created beings. This kind of distinction may be recognized with every other kind of knowledge as well, since the direct 'experience' of a thing suspends rational knowledge of it and direct 'perception' of a thing renders the 'conceptual knowledge' of it useless. By 'experience' (*peira*) I mean that knowledge, based on active engagement, which surpasses all reason. By perception

eschatological knowledge by analogy with sense knowledge.[51] The present text remains ambiguous on the cognitive function of the glorified body in the eschaton.

The doctrine of the glorified saints' knowledge presented in *Questions and Responses for Thalassios* 60 offers a clear parallel with mystical knowing in this life. Both eschatological and mystical knowledge in this life involve a transcending of two things: (1) all motions of reason and (2) the intellect's use of intelligible forms or representations. In both cases, one type of knowledge is excluded. Maximos follows "the wise" as he draws a twofold contrast: knowing by reasoning or by experience, and knowing by representation or by perception.

The text continues by returning to the theme of the whole of question 60, namely, knowledge of the Incarnate Word. This takes us beyond Dionysius, who says nothing about knowing any finite reality in the dark cloud or in the next life. Now, in this section of *Questions and Responses for Thalassios* 60, Maximos sets out two ways of knowing God, yet he does not mention the Incarnation. Still, this section helps to clarify our future knowledge of Christ in glory. If this section of question 60 does remain closely bound to the rest of the same question, then Maximos implies the following: the saints' noetic operation will no longer rely on the labor of reason and the content offered by intelligible forms, yet the object known includes a finite reality—namely, the humanity of the Logos—and this in a higher, more direct mode. For knowledge by participation involves direct access to the cognitive object. Maximos's discourse on perception would thus serve to clarify how we will know the whole Christ in the life to come. The language of perception may also recall the theme of the three Apostles with their transformed sense powers on Mt. Tabor.

If the previous exposition of *Questions and Responses for Thalassios* 60 is correct, then Maximos has opened a wide path for the saints' cognition of finite realities in glory, and not just a path for knowledge of Christ's humanity, but also the saints' knowledge of the whole of restored creation. It

---

(*aisthēsis*) I mean that participation in the known object which manifests itself beyond all conceptualization. This may very well be what the great Apostle is secretly teaching when he says, 'As for prophecies, they will pass away; as for tongues, they will cease; as for knowledge, it will disappear' (1 Cor 13:8). Clearly he is referring here to that knowledge which is found in reason and ideas." For the Greek text, see Maximos the Confessor, *Questions à Thalassios*, vol. 3, *Questions 56 à 65*, Sources Chrétiennes 569, ed. J.-L. Larchet and Françoise Vinel (Paris: Cerf, 2015), q. 60, pp. 86.60–87.89.

51. Hans Urs von Balthasar, *Cosmic Liturgy: The Universe According to Maximos the Confessor*, trans. Brian E. Daley (San Francisco: Ignatius Press, 2003), 286–87.

seems that Maximos's main concern is not to exclude knowledge of creatures from eschatological union, but rather to exclude an all-too-limited mode of cognition. Might something analogous be possible for cognitive union in this life? Could it be that, in passages such as *Questions and Responses for Thalassios* 25, the major aim behind the language of transcending all sense, reason, and things conceived is to highlight the cessation of our reliance upon the normal mode of acquiring knowledge of creatures? For this would allow the Apostles' experience at the Transfiguration to be on equal footing with the dark cloud. It would mean that the Transfiguration teaches not just on how to interpret Christ, Scripture, and the book of creation, but also about union's summit. In that case, we should not seek to ascend Mt. Tabor so as to then ascend Mt. Sinai.

Some confirmation for this reading of Maximos comes in *Ambigua to John* 19.[52] There, we find a fascinating discussion of Gregory the Theologian's prophetic vision. Maximos speaks by conjecture and invites those who have experienced this grace to correct him (for he has not received

---

52. *Amb. John* 19, pp. 403–7 (PG 91, 1233D–1236D): "Our blessed father Saint Gregory, being utterly purified by practical philosophy from all that habitually defiles human nature, and with his intellect thoroughly imbued with the qualities of the Holy Spirit (owing to his dedication to divine contemplations), through his true initiation into true knowledge, experienced the same things as the holy prophets, and with these words he enumerates for us the different forms of prophecy. Now if one must be so bold as to undertake an examination of these words, which were spoken with such brilliance and divine inspiration, and which are far beyond the grasp of anyone who is not himself like the teacher, it would seem best to do so conjecturally and not categorically. Now it seems to me (speaking conjecturally on account of my intellectual shortsightedness) that by an 'appearance during the day occurring in the imagination,' he was referring to the vision and audition of things and words, seen and heard by the saints, that were not caused by the presence of some other person, but spiritually, not unlike a kind of perception. For it is not right to claim that in the case of divine realities an actual image of them must necessarily be present in order to impress itself on the imagination, but rather that in such cases the imagination, in a manner that is paradoxical and beyond nature, operates without the presence of another person, and without audible sounds vibrating through the air, so that the one being initiated into divine realities truly hears and sees. For every mental image is either of things past or present, because there can be no object-based image formed of things that have not yet happened ... When he [Gregory] says 'a truthful vision in the night,' I take him to mean either the precise comprehension of future events by the soul during sleep ... or a certain vision of divine realities, which is visible to the bodily eyes of the saints, by virtue of their extreme purity and dispassion. And when he speaks of 'an impression made on the governing power,' I understand him to be stressing the forms of future events that are manifested to the saints, which occur in a unique manner, as if they were seeing a picture, according to a simple intellective intuition, which is without spatial or temporal extension. Though I myself have not received the grace of experience in these matters, I nevertheless was emboldened to speak of them conjecturally."

such a gift). Gregory refers to "an appearance during the day occurring in the imagination." Maximos proposes that this vision enjoyed by some saints does not involve an image impressed upon their imagination, but rather a paradoxical operation of the imagination that is beyond nature, which he compares to perception (*aisthēseōs*). Mental images concern present and past realities, and these are realities that we can comprehend. But divine realities cannot be comprehended.[53] Furthermore, there is an experience of divine realities as "visible to the bodily eyes of the saints," such that they know future events through "a simple intellective intuition."[54] Now this process is passive, in that God alone acts upon the imagination.

Ambiguum 19 draws no direct link with divinization or mystical theology, yet it shows how Maximos posits the elevation of the imagination's and the body's operative capacities in a way that transcends all other human ways of contemplating creatures. Such transcending parallels the intellect's passing beyond the contemplation tied to finite sensible or intelligible forms. In each case, mediations are overcome. This rare form of prophetic knowledge would seem to fulfill Maximos's Dionysian prerequisite that we cease to gaze upon all *images* derived from sense experience so as to enter the dark cloud. In *Questions and Responses for Thalassios* 60, the language of perception sets up an analogy between sense knowledge and eschatological knowledge, though I argued that the analogy ultimately serves to account for the eschatological knowledge of material creation, especially our future knowledge of Christ's glorified humanity. In the present text (*Ambiguum* 19), the term "perception" (*aisthēseōs*) clearly signals a higher way of bodily knowing, and the object perceived includes both God and some future aspects of the economy. Here, we find both the involvement of the sense powers and a multiplicity of cognitive objects.

In light of *Questions and Responses for Thalassios* 60 and *Ambiguum* 19, it would seem that Maximos's Christology and eschatology nuance his appropriation of the Evagrian/Dionysian structure of mystical ascent. The confessor's doctrine remains clearly distinct from that of Aquinas, for whom phantasms and intelligible forms *always* play some role in cognitive union during this life. Still, a partial parallel has begun to emerge.[55]

---

53. *Amb. John* 19, pp. 403–5 (PG 91, 1233D–1236C).

54. *Amb. John* 19, p. 407 (PG 91, 1236D).

55. Perhaps we have found one way of applying Paul M. Blowers's advice to see *praxis*, contemplation, and *theologia* in Maximos as a matter of "mutual co-inherence and perpetual cross-fertilization." Blowers refers to *Ambiguum* 10. See his *Maximus the Confessor*, 75.

But what of human cooperation in union? That is, what about the place of a properly human operation or energy in the dark cloud? Does Maximos grant it to either the intellect or the will? As Maximos is unclear on the intellect's active cooperation, I focus on the will.

The eastern Orthodox scholar Larchet has argued firmly against a synergistic reading of Maximos. He marshals a whole series of citations to show that the martyr sees only human passivity in divinization.[56] In my view, the most compelling evidence in favor of Larchet's stance is found in *Ambigua to John* 7. Much of this *Ambiguum* concerns the relation of rest and motion. All creatures are in motion, and God alone is their end: in him, they attain repose. For intelligent creatures, knowledge engenders love of what is known, and that love impels the creature toward the beloved until it is circumscribed by God, as air is filled with light and iron is penetrated by fire.[57] Maximos then invokes 1 Corinthians 15, where Paul speaks of all things being subjected to Christ and Christ subjecting all things to the Father (1 Cor 15:20–28). The confessor interprets this Pauline text to mean that we will surrender our wills to God, desiring nothing that is against his will.[58] The context is eschatological, but it has implications for Maximos's understanding of divinization here below. He states that (in the eschaton) the will shall be fixed, "so that henceforth it has neither the inclination nor the ability to be carried elsewhere ... for it will have received the divine energy."[59] Grace will render the human being impeccable. Yet Maximos insists that our freedom will also remain. He continues:

This occurs through the grace of the Spirit which has conquered it [the will], showing that it has God alone acting within it, so that through all there is only one sole energy, that of God and of those worthy of God, or rather of God alone, who in a manner befitting his goodness wholly interpenetrates all who are worthy. For all things without exception necessarily cease from their willful movement toward something else when the ultimate object of their desire and participation appears before them.[60]

The perfect repose given to the human being involves a radical work of grace. For Larchet, the phrases "one sole energy" and "God alone" are key. For the French patrologist, such language confirms that divinization is solely God's work, and that we receive it in a strictly passive mode. The

---

56. Larchet, *La divinisation de l'homme*, 540–608.
57. *Amb. John* 7, pp. 87–89 (PG 91, 1073D–1076B).
58. *Amb. John* 7, p. 89 (PG 91, 1076B–C).
59. *Amb. John* 7, p. 91 (PG 91, 1076D).
60. *Amb. John* 7, p. 91 (PG 91, 1076D–1077A).

saints renounce the activity of their own will, as they make an offering of their human powers to God.[61] The only operation or energy granted to human beings is one of disposition, of preparing ourselves for the reception of this gift.[62]

Larchet's argument seems compelling, yet some elements in *Ambiguum* 7 render his reading of the text problematic.[63] First, the most consistent theme in this part of the *Ambiguum* concerns the will's object. The human being surrenders or is subjected to Christ insofar as he or she no longer wills what displeases God. This theme both precedes and immediately follows the passage that refers to "one sole energy." By this phrase, Maximos seeks to emphasize that this perfection of human willing lies beyond our natural abilities. Yet this hardly excludes an abiding operation of the human will. Second, the language of interpenetration or *perichoresis* would seem to evoke a divine elevation of the creature's operation. This image probably nuances the earlier metaphors of light and fire, which express the abundant presence of divine energy in the human powers. The analogies and metaphors that Maximos uses complement each other, so that each gives a unique accent in the quest to make sense of divinization. Third, Maximos elsewhere uses the language of "one sole divine energy" with a specific aim. For example, in his *First Opusculum*, we read:

This energy, which has the power to divinize all the saints ... belongs to God by nature, but to the saints by grace. I added that this energy is of "God alone," for the divinization of the saints is exclusively the result of divine energy, and not a power found within our own nature.[64]

In other words, God alone can divinize by his natural power, whereas we can attain divinization only by participating in the divine energy. Maximos often uses such language to deny the idea that we possess a natural power of divinization. Several texts of Maximos that Larchet cites to exclude any human cooperation in divinization highlight the gifted or graced nature of divinization.[65] That is, Larchet attributes a meaning to these passages that they do not evidently bear.

61. Larchet, *La divinisation de l'homme*, 579–80.

62. Larchet, *La divinisation de l'homme*, 577, 581.

63. My interpretation of this text has benefited from the insight of Andrew Hofer.

64. Cited in Maximos the Confessor, *On Difficulties in the Church Fathers*, 480n16. Here, Constas translates PG 91, 33AB.

65. *Questions à Thalassios*, vol. 1, q. 22, p. 269 (PG 90, 321A) and scholia 5, p. 273; *Amb. John* 20, p. 409 (PG 91, 1237AB). For Larchet's use of these texts, see his *La divinisation de l'homme*, 540, 547, 552, 560–61, 568. See also Renczes, *Agir de Dieu*, 322, 328–29.

Philipp Gabriel Renczes has challenged Larchet's claims about mystical and eschatological passivity. He sees our own *hexis* or *habitus* of charity as the means whereby the divine operation brings about our divinization.[66] The most compelling passage that Renczes employs comes from *Questions and Responses for Thalassios* 59. This question takes up the issue of prophetic revelation. For Maximos, such revelation is received in a way that clearly differs from both eschatological knowledge and the peak of mystical theology. Maximos espouses the cooperation of the prophet's natural cognitive powers in the process of receiving and passing on divine revelation. Here, operative synergy has an evident place. This synergy makes possible the intelligible communication of the mystery received.[67] Maximos then turns to the finality of prophecy, or perpetual repose in the eschaton:

the participation in the divine realities which surpasses nature is the resemblance of the ones participating in the participated; the resemblance of the ones participating in the participated is the identity in act, received by the resemblance, of the ones participating in the very reality participated.[68]

Renczes rightly accentuates the language of "identity in act" or operation.[69] If there is identity, then we do not have the full cessation of the human energy, but rather its perfect harmony with the divine energy. The affirmation of such synergy renders more intelligible the language of "perpetually mobile repose," which we find just a few lines earlier. Interestingly, this part of *Questions and Responses for Thalassios* 59 does not specify which faculty or power enjoys identity of operation with God.

Larchet invokes a different part of the same question 59, only several lines after the passage cited above, to argue for utter human passivity in divinization.[70] Here, Maximos refers to an ineffable union beyond knowing enjoyed by "those who are acted upon."[71] But Maximos says nothing about God's energy substituting for ours. Rather, he highlights the eminence and immediacy of the divine operation in our divinization. Each Maximian passage on divinization has a specific doctrinal purpose.

But Larchet's exegesis of the Greek Father might contain another, subtle insight that concerns a key element in Maximos's doctrine of deifi-

66. Renczes, *Agir de Dieu*, 275–86, 333.
67. *Questions à Thalassios*, vol. 3, q. 59, pp. 57–63.
68. *Questions à Thalassios*, vol. 3, q. 59, p. 65.
69. Renczes, *Agir de Dieu*, 356.
70. Larchet, *La divinisation de l'homme*, 552.
71. *Questions à Thalassios*, vol. 3, q. 59, p. 67.150.

cation. For perhaps Larchet is best read as pointing toward a simultaneity and complementarity of passivity before God and human cooperation, so that the human being remains radically dependent on God's divinizing action, which occurs in the depth of his soul, all the while operating in a higher way thanks to the very gift received. If this is indeed Larchet's ultimate intention, then my own claims about Maximos may not be all that far from his.[72] Furthermore, it would give us a vision of Maximus's doctrine of divine action that bears striking similarities to Aquinas's teaching.

Conclusion

Overall, Maximos clearly excludes the contemplation of creatures and use of the imagination from most instances of noetic perfection. Yet he appears to open the door for a higher mode of gazing upon creatures that occurs simultaneously with divinization. Some radically transformed souls can obtain a rare prophetic gift. If this gift can go hand in hand with a new gift of divinization (a possibility for which Maximos's theology seems to remain open), then at least in some instances, the pilgrim who enjoys deep union with God can still gaze upon the glorified humanity of Christ. Still, both the imagination and the intellect would seem to be passive when such a gift is imparted. And yet Maximos likely suggests that God can activate properly human operations of the mind and the imagination during divinization. As for the will, there is good evidence that Maximos accepts the place of a properly human act of love for God in divinization, in other words, active cooperation at the zenith of perfection. Here, one might also consider Maximos's treatment of the gift of *hexis*. The saints' supernatural imitation of Christ by the action of their human hearts can thus mirror Christ's two wills with their full actualization.

As for Thomas, mystical cognition remains bound to concepts and phantasms. Hence we can still gaze upon the whole life of Christ and his paschal mystery from within the dark cloud. Aquinas's vision of mystical ascent remains highly attentive to the manifestive power of material creation, of Holy Scripture, and of the Incarnate Word. More specifically, his doctrinal principles imply that the historic words and deeds of Christ function as an indispensable mystical ladder, even at the summit of the spiritual life. In this way, the Gospel with all its illuminative power remains at the heart of graced cognition. Hence the mystic's knowledge im-

72. I thank my colleague David Dawson-Vasquez for this insight.

itates somewhat clumsily that of Christ, in whom the beatific vision did nothing to exclude knowledge of the economy. The mystic's knowledge also points toward the perfect both-and knowledge that the saints will enjoy after the resurrection of the body. As for a doctrine of union by love, the Christology of two operations does much to illumine it. The doctrine of noncompetitive divine action already implied in Constantinople III finds one form of genius expression in Thomas's theology of instrumental causality. As with Christ's humanity, the believer's heart retains its proper operation, one that need not pose any obstacle for or tension with God's operation. The graced activation of the human will and its abiding coop-eration with divine grace are essential for Aquinas, for only in this way can we speak of a properly human imitation of Christ. The fact that a theology of actual charity only emerges in Aquinas's comments on the fruits of eucharistic communion further points to the Christocentric and liturgical character of Thomas's mystical theology. The Eucharist is the normal site of loving union.[73] Yet, now, the mind's abiding gaze upon the symbols of the liturgy involves no mere disposition for union, but rather accompanies the divinization of the heart.

I close by returning to the underlying motive of this essay. For a long time, the typical reading of both Aquinas and Maximos has been that they are in broad agreement with the Dionysian schema of ascent, where the transcending of all sensible objects and intelligible forms constitutes an essential step toward union. Such a reading of Aquinas is no longer tenable. I suggested above that Maximos can also be read differently.

The question ultimately is this: When the Blessed Virgin Mary sensed the baby Jesus kicking in her womb, or when she gazed upon her new-born's body in Bethlehem, was she still one or two steps below the sum-mit of noetic union with her divine Son? Should we not rather posit her perfect union as occurring simultaneously with the contemplation of her Son's humanity?

The same question returns when we consider a remarkable pattern in the long and rich history of female mystical authors. So often, their most powerful encounters with God occur in the setting of a vision. Now, evidently, prophetic visions are formally distinct from the gift of sancti-fying or divinizing union, as Aquinas himself recognized. But does the bride's gaze upon an appearance of the suffering or glorified Bridegroom

---

73. The same can be said for Maximos, whose eucharistic theology closely links the themes of union with Christ, silence, and participation in the eschaton (see Blowers, *Max-imus the Confessor*, 171–95). Surely, the convergence of these three themes is no accident.

necessarily stand a step below her perfect union with him? Or must we restrict that union to the realm of the will, and look for perfect knowledge elsewhere? Could it be that the female mystics, often more at ease with their bodies than their male counterparts, have something important to teach us? In short, our theological account of noetic and loving union with God should be both Christocentric and Marian.[74]

74. Oddly, Hans Urs von Balthasar critiqued Aquinas's theology of prophecy for adopting problematic Platonic biases against the senses and the imagination. See his "Zur Ortsbestimmung christlicher Mystik," in *Grundfragen der Mystik*, ed. Werner Beierwaltes, H. u. von Balthasar, and Alois M. Haas (Einsiedeln: Johannes Verlag, 1974). A similar critique can be found in Balthasar's Notes to Thomas Aquinas, *Summa Theologica, II-II, 171–182: Besondere Gnadengaben und die Zwei Wege des Menschlichen Lebens*, by Thomas Aquinas, Die Deutsche Thomas-Ausgabe 22 (Heidelberg: Kerle, 1954), 351–53. Balthasar's study of Aquinas's treatise on prophecy and his own speculative theology of prophecy and union remain somewhat unexplored treasures.

9

Thomas Aquinas and John of Damascus on the Light of the Transfiguration

Can We Speak of a Greek Patristic Turn in Thomas?

MARCUS PLESTED

My interest in Aquinas and his patristic connections began to take root when teaching a course at Cambridge on late patristic and early medieval theology in the early years of this century. This particular course positively encouraged students to discern connections and continuities between Aquinas and the earlier patristic tradition.[1] Cambridge at that time was also rather alive with controversy over the appropriation of Aquinas proposed within the theological movement "Radical Orthodoxy." These two factors led me to revisit my take on Aquinas. My own education and reading in modern Orthodox theology had predisposed me to look at him as the representative of a sterile scholasticism foreign to the tradition of Greek patristic and Byzantine theology. But somehow this simple dichotomy didn't quite ring true. This realization led me, eventually, to the book *Orthodox Readings of Aquinas*. In that book I present, among other things, the "Byzantine Aquinas"—Aquinas as read and understood by his many Byzantine admirers and valued especially for his mastery of and immersion in the Greek philosophical and patristic tradition. Appreciation of this Byzantine Aquinas can, I suggest, open up some fascinating lines

---

1. The course was designed by my sometime colleague A. N. Williams.

of inquiry as we seek to understand better Aquinas's mode of theologizing and in particular to appreciate the nature and force of his patristic foundations.

Gustave Bardy wrote that research into Thomas's patristic roots had "hardly begun" almost one hundred years ago. It remains a domain that is, as Carmelo Conticello put it in 2004, "still rather under-explored."[2] There has been some fine work done—by Conticello, Martin Morard, and others—but this emerging field is one of the most exciting and relatively wide-open arenas of contemporary Thomist scholarship. I for one hope that this volume will greatly stimulate further research into Thomas's patristic roots, particularly his *Greek* patristic roots.[3]

Aquinas expresses an extraordinary and unusual devotion to the Greek Fathers (or Doctors, to use his preferred term).[4] A well-worn anecdote has him express his preference for a copy of St. John Chrysostom's *Commentary on Matthew* over the whole city of Paris—not that he was ever offered the city as such: he was no Henry IV.[5] This vivid tale nonetheless nicely encapsulates Thomas's debt to the patristic revival of the twelfth century. The Golden Mouth was among the Greek Fathers translated in the middle of that century by Burgundio of Pisa, one of the key figures in the remarkable recovery of Greek patristic material in the Latin West at this time. Burgundio produced excellent translations of such seminal works as St. John of Damascus's *Exact Exposition of the Orthodox Faith* and Nemesius of Emesa's *On the Nature of Man*.[6] John of Dasmascus (in Burgundio's translation) had an increasingly decisive impact on Thomas's theology from his early works onward, for instance, the *Commentary on the Sentences* (1252–57) with its 240 citations from John (a

---

2. Bardy, "Sur les sources patristiques grecques de saint Thomas," *Revue des Sciences Philosophiques et Théologiques* 12 (1923): 493–502; Conticello, "Théophylacte de Bulgarie, source de Thomas d'Aquin (*Catena aurea in Ioannem*)," in *Philomathestatos, Festschrift Jacques Noret* (Leuven: Peeters, 2004), 63–75.

3. This opening section borrows and reworks material from my *Orthodox Readings of Aquinas* (Oxford: Oxford University Press, 2012), 15–21.

4. The term "Greek," for Thomas, denotes anyone writing in that language; hence it is used interchangeably of classical philosophers, Church Fathers, and contemporary Byzantines. Thomas prefers the term "doctors" to "fathers" in obedience to scriptural precept (*Contra Errores Graecorum*, chap. 2.41).

5. Jean-Pierre Torrell, *Saint Thomas Aquinas: The Person and His Work* (Washington, DC: Catholic University of America Press, 1996), 140.

6. These were high-profile projects, the former done at the behest of Pope Eugenius III and the latter dedicated to the Emperor Frederick Barbarossa.

figure conditioned in part by the Lombard's own extensive use of John).[7] The Damascene opened to Thomas by way of constructive synthesis virtually the whole Greek patristic tradition.[8]

Thomas's interest in the Greek Fathers seems to become ever more intense from the 1260s being especially evident in that massive work of patristic erudition, the *Catena Aurea* (1262/63 to 1267/68). This substantial collection of patristic commentaries on the four Gospels was composed at the command of Pope Urban IV as part of the run-up to the reunion Council of Lyons (1274). The relative preponderance of Greek texts in the work is certainly related to this papal *Drang nach Osten* but is hardly reducible to it. Chrysostom is the single most often cited author, pushing even Augustine (usually Thomas's preferred patristic source) into second place.[9] Among other Greek authorities, a substantial place is given to Origen, with smaller contributions from Athanasius, Eusebius, Basil, the two Gregories (of Nazianzus and Nyssa), Cyril of Alexandria, Dionysius the Areopagite, John of Damascus, and others (in total, fifty-seven Greek writers are cited alongside twenty-two Latin ones). But perhaps the most striking feature of the *Catena* is the prominence given to Theophylact of Ochrid (ca. 1050/60 to ca.1125).[10] Theophylact was one of Byzantium's finest scholars, bishops, and exegetes but was virtually unknown in the West at the time. It was Thomas who commissioned the translation of his biblical commentaries.[11]

Production of the *Catena* was to provide Thomas with a wealth of material to draw upon in later works. It is also in the 1260s that Thomas

---

7. Torrell, *Saint Thomas Aquinas*, 41.

8. Richard Cross sums it up well when he writes that John of Dasmascus was "almost the sole means whereby the most theologically vital Patristic tradition was passed on to Western theologians of the Middle Ages." "Perichoresis, Deification, and Christological Predication in John of Damascus," *Mediaeval Studies* 62 (2000): 69.

9. According to the *Index Thomisticus*, 2,689 vs. 2,075 mentions. Mere numbers are a crude indicator of esteem but also give an idea of the sheer scale of the work.

10. The *Index Thomisticus* gives 1,033 mentions, of which 362 *in Marcum*, 423 *in Lucam*, and 248 *in Joannem*.

11. Thomas's express citations of Theophylact do not appear to extend far beyond the *Catena Aurea*. He mentions him by name only once outside elsewhere, in the *Commentary on John* 11, l. 2, 1490. In this work, dated by Torrell to 1270–72, he is introduced as *quidam Graecus, scilicet Theophylactus*. That said, Conticello has shown that the *Commentary on John* reworks material from the *Catena Aurea*, including considerable (and unattributed) chunks of Theophylact ("San Tommaso ed i Padri," 79–86). See further Jane Sloan Peters, "*Quidam Graecus*: Theophylact of Ochrid in the *Catena Aurea in Ioannem* and the *Lectura Super Ioannem*," chap. 11, this volume.

begins making extensive use of the *acta* of the Ecumenical Councils. Here again Thomas is something of a pioneer: none of his immediate Latin predecessors had made substantial use of this material, and still less made it so central to their Christology. This is a commitment that appears to have grown and intensified throughout the 1260s and into the 1270s, developing to take in Constantinople II (553) and III (680–81).[12] Thomas is the first Latin theologian to make use of the *acta* of these later Ecumenical Councils.

Thomas's increasing use of conciliar material went hand in hand with a thoroughgoing and ever-intensifying engagement with the Greek Fathers, not only in his exegetical works but also in his more overtly theological works. Thomas's Christology, for instance, is certainly greatly indebted to the Damascene with its precise dismissals of Christological heresies and its keen apprehension of the force of the hypostatic union and the instrumentality of Christ's humanity. Thomas's profound commitment to Greek patristic and conciliar sources and the practical steps he took to extend the volume of such material available in Latin are quite remarkable and stand out by comparison with his contemporaries. This ever-increasing engagement with the Greek patristic tradition from the 1260s onward can, I suggest, be labeled a *Greek patristic turn* in Aquinas.

The remainder of this essay discusses one specific instance of this Greek patristic turn: Thomas's account of the Transfiguration of our Lord. Here again it is John of Damascus who plays a decisive role in the development of Thomas's thinking. This will also involve some discussion of the Byzantine tradition of interpretation of the Transfiguration and also of the reception of Thomas in the Byzantine Hesychast controversy, a controversy that turned in large measure on the question of the character of the light of the Transfiguration.[13]

The Transfiguration had long been a central *topos* of Greek patristic theology—far more so than in the Latin tradition—and the specific issue of the character of the divine light (created or uncreated) became a bitterly contested issue in the Hesychast Controversy, which convulsed

12. See Martin Morard, "Une source de saint Thomas d'Aquin: Le deuxième concile de Constantinople (553)," *Revue des Sciences Philosophiques et Théologiques* 81 (1997): 21–56; idem, "Thomas d'Aquin, lecteur des conciles," *Archivum Franciscanum Historicum* 98 (2005): 211–365.

13. I am currently working on a longer and more detailed article, "The Light of the Transfiguration and the Being of God in Aquinas, Palamas, and the Byzantine Hesychast Controversy." Some of the material in what follows comes from that project.

fourteenth-century Byzantium. The victorious party, led by St. Gregory Palamas, strenuously upheld the uncreated character of the light that shone from Christ at the Transfiguration—all this within the context of a careful elaboration of the union and distinction between the unknowable and imparticipable divine essence (*ousia*) and the partly knowable and participable divine activities, operations, energies, powers, or actualizations (*energeiai*).[14] I note in passing that it is wholly misleading to think of this distinction as a *distinctio realis* or indeed as any one of the various distinctions proposed within medieval Latin theology. In another context, I have christened the distinction a *distinctio unificans*—a distinction that unites.[15]

Aquinas played an important if belated part in this controversy with the attempt of some anti-Palamites (most notably the Athonite Hieromonk Prochoros Kydones) to marshal Thomas against the perceived novelties and aberrations of Palamas. But notwithstanding Aquinas's own crystal-clear identification of the essence (*essentia*) and existence (*esse*) of God—an identification that would seem to preclude utterly the Palamite distinction—the anti-Palamites proved spectacularly unsuccessful in seriously denting the Palamite ascendency. And on the specific issue of the Transfiguration, they found Thomas most unhelpful in their attempt to show the light to be Thabor to be merely a created symbol. Thomas's most significant theological legacy in Byzantium was precisely in the Palamite party, for instance, in the monk-emperor John Cantacuzene, Metropolitan Theophanes III of Nicaea, and Patriarch Gennadios Scholarios. Is it simply an accident that Thomas proved more useful to the Palamites than the anti-Palamites in the last century of the Roman or Byzantine Empire? I think not. While it is not within the scope of this chapter to engage in any extensive exploration of the wider topic of Aquinas and Palamas, I suggest that on the decisive issue of the light of the Transfiguration there is a good deal of common ground between the two, and this is largely because of Thomas's Greek patristic turn.

Thomas Aquinas devotes more attention to the Transfiguration of

---

14. Note the phrase "union and distinction." It is wholly misleading to think of Palamas as a theologian of distinction without also recognizing him as a theologian of union. Palamas does not speak of the distinction between essence and energies without also emphasizing their absolute union, nor of God's self-revelation in multiplicity without emphasizing God's absolute simplicity. The Dionysian dialectic of union and distinction is the key to understanding the Palamite doctrine of God. See especially his treatise *On Union and Distinction*.

15. "St Gregory Palamas on the Divine Simplicity," *Modern Theology* (forthcoming).

Christ than any other Latin author of his era.[16] His treatment of the topic is deeply shaped and informed by his immersion in the Greek Fathers, above all St. John of Damascus. Given this notable intensity of interest, it is surprising that the topic has received relatively little attention in Thomas scholarship. Even in his early *Sentences* commentary, Aquinas chooses to comment on the Transfiguration despite the fact that Peter Lombard himself does not propose the topic for discussion.[17] In this commentary, Aquinas's main interest is in the relation between the light of the Transfiguration and the light of the resurrection—the *claritas gloriae*. His conclusion is that it the light that shone from Christ's mortal body was real, sensible, and a manifestation of the resurrection glory of the saints. The light was the light of his glorified soul communicated to his body by an act of divine power.

At the time of the *Sentences* commentary, however, there is little sign that Greek patristic sources are decisively shaping his work on the topic— they are rather counted among the various *auctoritates* (Greek and Latin) to be sifted and considered as one reaches a conclusion on a given topic. But Greek patristic texts do begin to decisively move and shape Thomas's thinking on the topic from the early 1260s onward. This Greek patristic turn in Aquinas is evident in the later books of the *Catena Aurea*, in the expositions on Mark and, especially, Luke. John of Damascus's *Homily on the Transfiguration* is decidedly Thomas's chief and most important witness for the Transfiguration narrative in Luke 9:28–31. The central passage reads as follows:

Moses indeed was arrayed with a glory, which came from without; our Lord, with that which proceeded from the inherent brightness of Divine glory (*ex innato gloriae divinae fulgore*). For since in the hypostatic union there is one and the same glory of the Word and the flesh, he is transfigured not as receiving what he was not, but manifesting to his disciples what he was ... And his raiment was white and glistening; that is, lighted up by its participation of the divine light (*illustratus scilicet per divinae lucis participationem*).[18]

---

16. This has been ably documented in Aaron Canty, *Light and Glory: The Transfiguration of Christ in Early Franciscan and Dominican Theology* (Washington, DC: Catholic University of America Press, 2011). See also Édouard Divry, *La transfiguration selon l'orient et l'occident: Grégoire Palamas, Thomas d'Aquin. Vers un dénouement oecuménique* (Paris: Téqui, 2009), and my *Orthodox Readings of Aquinas*, 80–83.

17. *Sent.* III, q. 16, aa. 1–2.

18. *Catena in Lucam* 9 l.6 (trans. in *Catena Aurea*, vol. III, *St. Luke*, ed. John Henry Newman [London: St. Austin Press, 1999], 319–20). John of Damascus, *Oration on the Transfiguration* 10–13 (Kotter V: 449–52). The extract given here extract corresponds to ll. 449.39–43; 450.13–15, 17–19; 452.36, 41–42.

The selection of this text and the prominence given it mark a significant shift in Thomas's account of the Transfiguration. Here, the emphasis is decidedly Christological: by virtue of the hypostatic union, the light of the Transfiguration is the very light of the divinity, a revelation of what he was—the uncreated Word—and, by implication, not merely a manifestation of the resurrection glory of the saints.

Thomas's most developed treatment of the topic comes in the *Tertia Pars* of the *Summa Theologiae* (q. 45). In this *Quaestio*, Thomas considers the fittingness of the Transfiguration, the relationship between the light of the Transfiguration and the light of glory, the fittingness of the witnesses (Moses, Elijah, Peter, James, and John), and the fittingness of the addition of the Father's voice. He begins by affirming the fittingness of the Transfiguration as a showing forth of Christ's inner glory and as foretaste of the glory to which his disciples will be configured at the resurrection. This was to strengthen the disciples for the trials ahead and to show them the promise that awaits them. Thomas proceeds to explain:

> The clarity which Christ assumed in his transfiguration was the light of glory as to its essence (*ad essentiam*), but not as to its mode of being (*ad modum essendi*). For the light of the glorified body is derived from that of the soul, as Augustine says in his *Epistle to Dioscorus*. And in like manner, the light of Christ's body in his transfiguration derived from his divinity, as the Damascene says, and from the glory of his soul. (*ST* III, q. 45, a. 2)

The light of the Transfiguration, as a temporary revelation permitted by divine dispensation, differs from the permanent state of luminosity vouchsafed to the saints in the resurrection. A further difference is that the glorification of the saints represents a change in state, whereas the Transfiguration manifests the inner state of Christ:

> But in Christ's transfiguration light overflowed from his divinity and from his soul into his body, not as an immanent quality affecting his very body, but rather after the manner of a transient passion, as when the air is lit up by the sun. (*ST* III,ª q. 45, a. 2)

The shining garments, moreover, serve as a prefiguration of the resurrection glory of the saints with the added qualification that this light of glory "will be surpassed by that of Christ, just as the brightness of the snow is surpassed by that of the sun" (*ST* III,ª q. 45, a. 2, ad 3).

Thomas is at pains to demonstrate not only the connection between the light of the Transfiguration and the light of glory (with the various differentiating factors noted above) but also the unfathomable superiority of the light of the Transfiguration, stemming as it does from both a glorified soul and, more importantly, the divinity. Here, Thomas is combining in an intriguing fashion the testimonies of Augustine (affirming that the light of glory comes from the soul) and John of Damascus (affirming that the light of the Transfiguration is the very light of the divinity). Thomas does not seem to see the need to reconcile these accounts, which are in fact dealing with different, if related, topics (Augustine's *Epistle to Dioscorus* treats of the outpouring of the soul's glory at the resurrection without reference to the Transfiguration). He contents himself with conjunctions: "the light of Christ's body in his transfiguration derived from his divinity, as the Damascene says, *and* from the glory of his soul" (*ST* III,ᵃ q. 45, a. 2) "light overflowed from his divinity *and* from his soul into his body" (*ST* III,ᵃ q. 45, a. 2).[19]

Thomas could hardly fail to offer some account of the connection between the light of the Transfiguration and the light of the resurrection given how central that question was to Latin treatments of the topic. But he also seems to be doing something rather more in his insistence, based unambiguously on John of Damascus, that the light of the Transfiguration is the very light of the Godhead shining forth from a mortal human body. Thomas is, in other words, combining insights from the Latin Augustinian tradition with the Greek patristic tradition encapsulated in the Damascene. These insights do not represent an "either-or" for Thomas but a "both-and": from the divinity *and* from the soul. Thomas does not enter into any great detail as to how the light of Christ's divinity is poured out on his body, although it appears that the soul performs some sort of mediating role. Nor does Thomas enter into any great detail into the question of how the disciples see and experience the uncreated light of the divinity within the confines of the created order. But, again, it is reasonable to suppose on the basis of other considerations in Thomas's works that while the light of the Transfiguration is unambiguously uncreated as to its origin and source, the vision and experience of that light requires some sort of change or transformation in the creature given that "the glory which was then being revealed surpasses in excellence the sense and faculty of all mortal beings" (*ST* III,ᵃ q. 45, a. 4, ad 4). In the context of this last remark, Thomas seems to have abandoned the contention of his *Sentences* commentary that the light of the Transfiguration was sen-

19. Emphasis mine.

sible to human eyes (*Sent.* III, d. 16, q. 2, a. 1, co.). In short, while the *Sentences* commentary would certainly seem to support the contention that the light of the Transfiguration was created, the same cannot be said so blithely of his mature works.

It is evident that the kind of questions beginning to be foregrounded here are not necessarily those most central to Thomas or his Latin contemporaries. Indeed, they bring us more obviously into Byzantine territory and specifically the territory of the Hesychast Controversy: the vexed question of the character of the light of the Transfiguration (created or uncreated) and the nature of the disciples' vision of that light. There is a certain anachronism here (akin to asking Origen why he is not more Nicene). Even at the time of the Hesychast Controversy, some of the more sophisticated anti-Palamites, such as Theodore Dexios, complained when asked to declare the light of the Transfiguration to be either created or uncreated, characterizing this as a false choice. That said, it is not inapposite to begin to raise such questions of Thomas, given that he was dragged into this controversy at a late stage by the anti-Palamite camp in the run-up to the last great Palamite synod, the Council of Constantinople (1368).

But before turning to the appropriation of Aquinas by anti-Palamites and Palamites alike in the latter phases of the Hesychast Controversy, a few words are needed on Byzantine tradition of interpretation of the Transfiguration. In the Greek patristic and ascetic tradition, interpretation of the Transfiguration is routinely bound up with mystical experience—the divine and deifying vision of God as light, a vision open to human beings not only in the next life but also in this life. The light of the Transfiguration is also frequently identified with the light that shone from the face of Moses and the visionary experiences of St. Paul. Perhaps the preeminent expositor of this tradition is the author of the Macarian Homilies (Macarius-Symeon; Pseudo-Macarius; hereafter simply "Macarius").[20]

As the body of the Lord was glorified when he ascended the mountain and was transfigured into the divine glory and the infinite light, so too are the bodies of

20. See further R. Staats, "Die Metamorphose des Christen: Die Wandlungslehre des Makarios-Symeon im Zusammenhang seiner Anthropologie, Christologie und Eucharistielehre," *Grundbegriffe christlicher Ästhetik: Beiträge des V. Makarios-Symposiums Preetz 1995*, ed. K. Fitschen and R. Staats (Wiesbaden: Harrassowitz 1997), 16–22; A. Golitzin, "A Testimony to Christianity as Transfiguration: The Macarian Homilies and Orthodox Spirituality," in *Orthodox and Wesleyan Spirituality*, ed. S. Kimbrough (Crestwood, NY: SVS Press, 2002), 129–56; and my *The Macarian Legacy* (Oxford: Oxford University Press, 2004), 33–34, 37–38, 216–23.

the saints glorified and resplendent. For as the glory that was within Christ covered his body and shone forth, in the same way the power of Christ that is [now] within the saints will overflow outwards upon their bodies.[21]

There are many other writers in the Greek tradition with an analogous mysticism of light (Evagrius of Pontus, St. Diadochus of Photice, St. Symeon the New Theologian), but rarely, before the Hesychast Controversy, do we find the same the kind of intensity coupled with a consistent connection with the Transfiguration.[22] This Macarian tradition was still very much alive at the time of the Hesychast Controversy. Early figures in the Hesychast revival, such as St. Gregory of Sinai and St. Theoleptos of Philadelphia, treat the vision of divine light as the summit of monastic experience and emphasize this light is the same divine light that shone from Christ at his Transfiguration.

Not everyone agreed, notably the celebrated monk and theologian Barlaam the Calabrian, who found such claims primitive and delusional. Barlaam had achieved a measure of fame in Byzantium as the Orthodox spokesperson in dialogue with the Latins in 1334. In those debates, he expressed disdain for Thomas Aquinas and his excessively rationalizing approach to theology, including his mistaken use of the language of substance and accidents in relation to God. Matters such as the *filioque* were, according to Barlaam, quite beyond any sort of demonstration. St. Gregory Palamas enters the fray at this time arguing precisely for the propriety of apodictic argumentation in theology and producing a creative approach to the *aporia* of the *filioque* in so doing.[23]

In his *First Letter to Palamas*, Barlaam begins to outline an understanding of illumination as essentially intellectual and cognitive—a gift of knowledge from God the "fount of immaterial and intellectual light."[24] Gregory leaps on Barlaam's rather jejune doctrine of illumination, immediately perceiving that it ran counter to Hesychast evocations of mystical experience, and in particular the experience of God as light. This strand

---

21. Collection II 15.38; Kallistos Ware observes that, in his evocations of the outpouring of the soul's glory onto the body at the Resurrection, Aquinas "writes in similar terms" to Macarius-Symeon, "The Transfiguration of the Body," *Sobornost* 4.8 (1963), 420–33.

22. See further H.-V. Beyer, "Die Lichtlehre der Mönche des vierzehnten und des vierten Jahrhunderts, erörtert am Beispiel des Gregorios Sinaïtes, des Evagrios Pontikos und des Ps.-Makarios/Symeon," *Jahrbuch der österreichischen Byzantinistik* 31 (1981): 473–512.

23. See my *Orthodox Readings of Aquinas*, 37–39.

24. *Epistle* 1.290. See further R. Sinkewicz, "The Doctrine of God in the Early Writings of Barlaam the Calabrian," *Mediaeval Studies* 44 (1982): 181–242.

of the debate was to assume increasing importance, soon utterly eclipsing the slightly tedious debate about apodictic demonstration. For Barlaam, there is no prospect of a vision of God as light (and certainly no prospect of any sort of sensible experience) but only a gift of knowledge. God may be named as light, but this is by virtue of this being the transcendent inaccessible and unknowable cause of light.[25]

What began as a somewhat recondite debate about theological knowledge and argumentation rapidly became a debate about the reality of mystical experience and particularly the possibility of a vison of God as light. In the process, the character of the light of the Transfiguration assumed increasing prominence in Gregory's assault on Barlaam, mostly in the third of his *Triads* and in the *Tome of the Holy Mountain* (both 1340).[26] Having instanced Maximus and Macarius as the chief patristic witnesses to the possibility of the vision of God as light and affirmed the reality of deification, the *Tome of the Holy Mountain* goes on to declare:

Whoever says that the light that shone around the disciples of Thabor was a phantasm and a symbol of the kind that comes into being and disappears, but has no real being, and is not beyond all cognition, but is an energy inferior to cognition, stands in clear contradiction to the opinions of the saints.[27]

The *Tome of the Holy Mountain* proceeds to underline the uncreated character of the divine energies, of which the light of Thabor was such a shining example. The question of the character of the light of the Transfiguration was to become a kind of cipher or shorthand for easy identification of theological proclivities.[28] To deem it created was to stand with Barlaam; to affirm it as uncreated was to side with Palamas (and, by extension, his teaching on the uncreated energies of God). Barlaam himself had no in-

---

25. *Against the Latins* A 4.12, ed. Fyrigos, *Opere contro i Latini* (Vatican City: Biblioteca Apostolica Vaticana, 1998).

26. The uncreated character of the Thaboric light remained a consistent feature of Gregory's teaching throughout his career. His two *Homilies on the Transfiguration* serve as precious instances of the pastoral and practical import of his teaching on the Transfiguration in a less obviously polemical and nontechnical mode.

27. *Tome of the Holy Mountain* (PG 150 1232B). St. John of Damascus's *Homily on the Transfiguration* is the chief source cited in support.

28. This was to prove remarkably enduring. A Jesuit visitor to Mt. Athos in the early seventeenth century reported that while the monks were a little hazy as to the details of the essence-energies distinction, they were adamant in viewing denial of the uncreated character of the Thaboric light as rank heresy. G. Hofmann, "Apostolato dei Gesuiti nell'Oriente greco, 1583–1773," cited in J. N. Cañellas, *La résistance d'Akindynos à Grégoire Palamas* (Leuven: Peeters 1996), xv–xvi.

tention of focusing the debate on the Transfiguration in this way, and it is a mark of Gregory's strategic gifts that he was able to push the debate in this direction.[29] This is the principal question on which Barlaam was indicted at the Council of Constantinople of June 1341. Barlaam's contention in his *Against the Messalians* that the light of Thabor was not the light of the divinity and was inferior to an act of human cognition was selected for particular censure.[30] Barlaam left the empire soon after and was rapidly disowned even by his erstwhile supporters.

There is no doubt that the anti-Palamite camp continued to struggle mightily with the question of the Transfiguration and much resented the created/uncreated axis onto which Palamas had successfully shifted the debate. Gregory Akindynos, leader of the anti-Palamite party following Barlaam's exit from the scene, regards Palamas's teaching with undisguised loathing. For Akindynos, it is clear that God alone is uncreated and that all that is outside him and effected by him is by definition created—whether these be men, angels, gods of some kind, graces, splendors, divinities, deifying gifts.[31] Concomitantly, all that properly belongs to him—life, wisdom, goodness, power—belongs to his uncreated essence.[32] Akindynos holds that the light of Thabor, while certainly a revelation of the divinity of Christ and a manifestation of the Logos, cannot be construed as uncreated because God is simple and invisible. Sources such as the Damascene, in his reading, do not warrant any such construal. He refuses to speculate as to the precise character of the light or the mode of the disciples' apprehension of that light. For him it suffices to say, in line with his reading of patristic and liturgical tradition, that Christ revealed his divinity to the disciples on the mountain as he wished and insofar as they were able to behold it.[33]

Akindynos's refusal to be pinned down on the character of the light of Thabor is telling. While his basic contention that all that is effected by God is created would seem to suggest that the light must be considered as creaturely, he is loath to admit this, emphasizing instead that the

---

29. See also his *Third Letter to Akindynos* (early 1341), ed. Chrestou (Thessaloniki: Kyromanos 1962), 296–312: Gregory argues that Barlaam's teaching makes a nonsense of the Transfiguration. If this light were not the revelation of the kingdom and power of God but merely some created effect, then God himself could be no more than a creature. If God's energies are not uncreated, then he is not God and not uncreated.

30. *Synodal Tome* (PG 151 682CD).

31. *Refutation* 1.39 (ed. Cañellas, p. 47). Note that, unlike Barlaam, Akindynos is not concerned to attack Hesychast practices and claims.

32. *Refutation* 3.15–16 (ed. Cañellas, pp. 188–90).

33. *Refutation* 1.40–42 (ed. Cañellas, pp. 48–50).

light is—somehow—a true, if necessarily limited, revelation of the Logos. Akindynos's hesitation here indicates what was to become a point of acute vulnerability for the anti-Palamite cause. After the death of Akindynos in 1348, the brilliant scholar Nikephoros Gregoras emerged as leader of the anti-Palamite party. Casting himself as the steadfast representative of Church tradition standing against the novelties of Palamas, Gregoras refuses to allow any distinction between God's simple essence and his supposedly uncreated energies. Gregoras had no hesitation in defining the light of Thabor as created, inferior to the angels, patently intelligible, and visible. The light was not God and not some uncreated divinity. God, being beyond mind and beyond essence, cannot be seen.[34]

A further council in 1351 quashed the anti-Palamite party and definitively canonized the essence-energies distinction. While opposition continued, it had little prospect thereafter of seriously challenging the Palamite ascendency. Moreover, the issue of the light of Thabor remained a central and defining question and one to which the anti-Palamite camp had yet to find a satisfactory answer. Up to this point, the debate was purely an intra-Byzantine affair. Barlaam, Akindynos, and Gregoras had no significant connections with contemporary developments in Latin theology. Indeed, they tended to be more hostile to Latin theology than the Palamite party. But from 1354, with the beginning of the translation of the works of Thomas Aquinas into Greek, this began to change.

The Athonite priest-monk Prochoros Kydones was, from the mid-1360s, the first to draw on contemporary Latin theology to challenge the Palamite settlement.[35] Brother to the illustrious Demetrios (chief minister to three emperors and translator of the *Summa contra Gentiles*, much of the *Summa Theologiae*, and many other works of Thomas), Prochoros produced a weighty tome in six books, *On Essence and Energy* (*De Essentia et Operatione*).[36] The first five books of *On Essence and Energy* are largely composed of assembled translations from the *Summa contra Gentiles, Summa Theologiae*, and *De Potentia*.[37] But by contrast, Book VI,

34. *Historia Romana* 3, ed. Bekker (Cambridge: Cambridge University Press, 1855), 434–45.

35. See my *Orthodox Readings of Aquinas*, 73–84. Some material from that section of the book is worked into the narrative here.

36. *De Essentia et Operatione* 1–2 (PG 151 1191–1242) (attributed to Akindynos), 6 (ed. Manuel Candal); M. Candal, "El libro VI de Prócoro Cidonio [sobre la luz tabórica]," *Orientalia Christiana Periodica* 20 (1954): 247–96.

37. Prochoros's own translation efforts were, by contrast to those of his brother, largely confined to texts he found useful in his struggle against Palamite theology.

On the Light of Thabor, is largely an original composition. While sticking closely to Thomas's methodology and some of his general principles, Prochoros produces an account of the light of the Transfiguration that is seriously at variance with that of his avowed master. In his long "response" section, Prochoros contends that while we may speak of God's essence as light, this is an analogy and not a homonym. The light of Thabor cannot be the light of the essence; because God cannot be the accidental cause of anything, the light is rather to be understood allegorically, as a natural symbol or type of a divine mystery. The response section concludes by reaffirming the created nature of the light of Thabor, a created light that shone from the body of Christ representing by analogy the light of his soul illumined by its contemplation of the divine essence.

Even though Prochoros had himself translated Thomas's *Quaestio* on the Transfiguration (*ST* III, q. 45), Prochoros's own take on the question is very much his own. In particular, he substantially downplays the testimony of the Damascene, so significant in Thomas's own account of outpouring of the light of the divinity at the Transfiguration. For Prochoros, the testimony of the Damascene and other Fathers seemingly supportive of the uncreated character of the Thaboric light must be interpreted in terms of a natural created symbol. All divine activity *ad extra* must be interpreted as created. While we do find points of contact with Thomas—for example, in the attention paid to the human soul's vision of the divine essence—there is little left in Prochoros of Thomas's overflowing of light "from the divinity and from the human soul" of Christ. And while Thomas does speak of the created effects of divine activity, that activity is not itself to be construed as created.

At his trial, conducted by Patriarch Philotheos Kokkinos, Prochoros appears to have abandoned the contention that the light of Thabor is simply created by adopting instead the position that it is somehow both created and uncreated, since Christ is dual—both God and man. This wavering position has none of either Palamas's or Aquinas's Christological clarity and rigor. In fact, by virtue of their common roots in Greek patristic and conciliar tradition, it is Patriarch Philotheos Kokkinos who is far closer to Aquinas here in his apprehension of the perfect union of divinity and humanity of Christ—and in his use of the Damascene as his prime witness to the character of the Thaboric light. Prochoros is also said to have likened the light that shone from Christ with that which shone from Moses, holding that both were temporary phenomena and simply came and went. Again, this is in direct contradiction to what we find in

Aquinas. Kokkinos, like Aquinas, draws once again on the Damascene to show that Moses's light was exterior to him, whereas Christ's divine light came from within.

Prochoros's position on the created character of the light of Thabor is essentially that of his anti-Palamite forebears Barlaam and Gregoras. Neither in *On Essence and Energy* nor at his trial in 1368 does Prochoros accurately represent the thinking of Thomas Aquinas. One is led to the conclusion that Thomas was useful to Prochoros principally as a source of anti-Palamite ammunition. Where Thomas was not helpful on this score, he was simply left aside. Thomas's own contributions on the specific matter of the Transfiguration do not substantially affect Prochoros's account precisely because they ran counter to Prochoros's preestablished position on the merely created and symbolic character of the light of the Transfiguration.

Prochoros's opponents were quick to recognize that Aquinas was not a natural ally of the anti-Palamite cause. Indeed, they moved to appropriate Aquinas to their own ends. This pattern of Palamite appropriation of Aquinas was already evident in the anti-Latin treatises of Neilos Kabasilas, focusing largely on the matter of the *filioque*, but it is applied specifically to the question of the light of Thabor in the refutations of Prochoros composed by the monk-emperor John Kantakuzene and Metropolitan Theophanes III of Nicaea.[38]

Given what I have said about Aquinas's debt to John of Damascus in the specific matter of the character of the light of the Transfiguration, I can only conclude that there is a certain justice in this Palamite appropriation of Aquinas. By virtue of his own Greek patristic turn, Aquinas came to stand closer to the Palamites than the anti-Palamites on the issue of the uncreated nature of the light of Thabor. In closing, I suggest that the Byzantine Aquinas—Thomas as received and admired by his many Byzantine readers—was indubitably a Palamite.

38. See my *Orthodox Readings of Aquinas*, 84–95.

10

Worshiping the Incarnate God

Thomas Aquinas on *Latria* and the Icon of Christ

JOHN SEHORN

Introduction

In *ST* III, q. 25, a. 3, Thomas Aquinas asks whether the adoration of *latria* should be directed to the image of Christ.[1] Thomas's answer, in short, is yes—the image of Christ is to be adored with the adoration of *latria*, that is, the worship due to God alone.[2] This jarring claim appears to run directly counter to the teaching of the Seventh Ecumenical Council in 787 (Nicaea II) and indeed to constitute outright idolatry.[3] How to explain

1. *ST* III, q. 25, prooemium. Unless otherwise noted, English translations of the *Summa Theologiae* are from St. Thomas Aquinas, *Summa Theologiae*, Works of St. Thomas Aquinas, vols. 13–20, trans. Fr. Laurence Shapcote, OP, ed. John Mortensen and Enrique Alarcón (Lander, WY: Aquinas Institute for the Study of Sacred Doctrine, 2012). Latin quotations of Thomas are from the Corpus Thomisticum website, accessed September 9, 2018, http://www.corpusthomisticum.org.

2. In common English usage, the word "worship" has come during the twentieth century to refer primarily or exclusively to the honor due to God alone. But until recently, "worship" had a wide range of meaning and referred appropriately to the veneration of saints, angels, and even living human beings. For instance, the 1662 Book of Common Prayer's matrimony service has the groom say to his bride, "With my body I thee worship." Even now, "Your Worship" can serve as a form of address for a magistrate. Throughout this essay I use "worship" in this broad, inclusive sense.

3. The *Catechism of the Catholic Church* implies that only by denying precisely what Thomas apparently affirms can one say that "Christian veneration of images is not contrary to the first commandment which proscribes idols.... The honor paid to sacred images is a 'respectful

this? The quick answer comes by way of appeal to the fourth-century Cappadocian Basil the Great, who taught that the honor paid an image is referred to its prototype. For Thomas and other scholastics, this provides the key to discerning the *kind* of reverence owed sacred images. Because the honor given the image passes over to the one depicted, the image is due an honor proportionate to its prototype. And because Christ is God and therefore honored with *latria*, so too should his image be honored with *latria*. Given the apparent straightforwardness of Thomas's view, what are we to make of its divergence from Nicaea II?

The following attempts to elucidate Thomas's teaching, its rationale, and its implications, especially in relation to the authoritative teaching of Nicaea II. Before turning to Aquinas's own teaching, I first offer a brief sketch of practices and attitudes surrounding sacred images in the Christian West to provide context for Thomas's teaching. A second piece of groundwork investigates Thomas's definition of three key terms: *latria*, *adoratio*, and *imago*. Third, I briefly review Thomas's understanding of the role of bodily things in the worship of God. There follows a careful examination of *ST* III, q. 25, a. 3, that attends particularly to how Thomas builds on his incarnational Christology and synthesizes his main authorities: the Third and Fifth Ecumenical Councils, Augustine, Basil, John of Damascus, and Aristotle. Finally, I discuss Thomas's divergences from the teaching of Nicaea II, particularly as developed in Byzantium by Theodore Studites, then close by reflecting on the significance of these divergences.

Images in the Christian West

While the popes immediately accepted the doctrine (if not the ecumenicity) of Nicaea II, its reception north of the Alps was cool.[4] Debates over sacred images effectively came to an end in the West with official papal recognition of Nicaea II as ecumenical at the Council of Constantinople in 879–880. Strikingly, the council's teaching appears to have fallen promptly into oblivion in the West.[5] Yet more strikingly, just after Con-

---

veneration' (*reverens veneratio*), not the adoration due to God alone [= *latria*]" (2132). Ironically, it immediately goes on to quote Aquinas, *ST* II-II, q. 81, a. 3, ad 3 (discussed below).

4. The best discussion of the image controversies among the Carolingians is Thomas F. X. Noble, *Images, Iconoclasm, and the Carolingians* (Philadelphia: University of Pennsylvania Press, 2009).

5. See Jean-Claude Schmitt, "L'Occident, Nicée II et les images du VIIIe au XIIIe siècle,"

stantinople IV, the Frankish aversion to image veneration began to give way to a cult of images that developed independently of Byzantine iconodulia. In the late ninth century, western European reliquaries began to take on representational form. Over the course of the next two centuries, the veneration of the relic contained in the statue migrated to the statue itself, until eventually statues that were not reliquaries were common objects of religious veneration.[6] From the tenth to the thirteenth centuries, the fundamental legitimacy of producing and venerating sacred images only elicited serious theological defense when it was occasionally challenged by Christian heretics or by Jews.[7]

Pope Innocent III (r. 1198–1216) enhanced the liturgical and devotional importance of sacred images through patronage of the arts,[8] through elaborate processions,[9] and through the attachment of an indulgence to a prayer in honor of the Veronica image at St. Peter's.[10] In 1289, Pope Nicholas IV promulgated an indulgence rewarding the veneration of the Veronica itself.[11] Processions with sacred images were a regular part of life in Italian villages.[12] In public devotions, "images were intended to arouse intense spirituality in the worshipping beholder. The effect was heightened as the images were often surrounded by banks of light—candelabra in the churches and torches in the streets."[13] Nor were sacred images only found in public liturgy. Western Christians in the High Middle Ages encountered sacred art in a wide variety of contexts and media: statuary, mosaics, paintings, murals, stained glass, reliquaries, vestments, manuscripts, doors, walls, columns, and so on.[14] In Thomas's era, especially in Italy, the lines between "Western" and "Eastern" art are often blurry

---

in *Nicée II, 787–1987: Douze siècles d'images religieuses. Actes du colloque international Nicée II tenu au Collège de France, Paris, les 2, 3, 4 octobre 1986*, ed. François Boispflug and Nicolas Lossky (Paris: Cerf, 1987), 272–82.

6. Schmitt, "L'Occident," 283–86.

7. Schmitt, "L'Occident," 286–90.

8. Brenda M. Bolton, "Advertise the Message: Images in Rome at the Turn of the Twelfth Century," in *The Church and the Arts*, ed. Diana Wood (Cambridge, MA: Blackwell, 1995), 118.

9. Bolton, "Advertise the Message," 125.

10. Flora Lewis, "Rewarding Devotion: Indulgences and the Promotion of Images," in *The Church and the Arts*, 179; Alain Besançon, *L'image interdite: Une histoire intellectuelle de l'iconoclasme* (Paris: Fayard, 1994), 211.

11. Lewis, "Rewarding Devotion," 180.

12. Bolton, "Advertise the Message," 125.

13. Bolton, "Advertise the Message," 124.

14. See, e.g., Herbert L. Kessler and Johanna Zacharias, *Rome 1300: On the Path of the Pilgrim* (New Haven, CT: Yale University Press, 2000).

owing to the common heritage of Late Antiquity, fresh Byzantine artistic influence,[15] and the influx of Eastern images and relics from to the Crusades, especially after the sack of Constantinople in 1204.[16]

While Thomas's theological consideration of sacred images is relatively brief, they occupy a prominent place during his lifetime in Western Christian worship and devotion, public and private. One need only recall the two stories told of Thomas hearing locutions from images of Christ Crucified. Despite reservations such as Bernard of Clairvaux's, Latin theology generally displayed an openness to the images' capacity to "transfer" the mind and affection of the devotee from the visible world to the invisible. While this represents material rapprochement with Greek thought, Western knowledge of Eastern theological explanations for image worship remained thin. Gratian does quote Nicaea II on images, but to my knowledge no scholastic follows suit.[17] Aquinas draws his sole citation of Nicaea II from Gratian, but on a question of canon law. He follows Gratian in referring to the canon in question as belonging to "the Seventh Synod" (*septime synodi*), suggesting his awareness of its ecumenical status, but he does not know the conciliar definitions.[18] Nor does Thomas know the standard Byzantine theological defenses of iconodulia from the First Iconoclasm (e.g., the Damascene's three *Orationes de imaginibus*) or from the Second (e.g., Theodore Studites). The sole Greek source on icons to which Thomas has access is the single relevant chapter of the Damascene's *De Fide Orthodoxa*, which was fully translated into Latin in the twelfth century by Burgundio of Pisa.[19]

15. See, e.g., Anne Derbes, "Images East and West: The Ascent of the Cross," in *The Sacred Image East and West*, ed. Robert Ousterhout and Leslie Brubaker (Chicago: University of Illinois Press, 1995), 110.

16. See Hans Belting, *The Image and Its Public in the Middle Ages: Form and Function of Early Paintings of the Passion*, trans. Mark Bartusis and Raymond Meyer (New Rochelle, NY: Aristide D. Caratzas, 1990), 214.

17. *Decreti*, pars 3, dist. 3, c. 28.

18. Martin Morard, "Thomas d'Aquin lecteur des conciles," *Archivum Franciscanum Historicum* 98 (2005): 317. Thomas's citation is at *Quodlibet* IX, q. 7, a. 2, obj. 2.

19. Cf. J.-P. Torrell, OP, *Le Verbe Incarné: Tome troisième. 3a, Questions 16–26* (Paris: Cerf, 2002), 450–51. E. M. Buytaert dates Burgundio's translation to 1153–54. Sometime before 1224, this translation was divided into four books, possibly by Philip the Chancellor, and likely on the model of the Lombard's *Sentences*. St. John of Damascus, *De Fide Orthodoxa: Versions of Burgundio and Cerbanus*, ed. E. M. Buytaert, OFM (St. Bonaventure, NY: Franciscan Institute, 1955), ix–xv, xviii. Throughout this chapter, I cite the text as Thomas will have read it, then provide the original citation in brackets. The Greek critical edition, which provides both systems of citation, is Bonifatius Kotter, ed., *Die Schriften des Johannes*

Thomas's Terminology

To comprehend Thomas's teaching, consideration of three key terms is necessary: *latria*, *adoratio*, and *imago*.

Latria

For both East and West, *latria* (λατρεία, or "service") denotes worship that is due to God alone.[20] In his *Scriptum*, Thomas distinguishes three more precise meanings of the term. The word *latria* can refer to a virtue, to that virtue's matter, or to an act of that virtue.[21] As a virtue, *latria* is synonymous with *religio*,[22] an equation that seems to have been introduced by William of Auxerre (d. 1231) in his *Summa Aurea* by means of a spurious quote from Cicero.[23] In the *Summa Theologiae*, Thomas drops one of the meanings he identifies in the *Scriptum*, leaving us with a distinction between *latria* considered as a virtue and *latria* as an act of that virtue.[24]

Latria is distinguished from *dulia*, the worship due to creatures of excellence. Although these are Greek terms, Eastern theologians did not use λατρεία and δουλεία as a technical pairing.[25] Rather, Thomas's authority for the distinction is Augustine's inquiry into the worship due to God alone in *City of God* 10.1, where Augustine concludes that Latin has no adequate term and resolves to rely on the Greek *latria*.[26] This passage provides the *sed contra* for *ST* II-II, q. 103, a. 3, which asks whether *dulia* is a special virtue distinct from *latria*. Interestingly, Augustine does not actually name *dulia* in the *City of God* passage, simply saying that this kind of service is called in Greek "by another name" (*alio nomine*). In his citation of the passage, Aquinas supplies *dulia* as if Augustine himself

---

von Damaskos, II: Expositio Fidei, Patristische Texte und Studien 12 (New York: Walter de Gruyter, 1973).

20. See, e.g., *Summa contra Gentiles*, trans. Vernon J. Bourke (Notre Dame, IN: University of Notre Dame Press, 1975), III, chap. 119; chap. 120.

21. *Scriptum* 3.9.1.1.1 co.

22. *ST* II-II, q. 94, a. 1, ad 2: as a virtue, "latria denotes the same as religion."

23. R. Jared Staudt, "Religion as a Virtue: Thomas Aquinas on Worship through Justice, Law, and Charity" (PhD diss., Ave Maria University, 2008), 72–73; cf. Odon Lottin, OSB, *Psychologie et morale aux XIIe et XIIIe siècles, tome III: Problèmes de morale*, part 2/1 (Gembloux, Belgium: J. Duculot, 1949), 318–19.

24. *ST* II-II, q. 94, a. 1, ad 2.

25. See Venance Grumel, s.v. "Images (Culte des)," in *Dictionnaire de théologie catholique*, vol. 7, pt. 1 (Paris: Letouzey et Ané, 1927), col. 809; *A Patristic Greek Lexicon*, ed. G. W. H. Lampe (New York: Oxford University Press, 1961), s.v. "δουλεία, ἡ."

26. CCSL 47:272.

used it.[27] There are in fact two passages where Augustine names *dulia* as the counterpart to *latria*.[28] One of these is quoted by the 825 Council of Paris, but the scholastics do not cite them.[29]

It is difficult to trace the details of how the *latria-dulia* pairing became standard, but a general picture emerges clearly enough. In the first half of the twelfth century, it appears in Hugh of St. Victor, who presumably gleaned it from Augustine.[30] Not long after, it is found in the *Enarrationes in Matthaeum* spuriously ascribed to Anselm of Laon.[31] According to Artur Michael Landgraf, if the attribution of this text to Gottfried of Babion (d. 1158) is accurate, it is the first appearance of the pairing in scholastic theology. Otherwise, he points to Peter Lombard's Psalms commentary and to Robert of Melun (d. 1167).[32] In any case, the inclusion of the pairing in the Lombard's *Sentences* secured its place in subsequent scholastic treatments.

For Aquinas, *latria* and *dulia* are not distinguished by degree, but by species.[33] As a virtue, *latria* is synonymous with *religio*; *dulia*, however, belongs to the virtue of *observantia*.[34] The infinite gap between their re-

---

27. As Ronald Thomas Bentley notes, the Greek of Eph 6:5, to which Augustine alludes here, does support the conclusion that he means *dulia*. "'Worship God Alone': The Emerging Christian Tradition of *Latreia*" (PhD diss., University of Virginia, 2009), 126. Thomas similarly supplies *dulia* when quoting the same passage (albeit slightly differently) at *Cat. in Matt.*, cap. 4, lect. 4. He does the same when quoting *City of God* 10.4 at *ST* II-II, q. 84, a. 1, ad 1. In this passage, Augustine uses *colere*, *venerari*, and *adorare*, but not *dulia*.

28. *Quaestiones Exodi* 94: "Hic [Ex 23:33] graecus δουλεύσῃς habet, non λατρεύσῃς. Vnde intelligitur, quia et δουλεία debetur deo tamquam domino, λατρεία uero nonnisi deo tamquam deo" (CCSL 33:117); *De Trinitate* 1.6.13: "Maxime uero illo loco satis claret quod spiritus sanctus non sit creatura ubi iubemur non seruire *creaturae* sed *creatori* [Rom 1:25], non eo modo quo iubemur *per caritatem* seruire *inuicem* [Gal 5:13], quod est graece δουλεύειν, sed eo modo quo tantum deo seruitur, quod est graece λατρεύειν" (CCSL 50:42–43).

29. For *City of God* 10.1 (which is correctly quoted without *dulia*) and *Trin.* 1.6.13 in the Council of Paris, see *Monumenta Germaniae Historica*, Concilia 2.2, 501–2, 519; cf. Noble, *Images, Iconoclasm, and the Carolingians*, 275–76.

30. *De Sacramentis* 1.12.6; see Staudt, "Religion as a Virtue," 66–67. *Pace* Schmitt, who credits Alain de Lille (ca. 1128–1202/3) with introducing the pairing into Western theology and claims he borrows it from the Greeks (Schmitt, "L'Occident," 296). In fact, Alain merely notes that *latria* and *dulia* are Greek words (*Contra Haereticos* 4.12; PL 210:428).

31. PL 162:1275.

32. Artur Michael Landgraf, *Dogmengeschichte der Frühscholastik, zweiter Teil: Die Lehre von Christus*, vol. 2 (Regensburg: Verlag Friedrich Pustet, 1954), 136n15a.

33. Some scholastics saw *dulia* as genus and *latria* as species. See, e.g., the Pauline commentary from the milieu of Robert of Melun quoted at Landgraf, *Dogmengeschichte der Frühscholastik*, 139.

34. *ST* II-II, qq. 102–19. *Dulia* is covered in q. 103.

spective terms, God and creatures, makes the two virtues, in a sense, incommensurable.[35] God's unique claim to *latria* is rooted in God's being Creator, a trait in no way shared by creatures.[36]

Adoratio

From the ninth century until the mainstreaming of the *latria-dulia* distinction in the twelfth century, Latin exegetes typically appear to take *adoratio* as equivalent to *latria*.[37] For Thomas, however, *adoratio* is roughly equivalent to Greek *proskynēsis*, primarily denoting an exterior act of homage. The meaning of an act of *adoratio* is determined by its term, so that there is no single virtue to which an exterior act of *adoratio* must be referred.[38] When Thomas considers *adoratio* within his treatise on the virtue of *religio* (= *latria*), he clearly establishes the relationship between the two. According to an objection, "It would seem that adoration is not an act of latria or religion. The worship of religion is due to God alone. But adoration is not due to God alone," and scriptural examples of Abraham paying *adoratio* to angels and the prophet Nathan to David follow. Thomas counters that "since external actions are signs of internal reverence, certain external tokens (*quaedam exteriora*) significative of reverence are offered to creatures of excellence, and among these tokens the chief is adoration."[39] Exterior acts of *adoratio* such as genuflections or prostrations may be manifestations of *latria*/*religio* or of *dulia*, depending on whether they are directed to God or to creatures, respectively.[40] This

---

35. Concerning a gloss on Ps 7:1 that reads "Lord of all by His power, to Whom dulia is due; God by creation, to Whom we owe latria," Thomas admits that "latria is called dulia by way of excellence, inasmuch as God is our Lord by way of excellence" (*ST* II-II, q. 103, a. 3, obj 1, ad 1; cf. III, q. 25, a. 2, co.). That is, *dulia* can be spoken of with reference to God in view of God's lordship since lordship is communicable to creatures (cf. Augustine, *Quaestiones Exodi* 94, quoted in note 28 above). Similarly, Thomas notes that *religio* can be called "piety" (honor rendered to parents and country) "by way of supereminence" (*ST* II-II, q. 102, a. 1, ad 1). But these are not strictly proper uses of *dulia* and piety. At *ST* II-II, q. 103, a. 4, co., and ad 2, Thomas denies that *hyperdulia*, the highest form of *dulia*, is the mean of *dulia* and *latria*.

36. *ST* II-II, q. 81, a. 1, ad 3.

37. See the authors considered by Landgraf, *Dogmengeschichte der Frühscholastik*, 133–35. For discussion of the varied and complex uses of *adoratio* in the Carolingian context, see Noble, *Images, Iconoclasm, and the Carolingians*, 181–83, 187–88, 274–76, 291–93, 301, 308–9, 315, 317–18, 321–23, 338, 351.

38. *ST* II-II, q. 3, a. 1, co.: "Outward actions belong properly to the virtue to whose end they are specifically referred."

39. *ST* II-II, q. 84, a. 1, obj. 1, ad 1.

40. Cf. *ScG* III, chap. 120: "genuflections, prostrations, and other manifestations of this

recognition clarifies the corpus of the same article: "Adoration is directed to the reverence of the person adored. Now it is evident from what we have said (Q. 81, AA. 2, 4) that it is proper to religion to show reverence to God. Hence the adoration whereby we adore God (*qua Deus adoratur*) is an act of religion."[41] *Qua Deus adoratur* is a limiting relative clause; there do exist other legitimate acts of *adoratio* than those by which God is reverenced.

While *adoratio* refers primarily to exterior acts and *latria* to a virtue, Thomas can use *latria* to refer to an *actus virtutis* as well as a *virtus*, and so *latria* can refer to an exterior act of divine worship. Additionally, *adoratio* sometimes signifies an interior act of *latria*. Thomas follows the Damascene (*De Fide Orthodoxa* 4.12 [89]) in holding that, "since we are composed of a twofold nature, intellectual and sensible, we offer God a twofold adoration; namely, a spiritual adoration, consisting in the internal devotion of the mind; and a bodily adoration, which consists in an exterior humbling of the body."[42] He even regards *adoratio* as "consist[ing] chiefly [*principaliter*] in interior reverence to God,"[43] though he uses it more frequently with reference to exterior adoration.

Imago

Following Augustine, Aquinas insists that for something to qualify as an *imago*, likeness (*similitudo*) is not enough, nor even intentional imitation: "Not every likeness, not even what is copied from something else, is sufficient to make an image.... But the nature of an image requires likeness in species; thus the image of the king exists in his son: or, at least, in some specific accident, and chiefly in shape (*figuram*); thus, we speak of a man's image in copper."[44] Thomas echoes here a distinction he has made earlier, explaining the difference between the Word as Image and human beings as made in the divine image:

---

kind of honor may also be shown to men, though with a different intention than in regard to God." Unlike prostrations and genuflections, however, Thomas follows Augustine (*City of God* 10.4) in asserting that sacrifice can only be directed to God (*ScG* III, chap. 120; *ST* II-II, q. 84, a. 1, ad 1).

41. *ST* II-II, q. 84, a. 1, co.
42. *ST* II-II, q. 84, a. 2, co.
43. *ST* II-II, q. 84, a. 2, ad 2.
44. *ST* I, q. 93, a. 2, co.; cf. *ST* I, q. 93, a. 1, co., which quotes Augustine, *83 Questions* 74: "Where an image exists, there forthwith is likeness; but where there is likeness, there is not necessarily an image."

The image of a thing may be found in something in two ways. In one way it is found in something of the same specific nature; as the image of the king is found in his son. In another way it is found in something of a different nature, as the king's image on the coin. In the first sense the Son is the Image of the Father; in the second sense man is called the image of God; and therefore in order to express the imperfect character of the divine image in man, man is not simply called the image, but *to the image* (*ad imaginem*), whereby is expressed a certain movement of tendency to perfection. But it cannot be said that the Son of God is *to the image*, because He is the perfect Image of the Father.[45]

In *ST* III, q. 25, a. 3, it is of course artificial images that are in view, but Thomas does not directly comment on their nature as images.[46] Still, one can agree with Torrell's remark: "If the bodily form is the specific marker (*signe de l'espèce*) necessary for one to be able to make an image,[47] it is clear that there is no longer any problem in representing Christ. Impossible though it is to paint his divinity, the reproduced exterior form does refer to the subject it evokes, the hypostasis in its two natures."[48]

Sensibles, Divine Cult, and the Incarnate God

If Scripture says that "God is spirit, and those who worship him must worship (προσκυνεῖν/*adorare*) in spirit and truth" (Jn 4:24),[49] why should Christian worship allot any role at all to material objects? Thomas offers a succinct answer: "The chief purpose of the whole external worship (*exterior cultus Dei*) is that man may revere God (*Deum in reverentia habeant*)."[50] Significantly, this line's context is the Old Testament cult. Christ's incarnation marks a watershed moment for divine worship, but Aquinas also perceives continuity in the economy of worship between the testaments. The principle Thomas provides at *ST* I-II, q. 102, for the presence and use of sacred objects in the worship of the Old Law holds true when one comes to the worship of the New Law. Thomas expands on it when clarifying the relationship between exterior and interior adoration of God: "exterior adoration is offered on account of interior adoration, in other words we exhibit signs of humility in our bodies in order to incite

---

45. *ST* I, q. 35, a. 2, ad 3.
46. See, however, *ST* III, q. 25, a. 3, ad 3, discussed below.
47. As per *ST* I, q. 93, a. 2, co.
48. Torrell, *Le Verbe Incarné*, 455.
49. Cf. *ST* I-II, q. 101, a. 2, obj. 4; II-II, q. 81, a. 7, obj. 1; III, q. 60, a. 4, obj. 2.
50. *ST* I-II, q. 102, a. 4, co.; trans. alt.

our affections to submit to God, since it is connatural to us to proceed through the sensible (*per sensibilia*) to the intelligible."[51] To reject the role of sensibles risks rejection of the goodness of our creation as embodied:

It is not astonishing if heretics who deny that God is author of our body condemn such manifestations [bodily acts of worship]. This condemnation shows that *they have not remembered that they are men* when they judge that the representation of sensible objects to themselves is not necessary for inner knowledge and love. For it is evident from experience that the soul is stimulated to an act of knowledge or of love by bodily acts. Hence, it is obvious that we may quite appropriately use even bodily things to elevate our mind to God.[52]

Divine cult is thus ordained "so that man may be reminded that he ought to refer both his own being and all his possessions to God as end, and thus to the Creator, Governor, and Lord of all."[53]

The relationship between exterior and interior worship works in both directions. Exterior cult is ordered to spiritual, interior adoration. As the soul is superior to the body, interior worship of God is superior to its outward expression, which is primarily meant to engender interior worship. But Thomas is careful to emphasize their close connection: "Even bodily adoration is done in spirit, insofar as it *proceeds from and is directed to* spiritual devotion."[54] In a cycle of mutual reinforcement, exterior cult incites the mind to inward adoration, which in turn seeks expression in outward actions.

Finally, it must be stressed that God has tailored the economy of worship *for us*. God has no need of our cult, exterior or interior. Both are ordered by God's goodness for the sake of human beings:

We pay God honor and reverence, not for His sake (because He is of Himself full of glory to which no creature can add anything), but for our own sake, because by the very fact that we revere and honor God, our mind is subjected to Him; wherein its perfection consists.[55]

---

51. *ST* II-II, q. 84, a. 2, co.; trans. alt. Cf. *ST* II-II, q. 81, a. 7, co.: "Now the human mind, in order to be united to God, needs to be guided by the sensible world, since *invisible things … are clearly seen, being understood by the things that are made*, as the Apostle says (Rom 1:20). Wherefore in the Divine worship it is necessary to make use of corporeal things, that man's mind may be aroused thereby, as by signs, to the spiritual acts by means of which he is united to God. Therefore the internal acts of religion take precedence of the others and belong to religion essentially, while its external acts are secondary, and subordinate to the internal acts."

52. *ScG* III, chap. 119; emphasis added.

53. *ScG* III, chap. 119.

54. *ST* II-II, q. 84, a. 2, ad 1; emphasis added.

55. *ST* II-II, q. 81, a. 7, co.

Thomas's general conviction that a corporeal, sensible dimension to divine cult is both beneficial and necessary for human beings provides important context for his approach to sacred images in particular.

Thomas's Teaching in *ST* III, q. 25, a. 3

To understand *ST* III, q. 25, a. 3, the article devoted to the adoration of the image of Christ, it is important to consider its immediate context, which is not a broader discussion of sacred art, but a two-question consideration of Christ in relation to us (*ST* III, qq. 25–26). *ST* III, q. 25, a. 3, builds on the two preceding articles, which depend in turn on the incarnational Christology developed earlier in the *Tertia Pars*, particularly in question 2. In *ST* III, q. 25, a. 1, Thomas considers "whether Christ's divinity and his humanity are to be adored with one and the same adoration."[56] By Thomas's time, the scholastic consensus replies in the affirmative. Yet early in his career, Thomas wonders whether this view can cohere with the Lombard's first opinion on the mode of union in the Incarnation.[57] In the corresponding passage in the *Scriptum*, Aquinas notes the potential awkwardness of rendering *latria* to Christ's humanity on the first opinion, according to which "it would be more proper to say that it is to be adored with *dulia*, since the first opinion posits another acting *suppositum* for the humanity, apart from the eternal *suppositum* to which *latria* is due."[58] By the time he writes the *Tertia Pars*, engagement with conciliar Christology has sharpened Thomas's view. He rejects the first and third opinions as subtle forms of Nestorianism, relying on the Councils of Ephesus and Constantinople II.[59] In *ST* III, q. 25, a. 1, s.c., Aquinas returns to Con-

---

56. *ST* III, q. 25, prooemium; my trans.

57. See *Sentences*, Book 3, d. 6, which lays out three views of the mode of union in the Incarnation. The first opinion holds that the Person of the Word assumed a human supposit (*homo assumptus*) in the Virgin's womb. The second holds that the Word assumed human nature and now subsists in both divine and human natures; there is no separate human supposit. The third suggests that the Word assumed body and soul separately and accidentally; Christ's human body and soul are never joined lest a second, human subject appear.

58. *Scriptum* 3, d. 9, q. 1, a. 2, qc. 1 co.; my trans. Some adherents to the first opinion do maintain that *latria* should be paid to Christ's humanity. Landgraf provides Robert of Melun as an example and remarks on the convergence of the scholastics' teaching with Constantinople II despite their ignorance of it (138–39). Conversely, Landgraf emphasizes that in no case can it be shown that a scholastic who held Christ's humanity only worthy of *dulia* had a "crypto-Nestorian reason" (*kryptonestorianischer Grund*) for doing so (Landgraf, *Dogmengeschichte der Frühscholastik*, 168–69). Nonetheless, Aquinas would argue this indicated an internal inconsistency.

59. *ST* III, q. 2, a. 3, co., 6 co.

stantinople II, which explicitly teaches that Christ must be adored in his two natures with a single adoration. This replaces the less robust language of his appeal in the *Scriptum* to the *Quicunque Vult*, which compares the unity of God and man in Christ with the unity of flesh and soul in a human being.[60] In *ST* III, q. 25, a. 1, co., Aquinas also refers to the teaching of Cyril of Alexandria as enshrined in the Council of Ephesus. These authorities establish the principle that "properly speaking honor is given to a subsistent thing in its entirety";[61] that is, adoration (whether expressive of *latria* or *dulia*) terminates in a *hypostasis* or a *suppositum*, not in a nature. Thomas thus goes on to argue in article 2 that Christ's humanity, body, or flesh must be adored with *latria*.[62] According to the *cause* of honor, as explained in article 1 and repeated in article 2, Christ's flesh could only be worshiped with *dulia*.[63] But this is only a secondary way of analyzing adoration. In the primary sense, because "adoration is due to the subsisting hypostasis, ... to adore the flesh of Christ is nothing else than to adore the incarnate Word of God."[64] The establishment of this point in the first two articles of question 25 is vital to Thomas's consideration of the Christ-icon in article 3, for it is precisely the bodily form of Christ's flesh that can be properly depicted in an image.

Building on the foundation of articles 1 and 2, the *sed contra* of *ST* III, q. 25, a. 3, is deceptively simple: "Damascene (*De Fide Orth.* iv, 16) quotes Basil as saying: *The honor given to an image reaches to the prototype*, i.e., the exemplar. But the exemplar itself—namely, Christ—is to be adored with the adoration of latria; therefore also His image." Thomas's conclusion appears straightforward, flowing directly from Basil's dictum once Christ's bodily form is recognized as inseparable from his divine Person as the term of adoration. Basil originally adduced this claim in the context of Trinitarian controversy to show that, owing to his identity as the image of God by nature (φυσικῶς), the Son's divine nature and reception of divine honor do not compromise the unity of the Godhead or of Christian worship. Yet the analogy Basil drew to illustrate his principle involved an imitative (μιμητικῶς) or artificial image: we recognize an image of a king as "the king" but do not thereby conclude that there are two kings.[65] The

60. *Scriptum* 3, d. 9, q. 1, a. 2, qc. 1 s.c. 1.
61. *ST* III, q. 25, a. 1, co.
62. *ST* III, q. 25, a. 2, co.
63. *ST* III, q. 25, a. 1, co., 2 co.
64. *ST* III, q. 25, a. 2, co.
65. *De Spiritu Sancto* 18.45 (PG 32:149).

principle was thus arguably applicable to sacred images, and when controversies broke out, iconophiles were not slow to exploit it.

Basil does not, however, speak of *latria* or *dulia*, nor does Thomas's direct source, John of Damascus's *De Fide Orthodoxa* 4.16 [89]. Burgundio's Latin translation refers to "adoring and honoring (*adorantes et honorantes*) the image of Our Savior and of Our Queen the Mother of God, and further of the rest of the saints and servants of Christ,"[66] which accurately renders the Damascene's original προσκυνοῦσί τε καὶ τιμῶσι.[67] From Thomas's point of view, these terms are insufficient to settle the question of *latria*. The Latin for *proskynēsis* is neither *latria* nor *dulia* but *adoratio*, and so for Thomas, it fundamentally denotes an exterior act without specifying the virtue to which it is ordered interiorly. The second term, *honor*,[68] "denotes a witnessing to a person's excellence" and can similarly express either *latria* or *dulia*.[69] Nor does the Damascene differentiate between the adoration offered to the icon of Christ and to those of the saints. Thomas does differentiate the two, implicitly, by means of the *latria-dulia* distinction, absent from the Damascene.[70] Augustine, not the Greeks, provides Thomas with this distinction. Thomas's *corpus* sets out to explain Basil's dictum through recourse to Aristotle:

As the Philosopher says (*De Memor. et Remin.* i), there is a twofold movement of the mind (*motus animae*) towards an image: one indeed towards the image itself as a certain thing (*secundum quod est res quaedam*); another, towards the image in so far as it is the image of something else (*inquantum est imago alterius*). And between these movements there is this difference; that the former, by which one is moved towards an image as a certain thing, is different from the movement

66. Buytaert, *De Fide Orthodoxa*, 330–31; my trans.

67. Kotter, *Schriften des Johannes von Damaskos*, 206.

68. Consistent with this, the Damascene's quotation of Basil uses τιμή, the substantive cognate of τιμῶσι, which is rendered *honor* in Thomas's quotation in *ST* III, q. 25, a. 3, sc.

69. *ST* II-II, q. 103, a. 1, co.; cf. q. 103, a. 2, ad 1.

70. See *ST* II-II, q. 103, a. 3, ad 3. Here, the images of the saints are not considered directly, but Thomas clarifies why the saints are worshiped with *dulia* and not *latria*, their status as images of God notwithstanding (cf. *ST* III, q. 25, a. 5, ad 2, ad 3). By applying Thomas's appropriation in *ST* III, q. 25, a. 3, of Basil's principle ("The honor given to the image reaches to the prototype") to the case of the saints in *ST* II-II, q. 103, a. 3, one concludes that the saints' images are to be adored with the adoration of *dulia*. This coheres with Thomas's only explicit reference in the *Summa Theologiae* to the icons of saints and angels: "Neither in the Tabernacle or Temple of the Old Law, nor again now in the Church are images set up that the worship of latria may be paid to them, but for the purpose of signification, in order that belief in the excellence of angels and saints may be impressed and confirmed in the mind of man. It is different with the image of Christ, to which latria is due on account of His Divinity" (*ST* II-II, q. 94, a. 2, ad 1).

towards the thing: whereas the latter movement, which is towards the image as an image, is one and the same as that which is towards the thing.[71]

In the case of the first motion of the soul, "no reverence is shown to Christ's image, as a thing—for instance, carved or painted wood: because reverence is not due save to a rational nature."[72] But when the image is considered precisely as an image, the soul's motion toward it is indistinguishable from the soul's motion toward the image's prototype; they are not two motions, but one. It follows that "the same reverence should be shown to Christ's image," considered *as image*, "as to Christ Himself."[73]

The influence of the Damascene's *De Fide Orthodoxa* 4.16 [89] resurfaces in three of Thomas's four replies to objections. In the first, Aquinas explicitly quotes John's admission of the "absurdity and impiety" of attempting to depict the Divine apart from the fact of the Incarnation. In the second, Thomas echoes John's distinction between Christian and pagan images, since the latter were depictions of demons. In the fourth, he repeats John's appeal to 2 Thessalonians 2:14 in support of unwritten apostolic tradition, and like John he alludes to an image of Christ from Christ's own lifetime.[74] These same dependencies on the Damascene are found in the *Scriptum*,[75] though in the reply to the second objection he adds an assist from Augustine (*City of God* 8.23). What will become the third objection in *ST* III, q. 25, a. 3 (discussed below) does not appear in the *Scriptum*. In the final objection, concerning the permissibility of practices not explicitly ordained in Scripture, Thomas omits the reference to 2 Thessalonians but includes the legend of the image given to Abgar.[76] Thomas adds the following in defense of the use of images:

There was a threefold reason for the establishment of images in the Church: first, for the instruction of the uninstructed, who are taught by them as if by so many books; second, so that the mystery of the Incarnation and the examples of the saints might be held more firmly in the memory as they are daily represented to the eyes; third, to stir up the affection (*affectum*) of devotion, which is incited more effectively by what is seen than by what is heard.[77]

71. *ST* III, q. 25, a. 3, co.
72. *ST* III, q. 25, a. 3, co.
73. *ST* III, q. 25, a. 3, co.
74. John refers to the legend of Abgar, Thomas to a Lukan image at Rome.
75. *Scriptum* 3, d. 9, q. 1, a. 2, qc. 2.
76. *Scriptum* 3, d. 9, q. 1, a. 2, qc. 2, ad 3. Thomas also attributes mention of the Lukan image to the Damascene, but John does not in fact speak of it.
77. *Scriptum* 3, d. 9, q. 1, a. 2, qc. 2, ad 3.

These reasons initially seem to reflect, in part, the emphasis on the didactic capabilities of images that dominated the field in eighth- and ninth-century Western reflection on images.[78] But this is only apparent. Thomas's proximate source is likely Bonaventure's *Scriptum*, which similarly says that images "were introduced for a threefold cause: namely, because of the lack of instruction (*ruditatem*) of the simple, because of the slowness of affections, and because of the slipperiness of memory."[79] Bonaventure expands on each one at length. Notably, all three of these rationales are present in *De Fide Orthodoxa* 4.16 [89], from which Bonaventure goes on to quote.[80] The best explanation seems to be that here, too, the Damascene provides the authority, but that Bonaventure has organized his teaching according to an Augustinian schema of intellect, memory, and will. Thomas follows suit in the *Scriptum* but abandons this line of argumentation in the *Summa*.[81] John of Damascus's *De Fide Orthodoxa* is thus the only significant patristic source for Thomas's teaching on images. Basil only appears as quoted by John, and Aristotle serves to bolster Basil's dictum. But Thomas, like other scholastics, maps the Damascene's teaching onto the twelfth-century scholastic reception of Augustine's *latria-dulia* distinction.

It is also clear, however, that Thomas sees his teaching on the image of Christ as closely related to his rejection of the first opinion on the authority of Ephesus and Constantinople II and from the careful linking of adoration, not to a nature, but to a person or *suppositum*. Following the Damascene (*De Fide Orthodoxa* 4.3 [76]), Thomas admits that, "understood as distinct from the Word of God, [the flesh of Christ] should be

---

78. This emphasis is usually traced to Gregory the Great's two letters to the iconoclast Serenus of Marseilles (*Ep.* 9.105, 11.13; PL 77:1027–28, 1128–30). For helpful challenges to the standard interpretation of Gregory, see Celia M. Chazelle, "Pictures, Books, and the Illiterate: Pope Gregory I's Letters to Serenus of Marseilles," *Word & Image* 6 (1990): 138–53; "Memory, Instruction, Worship: 'Gregory's' Influence on Early Medieval Doctrines of the Artistic Image," in *Gregory the Great: A Symposium*, ed. John C. Cavadini (Notre Dame, IN: University of Notre Dame Press, 1995), 184.

79. *Scriptum* 3, d. 9, q. 1, a. 2, conc.

80. See also *Summa Fratris Alexandri* lib. 3, pars 2, inq. 3, tract. 2, sect. 1, quaest. 2, tit. 1, dist. 3, cap. 3, art. 1 (Grottaferrata: Collegium S. Bonaventurae, 1983), which says images are set up "for our teaching and instruction and for remembrance of the passion of Christ, so that it might be present to our memory, and through this we might be instructed and enticed to the good." It goes on to quote *De Fide Orthodoxa* 4.16 [89] at length in defense of this claim.

81. A possible exception is in *ST* II-II, q. 94, a. 2, ad 1: images are set up in the Church "for the purpose of signification, in order that belief in the excellence of angels and saints may be impressed and confirmed in the mind of man."

adored with the adoration of 'dulia.'"[82] This would make the adoration of *latria* toward the icon, which properly images only the flesh, inappropriate. But such a posture requires that "by a subtle distinction you divide what is seen [i.e., the flesh] from what is understood [i.e., the divine nature]."[83] The first opinion's discernment of a human *suppositum* in Christ risks being just such a "subtle distinction."

The grounding of Thomas's thinking about icons in his incarnational Christology also bears on the place of sacred images within the economy of divine worship explored above. While Thomas perceives continuity between the Old and New Testaments in the purpose of sensibles to conduce to interior worship of God, the Incarnation also marks a crucial point of discontinuity between the testaments, one instantiated by the worship of the Christ-icon. Thomas obviously has the New Testament and not the Old Testament in mind when he writes, "The worship of religion (*religionis cultus*) is paid to images, not as considered in themselves, nor as things, but as images leading us to *God incarnate*."[84] Thomas appeals to this incarnational discontinuity in response to the prohibition of graven images in Exodus 20:4. The Old Law attended to circumstances *before* the Incarnation. At that time, "no corporeal image could be raised to the true God Himself, since He is incorporeal.... But *because in the New Testament God was made man*, He can be adored in His corporeal image."[85] The place of sensibles in worship, which spans both testaments, thus paves the way for the discontinuity wrought by the Incarnation of the Word. Thomas's teaching that the Christ-icon be worshiped with *latria* is predicated not only upon his synthesis of Augustine and the Damascene, but also upon his perception of the meaning of divine worship. At the heart of worship, we encounter the human, visible, and depictable Christ, the Mediator between God and human beings.[86]

Thomas and the Seventh Ecumenical Council

Is Thomas's teaching compatible with that of the Seventh Ecumenical Council? Nicaea II's *horos* (doctrinal definition) states that icons of Jesus, Mary, the angels, and the saints should be venerated because

---

82. *ST* III, q. 25, a. 2, ad 1.
83. *ST* III, q. 25, a. 2, ad 1, quoting John of Damascus, *De Fide Orthodoxa* 4.3 [76].
84. *ST* II-II, q. 81, a. 3, ad 3; emphasis added.
85. *ST* III, q. 25, a. 3, ad 1; emphasis added.
86. This will be the topic of *ST* III, q. 26.

each time that we see their representation in an image, each time while gazing upon them we are made to remember the prototypes, we grow to love them more, and we are even more induced to render them veneration of honour (τιμητικὴν προσκύνησιν) by kissing them and by witnessing our veneration, not the true worship (ἀληθινὴν λατρείαν) which, according to our faith, is proper only to the divine nature, but in the same way as we venerate the image of the precious and vivifying cross, the holy Gospel and other sacred objects which we honour with incense and candles according to the pious custom of our forefathers.[87]

Like the Damascene's *De Fide Orthodoxa* 4.16 [89], the *horos* does not explicitly distinguish the icon of Christ from those of Mary, the angels, or the saints; it is evidently included under the proscription of ἀληθινὴ λατρεία, and Thomas's position is ruled out. Many Thomists have argued that Thomas's language is compatible with the council because the *latria* that Thomas directs to the Christ-icon is not "true" or "absolute" *latria*, but "relative" *latria*.[88] In considering the icon, the only recipient of "true" *latria* is Christ. The icon qua material thing is due no honor. Because its worthiness of *latria* obtains only by virtue of its cultic function—that is, insofar as it is considered as an image—it seems clear that the *latria* of *ST* III, q. 25, a. 3, is not a precise equivalent of the ἀληθινὴ λατρεία of the council. Furthermore, the conciliar definition's opposition of *proskynēsis* (= *adoratio*) and *latria* would likely strike Thomas as a confusion of categories. *Adoratio* refers primarily to an outward act that may be configured *either* to the virtue of *dulia or* to that of *latria*. The problem with this line of argument is that, for the Byzantines, the term λατρεία is reserved precisely for the "absolute" worship of God and is contrasted with all that is "relative" (σχετική, κατὰ σχέσιν). In Eastern idiom, "relative *latria*" would be a contradiction in terms.[89] At this point, the import of Western scholasticism's reception of William of Auxerre's equation of *latria* with *religio* becomes clear. Basic agreement that *latria* designates the worship due

---

87. Quoted in Gennadios Limouris, ed., *Icons: Windows on Eternity: Theology and Spirituality in Colour* (Geneva: WCC, 1990), 1; Greek text in Mansi 13:377.

88. E.g., Reginald Garrigou-Lagrange, OP, *Christ the Savior: A Commentary on the Third Part of St. Thomas' Theological Summa*, trans. Bede Rose, OSB (St. Louis, MO: B. Herder, 1950), 520: "Relative but not absolute adoration of latria must be given to the image of Christ." Garrigou-Lagrange goes on to cite the Damascene's quotation of Basil and Nicaea II as authoritative proofs.

89. As Grumel remarks, "[Thomas's] 'absolute *latria*' is none other than their [the Greek Fathers'] '*latria*' *tout court*; his 'relative *latria*' is included in their προσκύνησις τιμητική and σχετική" (*Dictionnaire de théologie catholique*, col. 835). See Grumel's detailed discussion in coll. 827–31, 835–36.

to God alone masks a deeper divergence. For Greek theologians, *latria* retains its etymological sense of *servitus* and denotes the *act* of absolute worship of the divine Trinity; hence the contrast of *latreia* and *proskynēsis*. For Western scholastics, *latria* mainly denotes a virtue that can command a variety of acts referred to the worship of God. It is thus no surprise that it is used much less restrictively than in the East.

Another area of difference between Thomas and the East is the evaluation of the character of the image itself. While Byzantine theologians repeat Basil's dictum that the honor paid the image passes to the prototype with no less insistence than the Latins, Thomas's use of Aristotle to interpret it renders the icon rather more transparent than it is for the East. The image does no more than refer the viewer's mind to its prototype; as a thing, it disappears. According to Theodore Studites, in contrast, because the form of Christ's humanity is there in the icon, and humanity is hypostatically united to the Divine Word, Christ's divinity is truly present in the icon. But as Thomas Cattoi puts it in summarizing Theodore, "the divinity is not present in the image in virtue of a natural union (*physikē enōsei*) but in virtue of a relational participation (*schetikē metalēpsei*)," and thus cannot be worshiped with *latria*.[90] For Theodore and the Byzantines, the thingness of the icon asserts itself in a way it does not for Thomas.[91]

In *ST* III, q. 25, a. 3, obj. 3, an objection absent from the parallel in the *Scriptum*, Thomas entertains this argument: "to Christ the adoration of latria is due by reason of His Godhead, not of His humanity. But the ado-

90. Thomas Cattoi, "Introduction," in *Theodore the Studite: Writings on Iconoclasm*, Ancient Christian Writers 69, trans. Thomas Cattoi (New York: Newman Press, 2015), 34.

91. I therefore find myself in partial disagreement with Torstein Theodor Tollefsen, who seems to suggest that, for Theodore, "because of the common likeness the image itself is somehow absorbed into the prototype," and so we cannot deny that veneration of Christ in his icon is an act of *latria*. St *Theodore the Studite's Defence of the Icons: Theology and Philosophy in Ninth-Century Byzantium* (New York: Oxford, 2018), 147. While admitting that Thomas's treatment is, "at least on the face of it, quite similar to what Theodore said centuries earlier," he goes on to allege that Thomas "seems to argue that *the image itself* is adored if it is an image of Christ," while Theodore denies "that the material object as such is due any veneration" (147; emphasis original). But this is precisely what Aquinas denies. A partial explanation for the persistence of the icon's "thingness" may be provided by Christopher R. Sweeney's recent argument that in the pre-iconoclastic East cultic veneration of icons centered on their sacred materiality rather than their representational character. "Holy Images and Holy Matter: Images in the Performance of Miracles in the Age before Iconoclasm," *Journal of Early Christian Studies* 26 (2018): 111–38. This is obviously not true for theologians reacting to iconoclasm such as Theodore, who, as Tollefsen admirably shows, goes to great lengths to develop the icon's representational capacity (see esp. Tollefsen, St *Theodore the Studite's Defence of the Icons*, 95–97, 121–24), but it may provide illuminating cultural background.

ration of latria is not due to the image of His Godhead, which is imprint-
ed on the rational soul. Much less, therefore, is it due to the material image which represents the humanity of Christ Himself." It seems awkward,
in other words, to accord *latria* to an insensate image while denying it to
the *imago Dei* that human beings are. In reply, Thomas notes that rational
creatures are due reverence in themselves, so to adore the divine image
in them with *latria* would run the risk of the worship terminating in the
creature rather than God. But Thomas remarks, "This cannot happen in
the case of a graven or painted image in insensible material."[92] This seems
absurd unless the context of Christian worship is borne in mind. Thomas is thinking not of pagan nature worship but of insensate things that
have been somehow linked to Christian cult. In the next article, Thomas
explains that an insensate item can be linked to a rational nature in two
ways: through representation (as in the case of an icon) or through being
"united to it in any way whatsoever" (*ei quocumque modo coniungitur*).
The example he gives of the latter is a king's robe.[93] Earlier, Aquinas similarly explains why inanimate things can be the object of sacrilege:

a thing is called *sacred* through being deputed to the divine worship (*ex eo quod
ad divinum cultum ordinatur*). Now just as a thing acquires an aspect of good
through being deputed to a good end, so does a thing assume a divine character
(*efficitur quoddam divinum*) through being deputed to the divine worship, and
thus a certain reverence (*quaedam reverential*) is due to it, which reverence is
referred to God.[94]

What is this "certain reverence" due to the consecrated object? In *ST* III,
q. 25, a. 4, co., Thomas says that both an image of a rational nature and
any object "united to it in any way whatsoever" "are venerated by men
with the same veneration (*eadem veneratione*)." Thomas does not quote
Basil's dictum, but he seems to regard it as in principle applicable to objects that are not images but are otherwise associated with a venerable
rational nature.

Since all creatures bear the stamp of their Creator, are all things therefore to be worshiped with (relative) *latria*? Thomas carefully distinguishes *imago* from *vestigium*: any effect that indicates its cause constitutes a
"trace" (*vestigium*), while an image requires a likeness in form.[95] As imag-

92. *ST* III, q. 25, a. 3, ad 3.
93. *ST* III, q. 25, a. 4, co.
94. *ST* II-II, q. 99, a. 1, co.
95. *ST* I, q. 45, a. 7, co.; I, q. 93, a. 1, co.; I, q. 93, a. 2, co.; I, q. 93, a. 6, co.

es, depictions of Christ, the angels, and the saints bear a referential quality that activates, so to speak, the Basilian principle. Objects that are not images and that bear only the *vestigium Dei* are not to be venerated lest they cause error, for there is no automatic guarantee that they will be referred to the worship of God.[96] Nonetheless, as creatures bearing the *vestigia* of their Maker, they are radically available for deputation to the divine cult, as with the tabernacle in the Old Testament or sacred vessels in the New Testament.[97] This deputation has an objective character (*efficitur quoddam divinum*), so that one is no longer free to ignore its consecration and treat it as a mere thing.[98]

At the same time, in at least one text, Thomas leaves a cautious opening toward a nonerasure of the image as thing even when viewed as an image. Appearing to modify Aristotle's principle slightly, Aquinas suggests that "the movement towards an image is, after a fashion (*quodammodo*), towards the thing" with the result that "reverence paid to a person as the image of God redounds somewhat (*quodammodo*) to God: and yet this differs from the reverence that is paid to God Himself, for this in no way refers to His image (*pertinet ad eius imaginem*)."[99] While preserving Basil's conviction that the honor passes over to the prototype, this remarkable admission mitigates the transparency of the image's thingness, allowing for a sort of referential "drag" produced by the image as thing. While Thomas applies this only to human beings and not to insensate objects such as icons, he seems at least to gesture toward Theodore's position.

Conclusion

Icons do not occupy the privileged place in Thomas's understanding of sensibles in the divine cult that they do in the East. The different socioreligious history of images in the West means that there is no Western

96. Cf. *ST* II-II, q. 92, a. 2, co.

97. Grumel takes some later Thomists (the Salamancans, Vásquez, Cajetan) to task for reducing Thomas's use of Basil-cum-Aristotle to absurdity (coll. 825–26). Careful attention to the relevant texts, however, suggests that these commentators are concerned with upholding the fundamental availability of all creation for use in divine cult.

98. Cf. the insistence of the *Summa Fratris Alexandri* that God should only be adored through an irrational creature as his *vestigia* if it "has been made a sign through institution" (*efficitur signum per institutionem*) (lib. 3, pars 2, inq. 3, tract. 2, sect. 1, q. 2, tit. 1, dist. 3, cap. 3, art. 2). The examples provided are the tabernacle and the stone that Jacob anointed.

99. *ST* II-II, q. 103, a. 3, ad 3.

equivalent to the Christian East's annual reassertion of the centrality of images through the celebration of the Triumph of Orthodoxy of 843. Furthermore, Thomas takes a broad view of what counts as an "image" of Christ, considering even a bare cross of any material to constitute an *imago Christi*.[100] Nor does he mention any distinction between two- and three-dimensional representation, or among various representational media.[101] For Aquinas, sacred images fit seamlessly but relatively unremarkably into a schema of signification that encompasses all created reality. As Besançon comments, "The [Western] medieval aesthetic is simultaneously realist and symbolist, with each thing able to be regarded as a created thing and as an allegory of the divine."[102] Accordingly, Thomas's metaphysics "leads, in the spirit of Augustine, to seeing the world as an infinity of images, responding to one another in good order, illumined by the same light, and the human being, whose desire and intellect are turned toward the divine beauty—and thus toward all things—as capable of seeing the images and from them producing and deriving his joy."[103] Yet we should be quick to point out that John of Damascus, in his *Orationes de Imaginibus* (which Thomas did not have), also links his teaching on images with material creation's capacity to mediate worship[104] and with a Christologically transformed vision of all things.[105] Similarly, Theodore Studites hints at a cultic vision of all creation when he sees all Christian acts of *proskynēsis* as coordinated by their end in the worship of God: "it is because of the Trinity that other forms of venerations (*hai diaphoroi proskynēseis*) ultimately exist, and it is to the Trinity that all other venerations ultimately tend."[106]

The unavailability of Nicaea II and the works of associated Greek

---

100. *ST* III, q. 25, a. 4, co.

101. Thomas's contemporary William Durandus remarks on the Greeks' refusal to sculpt sacred images, but he appears to feel no need to address the difference or defend the Western acceptance of three-dimensional images. *Rationale Divinorum Officiorum* 1.3.2 (Naples: Joseph Dura, 1859), 23. Cf. Schmitt, "L'Occident," 298.

102. Besançon, *L'Image Interdite*, 214; my trans.

103. Besançon, *L'Image Interdite*, 226; my trans.

104. See *Orationes de Imaginibus* 1.16; 2.14.

105. See *Orationes de Imaginibus* 1.17. Like Thomas, John links the Incarnation of Christ and the use of sensibles in divine cult as accommodations to our constitution as human beings (see, e.g., *Orationes de Imaginibus* 3.12). See also Thomas's quotation of *De Fide Orthodoxa* 4.12 [85] to this effect at *ST* II-II, q. 84, a. 2, co.

106. "Letter to His Own Father Plato about the Veneration of the Sacred Images," in *Theodore the Studite*, 139.

theologians, combined with an Augustinian framework that by Thomas's time made *latria* into a virtue paired with *dulia*, led Thomas to propose a way of speaking about the icon of Christ incongruent with the Council's dogmatic definition. It seems clear that once this is understood, the ecumenical conciliar language of Nicaea II should take precedence over Thomas's. As Venance Grumel points out, the Council of Trent adopted such a course, carefully refusing to apply either *latria* or even the slippery term *adoratio* to the veneration of images (Session 25).[107] Not long after Trent, Robert Bellarmine was challenged by Báñez for failing to use Thomas's language concerning veneration of images. Bellarmine replied that "he does not speak like St Thomas because St Thomas does not speak like the Popes and the oecumenical Councils." This was due, Bellarmine (rightly) contended, to the unavailability of Nicaea II, Constantinople IV (under Pope Hadrian II, 869–70), and the Damascene's *Orations*, all of which were "only to be discovered and published in the present century." He blames the "novelty" of paying *latria* to images on Alexander of Hales.[108] Much more recently, Vatican II followed the same course. *Lumen Gentium* 67 exhorts that "those decrees, which have been given in the early days regarding the cult of images of Christ, the Blessed Virgin and the saints, be religiously observed." The footnote that identifies which "decrees" are meant cites Nicaea II and Trent exclusively.

Nonetheless, once allowances are made for differences in vocabulary and conceptual framework, Thomas's approximation of the content of Nicaea II should be appreciated. His teaching is responsive to the teaching of John of Damascus and is firmly rooted in a sound incarnational Christology, sharpened by his study of the Third and Fifth Ecumenical Councils. And like the Eastern Fathers whose work he did not know, Aquinas seeks to situate Christian use of sacred images within an incarnational economy that invites believers to a renewed experience of themselves and all creation, reconfigured in Christ to the glory of God: "pres-

---

107. Grumel, *Dictionnaire de théologie catholique*, col. 836.

108. Quoted in James Broderick, SJ, *Robert Bellarmine: Saint and Scholar* (Westminster, MD: Newman Press, 1961), 202–3. Broderick does not supply a citation, but the same passage is briefly noted by Stefania Tutino, *Empire of Souls: Robert Bellarmine and the Christian Commonwealth* (New York: Oxford University Press, 2010), 17, 296nn24–25. Tutino identifies its source as a "manuscript memo" titled "De sententia cujusdam, qui S. tum [sic] Thomam uno solo articulo exempt sequendum censuit," in X.-M. Le Bachelet, *Bellarmin avant son Cardinalat: Correspondance et documents* (Paris: Beauchesne, 1911), Appendix XI.

ent your bodies as a living sacrifice, holy and acceptable to God, which is your rational *latreia*" (Rom 12:1).

Acknowledgments

The author is grateful to Michael P. Barber, Douglas Bushman, J. Columcille Dever, Scott Hefelfinger, Fr. Andrew Hofer, OP, and Jordan Wales and for their indispensable encouragement and help.

11

Quidam Graecus

Theophylact of Ochrid in the *Catena Aurea in Ioannem* and the *Lectura Super Ioannem*

JANE SLOAN PETERS

Introduction

In the dedication of the *Catena Aurea in Marcum,* Thomas Aquinas writes, "In order that the exposition of the saints be whole and continuous, I have seen to it that certain passages from the Greek doctors were translated into Latin."[1] One such *doctor Graecus* was the Byzantine exegete Theophylact (d. 1125/26), Archbishop of Ochrid in the Byzantine province of Bulgaria. Prior to the publication of Aquinas's *Expositio Continua Super Evangelia,* popularly known as the *Catena Aurea,* Theophylact's works were unknown to the Latin West. Robert Grosseteste (d. 1253) incorporated fifty-six extracts from Theophylact's *Expositio in Epistolam ad Galatas* in his own commentary, though ignorant of the author. Aquinas himself quoted several passages from Theophylact in the *Contra Errores Graecorum,* though, following his source, Nicholas of Cotrone, he attributed them to John Chrysostom.[2] The translation of Theophylact's

---

1. Thomas Aquinas, *Catena Aurea in Quatuor Evangelia, 1: Expositio in Matthaeum et Marcum, II. Expositio in Lucam et Ioannem,* vol. 1, ed. A. Guarienti (Torino-Roma: Marietti, 1953), 429. Hereafter referred to as CA. I also consulted John Henry Newman, trans., "Thomas Aquinas: *Catena Aurea in Ioannem,* Gospel of Saint John," accessed September 10, 2018, https://www.dhspriory.org/thomas/CAJohn.htm.

2. Carmelo Giuseppe Conticello, "Théophylacte de Bulgarie, Source de Thomas

244

Gospel commentaries for use in the *Catena Aurea* effectively introduced him to the Latin-speaking world, where his writings—sometimes via the *Catena*—became an important source for Peter John Olivi, Erasmus, and others.[3]

Excerpts from Theophylact's Gospel commentaries make a significant contribution to the *Catena*: after John Chrysostom, he is the most frequently cited Greek Father in the final three volumes on Mark, Luke, and John.[4] Yet outside the *Catena*, Thomas mentions Theophylact by name only once, calling him *quidam Graecus* ("a certain Greek") in the *Lectura Super Ioannem*.[5] Understanding Thomas's overall reception of Theophylact's thought, then, requires identifying unattributed quotations and references. C. G. Conticello and L. J. Bataillon have already demonstrated that Thomas reemployed many texts from the *Catena Aurea* in his sermons and scriptural commentaries. Bataillon notes two places in the *Tertia Pars* where Thomas silently relies on Theophylact's text from the *Catena*.[6] Conticello identifies nineteen places in which Aquinas consults Theophylact's texts from the *Catena in Ioannem* for his *Lectura Super Ioannem*.[7] He notes correctly that most of these passages are employed to refute a heresy, but the scope of his analysis is limited to the Johannine prologue. The study of Aquinas's use of Theophylact, then, must advance

---

d'Aquin," in *Philomathestatos: Studies in Greek and Byzantine Texts Presented to Jacques Noret for His Sixty-Fifth Birthday*, ed. B. Janssens, B. Roosen, and P. Van Deun (Leuven: Peeters, 2004), 63–75, esp. 65n10.

3. Conticello, "Théophylacte," 65n11. The translator of Theophylact's texts is unknown, and, unfortunately, the Latin text Thomas used has been lost. James A. Weisheipl speculates that Thomas, who did not read Greek, obtained translation assistance from a linguist in Urban's court from 1263 to 1264. William of Moerbeke, a priest at the court of Clement IV in Viterbo in 1265, may also have helped; however, Moerbeke is known for translating philosophical works. James A. Weisheipl, *Friar Thomas d'Aquino: His Life, Thought, and Works* (Washington, DC: Catholic University of America Press, 1983), 173.

4. Conticello, "Théophylacte," 64n6.

5. Thomas Aquinas, *Commentary on the Gospel of John*, vol. 1, *Chapters 1–8*, and vol. 2, *Chapters 9–21*, trans. Fabian R. Larcher (Lander, WY: Aquinas Institute, 2013), 1, lect. 14, §259. Hereafter *Ioan*. I also consulted Thomas Aquinas, *Commentary on the Gospel of John*, vol. 1, *Chapters 1–7*, trans. James A. Weisheipl, and vol. 2, *Chapters 8–21*, trans. Fabian R. Larcher (Albany, NY: Magi Books), https://www.dhspriory.org/thomas/SSJohn.htm.

6. Louis-Jacques Bataillon, "Saint Thomas et les Pères: de la Catena a la Tertia Pars," in *Ordo Sapientiae et Amoris*, Studia Friburgensía 78, ed. C. J. Pinto de Oliveira and J. P. Mélanges (Fribourg: J. P. Torrell, 1993), 15–36.

7. Carmelo Giuseppe Conticello, "San Tommaso ed i Padri: La *Catena Aurea Super Ioannem*," in *Archives d'Histoire Doctrinale et Littéraire du Moyen Âge 57* (Paris: Librarie Philosophique J. Vrin, 1990), 31–92. See Conticello, "San Tommaso," 82, and Conticello, "Théophylacte," 70–74.

on two fronts. First, we must study Theophylact's overall presence in the *Catena in Ioannem* to clarify the kind of exegesis he contributes. Second, we must determine which of these passages reappear in Thomas's *Lectura Super Ioannem* to understand the impact of the Byzantine exegete on the Angelic Doctor's own exegesis.

In this chapter, I review Theophylact's contribution to the *Catena in Ioannem* and demonstrate that he contributes predominantly as an exegete of the literal sense of Scripture. Then, I examine Aquinas's redeployment of Theophylact in the *Lectura Super Ioannem*. In addition to the points of correspondence identified by Conticello, I list and classify eighty-seven other locations in which Thomas relies on passages from Theophylact for his own scriptural commentary. Again, Thomas draws primarily on Theophylact's exegesis of the literal sense for the *Lectura*. This study of Theophylact's contribution to the *Catena in Ioannem* and *Lectura Super Ioannem*, which extends far beyond Thomas's singular mention, highlights the importance and complexity of the literal sense of Scripture for Aquinas. In addition, this study advances our understanding of the influence of the *Catena Aurea*—particularly its Greek authorities—on Thomas's subsequent thought. Thomas's widespread use of Greek authorities for the *Catena*, Theophylact included, is a testament not only to his desire to acquire new sources, but also to the proximity of Greek and Latin theological worlds and the pressing question of reunion in the decade prior to the Second Council of Lyons (1274). For Thomas and his contemporaries, the membrane between East and West was perhaps more permeable than we suppose.[8]

Biography

Theophylact Hephaistos was born around the time popularly known today as the Great Schism (1054) in Euboea, in present-day Greece.[9] He

---

8. For an excellent monograph on the reception of Aquinas's writings in the Greek East, see Marcus Plested, *Orthodox Readings of Aquinas* (Oxford: Oxford University Press, 2012).

9. Most scholars place his birth between 1050 and 1060. For brief biographies of Theophylact, see Dimitri Obolensky, *Six Byzantine Portraits* (Oxford: Clarendon Press, 1988), 34–83, and Paul Gautier, *Théophylacte d'Achrida: Discours, Traités, Poésies*, vol. 1 (Thessalonique: Association de Recherches Byzantines, 1980), 11–37. See also Margaret Mullett, *Theophylact of Ochrid: Reading the Letters of a Byzantine Archbishop*, vol. 2, *Birmingham Byzantine and Ottoman Monographs*, ed. Anthony Bryer and John Haldon (New York: Routledge, 2016).

traveled to Constantinople to study under the eccentric polymath Michael Psellos, director of a new imperial school of philosophy that had been founded, along with a law school, by Emperor Constantine IX (1042–55).[10] In the heart of the empire, Theophylact grew into a prominent intellectual. He received the title "Master of Rhetoricians,"[11] served as a deacon at Hagia Sophia, and tutored the son of Emperor Michael VII Ducas (1071–78).[12]

Theophylact was a prolific writer; his works comprise four volumes of Migne's *Patrologia Graeca*. The large surviving collection of Theophylact's letters portray, according to Ernest W. Saunders, "a vigorous and well-informed mind, a strong-willed person who was quick to assert his authority in defense of his position, his rights, and the faith he held."[13] One of his most famous works, *On the Errors of the Latins*, vehemently opposed the addition of the *Filioque* to the Creed, yet graciously attributed the Latin position to the inferiority of the Latin language. He criticized fellow Greek theologians for confusing petty concerns, such as the length of beards, with weightier doctrinal matters, and reasoned that much of the disagreement between East and West was due to a "cooling of charity" that left Latin and Greek theologians eager to accuse one another of heresy.[14]

Theophylact produced biblical commentaries on the minor prophets and most books of the New Testament, and he wrote his *Explanation on the Four Gospels* while Archbishop of Bulgaria.[15] Theophylact's exegetical writings, like those of his contemporaries, rely heavily on patristic catenae and have been criticized for displaying little originality. He consulted a number of fathers, including Theodoret of Cyrus, the Cappadocians, Pseudo-Dionysius, and Cyril of Alexandria.[16] He follows John

---

Carmelo Giuseppe Conticello will publish a chapter on Theophylact in a forthcoming volume of *La Théologie Byzantine et sa Tradition* (Turnhout: Brepols, forthcoming).

10. Judith Herrin, *Byzantium* (Princeton, NJ: Princeton University Press, 2007), 76.

11. Mullett, *Theophylact of Ochrid*, 43.

12. Obolensky, *Six Byzantine Portraits*, 36.

13. Ernest W. Saunders, "Theophylact of Ochrid as Writer and Biblical Interpreter," *Research* 2 (1957): 31–44.

14. Tia M. Kolbaba, *The Byzantine Lists: Errors of the Latins* (Chicago: University of Illinois Press, 2000), 176.

15. There is no critical edition of *Theophylact's Explanation of the Four Holy Gospels*. One can consult Migne's *Patrologia Graeca*, vols. 123 and 124, for the Greek text. For the English volumes, see *Blessed Theophylact's Explanation of the New Testament*, trans. Fr. Christopher Stade (House Springs, MO: Chrysostom Press, 1992–2007).

16. Conticello, "San Tommaso," 77n323.

Chrysostom especially closely, leading some to view his Gospel commentaries as merely derivative of Chrysostom's.[17] Yet in the Middle Byzantine period it was not innovation but a faithful adherence to patristic tradition that was a sign of intellectual accomplishment.[18] Saunders has demonstrated further that while Theophylact draws heavily from Chrysostom's homilies, he is no slavish imitator. To take but one example, a synoptic reading of Theophylact's commentary and Chrysostom's homily on the Wedding Feast at Cana confirms Saunders's analysis. Theophylact wrote his commentary with Chrysostom's text (or a catena) close at hand, but the structure has been reworked, and passages have been adapted to his audience. Theophylact interprets John 2:7 with a lighter hand, omitting Chrysostom's condemnation of the Manichaeans, but retaining his insistence that the one who changed water to wine is the same Creator whose power always turns grapes into wine.[19] He then includes a mystical interpretation of the wedding as the union of God in the soul, and the six jars of water as the five senses and the faculty of reason. This interpretation is not present in Chrysostom's homily and has probably been taken from another source. Rather than viewing Theophylact's Gospel commentaries as unoriginal works of imitation, then, they should be viewed as works of craftsmanship undertaken with the best of resources. A Byzantine theologian would balk at Saunders's claim that Theophylact maintains a "certain independence from the patristic tradition." Still, his own voice emerges through the assembly of rich patristic materials in his commentary.

Theophylact's method of exegesis differs significantly from that of his teacher, Michael Psellos. Psellos was fascinated by the hidden symbolism of Scripture; his style, replete with allegorical interpretation, has been compared to Origen's.[20] Tia Kolbaba describes Psellos's own lectures on

17. Gautier observes that his Scripture commentaries were extremely popular from the beginning of the twelfth century "despite their lack of originality" (11). See also the suggestion from Staab in Saunders, "Theophylact," 37, to classify Theophylact's works as part of "Chrysostom and his school."

18. On the false assumption that Byzantine exegesis lacks originality, see Tia M. Kolbaba, "Byzantine Orthodox Exegesis," in *The New Cambridge History of the Bible 2*, ed. Richard Marsden and E. Ann Matter (Cambridge: Cambridge University Press, 2012), 485–504.

19. Theophylact, *Explanation* 4, chap. 2, vv. 5–8.

20. Michael Psellos's interests extended far beyond theology, and he has garnered greater attention from English-speaking academics than has Theophylact. Paul More has categorized his works in the *Iter Psellianum Subsidia Mediaevalia 26* (Toronto: Pontifical Institute of Medieval Studies, 2005). See the Michael Psellos in Translation Series, edited by Anthony Kaldellis at Ohio State University. See also *Reading Michael Psellos*, Medieval Mediterranean 61, ed. Charles Barber and David Jenkins (Leiden: Brill, 2006).

patristic exegesis as "idiosyncratic, possibly original and creative, and perhaps not entirely orthodox."[21] Theophylact's Gospel commentaries, however, position mystical interpretation within a comprehensive exegesis of the literal sense. He is eminently concerned with orthodoxy, naming and refuting heresies—usually Christological—as the Scripture gives occasion. This approach suits his Bulgarian flock, with their rudimentary catechesis and a basic knowledge of Scripture. For example, in the preface to the *Explanation of the Holy Gospel According to John*, Theophylact marvels that the Apostle, an illiterate fisherman, could rise to such spiritual heights. "Behold how a man like this—unlettered and unknown—acquired such spiritual power that he thundered forth doctrines taught by none of the other Evangelists."[22]

The transition from Constantinopolitan intellectual to rural archbishop was not an easy one. As *maistor ton rhetoron*, Theophylact delivered encomia for the Byzantine court, called *logoi basilikoi*.[23] Sometime after his last *logos basilikos* on January 6, 1088, Emperor Alexios I Komnenos appointed him Archbishop of Ochrid in Bulgaria (modern-day Macedonia).[24] The reason for this decision is unclear; perhaps the encomium was not well received, or perhaps the court disapproved of Theophylact's friendship with the ex-basilissa Maria.[25] More likely, the emperor viewed him as the perfect candidate for his burgeoning project: a corps of preaching clergy, trained to root out and correct heresy in a sprawling and diverse empire.[26] The province of Bulgaria, annexed to Byzantium in 1018, remained a sort of Slavic Wild West in comparison to Constantinople.[27] Whatever the reason for the appointment, Theophylact viewed the position as an *aeiphygia*, an "eternal exile" from his beloved intellectual hub to a brutish and uncatechized wasteland, from glittering courts and churches to an agrarian landscape populated by simple shepherds

---

21. Kolbaba, "Byzantine Orthodox Exegesis," 498.

22. Theophylact, *The Explanation of the Holy Gospel According to John*, trans. Fr. Christopher Stade (House Springs, MO: Chrysostom Press, 2007), 4.

23. Obolensky, *Six Byzantine Portraits*, 38–39. For the two speeches that survive from Theophylact's career as master rhetorician in Constantinople, see Mullett, *Theophylact of Ochrid*, 232–35.

24. Obolensky, *Six Byzantine Portraits*, 39. Gautier dates his departure between January 6, 1088, the day of his address to Emperor Alexius, and spring of 1092 (33–36).

25. Symeon, Metropolitan of Varna and Preslav, suggests that Alexius I condemned Theophylact to the archbishopric of Bulgaria because of his friendship with Maria. See Obolensky, *Six Byzantine Portraits*, 40n21.

26. Kolbaba mentions this project in "Byzantine Orthodox Exegesis," 498.

27. Saunders, "Theophylact," 33.

and farmers.[28] Letters written from Bulgaria by the bishop depict, with a flair for the dramatic, the depths of this feeling of exile. Margaret Mullett writes, "Bulgaria in the letters is Kedar of the Bible, a desert inhabited by scorpions, or a dismal swamp, these desolate places, where Laestrygonians and Cyclopes lurk and the harpies snatch away books."[29]

Despite viewing his appointment as an exile, Theophylact was fiercely dedicated to his flock and took responsibility for the welfare of the many Bulgarians under his care. Rhetorical flourishes once reserved for imperial encomia were now applied to letters complaining about complex Komnenian tax laws and their corrupt implementation in the outskirts of the empire.[30] Pope Francis once encouraged episcopal shepherds to smell like the sheep, and Theophylact knew this feeling.[31] "I descend among the Bulgarians," he wrote to the ex-basilissa Maria, "I who am a true Constantinopolitan, and strangely enough a Bulgarian, exuding like them the smell of sheepskin."[32] Theophylact would spend the rest of his life in Bulgaria, until about 1125/26.[33] Ochrid provided the fertile soil for his four Gospel commentaries, which, according to Saunders, "dominate[d] the exegetical theology of the Greek Church" for several centuries.[34] The surviving manuscripts attest to their popularity: 119 codices containing commentary on one or more of the Gospels remain.[35]

One hundred and fifty years after Theophylact's death, Thomas Aqui-

---

28. Margaret Mullett notes that in speaking of exile, Theophylact has taken up the motif of *xeniteia*, a prevalent concept in Greek and Byzantine literature from Homer to the letters of John Chrysostom. Chrysostom, who was twice exiled from his patriarchate in Constantinople, was a particularly important model for subsequent theologians in exile. Exile was such a prominent literary motif in the Middle Byzantine period that the instances may be categorized: politico-legal, monastic, non-episcopal official, episcopal (Theophylact falls here), and refugee clergy. See Mullett, *Theophylact of Ochrid*, 244.

29. Mullett, *Theophylact of Ochrid*, 274.

30. See Alan Harvey, "The Land and Taxation in the Reign of Alexios I Komnenos: The Evidence of Theophylakt of Ochrid," *Revue des Études Byzantines* 51 (1993): 139–54.

31. Pope Francis, "Chrism Mass Homily," March 28 2013, website of the Holy See, http://w2.vatican.va/.

32. Mullett, *Theophylact of Ochrid*, 261. Excerpt from letter G4 to Maria, II, 141.58–62 (see 261n197).

33. Saunders puts Theophylact's death in 1108. Gautier writes that Theophylact almost certainly lived until 1108, but questions the reliability of the date of 1125/26 found on Theophylact's Poem no. 4 (37). Plested and Mullett agree on the later date.

34. Saunders, "Theophylact," 34.

35. We can compare this with the known copies of the *Catena Aurea*, where between seventy-three and eighty-nine complete copies of each Gospel *catena* remain. See Conticello, "San Tommaso," 42.

nas was serving as the conventual lector at Orvieto in the papal court when Pope Urban IV commissioned of him a continuous patristic exposition of the Gospels.[36] This *Catena* was the occasion for the Latin world's official introduction to Theophylact. His commentary does not appear in the *Expositio Continua in Matthaeum,* likely completed before Urban's death in October of 1264, but appears over a thousand times (1,017) in the *Catena* on Mark, Luke, and John, about half as much as Chrysostom (2,044) and nearly twice as much as Origen (613).[37]

It is unclear how well Aquinas knew Theophylact's biography, but it appears that someone in the papal court saw the Byzantine exegete as the perfect candidate for the *Expositio Continua,* which was commissioned as the pope and Emperor Michael VIII Palaiologos discussed reunion between Rome and Constantinople.[38] While the possibility of reunion was a perennial question, the events of the thirteenth century heightened the significance of this conversation. Latin Crusaders had sacked Constantinople in 1204, and the city was occupied by Latins for fifty-seven years before, in July 1261, Michael VIII Palaiologos reclaimed it.[39] The new

36. For more on the commissioning of the *Catena Aurea,* which Weisheipl calls "the turning point in the development of Aquinas's theology," see *Friar Thomas d'Aquino,* 171–76, and Torrell, *Thomas Aquinas: The Person and His Work* (Washington, DC: Catholic University of America Press, 2005), 136–40.

37. Conticello, "Théophylacte," 64n6. A few times, Conticello notes, the *Catena* confuses Origen with John Scotus Eriugena.

38. According to Weisheipl, these discussions could have happened as early as August 1261 (*Friar Thomas d'Aquino,* 168). Despite the Constantinopolitan vitriol toward Westerners, which was only exacerbated by the sack of the city in 1204, the new emperor was aware of the empire's vulnerable status and the indispensability of Western military support. Three rival empires in Nicaea, Epiros, and Trebizond had emerged during the Latin occupation, and the latter two imperial claimants refused to submit to the victor from Nicaea. This meant that Michael VIII Palaiologos exercised limited control over Byzantium's land and sea territories. In addition to internal troubles, the threat of the Ottoman Turks loomed. See Herrin, *Byzantium,* 283.

39. Alexios Angelos, son of the recently deposed—and blinded—Isaac II Angelos (1185–95), had escaped from prison and entreated leaders of the Fourth Crusade to reroute their march to the Holy Land and help him reclaim the imperial throne from his uncle, Alexios III. The crusaders agreed on the condition that they be paid 200,000 silver marks and that the new emperor would ensure reunion with the Latin church. Alexios (IV) Angelos indeed acceded to the throne with the help of the Fourth Crusade, but the new emperor was unable to maintain the terms of the agreement. Crusaders camped outside the walls of Constantinople for a year, demanding payment, while inside the city, the citizens resented the emperor who had brought the Latins to their doorstep. In January 1204, citizens revolted against the emperor, and in April, crusaders sacked the city and established Latin rule. See Herrin, *Byzantium,* 262–63. See also George Ostrogorsky, *History of the Byzantine State,* trans. Joan Hussey (Oxford: Alden Press, 1968), 414–17.

emperor, in a weak position militarily, immediately initiated efforts to reunite the Eastern church with Rome. Thus momentum for the Second Council of Lyons was already building by the time Urban IV approached Thomas at Orvieto to request the *Expositio Continua*. In light of these events, Theophylact seems a felicitous candidate for the project: he was a popular Greek exegete, an even-handed critic of Latin theology, and a lover of Chrysostom. He lived only a century before Thomas, making him heir to most of Greek patristic tradition, including the sixth- and seventh-century conciliar Christology unavailable to many of his patristic predecessors. The incorporation of his commentaries would familiarize the Latin world with modern Greek exegesis or act as a conciliatory gesture toward the Greek church, or both.

Expositio Continua Super Ioannem

Two hundred and forty-nine excerpts from Theophylact's *Explanation of the Holy Gospel According to John* appear in the *Catena in Ioannem*, and they are roughly categorized here based on the type of exegesis that Theophylact contributes.[40] Examining all Theophylact's passages reveal that only a handful of the total number of passages—about twenty-five— are heresiological. Many such passages occur in the Johannine prologue, where he refutes the teachings of Apollinarius, Arius, Mani, and Nestorius. Beginning with the Book of Signs (Jn 1:19), however, Theophylact contributes primarily as an exegete of the literal sense. Almost three-fourths of Theophylact's passages in the *Catena in Ioannem*—about one hundred and seventy-eight—offer an interpretation of the letter.[41]

40. While Conticello counts 242 passages in his article "Théophylacte," I have counted 249 locations where Theophylact appears in the *Expositio Continua Super Ioannem*. The number 249 corresponds with that in the *Catena Aurea Electronica*, a project directed by Conticello and Martin Morard at the *Centre National de la Recherche Scientifique*. Conticello has noticed, however, that one passage attributed to Theophylact in the *Catena* does not appear in the text of his commentary in the *Patrologia Graeca*. For more information on this important project, visit the Sacra Pagina website, accessed September 10, 2018, https://big .hypotheses.org/catena-aurea.

41. Mark Johnson defines the literal sense as that which the author of Scripture intends the written words of Scripture to mean. "The literal sense of Scripture is what the author of Scripture intends to be understood by the words that are written. The author is twofold, for Thomas maintains that the Holy Spirit is the principal author of Scripture, while a human author operating under the Spirit's inspiration has the role of instrument. The medium of the words makes the literal sense different from the spiritual senses, since in the spiritual senses the medium of meaning is through the things signified by the words of Scripture as is intended by

This emphasis on the letter reflects Aquinas's own high regard for the literal sense. In *ST* I, q. 1, a. 10, Thomas explains that arguments about sacred doctrine must appeal only to the literal sense of Scripture. He writes, "All the senses are founded on one—the literal—from which alone can any argument be drawn, and not from those intended in allegory."[42] The spiritual senses cannot be used in an argument because, once untethered from the literal sense, they may be misunderstood or misapplied.[43] Thomas also grants that a scriptural text can sustain a variety of literal interpretations. While text that pertains to the faith per se, such as the doctrine of the Trinity, cannot admit many meanings, text pertaining per accidens to the faith can differ in interpretation while maintaining harmony with the substance of the doctrine.[44] Thomas warns against two errors: on the one hand, asserting something false about the literal sense, and on the other, limiting one's interpretation of the letter to the exclusion of other viable interpretations. Multiple interpretations of the letter facilitate the delight of the many readers and hearers of Scripture. Mark Johnson writes that for Thomas, "The ability of Scripture to admit of many meanings is part of its dignity ... for because of these many meanings it can happen that the different minds of human beings can grasp a truth found in Scripture, and that those human beings will accordingly marvel in that grasping."[45] Aquinas structures the *Catena Aurea* according to this appreciation for the multiplicity of the literal sense: he often includes interpretations of the letter from several authorities.

It is possible to roughly classify Theophylact's exegesis of the literal

---

the Holy Spirit alone, whereas in the literal sense the medium of meaning is the words alone, intended both by the human author and the Holy Spirit." See Mark Johnson, "Another Look at the Plurality of the Literal Sense of Scripture," *Medieval Philosophy and Theology* 2 (1992): 117–41, esp. 119. See also Leonard Boyle, "Authorial Intention and the *Divisio Textus*," in *Reading John with St. Thomas Aquinas* (Washington, DC: Catholic University of America Press, 2005), 3–8. In contrast to Johnson, yet citing the same article of the *Summa*, Boyle claims that for Thomas the literal sense "pertains to those things that the words of Scripture signify" and says that Thomas does not really consider what the human author meant. Boyle then proceeds to outline Thomas's search in the *De Potentia* for the *sensus auctoris* (6). Like Johnson, Boyle points out Aquinas's comfort with the multiplicity of the literal sense (7).

42. Thomas Aquinas, *Summa Theologiae*, trans. Fathers of the English Dominican Province (New York: Benziger Bros., 1947), I, q. 1, a. 10, ad 1, https://www.dhspriory.org/thomas/summa/index.html.

43. A lion, e.g., can be a symbol for Christ or the devil. I am indebted to Mark Johnson's article "Another Look," in which Johnson points out two passages where Thomas borrows this example from Augustine.

44. Johnson, "Another Look," 121–22.

45. Johnson, "Another Look," 127. See also Boyle, "Authorial Intention," 6.

sense in the *Catena in Ioannem*. About fifteen excerpts introduce a Scripture passage; these are simple remarks in which Theophylact acts almost as an emcee for other exegetes, usually Augustine, Chrysostom, or Origen.[46] Thomas's choice of Theophylact here suggests he finds the exegete quite reliable. His work is used for the architecture of the *Catena*, to move the commentary forward and link more esoteric passages.

Roughly fifteen excerpts provide some historical, religious, or cultural context. For example, Thomas prefaces Jesus's encounter with the Samaritan woman at the well with Theophylact's account of the history of Jacob's well.[47] In the account of the miracle of loaves and fishes, he invokes Theophylact to explain why the evangelist mentions that the multitude sit on green grass: the grass indicates that the miracle occurred in the first month of spring and the season of Passover.[48] He also quotes Theophylact to explain that the garment Christ wore during his passion was seamless because of a distinctive Palestinian style of weaving.[49] Theophylact's contextualization of the letter often grounds subsequent mystical or moral interpretation. In the case of the woman at the well, for example, Thomas quotes Theophylact again, after further commentary on the literal sense from Augustine and Chrysostom, to explain the significance of the well as a meeting place. The well is a reminder that what the patriarchs obtained by faith in God the Jews had lost by their impiety, thus making room for the salvation of the Gentiles.[50] And the seamless garment, woven from top to bottom, denotes Christ's humanity, which was "woven from above" as the power of the Holy Spirit overshadowed the Virgin Mary.[51]

Roughly forty excerpts, which Aquinas usually prefaces with *quasi dicat*, paraphrase the evangelist, Christ, or another figure to bring out the tone of a passage or clarify its meaning. For example, Theophylact rephrases Pilate's *Ecce, homo*, as a challenge to the Jews who insisted Christ be crucified. "As if to say, see the kind of man you suspect of aspiring to the throne, a humble person, who cannot have any such design."[52] In another place, Aquinas uses Augustine, Chrysostom, and Theophylact to explain the literal sense of Christ's words: "I have many things to say and to

---

46. See, e.g., 364A, *Quia Iudaei videbant ...*, 433B, *Quia dixerat dominus ...*, 467B, *Imbecilliores enim ...*, and 489A, *Decebat admirari ...*
47. CA 2, 382a.
48. CA 2, 415a.
49. CA 2, 571b.
50. CA 2, 382a.
51. CA 2, 572a.
52. CA 2, 569b.

judge of you, but he that sent me is true" (Jn 8:25). All three theologians speak in first person, as though rephrasing Christ's words. Augustine emphasizes the relationship of Christ to the Father: "I will be true in my judgment, because I am the truth, the Son of the true One ... My father is true, not by partaking of the truth, but by begetting truth."[53] Chrysostom distinguishes between Christ's present mission of salvation and his future advent as judge: "As my Father has sent me not to judge the world, but to save the world, and my Father is true, I accordingly judge no man now; but speak thus for your salvation, not your condemnation."[54] Finally, Theophylact contrasts the disbelief of Christ's Jewish interlocutors with the truth of the Father. Like Chrysostom, he emphasizes the impending judgment: "As if to say, though you are unbelievers, my father is true, who has appointed a day of retribution for you."[55]

Finally, roughly forty excerpts explain the motivation for a Gospel figure's words or actions, a method of interpretation that Thomas also ascribes to the literal sense.[56] Many such examples occur in the account of Christ's arrest in the Garden of Gethsemane. Judas led the guards to Gethsemane because he knew Christ was accustomed to teaching his disciples in such places.[57] The soldiers carried torches to guard against Christ escaping in the dark, yet Jesus asked the guards, "Whom are you looking for?" because they could not distinguish him from the others.[58] This showed that Jesus revealed himself by his own prerogative.[59] And why did Peter have a sword at hand with which to attack the high priest's servant? He had used it for sacrificing the paschal lamb and had carried it away from the supper.[60] Such passages from Theophylact flesh out the characters of Christ, the Apostles, the Pharisees, and even John the Evangelist.

Thomas quotes Theophylact on the moral and mystical meanings of Scripture as well, and though these passages are less frequent, they constitute some of the most beautiful of his contributions. In considering Christ bearing the Cross to Golgotha (Jn 19:16–18), Chrysostom observes that while Isaac carried the wood to his sacrifice, the sacrifice is

---

53. CA 2, 451b.
54. CA 2, 451b.
55. CA 2, 451b.
56. See, e.g., *Ioan* 1, lect. 16, §1310, wherein Thomas lists possible reasons Jesus left Judea for Galilee.
57. CA 2, 557b.
58. CA 2, 557b.
59. CA 2, 557b.
60. CA 2, 558b.

fully accomplished in Christ. Theophylact follows with a reflection on Christ's humanity and divinity: "But whereas Isaac was let go, and a ram offered, so here too the divine nature remains impassible, but the human, of which the ram was the type, the offspring of that straying ram, was slain."[61] Thomas also places Theophylact at the conclusion of lectio 11 of chapter 19, where he offers a moral reading of Christ's burial in the tomb of Joseph of Arimathea. He entreats his readers to see Christ in poor persons who are effectively being put to death by the greedy. This interpretation results in a call to prayer, rather than action: "Be therefore a Joseph, and cover Christ's nakedness, and, not once, but continually by contemplation, embalm Him in your spiritual tomb, cover Him and mix myrrh and bitter aloes, considering that bitterest sentence of all: Depart, ye cursed, into everlasting fire."[62]

Despite the richness of Theophylact's moral and mystical exegesis, he emerges primarily in Thomas's careful expansion and enlargement of literal sense exegesis throughout the *Catena in Ioannem*. This aspect of the *Catena* should not be overlooked, not only because Thomas values the letter as the backbone of apologetics, but also because he gathers various interpretations of the letter from respected *doctores*. Theophylact is a critical figure in this regard. The *Catena* does not cursorily clarify the letter to move beyond it. By proposing several literal interpretations of a passage, Thomas invites the reader to linger over the literal sense, to enter into a deeper consideration of the scriptural events as the Evangelist recounts them. This adds a valuable meditative dimension to the exegesis of the literal sense and confirms that, even at the level of the letter, the mystery of God's revelation is already at work. The letter contains, in a certain way, more than it is expected to hold, much like the humanity of Christ contains, in flesh and bone, a revelation of Christ's divinity.

Lectura Super Ioannem

Theophylact's presence in the *Catena* indicates Aquinas's willingness to include the exegesis of a near-contemporary Greek theologian alongside patristic and conciliar texts. What has been unrecognized until recently is that Theophylact also plays a significant, albeit largely unattributed, role in Aquinas's *Lectura Super Ioannem*. Originally delivered as a series of

61. CA 2, 570a.
62. CA 2, 576b.

lectures, the *Commentary on John* was composed during Aquinas's second Parisian regency between 1269 and 1272.[63] He had finished the final volume of the *Catena Aurea* in Rome between 1265 and 1268.[64] Thomas kept the *Catena* close at hand and had recourse to it when preparing the commentary: its texts were reorganized and redistributed throughout the *Lectura Super Ioannem*.[65] Along with John Chrysostom, Augustine, and Origen, Theophylact is one of the most frequently reused theologians,[66] though Thomas mentions him by name only once.[67] Conticello has identified fifteen locations in which Thomas silently draws on Theophylact's text from the *Catena* for his commentary on the Johannine prologue, and he has identified another four passages from chapter 19 that influence the *Lectura*.

The present study of the entire *Lectura Super Ioannem* shows eighty-seven additional locations in which Thomas either quotes Theophylact's text from the *Catena* or clearly relies on it for constructing his own commentary. Thus, Theophylact makes a tacit yet noteworthy contribution to Thomas's exegesis of the Gospel of John, appearing at least one hundred and seven times.[68] Exegetically, Aquinas's use of Theophylact in the *Lectura* is proportionate to that in the *Catena*. While about a dozen passages refute a heresy, the majority offer an interpretation of the literal sense, usually as one of several such interpretations. A handful of times, Aquinas implements one of his mystical or moral interpretations.[69] I have classified the eighty-seven passages I located into five categories according to their similarity to the text of the *Catena*: (1) direct attributions,

63. Torrell favors 1271–72 as the date of composition. There is some disagreement as to whether Thomas corrected the *reportatio* of the lectures. According to Weisheipl, Thomas probably wrote the first five chapters of the commentary himself and then corrected the *reportatio* of the remaining chapters, which were prepared by Reginald of Piperno (372). According to Torrell, "It seems hardly probable that Thomas himself reviewed the text" (339).

64. Weisheipl, *Friar Thomas d'Aquino*, 357.

65. Conticello, "San Tommaso ed i Padri," 83. Without identifying a source, Conticello also claims that the *Catena* was the only of Thomas's works that he always carried with him (87). Bataillon has also identified places where Thomas draws from the *Catena* for his sermons. See "Les Sermons de Saint Thomas et la Catena Aurea," in *Thomas Aquinas, 1274–1974: Commemorative Studies*, vol. 1 (Toronto: Pontifical Institute of Medieval Studies, 1974), 67–75.

66. Conticello, "San Tommaso," 69.

67. *Ioan.* 11, lect. 2, §1490.

68. It appears that Thomas relies on Theophylact's appearances in the *Catena* for his lecture material and does not consult the full text of the *Explanation of the Holy Gospel According to John*.

69. *Ioan.* 12, lect. 3, §1630.

(2) quotations without attribution, (3) passages with four or more shared words, (4) passages with shared key words and structural correspondence, and (5) passages with a common theme.

Direct Attributions

Catena in Ioannem	Lectura Super Ioannem
483a, *Quidam vero hunc ...*	chap. 11, lect. 2, §1490
590b, *Ex tunc etiam ...*	chap. 21, lect. 3, §2627

In one place, Thomas attributes an idea to *quemdam doctorem Graecum*,[70] and I classify this with the familiar *quidam Graecus, scilicet Theophylactus* as a direct attribution. Thomas is meticulous when it came to naming his sources, though he customarily refers to contemporaries and theologians of proximate generations with the moniker *quidam*.[71] It is not unusual to see Theophylact, only a century and a half Thomas's senior, referred to in this manner.

Quotations without Attribution

Catena in Ioannem	Lectura Super Ioannem
435b, *Quasi dicat: verax sum ...*	chap. 7, lect. 2, §1040
467a, *Quasi dicant: aut hoc falsum ...*	chap. 9, lect. 2, §1332
485b, *Sive etiam ipsam ...*	chap. 11, lect. 5, §1523
496a, *Ac si dicerent ...*	chap. 12, lect. 4, §1631
580b, *Timebat enim ...*	chap. 20, lect. 3, §2512

In five places, Aquinas directly quotes an entire passage of Theophylact's from the *Catena in Ioannem* without attribution. In the first example below (Jn 11:28), Aquinas draws on Augustine's and Theophylact's adjacent passages from the *Catena*. He mentions Augustine by name but attributes Theophylact's interpretation to "another." In the second example, Thomas enfolds Theophylact's contribution in with Chrysostom's. Aquinas considers the Pharisees' remark in John 12:19 as Christ enters

---

70. *Ioan.* 21, lect. 3, §2627.

71. According to Geenen, Thomas uses *quidam* not to hide an interlocutor's identity, but to demonstrate awareness of diverse currents or schools of theology (745). See Godfried Geenen, "Saint Thomas et les Pères," in *Dictionnaire de théologie catholique*, edited by A. Vacant et al. (Paris: Librairie Letouzey et Ané, 1946), 15.1, col. 738–61.

Jerusalem: "Behold, the whole world is gone after him." Thomas cites Chrysostom by name: certain Pharisees who believed in Jesus spoke these words privately among themselves, intending to prevent Christ's persecution. The text continues: "It is as though they were saying: no matter what snares you lay, he will grow in stature and his glory will increase. Why then not stop your plotting?"[72] The latter part of this text is Theophylact's from the *Catena*, and it occurs just after the passage containing Chrysostom's remarks. These two examples are typical of Thomas's use of Theophylact in the commentary; he frequently reuses portions of the *Catena* and cites certain Fathers by name while omitting Theophylact's name. He also frequently embeds Theophylact's text within another named source.

Catena

Augustinus: Advertendum etiam, quemadmodum Evangelista non dixerit ubi, vel quando, vel quomodo Mariam dominus vocaverit, ut hoc in verbis Marthae potius intelligeretur, narrationis brevitate servata.

Theophylactus: Sive etiam **ipsam** Christi **praesentiam vocationem reputavit,** quasi dicat: inexcusabile est ut eo praesente tu non exeas obviam ipsi.[73]

Lectura

Secundo dubitatur de hoc quod dicit *magister adest, et vocat te.* Videtur falsum dixisse: non enim dixit dominus Marthae quod vocaret Mariam. Responsio. Dicit Augustinus, quod Evangelista causa brevitatis dat intelligere quod in sua narratione intermiserat: nam forte dominus dixit Marthae quod eam vocaret. Alii autem dicunt, quod Martha **ipsam praesentiam vocationem reputavit; quasi diceret: inexcusabile est ut eo praesente tu non exeas obviam ipsi.**[74]

Catena

Chrysostomus: Mundum enim hic turbam dicunt. Videtur autem mihi hoc dictum esse eorum qui sani quidem erant, non audebant autem propalari: demum ab eventu deterrebant alios, quasi inconsummabilia tentantes.

Theophylactus: Ac si dicerent: **quantumcumque insidiemini, tanto hic augetur, et gloria eius intenditur: quis ergo** profectus de **tantis insidiis?**[75]

---

72. *Ioan.* 12, lect. 3, §1630.
73. CA 485b.
74. *Ioan.* 11, lect. 5, §1523.
75. CA 496a.

Lectura

Sed quid invidet caeca turba? Quia *post eum abiit mundus,* per quem factus est mundus. Sed tamen signatur per hoc, quod totus mundus eum secuturus erat; Oseae, VI, v. 3: *vivemus in conspectu eius, sequemurque, ut cognoscamus dominum.* Chrysostomus autem vult quod haec sint verba Pharisaeorum credentium, occulte tamen propter metum Iudaeorum. Et dicunt hoc, ut retraherent eos a persecutione Christi, **ac si dicerent: quantumcumque insidiamini, tanto hic augetur, et gloria eius intenditur. Quid ergo** non desistitis a tantis insidiis? Quod quidem quasi idem est cum consilio Gamalielis, de quo habetur Act. V, 34 ss.[76]

Four or More Common Words

Catena in Ioannem	*Lectura Super Ioannem*
349a, *Quia vero superius ...*	chap. 1, lect. 14, §260
349a, *Ausculta, o Ari ...*	chap. 1, lect. 14, §262
354b, *Non enim simpliciter ...*	chap. 1, lect. 15, §313
355a, *Non quia in ea natus ...*	chap. 1, lect. 15, §317
365b, *Ex hoc autem ...*	chap. 2, lect. 3, §413
370a–b, *Confundatur ergo ...*	chap. 3, lect. 2, §452
371b, *Cum vero filium ...*	chap. 3, lect. 2, §467
372a–b, *Videas ergo figuram ...*	chap. 3, lect. 2, §473
384b, *Quod autem dicit ...*	chap. 4, lect. 2, §583
389b, *In hoc autem ...*	chap. 4, lect. 3, §636
415a, *Idest herba viridis ...*	chap. 6, lect. 1, §858
417b, *Videm namque tria ...*	chap. 6, lect. 2, §883
420b–421a, *Seipsum dicit panem ...*	chap. 6, lect. 4, §914
426a, *Non enim puri ...*	chap. 6, lect. 7, §972
432a, *Secessit etiam nunc ...*	chap. 7, lect. 1, §1012
446b, *Ac si dicat ...*	chap. 8, lect. 2, §1150
447b, *Quidam vero notant ...*	chap. 8, lect. 2, §1159
458a, *Quasi dicat ...*	chap.8, lect. 3, §1191
458b, *Vel Samaritanum illum ...*	chap. 8, lect. 7, §1262
461b, *Tunc autem triginta ...*	chap. 8, lect. 8, §1289
469a, *Hoc autem dicit ...*	chap. 9 lect. 4, §1357
484a, *Intellexerunt autem quidam ...*	chap. 11, lect. 3, §1502
487a, *Hoc autem Martha ...*	chap. 11, lect. 6, §1557
501b, *Cum enim Verbum ...*	chap. 12, lect. 8. §1723

76. *Ioan.* 12, lect. 3, §1630.

517a, *Cum itaque activam ...*	chap. 14, lect. 2, §1871
560b, *Quidam tamen inanem*	chap. 18, lect. 3, §2309
563b, *Quasi dicat: quoniam ...*	chap. 18, lect. 5, §2329
564a, *Seorsum, eo quod ...*	chap. 18, lect. 5, §2344
578a, *Vel aliter. Hebdomadae ...*	chap. 20, lect. 1, §2471
579a–b, *Vel aliter. Intellige ...*	chap. 20, lect. 1, §2487
584b, *Qui prius infidelis ...*	chap. 20, lect. 6, §2562
592a, *Vel dicat: Christus ...*	chap. 21, lect. 5, §2647
593a, *Quod vero dicitur ...*	chap. 21 lect. 5, §2649

In thirty-three places, four or more key words from Thomas's text match a passage of Theophylact's from the *Catena*. These passages from the *Lectura*, in which Aquinas does not cite Theophylact verbatim, sometimes portray the Angelic Doctor adopting and shaping Theophylact's exegesis within his own system of thought. Commenting on John 3:13, for example, Thomas supplies the name Valentinus where Theophylact does not, yet clearly works from his text.

Catena

Theophylactus: Cum vero **filium hominis** descendisse de caelo audis, non putes **quod de caelo caro descenderit**: hoc enim haereticorum dogma est, qui docebant, quod Christus **de caelo corpus** sumpserat, et **per virginem transierat.**[77]

Lectura

Cum enim **filius hominis** designet humanam naturam, quae componitur ex anima et corpore, per hoc quod dicit quod filius **descendit de caelo**, Valentinus accipere voluit, quod etiam **corpus de caelo detulisset, et transisset per virginem,** nihil ex ea accipiens, sicut aqua per fistulam: ergo non de terrena substantia, nec sumptum de virgine: quod est contra apostolum.[78]

In another example, Aquinas uses Augustine's, Hilary's, and Theophylact's reflections on Christ's words, "I am the way, the truth, and the life" (Jn 14:6). Following the order of the *Catena*, he mentions Augustine and Hilary and then, anonymously, Theophylact. Theophylact's text in the *Catena* explains that Christ is "way" when one is engaged in action and "truth" when one is engaged in contemplation. "Life" signifies the importance of acting and contemplating with reference to the world to come. Aquinas retains this structure but augments the interpretation: "Holi-

77. CA 371b.
78. *Ioan.* 3, lect. 2, §467.

ness involves three things: action, contemplation, and one's intention."[79] Christ, who is way in action and truth in contemplation, directs the intention of both to eternal life. Aquinas is incorporating his own thought on contemplation from the *Secunda Secundae,* wherein the verb *intendo* and the noun *intentio* feature. Certain persons are especially intent upon the contemplation of truth, and others especially intent on external actions, and so life is fittingly divided into active and contemplative.[80] Intent is an act of the will regarding the end, which is the object of the will. As such, intention plays a role in motivating a person to desire the contemplative life.[81] Life, in the phrase "contemplative life," signifies that on which a person is chiefly intent.[82] So, Thomas fleshes out the dimension of desire for eternal life implicit in Theophylact's interpretation of *vita.*

Catena

Theophylactus: Cum itaque **activam exerces,** fit tibi **Christus via;** cum autem **in contemplativa perseveras,** efficitur tibi **veritas.** Adiecta autem **vita** est **activo et contemplativo:** decet enim ire et **praedicare pro futuro saeculo.**[83]

Lectura

Vel aliter. Tria sunt in homine quae ad sanctitatem pertinent, scilicet actio et contemplatio et intentio: et ista perficiuntur a Christo. Nam **activam exercentibus Christus est via; in contemplativa** vero **perseverantibus Christus** est **veritas:** sed **activorum et contemplantium** intentionem dirigit ad **vitam,** scilicet aeternam. Docet enim ire, et **praedicare pro futuro saeculo.** Sic ergo dominus est nobis via qua imus ad ipsum, et per ipsum ad patrem.[84]

Common Words and Structural Correspondence

Catena in Ioannem	*Lectura in Ioannem*
345b, *Vel quia veritatem…*	chap. 1, lect. 12, §237
346b, *Vel medius Pharisaeorum…*	chap. 1, lect. 13, §246
348b, *Sed quare non…*	chap. 1, lect. 14, §259
379a, *Sic ergo secundum…*	chap. 3, lect. 6, §545

79. *Ioan.* 14, lect. 2, §1871.
80. *ST* II-II, q. 179, a.1, co.
81. *ST* II-II, q. 180, a.1, co.
82. *ST* II-II, q. 180, a. 3, s.c.
83. CA 517a.
84. *Ioan.* 14, lect. 2, §1871.

382a, *Postquam autem filii* ...   chap. 4, lect. 1, §560
383a, *Congrue autem disputatio* ...   chap. 4, lect. 1, §569
405b, *Hoc enim dixit* ...   chap. 5, lect. 4, §779
414b, *Confundatur Manichaei* ...   chap. 6, lect. 1, §860
434b, *Nam in principio* ...   chap. 7, lect. 2, §1034
446a, *Uteris autem adversus* ...   chap. 8, lect. 2, §1143
469b, *Vel aliter. Si caeci* ...   chap. 9, lect. 4, §1363
486a, *Ad approbandam enim* ...   chap. 11, lect. 5, §1535
487b–488a, *Alta vero Salvatoris* ...   chap. 11, lect. 6, §1557–58
494a, *Quidam vero administrationem* ...   chap. 12, lect. 1, §1605
494a–b, *Visores enim susciati* ...   chap. 12, lect. 2, §1613
495b–496a, *Aspice autem* ...   chap. 12, lect. 3, §1629
524b, *Spiritus itaque sanctus* ...   chap. 14, lect. 6, §1960
557b, *Noverat etiam Iudas* ...   chap. 18, lect. 1, §2277
557b, *Faces autem afferunt* ...   chap. 18, lect. 1, §2278
561a, *Cum Iesus astantium* ...   chap. 18, lect. 4, §2319
561a, *Quasi dicat: si habes* ...   chap. 18, lect. 4, §2320
568b, *Dicit autem Qui* ...   chap. 19, lect. 2, §2396
576a, *Per hoc etiam* ...   chap. 19, lect. 6, §2468
591b, *Idest, numquid* ...   chap. 21, lect. 5, §2645

In two dozen places, Aquinas's commentary shares at least one key word or phrase with Theophylact's commentary in the *Catena*. Other features of the commentary, such as a structural similarity between the *Catena* and *Lectura*, confirm that Thomas is drawing from Theophylact.[85] To interpret John the Baptist's words in John 1:26, for example, "There is one standing in your midst whom you know not," Aquinas first cites the literal interpretations of Gregory, Chrysostom, and Augustine as they are listed in the *Catena*. He offers a second interpretation by Augustine that does not appear in the *Catena*. He skips Theophylact to give Origen's two interpretations and finally returns to Theophylact anonymously, writing simply that the passage can be explained "in a fourth way." The verbal similarities, along with traceable structural correspondence between the *Catena* and the *Lectura*, confirm Theophylact's contribution.

---

85. I am using Bataillon's method here. In his study of Thomas's use of the *Catena* in the *Tertia Pars*, Bataillon assumes Thomas had recourse to the *Catena* when texts by the same authors are regrouped in the same fashion in the *Summa* (22).

Catena

Theophylactus: Vel medius erat **Pharisaeorum** dominus; sed ignorabant eum, quia ipsi **Scripturas** se scire putabant: *et inquantum in illis* **praenuntiabatur** *dominus,* medius eorum erat, scilicet in cordibus eorum; *sed nesciebant eum,* eo quod Scripturas non intelligebant. Vel aliter. Medius quidem erat, inquantum mediator Dei existens et hominum Christus Iesus medius Pharisaeorum (3) extitit, volens illos Deo iungere; sed ipsi nesciebant eum.[86]

Lectura

Quarto modo exponitur ut referatur ad propheticam Christi praenuntiationem, ut sic respondeatur principaliter **Pharisaeis,** qui continue **Scripturas** veteris testamenti, *in quibus* **praenuntiabatur** *Christus,* inquirebant, *et tamen eum non cognoscebant.* Et secundum hoc dicitur *medius vestrum stetit;* idest, in sacra Scriptura, quam vos semper revolvitis; infra V, 39: *scrutamini Scripturas. Quem tamen vos nescitis,* quia cor vestrum induratum est propter infidelitatem et oculi vestri excaecati sunt, ut non agnoscatis praesentem, quem creditis futurum.[87]

Another noteworthy example comes from the fourth lecture on John, chapter 9, wherein Aquinas considers Christ's rebuke of the Jews after they questioned his healing of the blind man (Jn 9:41): "If you were blind, you would have no guilt; but now that you say, 'We see,' your guilt remains." Working from the *Catena,* he offers three interpretations of Christ's words. He distills a lengthy passage in which Augustine interprets Christ's words as referring to spiritual blindness. He then mentions Chrysostom, who believes Christ refers to physical blindness.[88] He includes a third interpretation that belongs to Theophylact: blindness is ignorance of the judgments of God and the sacraments of the law. Aquinas has expanded Theophylact's phrase *inscii Scriptuarum* but relies on his distinction between sin due to ignorance and the greater sin that comes from claiming one knows God's judgments. Once again, the structural similarities between *Catena* and *Lectura* confirm Thomas is drawing from Theophylact.

86. CA 346b.
87. *Ioan.* 1, lect. 13, §246.
88. Aquinas's claim that Chrysostom refers to a *caecitate corporali* is slightly different than Chrysostom's text in the *Catena,* which refers to a twofold blindness of sense and understanding (*sensibilis et intellectualis*). The Pharisees were ashamed of sensible blindness, and Christ wishes to show them that sensible blindness is preferable to a blindness of the understanding.

Catena

Theophylactus: Vel aliter. Si caeci essetis, **idest** *inscii Scripturarum*, nequaquam tam grande vobis peccatum incumberet, tamquam **ignorantia peccantibus**: nunc vero quia prudentes vos atque legisperitos asseritis, per vos ipsos condemnabiles estis.[89]

Lectura

Vel aliter, *si caeci essetis*, **idest** *ignorantes iudiciorum Dei et sacramentorum legis, non haberetis peccatum*; supple: tantum. Quasi dicat: si ex **ignorantia peccaretis**, peccatum vestrum non esset adeo grave. *Nunc vero quia dicitis, videmus*, idest arrogatis vobis scientiam legis et cognitionem Dei, et tamen peccatis, ideo *peccatum vestrum manet*, idest aggravatur; Lc. XII, 47: *servus qui scit voluntatem domini sui, et non fecit secundum voluntatem eius, vapulabit multis*.[90]

Common Theme with Probable Influence

Catena in Ioannem	*Lectura in Ioannem*
335b, *Si vero aliqui …*	chap. 1, lect. 4, §121
337b, *Vel quia in resurrectione …*	chap. 1, lect. 6, §150
353a, *Non frustra autem …*	chap. 1, lect. 15, §295
355b, *Sed Nathanaël laudatus …*	chap. 1, lect. 16, §324
364b, *Iudaei enim de …*	chap. 2, lect. 3, §406
384a, *Gratiam ergo spiritus …*	chap. 4, lect. 2, §577
399a, *Scilicet materialis …*	chap. 4, lect. 4, §645–46
411b, *Quasi dicat: ipse …*	chap. 5, lect. 7, §837
425a, *Per hoc scilicet …*	chap. 6, lect. 7, §957
439b, *Simul quidem, ut audibilis …*	chap. 7, lect. 5, §1086
480b, *Notandum autem …*	chap. 10, lect. 6, §1469
484b, *Primo itaque non …*	chap. 11, lect. 4, §1510
484b, *Quasi diffidens quoniam …*	chap. 11, lect. 4, §1511
504b, *Ex quo patet …*	chap. 13, lect. 2, §1754
516b, *Ac si dicat …*	chap. 14, lect. 1, §1852
522a, *Quasi dicat: et si mortem …*	chap. 14, lect. 4, §1924
529a, *Fructus autem Apostolorum …*	chap. 15, lect. 3, §2027
558b, *Vel ad opus …*	chap. 18, lect. 2, §2288
561a, *Reminiscitur autem hic …*	chap. 18, lect. 2, §2315

89. CA 469B.
90. *Ioan.* 9, lect. 4, §1363.

569b, *Quasi dicat: ecce ...*	chap. 19, lect. 3, §2407
574a, *Quidam vero hyssopum ...*	chap. 19, lect. 4, §2449
587b, *Quod vero se praecinxit ...*	chap. 21, lect. 2, §2593
590b, *Potest autem quis ...*	chap. 21, lect. 3, §2625
592b, *Vel aliter totum ...*	chap. 21, lect. 5, §2636

Finally, two dozen places share a common theme with Theophylact's text from the *Catena*. This category deserves caution, since it is possible that Theophylact and Thomas drew the same theme from a common source. Theophylact, writing in the late eleventh and early twelfth centuries, and Thomas, writing in the thirteenth, would have had access to some of the same texts, notably, John Chrysostom's *Homilies on the Gospel of John*. Further, Thomas was heir to centuries of rich Scripture commentary in the Latin West; patristic exegesis may have reached him through the Victorines, the *Glossa Ordinaria*, or various *florilegia* and *postillae* such as that of Hugh of St. Cher, another thirteenth-century Dominican.[91] Yet if it was the case that Thomas relied on the *Catena* for his later biblical commentaries, we can tentatively identify Theophylact's influence on these passages.

In one example, Thomas combines Chrysostom's and Theophylact's reflections on John 1:12 from the *Catena* to offer a threefold interpretation of sonship in the *Lectura*. In the *Catena*, Chrysostom focuses on the word *exousia* or *potestas* in the Evangelist's phrase "As many as received him, to them he gave power to become the sons of God, even to them that believe in his name."[92] The image of adopted sonship given in baptism must be cared for and preserved, and this is within the power of each baptized person. He writes, "The Evangelist wishes to show that this grace comes to us of our own will and endeavor: that, in short, the operation of grace being supposed, it is in the power of our free will to make

---

91. Given recent scholarship, it is evident that Thomas's reliance on the biblical commentaries and lectures of his predecessors requires much more attention. See the work of Alexander Andrée, Tristan Sharp, and Richard Shaw, who have demonstrated that Aquinas's citations of Alcuin of York did not derive directly from Alcuin, but from another *glossa* on John, perhaps by Anselm of Laon. Alexander Andrée et al., "Aquinas and 'Alcuin': A New Source of the *Catena Aurea* on John," *Recherches de Théologie et Philosophie Médiévales* 83, no. 1 (2016): 3–20. See also Mark Clark, "Peter Lombard, Stephen Langton, and The School of Paris: The Making of the Twelfth-Century Scholastic Biblical Tradition," *Traditio* 72 (2017): 171–274. See esp. Part 4, pp. 251–69, which proposes that Lombard's Scripture commentaries exercised a much greater influence on the Parisian school of scriptural interpretation than has heretofore been acknowledged.

92. CA 2, 337b.

us the sons of God."[93] Theophylact's interpretation follows, and the Byzantine exegete pairs John 1:12 with a paraphrase of Romans 8:23, a verse Thomas favors when writing about adopted sonship elsewhere. Perfect sonship will be attained at the resurrection, for as Paul says, we wait for adoption, the redemption of the body (Rom 8:23). He gave us power to become sons of God, that is, the grace to attain the fullness of adopted sonship at our future resurrection.[94] In the *Lectura*, Thomas ascribes to the sons of God a threefold likeness to God. They are like God by the infusion of sanctifying grace (*per gratiae infusionem*), by the perfection of action (*per operum perfectionem*), and by the attainment of glory (*per gloriae adoptionem*). Sonship *per gratiae infusionem* reflects Chrysostom's emphasis on the adoption through baptism, and *per operum perfectionem* reflects Chrysostom's emphasis on preserving this sonship through our own power with the grace of God. Finally, sonship *per gloriae adoptionem* reflects Theophylact's claim that sonship is attained at the Resurrection. Thomas, like Theophylact, supports this interpretation with Romans 8:23.

Catena

Chrysostomus: Non autem dixit, quoniam fecit eos filios Dei fieri; sed dedit eis potestatem filios Dei fieri; ostendens quoniam multo opus est studio, ut eam, quae in Baptismo adoptionis formata est, imaginem incontaminatam semper custodiamus: simul autem ostendens quoniam potestatem hanc nullus nobis auferre poterit, nisi nos ipsi auferamus. Si enim qui ab hominibus dominium aliquarum rerum suscipiunt, tantum habent robur quantum fere hi qui dederunt; multo magis nos qui a Deo potimur hoc honore. Simul autem ostendere vult quoniam haec gratia advenit volentibus et studentibus: etenim in potestate est liberi arbitrii et gratiae operatione filios Dei fieri.
Theophylactus: Vel quia in resurrectione filiationem perfectissimam consequemur, secundum quod apostolus dicit: **adoptionem filiorum Dei expectantes** redemptionem corporis nostri. Dedit ergo potestatem filios Dei fieri, idest hanc gratiam in futura gratia consequendi.[95]

Lectura

Dicit ergo *dedit eis potestatem filios Dei fieri*. Ad cuius evidentiam sciendum est, quod homines fiunt filii Dei per assimilationem ad Deum; et ideo secundum triplicem assimilationem hominum ad Deum homines sunt filii Dei. Primo enim per gratiae infusionem: unde quicumque habet gratiam gratum facientem, efficitur

93. CA 2, 337b.
94. CA 2, 337b.
95. CA 337b.

filius Dei; Rom. VIII, 15: *non enim accepistis spiritum servitutis* etc.; Gal. IV, 6: *quoniam estis filii Dei, misit Deus spiritum filii sui.*

Secundo assimilamur Deo per operum perfectionem, quia qui facit opera iustitiae, est filius; Matth. V, 44: *diligite inimicos vestros.*

Tertio assimilamur Deo per gloriae adeptionem, et quantum ad animam per lumen gloriae, I Io. III, 2: *cum apparuerit, similes ei erimus,* et quantum ad corpus, Phil. III, v. 21: *reformabit corpus humilitatis nostrae.* Unde de istis duobus dicitur Rom. VIII, 23: ***adoptionem filiorum Dei expectantes.***[96]

In a second example, Thomas seems to structure his commentary by appealing to several sources, including Theophylact's interpretation of Christ's commands to Peter, "feed my lambs" (Jn 21:15) and "tend my sheep" (Jn 21:16). Theophylact writes that Christ charges Peter with the care of both lambs and sheep; the lambs refer to those initiated into the faith, while sheep refer to those perfected in the faith. In the *Lectura,* Aquinas describes three types of people in the Church, based upon the distinction between lambs and sheep as well as Christ's thrice-given command. There are two types of lambs, *incipientum* and *proficientum,* who are still imperfect in the faith, while the sheep are the *perfectorum.* There is some evidence that Thomas needn't have relied on Theophylact for this interpretation. Theophylact is not the only exegete to propose this distinction between lambs and sheep; Ambrose of Milan employs it in his *Commentary on Luke.*[97] Aquinas's tripartite scheme might also rely on a passage from Augustine's fifth *Tractate on the First Epistle of John* that also appears in the *Secunda Secundae.*[98] Still, Thomas selected Theophylact to propose the interpretation in the *Catena,* and a quotation from Augustine, which follows in the *Catena* as well as the *Lectura,* strengthens the probability that Thomas had the *Catena* open alongside him as he prepared this portion of the commentary.

Catena

Theophylactus: Potest autem quis assignare differentiam inter agnos et oves: agni sunt qui introducuntur, oves vero **perfecti.**[99]

96. *Ioan.* 1, lect. 6, §150.

97. Ambrosius Mediolanensis, *Expositio Evangelii Secundum Lucam* [CSEL], 10, 176.

98. See *ST* II-II, q. 24, a. 9, sed contra, in which Aquinas quotes Augustine's *Tractates on the First Epistle of John* in classifying charity by degree according to beginners (*incipientes*), those who are progressing (*proficientes*), and those who are perfected (*perfectos*). Thomas does not include this passage in the *Catena in Ioannem* at the location in question, in spite of relying on other passages from Augustine.

99. CA 590b.

Lectura

Sed attende quod tertia vice dicit ei *pasce oves meas*. Cuius ratio est, quia in Ecclesia sunt tria genera hominum, scilicet incipientium, proficientium et **perfectorum**. Et primi quidem duo sunt agni, quasi adhuc imperfecti; alii autem sicut perfecti dicuntur oves. Ps. CXIII, 4: *montes*, scilicet perfecti, *exultaverunt ut arietes, et colles*, idest alii, *sicut agni ovium*. Et inde est quod omnes praelati debent custodire subditos ut oves Christi, et non proprias. Sed heu, quia, ut dicit Augustinus in sermone paschali, extiterunt quidam servi infideles, qui dimiserunt gregem Christi, et furtis suis peculia gregem sibi fecerunt, et audis eos dicere: oves meae sunt illae. Quid quaeris oves meas? Non te inveniam ad oves meas. Sed si nos dicamus meas, et illi dicunt suas: perdidit Christus oves suas.[100]

The 107 places Theophylact appears in the *Lectura Super Ioannem* comprise a little less than half of Theophylact's total passages from the *Catena in Ioannem*. All but one of these appearances are unattributed, but given the Bulgarian archbishop's status as a near contemporary of Aquinas, this is unsurprising. His contributions are usually distinguished from other authorities by an *alio modo, quidam dicunt quod,* or *vel dicendum*. Yet sometimes, curiously, Aquinas seems to elide Theophylact's contribution with that of another authority, usually Augustine or Chrysostom.[101] One example of such elision has been given above. Another occurs as Thomas considers Jesus's words regarding John, "I will have him remain till I come" (Jn 21:22). He cites an interpretation of Augustine in §2648, Chrysostom in §2349, then Jerome in §2650.[102] Enfolded in Chrysostom's interpretation of the passage is the observation that John did not leave Judea until Vespasian came to Judea and captured Jerusalem.[103] This historical detail does not occur in Chrysostom's *Homily 88*, however.[104] It seems to be part of an excerpt of Theophylact's from the *Catena*.

Catena

Theophylactus: Quod vero dicitur dum venero, quidam sic intellexerunt ac si diceret: quousque contra Iudaeos, qui me crucifixerunt, veniam percutiens illos

---

100. *Ioan.* 21, lect. 3, §2625.
101. Bataillon has also pointed out one such instance in the *Tertia Pars*, where Thomas blends a quotation from Theophylact with one attributed to Bede. According to Bataillon, "La citation de Bède a mordu sur celle de Théophylacte." See "Saint Thomas et les Pères," 21.
102. *Ioan.* 21, lect. 5, §§2648–2650.
103. *Ioan.* 21, lect. 5, §2649.
104. In addition, neither the *Glossa Ordinaria* nor Hugh of St. Cher's *Postilla* mention Vespasian at Jn 21:22.

baculo Romanorum. Aiunt enim, hunc apostolum usque ad **Vespasiani tempus,
cum Ierusalem capienda erat,** in locis illis conversatum. Vel dicit dum venero,
idest, dum hunc volens dirigam ad praedicandum, te namque nunc dirigo ad
orbis pontificatum; et in hoc sequere me: ipse vero maneat hic donec et eum
educam sicut te.[105]

Lectura

Sed, secundum Chrysostomum, legitur sic: *sic eum volo manere,* idest remanere
in Iudaea, et in hac terra ad praedicandum, et te volo me sequi habendo sollic-
itudinem totius orbis, et patiendo pro me, et hoc *donec veniam,* ad delendum
Iudaeos, *quid ad te?* Quasi dicat: meum est ordinare. Nam, sicut habetur in histo-
riis, Ioannes non recessit de Iudaea usque **ad tempus quo Vespasianus** veniens in
Iudaeam cepit Ierusalem, et tunc inde discedens venit ad Asiam.[106]

We might wrongly conclude that such elisions occur because Aquinas was wary of naming a schismatic in his lectures. The sheer number
of Theophylact's contributions, which Aquinas clearly harmonizes with
other patristic authorities, refutes this hypothesis. Given his audience for
the *Lectura*—students at the University of Paris—it is understandable
that Theophylact's exegesis should remain unattributed and sometimes
travel alongside the name of a better-known patristic authority such as
Chrysostom or Augustine.[107] Thomas was training aspiring theologians
and preachers who would profit from knowing the names of *doctores* and
auctoritates whose texts were readily available to them, and with whom
their audience might have been familiar. Theophylact was not a name
heard in the lecture halls at the University of Paris or among mendicant
communities, much less in Western Christian households.

Conclusion

This study has presented the first comprehensive examination of Theophylact of Ochrid's contribution to Aquinas's *Expositio Continua Super
Ioannem* and has examined the afterlife of many of these passages in the
Lectura Super Ioannem. The quantity of passages redeployed in the *Lectura* divests us of the notion that Theophylact was unimportant to Thomas
outside Pope Urban IV's commission; rather, he remained an important

---

105. CA 539a.
106. *Ioan.* 21, lect. 5, §2649.
107. For Aquinas's diligence in citing his sources, see Weisheipl, *Friar Thomas d'Aquino,*
172–73.

resource for Thomas well after the completion of the *Catena Aurea*. Aquinas's use of a Byzantine exegete enhances our understanding of his own historical milieu, suggesting that Greek East and Latin West enjoyed a more intimate relationship than is usually supposed. Readers of Aquinas must maintain a sense of the kinship of the Latin- and Greek-speaking worlds—theological as well as political—beyond the *Contra Errores Graecorum* and the Christological developments in the *Tertia Pars*. The Second Council of Lyons in 1274 may represent the height of Greek and Latin interaction during this period, but Aquinas's use of Theophylact for the *Catena* and subsequent works is perhaps a signal that conciliar momentum was already building in the 1260s.

Theophylact's presence also highlights Aquinas's personal investment in engaging exegetical sources from the Greek East. Thomistic scholarship tends to focus on Aquinas's appeal to Greek sources—such as Dionysius, John Damascene, and the Fifth and Sixth Ecumenical Councils—when it comes to matters of doctrine. The presence of Theophylact is a reminder that Thomas also valued the Greek contribution when it came to interpreting Scripture. Aquinas's redeployment of Theophylact in the *Lectura* is additionally remarkable because he relies on the archbishop predominantly for literal sense exegesis. Thomas is not content to explain the literal sense with the resources he already possesses; when he comes across Theophylact, he incorporates the newfound literal interpretations. This attests to the importance of the literal sense for Thomas, both as the ground of explaining sacred doctrine and as a locus of multiple distinct yet harmonious interpretations. Thomas invites the audience of the *Lectura* to linger over the meaning of the letter, thus amplifying their delight in the letter and drawing them to meditate more deeply on Gospel events. Theophylact's voice emerges again and again in this aspect of the *Lectura*.

The next step in my project is to see the forest through the trees, so to speak: to explore the theological content of Theophylact's contribution to the *Lectura* in greater depth in order to gain insight into how Aquinas used the Byzantine exegete to conduct his own explanation of sacred doctrine. Scholars acknowledge the synergy between Aquinas's exegesis and his speculative theology, and recent works—such as Dominic Legge's *The Trinitarian Christology of Thomas Aquinas* and Daria Spezzano's *The Glory of God's Grace*—demonstrate a methodological awareness of the complementarity between Thomas's biblical commentaries and his works of more straightforward speculative theology.[108] Appreciation for the role of patristic authorities in the development of his teaching is also increasing, as evidenced in part by Steve Brown's article on the role of the Fathers in the *Lectura Super Ioannem*.[109] Brown concludes, "Aquinas does indeed practice a declarative theology [in the *Lectura*] ... these declarative efforts are made by Aquinas himself, but to a very great extent, he was assisted and inspired in his efforts, especially in his *Commentary on John,* by the earlier efforts of the Fathers of the Church, especially Augustine, Chrysostom, Hilary, Gregory the Great, and John of Damascus."[110] Given the results of the present study, I suggest adding Theophylact to Brown's list. Aquinas finds such continuity between Theophylact and other Fathers that he can often quote them in the same breath. This must be the surest sign of Aquinas's respect for his authority.

Finally, in bringing Theophylact into conversation with patristic authorities, Thomas not only adds to his cadre of sources but also develops his predecessors' use of these sources. This deserves further study. To take but one example, I have shown how Aquinas constructs a threefold interpretation of sonship in John 1:12 that is inspired by Chrysostom and Theophylact. The description of sonship reflects Aquinas's interest in the role of adoptive filiation and deification found in the *Summa Theologiae* and the *Super Epistolam ad Romanos*.[111] Theophylact's contribution to the exegesis of John 1:12, with accompanying citation of Romans 8:23, invites further speculation into how the Byzantine exegete aids Thomas's articulation of this teaching. Hugh of St. Cher's *Postilla* includes the same excerpt from Chrysostom's *Homily 10* as is found in the *Catena Aurea* and

108. See the introduction to *Reading John with Thomas Aquinas,* which emphasizes the synergy of exegesis and speculative theology: "St. Thomas's biblical exegesis is constituted by his procedure of continually moving, within the exegetical task, from exegesis proper to speculative theological questioning and back again. In this dynamic process of exegesis, he brings to bear not only parallel interpretive texts from throughout the Bible, but also the accumulated insights of the Fathers" (xiii). See also Giles Emery, who calls Aquinas's biblical commentaries a "useful adjunct" to reading the *Summa.* "Though they differ in genre, they offer another access to Thomas's thought by means of direct contact with the biblical text whose words they explain and whose meaning they seek." Gilles Emery, "The Holy Spirit in Aquinas's Commentary on Romans," in *Reading Romans with Thomas Aquinas,* ed. Matthew Levering and Michael Dauphinais (Washington, DC: Catholic University of America Press, 2012), 127–62.

109. See Steve Brown, "The Theological Role of the Fathers: Aquinas's *Super Evangelium S. Ioannis Lectura,*" in *Reading John with Thomas Aquinas,* 9–21.

110. Brown, "Theological Role of the Fathers," 21.

111. See Emery, "Holy Spirit," esp. 144–49.

the *Lectura*.[112] This makes Aquinas's tripartite explanation all the more significant. He is not only synthesizing Greek authorities to articulate a dimension of his theology of grace but also building upon the Dominican tradition of biblical commentary. This is undoubtedly but one of many promising passages to be explored as we consider Theophylact's role in Aquinas's thought beyond the *Catena Aurea*.

112. Hugh of St. Cher, *Postilla* (1537 ed.), 259; available on Google Books, accessed September 10, 2018, https://books.google.com/books?id=ApQ4KzavfiYC&pg=PA259#v=onepage&q&f=true. I am indebted to Professor Jacob Wood for directing me to this passage.

12

The Greek Fathers in the Eucharistic
Theology of Thomas Aquinas

JOSEPH WAWRYKOW

In the *Summa Theologiae*, Thomas Aquinas offers a teaching about the
Eucharist that is detailed, textured, and richly documented. In composing
the treatise on the Eucharist,[1] Aquinas was resolute on being faithful to
the scriptural witness about Eucharist, and the recourse to Scripture is
frequent and constant. Aquinas also was intent on showing his continuity with those who had gone before him, similarly faithful to Scripture,
in proclaiming and interpreting Eucharist. In this chapter, I ask about
the contribution made to Aquinas's mature teaching about the Eucharist by the Greek Fathers. To what extent do the Greeks—that is, earlier
theologians writing in Greek—figure in Aquinas's mature teaching on
Eucharist? Or, otherwise put, in what ways has Aquinas woven into his
eucharistic teaching the insights and claims of select Greek Fathers? In
asking about the Greeks in Aquinas's eucharistic theology, I am especially

---

1. *ST* III, qq. 73–83. The eleven questions of the treatise fall under seven headings: on
the sacrament itself (q. 73); the matter of the sacrament (qq. 74–77); the form (q. 78); the
effects (q. 79); those who receive the sacrament (qq. 80–81); the minister (q. 82); and the rite
of the sacrament (q. 83). For the Latin: Thomas Aquinas, *Summa Theologiae*, cura et studio
Instituti Studiorum Medievalium Ottaviensis (Ottawa: Commissio Piana, 1941–). Quotations of the *Summa Theologiae* in English in this study are taken from the translation by the
English Dominicans, *The Summa Theologica of St. Thomas Aquinas*, rev. ed. (1920; reprint, 5
vols., Westminster, MD: Christian Classics, 1981), also available at the New Advent website,
accessed September 18, 2018, newadvent.org.

concerned with the place of Eucharist in the spiritual journey to God as beatifying end, with how the encounter with the Christ eucharistically present promotes growth toward God.

This study of the Greek Fathers in the eucharistic theology of Thomas Aquinas is in effect celebrating Aquinas in two ways. First, the treatise on the Eucharist in the *Summa*, while surely displaying Aquinas's skill as a theologian, very much underscores his religious commitments. The Eucharist stands at the center of Aquinas's spirituality, and we can learn much about his devotion to and discipleship to Christ, about communion with and participation in Christ, and about movement toward God through Christ, through the *Summa*'s questions on the Eucharist. And, second, this study is acknowledging Aquinas's deep commitment to the tradition, a tradition that for Aquinas takes its start and inspiration from Scripture and runs through the Fathers, East as well as West.[2]

Aquinas's effort as a "historian" and theologian in recovering the Tradition has received considerable scholarly attention in recent decades, although much work remains to be done. In terms of the East, there was a significant constraint on Aquinas's recovery efforts: Aquinas's own apparent lack of knowledge of the Greek language. But Aquinas was to be sure diligent in searching for the Greeks where available in Latin translation, and he enjoyed great success. Best known in this regard is Aquinas's discovery, midcareer, of early conciliar material in Latin translation. That discovery had a considerable impact on Aquinas's Christology, confirming him in his adherence to a single subject Christology and allowing a sharper appraisal of more recent Christologies that inclined to a twofold subject, with but an accidental union of the natures.[3]

And Aquinas also made his own contribution to the making available

---

2. I am echoing here Aquinas's teaching about sacred doctrine, as presented in *ST* I, q. 1). This is the truth, revealed by God in Scripture, that is needed for salvation. For Aquinas's comments about the various authorities that enter into the handing on of saving truth, see *ST* I, q. 1, a. 8, ad 2. He mentions there the Doctors of the Church. Their authority is intrinsic (for they are concerned with the saving truth revealed in Scripture) and probable (a gesture at human limitations, in interpreting and explaining and defending the faith). In contrast, the authority of the human authors of Scripture is intrinsic and certain, for God has revealed to them saving truth, and done so (a. 9, ad 2 adds) in a way that they cannot make mistakes in conveying that truth. For a statistical overview of Aquinas's use of earlier authorities in various writings throughout his career, see Walter Senner, "Thomas von Aquin und die Kirchenväter—eine quantitative Übersicht," in *Kirchenbild und Spiritualität: Dominikanische Beiträge zur Ekklesiologie und zum kirchlichen Leben im Mittlealter*, ed. Thomas Prügl and Marianne Schlosser (Paderborn: Ferdinand Schöningh, 2007), 25–42.

3. See, e.g., Joseph Wawrykow, "Hypostatic Union," in *The Theology of Thomas Aquinas*,

of Greek sources, through his work on the *Catena Aurea*.[4] In having certain commentaries and catenae translated into Latin, and then drawing on these translations in elucidating the last three Gospels, including their eucharistic verses, Aquinas in the process expanded the repertoire of authorities available to Western scholastics. Some of these authorities will, not incidentally, enter into the eucharistic theology of the *Summa*.[5]

---

ed. Rik van Nieuwenhove and Joseph Wawrykow (Notre Dame, IN: University of Notre Dame Press, 2005), 222–51.

4. Thomas Aquinas, *Glossa Continua Super Evangelia* (*Catena Aurea*), ed. A. Guarienti (Turin: Marietti, 1953). The Saint Austin Press reissued an English translation, edited by John Henry Newman and published in 1841, with an introduction by Aidan Nichols, 1997. Now in progress is *Thomae de Aquino Catena aurea: Editio scientifica electronica, fontibus repertis textuque emendato*, éd. Giuseppe Conticello and Martin Morard; available on the Sacra Pagina website, accessed May 7, 2018, https://big.hypotheses.org/catena-aurea. Paragraph numbering in citations of the *Catena* in later notes follows the electronic edition.

5. For a brisk orientation to Aquinas and the earlier Greek Fathers, see Gilles Emery, "A Note on St. Thomas and the Eastern Fathers," trans. J. Harms and Fr. John Baptist Ku, in *Trinity, Church, and the Human Person* (Naples, FL: Sapientia Press of Ave Maria University, 2007), 193–207. On Aquinas's knowledge and use of conciliar material, see Martin Morard, "Thomas d'Aquin lecteur des conciles," *Archivum Franciscanum Historicum* 98 (2005): 211–365, and "Une Source de Saint Thomas d'Aquin: Le Deuxième Concile de Constantinople (553)," *Revue des Sciences Philosophiques et Théologiques* 81 (1997): 21–56. On Aquinas's work on the *Catena Aurea*, see Carmelo Giuseppe Conticello, "San Tommaso ed I Padri: La Catena Aurea *Super Ioannem*," *Archives d'Histoire Doctrinale et Litteraire du Moyen Age* 57 (1990): 31–92, and "Théophylacte de Bulgarie, Source de Thomas d'Aquin (Catena Aurea in Ioannem)," in *Philomathestatos: Studies in Greek and Byzantine Texts Presented to Jacques Noret for His Sixty-Fifth Birthday*, Orientalia Lovaniensia Analecta 137, ed. B. Janssens, B. Roosen, and P. Van Deun (Leuven: Peeters, 2004), 63–75; see, too, Louis J. Bataillon, "Saint Thomas et les Pères: De la Catena à la *tertia pars*," in *Ordo Sapientiae et Amoris: Hommage au Professeur Jean-Pierre Torrell OP à l'occasion de son 65e anniversaire*, ed. Carlos-Josaphat Pinto de Oliveira (Fribourg: Éditions Universitaires Fribourg Suisse, 1993), 15–36. Conticello, "Théophylacte de Bulgarie," 64n6, provides some statistics about those cited in the *Catena*; there are more than two thousand citations of Chrysostom and more than three hundred and fifty of Cyril. For a description of what Aquinas had translated, see p. 65: commentaries by Theophylact on Mark, Luke, and John; a commentary on Mark by Victor of Antioch; catenae on John (seventh century); and by Nicetas (who died after 1117) on Luke and John.

While almost all the references to the Greek Fathers in the treatise on the Eucharist would seem due to Aquinas's work on the *Catena* and his recovery of conciliar material, there is another source that is to be mentioned here: Gratian, *De Consecratione*, in *Corpus Iuris Canonici*. Editio Lipsiensis Secunda. Richter/Friedberg. *Pars Prior: Decretum Magistri Gratiani* (Graz: Akademische Druck-U. Verlagsanstalt, 1959), Pars Tertia. The Greek Fathers are only rarely cited in *De Consecratione*, but as it happens, two of Aquinas's citations of the Greek theologians examined in this study are taken over from Gratian: one of Cyril and the other of Chrysostom. Each of these is interesting in its own way, and I address each below. For a general orientation to Eucharist as presented in canon law, see now Thomas M. Izbicki, *The Eucharist in Medieval Canon Law* (Cambridge: Cambridge University Press, 2015).

In this study, I am considering the contribution of the following four Greek theologians to the teaching on Eucharist in the *Summa*: these four are, in rough chronological order, John Chrysostom (d. 407), Cyril of Alexandria (d. 444), Pseudo-Dionysius, and John Damascene (d. 749).[6] All four are cited in the treatise on the Eucharist, with Pseudo-Dionysius leading the way in terms of explicit citation, and the Damascene, Chrysostom, and Cyril quoted less frequently but still to good effect. In terms of Aquinas's access to their eucharistic theologies, Aquinas was on the whole well served by the translations. Thanks to the efforts of Burgundio of Pisa in the second half of the twelfth century, Aquinas had available to him John Chrysostom's homilies on Matthew and on John;[7] Aquinas drew heavily on these homilies in the *Catena Aurea*. Aquinas also had available to him the Damascene's *de fide orthodoxa*, again thanks to the translating activity of Burgundio,[8] and given the range of his citations of John on Eucharist in the *Summa*, Aquinas would seem to have known well the chapter in *de fide* about Eucharist.[9] Aquinas also knew the Dionysian treatises, and epistles, in their integrity, through the "textbook" edition of Dionysius prepared at Paris in the 1240s, as well as through his studies with Albert, who commented on the Dionysian corpus. Of these writings, the *Ecclesiastical Hierarchy* is especially pertinent to Aquinas's account of Eucharist.[10]

6. Dates are not available for the pseudonymous Areopagite, but the scholarly consensus is that he was active in the late fifth / early sixth century.

7. Leo J. Elders, "Thomas Aquinas and the Fathers of the Church," in *The Reception of the Church Fathers in the West*, vol. 1, ed. Irena Backus (Leiden: Brill, 1997), 344, citing P. Classen's book on Burgundio. Chrysostom's other works had been translated much earlier. For an introduction to Chrysostom, including on the early translation of his works, see Wendy Mayer, "John Chrysostom," in *Wiley Blackwell Companion to Patristics*, ed. Ken Parry (Hoboken, NJ: Wiley, 2015), 141–54. For Chrysostom's homilies on John in English, see the translation by Sr. Thomas Aquinas Goggin (2 vols.) in the Fathers of the Church Series (Washington, DC: Catholic University of America Press, 2000).

8. For the Latin, see *Saint John Damascene, De Fide Orthodoxa: Versions of Burgundio and Cerbanus*, ed. Eligius M. Buytaert (St. Bonaventure, NY: Franciscan Institute, 1955). See, too, Frederic H. Chase Jr., trans., *Saint John of Damascus: Writings* (Washington, DC: Catholic University of America Press, 1958). In the Burgundio translation into Latin, the discussion of Eucharist comes in chapter 86 ("de sanctis et incoinquinatis Domini Mysteriis"); in the Chase translation of the *Orthodox Faith*, in Book IV, chap. 13. I have also consulted Jean Damascène, *La Foi Orthodoxe 45–100*, Sources Chrétiennes 540, ed. B. Kotter, trans. P. Ledrux with G.-M. Durand (Paris: Les Éditions du Cerf, 2011).

9. Gy's claim that Aquinas did not make use of the Damascene in his sacramental theology is hard to understand; see Pierre-Marie Gy, "La Documentation Sacramentaire de Thomas d'Aquin: Quelle Connaissance S. Thomas a-t-il de la Tradition Ancienne et de la Patristique?," *Revue des Sciences Philosophiques et Théologiques* 80 (1996): 425.

10. L. Michael Harrington, ed. and trans., *On the Ecclesiastical Hierarchy: The Thirteenth-*

Only when it comes to Cyril might Aquinas have been better served. Aquinas seems not to have had access to Cyril's *Commentary on John*, whether in its integrity or by extract. That offers, as is well known, striking witness, in a work predating the Nestorian controversy, to the importance for Cyril of Christ, of the eucharistic Christ, for spiritual energizing and growth. Aquinas, however, did have access to Cyril's exposition of Luke, at least in extract, and made use of that in the *Catena* on Luke, as well as in the *Summa*. And Aquinas could get a feel for Cyril's eucharistic teaching through the conciliar material that he had recovered. I have in mind here the Third Letter to Nestorius and the twelve chapters or anathemas (some of which echo the quote that now follows when it comes to Christ's life-giving flesh). The seventh paragraph of the Third Letter is worth quoting here:

This too we must add. We proclaim the fleshly death of God's only-begotten Son, Jesus Christ, we confess his return to life from the dead and his ascension into heaven when we perform in church the unbloody service, when we approach the sacramental gifts and are hallowed participants in the holy flesh and precious blood of Christ, savior of us all, by receiving not mere flesh (God forbid!) or flesh of a man hallowed by connection with the Word in some unity of dignity or possessing some divine indwelling, but the personal, truly vitalizing flesh of God the Word himself. As God he is by nature Life and because he has become one with his own flesh he rendered it vitalizing; and so, though he tells us "verily I say unto you, unless you eat the flesh of the Son of Man and drink his blood" [Jn 6:53], we must not suppose it belongs to one of men (how could man's flesh be vitalizing by its own nature?) but that it was made the truly personal possession of him who for us has become and was called the "Son of Man."[11]

Aquinas's Christology stands in continuity with Cyril's; so too he is in agreement with Cyril about the saving effects of engagement with Christ in the Eucharist.[12] And in fact Aquinas quotes from this letter, from this paragraph, in the treatise on the Eucharist.

Century Paris Textbook Edition (Paris-Leuven-Walpole, MA: Peeters, 2011. For Aquinas's work as secretary to Albertus Magnus as he lectured on Dionysius, see Jean-Pierre Torrell, *Saint Thomas Aquinas*, vol. 1, *The Person and His Work*, trans. Robert Royal (Washington, DC: Catholic University of America Press, 1996), 21.

11. Cyril of Alexandria, *Select Letters*, ed. and trans. Lionel R. Wickham (Oxford: Clarendon Press, 1983), 23. For anathemas that have eucharistic implications, see, e.g., 10 and 11. The Third Letter was read at Ephesus; it, with the twelve chapters, was read and formally approved at Constantinople II. See Morard, "Thomas d'Aquin lecteur des conciles," 282–83.

12. Aquinas gives striking expression to his conviction about the saving importance of

The texts that are in play here are of different kinds, and we should not overlook the differences in form. Aquinas's *Summa* is an exercise in systematic theology, which aims at a kind of comprehensiveness in proclaiming, interpreting, explaining, and defending the truths of the Christian faith. Of the other writings that figure in this account, the Damascene's stands closest to the *Summa*. But expositions of, or homilies on, Scripture (such as Cyril on Luke, John Chrysostom on Matthew and John) are not systematic exercises and are more directly and obviously tied to particular scriptural passages. And one would never confuse the *Ecclesiastical Hierarchy* with the *Summa*.

Nonetheless, despite differences in genre, purpose, and rhetorical style, there is considerable agreement among Aquinas and his Greek interlocutors. The insight of Cyril is shared by all treated in this study: Christ, construed incarnationally, and salvation are intimately linked, and the eucharistic Christ provides for growth toward God.[13] The four Greeks, then, are congenial interlocutors, and in drawing on them in putting forward his own eucharistic teaching, Aquinas would seem far from doing violence to their thought.

It is time now for a closer look at the eucharistic teaching of Thomas Aquinas in its main features, which is followed by a more detailed examination of how Chrysostom and the Damascene, Dionysius, and Cyril enter into that teaching.

---

the Eucharist at the head of *ST* III, q. 83, a. 4c: "the whole mystery of our salvation is comprised in this sacrament" ("in hoc sacramento totum mysterium nostrae salutis comprehenditur"). Aquinas's assessment, not incidentally, is repeated in Pope John Paul II's Encyclical Letter *Ecclesia de Eucharistia*, 61.

13. The five authors discussed in this essay can be said to share an account of salvation that takes "divinization" seriously. In terms of the four Greeks, that claim probably isn't overly controversial, but while there might be some disputing when said of Aquinas, it holds of Aquinas as well. He thinks of human being, operation, and fulfillment in terms of an elevation into and participation in God, made possible by God through Christ. For a sound orientation to Aquinas on divinization, see Daria Spezzano, *The Glory of God's Grace: Deification According to St. Thomas Aquinas* (Naples, FL: Sapientia Press of Ave Maria University, 2015). Her "Conjoined to Christ's Passion: The Deifying Asceticism of the Sacraments According to Thomas Aquinas," *Antiphon* 17, no. 1 (2013): 73–86, offers a brisk and insightful review of the role of sacraments in deification according to Aquinas. See, too, Andrew Hofer, "Aquinas, Divinization, and the People in the Pews," in *Divinization: Becoming Icons of Christ through the Liturgy*, ed. Andrew Hofer (Chicago: Hillenbrand, 2015), 54–72, esp. 65*ff.*, on Eucharist.

The Eucharist in the *Summa*

In the questions on the Eucharist in the *Summa*, Aquinas asserts: the presence in truth of Christ in the Sacrament;[14] a change, transubstantiation, that accounts for that presence;[15] and the great spiritual benefits of engaging the eucharistic Christ for those who are properly disposed for that reception.[16]

Prominent in affirming the presence in truth are the words of institution: they describe what, in a eucharistic setting, is the case. This *is* Christ's body, Christ's blood. The words of institution also occasion the teaching about transubstantiation, as accounting for that presence. By God's power, what was bread at the beginning of the consecratory formula is body when the entire statement is uttered, what was wine, blood. Only God can change the fundamental reality of things, make one thing something else.[17] But in changing substance into substance, God makes use of secondary causes, here construed instrumentally. In instituting the sacrament, Christ has promised his presence; a created power, in this sense, is attached to the words of institution, the consecratory formula, by the promise of Christ.[18] And when these words of Christ are uttered by Christ's due representative—the ordained minister who by virtue of his ordination and the imprinting attendant on that, of priestly character—

---

14. *ST* III, q. 75, a. 1; q. 76.

15. The change of substance into substance is termed "transubstantiation" at, e.g., *ST* III, q. 75, a. 4c. For Aquinas, Christ's distinctive, irreducible eucharistic presence and transubstantiation are two sides of the same coin, both authorized and called for by the words of institution. While he can adapt philosophical terms to expressing eucharistic truth, the change that is transubstantiation is biblically warranted.

16. The spiritual benefits of this sacrament, and the spiritual characteristics of those who receive fruitfully, are the especial concern of qq. 79 and 80. I have discussed Aquinas's eucharistic theology in "Luther and the Spirituality of Thomas Aquinas," *Consensus* 19 (1993): 77–107; and in the second half of my "The Sacraments in Thirteenth Century Theology," in *The Oxford Handbook of Sacramental Theology*, ed. Hans Boersma and Matthew Levering (Oxford: Oxford University Press, 2015). For a recent overview of Aquinas on the Eucharist, in both his systematic writings and in his poetry, see Jan-Heiner Tück, *A Gift of Presence: The Theology and Poetry of the Eucharist in Thomas Aquinas*, trans. Scott G. Hefelfinger (Washington, DC: Catholic University of America Press, 2018). Roger Nutt, *General Principles of Sacramental Theology* (Washington, DC: Catholic University of America Press, 2017), provides a sound introduction to a sacramental theology that is rooted in the teaching of Thomas Aquinas.

17. See, e.g., *ST* III, q. 75, a. 4c: "haec ... conversio ... est omnino supernaturalis, sola Dei virtute effecta."

18. For the causality of the words of institution/consecration, see *ST* III, q. 78, a. 4.

the priest is speaking in a eucharistic setting *in persona Christi*.[19] God works the change of substance; God employs the consecratory formula and, in the way appropriate to the priest, to work the change.

It is the "whole Christ," the *totus Christus*, who is present in the sacrament.[20] Body and blood are important, but there is more to Christ than body and blood. Here, Aquinas is linking his eucharistic theology to his incarnational Christology. The fully divine Word, the second person of God, became incarnate; without loss to itself as fully divine second person, the Word has taken up and expressed, instantiated, all that pertains to human nature, to being human. In the incarnate Word, the two natures—the divine and the human—have been united. And what is joined in reality will not be separated. In this regard, Aquinas articulates a teaching on concomitance. By the power of the sacrament (*ex vi sacramenti*), the substance of the bread is changed into the substance of the body, the substance of the wine into the substance of blood. By the power of concomitance (*ex reali concomitantia*), all that is "attached" to the substance of body, substance of blood, also becomes present—divinity and soul, to be sure, but the accidents of body and blood as well, although, Aquinas inserts, not in their proper mode but in the mode of substance.[21]

Throughout the treatise on the Eucharist, Aquinas insists on the deep connection between Eucharist and the Passion. Christ instituted the sacrament to recall the Passion and to convey its benefits.[22] In celebrating the Eucharist, it is the crucified Christ (*Christus passus*[23]) who is present. A favorite designation for the Eucharist is as "the sacrament of charity."[24] This is apt, pointing to the love in which Christ instituted the sacrament for his "friends,"[25] to encourage their love and to provide them with sustenance in the journey to eternal life when he and his friends would be finally, irrevocably united in the presence of God. The designation, "sacra-

---

19. For the priest, acting *ex persona Christi*, as cause, see, e.g., *ST* III, q. 78, a. 1c, and *ST* III, q. 82, a. 1.

20. See *ST* III, q. 76, aa. 1–4, for what follows in the text.

21. For the insight that Christ's bodily accidents are present eucharistically *ex vi realis concomitantiae*, see *ST* III, q. 76, a. 4c; that they are present not in their proper mode but in the mode of substance is stated in *ST* III, q. 76, a. 4, ad 1.

22. For representative statements that the Eucharist was instituted to recall the Passion, see, e.g., *ST* III, q. 73, aa. 5c, 6c; q. 79, aa. 1c, 2c; q. 83, a. 1c.

23. See, e.g., *ST* III, q. 73, a. 5, ad 2; 6c; q. 75, a. 1c, for *Christus passus*.

24. For the Eucharist as "sacrament of charity," see, e.g., *ST* III, q. 73, a. 3, ad 3; q. 74, a. 4, ob 3; q. 78, a. 3, ad 6; q. 79, a. 4, ob 1; q. 79, a. 6, ob 2; q. 80, a. 3, ob 2.

25. The language of friendship is used in the treatise at, e.g., *ST* III, q. 73, a. 5c, and q. 75, a. 1c.

ment of charity," also testifies to the love that the incarnate Word showed in dying for sins and providing access to eternal life.

In teaching the Eucharist, Aquinas makes considerable use of a three-fold sacramental formula that ultimately derives from Augustine: *sacramentum tantum, res et sacramentum*, and *res tantum*.[26] The *res et sacramentum* is the Christ who is truly present at the term of the consecration, at the term of the change. The *res tantum* summarizes the spiritual benefits that the eucharistic Christ brings. Aquinas can describe these spiritual benefits variously: as grace, and charity, as participation and incorporation in the body of Christ that is church, as access to eternal life. The consecrated bread and wine are the *sacramentum tantum*. Transubstantiation does not involve a transaccidentation, a changing of accidents into other accidents. The accidents of the bread and wine "remain" after the change of substance,[27] and these remaining accidents sign, point beyond themselves. They point to the *res et sacramentum*, to the Christ who is present as spiritual food. They point as well to the *res tantum*: just as out of many grains one bread is made, and out of many grapes one wine, so in the reception of the Eucharist, grace and charity are increased, and the recipient who engages Christ worthily is further incorporated into the body of Christ that is church.

For Aquinas, not all who receive the sacrament benefit from that reception.[28] Spiritual disposition is important, and those who lack the proper disposition will eat, as 1 Corinthians puts it, unto their condemnation. Much on the part of the recipient goes into worthy, fruitful, reception. Spiritual food is nourishment, and nourishment is only for the living, in this case, for those who are alive in Christ, who have received new life in baptism, by which they are oriented to the Eucharist. The worthy recipient is marked by grace, and by the faith and charity of one who already belongs

---

26. See, e.g., *ST* III, q. 73, a. 6c, and q. 80, a. 4c, where all three parts of the formula are invoked.

27. See *ST* III, q. 75, a. 5, for a discussion of the accidents of bread and wine remaining after the conversion. That the accidents of bread and wine remain, without a subject, is explored in *ST* III, q. 77, a. 1. See now Jörgen Vijgen, *The Status of Eucharistic Accidents 'sine subjecto': An Historical Survey Up to Thomas Aquinas and Selected Reactions* (Berlin: Akademie Verlag, 2013). By this point in the treatise, Aquinas will have made clear how important signing is in this sacrament, including by the remaining accidents of bread and wine. For one bread from many grains and one wine from many grapes, see, e.g., *ST* III, q. 74, a. 1c. On spiritual food, spiritual drink, see, e.g., *ST* III, q. 73, a. 2c.

28. For what follows in the text, in this and the next paragraph (on kinds of eating), see, e.g., *ST* III, q. 80, aa. 1–3; for unworthy reception and its consequences, see the use of Paul at *ST* III, q. 80, a. 4, *sed contra*.

to Christ; Christ's love in the Eucharist is to be met by the love of those who are Christ's. And the worthy recipient is aware, in approaching the altar, that this is sacrament and that Christ is present, and is present for spiritual benefit. To the person marked by formed faith who receives in devotion and reverence, the spiritual benefits of the sacrament are granted. That person, already alive in Christ, is granted more grace, more charity, and is further incorporated into the body of Christ that is church.

To secure the teaching about apt disposition, Aquinas can refer to different kinds of eating, again drawing on, ultimately, Augustine. There is a sacramental eating that is merely sacramental. There is a spiritual eating that is merely or only spiritual. There is a sacramental eating that is also spiritual. A merely sacramental eating is that of a person who is not spiritually alive and so cannot receive "more" grace, "more" charity. This is the eating of someone who is mired in mortal sin. That person eats only the *sacramentum tantum* and the *res et sacramentum* (the Christ truly present does not recede at the approach of a mortal sinner).[29] A spiritual eating is one in which the spiritual benefits of the Passion are in fact received; this can occur outside of a sacramental setting, as when it is impossible to actually receive.[30] And a sacramental eating that is spiritual is one in which a person receives the consecrated elements, encounters the Christ truly present, *and* does so to the recipient's spiritual benefit, receiving more grace, more charity, new access to eternal life, further incorporation into the body of Christ that is church. Fruitful reception is in sum a deepening assimilation to Christ, a point that Aquinas can make in striking fashion, again with the help of Augustine.[31] As Augustine puts it in the *Confessions*, there is a difference between bodily and spiritual food. The eater transforms bodily food into himself. Spiritual food transforms the eater into itself. Eucharistic recipients are changing into Christ.

The Eucharist, finally, is sacrifice as well as sacrament. A sacrament is received; a sacrifice is offered.[32] A sacrifice is offered by someone, to

---

29. Aquinas denies that the eucharistically present Christ recedes at the approach of the mortal sinner at *ST* III, q. 80, a. 3c. To say that he does recede would derogate from the truth of the sacrament, that is, that Christ is present in truth.

30. On reception by desire (*ex voto*), see *ST* III, q. 73, a. 3c.

31. The Augustine of *Confessions*, Book VII, 10, is quoted about the difference between corporeal and spiritual food (and incorporation) at *ST* III, q. 73, a. 3, ad 2. As becomes clear in the discussion later in this study of the eucharistic teaching of the *Scriptum* on the Lombard's *Sentences*, Aquinas can use this Augustine in combination with Pseudo-Dionysius to striking effect.

32. *ST* III, q. 79, a. 5c.

someone, for someone. A sacrifice is assessed according to the value of what is offered, but also according to the spirit in which it is offered. The eucharistic sacrifice is rooted in Christ's sacrifice on the Cross, memorializing it, participating in it, conveying its spiritual power to those for whom the sacrifice to God is offered. On the Cross, Christ is both priest and victim.[33] In the eucharistic sacrifice, the "invisible priest,"[34] who is the principal priest, is also active, and as Christ's, the eucharistic sacrifice is spiritually rich. Others participate in the offering; the eucharistic offering is at the same time, in a participatory way, the offering of the Church. The ordained minister is important here. In consecrating, he acts *in persona Christi*;[35] in the eucharistic sacrifice, he acts *in the person of the Church*, of the body of Christ that is engaged in the eucharistic offering, offering Christ its prayers. But in the treatise on the Eucharist, Aquinas acknowledges yet another priesthood, a "spiritual priesthood" exercised by those who are in fact joined to Christ as their head by their faith and charity.[36] It is their formed faith that qualifies them as spiritual priests, and they enter into the Eucharistic sacrifice by the prayers that they offer out of the charity and devotion that they have received from Christ through the Spirit.

In constructing his teaching about the Eucharist, Aquinas is attentive to Scripture. He also draws on the tradition to teach the Eucharist. The debt to Augustine is already apparent. But Aquinas is in dialogue with other Fathers—with others in the West, not least Ambrose, but also with the Greeks. It is to the Greeks that I now turn.

The Contribution of the Greeks

How, then, do the Greeks enter into the eucharistic theology of Thomas Aquinas?[37]

33. For Christ as priest and victim, see *ST* III, q. 22, a. 2.

34. The designation of Christ as "invisible priest" comes in a citation of Eusebius Emissenus, quoted at *ST* III, q. 78, a. 1, ob 1. Aquinas has received this quotation through Gratian, *De Consecratione*, d. II, can. XXXV (col. 1325).

35. For the ordained minister acting *in persona totius ecclesiae*, see *ST* III, q. 82, a. 6c.

36. The just laity is said to exercise a spiritual priesthood at *ST* III, q. 82, a. 1, ad 2. A quote ascribed to Chrysostom is found in ob 2, to the effect that every holy person is a priest. That quote is from the *Opus Imperfectum*, however, which is not by Chrysostom. For a similar claim in Augustine about the priesthood enjoyed by all Christians, by virtue of their relation to Christ, who is the one priest, see *De Civ. Dei* 20.10.

37. For a general introduction to Greek patristic eucharistic teaching, see Johannes

In terms of simple statistics, John Damascene is quoted or paraphrased seven times in these questions, Pseudo-Dionysius fourteen times, Cyril four times, and John Chrysostom eight times.[38] Some of these quotes are on the long side, and some are relatively brief. Some of the references are made simply to confirm some point or other that Aquinas is intent on. Some are made to nuance some aspect of Aquinas's own eucharistic teaching, by "showing" what a Father does and does not mean. And some of the quotes of these Fathers are extraordinarily powerful, lending a distinctive cast to Aquinas's teaching. The reception of these Fathers is in the main localized, connected, that is, to specific topics of significance. These Greek Fathers are invoked in particular to uphold Christ's distinctive, irreducible presence in the Eucharist; to affirm a change that accounts for that presence (although that change is not explicitly designated "transubstantiation," nor attached so resolutely to the words of institution[39]);

Betz, *Eucharistie in der Schrift und Patristik*, Handbuch der Dogmengeschichte, Band IV, Faszikel 4a (Freiburg: Herder, 1979). For Chrysostom, see J. Marsaux, "Pour une nouvelle approche de l'eucharistie chez Jean Chrysostome à partir de la pragmatique," *Studia Patristica* 37 (2001): 565–70; for Cyril of Alexandria, see Henry Chadwick, "The Eucharist and Christology during the Nestorian Controversy," *Journal of Theological Studies*, new ser., 2 (1951): 145–64; Ezra Gebremedhin, *Life-Giving Blessing: An Inquiry into the Eucharistic Doctrine of Cyril of Alexandria* (Stockholm: Almqvist & Wiksell, 1977); Lawrence J. Welch, *Christology and Eucharist in the Early Thought of Cyril of Alexandria* (Lanham: Catholic Scholars Press, 1994); Marie-Odile Boulnois, "L'eucharistie, mystère d'union chez Cyrille d'Alexandrie: Les modèles d'union trinitaire et christologique," *Revue des Sciences Religieuses* 74, no. 2 (2000): 147–72; Ellen Concannon, "The Eucharist as Source of St. Cyril of Alexandria's Christology," *Pro Ecclesia* 17, no. 3 (2009): 318–36; for Pseudo-Dionysius, see A. Golitzin, *Mystagogy: A Monastic Reading of Dionysus Areopagita* (Collegeville, MN: Cistercian, 2013), 261–71; for John Damascene, see C. N. Tsirpanlis, *Introduction to Eastern Patristic Thought and Orthodox Theology* (Collegeville, MN: Liturgical Press, 1991), 133–40.

38. For quotations or paraphrases of Cyril, see *ST* III, q. 75, a. 1c; q. 76, a. 1, ad 1; q. 76, a. 6, ad 2; q. 79, a. 1c. Of the Damascene, see *ST* III, q. 73, a. 4c (bis); q. 75, a. 2, ob 1; q. 78, a. 4, ob 1; q. 79, a. 1, ad 2; q. 79, a. 8, sed contra; q. 82, a. 5, ob 2. Of Pseudo-Dionysius, see *ST* III, q. 73, a. 1, ob 1; q. 73, a. 5, ob 1; q. 75, a. 1c; q. 78, a. 3, ad 9; q. 80, a. 9, ob 2; q. 80, a. 9, ob 3/ad 3; q. 81, a. 2c; q. 82, a. 3, ob 3; q. 82, a. 4c; q. 82, a. 5, ob 3; q. 83, a. 4c; q. 83, a. 5, ad 1; q. 83, a. 5, ad 7. And of Chrysostom, see *ST* III, q. 73, a. 1, ad 2; q. 75, a. 4c; q. 79, a. 1c (bis); q. 79, a. 6c; q. 81, a. 2 *sed contra*; q. 83, a. 1c and ad 1. In terms of Chrysostom, the citations in q. 83, a. 1, are ascribed wrongly, to Ambrose. This is discussed in the text and at notes 54, 55, and 88 below.

39. For Aquinas, the being present of Christ eucharistically is tied to the words of consecration and their utterance by the due representative of Christ. See *ST* III, q. 78. While his early Greek interlocutors are attentive to the words of consecration, they and their Eastern successors appear less inclined to tie the presence to these words, at least exclusively. See, e.g., the Damascene's references to the invocation of God, of the Spirit, along with his comments on the words of institution, which promise presence; the Damascene's "invocation" in the *de fide* is discussed later in this study. For points of controversy noted by Aquinas in his handling

and, most notably, to portray the encounter with the eucharistic Christ in striking fashion, to make clear the immediacy and poignancy of the encounter and the spiritual benefits of fruitful reception. The use of Cyril is apt and deft, and I review briskly all four of the references. The first three show Cyril's commitment to an irreducible, distinctive, eucharistic presence of Christ; the second and the fourth play up nicely the saving benefits that Christ conveys through his presence.

Cyril's first appearance comes in *ST* III, q. 75, a. 1, which prefaces the detailed account of transubstantiation in the rest of q. 75. Here, the topic is the presence of Christ's body in the sacrament in truth, not merely in sign. For Aquinas, this is the common witness of both West and East (whatever Berengar might think). Hence, in the *sed contra* of this article, Aquinas quotes Ambrose and Hilary, who both proclaim Christ's eucharistic presence in truth, and then in the corpus quotes Cyril's words on Luke 22:19, the words of institution. Cyril, too, is witness to the presence: "doubt not," Cyril is quoted, "whether this be true; but take rather the Savior's words with faith; for since He is the Truth, He lieth not."[40]

The second use in the treatise of Cyril similarly leaves no doubt about Cyril's commitment to a presence in truth: the citing of the Third Letter to Nestorius quoted at length above.[41] In *ST* III, q. 76, a. 1, ad 1, Aquinas

---

of Eucharist, see below on the use of leavened or unleavened bread and on infant reception. He does not make the point in the liturgy at which Christ becomes eucharistically present a matter of dispute with either his earlier interlocutors or his contemporaries. The "timing" of presence only became a matter of controversy for the churches in the next century; see M. H. Congourdeau, "L'Eucharistie à Byzance du XIe au XVe Siècle," in *Eucharistia: Encyclopédie de l'Eucharistie* (Paris: Les Éditions du Cerf, 2002), 153. Aquinas, incidentally, would seem to acknowledge an invocation or epiclesis, which prays for the effect of the consecration, to be received by those who are well prepared; see Tück, *Gift of Presence*, 153, following Jungmann. See *Quam oblationem*, as discussed in *ST* III, q. 83, a. 4, ad 7, as part of Aquinas's commentary on the words of the eucharistic liturgy.

40. "Non dubites an hoc verum sit, sed potius suscipe verba Salvatoris in fide; cum enim sit veritas, non mentitur." This comment from Cyril's *Commentary on Luke* is found as well in Aquinas's *Catena* on Luke, on 22:19, at 3283. This passage has made its way into more recent ecclesial documents. Aquinas's word on the need for faith to apprehend the presence, with this quotation from Cyril, is cited in the *Catholic Catechism* Part Two, Section Two, chapter 1, article 3, 1381, which is here apparently following *Mysterium Fidei*, the Encyclical of Pope Paul VI on the Holy Eucharist (1965), 18.

41. This is the first of the two citations of my four Greek Fathers that are taken over from Gratian. Aquinas did know in its entirety the Third Letter and the twelve chapters and quotes them directly in a different translation elsewhere; see Morard, "Thomas d'Aquin lecteur des conciles," 262–63. Here, however, Aquinas introduces the quotation by referring to the "Ephesine symbol," not to "Cyril"; he is taking over the saying as found in Gratian, *De Consecratione*,

points to Cyril's insistence that the flesh that gives life is precisely the flesh of the Word, who does not remain apart from the flesh, in support of the claim that the whole Christ (not simply substance of body, substance of blood) is present in the sacrament. As Aquinas puts it after quoting the Third Letter, substance has been changed into substance, and what in reality is joined to the substance is present concomitantly. The language of "concomitance" is Aquinas's, to be sure, but the teaching about the who (the whole Christ) that is eucharistically present is Cyril's as well.

The quote is even richer, underscoring the deep connection between Christ and salvation, the soteriological point of the eucharistic presence: "We are made partakers of the body and blood of Christ, not as taking common flesh, nor as of a holy man united to the Word in dignity, but the truly life-giving flesh of the Word Himself."[42] Aquinas would appreciate the dig at Nestorius ("nor as of a holy man united to the Word in dignity"), but even more the stress on the life-giving power of the eucharistic Christ. On presence and on the point of that presence, Aquinas is in complete agreement with Cyril.

The third Cyril reference, which comes in *ST* III, q. 76, a. 6, ad 2, is also concerned with presence. This is taken from Cyril's Epistle 83 and, as Aquinas notes, has to do with the "duration" of the presence in truth: Cyril observes, "Some are so foolish as to say that the mystical blessing departs from the sacrament, if any of its fragments remain until the next day: [that is foolish] for Christ's consecrated body is not changed, and the power of the blessing, and the life-giving grace is perpetually in it."[43] "Perpetually" might be pushing it; Aquinas would set a limit on the presence, to correspond with how long what is bread remains bread as subject to corruption, to digestion.[44] But with the main point he would agree:

---

d. II, c. LXXX (col. 1346), where, quoted at length, it is introduced similarly. It is hard to discern why he would quote this Cyril via Gratian when he has the entire letter to hand.

42. *ST* III, q. 76, a. 1, ad 1: "Unde in Symbolo Ephesino legitur: 'Participes efficimur corporis et sanguinis Christi, non ut commune carnem percipientes, nec viri sanctificati et Verbo coniuncti secundum dignitatis unitatem, sed vere vivificatricem, et ipsius Verbi propriam factam.'"

43. *ST* III, q. 76, a. 6, ad 2: "Cyrillus dicit: 'Insaniunt quidam dicentes mysticam benedictionem cessare a sanctificatione, si quae eius reliquiae remanserint in diem subsequentem. Non enim mutatur sacratum corpus Christi, sed virtus benedictionis et vivificativa gratia iugis in eo est.'" This saying is found in the *Catena* on Luke, at 3284. The "perpetually" in the translation in the text, found in the English Dominican translation, may be stretching it; all Cyril need be committed to, with the *iugis*, is a presence that is not transient.

44. Aquinas considers the "duration" of the presence in *ST* III, q. 76, a. 6, ad 3: that

Christ *is* eucharistically present. Implied here, one might add, in this talk of continued presence in the elements, is a change of the elements.

The final citation of Cyril comes in *ST* III, q. 79, a. 1, co, and returns to the theme of the point of Christ's eucharistic presence. Again, as in the first Cyril reference, it is Cyril on Luke 22:19 (but a different line of Cyril) that is cited: "God's life-giving Word by uniting Himself with His own flesh, made it to be productive of life. For it was becoming that He should be united somehow with bodies through His sacred flesh and precious blood, which we receive in a life-giving blessing in the bread and wine."[45] In sum, then, to state the obvious, Christ's becoming present eucharistically is not for its own sake, but to give life, to facilitate assimilation to Christ and the movement to the end of eternal life.[46]

In including John Chrysostom in his own teaching, Aquinas draws anew on homilies employed in the *Catena Aurea*. He cites in the treatise on the Eucharist homilies of John on the Bread of Life discourse in John 6 and on the flowing of the blood from the side of Christ (in Jn 19), as well as a homily on Matthew. While in one of the citations[47] John is acknowl-

---

presence endures for as long as the sacramental species remain. Cyril's saying can be read in a way compatible with that position.

45. *ST* III, q. 79, a. 1c: "Unde et Cyrillus dicit: 'Vivificativum Dei Verbum, uniens seipsum propriae carni, fecit ipsam vivificativam ... Decebat ergo eum nostris quodammodo uniri corporibus per sacram eius carne et pretiosum sanguinem, quae accipimus in benedictionem vivificatativam in pane et vino.'" This is also found in the *Catena* on Luke 22:19, a few lines after what is cited in note 43 above.

46. For Aquinas, there is a wisdom to the Incarnation, and to the eucharistic presence of the whole Christ. Both divinity and humanity are pertinent to the account of the Savior. It is God who saves; humans need saving; by sin, humans have lost sight of God; the Word who is Wisdom becomes human to reach fallen humans and accomplish their salvation suavely, through the humanity taken up and through the acts and undergoings of the Word incarnate, perfected in grace. The incarnate Word present in the sacrament also "speaks" to people where they are, facilitating their ascent to God. For a discussion of the wisdom motif as found in Aquinas's *Commentary on John*, see Michael Dauphinais, "'And They Shall All Be Taught by God': Wisdom and the Eucharist in John 6," in *Reading John with St. Thomas Aquinas: Theological Exegesis and Speculative Theology*, ed. Michael Dauphinais and Matthew Levering (Washington, DC: Catholic University of America Press, 2005), 312–17. What holds of Aquinas holds of Cyril, who also knows the importance of the humanity of the Word for the achievement of human salvation. For more on the Wisdom Christology of Thomas Aquinas, see my "Wisdom in the Christology of Thomas Aquinas," in *Christ among the Medieval Dominicans: Representations of Christ in the Texts and Images of the Order of Preachers*, ed. Kent Emery Jr. and Joseph Wawrykow (Notre Dame, IN: University of Notre Dame Press, 1998), 175–96.

47. The saying of Chrysostom in *ST* III, q. 75, a. 4c, is taken from a homily (47) on John [6:54]: "Idest, spiritualia sunt, nihil carnale neque consequentiam naturalem, sed eruta sunt ab omni tali necessitate quae in terra, ete a legibus quae hic positate sunt."

edging that what occurs in the Eucharist is not to be assimilated to some natural occurrence—what happens in Eucharist in the becoming present of Christ is above nature—John's contributions have more to do with the recipient, with how the recipient should approach the altar, with what should be avoided in eucharistic reception. Negatively put, the warning of 1 Corinthians against eating unto one's condemnation is kept in mind, and one should avoid the example of Judas. There was some disagreement among the Fathers about whether Judas had received at the Last Supper; John is cited[48] as among those who affirmed that reception, although, to Judas's condemnation, against those such as Hilary who had denied that Judas had received.

The comments of John that Aquinas retrieves in discussing worthy reception, fruitful reception, are striking, impressive testimony to John's skill as homilist. The blood that one drinks in the Eucharist is the blood of Christ, and one should approach the chalice as if one were about to drink from the side of Christ.[49] In that same article (*ST* III, q. 79, a. 1), John is quoted again about what occurs in eucharistic reception. The Eucharist, Aquinas observes, is spiritual food and does for the spiritual life all that material food does for bodily life—sustaining, giving increase, restoring, and giving delight. Accordingly, Aquinas continues, Ambrose says, "This is the bread of everlasting life, which supports the substance of our soul," and Chrysostom says, "When we desire it, He lets us feel Him, and eat Him, and embrace Him."[50] It is probably out of place to quibble with John's depiction, although given that the accidents of the body of Christ are not present in the Eucharist, according to Aquinas, in their proper mode but in the mode of substance,[51] there is not, literally, a bodily encounter, a touching of one body of another. What matters here— and Aquinas quotes John without reservation, without my quibble—is the intimacy of the encounter that Eucharist provides: one is eating him, embracing Christ. In another use of John, elsewhere,[52] Aquinas employs

---

48. *ST* III, q. 81, *sed contra*.

49. *ST* III, q. 79, a. 1c: "dicit Chrysostom: 'Quia hinc suscipiunt principium sacra mysteria, cum accesseris ad tremendum calicem, ut ab ipsa bibiturus Christi costa, ita accedes.'" This is from John's Homily 85; Aquinas also quotes this in the *Catena* on John (19:34), at 2531.

50. *ST* III, q. 79, a. 1c, quoting from Homily 46 on John: "Praestat nobis desiderantibus et palpare et comedere et amplecti."

51. Recall *ST* III, q. 76, a. 4, ad 1, cited in note 21 above.

52. *ST* III, q. 79, a. 6c. This is taken from Chrysostom's Homily 46 on John. That is also quoted, but at greater length, in Aquinas's *Catena* on Luke (on 22:19–20), at 3285. The saying as quoted there is quite stirring. Protection from sin at the same time is a call to action, action

John to add to the list of what this spiritual food supplies; as John says, along with the sustaining, giving increase, restoring, giving delight of the previous article, the Eucharist can be said as well to preserve from sin, protecting the one who has eaten fruitfully from the attacks of devils. "We leave the table," John observes, "made fierce-some to the devil."

Chrysostom makes a final appearance, in *ST* III, q. 83, a. 1. Question 83 offers reflections on the liturgy of the Eucharist, playing up the symbolism of place, time, words, and actions, and noting how the entire Church (ordained ministers, the faithful laity) is engaged in the eucharistic offering. The first article asks about the sacrifice, the *immolatio*, of the Eucharist. As previously noted in the treatise,[53] the Eucharist is indeed a sacrifice, one that is not of itself but rather stands in close relationship to and dependence on the sacrifice of Christ on the cross. Here, Chrysostom, on Hebrews, is invoked to stress the symbolism and the connection between Passion and Eucharist, and to assert that by the Eucharist, Christ's sacrifice is recalled and brought to memory and ritually enacted.[54] But in the quoting of Chrysostom, Aquinas is unaware of the author's identity. The saying is ascribed, mistakenly, to Ambrose. The quotation in fact is taken over by Aquinas from Gratian, where the saying is similarly misascribed; this is one of the two places in the treatise where these Greeks enter via Gratian.[55]

John might have figured in Aquinas's eucharistic teaching in the

---

that is in keeping with the Eucharist, in loving service to others: "hoc fecit Christus ducens nos ad maius amicitie foedus, suamque caritatem declarans erga nos, prestans se non solum videri desiderantibus, sed et palpare, et comedere, et amplecti, et totum affectum explere. Igitur ut leones flammam spirantes, sic ab illa mensa discedimus terribiles facti diabolo." This goes well with the characterization of the Eucharist as the sacrament of charity. In *ST* III, q. 79, a. 6c, Aquinas is content to quote only the final line of that passage.

53. For earlier mentions of Eucharist as sacrifice, see, e.g., *ST* III, q. 79, aa. 5 and 7; q. 82, aa. 4 and 6.

54. "Ambrose" (= Chrysostom) is quoted on Hebrews in both the corpus and of *ST* III, q. 83, a. 1, ad 1. *ST* III, q. 83, a. 1c: "Unde Ambrosius dicit, Super Epistolam ad Hebraeos: 'In Christo semel oblata est hostia ad salutem sempiternam potens. Quid ergo nos? Nonne per singulos dies offerimus, sed ad recordatioem mortis eius?'" *ST* III, q. 83, a. 1, ad 1: "sicut Ambrosius ibidem dicit, 'una est hostia,' quam slicet Christus obtulit et nos offerimus, 'et non multae, quia semel oblatus est Christus, hoc autem sarificium exemplum est illius, sicut enim quod ubique offertur unum est corpus et non multa corpora, ita et unum sacrifium.'" This is from Chrysostom's Homily 17 on Hebrews. See also note 55 below.

55. For the entire quote as ascribed to Ambrose in Gratian, see *De Consecratione*, d. II, c. LIII (col. 1333). For the other Gratian-sourced quotation of a Greek Father, see note 41 above. The quoting of this "Ambrose" is also made by Peter Lombard in his *Sententiae*, Book IV, d. 12, chap. 5. See also note 88 below.

Summa in another way but doesn't. The *Contra Errores Graecorum* is an interesting work.[56] The "Greeks" in question are not the Fathers but contemporary Greeks, that is, the Byzantines. Texts of the Greek Fathers on various issues in dispute between Latins and Byzantines had been put together, and Aquinas had been asked to comment on these issues and early texts. One of the chapters of the *Contra Errores Graecorum* (Part 2, chap. 39) is given over to a eucharistic matter, to be precise, to the use or nonuse of unleavened bread in the sacrament. Here, the practices of the churches differ. John Chrysostom is prominent among the handful of early authorities cited in the chapter, providing two of the sayings (at least one of which is in fact authentic, taken from the homilies on Matthew [84]). Now, Aquinas includes a discussion of leavened and unleavened bread in the *Summa*'s treatise on the Eucharist,[57] reviewing the symbolism of the different breads, indicating his preference for the Latin practice but insisting that a priest in celebrating must follow the usage of his own rite. In the *Summa*'s treatment, John is not cited; for that matter, no early Greek Father is brought into this discussion (and only Gregory the Great comes into play, to help in presenting the symbolism). Here, in sum, Aquinas has refrained from playing the "modern" Greeks off against the early Fathers, to whom they, with Aquinas, are heir.

John Damascene for his part offers Aquinas the opportunity to finesse his teaching, to comment further about what is involved in eucharistic change and the irreducible eucharistic presence of Christ. Two sayings in particular call out to Aquinas for comment. The first[58] is the Damascene's statement that "Since it is customary for men to eat bread and drink wine, God has wedded his Godhead to them, and made them His body and blood," and further on that "The bread of communication is not simple bread, but is united to the Godhead." Doesn't this mean that for John what was bread prior to the change remains bread, with the difference simply being that now the Word in the Word's divinity is joined to that bread? Two "things"—bread and divinity—exist; they are

---

56. Thomas Aquinas, *Contra Errores Graecorum*, in *Sancti Thomae Aquinatis doctoris angelici Opera omnia iussu Leonis XIII.O.M. edita* (Rome, 1882–), Tome 40, Pars A.

57. Aquinas discusses the use of leavened or unleavened bread in *ST* III, q. 74, a. 4.

58. This Damascene is cited in *ST* III, q. 75, a. 2, ob 1: "Quia consuetudo est hominibus comedere panem et vinum bibere, coniugavit eis divinitatem, et fecit ea corpus et sanguinem." [Et ita] "panis communicationis non panis simplex est, sed unitus divinitati." In *de fide*, the two quotes that have been conjoined by Aquinas in ob 1 are about a page apart. The first, *quia consuetudo*, is found in the Buytaert at c. 86, 6, ll. 94–96 (p. 312); the second, *panis communicationis*, is found at c. 86, 10, ll. 136–37 (p. 314).

joined, and each continues to exist in the union. Aquinas's handling of this saying in his response, however, calls on the distinction that Aquinas observes, between substance and accident. Substance has been changed into substance, and what was bread is now the substance of Christ's body. The accidents of the bread have not been changed (into the accidents of Christ's body), and thus what John means (without himself making use of the substance-accident distinction) is that while the reality of the bread has been changed, the accidents remain, to signify the presence of Christ. That is the sense, at least according to Aquinas, in which there is here a "union" of "two things."

The other saying of the Damascene that comes in for closer inspection by Aquinas has to do with the Holy Spirit. It is by the Holy Spirit, by the coming of the Holy Spirit, that Christ becomes present. Actually, in the Damascene's saying, there is, apparently, an exclusivity here: it is by the Holy Spirit *alone*, John is quoted as saying, that the change occurs, that Christ is present.[59] Aquinas agrees about the work of the Holy Spirit in the sacrament. It *is* by the power of the Holy Spirit that Christ is present. That is not what needs nuancing. Aquinas suggests, however, the alleged exclusivity in John's statement (as he has reported it) pertains only to the *principal* causality in the change and presence. Only God can work the radical change of one substance into another, and only God can work eucharistic presence. But that does not exclude instrumental causality, the use of secondary causes to bring about that change. And in the Eucharist,

---

59. *ST* III, q. 78, a. 4, ob 1: "sola virtute Spiritus Sancti fit conversio panis in corpus Christi." The exact wording appears to be absent from the Latin of Buytaert. The principal ideas here expressed, however, are surely the Damascene's. He mentions more than once that it is by the Holy Spirit that a change of bread into body, of wine into blood, occurs (see, e.g., Buytaert, c. 86, 5 [p. 311]; c. 86, 7 [p. 313]), and he does think that something happens, that bread becomes or is made (*fit*, e.g., c. 86, 5, l. 84 [p. 311]) into something else, that bread is changed (*transmutatur*, c. 86, 7, ll. 107–8). See also note 61 below. The *sola* has been introduced into this summary of the Damascene's teaching, for effect. He has focused on the power of the Holy Spirit, which is invoked, and basically leaves it at that. The insertion of the *sola*, whether by Aquinas himself or by someone who also makes use of the Damascene on whom Aquinas might be drawing, is useful. It does not change John's teaching but states it more bluntly—the change is by the power of the Spirit—to set up for the additional, explicit claim, about instrumental causality, made by Aquinas. Thomas, not incidentally, can refer to the change according to God's power "only" (see *ST* III, q. 75, a. 4c, quoted in note 17 above). Aquinas's additional assertion of secondary causality is seemingly compatible with John's teaching. John does refer to an invocation of the Spirit (c. 86, 5, l. 77 [p. 311]; 86, 7, l. 109 [p. 313]); someone at the celebration is doing the invoking; that invoking, Aquinas specifies, is causal instrumentally. At the conference, I had a helpful exchange with Melissa Eitenmiller about the *sola* and its implications.

that is in fact the case. As Aquinas observes, by the promise of Christ in the institution, there is a created power attached, as it were, to the consecratory formula and thus the Holy Spirit, who works the change of substance into substance, works through the instrumentality of the consecratory formula as uttered by the officiant acting in the person of Christ.

Aquinas continues this discussion in a later article[60] where the topic is the consecration of a wicked priest. Is that consecration effective? In the second objection in that article, John is again quoted about the activity in the sacrament of the Holy Spirit, who is invoked by a priest; that quotation[61] is then followed by one from a pope, Gelasius, who asks why the invocation of the Spirit by a wicked priest would be heard, thus putting into doubt the consecration.[62] In his response, Aquinas puts the comment of that pope in its proper context: the pope is urging priests not to be wicked, to approach their work in the sacrament without sin. And, Aquinas adds, the personal merits of a priest are of no account in the consecration and do not determine the "success" of the consecration. For it is the Holy Spirit (as John has said) who is the principal agent, making use of the consecratory formula, to which Christ has attached a created power, as uttered by the priest acting in Christ's person. From both discussions in which the recognition of the Holy Spirit by the Damascene figures, it is clear that there is, in a word, no disagreement between John and Thomas about the Holy Spirit; all Aquinas has done is extend the discussion to make the further point about instrumental causality.

John's other comments about Eucharist, as retrieved by Aquinas, speak nicely, and in a straightforward way, to the themes of engagement with the eucharistic Christ and the spiritual benefits of fruitful reception. Thus, in *ST* III, q. 73, a. 4c, Aquinas quotes the Damascene with approval for two of the names given to the Eucharist. This sacrament is called "Communion" or *synaxis*, writes John, "because we communicate with Christ through it, both because we partake of His flesh and Godhead, and because we communicate with and are united to one another through it."[63] And it is also called in Greek *metalepsis* because, as John says, "we

60. *ST* III, q. 82, a. 5.

61. Here, the Damascene is quoted as stating, "panis et vinum, per adventum Sancti Spiritus, supernaturaliter transit in corpus et sanguinem Domini." See Buytaert, c. 86, 7, ll. 109–11 (p. 313).

62. For the eucharistic theology of Pope Gelasius, see Edward J. Kilmartin, *The Eucharist in the West: History and Theology*, ed. Robert J. Daly (Collegeville, MN: Liturgical Press, 2004), 31–58.

63. *ST* III, q. 73, a. 4c: "secundum hoc nominatur communio vel synaxis; dicit enim

thereby [in the sacrament] assume the Godhead of the Son."[64] Aquinas is not disconcerted by language of participation, of deification; in quoting John to name the sacrament, he is embracing this language.

The Damascene's likening of the Eucharist to the burning coal that Isaiah saw also meets with Aquinas's approval; Aquinas makes use of that image, and John's words about the burning coal and what it does, in two articles in the treatise. In the one article,[65] John's words have a particular force when considered in the context of Aquinas's affirmation of Eucharist as sacrament of charity, of Christ's love for those who are his, and their love of him. As John states, "The fire of that desire which is within us, being kindled by the burning coal," that is, this sacrament "will consume our sins, and enlighten our hearts, so that we shall be inflamed and made godlike (*deificemur*)."[66] The Eucharist, then, stimulates love, purges of (venial) sin, illumines, and perfects; again, we meet the language of divinization through the loving participation in the sacrament. In the other article in which the Damascene's burning coal appears,[67] the notion of bread united with the Godhead comes up again, here asserted to make the point of the spiritual power of the Eucharist. The entire passage in which the Damascene is here quoted is a marvel, testimony to Aquinas's skill as a writer who is firmly rooted in Scripture and tradition; the Damascene, in Aquinas's hands, quoted along with others, becomes part of a chorus about what Christ has done and is doing in this sacrament.

This sacrament confers grace spiritually together with the virtue of charity. Hence Damascene compares this sacrament to the burning coal which Isaias saw (Isa 6:6): "For a live ember is not simply wood, but wood united to fire; so also the bread of communion is not simple bread but bread united with the Godhead." But as Gregory [the Great] observes in a Homily for Pentecost, "God's love is never idle; for, wherever it is it does great works." And consequently through this sacrament, as far as its power is concerned, not only is the habit of grace and

---

Damascenus quod 'dicitur communio, quia communicamus per ipsam Christo; et quia participamus eius carne et deitate; et quia communicamus et unimur ad invicem per ipsam.'" See Buytaert, c. 86, 15, ll. 174–77 (p. 317).

64. *ST* III, q. 73, a. 4c: "dicitur graeco metalepsis, quia, ut Damascenus dicit, 'per hoc Filii deitatem assumimus.'" See Buytaert, c. 86, 15, ll. 173–74 (p. 317).

65. *ST* III, q. 79, a. 8 *sed contra*.

66. *ST* III, q. 79, a. 8 *sed contra*: "est quod Damascenus dicit ... 'Ignis eius quod in nobis est desiderii, asssumens eam quae ex carbone,' idest ex hoc sacramento 'ignitionem, comburat nostra peccata, et illuminet corda nostra, ut participatio divini ignis igniamur et deificemur.'" See Buytaert, c. 86, 10, ll. 132–34 (p. 314).

67. *ST* III, q. 79, a. 1, ad 2.

of virtue bestowed, but it is furthermore aroused to act, according to 2 Corinthians 5:14: "The charity of Christ presseth us." Hence it is that the soul is spiritually nourished through the power of this sacrament, by being spiritually gladdened, and as it were inebriated with the sweetness of the Divine goodness, according to Canticles 5:1: "Eat, O friends, and drink, and be inebriated, my dearly beloved."[68]

The spirituality of Aquinas has here come to quite lyrical expression.

The final of the Greek Fathers to be considered here is the one most frequently cited by Aquinas in discussing Eucharist. References to Pseudo-Dionysius are scattered throughout the treatise on the Eucharist, to make a variety of points. Dionysius confirms that the Eucharist is a sacrament, one that aims at perfecting, and perfecting in a way different from chrismation.[69] Dionysius is also named among those who have proclaimed the eucharistic presence of Christ, joining Cyril, Hilary, and Ambrose, in *ST* III, q. 75, a. 1, in testifying to the presence of Christ in this sacrament in truth; Aquinas, however, in ascribing an affirmation of eucharistic presence to Dionysius, simply gestures at the *Ecclesiastical Hierarchy* without actually quoting Dionysius in his own words to this effect. Aquinas's Dionysius also knows how closely linked are the eucharistic Christ and human salvation, and movement toward God. Thus in asking, in *ST* III, q. 82, a .3, to whom dispensing of the sacrament pertains—bishop, priest, deacon?—Aquinas observes, in the response to the third objection (a response in which the *Ecclesiastical Hierarchy* is alluded to twice, with regards to perfecting), that in this sacrament "a man is perfected by union with Christ."[70]

These as well as the other references to Dionysius in the treatise show a nice sensitivity to the movement of the *Ecclesiastical Hierarchy*, an awareness of Dionysius's attentiveness to the perfecting work, in word and action, of the hierarch, as well as of Dionysius's attentiveness to the disposition and activity of the one being perfected. In terms of the hierarch, two of the references call for mention here. First, Dionysius is prominent in the discussion of whether the priest who consecrates should receive.[71] The Eucharist is sacrament and sacrifice. By dispensing the sacrifice to

---

68. *ST* III, q. 79, a. 1, ad 2, for the words of the Damascene: "'Carbo enim lignum simplex non est, sed unitum igni; ita et panis communionis non simplex panis est, sed unitus divinitati.'" See Buytaert, c. 86, 10, ll. 135–37 (p. 314); there, the final word of the quote from the Damascene is *deitati*.

69. *ST* III, q. 73, a. 1, ob 1.

70. *ST* III, q. 82, a. 3, ad 3: "inquantum dispensat hoc sacramentum, quo perficitur homo secundum se per comparationem ad Christum."

71. *ST* III, q. 82, a. 4c.

the people, the consecrating priest shows, as Dionysius says, that he is the dispenser of Divine gifts, of which he ought himself to be the first to partake. Aquinas repeats this Dionysian point in the corpus of the fourth article of question 83, which is in effect Aquinas's commentary on the liturgy, in its words, actions, and setting (this is, incidentally, one of the three references to Dionysius that Aquinas makes in q. 83).[72]

Second, Aquinas refers to Dionysius in the discussion of the consecration of the sinful priest.[73] As a reminder, in the *Ecclesiastical Hierarchy*, Dionysius is clear that the hierarch, who dispenses divine gifts, who perfects, is himself purged of sin, illumined, and perfected, and as such lifts up the one who is to be perfected. But what about the sinful priest? Does such a one perfect? In the third objection of this article (q. 82, a.5), Aquinas quotes another writing of Dionysius, Epistle 8, to Demophilus, in which Dionysius takes a hard line: "He who is not enlightened has completely fallen away from the priestly order; and I wonder that such a man dare to employ his hands in priestly actions, and in the person of Christ to utter, over the Divine symbols, his unclean infamies, for I will not call them prayers."[74] The Damascene, along with Pope Gelasius, had been cited in the objection immediately prior to this objection, similarly expressing doubt about the work of the "hierarch" (who in this telling is in fact not a hierarch). And Aquinas's answer (ad 3) to this saying of Dionysius echoes the prior response to the Damascene and the pope: "the blessing of a sinful priest, inasmuch as he acts unworthily is deserving of a curse, and is reputed an infamy and a blasphemy, and not a prayer; whereas, inasmuch as it is pronounced in the person of Christ, it is holy and efficacious." This is not to provide warrant for anyone continuing in sin. Rather, it is to provide assurance, based on the power of the Holy Spirit, the promise of Christ and the (merely) instrumental contribution of a priest.

What about the recipient? Dionysius had weighed in, in the *Ecclesiastical Hierarchy*, about Judas; with Augustine and Chrysostom (and against Hilary), Dionysius, Thomas notes, also thinks that Christ did give the sac-

---

72. For the other two in *ST* III, q. 83, see a. 5, ad 1 (on the signification of the washing of hands), and, a. 5, ad 7 (on the signification of the breaking of the host).

73. *ST* III, q. 82, a. 5.

74. *ST* III, q. 82, a. 5, ob 3: "Et Dionysius dicit in epistola *Ad Demophil. Mon.*: 'Perfecte cecidit a sacredotali ordine, qui non est illuminatus: et audax quidem nimium mihi videtur talis, sacerdotalibus manum apponens; et audet immundas infamias, non enim dicam orationes, super divina symbola Christiformiter enuntiare.'"

rament to Judas at the Last Supper.[75] In Dionysius's terms, I should add, such reception would of course not be perfective, for by his sin, Judas lacked the disposition to benefit from reception. Dionysius also contributes to the consideration of who, now, should receive, in an article that asks about those who lack the use of reason and are incapable of forming the devotion typically called for in eucharistic reception.[76] The discussion of infants (in the third objection and response) is especially informative. Should infants receive this sacrament? Infant reception is the practice, Aquinas acknowledges, among "certain Greeks" (i.e., contemporaries), and for this practice, Aquinas notes, the authority of Dionysius has been alleged. As in the second chapter of the *Ecclesiastical Hierarchy*, in the telling of these "certain Greeks," Dionysius sanctions infant reception as the culmination of the process of initiation. In this case at least, the use of reason, the actual forming of devotion, any act of the person himself, is not germane.

In his response, Aquinas, of course, is not quibbling with infant baptism; by his time, that is the norm in his church. He is calling infant reception into question.[77] There is, he says, no damage to the baptized child's well-being in not actually receiving. By baptism, the child is made a member of Christ's body (church), and qualified for eucharistic reception and ordered/ordained to it, and thus in that sense participating, spiritually, in Christ's life-giving body and blood. And once the infant comes of age and is able to use reason to form the requisite devotion, the child can actually receive the body and blood *sacramentally* as well as spiritually.

For our purposes, as interesting is what Aquinas says in this response about what Dionysius does and does not sanction. For Aquinas, the comments in *Ecclesiastical Hierarchy*, chapter 2, do not have to do with an infant or child. They have to do with the process of initiation of an *adult*. Otherwise put, Dionysius has been misunderstood by those "Greeks." In this case, there is a playing off of a Father against his Greek heirs.

As a reading of chapter 2 of the *Ecclesiastical Hierarchy*, Aquinas's interpretation—that is, that this has to do with an *adult*, an adult who has repented of sin and undergone instruction, and is consciously and

---

75. *ST* III, a. 81, a. 2c.

76. *ST* III, q. 80, a. 9.

77. Infant reception was not practiced in the West at Aquinas's time. For a discussion of earlier Western practice, see Pierre-Marie Gy, "Die Taufkommunion der kleinen Kinder in der lateinischen Kirche," in *Zeichen des Glaubens: Studien au Taufe und Firmung Balthasar Fischer zum 60. Geburtstag*, ed. Hansjörg auf der Maur and Bruno Kleinheyer (Zurich: Benziger Verlag, 1972), 485–91.

purposefully undergoing sacramental initiation—is not implausible. But there is much more to Dionysius on the eucharistic reception of infants, and Aquinas here simply leaves that out of account. Dionysius explicitly discusses infant baptism and infant reception in the final chapter of the *Ecclesiastical Hierarchy*, and Dionysius supports both.[78] To the impure, to be sure, such practice seems laughable. "It is as if the high priests teach what is divine to those who are unable to hear, and as if they hand down the sacred traditions to those who cannot think in images." And what is as laughable, from the perspective of the impure, is that others say the renunciations and sacred avowals on behalf of these infants.

Yet infant baptism and infant reception are practiced and should be practiced. Not everything divine, Dionysius notes, is encircled by our understanding. "Much that is unknown to us has a divine cause, unknown to us, but known to the ranks that are better than ours." And this has been passed on to the holy deiform perfectors, and they have passed this on to "us." To wit, the divine leaders "agreed that babies be received in this sacred way, so that the natural parents of the initiated child might hand the child down to a good tutor, learned in what is divine." The child would be perfected under the good tutor, as under a divine father. In sacramental initiation, that one (the good tutor) vows before the high priest to bring up the child in the divine life, and vows the renunciation and the sacred avowals. The child will be brought up according to a divine anagogy, having a leader who will suggest in him a divine character, and will be an experienced guard against its opposite. The child, initiated sacramentally, will be formed in a life that always contemplates what is divine, and made a fellow of those who are advanced in what is sacred, will be of sacred character. The practice of Thomas's contemporaries, then, clearly has plenty of Dionysian support, and the omission of this passage from Thomas's discussion is regrettable.

The Greeks in the Eucharistic Teaching of the *Scriptum*

A glance at the early *Scriptum* is instructive in concluding this discussion of the Greeks in the eucharistic theology of Thomas Aquinas.[79] On the

---

78. For what follows in the text, see *On the Ecclesiastical Hierarchy*, chap. 7, pp. 266–67ff.; the quotes in the text come from the translation found on the odd-numbered pages of this bilingual (Latin-English) edition.

79. St. Thomas Aquinas, *Commentary on the Sentences Book IV, Distinctions 1–13*, vol. 7,

whole, the theology of Eucharist of the *Summa* is anticipated nicely in the *Scriptum*. We meet in the distinctions on the Eucharist in the fourth book of the *Scriptum*, for example, the same affirmations of: a distinctive eucharistic presence;[80] the presence of the whole Christ, indeed of the "incarnate Word";[81] the linking of presence to the change that is transubstantiation;[82] the notion of concomitance;[83] the characterization of this sacrament as the sacrament of charity;[84] the eatings that can be sacramental, spiritual, or both;[85] and the profound spiritual benefits of worthy reception.[86] One way in which the early writing differs from the later,[87] however, has to do with the Greek Fathers. Cyril is completely missing from the *Scriptum*'s distinctions on the Eucharist; so, too, is John Chrysostom, with one exception.[88] This underscores the importance of the recovery of conciliar material, and of the work on the *Catena Aurea*, subsequent to the *Scriptum*. In terms of Chrysostom, while Burgundio's translations of the homilies had long been available, and might have been drawn on in teaching Eucharist in the *Scriptum*, Aquinas's work on the

---

Latin/English Edition of the Works of St. Thomas Aquinas, trans. Beth Mortensen (Green Bay, WI: Aquinas Institute, 2017). In the citations that follow, I list the work as *In IV Sent.*, followed by the distinction number, question number, article number, and questiuncula number (if there is a qc). The discussion of Eucharist comes in *In Sent. IV*, dd. 8–13.

80. See, e.g., *In IV Sent.*, d. 10, q. 1, a. 1.

81. That is the whole Christ who is present is affirmed in, e.g., *In IV Sent.*, d. 10, q. 1, a. 2, qc. 1–4. The presence of the "Incarnate Word" is affirmed, e.g., at d. 8, q. 1, a. 3, qc. 2, *sed contra* (1); and in qc. 1, resp.

82. Transubstantiation is discussed in *In IV Sent.*, d. 11, q. 1.

83. We meet in *In IV Sent.*, d. 10, q. 1, a. 2, resp., the distinction between what is present *ex vi sacramenti*, what *ex naturali concomitantia*.

84. For designations of this as the sacrament of charity, see, e.g., *In IV Sent.*, d. 8, q. 1, a. 3, qc. 1, *sed contra* (2); d. 8, q. 2, a. 2, qc. 3, ad 5.

85. On the eatings, see *In IV Sent.*, d. 9, a. 1.

86. See *In IV Sent.*, d. 12, q. 2, on the spiritual benefits of worthy reception.

87. For a brisk review of several ways, large and small, in which the discussion of the Eucharist in the *Summa* may mark an advance on that in the *Scriptum*, see Pierre-Marie Gy, "Avancées du traité de l'eucharistie de S. Thomas dans la *Somme* par rapport aux *Sentences*," *Revue des Sciences Philosophiques et Théologiques* 77, no. 2 (1993): 219–28. Among the advances noted by Gy are a deepened meditation on the scriptural witness, including John 6, and a more ample patristic dossier; he mentions in this regard the importance of the *Catena Aurea*, as well as the subsequent reading of Gratian's *De Consecratione*. At least in terms of the Greek Fathers here studied, that is, however, to overstate the importance of *De Consecratione*.

88. The quote of Chrysostom, wrongly ascribed to Ambrose, that is found in *ST* III, q. 83, a. 1 (see notes 54 and 55 above) is also found in the *Sentences* of Peter Lombard, on which Aquinas is commenting in the *Scriptum*. Lombard, too, ascribes it to Ambrose; *Sent.* IV, d. 12, chao. 5. In *In IV Sent.*, d. 12, Exposition of the Text, Aquinas only lightly treats that saying of "Ambrose."

Catena Aurea apparently provided the impetus for their engagement and incorporation into his later account of Eucharist.[89]

As for the Damascene, there are some citations in the *Scriptum*, but fewer than in the *Summa*. Again, the statement about the conversion happening by the power of the Holy Spirit "alone" is quoted,[90] and Aquinas's handling of that saying parallels what he will do in the *Summa*.[91] We meet again John's statement of the divinity *joining* the bread and wine to itself;[92] familiar, too, is Aquinas's response, that John is thinking here of the appearances of the bread and wine, that what was bread is no longer bread. And John is cited[93] to confirm that there is a change, that bread and wine have passed into (*transit*) the body and blood of Christ. But the Damascene is otherwise silent; Aquinas does not invoke him, as with the burning coal, to talk about the sacrament as stimulating charity and bringing spiritual delight.

Pseudo-Dionysius, in contrast, pops up relatively frequently in these distinctions in the *Scriptum*; indeed there are more references to Dionysius in these distinctions than in the corresponding questions in the *Tertia Pars*. The use of Dionysius here parallels the use in the *Summa*: this sacrament is perfective,[94] and, it can be added, the perfection of all the sacraments;[95] Christ is (truly) present;[96] Judas was given the Eucharist at the Last Supper;[97] and the consecrator should always receive.[98] The discussion of infant reception[99] is similarly restricted in the *Scriptum* to the second chapter of the *Ecclesiastical Hierarchy*; here, too, there is no reference to the final chapter of that writing.

89. The quote in *ST* III, q. 82, a. 1, ob 2 (see note 36 above) from the *Opus imperfectum*, falsely ascribed to Chrysostom, that every holy person is a priest, is also found in the *Scriptum*: *In IV Sent.*, d. 13, a. 1, qc. 1, ob 1.

90. *In IV Sent.*, d. 8, q. 2, a. 3, ob 1.

91. *In IV Sent.*, d. 8, q. 2, a. 3, ad 1: "dictio exclusive adjuncta principali agenti non excludit agens instrumentale: non enim sequitur: solus hic faber facit cultellum; ergo martellus nihil est operatus est. Virtus enim instrumenti non est nisi quaedam redundantia virtutis agentis principalis; unde in toto actio non attribuitur instrument, sed principali agenti, secundum Philosophum; et propter hoc, ex hoc quod dicitur, quod sola virtute Spiritus Sancti fit huiusmodi conversio, non excluditur virtus instrumentalis, quae est in verbis praemissis."

92. *In IV Sent.*, d. 11, q. 1, a. 1.

93. *In IV Sent.*, d. 11, q. 1, a. 3, qc. 1, *sed contra*.

94. *In IV Sent.*, d. 8, q. 1, qc. 1, ob 1/ad 1.

95. *In IV Sent.*, d. 8, q. 1, a. 2, qc. 1, *sed contra*.

96. *In IV Sent.*, d. 11, q. 3, a. 2, qc. 1, *sed contra*.

97. *In IV Sent.*, d. 9, q. 1, qc. 1, *sed contra*; d. 11, q. 3, a. 2, qc. 1, *sed contra*.

98. *In IV Sent.*, d. 12, q. 3, a. 2, qc. 2, resp.

99. *In IV Sent.*, d. 9, q. 1, a. 5, qc. 4, ob 1/ad 1.

In the *Summa*, the *Ecclesiastical Hierarchy* is the main text of reference, supplemented by Epistle 8. In the *Scriptum*, the *Ecclesiastical Hierarchy* continues to be prominent, providing the overwhelming majority of the references. But in the *Scriptum*, Aquinas also makes use of the *Divine Names* to teach the Eucharist. For Dionysius, as in chapter 4 of the *Divine Names*, love is transformative, unitive, drawing the lover out of himself and into the beloved.[100] In a few places in the *Scriptum*,[101] Aquinas neatly juxtaposes these thoughts about love with the Augustine of the *Confessions* (Book VII) on spiritual food. Spiritual food is unlike bodily food. Bodily food is taken into the eater, is transformed into the eater. Spiritual food changes the one who eats into itself. And so in the Eucharist, the recipient in love passes into Christ, is assimilated to the beloved. Aquinas does not cite the *Divine Names* in treating Eucharist in the *Summa*, but he surely has retained its insight in describing in the *Summa* the sacramental eating that is spiritual.

Conclusion

In 2007, Pope Benedict issued a letter on the occasion of the sixteenth centenary of the death of St. John Chrysostom.[102] The pope's appreciation of this great bishop and homilist is deep and wide ranging, praising John for his doctrinal orthodoxy, for his skill in making Scripture accessible to the faithful, and for his commitment to peace and ecclesiastical unity. As is fitting of one whom the pope esteems as the "Doctor of Eucharist," Pope Benedict in this letter singles out John's eucharistic teaching for especial praise—for its stress on love, worthiness, unity, and a commitment to an ethics of love that issues from eucharistic belief and practice. In the conclusion to this letter, the pope also includes his oft-stated hope that today's theologians will make the Fathers their ever-firmer reference point, that is, that they will read the Fathers, learn from them, build on them.

100. *In IV Sent.*, d. 13, q. 2, a. 1, ob 1.

101. For the quote from the *Confessions*, see, e.g., *In IV Sent.*, d. 8, q. 1, a. 3, qc. 1, resp.; for the combination of Pseudo-Dionysius on love, and being drawn into God, and Augustine's insight about incorporation into Christ, see d. 12, q. 2, a. 1, qc. 1, ad 3; d. 9, q. 1, a. 1, qc. 1, ob 2/ad 2.

102. "Letter of his Holiness Benedict XVI on the Occasion of the 16th Centenary of the Death of St. John Chrysostom," Accessed May 8, 2018, https://w2.vatican.va/content/benedict-xvi/en/letters/2007/documents/hf_ben-xvi_let_20070810_giovanni-crisostomo .html.

With all this, Thomas Aquinas would most assuredly agree.[103] He has listened attentively to the Fathers, East as well as West, and has rooted his own teaching firmly in the tradition, in the process constructing a theology that is distinctive and still itself worthy of our attention. Thomas's practice as theologian, anticipating as it does the pope's instructions and showing how fruitful the engagement with the Fathers can be, gives further resonance to the pope's words and may itself inspire today's theologians.

103. Recall in this regard Aquinas's view of the Eucharist as sacrament of charity. The loving encounter with Christ in the sacrament will promote further love of God as well as love of neighbor. For the Eucharist as stimulating loving action, see *ST* III, q. 79, a. 1, ad 2, quoted above in the text (in particular for the comment of Pope Gregory the Great and the quoting of 2 Cor 5:14); for the agreement with Chrysostom in particular, see *ST* III, q. 79, a. 6c, quoted above in the text (and in note 52).

Conclusion

Reading Thomas Aquinas and the Greek Fathers Together for the Renewal of Theology

ANDREW HOFER, OP

Someone could object, even after reading this volume's chapters, that pairing Thomas Aquinas and the Greek Fathers seems to be an odd juxtaposition. To state the obvious, Thomas Aquinas is only one theologian, a Latin theologian who lived in Italian, French, and German cities in the thirteenth century, and the many Greek Fathers are found throughout the first several centuries of Christianity on three continents. Who can even give a list of all the Greek Fathers? Various outstanding Fathers can be quickly named. But there is no exhaustive, commonly accepted list of who counts as a Greek Father. Thomas Aquinas is singular, and the Greek Fathers are, in a certain sense, innumerable.

Pairing them for study is not meant to suggest that the two terms are equivalent in their stature or work. The Greek Fathers, who continued to reflect on revelation in the same language as that of the New Testament writers, give an incalculable contribution to Christian thinking by their early witness to Sacred Tradition, such as through the ancient ecumenical councils. Among all teachers, Thomas Aquinas has an unparalleled influence according to Rome's judgments on theology, such as articulated at the Second Vatican Council and in the Code of Canon Law for the theological formation of future priests.[1] The individual studies in this volume

---

1. Second Vatican Council, *Optatam Totius*, Decree on Priestly Training (1965), no. 16, *Codex Iuris Canonici* (CIC) 252 §3. All quotations of official ecclesial documents are taken from the Vatican website, www.vatican.va, when available.

can excite us to do further work in focused areas of research in Aquinas and the Greek Fathers. These studies can also raise larger questions about Greek patristic and Thomistic study in the theological enterprise today. Because of the mid-twentieth-century tensions in the history of theological discourse, some may wonder whether such considerations would fit within the parameters of the debates among French neo-scholastic and *ressourcement* theologians, evidenced by articles from 1946. At that time, Marie-Michel Labourdette, Dominican editor of *Revue Thomiste*, wrote an essay on two projects of the Jesuits of Fourvière recently begun that he considered important in raising fundamental questions about the nature of theology.[2] These two projects were *Sources Chrétiennes*, a series of accessible editions and French translations of early works such as Gregory of Nyssa's *Life of Moses*, and *Théologie*, a series of studies that included Henri Boulliard's *Conversion et grâce chez saint Thomas d'Aquin: Étude historique*, Jean Daniélou's *Platonisme et Théologie mystique: Essai sur la doctrine spirituelle de saint Grégoire de Nysse*, and Henri de Lubac's *Corpus mysticum: L'Eucharistie et l'Église au Moyen-Âge* and *Surnaturel: Études historiques*. Although appreciative of much of their work, Labourdette also expressed grave reservation. He thought that the Jesuits threatened the permanency of the truth. For example, he singles out for censure a passage from Bouillard that includes this warning: "A theology that is not current is a false theology."[3] The Jesuits quickly replied with a passionate appeal.[4] They charge Labourdette with such offenses as: "He feared just now that a certain exaltation of the Fathers might occur to the detriment of the great Doctor."[5] From Rome, Reginald Garrigou-Lagrange famously contributed to the debate in 1946 by dropping what Aidan Nichols has called "his atom bomb," an article alleging that the *nouvelle théologie* takes us back to the heresy of modernism.[6]

2. Marie-Michel Labourdette, OP, "La théologie et ses sources," *Revue Thomiste* 46 (1946): 353–71.
3. "*Une* théologie qui ne serait pas actuelle serait une théologie fausse" (emphasis original). See Labourdette, "La théologie et ses sources," 365, citing Henri Bouillard, SJ, *Conversion et grâce chez saint Thomas d'Aquin: Étude historique* (Paris: Aubier, Éditions Montaigne, 1944), 26.
4. The Jesuits of Fourvière, "La théologie et ses sources: Réponse aux Études critiques de la *Revue Thomiste* (mai-août 1946)," *Recherches de Science Religieuse* 33 (1946): 385–401.
5. "Il craignait tout à l'heure qu'une certaine exaltation des Pères ne se fît au détriment du grand Doctor." See Jesuits of Fourvière, "La théologie et ses sources," 389.
6. Réginald Garrigou-Lagrange, "La nouvelle théologie, où va-t-elle?," *Angelicum* 23 (1946): 126–45. For a revised English version, see Suzanne M. Rini, trans., "Where Is the New Theology Leading Us?," *Josephinum Journal of Theology* 18 (2011): 63–78. For analysis, see Aidan Nichols, OP, "Thomism and the *nouvelle théologie*," *The Thomist* 64 (2000): 1–19,

Garrigou-Lagrange selects the same line from Bouillard to begin his attack. The neo-scholastic battle against the *nouvelle théologie* seemed to be won in Rome by Pius XII's encyclical *Humani Generis* (1950) and in the various silencings and exiles of the *ressourcement* theologians in the following years. Yet people did not know that John XXIII on January 25, 1959, would call for a new ecumenical council at the Vatican, one that would see the prominence of the *ressourcement* and also be the first time that an ecumenical council would single out one theologian for priestly formation: "the students should learn to penetrate them [the mysteries of salvation] more deeply with the help of speculation, with St. Thomas as teacher [*S. Thoma magistro*], and to perceive their interconnections."[7] The conflict between *ressourcement*, which sounded a call for *aggiornamento* to address the changing needs of a time beyond neo-scholasticism, and its neo-scholastic foes does not adequately provide a framework for addressing the opportunities to read Thomas Aquinas and the Greek Fathers for renewing theology immediately after the Council, and still less today.

Now, about sixty years after Pope John XXIII's surprise of calling for the Second Vatican Council, much work needs to be done to renew theology. Some tasks of theology's renewal pertain to its discourse as theocentric and reliant on the Word of God, its unity in the face of the fracturing of theology into subdisciplines and use of methodologies ill-suited to properly theological work, its need for sound philosophy, its ecclesial home, its openness to the new questions of the times, and its pastoral benefit for people's growth in holiness, especially in protecting and promoting the faith of those who are poor, marginalized, or unable to under-

---

at 11. Also, see Brian E. Daley, SJ, "The Nouvelle Théologie and the Patristic Revival: Sources, Symbols, and the Science of Theology," *International Journal of Systematic Theology* 7 (2005): 362–82. For a broad collection of essays, see Gabriel Flynn and Paul D. Murray, eds., *Ressourcement: A Movement for Renewal in Twentieth-Century Theology* (New York: Oxford University Press, 2012). For a new study that sets the movement in its historical context, see Jon Kirwan, *An Avant-Garde Theological Generation: The Nouvelle Théologie and the French Crisis of Modernity*, Oxford Theology and Religion Monographs (Oxford: Oxford University Press, 2018). For an argument in analyzing the extremes and proposing Dominican theology today, see Thomas Joseph White, OP, "The Precarity of Wisdom: Modern Dominican Theology, Perspectivalism, and the Tasks of Reconstruction," in *Ressourcement Thomism: Sacred Doctrine, the Sacraments and the Moral Life*, ed. Reinhard Hütter and Matthew Levering (Washington, DC: Catholic University of America Press, 2010), 92–123.

7. *Optatam Totius*, no. 16 (translation of Latin given in the text altered to be more literal); cf. Second Vatican Council, *Gravissimum Educationis*, Declaration on Christian Education, no. 10. Pope Paul VI noted that never before had an ecumenical council singled out a theologian in this way. See his Apostolic Letter *Lumen Ecclesiae* (November 20, 1974), no. 24.

take theological work. This conclusion hazards an attempt at considering Aquinas and the Greek Fathers together from wide perspectives for the renewal of theology.

Below I sketch some proposals under four headings: how pairing Aquinas and the Greek Fathers can assist in renewing (1) Thomistic studies, (2) the study of Greek patristics, (3) the Orthodox-Catholic or Greek-Latin theological dialogue, and (4) postconciliar developments in the Catholic Church's theology, especially for priestly formation. Then, after noting the nineteenth-century example of Matthias Scheeben's own Thomistic appreciation of the Greek Fathers, I ultimately conclude that continuing to read Thomas Aquinas and the Greek Fathers together can assist the renewal of theology today. While I do not presume that the contributors to this volume agree with my proposals, at times I cite specific chapters to illustrate my argument.

Renewing Considerations of Thomas Aquinas's Theology

The icon of the Madonna and Child that graces this book's cover, probably by Coppo di Marcovaldo around the year 1265 in Orvieto, can be taken as a symbol of Aquinas's Orvieto period of 1261–65.[8] In 1997, Martin Morard proved Aquinas's access to acts of Constantinople II (553) during his Orvieto period, and Morard went on to publish a detailed study of Aquinas's pioneering use in the West of the councils, especially in his work at Orvieto and until the end of his life in 1274.[9] Even before Morard's studies, which significantly expanded our knowledge of Aquinas's research on the Greek Fathers, it was said that Aquinas's compilation of the *Catena Aurea* was a "turning point in the history of Catholic dogma."[10] Aquinas's Orvieto period includes initiating and completing much of the *Catena Aurea*, which cites (according to one scholar's count) fifty-seven Greeks and twenty-two

8. For information on the painting and its changes subsequent to the original work, see Susan Barahal, "Repaint, Reframe, Renew: Updating Sacred Images during the Early Italian Renaissance" (PhD diss., Boston University, 2016, 17, 130–32, and 140–47; see also fig. 44 on p. 341, and fig. 59 on p. 356).

9. Martin Morard, "Une source de saint Thomas d'Aquin: Le deuxième concile de Constantinople (553)," *Revue des Sciences Philosophiques et Théologiques* 81 (1997): 21–56, and idem, "Thomas d'Aquin lecteur des conciles," *Archivum Franciscanum Historicum* 98 (2005): 211–365.

10. See I. T. Eschmann, "A Catalogue of St. Thomas's Works: Bibliographical Notes," in Etienne Gilson, *The Christian Philosophy of St. Thomas Aquinas*, trans. L. K. Shook (New York: Random House, 1956), 397.

Latins.[11] Based upon his own introduction to the *Catena* on Mark, and the historical context, we see that the compilation of the *Catena* was the occasion for Aquinas to commission translations of Greek commentaries, including those by Origen and Theophylact of Ochrid.[12] Now, just as this large Orvieto painting of the Mother of God (almost eight feet by four and a half feet wide) clearly follows the Greek Christian tradition of icons, but has a Western and specifically thirteenth-century Italian form, so too Aquinas became immersed in the Greek Fathers and first ecumenical councils, and expressed their teaching on a vast literary canvas appropriate to his time and place. Moreover, the purpose of Aquinas's theology and this Orvieto icon is the same: right thinking and worship of the living God come close to us in the Incarnation. Aquinas received the Christian tradition from the best sources, and passed on what he received with a distinctively magisterial contribution.

In his *Orthodox Readings of Aquinas*, Marcus Plested perceptively writes, "Taken in the round, Thomas's profound commitment to Greek patristic and conciliar sources and the practical steps he took to extend the volume of such material available in Latin stand out by comparison with his contemporaries. One might even go so far as to characterize his theology as being *ad mentem patrum*."[13] Plested's suggestion that Thomas's theology could be called "to the mind of the fathers" applies to Aquinas what Georges Florovsky held about his own neo-patristic synthesis.[14] Florovsky was adapting the phrase *ad mentem Thomae*, which became popular through the Thomistic movement inaugurated by Pope Leo XIII's *Aeterni Patris* (1879), also given the title *De philosophia christiana ad mentem Sancti Thomae Aquinatis Doctoris Angelici in scholis catholicis instauranda*.[15] Rather than *ad mentem Thomae*, Florovsky proposed *ad mentem patrum*. This contrast between the two also, in certain but not all ways, played out

11. See C. G. Geenen, "Saint Thomas et les Pères," *Dictionnaire de Théologie Catholique* 15, no. 1 (1946): cols. 738–61, at col. 743.

12. See chap. 2 on Origen and chap. 11 Theophylact, by Jörgen Vijgen and Jane Sloan Peters, respectively, in this volume.

13. Marcus Plested, *Orthodox Readings of Aquinas*, Changing Paradigms in Historical and Systematic Theology (Oxford: Oxford University Press, 2012), 20.

14. Plested, *Orthodox Readings of Aquinas*, 20n43. For a brief analysis of what Florovksy called in his theological testament "the Neo-Patristic Synthesis," which explicitly includes the need to be *ad mentem patrum*, see Paul Gavrilyuk, *Georges Florovsky and the Russian Religious Renaissance*, Changing Paradigms in Historical and Systematic Theology (Oxford: Oxford University Press, 2014), 261–63.

15. For a study of the title of this encyclical, see Georges Van Riet, "Le titre de l'encyclique 'Aeterni Patris': Note historique," *Revue Philosophique de Louvain* 1982 (45): 35–63.

in those mid-twentieth-century Roman Catholic debates between *ressourcement* theologians and neo-scholastics.[16] Plested's idea that Thomas himself taught *ad mentem patrum* has much merit. In fact, Leo XIII's *Aeterni Patris* suggests as much in quoting Cardinal Cajetan's statement: "because [Aquinas] most venerated the ancient doctors of the Church, in a certain way he seems to have inherited the intellect of all."[17] Moreover, it should not be missed that *Aeterni Patris*, which did in fact inaugurate a renewal of Christian philosophy *ad mentem Thomae*, has more references to the early Greek Father Clement of Alexandria's *Stromata* than to Aquinas's works.[18]

If we have an emphasis on Thomas himself being *ad mentem patrum*, could we say that Thomas's theology is *ad mentem doctorum Graecorum*? In some sense, yes, most certainly. We ought to be true to his own vision. If generations have interpreted Thomas's theology with one Greek in mind—a fourth-century BC pagan philosopher by the name of Aristotle—how much more could we say that Thomas's theology is indebted to early Greek Christian thinkers?[19] In his *Summa Theologiae*, Thomas clearly ranks the holy Doctors of the Church ahead of the philosophers, and both Doctors and philosophers contribute to the work of interpreting the Bible. Consider Aquinas's treatment of authorities in the work of *sacra doctrina*:

> Sacred doctrine makes use also of the authority of philosophers in those questions in which they were able to know the truth by natural reason, as Paul quotes a saying of Aratus: "As some also of your own poets said: For we are also his offspring" (Acts 17:28). Nevertheless, sacred doctrine makes use of these authorities as extrinsic and probable arguments; but properly uses the authority of the canonical Scriptures as an incontrovertible proof, and the authority of the doctors of the Church as one that may properly be used, yet merely as probable. For our faith rests upon the revelation made to the apostles and prophets who wrote the canonical books, and not on the revelations (if any such there are) made to other doctors.[20]

16. Hans Urs von Balthasar protests: "We are not ingenuous enough to prefer a 'neopatristic theology' to a 'neoscholastic' theology!" See his *Presence and Thought: An Essay on the Religious Philosophy of Gregory of Nyssa*, trans. Mark Sebanc (San Francisco: Ignatius Press, 1995), 10.

17. Cajetan's commentary on *ST* II-II, q. 148, a. 4; Leonine edition., vol. 10, 174. Quoted in *Aeterni Patris*, no. 17.

18. See note 6 referring to *Stromata* 1.16 (*Patrologia Graeca* [PG] 8.795) and 7.3 (PG 9.426), note 8 referring to *Stromata* 1.5 (PG 8.718–19), and note 22 referring to *Stromata* 1.20 (PG 8.818).

19. For the importance of still studying Aristotle in Aquinas, see the preface and collection of essays in Gilles Emery, OP, and Matthew Levering, eds., *Aristotle in Aquinas's Theology* (Oxford: Oxford University Press, 2015).

20. *ST* I, q. 1, a. 8. All translations of the *Summa Theologiae* are taken, with some slight

Within this passage from Aquinas we find what our faith rests upon, and it is not the Fathers, although they are indispensable. As Aquinas says in commenting on Pseudo-Dionysius, "It is necessary to preserve not only those things which are handed down in the holy Scriptures, but also those things which are said by the sacred Doctors, who have preserved Sacred Scripture unblemished."[21] This centering of Aquinas on the written word of God helps us to think of what his theology is all about: God. More important than *ad mentem Thomae*, or *ad mentem patrum*, or more specifically *ad mentem doctorum Graecorum*, is what we could call *ad mentem Dei cum sanctis*. Furthermore, the *sancti* of the *ad mentem Dei cum sanctis* can be considered in two respects: *in via* and *in patria*.

First, considering the saints *in via*, when we study Thomas in terms of the Greek Fathers, we find that he is working not simply on them, as if they were the object of his science, but working with them in approaching the mind of God, who is the object of *sacra doctrina*.[22] The *sancti*, such as the Greek Fathers, lived here on earth and were graced to have insight into the mysteries *in via*. Thomas allows them to be his *doctores* in a process where he learns from them; together, across different times, they travel through this era of faith. Often in the *Summa Theologiae*, in his scriptural commentaries, and elsewhere, Thomas pursues the truth with their explicit guidance. Also, even where Thomas is not invoking their authority, it does not mean that Thomas's reliance upon them is nil. For example, Gilles Emery has noted that in the treatise on the Trinity in *Summa contra Gentiles*, Book IV, Thomas has few authorities beyond Scripture, not in the sense of excluding the Fathers, but of continuing the scriptural work that they were doing.[23]

Second, the *sancti* now participate in the happiness of heaven, sharing in the beatific vision that is the source and end of sacred doctrine. Aquinas writes about the scientific character of *sacra doctrina* in the second article of the *Summa*: "sacred doctrine is a science because it proceeds

---

alterations, from *Summa Theologica*, trans. Fathers of the English Dominican Province (New York: Benziger, 1947).

21. *In Divinis Nominibus* 2.1. My translation.

22. *ST* I, q. 1, a. 7.

23. Emery writes, "It would seem appropriate at this point to suggest that Thomas is here setting out *to provide his own, personal account of Patristic and Conciliar writings, based on scriptural and doctrinal sources. If therefore the heresies are dispelled, it is because the doctrines involved are not what Scripture teaches*" (emphases original). See Gilles Emery, OP, "The Treatise of St. Thomas on the Trinity in the Summa contra Gentiles," in *Trinity in Aquinas*, trans. Heather Buttery (Ypislanti, MI: Sapientia Press, 2003), 71–120, at 93.

from principles established by the light of a higher science, namely, the science of God and the blessed."[24] Aquinas could have simply stopped at saying "the science of God," but he added "and the blessed." *In patria*, the saints already share, by the light of glory, in the knowledge of God according to the degree of their own fullness in charity.[25] Our work here in approaching *ad mentem Dei cum sanctis* recognizes that the holy ones are in heaven, and our knowledge of this sacred teaching is aimed utterly at sharing their joy in beholding God. Aquinas keenly knew the power of the prayer of the saints in the divine plan of predestination.[26] Just as John Chrysostom is said to have been seen by the young Proclus to have St. Paul whispering into his ear at night, so too Aquinas is said to have been assisted by SS. Peter and Paul at night.[27] According to Bernard Gui, Aquinas revealed to his socius Reginald of Piperno:

My son, you have seen the distress I have suffered lately because of that text [from the prophet Isaiah] which I have only now finished explaining. I could not understand it, and I begged our Lord to help me, and tonight he sent his blessed Apostles to me, Peter and Paul, whose intercession I had also begged for; and they have spoken with me and told me all I desire to know.[28]

Gui later comments about Thomas: "O happy master, to whom heaven's Key-bearer opened the gate of the Scriptures, to whom the heaven-climbing master of marvels, Paul, showed secrets of heavenly truth! Happy teacher, already a citizen of heaven while still a wayfarer on earth, conversing with your fellow-citizens while still a pilgrim in the body!"[29] While Chrysostom and Aquinas are both said to have been granted highly unusual heavenly visitors, the power of intercession of those already at rest in heaven is something that those who work in *sacra doctrina* can commonly enjoy.

24. *ST* I, q. 1, a. 2.

25. *ST* I, q. 12, a. 6.

26. See, e.g., *ST* I, q. 23, a. 8.

27. For an analysis of this John Chrysostom story found first in the seventh-century Vita by George of Alexandria and for a catalogue of its reproductions in Byzantine art, see Margaret M. Mitchell, *The Heavenly Trumpet: John Chrysostom and the Art of Pauline Interpretation* (Louisville, KY: Westminster John Knox Press, 2002), 489–93. For a depiction, I recommend especially the Vatican's *Cod. Gr. 766*, fol. 2v, found as plate 1 in Mitchell, *Heavenly Trumpet*, 502.

28. Bernard Gui, *Vita Sancti Thomae Aquinatis*, no. 16, translated in Kenelm Foster, OP, *The Life of Saint Thomas Aquinas: Biographical Documents* (Baltimore: Helicon Press, 1959), 39.

29. Gui, *Vita*, no. 16, in Foster, *Life of Saint Thomas Aquinas*, 39. For an appreciation of this scene by a leading Protestant biblical scholar under the aspect of the wisdom of the implied exegete, see Markus Bockmuehl, *Seeing the Word: Refocusing New Testament Study*, Studies in Theological Interpretation (Grand Rapids, MI: Baker Academic, 2006), 96–99.

Research into Aquinas's sensitivity to the Greek patristic inheritance will continue to yield tremendous results. So many of this volume's chapters are dedicated precisely to what Aquinas learned from the Greek Fathers and how he continued their work. For example, in his chapter, Dominic Legge, shows how Aquinas is able to build on the Greek patristic achievement and continue that work with even more insight into what the Trinity has done for us in the mysteries of Christ. The continued emphasis on the presence of the Greek Fathers in Aquinas's theology, I believe, helps us to present a truer vision of his theology. Even pairing his theology with a Greek Father with whom he had little familiarity, as in the case of Maximus the Confessor, can be helpful to appreciate his contribution to theology, as we see in chapter 8, by Bernhard Blankenhorn.[30] His theology is not about himself or about those upon whom he relies for assistance, but it is about God. We come by faith to the mind of God with the saints now, so as to approach the mind of God with the saints in heaven.

Renewing the Field of Greek Patristic Study

It might seem strained to propose to have a thirteenth-century Latin theologian assist in the renewal of Greek patristic study. Aquinas knew little Greek, and he simply did not have the vast resources, such as the critical editions and learned studies, that we have today in Greek patristics. He makes mistakes that would be understandable in his time but unacceptable in ours. He, like others of his age, thinks that Nemesius of Emesa's *De Natura Hominis* is a work by Gregory of Nyssa, and that the treatises and letters passing under the name of Dionysius the Areopagite were really by Paul's convert in Athens rather than by someone writing around 500 AD. He is ignorant of so much that modern scholars of Greek patristics take for granted. For example, chapter 10, by John Sehorn, displays a significant lacuna of Aquinas's knowledge of the ancient ecumenical councils, as Aquinas did not have access to the teaching of

---

30. Aquinas uses Maximus's name several times and knows him as a "commentator of Dionysius." See *ST* I-II, q. 50, a. 6, arg. 1; cf. *De Veritate*, q. 8, a. 15, sed contra 5, and *De Veritate*, q. 21, a. 2, arg. 2. Scholia on Dionysius sometimes went under the name of Maximus, who may have contributed some of the comments. See Marek Jankowiak and Phil Booth, "A New Date-List of the Works of Maximus the Confessor," in *The Oxford Handbook of Maximus the Confessor*, ed. Pauline Allen and Bronwen Neil (Oxford: Oxford University Press, 2015), 19–83, at 30–31.

Nicaea II (787) on icons. But the following argues that Aquinas can help renew the study of the Greek Fathers, both in terms of our thinking about how to approach the field of Greek patristics and in interpreting individual thinkers and themes from early Christianity.

Aquinas demonstrates the principle, strongly advocated today, of letting ancient authors speak for themselves when commenting on them, as exemplified in his commentary on the *De Divinis Nominibus*, which takes pains to interpret Pseudo-Dionysius through Pseudo-Dionysius. Thomas probably would have been confused by the modern academy's division of "historical theology," as all theology for him is reliant upon the Christian tradition. He rescues Greek patristic study for speculative theology from the dustbin of merely historicist thinking, as he finds a need for the presence of Greek patristics in ongoing Christian thinking. For example, the ancient heresies, the preoccupation of so many doctrinal texts of the Fathers, are options that still need to be addressed. Often when the Fathers write about the heresies of their day, they see those heresies within a genealogy of heresies or imagine their future harm to the faith.[31] Aquinas continues their way of thinking, and carries out the twofold office of the wise not only in propounding the truth, but also in refuting error.[32] The errors that the Fathers fought need to be denounced in every age, as they still have a destructive force. Aquinas says that one reason why there is a general judgment after the particular judgment is that we will not know until the end of the world the extent of the goodness of the preaching of the Apostles and the extent of the harm caused by Arius's error.[33] Thus he wants to ensure that the voices of the Fathers can still be heard over the din of errors that also sprang up in early Christianity.

But whose voices should be heard? Those who teach early Christianity usually have a canon, even if only implicit, that privileges certain writers. Those of greatest prominence today for courses in early Christian studies would include Origen, Gregory of Nyssa, and Maximus the Confessor. These three came to particular prominence as the representative Fathers through the twentieth-century *ressourcement*. None of these is considered a Doctor of the Church, a classification begun in Boniface VIII's pontificate (1294–1303) with the four Latin Doctors of Ambrose, Jerome,

---

31. For a study of the earliest Christian heresy lists, see Geoffrey S. Smith, *Guilt by Association: Heresy Catalogues in Early Christianity* (New York: Oxford, 2015).

32. See the use of Prov 8:7 as the *thema*, or epigraph, at the beginning of *Summa contra Gentiles* and comments on it in *ScG* I, chap. 1.

33. *ST* III, q. 59, a. 5.

Augustine, and Gregory the Great. The classification was broadened in Pius V's pontificate (1566–72) to include four Greek Doctors: Athanasius, Basil the Great, Gregory of Nazianzus, and John Chrysostom. That same pope, the third Dominican friar to be the bishop of Rome, also declared someone who was not a Father of the Church to be a Doctor of the Church. Thus it was that Thomas Aquinas and these four Greek Fathers were added in the same pontificate to expand a liturgical category of commemorating saints as Doctors. By referring back to Thomas's own way of studying Greek patristics, we can have a better sense of the fluidity of the field, as there has never been an official list of Fathers of the Church, unlike Rome's list of Doctors of the Church.

For Aquinas, some of the most important *sancti* are those that he wrote commentaries on: Dionysius, whose *De Divinis Nominibus* gave Aquinas the opportunity to follow in the footsteps of his teacher Albert the Great, who commented on the entire Dionysian corpus, and Boethius, also known as the martyr St. Severinus, a translator and writer so learned about both Greek and Latin traditions, whose *De Trinitate* and *De Hebdomadibus* were of unparalleled interest to Aquinas in the thirteenth century.[34] With the Angelic Doctor as a reference, we are better able to judge who counts, and who does not count, as worthy of study in Greek patristics in times past and present as well as future.

Aquinas usually uses the term *sancti patres* for the saints of the Old Testament, and for those Fathers of the Church who were present at ecumenical councils.[35] Other expressions for invoking the Fathers include *sancti doctores*, *antiqui doctores*, *doctores Ecclesiae*, or simply *sancti* or *doctores* (not to be confused with the scholastic *magistri*).[36] He disapproves of the expression *patres fidei*, as these *sancti* are the faith's Doctors or ex-

---

34. For a single book on each of these figures in Aquinas, see Fran O'Rourke, *Pseudo-Dionysius and the Metaphysics of Aquinas* (Notre Dame, IN: University of Notre Dame Press, 2005), and Ralph McInerny, *Boethius and Aquinas* (Washington, DC: Catholic University of America Press, 1990). See in this volume chap. 7, by Stephen Fields, SJ, for a study of Pseudo-Dionysius and Aquinas on analogy and the importance of their teachings for today. For a study of the Dionysian presence in Aquinas's thinking on Christ, see my "Dionysian Elements in Thomas Aquinas's Christology: A Case of the Authority and Ambiguity of Pseudo-Dionysius," *The Thomist* 72 (2008): 409–42.

35. To take examples from a single question, see *ST* III, q. 2, a. 3, for an example of *sancti patres* as Fathers of the Church present at an ecumenical council and *ST* III, q. 2, a. 11, for an example of reference to the Old Testament saints.

36. For Aquinas's historical sensitivity to which Fathers were writing before Augustine, the scholastic masters following Augustine, and how the teaching of these masters should be considered, see the example of *De Malo* q. 3, a. 14.

positors, not its Fathers.[37] By holding that the authority of the Fathers is intrinsic to the work of *sacra doctrina*, but only probable, as we saw above in *ST* I, q. 1, a. 8, Aquinas avoids some of the exaggeration that would establish the Fathers as the principal authority on theological matters.[38] As bears repeating, he does not think their authority is the same as the Bible's. But he also has a profound respect for their thinking. He gives what is famously called a reverential exposition to writing that makes for difficult interpretation. He says, "If there are found some points in statements of the ancient Fathers not expressed with the caution moderns find appropriate to observe, their statements are not to be ridiculed or rejected; on the other hand neither are they to be overextended, but reverently interpreted."[39]

Always the question in study is the pursuit of truth. What is true? Thomas here follows a venerable tradition. In critiquing Plato, Aristotle says, "it would seem to be obligatory, especially for a philosopher, to sacrifice even one's closest personal ties in defense of the truth. Both are dear to us, yet it is our duty to prefer the truth."[40] Aquinas comments, "While reason prescribes that all men should prefer truth to their friends, this holds in a special way for the philosophers whose calling is to study wisdom, which is knowledge of the truth."[41] While he does not here explicitly take this principle to the next level of *sacra doctrina*, one can think how those who work in theology have a special duty of what is called "obedience to the truth" (1 Pt 1:22). Aquinas found this truth in all sorts

37. *Contra Errores Graecorum* II 41 (epilogue).

38. For one of many examples where theology is considered to be compiling what the Fathers say, see Peter Lombard's prologue to his *Four Books of the Sentences (of the Fathers)*. Some teachers, in both the East and West, do not avert to a possible tension in authority between the Fathers and the Scriptures. For instance, see how the phrase "in accordance with the Scriptures" (1 Cor 15: 3–4) becomes practically replaced with "in accordance with the Fathers," such as at the Lateran Synod of 649 and Constantinople III (680–81), to take two seventh-century examples. For an argument about a gradual scholasticization in early Christological exegesis, which includes an increasing place for the authorities of the Fathers, see my essay "Scripture in the Christological Controversies," in *The Oxford Handbook of Early Christian Biblical Interpretation*, ed. Paul Blowers and Peter Martens (Oxford: Oxford University Press, forthcoming in 2019).

39. *Contra Errores Graecorum* I, prologue, trans. Peter Damian Fehlner, FI, accessed August 22, 2018, https://dhspriory.org/thomas/english/ContraErrGraecorum.htm. Cf. *ST* I, q. 31, a. 4, co.; I, q. 39, a. 5, ad 1.

40. Aristotle, *Nicomachean Ethics*, Book 1, chap. 6 (1096a), trans. W. D. Ross, in *The Basic Works of Aristotle*, ed. Richard McKeon (New York: Random House, 1941), 939.

41. *Commentary on the Nicomachean Ethics*, Book 1, lecture 6, no. 76 in *Commentary on the Nicomachean Ethics*, vol. 1, trans. C. I. Litzinger, OP (Chicago: Henry Regnery, 1964), 34.

of places, and his practice of theology witnesses to this patristic adage he loved: "Truth by whomever it is spoken comes from the Holy Spirit."[42]

Take the examples of Aquinas's uses of Origen and John Chrysostom, two of his most frequently cited authors in the Greek Christian tradition. Origen's legacy is, to put it mildly, mixed, as we see in Jörgen Vijgen's thorough essay in this volume (chap. 2). For instance, Aquinas classifies Origen a "doctor of the Church," but rebukes him harshly in his commentary on John,[43] and knows that another early Greek writer, Epiphanius of Salamis, names Origen the "father of Arius."[44] Origen has both ardent supporters and fierce detractors through history. But was what he said true? Aquinas finds repeatedly in many writings that what Origen said at times was true and what he said at other times was not true. Aquinas is willing to praise and to condemn Origen's thinking precisely because he is a greater friend of truth than of any single writer. John Chrysostom certainly holds a higher reputation than Origen for orthodoxy. Yet Aquinas will even criticize John Chrysostom, whose importance to Aquinas's thinking is seen in chapters 5 and 6, by Gerald Boersma and Brian Dunkle, respectively, when Chrysostom suggests that the Virgin Mary had vainglory and succumbed to human frailty.[45]

Or consider another Greek Doctor, but one not nearly as frequently cited by Aquinas, Gregory of Nazianzus. Gregory holds an eminent authority in the Greek and Latin traditions. Aquinas was so respectful of Gregory's authority that in the *Summa* he repeats the ancient Latin appreciation found in different expressions in the contemporaries Jerome and Rufinus, as chapter 4, by John Baptist Ku, indicates. We focus here on a famous formulation from Gregory of Nazianzus's writing on Christ in *Ep.* 101, one of two Theological Letters to the priest Cledonius. This letter became one of the most celebrated documents in the history of Christology. Gregory writes: "And if it is necessary to speak concisely, something and another are the things from which the Savior is (since the invisible is not the same as the visible and the timeless is not bound by time), but not someone and another. Certainly not! For both things are

---

42. For a study of the sixteen appearances of this comment by Ambrosiaster on 1 Cor 12:3, with variations of text and context, see Serge-Thomas Bonino, OP, "'Toute vérité, quel que soit celui la dit, vient de l'Esprit Saint,' Autour d'une citation de l'*Ambrosiaster* dans le corpus thomasien," *Revue Thomiste* 106 (2006): 101–47.

43. *In Ioannem* 1:1 (lec. 1, no. 58) and 1:3 (lec. 2, no. 76).

44. For an example of Origen as listed among the doctors of the Church, see *ST* I, q. 70, a. 3. For being "the father of Arius," see the *Commentary on Boethius's De Trinitate*, q. 3, a. 4.

45. See *ST* III, q. 27, a. 4, arg. 3 and ad 3.

one thing by the blending together (Τὰ γὰρ ἀμφότερα ἓν τῇ συγκράσει): of God and humanization, of the human and divinization, or however one should call this."[46] The two widely used English translations, where I translate "both things are one thing by the blending together," have simply "one," not "one thing," an ambiguity that hides Gregory's conclusion.[47] By differentiating only the gender of the pronoun (neuter = "something"; masculine = "someone"), Gregory teaches that Christ is from two different "somethings" but is not two different "someones." One might expect him to conclude that Christ is one in the masculine, but he says that Christ is one in the neuter according to the blending together.

But how is Gregory's teaching on this matter received in modern times? Joseph Tixeront, a leading Catholic scholar of the history of dogmas in the early twentieth century, in writing about this passage in Gregory's *Ep.* 101, simply said that Gregory's teaching was not correct.[48] At least he bothered to address the question, which is different from what we find in the gold standard of twentieth-century scholarship on patristic Christology by Aloys Grillmeier. In his influential survey of Christology before Chalcedon, Grillmeier has little time for Gregory's thinking on Jesus.[49] He lumps Gregory together with Basil of Caesarea and Gregory of Nyssa, and writes that their Cappadocian Christology suffers two failures: the use of the Stoic concepts of mixture language for the Incarnation, suggesting to Grillmeier that the unity is on the level of nature, and an insufficient understanding of the distinction between substance and hypostasis. Grillmeier laments that this Cappadocian Christology has neither its path nor its goal stated clearly.[50]

Aquinas treats Gregory more respectfully, and, I would argue, more accurately, than either Tixeront or Grillmeier does. He also provides an

---

46. *Ep.* 101.20–21. My translation. For the Greek text, see Paul Gallay, ed., *Grégoire de Nazianze, Lettres Théologiques*, Sources Chrétiennes 208 (Paris: Cerf, 1974), 36–68, at 44.

47. Translation of *Ep.* 101 by Charles Gordon Browne and James Edward Swallow in *Nicene and Post-Nicene Fathers*, vol. 7, *Cyril of Jerusalem and Gregory of Nazianzus* (Peabody, MA: Hendrickson, 2012 [reprint]), 439–43, at 439–40, and by Lionel Wickham, *On God and Christ: The Five Theological Orations and Two Letters to Cledonius*, Popular Patristics Series (Crestwood, NY: St. Vladimir's Seminary Press, 2002), 155–66, at 157.

48. Joseph Tixeront, *History of Dogmas*, vol. 2, *From St. Athanasius to St. Augustine (318–430)*, trans. Henry L. Brianceau (St. Louis, MO: Herder, 1914), 127.

49. Aloys Grillmeier, SJ, *Christ in Christian Tradition*, vol. 1, *From the Apostolic Age to Chalcedon (451)*, 2nd ed., trans. J. S. Bowden (New York: Sheed and Ward, 1975), 368–70.

50. Grillmeier, *Christ in Christian Tradition*, 1.370. Cf. my *Christ in the Life and Teaching of Gregory of Nazianzus*, Oxford Early Christian Studies (Oxford: Oxford University Press, 2013), 4.

insight into a truth only implicit in Gregory's formulation. After compiling the *Catena Aurea*, where Gregory appears twenty-five times in patristic comments on Luke's Gospel alone, Aquinas wrote the *Tertia Pars* of the *Summa*.[51] Here Aquinas cites Gregory's authority ten times on Christological questions.[52] Most interestingly, in *ST* III, q. 17, a. 1, Aquinas shows that Christ is not only one in the masculine (*unus*), but also one in the neuter (*unum*). Aquinas quotes the *Ep.* 101 passage where Gregory exploits the masculine and neuter genders without offering technical substantives such as nature, person, or supposit. How is Christ one in the neuter for Aquinas? Aquinas interprets the oneness of Christ in the neuter to refer to the one supposit. This demonstrates Aquinas's reliance upon Gregory for precision in explaining the grammar of the Incarnation in his pressing concern to ward off the threat of Nestorianism's dualism.[53]

For one theme in early Christianity that Aquinas sheds light upon, take the example of his treatment of Nestorianism. In a penetrating analysis, Aquinas reviews the three opinions of Peter Lombard on the Incarnation.[54] Aquinas finds that the second opinion is not a mere opinion, but the truth of the Catholic faith, whereas the first and third opinions are forms of Nestorianism; in fact, the last opinion is worse than what Nestorius himself held. When you know what Nestorianism is, you can see how Christologies developed many centuries after Nestorius's fall into his error or something even worse.[55]

51. Cf. a *Corpus Thomisticum* tabulation in Leo J. Elders, SVD, "Santo Tomás de Aquino y los Padres de la Iglesia," *Doctor Communis* 48 (1995): 55–80, at 66. For a brief chronology of Thomas's works, see Jean-Pierre Torrell, OP, *Saint Thomas Aquinas*, vol. 1, *The Person and His Work*, trans. Robert Royal (Washington, DC: Catholic University of America Press, 1996), 327–28. Cf. Louis J. Bataillon, OP, "Saint Thomas et les Pères: De la Catena à la *Tertia Pars*," in *Ordo Sapientiae et Amoris: Image et Message de Saint Thomas d'Aquin*, ed. Carlos-Josaphat Pinto de Oliveira (Fribourg: Éditions Universitaires, 1993), 15–36.

52. *ST* III, q. 2., a. 3, ad 1; q. 16, a. 7, arg. 3; q. 17, a. 1, ad 2 (referring to *Ep.* 101); q. 39, a. 1, co.; q. 39, a. 2, co.; q. 39, a. 3, ad 3 (referring to *Or.* 39); q. 39, a. 3, ad 1 (referring to *Or.* 40); and q. 31, a. 2, ad 2 (referring to *Carm.* 1.1.28). As for the two remaining citations, Aquinas appeals to Gregory in *ST* III, q. 31, a. 3, ad 2, but no text can be found from Gregory to support this position. Also, Aquinas mentions in *ST* III, q. 2, a. 1, arg. 3, that it is clear through John Damascene that Gregory understands Christ's humanity to be deified.

53. See esp. *ST* III, q. 2, a. 6, and III, q. 17, a. 1, co. For Aquinas, Nestorians thought of Christ not only as two in the neuter, but also as two in the masculine.

54. *ST* III, q. 2, a. 6.

55. For analysis of Aquinas on Nestorianism in *ST* III, q. 2, a. 6, see Joseph Wawrykow, "Hypostatic Union," in *The Theology of Thomas Aquinas*, ed. Rik van Nieuwenhove and Joseph Wawrykow (Notre Dame, IN: University of Notre Dame Press, 2005), chap. 10, 222–51, at 234–37. For an application of Aquinas's work on Nestorianism to various modern theologies,

Moreover, something remains inadequate in theology if the work is only about the Fathers of the Church, without reference to future theological achievement, not least of which is that of Thomas Aquinas. Khaled Anatolios provides us with an example in his penetrating study in chapter 3 in this volume. He discusses the commonality and complementarity of Athanasius and Thomas Aquinas on their ontological grammar and the saving work of Christ, against an all-too-common way of contrasting Eastern and Western soteriologies. On Aquinas's attention to Christ's psychological interiority on the Cross, Anatolios writes, "Aquinas's development of this more interiorized and more concretely existential conception of Christ's sacrifice not only may but also must be considered as a necessary extension and elaboration of Athanasius's ontological framework." Such an insight could be applied to other theological areas where Aquinas's work must be considered as a necessary extension and elaboration of what the Greek Fathers achieved. Aquinas repeatedly brings out the insights of the Fathers and gives his elaborations upon those insights, allowing us to share in their mutual vision.

In renewing Thomistic study with an emphasis on the Greek Fathers, we should not have as the object of our contemplation Thomas Aquinas, but God. So, too, in renewing the study of Greek patristics with an emphasis on Thomas as a guide, we find that the study of Greek patristics itself should be reoriented to questions concerning truth in the study of God.

Renewing Orthodox-Catholic, Greek-Latin Theological Conversations

Gilles Emery has written a marvelous brief article on Aquinas and the Greek Fathers, in which he says: "For St. Thomas, the ressourcement of theology necessarily requires the study of the Greek Fathers as much as the Latin Fathers. He proposes to develop neither a 'Western' nor an 'Eastern' theology, but a Catholic theology that benefits from the foundations laid by the patristic tradition recognized in its fullness." Emery then shows the opportunity that Aquinas gives for our own work: "The objective of ecumenical Catholic fullness is at the heart of the project to

---

especially that of Karl Rahner, see Thomas Joseph White, OP, "The Ontology of the Hypostatic Union," in *The Incarnate Lord: A Thomistic Study in Christology*, Thomistic Ressourcement 5 (Washington, DC: Catholic University of America Press, 2015), chap. 1, 73–125.

which St. Thomas continues even today to invite his readers."[56] Aquinas was interested in the Greek Fathers in part because of his concern for what we also could call his "ecumenical Catholic fullness."[57]

In her essay in this volume (chap. 11), Jane Sloan Peters connects the impetus for Aquinas's commissioned translations of Theophylact's commentaries on the Gospel accounts of Mark, Luke, and John with the contemporary Latin efforts for union with the Greeks. Aquinas's interest can be considered an example of how he thinks a common ground is paramount for having a fruitful theological conversation. In an important Quodlibetal question, he writes concerning authorities: "And if disputing with schismatics, who accept Old and New Testament, but not the teaching of our saints (such schismatics as the Greeks, for example), it is necessary to dispute from the authorities of the New and Old Testaments and of those doctors whom they accept."[58] Aquinas does not state that this is a merely linguistic problem or a theological variance in ways of speaking among Greeks and Latins (that may go beyond simply saying the same things but in different words), both of which he does elsewhere many times.[59] Rather, he states a fact about the need for interlocutors having a common ground. Aquinas perhaps most clearly articulates the common ground approach in Book 1 of the *Summa contra Gentiles*, as he wants to emphasize that humans, even without revelation, still have reason and can think.[60] Yet, in Christian theology, it is important to have authorities. So, who are the Doctors that the Greeks accept? One should not quickly conclude only Greek Doctors.

A keen proponent of Constantinople II (553), Aquinas develops an argument in the *Summa contra Gentiles*, Book IV, based upon the authorities that this ecumenical council accepts.[61] He quotes the fifth synod in

---

56. Gilles Emery, OP, "A Note on St. Thomas and the Eastern Fathers," in *Trinity, Church, and the Human Person: Thomistic Essays*, trans. John Baptist Ku, OP (Naples, FL: Sapientia Press, 2007), 193–207, at 207.

57. For an emphasis on the author's intention in arriving at the truth in ecumenical fullness, see the 1973 article by Yves Congar, OP, translated as "The Ecumenical Value and Scope of Some Hermeneutical Principles of Saint Thomas Aquinas" by Andrew Jacob Cuff and Innocent Smith, OP, *Pro Ecclesia* 26 (2017): 186–201.

58. *Quodlibet* IV, q. 9, a. 3.

59. See the examples of: *De Veritate* q. 4, a. 3, co.; *ST* I, q. 29, a. 2, ad 2; and *ST* I, q. 33, a. 1, ad 1.

60. *ScG* I, chap. 2.3.

61. For an analysis of Aquinas on the fifth ecumenical council, see Morard, "Une source de saint Thomas d'Aquin." Some theologians today like to speak of the "Chalcedonian faith." Thomas cites sources from Ephesus (431) twice as frequently as he cites from Chalcedon

its declaration: "In all matters we follow the holy Fathers and Doctors of the Church: Athanasius, Hilary, Basil, Gregory the theologian, and Gregory of Nyssa, Ambrose, Augustine, Theophilus, John of Constantinople, Cyril, Leo, Proclus; and we accept what they have set down on the correct belief and the condemnation of heretics."[62] Notice how Constantinople II gives a list of "fathers and doctors," and makes no discrimination between the Greeks and Latins. Aquinas then goes on to single out one Latin Doctor from this Greek council's list for his argument: "But it is manifest from many testimonies of Augustine, especially in his *On the Trinity* and his *Exposition of John*, that the Holy Spirit is from the Son. It must, then, be conceded that the Holy Spirit is from the Son just as he is from the Father."[63] From that appeal to authority, Aquinas goes on to argue from evident reasons (*evidentibus rationibus*).[64]

Let us consider for a moment the significance of this line of thought. Aquinas's appeal to both Greek and Latin Doctors does not come as the fruit of a merely thirteenth-century Western perspective. He turns to an ancient ecumenical council held in Constantinople, and thinks that this is the approach of the Church. His frustration is that he does not understand why some Greeks of his day would not accept the authority of Doctors that are Latin, when Constantinople II follows certain Greek and Latin Fathers "in all matters." Of course, in Thomistic fashion, one could apply Thomas's own principle of preference for the truth regardless of who is saying it, as even the authority of a Doctor does not have the surety of Sacred Scripture.

Aquinas knows that theology is not simply a matter of quoting authorities. To quote a common authority may determine what the right answer is, but it does not mean that people are led to understand. This is why he continues in this Quodlibetal question quoted above with the following stress with respect to arguments: "Also, a certain kind of teaching disputation in the schools is not for removing error, but for instructing hearers so that they may be led to an understanding of the truth which is proposed, then it is necessary to rely on arguments which investigate

---

(451) in the *Summa Theologiae*'s questions on Christ (*ST* III, qq. 1–59). Constantinople II continued Chalcedon's teaching in a more explicitly Cyrillian, and thus Ephesian, way. Aquinas cites this fifth synod five times in *ST* III, qq. 1–59: *ST* III, q. 2, a. 1, ad 1; *ST* III, q. 2, a. 3, twice in *ST* III, q. 2, a. 6, and *ST* III, q. 25, a. 1, sed contra.

62. *ScG* IV, chap. 24.6, trans. Charles J. O'Neil, in *Summa Contra Gentiles Book Four: Salvation* (Notre Dame, IN: University of Notre Dame Press, 1975 [reprint]), 136.

63. *ScG* IV, chap. 24.6.

64. *ScG* IV, chap. 24.7.

the foundation of the truth, and which make known how what is said is true." Aquinas thinks that it is important to get to the foundation, or very depth, of the truth (*veritatis radicem*) through argumentation. "Otherwise," he concludes, "if a teacher answers a question with mere authorities, some hearer will be certain that it is so, but he will acquire nothing of knowledge and of understanding, and he will go away empty."[65]

This way of thinking can be helpful in the Catholic-Orthodox dialogue on issues that need more scholarly attention. Aquinas used his argument in *Summa contra Gentiles*, Book IV, quoted above, to support the teaching of the *filioque*, which is clearly taught by Augustine and, Aquinas maintains, has compatibility with the teachings of the Greeks.[66] He also turns repeatedly in his studies of Eastern and Western differences to sacramental practices, such as regarding the matter of the bread used for the Eucharist or the rite of Baptism.[67] One example of an important theological inquiry needing more attention to authorities and argumentation regards the conflicting Orthodox and Catholic theological accounts of marriage and how either divorce or the death of a spouse affects the possibility of a future marriage, penance, and reception of Holy Communion.

In a section of *A Pastoral Statement on Orthodox/Roman Catholic Marriages* (1990), titled "The Enduring Nature of Marriage," the Joint Committee of Orthodox and Catholic Bishops shows that the Orthodox Church treats subsequent marriages in similar terms—whether or not the spouse in the previous marriage is deceased. The bishops write that for the Orthodox Church, "perpetual monogamy is upheld as the norm of marriage, so that those entering upon a second or subsequent marriage are subject to penance even in the case of widows and widowers." This is compared with what is called "absolute prohibition of divorce" in the Catholic Church. The bishops go on to say: "Out of pastoral consideration and in order better to serve the spiritual needs of the faithful, the Orthodox Church tolerates remarriage of divorced persons under specific circumstances as it permits the remarriage of widows and widowers under specific circumstances." This is compared with the following: "While it is true that the Roman Catholic Church does not grant dissolution of the bond of a consummated sacramental marriage, it remains a question among theologians whether this is founded on a prudential judgment or on the Church's

---

65. *Quodlibet* IV, q. 9, a. 3.

66. For Aquinas's position of compatibility, see esp. *ST* I, q. 36, a. 2.

67. For examples from the *Summa*, see *ST* III, q. 65, a. 5, ad 2 and 3, and *ST* III, q. 74, a. 4.

perception that it lacks the power to dissolve such a bond." Immediately after this statement, the bishops draw this conclusion to the enduring nature
of marriage regarding a revision of the Catholic understanding—without
reference to a revision of the Orthodox understanding:

Study of the history of our various traditions has led us to conclude that some
at times may raise a particular theological explanation of relatively recent origin
to the level of unchangeable doctrine. The Second Vatican Council's "Pastoral
Constitution on the Church in the Modern World" stated that there was need
for a renewal of the Roman Catholic Church's understanding and approach to
its teaching on marriage. That council implicitly recognized that teaching on
marriage had frequently proceeded from a biological and juridical point of view
rather than from an interpersonal and existential one.[68]

This conclusion seems rather lopsided, and the brief statement does
not proceed from either sufficient authorities or argumentation. A return
to the Greek Fathers, before the Byzantine Church's concessions to imperial laws, could assist in showing the greater complexity of early Christianity than is sometimes thought.[69] For example, after relating that Christian
emperors gave many divorce laws, John Meyendorff writes: "No Father
of the Church ever denounced these imperial laws as contrary to Christianity."[70] To take one example, however, Meyendorff seems unaware that
Gregory of Nazianzus rails against the divorce laws of the emperor during
the time of Theodosius I. Gregory calls divorce "completely disagreeable
with our laws, even if those of the Romans [of the empire] judge otherwise."[71] Meyendorff finds that after Emperor Leo VI (d. 912), "the Church

68. Joint Committee of Orthodox and Catholic Bishops, "A Pastoral Statement on Or-
thodox/Roman Catholic Marriages," October 5, 1990, Johnstown, PA, http://www.usccb
.org/beliefs-and-teachings/ecumenical-and-interreligious/ecumenical/orthodox/pastoral
-orthodox-catholic-marriage.cfm.

69. For an important work on the marriage and divorce in the early Church, see Henri
Crouzel, SJ, L'Église primitive face au divorce: Du premier au cinquième siècle (Paris: Beauchesne, 1971). For his reply to his opponents regarding the proper use of history on the question
of remarriage after divorce, see his "Divorce et remariage dans l'Église primitive," Nouvelle
Revue Théologique 98 (1976): 891–917, translated by Michelle K. Borras as "Divorce and Remarriage in the Early Church: Some Reflections on Historical Methodology," Communio 41
(2014): 472–503.

70. John Meyendorff, Marriage: An Orthodox Perspective, 2nd ed. (Crestwood, NY:
St. Vladimir's Seminary Press, 1975), 63.

71. Gregory of Nazianzus, Ep. 144.4. Cf. Gregory of Nazianzus, Or. 37.7–8. Cf. John M.
Rist, "Divorce and Remarriage in the Early Church: Some Historical and Cultural Reflections," in Remaining in the Truth of Christ: Marriage and Communion in the Catholic Church,
ed. Robert Dodaro, OSA (San Francisco: Ignatius Press, 2014), 64–92.

was obliged not only to bless marriages which it did not approve, but even to 'dissolve' them (i.e., give 'divorces')."[72] A return to Aquinas would similarly shed light on the indissolubility of marriage.[73] A greater emphasis on the arguments and authorities regarding the permanence of marriage in both East and West, with the help of the Greek Fathers and Aquinas, could be advantageous to the present Orthodox-Catholic dialogue.

Aquinas died on the way to the Second Council of Lyons (1274), where he would have met representatives from Constantinople and heard the Profession of Faith of Emperor Michael VIII Paleologus that included teaching on marriage.[74] Some of Aquinas's writings were translated into Greek in the following century and influenced various efforts for union between East and West.[75] One writing that Aquinas offered in support of union efforts, his *Contra Errores Graecorum*, is, on the one hand, of limited value owing to spurious authorities in the text he was given. But, on the other hand, his work does importantly evince his concern for correct translation and what could be called cross-cultural theology.[76] In its two parts, Aquinas sets forth authorities either to be clarified or to be cited in confirmation of the true faith. Aquinas's project of clarifying and confirming the faith are two tasks that are much needed in the present ecumenical project of the East-West dialogue. Moreover, the two sides need to hear argumentation so as not to go away empty. Ecumenists who engage in the writings of the Greek Fathers and Aquinas have the chance to be well prepared for serious argumentation, without which there will not be understanding.[77]

---

72. Meyendorff, *Marriage*, 29.

73. E.g., *ST Suppl.* q. 67, a. 1, and his *Commentary on the Gospel of St. Matthew*, chap. 19, lect. 1, no. 1559.

74. Found in Heinrich Denzinger, *Compendium of Creeds, Definitions, and Declarations on Matters of Faith and Morals*, 43rd ed., ed. Peter Hünermann (San Francisco: Ignatius Press, 2012), no. 860.

75. See Plested, *Orthodox Readings of Aquinas*, for the reception of Aquinas's works in the Greek East.

76. For a pertinent argument on (1) translation as difference, (2) translation as discovery, (3) translation and pedagogical structures, and (4) translation and emblems, see Mark D. Jordan, "The 'Greeks' and Thomas Aquinas's Theology," *Journal of Orthodox Christian Studies* 1 (2018): 155–66.

77. For an argument regarding deification and the Trinity, see Bruce D. Marshall, "Ex Occidente Lux? Aquinas and Eastern Orthodox Theology," *Modern Theology* 20 (2004): 23–50.

Renewing the Catholic Church's Practice of Theology, Especially for Priestly Formation

In a strange twist of twentieth-century Catholic theology, the *ressource-ment* movements that prepared for the Second Vatican Council gave way to theologies that neglect the significance of the patristic and Thomistic traditions. Here I would like to consider some aspects of postconciliar Catholic theology, as seen in: the example of Karl Rahner (arguably the most influential Catholic theologian after the Second Vatican Council), the Congregation for Catholic Education's *Instruction on the Study of the Fathers of the Church in the Formation of Priests* (1989), the International Theological Commission's *Theology Today: Perspectives, Principles, and Criteria* (2011), and the Congregation for Clergy's new *Ratio Fundamentalis Institutionis Sacerdotalis* (2016).

In 1970, Karl Rahner writes: "in contemporary theology regarded as a whole, there is a strange silence on the subject of Thomas." Interestingly, Rahner finds that Thomas has receded to being ... a Father of the Church. He comments on this twentieth-century change: "From being, in this peculiarly direct sense, *the* teacher of theology in the theological schools themselves, Thomas has acquired the status of a Father of the Church."[78] In developing his argument about Aquinas, Rahner continues: "From having formerly been a teacher in this direct sense he has become a Father of the Church, an authority belonging to the same dimension as the great philosophers such as Plato or Aristotle, or the great theologians such as Augustine or Origen, more remote, less readily accessible, more isolated than he was before."[79]

Although written some years later, the Congregation for Catholic Education's *Instruction on the Study of the Fathers of the Church in the Formation of Priests* (1989), which refers several times to Thomas Aquinas, whose work is acclaimed as "in complete fidelity to the doctrine of the fathers," perhaps gives a window into that remoteness with which the

---

78. Karl Rahner, "On Recognizing the Importance of Thomas Aquinas," lecture of December 29, 1970, translated in *Theological Investigations*, vol. 13 (New York: Seabury Press, 1975), 3–12, at 3. Emphasis original.

79. Rahner, "On Recognizing the Importance of Thomas Aquinas," 4. For Rahner, Aquinas still has a uniqueness that theologians must take into account, but Rahner does not predict that "some spectacular Thomist renaissance is on the point of breaking out in the Church" (12).

Fathers are seen.[80] The congregation observes: "Today there are many theological concepts or tendencies which, contrary to the indications of *Optatam Totius* (No. 16), pay little attention to the fathers' witness and in general to ecclesiastical tradition, and confine themselves to the direct confrontation of biblical texts with social reality and life's concrete problems with the help of the human sciences." The congregation criticizes that the patristic and medieval achievements are discarded as if they had no real importance: "In such cases, study of the fathers is reduced to a minimum, practically caught up in the rejection of the past."[81] The congregation continues its lament, saying such things as how theologians "think that they are doing theology but are really doing only history, sociology, etc., flattening the contents of the Creed to a purely earthly dimension."[82] The congregation knows that many excellent studies of the Fathers were being produced by scholars, but it finds that such scholarship did not sufficiently influence seminarians.

Perhaps one theoretical model of this dismissal of Thomas can be found in what Karl Rahner came to formulate, about nine years after his address on Aquinas, as his hermeneutics for interpreting the Second Vatican Council.[83] When he received an honorary Doctorate of Humane Letters at the Jesuits' pontifical faculty at Weston, Massachusetts, on April 8, 1979, he divided the history of the Church up into three periods with breaks between each period: from Jesus to Paul, with Paul's mission to the Gentiles, then from Paul to the Second Vatican Council, with the council's birth of the "World Church," and then after the council. Rahner concludes his address in these words:

I tried to make clear with a few problematic considerations that the coming-to-be of a world Church precisely as such does not mean just a quantitative increase in the previous Church, but rather contains a theological break in Church history

---

80. For the reference to Aquinas's fidelity to the Fathers, see *Instruction on the Study of the Fathers of the Church in the Formation of Priests*, II.2.

81. *Instruction on the Study of the Fathers of the Church in the Formation of Priests*, I.1.c. Antonio Orbe, SJ, makes a distinction between the *theoretical* assent of a theologian to the importance of the Fathers and the *practical* neglect of communicating their teaching. See his "The Study of the Fathers of the Church in Priestly Formation," trans. Louis-Bertrand Raymond, *Vatican II: Assessment and Perspectives Twenty-Five Years After (1962–1987)*, vol. 3, ed. René Latourelle, SJ (New York: Paulist Press, 1989), chap. 55, 361–77.

82. *Instruction on the Study of the Fathers of the Church in the Formation of Priests*, I.1.c.

83. Karl Rahner, SJ, "Towards a Fundamental Theological Interpretation of Vatican II," trans. Leo. J. O'Donovan, SJ, *Theological Studies* 40 (1979): 716–27.

that still lacks conceptual clarity and can scarcely be compared with anything except the transition from Jewish to Gentile Christianity. This was the caesura or break which occupied Paul, although one need not think that he reflected with theological adequacy on this transition whose protagonist he was. This is all I really wanted to say. Everything else is but dimly envisaged, and developed perhaps without the necessary systematic clarity. But I did want to draw attention to problems that have scarcely been noticed in previous theology.[84]

Whatever Rahner's intent, his proposal is disastrous for a unified vision of theology.[85] Written as a corrective to theologies that no longer have a distinctive unity as Catholic theology, *Theology Today*, from the International Theological Commission (ITC), is a valuable document and rightly has several emphases on the Fathers of the Church, especially from the Greek tradition, such as when stating: "Great Eastern theologians used the encounter between Christianity and Greek philosophy as a providential opportunity to reflect on the truth of revelation, i.e. the truth of the *logos*." The ITC continues that such Eastern theologians "critically adopted philosophical notions" for the service of the faith, all while they insisted on theology's apophatic dimension.[86] But the ITC could have been clearer when saying that the Fathers of the Church, both East and West, and St. Thomas "remain as reference points for theology today. It is true," continues the ITC, "that certain aspects of prior theological tradition can and must some-

---

84. Rahner, "Towards a Fundamental Theological Interpretation of Vatican II," 726–27. For a comparable essay by Rahner, see his "Dogmen—und Theologiegeschichte—gestern und morgen," *Zeitschrift für katholische Theologie* 99 (1977): 1–24, found in English as "Yesterday's History of Dogma and Theology for Tomorrow," in *Theological Investigations*, vol. 18, trans. Edward Quinn (New York: Crossroad, 1983), 3–34. For an article that sees Rahner and Aquinas as two different options as principal teachers after the council, with an argument for Aquinas, see my "St. Thomas as Teacher in the Introduction to Theology," *Josephinum Journal of Theology* 21 (2014): 146–63. In that article, I also consider what Rahner does in his influential *Foundations of Christian Faith*.

85. See Benedict XVI, "Address to the Roman Curia Offering Them His Christmas Greetings," December 22, 2005, wherein he offers a contrasting approach: "On the one hand, there is an interpretation that I would call 'a hermeneutic of discontinuity and rupture'; it has frequently availed itself of the sympathies of the mass media, and also one trend of modern theology. On the other, there is the 'hermeneutic of reform,' of renewal in the continuity of the one subject-Church which the Lord has given to us. She is a subject which increases in time and develops, yet always remaining the same, the one subject of the journeying People of God."

86. *Theology Today*, no. 66. For other passages on the Fathers, see nos. 23, 27, 28, 32, 65, 75, 81, and 90.

times be abandoned, but the work of the theologian can never dispense with a critical reference to the tradition that went before."[87]

The Fathers do not merely remain in the common memory for the "critical reference" of theologians today as "the tradition that went before." They are authorities who give witness to Sacred Tradition in the first centuries of the Church.[88] Moreover, the Common Doctor has a privileged place in Catholic thought as *magister*, guiding the speculative task of theology, if we want to follow the lead of the Second Vatican Council's *Optatam Totius*, no. 16, and the Code of Canon Law concerning priestly formation. But do we? The ITC's *Theology Today* cites *Optatam Totius*, no. 16, several times, but neglects to mention Thomas's unique place there.

Ratio Fundamentalis Institutionis Sacerdotalis, known also as *The Gift of the Priestly Vocation*, issued in December 2016, carries forward much of the famous paragraph of *Optatam Totius*, no. 16, but it has one significant omission. Compare these two texts, first *Optatam Totius*, no. 16:

Dogmatic theology should be so arranged that these biblical themes are proposed first of all. Next there should be opened up to the students what the Fathers of the Eastern and Western Church have contributed to the faithful transmission and development of the individual truths of revelation. The further history of dogma should also be presented, account being taken of its relation to the general history of the Church. Next, in order that they may illumine the mysteries of salvation as completely as possible, the students should learn to penetrate them more deeply with the help of speculation, under the guidance of St. Thomas [more literally from *S. Thoma magistro*, "with St. Thomas as teacher"], and to perceive their interconnections.[89]

Ratio Fundamentalis Institutionis Sacerdotalis, no. 168:

Dogmatic theology, including sacramental theology, should be taught in a systematic and orderly way. It should begin with the examination of biblical texts. Then the contributions of the Fathers of the Church, from both East and West, should be

---

87. *Theology Today*, no. 79.

88. Cf. *Theology Today*, no. 27.

89. For "A note on the controversy about the place of St. Thomas in ecclesiastical studies," within a commentary on this conciliar document, see Josef Neuner, SJ, "Decree on Priestly Formation," in *Commentary on the Documents of Vatican II*, vol. 2, trans. William Glen-Doepel (New York: Herder and Herder, 1967), 371–404, at 395. Cf. Anthony A. Ankinwale, OP, "The Decree on Priestly Formation, *Optatam Totius*," in *Vatican II: Renewal within Tradition*, ed. Matthew L. Lamb and Matthew Levering (Oxford: Oxford University Press, 2008), 229–50.

studied, in order to illustrate the transmission and development of the understanding of revealed truths. The historical progress of dogmas should be shown. Finally, the seminarians should learn how to penetrate more deeply into the mysteries of salvation and to grasp the connection between them by speculative investigation.

The Congregation for Clergy dropped the reference to St. Thomas.[90] One wonders what will happen in the revised programs of priestly formation throughout the Church's episcopal conferences, as the *Ratio Fundamentalis* serves as the basis for bishops to plan priestly formation. I do not think that omitting Aquinas will increase the seminarians' exposure to the Church's patristic heritage, or that this omission enables priests better to lead people to worship the living God and be transformed in deification, the twofold goal of the sacred liturgy.[91]

The Catholic Church can ill afford to neglect such learned saints as the Greek Fathers and Aquinas in theological work and the care of souls, especially regarding the Holy Eucharist, which—as Thomas notes—Pseudo-Dionysius calls the "sacrament of sacraments."[92] Chapter 12 in this volume, by Joseph Wawrykow, shows how Aquinas, with the help of the Greek Fathers, is highly alert to the mystery of Christ present in the Eucharist. Future priests need the instruction and example of the Greek Fathers and Aquinas for help in studying Sacred Scripture, celebrating the liturgical mysteries, meditating rightly, and communicating the truth in a world that abounds in information of all kinds but sorely lacks wisdom for guidance to heaven's happiness.

90. Cf. both the old and the new apostolic constitutions on ecclesiastical universities and faculties. Neither John Paul II's *Sapientia Christiana* (1979) nor Francis's *Veritatis Gaudium* (2017) mentions St. Thomas in treating theology. This has significance for their modeling of priestly formation, as John Paul II writes: "In the first place, the Church has entrusted to these Faculties the task of preparing with special care students for the priestly ministry, for teaching the sacred sciences, and for the more arduous tasks of the apostolate." See *Sapientia Christiana*, foreword, sec. III.

91. For an argument for Aquinas's pastoral benefit for deification, see my "Aquinas, Divinization, and the People in the Pews," in *Divinization: Becoming Icons of Christ through the Liturgy*, ed. Andrew Hofer, OP (Chicago: Liturgy Training, 2015), 54–72. For a deeper and broader examination of Aquinas on deification, see the erudite work of Daria Spezzano, *The Glory of God's Grace: Deification According to St. Thomas Aquinas* (Ave Maria, FL: Sapientia Press, 2015).

92. Pseudo-Dionysius says that the title "sacrament of sacraments" comes from his teacher; presumably, here he means the same Hierotheus he mentions elsewhere. See *The Ecclesiastical Hierarchy*, chap. 3, at the beginning (PG 3.424). For a quotation of it by Aquinas, see *Super Sent. Lib.* 4., d. 24, q. 2, a. 1, qc. 2, co. For two references to *The Ecclesiastical Hierarchy*, chap. 3, but without a direct quotation of our phrase, see Aquinas's discussion of the question regarding whether the Eucharist is the greatest of sacraments, in *ST* III, q. 65, a. 3.

Conclusion: Renewing Theology Today

In a fervent appeal, Bruce Marshall has recommended that dogmatic theology be renewed by returning to the virtuous example of the nineteenth-century Catholic theologian Matthias Scheeben.[93] Scheeben is a fine model of reading Thomas Aquinas and the Greek Fathers together for the renewal of theology. His impressive *The Mysteries of Christianity* gives a Thomistic exploration of the subject, with a special regard for the Greek Fathers, especially Cyril of Alexandria. In his chapter "The Significance of the Eucharist," for instance, Scheeben writes: "We have mentioned several times that St. Cyril, the champion raised up by God to do battle with Eastern rationalism, had an extraordinarily clear insight into the meaning and connection of the cardinal mysteries, and pressed home his views with vigor."[94] Scheeben then proceeds to quote and summarize for some pages comments from Cyril on John 17, the Lord's high priestly prayer of unity. He concludes this chapter with a brief reflection on how Cyril shows us that "the three mysteries of the Trinity, the Incarnation, and the Eucharist are connected with one another in perfect harmony."[95] Understanding Scheeben's work, Marshall comments, "calls into question the common assumption that an interest in the Eastern tradition, and in the Fathers more generally, entered Catholic theology only with the *ressourcement* theologians of the mid-twentieth century."[96]

Today, when thinking of Thomas Aquinas and the Greek Fathers together, scholars may be mindful of the battle between the *ressourcement* theologians and those committed to neo-scholasticism before the Second Vatican Council. But there are other ways of thinking about theology's debts to the Greek Fathers and Aquinas, without all the contention of that bitter rivalry. Scheeben was not at all influenced by the *ressourcement* of the twentieth century, nor, for that matter, was Thomas when he did his work in *sacra doctrina* with the indispensable assistance of such theologians as John Chrysostom, Cyril of Alexandria, Pseudo-Dionysius, John of Damascus, and the decisions of the first ecumenical councils. It is time to look at these sources, these teachers, with fresh eyes. By doing so,

93. Bruce Marshall, "Renewing Dogmatic Theology: Matthias Scheeben Teaches Us the Virtues Theologians Need," *First Things* 223 (May 2012): 39–45.

94. Matthias Joseph Scheeben, *The Mysteries of Christianity*, trans. Cyril Vollert, SJ (St. Louis, MO: Herder, 1946), no. 76, p. 530.

95. Scheeben, *Mysteries of Christianity*, no. 76, p. 534.

96. Marshall, "Renewing Dogmatic Theology," 42.

we can strive in our own time to have a properly sapiential theology that, as Reinhard Hütter advocates, "liberates the theologian for a genuine engagement of all kinds of intellectual disciplines of enquiry—historical, hermeneutical, and empirical."[97] The challenge to have wisdom's vision is daunting. Given the complexity of the disciplines today, it would be impossible to specialize in every subfield of theology. But by returning to Aquinas and the Greek Fathers, we can be free to think with these holy Doctors on the mysteries of God for our needs today.

It is my hope that the essays of this volume, in their variety of historical and theological perspectives, help readers envision a renewal in Thomistic study, the study of Greek patristics, the Eastern Christian–Western Christian conversation, and Catholic teaching on the task of theology, particularly for priestly formation. One cannot study Aquinas's theology well without a sensitive recourse to the Greek Fathers, so indebted is he to them. Moreover, a theologian who reads the Greek Fathers would greatly benefit from also reading Aquinas's way of thinking about what they themselves thought about, which is principally God. By reading Aquinas and the Greek Fathers together, we may attain new outlooks on such topics as ecumenical dialogues or theology's role in priestly formation. It is best to hear the voices of these saints, like the heavenly chorus where they now sing in praise of God, together. As we listen, we occasionally find solos, and certain voices will be stronger than others as dissonance will be resolved into a more pleasing sound, but to hear them rightly is necessary for our own theological work to be in tune with the faith of our Fathers.

Acknowledgments

The author is grateful to Peter Joseph Gautsch, OP; Reginald Hoefer, OP; John Baptist Ku, OP; Matthew Levering; the participants of a panel presentation at Ave Maria University's conference on Thomas Aquinas and the Greek Fathers, co-sponsored by the Aquinas Center for Theological Renewal and the Thomistic Institute, on January 26, 2018; and also the participants of the two-hour historical and systematic theology area seminar on an earlier version of this essay, organized by Nicholas Lombardo, OP, at the Catholic University of America on April 9, 2018.

97. Reinhard Hütter, "Theological Faith Enlightening Sacred Theology: Renewing Theology by Recovering Its Unity in *Sacra Doctrina*," *The Thomist* 74 (2010): 369–405. See also his "God, the University, and the Missing Link—Wisdom," *The Thomist* 73 (2009): 241–77.

Contributors

KHALED ANATOLIOS is the John A. O'Brien Professor of Theology at the University of Notre Dame. His writings include: *Retrieving Nicaea: The Development and Meaning of Trinitarian Doctrine* (2011, 2018); the *Athanasius* volume of the Routledge Early Church Fathers Series (2004); and *Athanasius: The Coherence of His Thought* (1998, 2004). He is presently completing a manuscript on soteriology from the perspective of the Byzantine Christian tradition.

BERNHARD BLANKENHORN, OP, is aggregate professor of theology at the Pontifical University of St. Thomas Aquinas (Angelicum) in Rome. He is the author of *The Mystery of Union with God: Dionysian Mysticism in Albert the Great and Thomas Aquinas* (2015).

GERALD P. BOERSMA is an associate professor of theology at Ave Maria University. He is author of *Augustine's Early Theology of Image* (2016). His research focuses on Latin patristic theology.

BRIAN DUNKLE, SJ, is an assistant professor of historical theology at the Boston College School of Theology and Ministry. He is the author of *Enchantment and Creed in the Hymns of Ambrose of Milan* (2016) and the translator of works by Ambrose of Milan and Gregory of Nazianzus.

STEPHEN M. FIELDS, SJ, is a professor of the philosophy of religion and systematic theology at Georgetown University. He is the author of *Being as Symbol: On the Origins and Development of Karl Rahner's Metaphysics* (2000) and *Analogies of Transcendence: An Essay on Nature, Grace and Modernity* (2016). He recently contributed essays on Benedict XVI's conciliar hermeneutics and *Deus Caritas Est* to a special edition of *Nova et Vetera* that he guest edited (August 2017).

ANDREW HOFER, OP, is an associate professor of patristics and ancient languages and the director of the doctoral program at the Pontifical Faculty of the Immaculate Conception at the Dominican House of Studies in Washington, DC. He is the author of *Christ in the Life and Teaching of Gregory of Nazianzus* in Oxford Early Christian Studies series and of articles in several journals.

JOHN BAPTIST KU, OP, is an assistant professor at the Pontifical Faculty of the Immaculate Conception in Washington, DC. He is the author of *God the Father in the Theology of St. Thomas Aquinas* (2012).

DOMINIC LEGGE, OP, is the director of the Thomistic Institute and an assistant professor in systematic theology at the Pontifical Faculty of the Immaculate Conception in Washington, DC. He is the author of *The Trinitarian Christology of St. Thomas Aquinas* (2016).

MATTHEW LEVERING holds the James N. and Mary D. Perry Jr. Chair of Theology at Mundelein Seminary. He has authored or edited a number of studies of Thomas Aquinas's theology. He serves as coeditor of two quarterly journals, *Nova et Vetera* and *International Journal of Systematic Theology*.

ROGER W. NUTT is vice president for academic affairs and dean of faculty at Ave Maria University, where he also serves as an associate professor of theology, co-director of the Aquinas Center for Theological Renewal, and editor-in-chief of Sapientia Press. He is the author of *General Principles of Sacramental Theology* (2017) and *Thomas Aquinas: De unione verbi incarnati* (2015).

JANE SLOAN PETERS is a doctoral candidate in historical theology at Marquette University. Her dissertation is titled "Greek Patristic and Byzantine Exegesis in the Works of Thomas Aquinas, 1261–1274."

MARCUS PLESTED is a professor of theology at Marquette University. He is the author of two books to date, *The Macarian Legacy: The Place of Macarius-Symeon in the Eastern Christian Tradition* (2004) and *Orthodox Readings of Aquinas* (2012). His current book project is on the theme of wisdom in patristic, medieval, and modern Orthodox theology.

JOHN SEHORN earned his PhD at the University of Notre Dame and is an assistant professor of theology at the Augustine Institute in Greenwood Village, Colorado. Focusing on Greek and Latin patristics, he has translated Origen's Homilies on Ezekiel and published on Augustine. With Timothy C. Gray, he is currently coediting the forthcoming Baker Academic series *From the Side of Christ: A Biblical Theology of the Sacraments*.

JÖRGEN VIJGEN is a professor of philosophy at the Philosophical-Theological Institute St. Willibrord in the Netherlands, research fellow of Faculty of Theology (Nicolaus Copernicus University) in Poland, and an ordinary member of the Pontifical Academy of St. Thomas Aquinas. He is the author of *The Status of Eucharistic Accidents "sine subiecto"* (2013) and coeditor with Piotr Roszak of *Reading Sacred Scripture with Thomas Aquinas* (2015) and *Towards a Biblical Thomism* (2018).

JOSEPH WAWRYKOW is a professor of theology at the University of Notre Dame. In his teaching and his research, Wawrykow focuses on thirteenth-century theology in the West. He is perhaps best known for his study of "merit" in the theology of Aquinas. His more recent work has been on the Christology of Aquinas, especially with regard to the perfections and vulnerabilities of the Word incarnate in the Word's assumed humanity.

Select Bibliography

COMPILED BY ELLY A. BROWN

This select bibliography gives only modern works of scholarship. The exact editions and translations of primary sources and magisterial ecclesial documents consulted vary according to the individual contributors of this volume.

Alexandre, Monique. "La redécouverte d'Origène au XX siècle." In *Les Peres de l'Église dans le monde d'aujourd'hui*, edited by Cristian Badilita and Charles Kannengiesser, 54–94. Paris: Beauchesne, 2006.

Anatolios, Khaled. *Athanasius*. Early Church Fathers. New York: Routledge, 2004.

———. *Athanasius: The Coherence of His Thought*. London: Routledge, 1998.

———. "*Creatio ex nihilo* in Athanasius of Alexandria's *Against the Greeks-On the Incarnation*." In *Creation ex nihilo: Origins, Development, Contemporary Challenges*, edited by Gary Anderson, 119–49. Notre Dame, IN: University of Notre Dame Press, 2017.

———. "Creation and Salvation in St. Athanasius of Alexandria." In *On the Tree of the Cross: George Florovsky and the Patristic Doctrine of Atonement*, edited by Matthew Baker, Seraphim Danckaert, and Nicholas Marinides, 59–72. Jordanville, NY: Holy Trinity Seminary Press, 2016.

———. *Retrieving Nicaea: The Development and Meaning of Trinitarian Doctrine*. Grand Rapids, MI: Baker Academic, 2011.

———. "The Soteriological Grammar of Conciliar Christology." *The Thomist* 78, no. 2 (2014): 165–88.

Andrée, Alexander, Tristan Sharp, and Richard Shaw. "Aquinas and 'Alcuin': A New Source of the Catena Aurea on John." *Recherches de Théologie et Philosophie Médiévales* 83 (2016): 3–20.

Ankinwale, Anthony A. "The Decree on Priestly Formation, *Optatam Totius*." In *Vatican II: Renewal within Tradition*, edited by Matthew L. Lamb and Matthew Levering, 229–50. Oxford: Oxford University Press, 2008.

Ayres, Lewis. *Nicaea and Its Legacy: An Approach to Fourth-Century Trinitarian Theology*. Oxford: Oxford University Press, 2004.

Backes, Ignaz. *Die Christologie des hl. Thomas v. Aquin und die griechischen Kirchen-väter.* Paderborn: Schöningh, 1931.

Balthasar, Hans Urs von. *Cosmic Liturgy: The Universe According to Maximos the Confessor.* Translated by Brian E. Daley. San Francisco: Ignatius Press, 2003.

————. "Denys." In *Studies in Theological Styles: Clerical Styles,* edited by John Riches, translated by Andrew Louth et al. Vol. 2 of *The Glory of the Lord: A Theological Aesthetics,* 7 vols., edited by Joseph Fessio et al., 144–210. San Francisco, CA: Ignatius Press, 1984–91.

————. *Notes to Thomas Aquinas, Summa Theologica, II-II, 171–182: Besondere Gnadengaben und die Zwei Wege des Menschlichen Lebens.* Die Deutsche Thomas-Ausgabe 22. Heidelberg: Kerle, 1954.

————. "Plato." In *The Realm of Metaphysics in Antiquity,* translated by Brian McNeil. Vol. 4 of *The Glory of the Lord: A Theological Aesthetics,* 7 vols., edited by Joseph Fessio et al., 166–215. San Francisco, CA: Ignatius Press, 1984–91.

————. "Plotinus." In *Realm of Metaphysics in Antiquity,* translated by Brian McNeil. Vol. 4 of *The Glory of the Lord: A Theological Aesthetics,* 7 vols., edited by Joseph Fessio et al., 280–313. San Francisco, CA: Ignatius Press, 1984–91.

————. *Presence and Thought: An Essay on the Religious Philosophy of Gregory of Nyssa.* Translated by Mark Sebanc. San Francisco: Ignatius Press, 1995.

————. "Umrisse der Eschatologie," In *Verbum caro: Skizzen zur Theologie 1,* 276–300. Einsiedeln: Johannes Verlag, 1960.

————. "Zur Ortsbestimmung christlicher Mystik." In *Grundfragen der Mystik,* edited by Werner Beierwaltes, Hans Urs von Balthasar, and Alois M. Haas. Einsiedeln: Johannes Verlag, 1974.

Barahal, Susan. "Repaint, Reframe, Renew: Updating Sacred Images during the Early Italian Renaissance." PhD diss., Boston University, 2016.

Bardy, Gustave. "Sur les sources patristiques grecques de saint Thomas." *Revue des Sciences Philosophiques et Théologiques* 12 (1923): 493–502.

Barnes, Corey L. *Christ's Two Wills in Scholastic Thought: The Christology of Aquinas and Its Historical Contexts.* Toronto: Pontifical Institute of Medieval Studies, 2012.

————. "Thomas Aquinas's Chalcedonian Christology and Its Influence on Later Scholastics." *The Thomist* 78, no. 2 (2014): 189–217.

Bataillon, Louis. "La diffusione manoscrita e stampata dei commenti biblici di San Tommaso d'Aquino." *Angelicum* 71 (1994): 579–90.

————. "Note sur la documentation patristique de Saint Thomas à Paris en 1270." *Revue des Sciences Philosophiques et Théologiques* 47 (1963): 403–6.

————. "Saint Thomas et les Pères: De la Catena a la Tertia Pars." In *Ordo Sapientiae et Amoris: Image et Message de Saint Thomas d'Aquin,* edited by Carlos-Josaphat Pinto de Oliveira, 15–36. Fribourg: Éditions Universitaires, 1993.

————. "Les Sermons de Saint Thomas et la Catena Aurea." In *Thomas Aquinas, 1274–1974: Commemorative Studies,* 1:67–75. Toronto: Pontifical Institute of Medieval Studies, 1974.

Baur, Chrysostome. *S. Jean Chrysostome et ses oeuvres dans l'histoire littéraire.* Louvain: Bureaux du Recueil, 1907.

Beeley, Christopher. "Divine Causality and the Monarchy of God the Father in Gregory of Nazianzus." *Harvard Theological Review* 110, no. 2 (2007): 199–214.

Bellamah, Timothy F. "The Interpretation of a Contemplative: Thomas' Commentary Super Iohannem." In *Reading Sacred Scripture with Thomas Aquinas: Hermeneutical Tools, Theological Questions and New Perspectives*, edited by J. Vijgen and Piotr Roszak, 229–55. Turnhout: Brepols, 2015.

Belting, Hans. *The Image and Its Public in the Middle Ages: Form and Function of Early Paintings of the Passion*. Translated by Mark Bartusis and Raymond Meyer. New Rochelle, NY: Aristide D. Caratzas, 1990.

Bentley, Ronald Thomas. "'Worship God Alone': The Emerging Christian Tradition of *Latreia*." PhD diss., University of Virginia, 2009.

Besançon, Alain. *L'image interdite: Une histoire intellectuelle de l'iconoclasme*. Paris: Fayard, 1994.

Betz, Johannes. *Eucharistie in der Schrift und Patristik*. Handbuch der Dogmengeschichte, Band IV, Faszikel 4a. Freiburg: Herder, 1979.

Beyer, Hans-Veit. "Die Lichtlehre der Mönche des vierzehnten und des vierten Jahrhunderts, erörtert am Beispiel des Gregorios Sinaïtes, des Evagrios Pontikos und des Ps.-Makarios/Symeon." *Jahrbuch der österreichischen Byzantinistik* 31 (1981): 473–512.

Blankenhorn, Bernhard. *The Mystery of Union with God: Dionysian Mysticism in Albert the Great and Thomas Aquinas*. Thomistic Ressourcement 4. Washington, DC: Catholic University of America Press, 2015.

———. "Mystical Theology and Christology in Aquinas." Leuven University Press, forthcoming.

Blowers, Paul M. *Maximus the Confessor: Jesus Christ and the Transfiguration of the World*. Christian Theology in Context. Oxford: Oxford University Press, 2016.

Bockmuehl, Markus. *Seeing the Word: Refocusing New Testament Study*. Studies in Theological Interpretation. Grand Rapids, MI: Baker Academic, 2006.

Bolton, Brenda M. "Advertise the Message: Images in Rome at the Turn of the Twelfth Century." In *The Church and the Arts*, edited by Diana Wood. Cambridge, MA: Blackwell, 1995.

Bonino, Serge-Thomas. "'Toute vérité, quel que soit celui la dit, vient de l'Esprit Saint,' Autour d'une citation de l'*Ambrosiaster* dans le corpus thomasien." *Revue Thomiste* 106 (2006): 101–47.

Bouillard, Henri. *Conversion et grâce chez saint Thomas d'Aquin: Étude historique*. Paris: Aubier, Éditions Montaigne, 1944.

Boulnois, Marie-Odile. "L'eucharistie, mystère d'union chez Cyrille d'Alexandrie: Les modèles d'union trinitaire et christologique." *Revue des Sciences Religieuses* 74, no. 2 (2000): 147–72.

Boyle, Joseph. "The Twofold Division of St. Thomas's Christology in the Tertia Pars." *The Thomist* 60 (1996): 439–47.

Boyle, Leonard. "Authorial Intention and the *Divisio Textus*." In *Reading John with St. Thomas Aquinas*, 3–8. Washington, DC: Catholic University of America Press, 2005.

Broderick, James. *Robert Bellarmine: Saint and Scholar*. Westminster, MD: Newman Press, 1961.

Brown. Steven. "The Theological Role of the Fathers: Aquinas's *Super Evangelium S. Ioannis Lectura*." In *Reading John with Thomas Aquinas*, 9–21. Washington, DC: Catholic University of America Press, 2005.

Bulgakov, Sergius. *The Lamb of God*. Translated by B. Jakim. Grand Rapids, MI: Eerdmans, 2008.

Canty, Aaron. *Light and Glory: The Transfiguration of Christ in Early Franciscan and Dominican Theology*. Washington, DC: Catholic University of America Press, 2011.

Carruthers, Mary. *The Book of Memory: A Study of Memory in Medieval Culture*. Cambridge: Cambridge University Press, 1990.

Cattoi, Thomas. "Introduction." In *Theodore the Studite: Writings on Iconoclasm*. Ancient Christian Writers 69. Translated by Thomas Cattoi. New York: Newman Press, 2015.

Cessario, Romanus. *The Godly Image: Christ and Salvation in Catholic Thought from St. Anselm to Aquinas*. Petersham, MA: St. Bede's, 1990.

Chadwick, Henry. "The Eucharist and Christology during the Nestorian Controversy." *Journal of Theological Studies*, new ser., 2 (1951): 145–64.

Chauvet, Louis-Marie. *Symbole et sacrement: Une relecture sacramentelle de l'existence chrétienne*. Paris: Éditions du Cerf, 1987. [Translated by Patrick Madigan and Madeleine Beaumont as *Symbol and Sacrament: A Sacramental Reinterpretation of Christian Existence*. Collegeville, MN: Liturgical Press, 1995.]

Chazelle, Celia M. "Memory, Instruction, Worship: 'Gregory's' Influence on Early Medieval Doctrines of the Artistic Image." In *Gregory the Great: A Symposium*, edited by John C. Cavadini. Notre Dame, IN: University of Notre Dame Press, 1995.

————. "Pictures, Books, and the Illiterate: Pope Gregory I's Letters to Serenus of Marseilles." *Word & Image* 6 (1990): 138–53.

Clark, Elizabeth A. *The Origenist Controversy: The Cultural Construction of an Early Christian Debate*. Princeton, NJ: Princeton University Press, 1992.

Clark, Mark. "Peter Lombard, Stephen Langton, and the School of Paris: The Making of the Twelfth-Century Scholastic Biblical Tradition." *Traditio* 72 (2017): 171–274.

Concannon, Ellen. "The Eucharist as Source of St. Cyril of Alexandria's Christology." *Pro Ecclesia* 17, no. 3 (2009): 318–36.

Congourdeau, M. H. "L'Eucharistie à Byzance du XIe au XVe Siècle." In *Eucharistia: Encyclopédie de l'Eucharistie*. Paris: Les Éditions du Cerf, 2002.

Conticello, Carmelo G. "San Tommaso ed i Padri: La '*Catena aurea super Ioannem*.'" *Archives d'Histoire Doctrinale et Littéraire du Moyen Âge* 57 (1990): 31–92.

————. "Théophylacte de Bulgarie, Source de Thomas d'Aquin." In *Philomathestatos: Studies in Greek and Byzantine Texts Presented to Jacques Noret for His Sixty-Fifth Birthday*, edited by B. Janssens, B. Roosen, and P. Van Deun, 63–75. Leuven: Peeters 2004.

Cordonier, Valérie. "Sauver le Dieu du Philosophe: Albert le Grand, Thomas d'Aquin, Guillaume de Moerbeke et l'invention du 'Liber de bona fortuna.'" In *Christian*

Readings of Aristotle from the Middle Ages to the Renaissance, edited by L. Bianchi, 65–114. Brepols: Turnhout, 2011.

Cordonier, Valérie, and Carlos Steel. "Guillaume de Moerbeke traducteur du 'Liber de bona fortuna' et de l'Ethique à Eudème." In *The Letter before the Spirit: The Importance of Text Editions for the Study of the Reception of Aristotle*, edited by A. M. I. van Oppenraay, 401–46. Leiden: Brill, 2012.

Cross, Richard. "Divine Monarchy in Gregory of Nazianzus." *Journal of Early Christian Studies* 14, no. 1 (2006): 105–16.

————. "Perichoresis, Deification, and Christological Predication in John of Damascus." *Mediaeval Studies* 62 (2000): 69–124.

Crouzel, Henri. "Divorce et remariage dans l'Église primitive." *Nouvelle Revue Théologique* 98 (1976): 891–917. [Translated by Michelle K. Borras as "Divorce and Remarriage in the Early Church: Some Reflections on Historical Methodology," *Communio* 41 (2014): 472–503.]

————. *L'Église primitive face au divorce: Du premier au cinquième siècle.* Paris: Beauchesne, 1971.

————. "Origène est-il la source du Catharisme?" *Bulletin de littérature ecclésiastique* 80 (1979): 3–28.

Dahan, Gilbert. *Lire la Bible au Moyen Âge: Essais d'herméneutique médiévale.* Geneva: Droz, 2009.

————. "Les Pères dans l'exégèse médiévale de la Bible." *Revue des Sciences Philosophiques et Théologiques* 91 (2007): 109–27.

————. "Tradition patristique, autorité et progrès dans l'exégèse médiévale." In *Les réceptions des Pères de l'Église au Moyen Âge*, vol. 1, edited by Rainer Berndt and Michel Fédou, 349–68. Münster: Aschendorff Verlag, 2013.

Daley, Brian E. *Light on the Mountain: Greek Patristic and Byzantine Homilies on the Transfiguration of the Lord.* Yonkers, NY: St. Vladimir's Seminary Press, 2013.

————. "The Nouvelle Théologie and the Patristic Revival: Sources, Symbols, and the Science of Theology." *International Journal of Systematic Theology* 7 (2005): 362–82.

Daly, C. B. "The Knowableness of God." *Philosophical Studies* 9 (1959): 90–133.

Dauphinais, Michael. "'And They Shall All Be Taught by God': Wisdom and the Eucharist in John 6." In *Reading John with St. Thomas Aquinas: Theological Exegesis and Speculative Theology*, edited by Michael Dauphinais and Matthew Levering, 312–17. Washington, DC: Catholic University of America Press, 2005.

de Andia, Ysabel. "Transfiguration et théologie négative chez Maxime le Confesseur et Denys l'Aréopagite." In *Denys l'Aréopagite: Tradition et Métamorphoses.* Paris: Vrin, 2006.

de Lubac, Henri. *Histoire et esprit: L'intelligence de l'écriture d'après Origène.* Paris: Aubier Montaigne, 1950.

————. "The Latin Origen." In *Medieval Exegesis*, vol. 1, translated by M. Sebanc, 161–224. Grand Rapids, MI: Eerdmans, 1998.

Denzinger, Heinrich. *Compendium of Creeds, Definitions, and Declarations on Matters of Faith and Morals*, 43rd ed., edited by Peter Hünermann. San Francisco: Ignatius Press, 2012.

Derbes, Anne. "Images East and West: The Ascent of the Cross." In *The Sacred Image East and West*, edited by Robert Ousterhout and Leslie Brubaker. Chicago: University of Illinois Press, 1995.

Divry, Édouard. *La transfiguration selon l'orient et l'occident: Grégoire Palamas, Thomas d'Aquin. Vers un dénouement oecuménique*. Paris: Téqui, 2009.

Dodds, Michael J. *Unlocking Divine Action: Contemporary Science and Thomas Aquinas*. Washington, DC: Catholic University of America Press, 2012.

Dulles, Avery. "The Cognitive Basis of Faith." *Philosophy and Theology* 10, no. 1 (1998): 19–31.

———. "Criteria of Catholic Theology," *Communio: International Catholic Review* 22 (1995): 305–15.

Durand, Emmanuel. *L'offre universelle du salut en Christ*. Cogitatio Fidei 285. Paris: Cerf, 2012.

———. *Le Père, Alpha et Oméga de la vie trinitaire*. Paris: Cerf, 2008.

Edwards, Dennis. "Roman Catholic Theologies." In *Creation and Salvation*, vol. 2, *A Companion on Recent Theological Movements*, edited by Ernst M. Conradie. Zürich: Lit Verlag, 2012.

Egan, John P. "αἴτιος/'Author,' αἰτία/'Cause' and ἀρχή/'Origin': Synonyms in Selected Texts of Gregory Nazianzen." *Studia Patristica* 32 (1997): 102–7.

Elders, Leo. *Autour de saint Thomas d'Aquin: Recueil d'études sur sa pensée philosophique et théologique, tome II. L'agir moral; Approches théologiques*. Paris: Fac-Editions, Uitgeverij Tabor, 1987.

———. "Les destinataires de la Somme contre les gentils." In *S. Tommaso Filosofo: Ricerche in occasione dei due centenari accademici*, edited by Antonio Piolanti, 287–304. Vatican City: Libreria Editrice Vaticana, 1995.

———. "Santo Tomás de Aquino y los Padres de la Iglesia." *Doctor Communis* 48 (1993): 55–80.

———. "Structure et fonction de l'argument Sed contra dans la Somme théologique." *Divus Thomas* 80 (1977): 245–60.

———. "Thomas Aquinas and the Fathers of the Church." In *Theological Innovation and the Shaping of Tradition: The Reception of the Church Fathers in the West from the Carolingians to the Maurists*, edited by Irena Backus, 337–66. Leiden: Brill, 1996.

———. *Thomas Aquinas and His Predecessors: The Philosophers and the Church Fathers in His Works*. Washington, DC: Catholic University of America Press, 2018.

Emery, Gilles. "The Holy Spirit in Aquinas's Commentary on Romans." In *Reading Romans with Thomas Aquinas*, edited by Matthew Levering and Michael Dauphinais, 127–62. Washington, DC: Catholic University of America Press, 2012.

———. "Missions invisibles et missions visibles: Le Christ et son Esprit." *Revue Thomiste* 106 (2006): 51–99.

———. "A Note on St. Thomas and the Eastern Fathers." In *Trinity, Church, and the Human Person*, translated by J. Harms and Fr. John Baptist Ku, 193–207. Naples, FL: Sapientia Press of Ave Maria University, 2007.

———. "Saint Thomas d'Aquin et l'Orient chrétien." *Nova et Vetera* 74, no. 4 (1999): 19–36.

―――――. "*Theologia* and *Dispensatio*: The Centrality of the Divine Missions in St. Thomas's Trinitarian Theology." *The Thomist* 74 (2010): 515–61.

―――――. *Thomas d'Aquin, Traités: Les raisons de la foi; Les articles de la foi et Les sacraments de l'Eglise.* Paris: Cerf, 1999.

―――――. "The Treatise of St. Thomas on the Trinity in the Summa contra Gentiles." In *Trinity in Aquinas*, translated by Heather Buttery, 71–120. Ypislanti, MI: Sapientia Press, 2003.

―――――. "Trinitarian Theology as Spiritual Exercise in Augustine and Aquinas." In *Aquinas the Augustinian*, edited by Michael Dauphinais, Barry David, and Matthew Levering, 1–40. Washington, DC: Catholic University of America Press, 2007.

―――――. *The Trinity: An Introduction to Catholic Doctrine on the Triune God.* Translated by Matthew Levering. Washington, DC: Catholic University of America Press, 2011.

Emery, Gilles, OP, and Matthew Levering, eds. *Aristotle in Aquinas's Theology.* Oxford: Oxford University Press, 2015.

Eschmann, I. T. "A Catalogue of St. Thomas's Works: Bibliographical Notes." In Etienne Gilson, *The Christian Philosophy of St. Thomas Aquinas*, translated by L. K. Shook. New York: Random House, 1956.

Evdokimov, Paul. *Orthodoxy.* London: New City Press, 2011.

Fairbairn, Donald. "Patristic Theology: Three Trajectories." *Journal of the Evangelical Theological Society* 50, no. 2 (2007): 289–310.

Ferraro, Giuseppe. "San Giovanni Crisostomo come fonte de san Tommaso: La sua esposizione dei testi pneumatologici nel commento del questo vangelo." *Angelicum* 62 (1985): 194–244.

Ferré, Frederick. "The Logic of Analogy." In *The Challenge of Religion: Contemporary Readings in Philosophy of Religion*, edited by Frederick Ferré et al., 104–13. New York: Seabury Press, 1982.

Fichtenau, Heinrich. *Heretics and Scholars in the High Middle Ages, 1000–1200.* University Park: Pennsylvania State University Press, 1998.

Fields, Stephen M. *Analogies of Transcendence: An Essay on Nature, Grace and Modernity.* Washington, DC: Catholic University of America Press, 2016.

―――――. "From Classic to Patristic: Balthasar, Rahner, and the Origins of Analogy." In *Ressourcement after Vatican II: Essays in Honor of Joseph Fessio, SJ*, edited by Nicholas J. Healy Jr. and Matthew Levering. San Francisco, CA: Ignatius Press, in press.

―――――. "Contraries in One: Contingency, Analogy, and God in Transcendental Thomism." In *The Discovery of Being: Philosophical and Theological Perspectives on Thomas Aquinas*, edited by Christopher M. Cullen and Franklin T. Harkins. Washington, DC: Catholic University of America Press, in press.

―――――. "The Reception of Aquinas in Twentieth-Century Transcendental Thomism." In *The Oxford Handbook to the Reception of Aquinas*, edited by Marcus Plested and Matthew Levering. Oxford: Oxford University Press, in press.

Florovsky, Georges. "Redemption." In *Collected Works*, vol. 3, *Creation and Redemption.* Belmont: Nordland, 1976.

Flynn, Gabriel, and Paul D. Murray, eds. *Ressourcement: A Movement for Renewal in Twentieth-Century Theology.* New York: Oxford University Press, 2012.

Gaine, Simon. *Did the Saviour See the Father? Christ, Salvation and the Vision of God.* London: T&T Clark, 2015.

Garrigou-Lagrange, Réginald. *Christ the Savior: A Commentary on the Third Part of St. Thomas' Theological Summa.* Translated by Bede Rose. St. Louis, MO: Herder, 1950.

—————. "La nouvelle théologie, où va-t-elle?" *Angelicum* (1946): 126–45. [Translated by Suzanne M. Rini as "Where Is the New Theology Leading Us?" *Josephinum Journal of Theology* 18 (2011): 63–78.]

Gauthier, René-Antoine. "Introduction." In *Saint Thomas d'Aquin, Somme contre les gentils.* Paris: Cerf, 1993.

Gautier, Paul. *Théophylacte d'Achrida: Discours, Traités, Poésies*, vol. 1. Thessalonique: Association de Recherches Byzantines, 1980.

Gavrilyuk, Paul. *Georges Florovsky and the Russian Religious Renaissance.* Changing Paradigms in Historical and Systematic Theology. Oxford: Oxford University Press, 2014.

Gebremedhin, Ezra. *Life-Giving Blessing: An Inquiry into the Eucharistic Doctrine of Cyril of Alexandria.* Stockholm: Almqvist & Wiksell, 1977.

Geenen, Gottfried. "En marge du concile de Chalcédoine: Les texts du Quatrième Concile dans les oeuvres de Saint Thomas." *Angelicum* 29 (1952): 43–59.

—————. "Saint Thomas d'Aquin et ses sources pseudoépigraphiques." *Ephemerides Theologicae Lovaniensis* 20 (1943): 71–80.

—————. "Thomas d'Aquin et les Pères." In *Dictionnaire de théologie catholique*, vol. 15, pt. 1, col. 738–61. Paris: Letouzey et Ané, 1946.

Gilby, Thomas. "Introduction." In Thomas Aquinas, *Summa Theologiae*, vol. 3, *Knowing and Naming God, 1a. 12–13*, edited by Herbert McCabe. Cambridge: Cambridge University Press, 2006.

Gilson, Étienne. "Cajétan et existence." *Tijdschrift voor Philosophie* 15 (1953): 267–86.

Golitzin, Alexander. *Mystagogy: A Monastic Reading of Dionysus Areopagita.* Collegeville, MN: Cistercian, 2013.

—————. "A Testimony to Christianity as Transfiguration: The Macarian Homilies and Orthodox Spirituality." In *Orthodox and Wesleyan Spirituality*, edited by S. Kimbrough, 129–56. Crestwood, NY: SVS Press, 2002.

Grillmeier, Aloys. *Christ in Christian Tradition*, vol. 1, *From the Apostolic Age to Chalcedon (451)*, 2nd ed. Translated by J. S. Bowden. New York: Sheed and Ward, 1975.

Grumel, Venance. "Images (Culte des)." In *Dictionnaire de théologie catholique*, vol. 7, pt. 1, col. 809. Paris: Letouzey et Ané, 1927.

Guillén, Domingo García. *Padre es Nombre de Relación: Dios Padre en la teología de Gregorio Nacianceno.* Rome: Gregorian and Biblical Press, 2010.

Gwynn, David M. *The Eusebians: The Polemic of Athanasius of Alexandria and the Construction of the "Arian Controversy."* Oxford: Oxford University Press, 2007.

Gy, Pierre-Marie. "Avancées du traité de l'eucharistie de S. Thomas dans la *Somme* par rapport aux *Sentences*." *Revue des Sciences Philosophiques et Théologiques* 77, no. 2 (1993): 219–28.

————. "La Documentation Sacramentaire de Thomas d'Aquin: Quelle Connaissance S. Thomas a-t-il de la Tradition Ancienne et de la Patristique?" *Revue des Sciences Philosophiques et Théologiques* 80 (1996): 425–31.

————. "Die Taufkommunion der kleinen Kinder in der lateinischen Kirche." In *Zeichen des Glaubens: Studien au Taufe und Firmung Balthasar Fischer zum 60. Geburtstag*, edited by Hansjörg auf der Maur and Bruno Kleinheyer, 485–91. Zurich: Benziger Verlag, 1972.

Habra, Georges. *La transfiguration selon les pères grecs*. Paris: Editions S.O.S., 1973.

Haight, Roger. *Jesus, Symbol of God*. Maryknoll, NY: Orbis, 1999.

Hanson, R. P. C. *The Search for the Christian Doctrine of God: The Arian Controversy 318–381 AD*. Edinburgh: T&T Clark, 1988.

Harnack, Adolph von. *History of Dogma*, vol. 5. Translated by J. Millar. Boston: Roberts, 1897–99.

Harvey, Alan. "The Land and Taxation in the Reign of Alexios I Komnenos: The Evidence of Theophylakt of Ochrid." *Revue des Études Byzantines* 51 (1993): 139–54.

Heine, Ronald E. *Homilies on Genesis and Exodus*. Washington, DC: Catholic University of America Press, 1981.

Herrin, Judith. *Byzantium*. Princeton, NJ: Princeton University Press, 2007.

Hofer, Andrew. "Aquinas, Divinization, and the People in the Pews." In *Divinization: Becoming Icons of Christ through the Liturgy*, edited by Andrew Hofer, 54–72. Chicago: Hillenbrand, 2015.

————. *Christ in the Life and Teaching of Gregory of Nazianzus*. Oxford Early Christian Studies. Oxford: Oxford University Press, 2013.

————. "Dionysian Elements in Thomas Aquinas's Christology: A Case of the Authority and Ambiguity of Pseudo-Dionysius." *The Thomist* 72 (2008): 409–42.

————. "Scripture in the Christological Controversies." In *The Oxford Handbook of Early Christian Biblical Interpretation*, edited by Paul Blowers and Peter Martens. Oxford: Oxford University Press, forthcoming.

————. "St. Thomas as Teacher in the Introduction to Theology." *Josephinum Journal of Theology* 21 (2014): 146–63.

Hofmann, G. "Apostolato dei Gesuiti nell'Oriente greco, 1583–1773." In *La résistance d'Akindynos à Gregoire Palamas*, edited by J. Nadal Cañellas. Leuven: Peeters, 1996.

Horst, Ulrich. *Evangelische Armut und Kirche: Thomas von Aquin und die Armutskontroversen des 13. und beginnenden 14. Jahrhunderts*. Berlin: Akademie Verlag, 1995.

Houghton, H. A. G., ed. *Commentaries, Catenae, and Biblical Tradition: Papers from the Ninth Birmingham Colloquium on the Textual Criticism of the New Testament in Conjunction with the COMPAUL Project*. Piscataway, NJ: Gorgias Press, 2016.

Hütter, Reinhard. "God, the University, and the Missing Link—Wisdom." *The Thomist* 73 (2009): 241–77.

————. "Theological Faith Enlightening Sacred Theology: Renewing Theology by Recovering Its Unity in *Sacra Doctrina*." *The Thomist* 74 (2010): 369–405.

Inglis, John. "Emanation in Historical Context: Aquinas and the Dominican Response to the Cathars." *Dionysius* 17 (1999): 95–128.

Izbicki, Thomas M. *The Eucharist in Medieval Canon Law*. Cambridge: Cambridge University Press, 2015.

Jesuits of Fourvière. "La théologie et ses sources: Réponse aux Études critique de la *Revue Thomiste* (mai-août 1946)." *Recherches de Science Religieuse* 33 (1946): 385–401.

Johnson, Junius. *Christ and Analogy: The Christocentric Metaphysics of Hans Urs von Balthasar.* Minneapolis, MN: Fortress Press, 2013.

Johnson, Mark. "Another Look at the Plurality of the Literal Sense of Scripture." *Medieval Philosophy and Theology* 2 (1992): 117–41.

Jordan, Mark D. "The 'Greeks' and Thomas Aquinas's Theology." *Journal of Orthodox Christian Studies* 1 (2018): 155–66.

Journet, Charles. *Connaissance et inconnaissance de Dieu.* Paris: Egloff, 1943.

Kannengieser, Charles. *Handbook of Patristic Exegesis.* Leiden: Brill, 2006.

Keaty, Anthony W. "Thomas's Authority for Identifying Charity as Friendship: Aristotle or John 15?" *The Thomist* 62 (1998): 581–601.

Kessler, Herbert L., and Johanna Zacharias. *Rome 1300: On the Path of the Pilgrim.* New Haven, CT: Yale University Press, 2000.

Kilmartin, Edward J. *The Eucharist in the West: History and Theology.* Edited by Robert J. Daly. Collegeville, MN: Liturgical Press, 2004.

Kirwan, Jon. *An Avant-Garde Theological Generation: The Nouvelle Théologie and the French Crisis of Modernity.* Oxford Theology and Religion Monographs. Oxford: Oxford University Press, 2018.

Klubertanz, George P. *St. Thomas Aquinas on Analogy: A Textual Analysis and Systematic Synthesis.* Chicago: Loyola University Press, 1960.

Kolbaba, Tia M. *The Byzantine Lists: Errors of the Latins.* Chicago: University of Illinois Press, 2000.

———. "Byzantine Orthodox Exegesis." In *The New Cambridge History of the Bible 2*, edited by Richard Marsden and E. Ann Matter, 485–504. Cambridge: Cambridge University Press, 2012.

Ku, John Baptist. *God the Father in the Theology of St. Thomas Aquinas.* New York: Peter Lang, 2013.

———. "Thomas Aquinas's Careful Deployment of *auctor* and *auctoritas* in Trinitarian Theology." *Angelicum* 90 (2013): 677–710.

Kugel, James L. *The Bible as It Was.* Cambridge, MA: Harvard University Press, 1999.

Labourdette, Marie-Michel. "La théologie et ses sources." *Revue Thomiste* 46 (1946): 353–71.

Lampe, G. W. H. *A Patristic Greek Lexicon.* New York: Oxford University Press, 1961.

Landgraf, Artur Michael. *Dogmengeschichte der Frühscholastik, zweiter Teil: Die Lehre von Christus*, vol. 2. Regensburg: Verlag Friedrich Pustet, 1954.

Lapierre, Michael J. *The Noetical Theory of Gabriel Vasquez, Jesuit Philosopher and Theologian (1549–1604): His View of the Objective Concept.* Lewiston, NY: Mellen Press, 1999.

Larchet, Jean-Claude. *La divinisation de l'homme selon saint Maxime le Confesseur.* Cogitatio Fidei 194. Paris: Cerf, 1996.

———. *Introduction to Maximos the Confessor, Questions à Thalassios*, vol. 1, *Questions 1 à 40*. Sources Chrétiennes 529. Edited by J.-L. Larchet and Françoise Vinel. Paris: Cerf, 2010.

————. "The Mode of Deification." In *The Oxford Handbook of Maximus the Confessor*, edited by Pauline Allen and Bronwen Neil. Oxford: Oxford University Press, 2015.

Lawrenz, Mel. *The Christology of John Chrysostom*. Lewiston, NY: Mellen Press, 1996.

Le Bachelet, X.-M. *Bellarmin avant son Cardinalat: Correspondance et documents*. Paris: Beauchesne, 1911.

Le Brun-Gouanvic, Claire, ed. *Ystoria sancti Thome de Aquino de Guillaume de Tocco (1323)*. Toronto: Pontifical Institute of Mediaeval Studies, 1996.

Legge, Dominic. *The Trinitarian Christology of St. Thomas Aquinas*. Oxford: Oxford University Press, 2017.

Lévy, Antoine. *Le créé et l'incréé: Maxime le Confesseur et Thomas d'Aquin, Aux sources de la querelle palamienne*. Bibliothèque Thomiste 59. Paris: Vrin, 2006.

Lewis, Flora. "Rewarding Devotion: Indulgences and the Promotion of Images." In *The Church and the Arts*, edited by Diana Wood. Cambridge, MA: Blackwell, 1995.

Limouris, Gennadios, ed. *Icons: Windows on Eternity: Theology and Spirituality in Colour*. Geneva: WCC, 1990.

Long, Steven A. *Analogia Entis: On the Analogy of Being, Metaphysics, and the Act of Faith*. Notre Dame, IN: University of Notre Dame Press, 2011.

————. "Obediential Potency, Human Knowledge, and the Natural Desire for God." *International Philosophical Quarterly* 37 (1997): 45–63.

Löser, Werner. *Im Geiste des Origenes: Hans Urs von Balthasar als Interpret der Theologie der Kirchenväter*. Frankfurt: Josef Knecht Verlag, 1976.

Lossky, Vladimir. *The Vision of God*. Bedfordshire: Faith Press, 1973.

Lottin, Odon. *Psychologie et morale aux XIIe et XIIIe siècles, tome III: Problèmes de morale, part 2/1*. Gembloux, Belgium: J. Duculot, 1949.

Louth, Andrew. *Introducing Eastern Orthodox Theology*. Downers Grove, IL: InterVarsity Press, 2013.

————. *Maximus the Confessor*. Early Church Fathers. London: Routledge, 1996.

Luomanen, Petri. *Recovering Jewish-Christian Sects and Gospels*. Leiden: Brill, 2012.

Maier, Jean-Louis. *Les missions divines selon saint Augustin*. Fribourg: Editions Universitaires Fribourg Suisse, 1960.

Mali, Franz. *Das "Opus imperfectum in Matthaeum" und sein Verhältnis zu den Matthäuskommentaren von Origenes und Hieronymus*. Innsbruck: Tyrolia, 1991.

Maréchal, Joseph. *A Maréchal Reader*. Edited and translated by Joseph Donceel. New York: Herder and Herder, 1970.

————. *Le Thomisme devant la philosophie critique*, vol. 5, *Le point de départ de la métaphysique*. 2nd ed. Brussels: Édition universelle, 1949.

Marion, Jean-Luc. *Essential Writings*. Edited by Kevin Hart. Translated by B. Gendreau et al. New York: Fordham University Press, 2013.

Marsaux, J. "Pour une nouvelle approche de l'eucharistie chez Jean Chrysostome à partir de la pragmatique." *Studia Patristica* 37 (2001): 565–70.

Marshall, Bruce D. "Ex Occidente Lux? Aquinas and Eastern Orthodox Theology." *Modern Theology* 20 (2004): 23–50.

————. "Renewing Dogmatic Theology: Matthias Scheeben Teaches Us the Virtues Theologians Need." *First Things* 223 (May 2012): 39–45.

Mayer, Wendy. "John Chrysostom." In *Wiley Blackwell Companion to Patristics*, edited by Ken Parry, 141–54. Hoboken, NJ: Wiley, 2015.

McCabe, Herbert. "Analogy." Appendix 4 in Thomas Aquinas, *Summa Theologiae*, 60 vols., vol. 3, translated and edited by English-Speaking Dominican Provinces, 106–7. New York: McGraw-Hill, 1964–66.

Mcguckin, John Anthony, ed. *The Path of Christianity: The First Thousand Years*. Downers Grove, IL: IVP Academic, 2017.

————. *The Transfiguration of Christ in Scripture and Tradition*. Lewiston, NY: Mellen Press, 1986.

————. *Westminster Handbook to Origen*. Louisville, KY: Westminster John Knox Press, 2004.

McInerny, Ralph. *Boethius and Aquinas*. Washington, DC: Catholic University of America Press, 1990.

Meijering, Eginhard Peter. *Athanasius, Contra Gentes: Introduction, Translation, and Commentary*. Philosophia Patrum 7. Leiden: Brill, 1984.

Meyendorff, John. *Marriage: An Orthodox Perspective*. 2nd ed. Crestwood, NY: St. Vladimir's Seminary Press, 1975.

Mitchell, Margaret M. *The Heavenly Trumpet: John Chrysostom and the Art of Pauline Interpretation*. Louisville, KY: Westminster John Knox Press, 2002.

Morard, Martin. "Thomas d'Aquin, lecteur des conciles." *Archivium Franciscanum Historicum* 98 (2005): 211–365.

————. "Une source de Saint Thomas d'Aquin: Le deuxième concile de Constantinople (553)." *Revue des Sciences Philosophiques et Théologiques* 81 (1997): 21–56.

Mullett, Margaret. *Theophylact of Ochrid: Reading the Letters of a Byzantine Archbishop*, vol. 2, *Birmingham Byzantine and Ottoman Monographs*. Edited by Anthony Bryer and John Haldon. New York: Routledge, 2016.

Murray, Paul. *Aquinas at Prayer: The Bible, Mysticism and Poetry*. London: Bloomsbury, 2013.

Neuner, Josef. "Decree on Priestly Formation." In *Commentary on the Documents of Vatican II*, vol. 2, translated by William Glen-Doepel, 371–404. New York: Herder and Herder, 1967.

Nichols, Aidan "Introduction." In *Catena Aurea of St. Thomas Aquinas*. Southampton: St. Austin, 1997.

————. "Thomism and the *Nouvelle Théologie*." *The Thomist* 64 (2000): 1–19.

Noble, Thomas F. X. *Images, Iconoclasm, and the Carolingians*. Philadelphia: University of Pennsylvania Press, 2009.

Norris, Frederick. *Faith Gives Fullness to Reasoning*. New York: Brill, 1991.

Nutt, Roger. *General Principles of Sacramental Theology*. Washington, DC: Catholic University of America Press, 2017.

Oblensky, Dimitri. *Six Byzantine Portraits*. Oxford: Clarendon Press, 1988.

Orbe, Antonio. "The Study of the Fathers of the Church in Priestly Formation." Translated by Louis-Bertrand Raymond. In *Vatican II: Assessment and Perspectives Twenty-Five Years after (1962–1987)*, vol. 3, edited by René Latourelle, 361–77. New York: Paulist Press, 1989.

O'Rourke, Fran. *Pseudo-Dionysius and the Metaphysics of Aquinas*. Leiden: Brill, 1992.

Ostrogorsky, George. *History of the Byzantine State*. Translated by Joan Hussey. Oxford: Alden Press, 1968.

Pera, Ceslao. *Le fonti del pensiero di S. Tommaso d'Aquino nella Somma Theologica*. Turin: Marietti, 1979.

Plested, Marcus. *The Macarian Legacy*. Oxford: Oxford University Press, 2004.

————. *Orthodox Readings of Aquinas*. Oxford: Oxford University Press, 2012.

————. "St Gregory Palamas on the Divine Simplicity." In *Modern Theology* (forthcoming).

Porro, Pasquale. *Thomas Aquinas: A Historical and Philosophical Profile*. Translated by Joseph G. Trabbic and Roger W. Nutt. Washington, DC: Catholic University of America Press, 2016.

Portaru, Marius. "Classical Philosophical Influences: Aristotle and Platonism." In *The Oxford Handbook of Maximus the Confessor*, edited by Pauline Allen and Bronwen Neil. Oxford: Oxford University Press, 2015.

Power, David. *Sacrament: The Language of God's Giving*. New York: Crossroad, 1999.

Prügl, Thomas. "Thomas Aquinas as Interpreter of Scripture." In *The Theology of Thomas Aquinas*, edited by Rik Van Nieuwenhove and Joseph Wawrykow, 386–415. Notre Dame, IN: University of Notre Dame, 2005.

Rahner, Karl. *The Christian Commitment: Essays in Pastoral Theology*. Translated by Cecily Hastings. New York: Sheed and Ward, 1963.

————. "Dogmatic Questions on Easter." In *Theological Investigations*, vol. 4, translated by K. Smyth. London: Darton, Longman and Todd, 1966.

————. "Dogmen—und Theologiegeschichte—gestern und morgen." *Zeitschrift für katholische Theologie* 99 (1977): 1–24. [Translated by Edward Quinn as "Yesterday's History of Dogma and Theology for Tomorrow." In *Theological Investigations*, vol. 18, 3–34. New York: Crossroad, 1983.]

————. *Hearer of the Word: Laying the Foundation for a Philosophy of Religion*. Translated by Joseph Donceel. New York: Continuum, 1994.

————. "On Recognizing the Importance of Thomas Aquinas." December 29, 1970. [Translated in *Theological Investigations*, vol. 13, 3–12. New York: Seabury Press, 1975.]

————. "Towards a Fundamental Theological Interpretation of Vatican II." Translated by Leo J. O'Donovan. *Theological Studies* 40 (1979): 716–27.

Ramelli, Ilaria L. E. "Origen, Patristic Philosophy, and Christian Platonism Re-Thinking the Christianisation of Hellenism." *Vigiliae Christianae* 63 (2009): 217–63.

Renczes, Philippe Gabriel. *Agir de Dieu et liberté de l'homme: Recherches sur l'anthropologie théologique de saint Maxime le Confesseur*. Cogitatio Fidei 229. Paris: Cerf, 2003.

Riches, Aaron. "Theandric Humanism: Constantinople III in the Thought of St. Thomas Aquinas." *Pro Ecclesia* 23 (2014): 195–218.

Rist, John M. "Divorce and Remarriage in the Early Church: Some Historical and Cultural Reflections." In *Remaining in the Truth of Christ: Marriage and Communion in the Catholic Church*, edited by Robert Dodaro, 64–92. San Francisco: Ignatius Press, 2014.

Roszak, Piotr. "Between Dialectics and Metaphor: Dynamics of Exegetical Practice of Thomas Aquinas." *Angelicum* 90 (2013): 507–34.

Rouse, Mary, and Richard Rouse. *Authentic Witnesses: Approaches to Medieval Texts and Manuscripts*. Notre Dame, IN: University of Notre Dame, 1991.

Saunders, Ernest W. "Theophylact of Ochrid as Writer and Biblical Interpreter." *Research* 2 (1957): 31–44.

Scheeben, Matthias Joseph. *The Mysteries of Christianity*. Translated by Cyril Vollert. St. Louis, MO: Herder, 1946.

Scheffczyk, Leo. "Die Stellung des Thomas von Aquin in der Entwicklung der Lehre von den *Mysteria vitae Christi*." In *Renovatio et Reformatio (Festschrift für Ludwig Hödl)*, edited by Manfred Gerwing and Godehard Ruppert. Münster: Aschendorff, 1985.

Schenk, Richard. "Omnis Christi Actio Nostra Est Instructio: The Deeds and Sayings of Jesus as Revelation in the View of Thomas Aquinas." In *La doctrine de la révelation divine de Saint Thomas d'Aquin*, edited by Arturo Blanco and Leo Elders, 104–31. Vatican City: Pontificia Accademia di S. Tommaso d'Aquino, 1990.

———. "From Providence to Grace: Thomas Aquinas and the Platonisms of the Mid-Thirteenth Century." *Nova et Vetera* 3 (2005): 307–20.

Schmitt, Jean-Claude. "L'Occident, Nicée II et les images du VIIIe au XIIIe siècle." In *Nicée II, 787–1987: Douze siècles d'images religieuses. Actes du colloque international Nicée II tenu au Collège de France, Paris, les 2, 3, 4 octobre 1986*, edited by François Boispflug and Nicolas Lossky, 272–82. Paris: Cerf, 1987.

Schroeder, Ed. *Gift and Promise: The Augsburg Confession and the Heart of Christian Theology*. Edited by Ronald Neustadt and Stephen Hitchcock. Minneapolis: Fortress Press, 2016.

Seidl, Horst. "Über die Erkenntnis erster, allgemeiner Prinzipien nach Thomas von Aquin." In *Thomas von Aquin: Werk und Wirkung im Licht neuerer Forschungen*, edited by Albert Zimmermann, 103–16. Berlin: De Gruyter, 1988.

Senner, Walter. "Thomas von Aquin und die Kirchenväter—eine quantitative Übersicht." In *Kirchenbild und Spiritualität: Dominikanische Beiträge zur Ekklesiologie und zum kirchlichen Leben im Mittlealter*, edited by Thomas Prügl and Marianne Schlosser, 25–42. Paderborn: Ferdinand Schöningh, 2007.

Sinkewicz, R. E. "The Doctrine of God in the Early Writings of Barlaam the Calabrian." *Mediaeval Studies* 44 (1982): 181–242.

Smalley, Beryl. *The Gospels in the Schools*. London: Hambledon, 1985.

Smith, Geoffrey S. *Guilt by Association: Heresy Catalogues in Early Christianity*. New York: Oxford, 2015.

Spezzano, Daria. "Conjoined to Christ's Passion: The Deifying Asceticism of the Sacraments According to Thomas Aquinas." *Antiphon* 17, no. 1 (2013): 73–86.

———. *The Glory of God's Grace: Deification According to St. Thomas Aquinas*. Naples, FL: Sapientia Press of Ave Maria University, 2015.

Staats, R. "Die Metamorphose des Christen: Die Wandlungslehre des Makarios-Symeon im Zusammenhang seiner Anthropologie, Christologie und Eucharistielehre." In *Grundbegriffe christlicher Ästhetik: Beiträge des V. Makarios-Symposiums Preetz 1995*, edited by K. Fitschen and R. Staats, 16–22. Wiesbaden: Harrassowitz 1997.

Staudt, R. Jared. "Religion as a Virtue: Thomas Aquinas on Worship through Justice, Law, and Charity." PhD diss., Ave Maria University, 2008.

Sweeney, Christopher R. "Holy Images and Holy Matter: Images in the Performance of Miracles in the Age before Iconoclasm." *Journal of Early Christian Studies* 26 (2018): 111–38.

Tillich, Paul. "Theology and Symbolism." In *Religious Symbolism*, edited by F. Ernest Johnson, 107–16. New York: Institute for Religious and Social Studies, 1955.

Tixeront, Joseph. *History of Dogmas*, vol. 2, *From St. Athanasius to St. Augustine (318–430)*. Translated by Henry. L. Brianceau. St. Louis, MO: Herder, 1914.

Tollefsen, Torstein Theodor. *St Theodore the Studite's Defence of the Icons: Theology and Philosophy in Ninth-Century Byzantium*. New York: Oxford, 2018.

Torrell, Jean-Pierre. *Le Christ en ses mystères: La vie et l'oeuvre de Jésus selon saint Thomas d'Aquin*, vol. 2. Paris: Desclée, 1999.

————. *Notes to Thomas Aquinas, Encyclopédie Jésus le Christ chez saint Thomas d'Aquin*. Paris: Cerf, 2008.

————. *Pour nous les hommes et pour notre salut: Jésus notre redemption*. Paris: Cerf, 2014.

————. *Saint Thomas Aquinas: The Person and His Work*. Washington, DC: Catholic University of America Press, 1996.

————. *Le Verbe Incarné: Tome troisième. 3a, Questions 16–26*. Paris: Cerf, 2002.

Tsirpanlis, C. N. *Introduction to Eastern Patristic Thought and Orthodox Theology*. Collegeville, MN: Liturgical Press, 1991.

Tück, Jan-Heiner. *A Gift of Presence: The Theology and Poetry of the Eucharist in Thomas Aquinas*. Translated by Scott G. Hefelfinger. Washington, DC: Catholic University of America Press, 2018.

Tutino, Stefania. *Empire of Souls: Robert Bellarmine and the Christian Commonwealth*. New York: Oxford University Press, 2010.

Tzamalikos, Panayiotis. *Origen: Cosmology and Ontology of Time*. Leiden: Brill, 2006.

Urban, Wilbur M. *Language and Reality: The Philosophy of Language and the Principles of Symbolism*. London: Allen and Unwin, 1939.

Vaggione, Richard Paul. *Eunomius of Cyzicus and the Nicene Revolution*. New York: Oxford University Press, 2000.

Valkenberg, Wilhelmus. *Did Not Our Heart Burn? Place and Function of Holy Scripture in the Theology of St. Thomas Aquinas*. Utrecht: Thomas Instituut te Utrecht, 1990.

————. *Words of the Living God Place and Function of the Holy Scripture in the Theology of St. Thomas Aquinas*. Leuvens: Peeters, 2000.

Van Banning, J. "Saint Thomas et l'Opus Imperfectum in Matthaeum." In *Atti dell' VIII Congresso Tomistico Internazionale*. Studi Tomistici 17. Vatican City: Congresso Tomistico Internazionale, 1982.

Van Riet, Georges. "Le titre de l'encyclique 'Aeterni Patris': Note historique." *Revue Philosophique de Louvain* 1982 (45): 35–63.

Vidu, Adonis. *Atonement, Law, and Justice: The Cross in Historical and Cultural Contexts*. Grand Rapids, MI: Baker Academic, 2014.

Vijgen, Jörgen. *The Status of Eucharistic Accidents "sine subjecto": An Historical Survey Up to Thomas Aquinas and Selected Reactions*. Berlin: Akademie Verlag, 2013.

Waddell, Michael. "Aquinas on the Light of Glory." *Tópicos* 40 (2011): 105–32.

Wagner, M. Monica. "Rufinus the Translator: A Study of His Theory and His Practice as Illustrated in His Version of the *Apologetica* of St. Gregory Nazianzen." PhD diss., Catholic University of America, 1945.

Ware, Kallistos. "The Transfiguration of the Body." *Sobornost* 4, no. 8 (1963): 420–33.

Wawrykow, Joseph. "Hypostatic Union." In *The Theology of Thomas Aquinas*, edited by Rik van Nieuwenhove and Joseph Wawrykow, 222–51. Notre Dame, IN: University of Notre Dame Press, 2005.

———. "Luther and the Spirituality of Thomas Aquinas." *Consensus* 19 (1993): 77–107.

———. "The Sacraments in Thirteenth Century Theology." In *The Oxford Handbook of Sacramental Theology*, edited by Hans Boersma and Matthew Levering. Oxford: Oxford University Press, 2015.

———. "Wisdom in the Christology of Thomas Aquinas." In *Christ among the Medieval Dominicans: Representations of Christ in the Texts and Images of the Order of Preachers*, edited by Kent Emery Jr. and Joseph Wawrykow, 175–96. Notre Dame, IN: University of Notre Dame Press, 1998.

Wéber, Édouard. *La personne humaine au XIIIe siècle*. Bibliothèque Thomiste 46. Paris: Vrin, 1991.

Weisheipl, James. *Friar Thomas d'Aquino*. New York: Doubleday, 1974.

———. *Friar Thomas d'Aquino: His Life, Thought, and Works*. Washington, DC: Catholic University of America Press, 1983.

Welch, Lawrence J. *Christology and Eucharist in the Early Thought of Cyril of Alexandria*. Lanham: Catholic Scholars Press, 1994.

White, Thomas Joseph, OP. *The Incarnate Lord: A Thomistic Study in Christology*. Thomistic Ressourcement 5. Washington, DC: Catholic University of America Press, 2015.

———. "The Precarity of Wisdom: Modern Dominican Theology, Perspectivalism, and the Tasks of Reconstruction." In *Ressourcement Thomism: Sacred Doctrine, the Sacraments and the Moral Life*, edited by Reinhard Hütter and Matthew Levering, 92–123. Washington, DC: Catholic University of America Press, 2010.

Williams, Rowan. *Arius: Heresy and Tradition*, rev. ed. Grand Rapids, MI: Eerdmans, 2001.

Wippel, John F. *Metaphysical Themes in Thomas Aquinas*. Washington, DC: Catholic University of America Press, 1984.

Index

Abelard, Peter, 35
accident, 25, 45, 215, 228, 281–82, 281n21, 282n27, 289, 292; accidental, 43–45, 43n65, 76, 275; accidental cause (*see* cause)
act, 44, 49n88, 52, 54, 57, 69, 90n4, 94–96, 98–100, 103, 105n34, 108, 113n7, 120n37, 125, 131, 139n29, 143n41, 146, 146n56, 147n60, 148n63, 165, 168, 170, 173–74, 176, 178–80, 186–93, 199, 202–3, 211, 217, 225, 227–28, 230, 230n51, 233, 237–38, 238n91, 241, 262, 284, 288n46, 293, 295; action, 6, 54n112, 104, 121, 138, 142nn37–38, 148n63, 153, 161, 166, 185, 187, 189–93, 203–4, 227, 227n38, 230, 255–56, 261–62, 267, 289n52, 290, 295–96, 302n103
acts and sufferings (*acta et passa*), 153, 157–60, 164
Adam and Eve, 55, 90n1, 90n4
adoration, 221, 222n3, 227–33, 233n70, 235–36, 237n88, 238; *adoratio*, 222, 225, 227–28, 227n37, 233, 237, 242
Akindynos, Gregory, 217–18, 217n31
Albert the Great / Albertus Magnus, xi, 2, 77n211, 186, 277, 278n10, 313
allegory, 241, 253
Ambrose / Ambrosius of Milan, 10, 153n12, 158n39, 268, 284, 285n38, 286, 289–90, 290nn54–55, 295, 299n88, 312, 320
anagogical sense, 78
analogy, xvi, 6, 164, 166–69, 171–76, 178–81, 190–91, 190n33, 196–99,

196n50, 201, 219, 232, 313n34; analogous, 113, 120n37, 170, 172–73, 177, 215; prime analogate, 171–74
angel, 40, 42, 42–43n65, 48n88, 50, 52–53, 67–70, 72–74, 74n197, 78, 83, 86, 112n5, 130, 133, 136–38, 141–43, 141n34, 145, 217–18, 221n2, 227, 233n70, 235n81, 236–37, 240
Anselm of Laon, 82n236, 226, 266n91
anthropology, xvi, 138, 184
anti-Palamite. *See* Palamas, Gregory
apokatastasis, 76, 86
Apollinarius, 252; Apollinarians, 163–64; Apollinarianism, 64n152
apophatic/apophasis, 6, 165–67, 169–71, 173–74, 176–78, 180–81, 326
archetype, 171, 174, 176–77
Aristotle, xi, 43–44, 54n112, 57n124, 59, 69, 72, 96, 171, 175, 184, 222, 233, 235, 238, 240, 240n97, 308, 308n19, 314, 324; radical Aristotelianism, 47
Arius, 37–41, 47n82, 125n65, 252, 312, 315; Arian, 12–13, 121, 127n73, 135, 152, 163
Athanasius of Alexandria, xiv, xvi, 5–7, 12–13, 13n11, 16, 22, 33, 92–104, 94n9, 108–9, 113, 122n43, 125n65, 177, 208, 313, 318, 320
atonement, 90n1, 101–2
Augustine, xvi–xvii, 2, 11–13, 16, 22–23, 27, 32, 37, 47, 52, 55–56, 55n115, 66–68, 71, 75, 77, 79–80, 82, 84–85, 106, 128, 137, 152, 154n16, 157, 161n50, 166, 192, 208, 212–13, 222, 225–26, 226n27, 228, 228n40, 228n44, 233–36, 241, 253n43,

Thomas Aquinas and the Greek Fathers was designed in Garamond Premier Pro and composed by Kachergis Book Design of Pittsboro, North Carolina. It was printed on 60-pound House Natural Web and bound by Sheridan Books of Chelsea, Michigan.